JAYAPRAKASH NARAYAN

SELECTED WORKS

Volume Six (1950-1954)

First published 2005

ISBN 81-7304-353-1 (Series)
ISBN 81-7304-642-5

Published by
Ajay Kumar Jain for
Manohar Publishers & Distributors
4753/23 Ansari Road, Daryaganj
New Delhi 110002

Typeset by
A J Software Publishing Co. Pvt. Ltd.
New Delhi 110005

Printed at
Lordson Publishers Pvt. Ltd.
Delhi 110007

Distributed in South Asia by
FOUNDATION BOOKS
4381/4 Ansari Road, Daryaganj
New Delhi 110002
and its branches at Mumbai, Hyderabad, Bangalore, Chennai, Kolkata

CONTENTS

Appendices

ILLUSTRATIONS

FOREWORD

We are happy to present before the reading public Volume 6 of the *Selected Works of Jayaprakash Narayan* edited by Professor Bimal Prasad. It covers a period of four years from the end of Madras Conference of the Socialist Party (1950) to the announcement of *Jeevandan* by J.P. for the cause of the Bhoodan-Gramdan movement (1954). These four years witnessed several important political developments, such as the holding of the first general elections in India (1952), the formation of the Praja Socialist Party as a result of the merger of the Socialist Party and the Kisan Mazdoor Praja Party (1952), the failure of the talks between Nehru and J.P. (initiated by the former) in order to ensure cooperation between the Congress and the PSP (1953), controversy among the ranks of the PSP on J.P.'s open appreciation for Nehru's initiative, the growing involvement of J.P. in the Bhoodan-Gramdan movement, and his announcement of *Jeevandan*.

This volume gives the readers an insight into these developments while bringing out in full the nature of J.P.'s role in them. J.P.'s deep interest in the struggles of railwaymen and the post and telegraph workers (whose unions continued to be headed by him till 1952), workers in the coal mines around Dhanbad, the steel factory at Jamshedpur and the sugar factory at Dalmianagar, whose unions were controlled by the Socialist Party, are fully covered through his correspondence with the officials and Cabinet Ministers, at the Centre as well as in Bihar. The writings of this period also highlight J.P.'s deep interest in the fight for democracy in Nepal.

Nehru Memorial Museum &
Library, New Delhi

K. JAYAKUMAR
Director

ACKNOWLEDGEMENTS

It is a pleasure to thank all those who have helped me in preparing this volume.

First and foremost, I must thank Srimati Sonia Gandhi for her gracious permission to use certain sections of J.P.'s correspondence with Nehru which were not available in the former's own papers, but were available in Nehru Papers for the closed period, particularly in the folio marked 'Files at Home'.

I must also thank Sri K. Jayakumar, Director, Nehru Memorial Museum & Library for his deep interest in the work relating to this volume and his willingness to help as and when required. The same can be said about Dr N. Balakrishnan, Deputy Director, NMML, and I am thankful to him.

The members of the research team who worked with me in preparing this volume, namely, Sri J.L. Gera, Dr Maya Gupta and Mrs Sangita Mallik (Research Officers) and Sri S.A. Abidi, Dr Kapileshwar Labh and Sri Vas Dev Lakhanpal (Assistant Research Officers) enthusiastically helped me in collecting and arranging the materials that appear in this volume as also in seeing it through the press. I am thankful to all of them.

I also thank Sri Deshraj, Administrative Officer of the NMML for his helpful attitude on all occasions. Ms Neha Bhardwaj and Ms Bhawana Pandey handled the typing work for this volume. They also deserve my thanks.

BIMAL PRASAD

INTRODUCTION

This volume, covering the period 1950-4, illustrates a major transition in J.P.'s political life and thought. In the beginning of this period, while already attracted towards certain aspects of Gandhi's teachings and making it a point to draw the attention of his colleagues and followers towards them, he was functioning primarily as a leader of the Socialist Party and was not in any way connected with the Gandhian or Sarvodaya movement. However, he was highly impressed by the Bhoodan movement started in 1951 under the leadership of Vinoba Bhave, resulting in voluntary gift of land on a fairly large scale in different parts of the country for distribution among the landless. J.P. looked upon it as a peaceful way of achieving radical social change, which is what the Socialist Party had been aiming at. He indeed considered the Bhoodan movement as a revolution in action and openly supported it. This, combined with his growing disillusionment with party and power politics paved the way for his whole-heartedly joining the Sarvodaya Movement and indeed offering his whole life to it in April 1954. This became famous as *Jeevandan*.

I

Before coming to that stage, J.P., for some time, continued with his usual activities as the General Secretary of the Socialist Party—explaining and spreading the gospel of socialism through his speeches and writings, seeking to strengthen the organization of the Socialist Party, lending his hand to the strengthening of labour and peasant organizations and inculcating socialist ideals among the youth, particularly students. At the same time he continued to be the president of several large unions of government employees such as the All-India Railwaymen's Federation, the All-India Post and Lower Grade Staff Union and the Union of the Civilian Employees of the Defence Ministry. The readers will have an idea of his relentless effort on their behalf from the texts of his speeches before some of their conferences and his letters pleading their cases to the Prime Minister, Jawaharlal Nehru, as well as to the other Cabinet Ministers in charge of the concerned Departments. These documents will also be useful in understanding the state of the trade union movement in India in the 1950s. The same applies to many of J.P.'s speeches at the gatherings of peasants, particularly at Dekuli in the Darbhanga District of Bihar (12 March 1952), where he emphasized the importance of constructive work in the villages for rural uplift. What is remarkable is that while addressing the representatives of these groups he not only talked of their rights and demands, but also reminded them of their duties not only to the people on behalf of whom they were working, but to the nation at large. This is best illustrated by his role in the All-India Railwaymen's Federation in 1950-1. While, in the face of the unsympathetic attitude of the authorities, a decision to go on strike had been taken with his full support, he did not hesitate at a later stage—when Nehru drew attention to the impending danger of a war with Pakistan—to advise the Railway workers to revise their decision and desist from going on strike. For this he was strongly criticized by the communist leaders, both inside the Federation and outside, but he stood firm on his advice.

One of the main preoccupations of J.P. since the end of the Madras Conference of his party (1950) was preparing for the first general elections in the country which were held in the beginning 1952. He did his best in order to galvanize public opinion in favour of free and fair elections and convened a conference of the leaders of the various opposition parties with that end in view, which resulted in the adoption of a number of suggestions for ensuring such elections. Some of his speeches and letters in this connection, included in this volume, show his deep concern with this problem. So far as he himself was concerned, however, he refused to become a candidate in the elections. When the national executive of the Socialist Party, disregarding his advice, adopted a resolution affirming that all the top leaders of the Party should contest the elections, J.P. wrote to its members on 28 August 1951, begging to be excused from this task. He, of course, acknowledged the importance of parliamentary work, but affirmed that it was not necessary for everyone to be engaged in such work. The sphere of one's work in the party should depend upon his or her inclinations. So far as he himself was concerned he wanted to be left free to work among the masses.

Though not contesting the elections himself, J.P. worked as hard in them as he had ever worked for the building up of his Party. The election results were not at all upto his or other leaders' expectations. Out of about five hundred members in the Lok Sabha, the Socialist Party could win only twelve seats. It did not do any better in the elections to the State Assemblies. Although deeply disappointed, J.P. was not disheartened. As in the past, he continued to exhort peasants and workers to join the Party in large numbers and strengthen it in order to lay the foundations of a new social order, free from exploitation and injustice. However, the poor showing in the elections reduced his hold over certain sections in the leadership of the Party who began, privately or publicly, to describe J.P.'s leadership as being primarily responsible for the massive electoral defeat of the Party. The first indication of this attitude became visible at the Conference of the Bihar Socialist Party at Paṭna in early April 1952. Ramanandan Mishra, one of the prominent leaders of the Party in Bihar, issued a pamphlet on that occasion which without naming J.P., attacked the leadership for its failure to follow a revolutionary path, thereby creating a feeling among the people that the Socialist Party was not very different from the Congress. He also spoke before the conference in the same vein. Even though it was clear that Mishra enjoyed only a limited following in the Party and that most of those present at the conference did not share his views and remained firmly loyal to J.P., the latter was quite upset and left the conference announcing that he would no longer take any interest in the work of the Party in Bihar. Mishra, of course, received such severe bashing at the conference that he soon left Patna for his home-town, ceased to take any interest in the Party, and turned towards spiritual pursuits.

This was merely a prelude to more of such attacks which J.P. had to face within the Party in the following months. This is fully borne out by proceedings of the Special Convention of the Socialist Party held at Pachmarhi in the last week of May 1952. Rammanohar Lohia, delivering his presidential address—a brilliant performance full of several radical formulations regarding the need to develop a socialist doctrine based on Indian conditions—emphasized that one of the major causes of the poor performance of the Socialist Party in the elections was the lack of keenness on its part to launch struggles of peasants and workers from time to time. This was a veiled attack on J.P., but he took it in his stride, referring to some of the struggles launched by Lohia—as Lohia too was a part of the leadership—and defending his own personal failing by pointing to the heavy burden of organization which he had had to carry. Further, he strongly commended most of the points made by Lohia and asked his partymen to ponder over them and modify their pattern of work accordingly.

II

As in the past, J.P. also continued to bear for some time the main responsibility of leading the Socialist Party. As he saw it, one of the main reasons for the debacle of the Party in the elections was its decision to put up candidates in as many constituencies as possible. The Communists had done better by concentrating on areas where they were really powerful. The result was that while they secured a much smaller proportion of the total votes cast in the elections than the Socialists, they obtained about double the number of seats. The strategy followed by the Socialists had, however, achieved some good: their message had been broadcast and some followers secured in all parts of the country. This, J.P. thought, could be made the foundation for further, more intensive work in selected areas. Another reason, according to him, for the setback suffered by the Socialist Party lay in its having had to share the votes of those opposed to the Congress with a number of opposition parties. He therefore thought it would be to the good if those of the non-Congress and non-Communist parties which had a broadly similar outlook were brought together so as to avoid splitting the opposition votes. This led to the birth of the Praja Socialist Party as a result of the merger of the Socialist Party and the Kisan Mazdoor Praja Party, which had been formed shortly before the elections when some Congress leaders had left their old organization. Since the Socialist Party, under J.P.'s leadership, had already adopted some of the tenets of Gandhism and the strongly Gandhian KMPP, under the leadership of J.B. Kripalani, was prepared to accept the principles of Democratic Socialism, the merger of these two was in a sense natural and considered likely to prove helpful to the functioning of parliamentary democracy as well as to the cause of socialism. In any case, it was not motivated by any desire for quick political returns in terms of sharing power. J.P. was not the type of leader to be moved by such considerations.

An opportunity for sharing power, with bright prospects for occupying the top position in the future, came to J.P. shortly after the merger, but he spurned it without any hesitation. Early in 1953 Nehru invited him to join the Cabinet, along with some of his colleagues, in order to strengthen the progressive forces in the Government. Here it may be mentioned that both in personal relationship and in political and economic outlook J.P. was much closer to Nehru than any member of the Cabinet. In 1948, when, after the assassination of Gandhi, J.P. was being assailed by many Congress leaders for his attack on Sardar Vallabhbhai Patel, the then Home Minister and Deputy Prime Minister, for negligence of Gandhi's security, Nehru had used the opportunity provided by a broadcast to the nation to pay a tribute to J.P. and throw a hint about his future role in Indian politics. 'I have never had any doubt', said Nehru, 'about the integrity and ability of Jayaprakash whom I value as a friend and I am sure that a time will come when he will play a very important role in shaping India's destiny'. Besides, in the matter of popularity among the elite as well as the masses, J.P. stood only second to Nehru and, in spite of the electoral debacle of the Socialist Party in the last elections, was widely regarded as a natural successor to the latter. His inclusion in the Cabinet at that stage was likely to strengthen this trend of thinking. Indeed Nehru had mentioned to him orally the desirability of his gaining some administrative experience if he was to lead the country in the future, as he then appeared destined to do. But such a prospect held no allurement for J.P., though it did create opposition to Nehru's move inside the leadership of the Congress party. On the other hand, the top socialist leaders too were divided, some, notably Lohia, thinking that cooperation with the Government at that stage would weaken the socialist movement in the country. Although appreciative of Nehru's move, J.P. too did not consider it desirable to accept Nehru's offer without being assured that his Government was keen to work for socialism. In his letter to Nehru on 4 March 1953, he paid a tribute to the former for his bold and unusual proposal, for the Congress had an absolute majority in the legislatures both at the centre and in the states and did not need the support of any other party to stay in office. He also recognized that it was the common people's wish that their leaders, irrespective of the parties to which they belonged, should join hands to serve them and make their lot better. But he made it clear that he was not interested in joining the Government unless he was sure that it would move swiftly in the direction of socialism. He wrote to Nehru:

> Therefore, a great deal would depend on how you conceived your own move in asking for our co-operation. If it means only this that a few of us are to be added to your Cabinet and some of the state cabinets to strengthen the Government and your hands in carrying out your present polices, the attempt would not be worth making. But if it means launching upon a bold joint venture of national re-construction, it might well have been a historic move.

For this purpose J.P. put forward a fourteen-point programme involving certain constitutional, legal, administrative, fiscal and economic reforms in the direction of socialism, including such items as redistribution of land, nationalization of banks, insurance companies and coal and other mining industries, progressive development of state trading, and scaling down the higher salaries and emoluments in government service. Nehru, though not opposed to these reforms, did not find it prudent to commit himself to carry them out in the next four years as J.P. wanted. So the talks on cooperation between the Congress and the PSP did not produce any constructive result.

J.P.'s letter to Nehru dated 4 March 1948, included in this volume, is important not only for the light it throws on one of the principal causes for the breakdown of talks between the two leaders, but also for the insight it provides into the former's political philosophy at that point of time. 'I assure you,' he wrote to Nehru, 'our approach to socialism is not doctrinaire, hidebound or conservative. But I must make one point clear. No matter how empirical or experimental may be our approach, the goals and values of socialism are unalterably fixed before us.' This ardour for socialism went hand in hand with an equally strong ardour for Gandhism. 'We have all,' added J.P., 'been influenced by Gandhiji. I do not mind saying that I have been rediscovering him lately and reunderstanding him. I believe he was one of the most vital thinkers of the modern age. . . . I feel sure that the Gandhians and the socialists, dropping their respective jargons, must work together.'

III

J.P. had been trying to bridge the gap between the Gandhians and socialists for quite some time. Thus in an article entitled 'Socialism and Sarvodaya', published in *Janata* in 1951, he had asked the socialists to make a careful study of the Sarvodaya plan for economic development prepared by Gandhian workers a year earlier, describing it as 'no wishy washy sentimentalism, but a concrete programme of basic social revolution'. After discussing its salient features he had expressed the hope that the Gandhians and the socialists would join hands to found a new social order on its basis. He had also warned that socialism in India would neglect Gandhism only at its peril and added: 'Far from being reactionary, Gandhiji was a social revolutionary of an exceptionally revolutionary kind, and he has made contributions to social thought and the methodology of social change that constitute imperishable contributions to human progress and civilization.' He found three aspects of Gandhism particularly significant: its moral or ethical basis and its insistence on values; its great contribution to revolutionary technology in the shape of civil disobedience or *satyagraha*; and its insistence on political and economic decentralization.

In June 1952, shortly after the first general elections, J.P. undertook a self-purificatory fast at Poona for twenty-one days in atonement of the supposed mistake he had made in interpreting the Government's assurances regarding the payment of salary to the post and telegraph workers for a strike-period, on the basis of which the latter had desisted from going on strike, but which the Government later denied having made at all. J.P. had, of course, fasted longer in the Deoli camp jail in 1941, but that was in support of certain demands. This 'self-purificatory' fast had a peculiarly Gandhian flavour and showed that J.P. had moved much closer to Gandhism than before. It was during this fast also that the long process of questionings and doubts which had started with the Stalinist purges in the Soviet Union in the 1930s, reached its culmination. J.P. now finally realized that he no longer believed in Dialectical Materialism, the goddess at whose shrine he had worshipped for so many years. In an article entitled 'Incentives to Goodness', written shortly after the fast and published in *Freedom First* (ed. M.R. Masani), and included in this volume, J.P. affirmed that 'man must go beyond the material to find the incentives to goodness' and further that 'the task of social reconstruction cannot succeed under the inspiration of a materialist philosophy'. He, of course, clarified that he did not mean to imply that all those who professed a materialist philosophy were necessarily vicious or that all non-materialists were necessarily good. But he did emphasize that there was nothing in materialism, which impelled man towards goodness:

[Man] asks naturally why he should be virtuous. Our social forms of today and the materialist philosophy, which rules the affairs of men, answer back: he need not. The cleverer he is, the more gifted, the more courageously he practices the new amorality; and in the coils of this amorality the dreams and aspirations of mankind become warped and twisted.

The final break with Dialectical Materialism cleared the way for a fuller understanding and adoption of Gandhism. But, as borne out by J.P.'s letter to Nehru in March 1953, referred to above, the old goals of socialism were not given up. On the contrary, Gandhism was adopted primarily because those goals appeared more likely to be reached through the Gandhian path. Besides, the goals themselves became nobler and more inspiring because of the association of Gandhism with socialism. This should become clear from a perusal of 'The Ideological Problems of Socialism', included in this volume, based on his address to the First Asian Socialist Conference held in Rangoon early in 1953.

The first problem dealt with here by J.P. is what he describes as the problem of socialist axioms. This problem, he points out, had arisen as a result of the failure of the Soviet leaders to build up a truly socialist society in spite of their success in laying down the economic foundations of such a society, largely because of the amoral philosophy of Marxism and the struggle for power within the ruling party. It had also arisen as a result of the weakness of human beings, 'the weakness of individual man everywhere, his ambition, his selfishness, his stupidity, his hate, his fear'. J.P., therefore, pleaded that all those who might be engaged in working for socialism, whatever their conception of the path to socialism, whatever their interpretation of socialist theories, must subscribe to certain values, which they would not consider relative in the sense that they could be sacrificed for an immediate end, however laudable. Thus the socialist movement, along with its economic, social and political programmes, must also have a programme based on vlaues, which can never be sacrificed.

Proceeding to deal with the problem of creating a proper political framework for the development of a socialist society, J.P. not only rejected the system of one-party dictatorship then in vogue in the Soviet Union, but also founded drawbacks in the system of parliamentary democracy established in some countries of Western Europe. To do away with those drawbacks, he advocated decentralization of political power so that the people might directly participate in the management of their affairs. Allied to this problem was that of the economic structure for a socialist society. J.P. warned that the old belief that nationalization of industries would solve all problems in the economic field was no longer valid. This was shown by what had happened in the Soviet Union: all the industries there had been nationalized, but this had not led to the establishment of socialism in the true sense of the term. The chief defects of the Soviet system, according to J.P., were 'centralization, bureaucratization, lack of industry, in short, lack of popular control over the economic process'. One solution to this problem was the dispersal of ownership of industries at different levels down to the village organization and municipal corporation, instead of concentration of ownership of all industries in the hands of the central government. Thus political decentral-ization would have to be accompanied by economic decentralization.

Turning to the technique of struggle for bringing about socialism, J.P. emphatically repudiated the view that though democratic methods might take us forward to a certain extent, at the final stages of the struggle for socialism, violence would be absolutely necessary. On the contrary, since the objective is the establishment of a democratic socialist society, the means adopted to bring such a society into existence must also be democratic, provided, of course, such means are available. By democratic methods, however, J.P. did not mean only parliamentary or constitutional methods, but also included in them mass movements and actions of a non-violent character, which might be unconstitutional, yet peaceful. In the end, he took up the question of relationship between two socialist countries, a question brought into prominence by the strained relationship between the Soviet Union and Yugoslavia. Here he emphasized that the relationship between one socialist country and another must be based on equality and mutual aid. If there had to be any tilting of the balance, it should be in favour of the backward and weaker country and not in favour of the more developed and stronger one.

In his address to the foundation conference of the Praja Socialist Party during the same year (1953), which was published in *Janata* under the title 'A Plea for Gandhism', J.P. was more emphatic on the use of Gandhism to enrich Socialism. Rejecting the view that to mix Gandhism and Socialism was a sign of ideological confusion, he suggested that Gandhism should be used to develop the ideology of Socialism in India. According to him both Communism and Socialism (as practised in the West) were facing failure. While Communism had ended up in State capitalism and dictatorship, Socialism had become only a parliamentary or legalistic creed. Gandhism offered the third alternative, that of 'revolution by non-violent mass action'. There was nothing wrong with the goals of Socialism, but those goals were more likely to be reached by following the methods of Gandhism. As J.P. put it:

> Socialism ultimately aims at creating a stateless society, but it wishes to make the State all powerful by making the social revolution itself dependent upon State action. Gandhism, too, like Socialism, aims at a stateless society. But on that account it proceeds more consistently by making the social process as little dependent upon

the State as possible. The creation of the stateless society begins here and now, and is not relegated to a remote and imaginary period in the future. It is, therefore, a more truly revolutionary process and is more likely to reach the goal than the other processes.

IV

Behind such assertions lay J.P.'s assessment of the nature and significance of the Bhoodan or land-gift movement being carried on in India since 1951, under the leadership of Vinoba Bhave, widely acclaimed as the spiritual heir of Gandhi. As the latter proceeded on foot from one village to another, people with big holdings and small enthusiastically responded to his call and offered portions of their land for distribution among the landless. To J.P., who had already been gradually moving towards Gandhism, this appeared not merely a movement for the redistribution of land, but as the beginning of a great human as well as social revolution. After the general elections of 1952, therefore, he plunged whole-heartedly into it. As he moved from one village to another with the message of *Bhoodan* he, too, had an experience similar to Vinoba's and was able to secure donations amounting to thousands of acres of land in the course of a few weeks. Here was, he thought, 'revolution by non-violent mass action' taking place before his own eyes. Soon his fascination for this movement and even more for the philosophy behind it became so strong that he decided to devote all his time and attention to it, to the exclusion of everything else. This decision was announced at the Sarvodaya Conference held at Bodh Gaya in 1954, and became famous as *Jeevandan* (meaning dedication of one's life to a cause).

This involved J.P.'s withdrawal from the field of party and power politics, in particular from the leadership of the PSP, though not yet from its membership. When it is remembered that J.P. had been the chief source of inspiration for most socialists in India ever since 1934, and was, next only to Nehru, the most popular and respected political leader in the country, the gravity of this decision can easily be imagined. The fact that only a year earlier he had been invited to join Nehru's cabinet and that, in spite of his refusal to do so, was generally considered the most likely and natural successor to Nehru as Prime Minister, gave to his *Jeevandan* the aura of a great renunciation. It is not, therefore, surprising that Vinoba Bhave, the founder of the Bhoodan movement and the chief source of inspiration to all Gandhian workers, thought it proper to mark the solemnity of that moment by re-dedicating his own life also to the cause of *Bhoodan*, 'in response', as he put it, to J.P.'s call.

V

However, what has been written in the earlier section gives only one half of the background behind J.P.'s announcement of *Jeevandan* and the consequent distancing from the leadership of the Praja Socialist Party. The fact is that he moved in that direction also by the goings on in the Party. He was deeply hurt by the attacks after the debacle of the Socialist Party in the first general election—both open and veiled—on his leadership of the Party. For some time—except for Ramanandan Mishra's outburst at Patna (April 1952)—these attacks remained subdued. However, they came into the open and in a much more serious form, at the time of the Betul Convention (1953) of the Praja Socialist Party held after the failure of the Nehru-J.P. talks on cooperation between the Congress and the PSP. In the discussions at Betul it became clear that an overwhelming opinion in the Party felt that its position had been harmed by the talks and in particular by J.P.'s attitudes towards them. What was said outside the Convention was much more hurting than what was said at the Convention. There was a whispering campaign that J.P.'s interest in the talks with Nehru was primarily motivated by his desire to acquire a strategic position in the Cabinet so as to emerge as Nehru's successor and become Prime Minister in due course. His position in the Party was made much worse by Asoka Mehta's report as General Secretary, where he propounded his famous thesis on the 'Compulsions of a Backward Economy' emphasizing the necessity of muting rivalries among democratic parties and working unitedly for economic advance. Although J.P. had had nothing to do with that thesis, it was widely whispered that it had been presented at his suggestion. All this deeply heart J.P., who had till then nourished the party through its various stages—Congress Socialist Party, Socialist Party and Praja Socialist Party—with singular devotion, and he indeed offered his resignation from the national executive of the Praja Socialist Party. Although at the persuasion of Lohia he withdraw that resignation, the happenings at Betul further deepened his distaste for party and power politics, already ingrained in him. He now began to concentrate more and more on his work in connection with the Bhoodan Movement. He did not speak at all at the first all India conference of the Praja Socialist Party held at Allahabad in January 1954. The announcement of *Jeevandan* followed in April 1954. It is, therefore, necessary to follow closely the proceedings of the Pachmarhi Convention (1952) and the Betul Convention (1953)—to which we have devoted considerable space in this volume—in order to fully understand the background of J.P.'s historic announcement of 1954. It may here be added that although in 1954 J.P. did not say a world about the happenings in the PSP, which also constituted a factor in his decision to give up all power and part politics, years later (in 1969), while writing a foreword to a biography of his senior and very highly esteemed colleague in the socialist movement right from 1934, Narendra Deva, J.P. mentioned them as a factor. If so inclined, J.P. could certainly have suppressed dissent in the Party, for everyone knew that, in spite of the debacle in the elections of 1952 and the talks with Nehru for cooperation in 1953, J.P. still commanded the overwhelming support of the majority in it. However, since he had never been interested in seeking power for himself and had been building up the Party so as to use it as an instrument for bringing about a social revolution in India, he now came to the conclusion that the Bhoodan-Gramdan movement would provide a much more effective instrument for it than a faction-ridden party, with prominent members at loggerheads among themselves for occupying prominent positions in the Party.

VI

Needless to add, this volume should be useful not only in understanding the evolution of J.P.'s thinking and his changing role in Indian politics, but also in indicating his myriad interests in so many problems facing India and even some countries outside India. To take just Nepal, J.P.'s letter to the socialist leaders of Burma who were in control of the Government there in December 1950 will illustrate J.P.'s role in securing arms-aid to the Nepali Congress, then engaged in spearheading an armed insurrection in Nepal against Rana rule. Similarly, his letters to Nehru and statements regarding Nepal show J.P.'s keenness to influence the Government of India's role in Nepal, turning it more and more favourable towards the democratic forces struggling there. On the other hand, some of the letters to B.P. Koirala in 1952, chastising him for not fully cooperating with his elder brother, M.P. Koirala, who had been made Prime Minister by King Tribhuwan, shows the depth of his interest in the cause of democracy in Nepal.

1. To B.R. Ambedkar, 17 July 1950[1]

Dear Dr. Ambedkar,

At the Opposition Parties' Conference held here [Bombay] on July 1 and 2, I had occasion to have certain talks with Shri P.N. Rajbhoj and Shri Subbiah of Hyderabad. They were anxious to know what the Socialist Party's programme was to be with regard to the Scheduled Castes. They were particularly anxious to have definite guarantees on three points. As a result of these talks I issued a statement on the subject from Madras which was published in full in the *Hindu* of 7th July. I understand it was published in other papers also. I am enclosing a copy for your information.

Apart from the statement, a paragraph on the same lines as the statement has been added to the Party's Programme for National Revival that was adopted at the Madras Conference recently concluded. I shall send you a copy of the Programme as soon as it is printed.

I feel it is time now that we come to a definite understanding as to our work in the future and the relations between the Scheduled Castes Federation[2] and the Socialist Party and the Scheduled Castes' Labour unions and our own Labour movement. I hope to be in Delhi in the 3rd week of August and should like to talk over the matter with you.

Hoping you are well and with kind regards,

Yours sincerely,
Jayaprakash Narayan

[1]*J.P. Papers* (NMML).

[2]All India Scheduled Castes Federation had been formed at the Conference of All India Depressed Classes held at Nagpur from 18 to 19 July 1942. Dr. B.R. Ambedkar and P.N. Rajabhoj had been its prime sponsors.

2. Address at the Rotary Club, Bombay, 18 July 1950[1]

The policy being followed by the Indian National Congress has led the country to stagnation. The only alternative to Congress Government in the country is a Socialist Government. There is the Communist alternative, but the country knows what that alternative would mean.

The Socialist Party has laid in the forefront of its programme the equitable distribution of what we have. As long as inequalities are there, it will never be possible for the people to see that a new order of society or a new life is being created for them. The range between the highest and the lowest income, earned or unearned, should not be more than between one and ten.

[1]Adapted from *Hindu*, 20 July 1950.

Legislation will be necessary to bring about all the incomes in the country within this range. Drastic economic measures will have to be undertaken and a small number of people may have to suffer in this process.

Redistribution of land is another important part of the Socialist new deal for the people. In certain parts of Bihar, it has been found that often there are 56 intermediaries between the tiller and Government. The number of cultivators may be about 60 millions. There are other millions and millions who work on the land but have no right on it and are poorly paid for their labour. They are the landless labourers.

The Socialist Party plans to reclaim waste lands and distribute it to the landless. The Congress Government has been in power for some years, but there is no evidence of any drastic agrarian reforms in any of the States.

I appeal to industrialists and businessmen to be content with lesser incomes and co-operate in bringing about a "New Deal", in which justice would be done to all. In a Socialist India, there would be cooperative trading, co-operative finance corporations, cooperative farming and irrigation.

There is the need for an immediate programme which promises the people a new order of society. Unless this is done there would be no enthusiasm among the people. I want Government to impress on the people that the present set-up of society is changing and a Socialist order is being created in which there would be better opportunities for all.

3. To the Secretary, Ministry of Defence, 28 July 1950[1]

Dear Shri Patel,[2]

I wish to remind you of the conference I had with you on the 17th April 1950. I along with my colleagues of the AIDSCE (All India Defence Services Civil Employees) Federation had placed before you then the outstanding grievances of the civilian employees of the Defence Ministry. The grievances mainly related to the implementation of the RPC and its anomalies, implementation of the letter of August 19, conditions of service, retrenchment, conveyance allowance, recovery of supposed over-payments from the monthly pay, etc. In the course of our talks, we were assured that several of the issues raised would be examined while certain others would

[1]*J.P. Papers* (NMML).

[2]H.M. Patel (1904-80); joined ICS, 1927; Secretary, Union Ministry of Defence, 1947-53; Food and Agriculture, 1953-4 and Economic Affairs, 1955-6; Principal Finance Secretary, 1957-9; Chairman, LIC, 1956-7; member, Gujarat Assembly, 1967-71; member, Lok Sabha, 1971-80; President Gujarat Unit of Swatantra Party, 1967-72 and All India Swantra Party 1971-2; Union Minister for Finance, 1977-9, and Home Affairs, 1979-80.

be favourably considered. For example, we were told in regard to conveyance allowance that the question had already been taken up and that order would be issued shortly. About the recovery of arrears it was promised that the Federation's suggestion in the matter would be waived. In regard to the merger of different categories you agreed that although there were difficulties in the way of preparing a common roster in DOS, it could be done at least on the area basis. It was further agreed that difficulties arising out of retrenchment would be carefully scrutinised and that an effort would be made to avoid them. You were also good enough to say that the memorandum submitted by the Federation concerning the factory workers would be studied and a conference of experts would be convened to discuss the question with the Federation.

In view of these assurances, I advised the Federation to wait for some time and not proceed with the strike ballot in accordance to the resolution of the Poona Convention. More than three months have elapsed since and I am surprised that practically nothing has been done to solve these outstanding issues. Thousands of rupees are still being recovered, in the name of over-payment, from the monthly pay. Not only has conveyance allowance not been granted, even the charge for the military transport provided to the workers in the past, is being recovered now.

The Executive Committee of the AIDSCE. Federation met in Bombay on the 23rd July and after a careful consideration of the whole issue and the unjustifiable delay on the part of the Government, decided that a special session of the General Council of the Federation should be called in the first week of September to map out the future course of action. I need not say that the Federation is anxious to settle every question through negotiation. But yet I am constrained to say that if the outstanding issues are not speedily settled, say, within a month from today, there will be no alternative left for me but to advise the Federation to take a strike ballot. Considering the time already taken another month should be enough for Government to reach final decisions. I hope this matter will receive your urgent attention.

Yours sincerely,
Jayaprakash Narayan

4. To Rafi Ahmed Kidwai, 28 July 1950[1]

My dear Rafi Saheb,

After I met you in Bombay, I had further talks with Union representatives there. Some representatives of other P&T unions also came with their

[1]*Brahmanand Papers* (NMML).

troubles. May I bring some of these issues to your notice, none of which is new or has been raised for the first time. As I expect to be in Delhi on the 17th August, I shall be obliged if definitive decisions are taken before then.

1. *Pre-1931 Officials*: We have several times discussed this question and there is no need to restate the case for this category of staff. At the time we had seen the Prime Minister in this connection (among other things), this demand was rejected I believe on the ground that if appropriate monetary benefit was granted to the pre-31 staff, the estimated increase in cost would come to Rs. 15 lacs. My Union, however, does not believe that the cost would be so high. The question is peculiar mainly to the two cities of Bombay and Calcutta. According to the information of the Bombay Branch of my Union there are about 640 officials in Bombay who come under this category and there may be an equal number in Calcutta. If the benefit sanctioned to these officials is at the rate of Rs. 20/- per month, the total cost may not be more than three lakhs of rupees per year. Thus the figure is not so high as estimated by your Department and perhaps it may be possible for you to sanction the amount.

2. *Old (pre-1931) Lower Dn. Clerks*: Prior to 1935 there existed a category of officials in the post offices, called the Lower Dn. Clerks, whose scale was Rs. 60-4-100. In 1935 two grades were introduced into the clerical cadre of the post offices and these officials were merged in the second Grade (scale Rs. 45-45-3-90). But they were allowed to retain their own scale of Rs. 60-4-100. Most of these lower Dn. clerks reached the maximum of their scales in 1939 and since then drew no increments, as promotion to the first grade (scale Rs. 100-5-160) could be made only when the strengths of the two cadres reached 50 : 50 ratio. In 1945, the first and second grades were merged into one running grade (scale Rs. 45-45-3-90-5-120 and 60-4-100-5-160). It was only then that the officials in question got their first increment after being stagnated at Rs. 100/- for six years. The Pay Commission too had not conferred any material benefit on them. The Rajadhyaksha Award of 1946 also excluded them from its benefit as it did not apply to pre-1931 officials.

Now the Department has recently issued orders (vide letter No. AI-31-63/47 dated 17.2.1950 issued by the Minister of Communications to the DGPT) according to which the relief of 15 per cent of the pay granted by the Rajadhyaksha Award to the clerical cadre should be added to their Basic pay for the purpose of fixation of their initial pay in the revised scales introduced in 1947. This has created an anomalous situation in which the above-mentioned pre-1931 officials are drawing less pay than their juniors recruited after 1931. This is due to two factors. Firstly, these officials were denied increments for six years, and secondly they have been excluded from the benefit of the Rajadhyaksha Award, whereas the post-1931 officials, though their juniors, drew continuous increment every year and in addition got an addition of 15 per cent to their basic pay on account of the Rajadhyaksha Award. I am citing below concrete instances illustrating the anomaly:

Old Lower Divn. Clerks of pre-1931 Scale 60-4-100-5-160			2nd grade of post 1931 (scale 45-45-3-90-4-120)		
Name	Date of entry in the grade	pay now drawn Rs.	Name	Date of entry in the grade	pay now drawn Rs.
1. M.R. Savant	11-7-29	125	1. N.D. Nemani	1-10-32	145
2. Sk. Yakub Sk. Ismail	20-7-31	125	2. R.N. Joshi	1-10-32	145
3. B.S. Sathe	1-7-32	125	3. S.N. Malt	13-12-32	135
4. N.G. Vaze	6-5-32	125	4. J.H. Nurzhelol	1-7-33	135
5. N.V. Sail	14-2-33	125	5. A.H. Darasalamwala	4-8-33	130

I am sure you will agree with me that a grave injustice is being done to these officials. Equity and justice demand that a senior person should draw more, or at least not less, pay than his junior in the same cadre. I hope this anomaly will receive your attention.

3. *Task-Work Messengers Promoted as Postmen*: The pay of task work messengers, who are promoted to the postmen cadre is fixed in the latter grade on the basis of their average earnings as task work messengers. As the maximum of the postmen's cadre was Rs. 34/- only officials promoted before 1947 got their pay fixed at Rs. 34/-. But after 1947 the maximum of postmen scale has been Rs. 50/- and as a result officials now promoted get their pay fixed at Rs. 50/-. Thus a junior draws about Rs. 15/- more than his senior in the same grade which is again a serious anomaly. This anomaly too deserves your attention.

4. You will recall that the Union had once demanded a joint anomalies committee, such as on the railways, to deal with all the anomalies that have been created by the revision of scales, fixation, etc. But you had assured us that you would deal with the anomalies yourself. It appears, however, that even after so many months, the anomalies do continue. Should you not therefore consider the appointment of a joint committee to deal with this matter? On the railways, the Joint Advisory Committee was originally meant to be only an anomalies committee, but its scope was extended with the consent of Labour, and it now deals with other matters too that are in dispute. Likewise in the P&T you could have a joint committee with a wider scope. In any case a committee to dispose of the anomalies seems urgently to be called for. The advantage of a committee would be that the representatives

of the Department and of Labour could sit together and thrash out their differences. The committee would have to have a neutral chairman.

5. *Economy Measures:* Recently the Department has adopted a number of measures in its campaign for economy such as those mentioned below:

1. Vacancies caused by retirement etc. are not filled.
2. No substitute is allowed for officials proceeding on leave.
3. No officiating promotion is given to a man in the lower cadre when he acts in a higher cadre in leave vacancy.
4. Officials are not made permanent for years together.
5. No additional staff is assigned even when justified.

These measures are causing a great deal of hardship, both physical and monetary. The staff would have willingly put up with these hardships had they been convinced that the Department was in serious difficulties and was earnest about economy. But they find that while economy is exercised in the lower cadres, unnecessary posts like those of Labour Officers, Assistant Registrar of Cooperative Societies, Regional Complaint Officers, etc. are being retained. I also learn that very recently 10 posts of Directors were upgraded (from Rs. 1,000 to Rs. 1,300 and from Rs. 1,300 to Rs. 1,800). In the face of such incongruous policy the staff cannot have any enthusiasm for an economy drive.

6. *Indirect Retrenchment*: Recently Government had announced that they would avoid retrenchment of any kind, but I am informed that there is a kind of indirect retrenchment carried on in Bombay by the authorities who set very stiff papers and conduct examinations for recruitment and confirmation in certain grades in such a manner that the percentage of passed candidates is necessarily very low and the unsuccessful staff is discharged. This needs to be looked into.

7. I had discussed with you recently the question of supply of umbrellas and you had told me that you were considering whether some cash allowance could not be given in lieu of umbrellas, chapples, etc. I think in such matters the Department would be well advised to consult the Unions before passing orders in order to avoid adverse reactions of the staff at a later stage.

With kind regard,

Yours sincerely,
Jayaprakash Narayan

5. Address at the Journalists Association, Gorakhpur, 31 July 1950[1]

Indian journalists have contributed enormously to the political emancipation of the country, are playing well their role in the reconstruction of the country today, and are expected to do a great deal in future. It is most unfortunate, therefore, that their economic conditions are quite unsatisfactory.

It may be that like education, young men come to the profession as a last resort; but there are others also, who join journalism inspired by motives of service to the country and humanity and their aptitude for the work, and it is this type that really adorn the profession and render service to the cause. Today profit motive had entered the newspaper industry, which is attracting capitalists in large numbers. Under such conditions dangers for exploitation of journalists, particularly in the absence of a powerful union of theirs, are increasing. While in other professions through organized agitation they have gained much in respect of salaries and living conditions, journalists have achieved nothing and I would be always with the journalists in their endeavours in this direction. To me journalists are like other labouring classes of the country and their struggle is part of the countrywide labour agitation and my good wishes are with the journalists.

The present wages of journalists are most unsatisfactory although their work, particularly during night, is so exacting. While their present salaries are hardly three times of pre-war days, dearness at some places is eight to ten times. It has thus become imperative for the Government to legislate for the working conditions of the journalists and for their protection from undue competition and unemployment, at a time when unemployment is on the increase amongst the middle classes.

I have no hopes that justice would be done to journalists with regard to working conditions such as leave and provident fund rules, unless legal protection is accorded to them. Therefore, I give full support to their demands and hope that those working journalists who are not with those fighting for the cause today, would also join them.

In such a legislation, I foresee one more advantage from a political worker's viewpoint, besides the economic betterment of journalists, inasmuch as the journalists would find better security while working independently. I regret the deterioration in the high standard of news reporting that was found before the achievement of freedom, particularly in the Indian language papers. News are now interpreted in the light of the proprietors of the newspapers. Newspapermen would enjoy greater freedom after legislation covering their salaries and working conditions, and I welcome the demand for such legislation from this viewpoint too.

[1]Adapted from *National Herald*, 1 August 1950.

6. On Famine Conditions in Parts of Northern Bihar, 6 August 1950[1]

During the past few days, while on tour outside Bihar, I could gather from reports in the papers that severe scarcity of food had produced a famine situation in many parts of Purnea, Saharsa, Bhagalpur, Monghyr and Darbhanga. Reports speak of villages in which 99 per cent of the inhabitants have no corn left with them and of dozens of them having died due to starvation.

There are reports of people living on *Patua* and *Karmi* leaves. So many of them have sold ornaments of their women-folk in order to get a few morsels of food. Large numbers of small holders are said to have sold their lands and cattle to money bags at very low prices. Considerable numbers of the village poor have been forced to migrate to the towns in search of food. I gathered from the papers that this fearful situation has been produced by the failure, during the past few months, of the *bhadai* crops due to untimely as well as excessive rains in these areas.

Back in Patna, I was informed by my colleagues that this terrible situation did not develop suddenly; it had in reality been maturing for the past few months, accompanied with grave forebodings and warnings from various quarters.

The Socialist Party and the Hind Kisan Panchayat of Bihar, have for months past been trying to draw the attention of the Government to the fast deteriorating food situation in these areas. But the Government has remained unmoved. So far as the district of Saharsa is concerned, as early as April, two leaders of the Socialist Party, Comrades Bhupendra Narayan Mandal and Ramesh Jha depicted the terrible situation in the district in their statements in the *Janata*[2] and the *Indian Nation*[3] and appealed to the Government to take early measures to control the situation there, otherwise they would be faced with famine conditions in these parts. But the Government refused to accept this reality and issued a press note contradicting these statements.

In April again, at a meeting held at Dhalbajja on the borders of Purnea, Bhagalpur and Saharsa, under the auspices of the Socialist Party, Bihar and attended by Shri Karpoori Thakur, General Secretary of the Hind Kisan Panchayat, Bihar, attention of the Government was drawn to the serious food situation in the thanas of Alamnagar, Rupauli and Gopalpur. The *Janata* of April 23, wrote an editorial note on the situation in these areas. Near about this time the Bangawan Thana Kisan Sammelan also, by a resolution,

[1]Adapted from *Janata*, 6 August 1950. The statement had been issued in late July.

[2]A Hindi weekly published from Patna; organ of the Socialist Party.

[3]An English daily published from Patna.

drew the attention of the Government to the situation in the district of Saharsa.

In the course of a long article, published in the *Janata* dated May 27, Shri Karpoori Thakur gave full facts about the situation in these four districts of North Bihar. Giving his reasons for the serious food situation that had developed, he had mentioned the failure of the *rabi* crop last year owing to the rains starting before time, the destruction of the *bhadai* and paddy crops owing to excessive rain and floods and the fact that the "Hathia" rains wiped out what remained of the paddy crops as well as the cash crops of chillies and tobacco leaves. Shri Karpoori Thakur had ended this article with an appeal to the Government to declare these areas as famine-stricken areas and provide assistance to people of these areas.

The Bihar Provincial Kisan Conference which met at Muktapur (Darbhanga) on May 27 and 28, also appealed to the Government by a resolution to give immediate help to these famine-stricken areas. Shri Karpoori Thakur through a statement on June 14, again appealed to the Government to give immediate assistance to the famine affected areas in Bhagalpur, Saharsa and Purnea.

In view of these facts, it is perfectly clear that the Government has had previous information about the terrible situation that has arisen, but refused to take any notice. If the Government had paid attention to the appeals of the Socialist Party and the Hind Kisan Panchayat such an ugly situation would undoubtedly have not developed.

The most distressing part of this sad affair is that the Food Minister of Bihar still maintains that there have been no deaths due to starvation, and this in face of the fact that Shri Krishna Ballabh Sahay (Revenue Minister Bihar) accepted only a few days ago that the District Magistrate of Purnea had reported 6 deaths due to starvation.

But the question now is: what can we do to remedy the situation? It is no use now pointing out the delays and the shirking of responsibility by the Bihar Government. The food problem is a national problem. When people are dying of hunger it is hardly helpful to talk of past mistakes. But the Bihar Government must certainly stop refusing to accept facts. It is distressing and disgraceful that, face to face with famine and deaths due to starvation, Government should be trying to make up its mind whether the deaths are due to starvation or under-nourishment and poor dieting. Such regrettable mental effort in Government circles has resulted in very insufficient relief being given to forty or fifty lakhs of distressed people in Saharsa, Purnea, Bhagalpur, Monghyr and Darbhanga.

It is the time Government should realise the seriousness of the situation and accept the facts staring them in the face or else the people will have to give it a good shaking and bring it back to reality. The Socialist Party has all along taken up a constructive attitude about this matter and nothing would please it more than to go on doing so.

I, therefore, appeal to the Government to act quickly and to throw all its resources into the work of providing immediate relief to these distressed people. It should, to begin with, declare the entire starved areas of Purnea, Saharsa, Bhagalpur, Monghyr and Darbhanga as famine-stricken areas. Arrangements should be made to distribute grain free to agricultural labourers and very poor peasants. Other needy persons should receive *takkavi* loans [usually given by Government to agriculturists in distress] on large scale. *Takkavi* loans should preferably be given in the shape of grains.

Over and above securing grain from outside, grain can be obtained easily and locally from the large stocks running into lakhs of *maunds* possessed by big peasants and zamindars in these distressed areas. Government should use strong measures for procuring grain from these stocks and relieve the suffering of the people.

It would also be necessary to provide work on a large scale to agricultural workers to provide them the much needed relief. Medical treatment and food should be provided for those who have been, for months or weeks, trying to live on *Patua* or *Karmi* leaves, mango seeds and roots and plants, and have thus ruined their health or are nearing their end.

Government should also give their attention to measures for protecting poor village people from the rapacious claws of moneyed people trying to get hold of people's land or cattle or ornaments at nominal prices during this period of distress.

7. Report to the People of Bihar on Famine Conditions in Purnea District, 8 August 1950[1]

It is not possible to appreciate the situation in the affected areas except through a first-hand study. All the press reports and statements could not have given me such a picture of the reality as even a hurried visit to the spot did. Owing to transport difficulties, it was not possible to visit all the stricken areas. Yet I was able to visit the Dhamdaha area, and to talk to scores of people—peasants, *bataidars*, agricultural labourers, teachers, students. This is the situation as I found it.

My report is confined at present to Purnea district. I shall report on the other affected areas, where the situation as I have been told, is no less serious, after a personal study which I hope to undertake in a few days.

[1]*J.P. Papers* (NMML). The report was published in an abridged form in almost all newspapers in India on 9 August; the full text was later reproduced in *Janata* on 20 August 1950.

The area of Purnea that is badly affected covers roughly the area that is known as Dharampur paragana, i.e. the thanas of Rupauli, Dhamdaha, Dharahara, Kodaha and Berari. To these may be added the thanas of Manihari, Katihar, Kadwa and part of Sadar thana. Strangely enough, it is exactly this area that has traditionally been known as the granary of Purnea, if not of the entire State. That such a fertile area should be stricken with famine, and that there should be starvation deaths there, would have been unbelievable, had it not been for the tragic truth. All the persons I met were unanimous that such a calamity as the present one had never afflicted the land in living memory.

Let me describe briefly this calamity that has stricken this fair land. There are two aspects of it: one economic and the other physical.

For the last three years the economy of the district had been undergoing a change. The partition of Bengal had given a fillip to jute-growing in Purnea. As a result a considerable part of the acreage sown to paddy has passed under jute. The popular estimate, for the accuracy of which I cannot vouch, is 25 per cent. Whatever may be the accurate figure, it is undeniable that the spread of jute-cultivation has led to a considerable reduction in the district's output of rice. Purnea, long regarded as a surplus district, is surely no longer such. Indeed it might already have become a deficit area. This factor has considerable bearing on the food situation in the district.

Another element of the economic aspect is the arrangement that the Bihar Government had made with the rice mills in Purnea. According to that arrangement a portion of the rice milled was bought by the Government at fixed prices and the mills were left free to sell the remaining rice anywhere and at any price they wished. In this manner, lakhs of maunds of rice were exported from Purnea.

The physical aspect of the present calamity is the successive failure of crops due to natural causes. The last year's *agahani* crops of rice, as well as the *rabi* crop, was considerably damaged owing to untimely rains. The partial failure of these crops had already caused some distress to the poor and middle sections of the population. On top of it all came the present calamity; namely the total (this word needs to be emphasised) destruction of the standing maize crop, both *jethua* and *bhadai*, due to untimely and unprecedently heavy rains. It should be remembered that it is this maize crop that has always been the mainstay of the villagers and that tided them over till next *agahani* paddy crop. Indeed a large part of this maize used to be exported to the deficit areas of Bihar. The rains which destroyed the maize crop have also damaged the standing jute crop, the extent of the damage being estimated by the villagers as 25 per cent to 50 per cent from area to area.

The total destruction of the maize crop on top of the partial failure of previous *agahani* and *rabi* crops has created an acute situation of deprivation affecting agricultural labourers, *bataidars*, small and medium peasants, who together constitute 90 per cent if not more of the village population. The approximate population of the affected area of Purnea would be roughly ten lakhs. Of these nine lakhs have surely been severely hit.

Mr. K.M. Munshi Food and Agriculture Minister, Government of India and the State Government have been at some pains to assure the people that there is no famine and that there is enough grain to keep the wolf away from the door. I am afraid they have completely failed to appreciate the situation. Speaking for Purnea alone, it is likely that there is enough rice for some months in the district. But this rice is with the rice-mills, the dealers and the prosperous peasants and landlords. Therefore this does not help the agricultural labourers, the *bataidars*, the small peasants, who have no money to buy the rice. Thus we have a situation in which there is enough food on one side and starvation on the other. It is as if the wheels of the economy of the district have stopped.

This exactly is the crux of the situation. The wheels of the economic life of the people in the affected areas have actually come to a stop; and the main task of the Government is to set these wheels going again. If this is not done, in another couple of months the situation would become far graver than today.

The wheels of economy in the affected parts of Purnea have stopped because owing to the successive failure of crops and particularly the total failure of the maize crop, small and medium peasants, who constitute the bulk of the peasantry there, have no resources left to finance their agricultural operations. This is the season for sowing of the *agahani* [winter] paddy crop, but except for a handful of the prosperous peasants, the rest are not in a position to undertake these operations. The normal channels of agricultural financing have dried up, because the *mahajans* are reluctant to lend money to the peasants, who in normal years were able to borrow on the strength of their maize and jute crops. When the peasants are unable to borrow the *bataidars* and agricultural labourers are forced to ramian idle, and the wheel of agriculture does not turn. Thus while there may be enough rice in Purnea with the mills, the prosperous peasants and the dealers, the people may still starve because there is no employment and economic activity.

The main problem in Purnea, therefore, is to help the agriculturists to carry on their normal agricultural operations of this season, so that there may be current employment and circulation of money and also that the next *agahani* paddy crop may be produced.

1. The solution is obvious. Timely and adequate *takkavi* loans must be given by the Government. An effort in this direction has actually been made. But as is the tragedy with all offical measures, the *takkavi* granted so far is

far from being adequate and there is every fear that further loans would be given when the time would have passed. I had heard on my visit that generally small loans had been given which were insufficient to finance agricultural operations, with the result that the money was spent on personal consumption. On the other hand, I also heard that loans were sometimes given to persons who did not need them so that money obtained from the Government was loaned out on usurious interests. What is required is not tinkering, but a bold and imaginative step. To do too little is worse than doing nothing.

In connection with *takkavi*, there was another serious objection of which I was told by peasants themselves. It appears that these loans are given only when five agriculturists, make a joint application. This is an unnecessary impediment and must be removed. If there is a legal difficulty, an ordinance might be passed to remove it. Surely such an ordinance would be far more justifiable than many others.

In Purnea the far larger part of cultivation is carried on by *bataidars* or tenants at will. These have no rights in the lands they cultivate and so cannot offer any landed security. But unless the *bataidars* are enabled to carry on, cultivation would suffer greatly. Therefore these cultivators too must be included in the scope of the *takkavi* loans.

2. Apart from *takkavi* loans, certain other steps would be needed to ease the distress in the district. Fair price grain shops must be opened in every circle and to prevent black-marketing, ration cards should be introduced. I was told that in the few control shops that had been opened, a part of the grain supplied was being black-marketed.

3. The Government have already frozen the rice with the mills. It is further necessary to freeze the grain with the prosperous peasants, landlords and the big jotadars and to buy it all at fixed prices.

4. Public works on a big scale should be started to provide employment. Among such works may be road and bund building, digging of canals and other irrigation works, tilling of *parati* lands, roap-making, etc. I was told that a few hundred labourers had been employed in road-building in Purnea. But this work was being executed through contractors who were pocketing a substantial part of the benefit. Wages should be paid in grain as far as possible.

5. In specially severe cases, relief in the shape of free distribution of grains should be undertaken.

6. Enough medical units should be detailed in every thana to cope with epidemics and diseases that are bound to accompany famine conditions.

7. A proper machinery should be devised to carry out these measures. Representative and all-parties relief committees should be set up at the district headquarters and in every thana. The district committee should be

presided over by the District officer and the thana committees by magistrates nominated by the latter. In every thana as many relief centres as possible should be opened to coordinate all the relief operations in the area, such as distribution of relief, running of fair-price shops, public works, medical relief etc.

The few committees that have been set up are largely one-party bodies not that has led to corruption, discrimination and inefficiency. It is necessary that all these committees and centres are representative of all organizations and sections of the public.

8. In order that the gravity of the situation is realised and adequate steps are taken with requisite speed and effectiveness and the required relief rendered, *it is necessary to declare the entire affected area of the State (and not only the area in Purnea) a famine area.*

I am sure that if these steps are taken with energy and speed, the situation in Purnea at least can be mended and distress alleviated to a large extent.

Before I close, I should like to protest against the repression of socialist workers in the district. Even much a prominent worker as Shri Mohit Pandit has been imprisoned. I understand he is being implicated in the grain looting case in the Rupauli thana. This is a fantastic charge to be made against such a fine public worker. I hope the authorities will release him immediately so that he might help in the solution of the difficult problem facing the district.

Finally, it is a matter of great pity that ministerial pronouncements have so far been extremely light-hearted and complacent. One hopes that it would not be necessary for thousands of innocent lives to be lost before those in power shall wake up to the realities and to their responsibilities. So far the people have been very patient with their masters, but their patience is fraying now and it may soon be too late to act.

8. To Asoka Mehta, 10 August 1950[1]

Dear Asoka,

You may be wondering what has happened to me. I shall give you a brief report of what I have been doing since I left Bombay.

I arrived here [Patna] on the 27th of last month. The next day I called a meeting of comrades present here to consider the food situation in the Province. Among those present were: Ramanandan, Benipuri, Chand and the Provincial Secretaries. As a result of the discussions a statement was prepared in Hindi which was issued in my name. Its English translation was made by B.P. Sinha and it appeared in full in the local papers.[2] Copies

[1]*J.P. Papers* (NMML).

[2]For the text of the statement see *ante* item 6.

of the statement were sent to you and the *Janata*. It was also decided at the meeting that I should leave the very next day to visit some of the affected areas. I accordingly went to Purnea. I have published a report on Purnea on my return,[3] copies of which too have already been sent to you and the *Janata.* I am asking Shanker[4] to send you press cuttings from the local papers so that you may have an idea of the publicity that we are able to get on this question. The third decision that was taken at the preliminary meeting of the 28th was that the Provincial Party Executive and the Kisan Panchayat Executive and district secretaries should be called to Patna for a meeting on the 7th and 8th of August. This meeting has already been held and the whole work has been organized. I am asking the Provincial Secretary to send you minutes of the meeting. One result of this meeting was that I was asked to give some time to Bihar to tour the affected areas. I also was feeling since I returned that it would not be right for me to leave the province so abruptly at a time like this. So my tour has been fixed up from the 28th of August to the 11th of September. Among other things this means that my Andhra tour will have to be postponed by almost a month. I am writing to Annapurnaiah[5] about it.

I am in Patna till the 16th morning when I would be leaving for Delhi. I hope, in the next few days, to be able to write a few articles which I was asked to do by Secretaries' meeting. On my return from Jaipur I shall stop for a day at Banaras to address the students of the Hindu University and Vidyapith.

Among the decisions of the Provincial meeting of the 7th and 8th August was one to observe August 10 to 25 as a famine fortnight during which hunger marches, famine conferences, etc. would be held throughout the affected area. On the 27th when I return to Patna a public meeting will be held on the famine situation.

Another decision was that the Provincial Party and the Kisan Panchayat should jointly place a memorandum before the Provincial Government and see the Chief Minister or the Food Minister in a deputation. The statement prepared at the meeting of the 7th and 8th August is being released today and copies of it are being sent to you.

More about my programme. From Purnea I went to Gorakhpur to attend the first annual conference of the O.T. Railway Employees Union. The Conference was a great success inspite of Bholanath Chowdhry's[6] effort to create mischief. I also addressed a very largely attended Party workers'

[3] See *ante*, item 7

[4] Shanker Shetty; J.P.'s Private Secretary at that time.

[5] Madduri Annapurnayya (1900-53); General Secretary of the Socialist Party in Andhra.

[6] Bholanath Chowdhry; leader of a section of railwaymen, opposed to the All India Railwaymen's Federation, and hostile to J.P. and the Socialist Party.

meeting at Gorakhpur and a public meeting in the evening which had to be abandoned after some time due to heavy downpour. From Gorakhpur I went to Deoria which is the district of Genda Singh, the Provincial Secretary. There too there was a good workers' meeting and a public meeting. From Deoria I went to Mau in Azamgarh district where the main function was a workers' meeting. Workers from all the neighbouring districts, i.e. Jaunpore, Ballia, Ghazipur in addition to that of Azamgarh had assembled. At all these meetings I spoke about Madras Conference and the Party programme. The longest I spoke was at Mau which was for 4 hours! At Deoria a purse of Rs. 1,200/- was presented to me, but due to the financial situation of the Province, I did not take the Centre's share from it. The money was left behind with Genda Singh. From Mau I went to Calcutta via Benaras to attend the Bengal Provincial Party Conference. There was a better spirit prevailing at this conference than in previous years and mutual wranglings and recriminations were far less marked. You would be happy to know that the election of office-bearers and the Executive was held without any contest. This was largely due to improved relations among Bengal comrades and Prem's[5] efforts to smoothen out things. Lohia also attended the Conference and addressed both the delegates and the open session. Sibnath [Banerjee] was elected Chairman and Shakti Provincial Secretary.

At Calcutta I took an opportunity of meeting Mr. Hemanta Basu who was Secretary of the Congress Parliamentary Party in the Bengal Assembly and who has always been a sort of right-hand man of Suresh Mazumdar.[7] Hemanta Basu resigned from the Congress a month ago. I shall tell you about my talk with him when we meet at Jaipur.

I hope you have been able to collect some of the amounts that had been promised. You need not write to me about them. We shall discuss that at Jaipur. I am sorry, I was not able to collect as much as I should have in Bombay. But due to the fact that just before going to Madras I had to collect something like Rs. 15,000/-, I found it difficult to make a large collection so soon after. However, if the promises made are carried out, you should have no worry for the next couple of months at least. I am writing to Rameshwar Rao again about the promised amount in Hyderabad.

At Calcutta the annual general meeting of the Khoj Parishad was held where the decisions taken at the Lucknow Governors' meeting were ratified.

[7]Suresh Chandra Majumdar (1888-1954); political leader and journalist, assciated with Jugantar Group, a secret revolutionary organization of Bengal in early twentieth century; took part in Non-Cooperation Movement, 1921; President North Calcutta Congress Committee, 1927-37; helped Subhas Bose in leaving the country, 1941; imprisoned in Quit India Movement, 1942; elected to Bengal Legislative Assembly twice in 1943 and 1952. Started *Anand Bazar Patrika* 1922 along with Prafulla Kumar Sarkar, floated a Bengali weekly, *Desh* 1933 followed by an English daily *Hindustan Standard* in 1937.

It was decided *inter alia* that the head office should be shifted to Bombay. Satyabrota Sen has applied to the Registrar in Calcutta to make the necessary change in the Articles, etc. of the Parishad. According to those articles, three governors have to retire periodically. The three who retired at Calcutta were: Suren Dwivedy,[8] Satyabrota Sen and Prof. S.N. Ray. In their places the following new governors were appointed: yourself, Dantwala and D.P. Mookerjee of Lucknow. It was also decided that a meeting of the Council of Governors should be called at Jaipur on the 23rd of August at 4 p.m. Satu Sen having been retired from the governorship, he is no longer the General Secretary of the Parishad and therefore in the absence of a secretary I undertook to issue notices for this meeting. You must persuade Dantwala to attend this meeting because it will be there that the future policy and programme of the Parishad will be decided.

More when we meet.

Yours affectionately,
Jayaprakash

[8]Surendranath Dwivedy (1913-); joined Indian National Congress in 1930; was arrested and imprisoned several times; one of the founder members of Congress Socialist Party in 1934; founded and edited an Oriya weekly entitled "Krishak"; he was a prolific writer; Deputy Chairman P.S.P., 1956-62; M.P. Rajya Sabha, 1952-6, M.P. Lok Sabha 1962-7; Governor of Arunachal Pradesh, 1991-3.

9. To Asoka Mehta, 11 August 1950[1]

Dear Asoka,

This is a sort of a postscript to the letter I wrote you yesterday. In view of the change in my Andhra programme, it would not be possible for me any more to undertake the Cochin-Travancore tour. I am sorry about this, but after 40 days in Andhra I must go back to Bihar and also take a little rest. The U.P. Party in view of its financial position was anxious to arrange a month's tour for me. If you approve of this I will have to give the whole of December to that Province. In any case you should write to Wilson that my tour programme must be cancelled or that some one else would do the job in my place. I am also writing to Wilson about this.

Shanker has posted today a copy of an article which I had to write under Murlibabu's persistent pressure for the *Spark*. It is not exactly the kind of article that I should like to write for the *Janata*, but you and Rohit may make such use of it as you wish.

[1]*J.P. Papers* (NMML).

Please don't forget to bring with you "Socialised Agriculture in the USSR".

Yours,
J.P.

P.S. After I wrote the above I read your letter of August 8, about Suren Dwivedy's demand. Arrears on account of subventions which could not be remitted can hardly be claimed as a matter of right. However, in view of the financial position of the Orissa Party and of its fine work I would advise you if you can to send them Rs. 500/- a month for the next 3 or 4 months. We can further discuss this matter with Dwivedy at Jaipur.

10. Statement at Press Conference regarding Starvation Deaths in North Bihar, Patna, 11 August 1950[1]

I have been deeply disappointed at India's Food Minister K.M. Munshi's statement that there is no famine nor starvation in Bihar.

I can say from personal knowledge that the situation in a very big area in North Bihar is grave, and unless proper steps are taken immediately to help the cultivators for raising the next crops by distributing *takkavi* loans and seeds on a large scale, there will be repetition of the Bengal famine of 1943.

Ninety cases of what I call authentic starvation deaths have been reported to the Socialist Party from the famine areas of Bihar and the names and addresses of 87 persons who died are with me.

Figures of dead are as follows:

Saharsa 1, Kishanganj thana 15, Alamnagar 3, Madhepura 3, Purnea Rupauli and Dhamdaha 58, Bhagalpur (Naugachchia thana) 7.

I regret that Government are still showing an unwillingness to declare the affected areas as famine areas due to a false sense of prestige, while admitting themselves that acute scarcity is prevailing. If these areas are declared famine areas, aid from international organizations can also be sought and obtained.

I also criticise the Bihar Government's attitude of throwing the blame on the Centre for not rendering adequate assistance. Had the Bihar Government informed the Centre of the extent of the deficit earlier and made a strong representation with facts and figures, the Government of India would not have ignored it.

Besides rendering relief, Government should also take drastic measures

[1]Adapted from *Tribune*, 13 August 1950.

to control the prices and unearth hoarded stocks. The C.I.D. can easily detect hoarders and profiteers.

11. To Rafi Ahmed Kidwai, 18 August 1950[1]

My dear Rafi Saheb,

In the course of our talk yesterday I referred to another case of anomaly the details of which I did not remember and which you promised to consider.

The anomaly is in regard to the fixation of pay of some clerks in the office of the Postmaster General, Bombay. I am enclosing herewith copies of two letters addressed to you by the General Secretary of the Union to which these officials belong. The letters are fully self-explanatory. Two factors primarily contribute to the anomaly. (1) The officials are denied the benefit of their service to the extent of about 5 years in the Second Division cadre. This seems to me to be very unfair, especially in view of the fact that similar service of the officials promoted from the subordinate P.& T. offices to the First Division cadre in the P.M.G.'s office, is allowed to be counted after deducting two years, in lieu of the benefit they get in the higher initial pay in the First Division scale. (2) The second factor is the comparatively smaller relief granted to these officials by the Adjudicator in 1946, viz. 5 per cent awarded to other clerical staff. The Adjudicator's presumption that all First Division clerks in the P.M.G.'s office were direct recruits and get the advantage of a higher initial pay and higher rate of increments, was obviously incorrect. The injustice done to these officials on this account ought to be removed as early as possible. After going through their case I feel convinced that they have a genuine grievance which requires to be redressed immediately.

I may add that the cost involved in conceding the request will not be much, as the member of officials affected is hardly about fifty in the whole of India, only those recruited before 1938 being hit the hardest. Those recruited after that get the benefit of officiating promotion in the First Division cadre almost from the beginning of their service and also a sudden lift in their pay on account of the unified scales of pay.

I shall be glad if you will be good enough to give your personal attention to this case and issue early orders so as to ensure that justice is done to these officials and that they get at least as much as their juniors, if not more.

Yours sincerely,
Jayaprakash

[1]*Brahmanand Papers* (NMML).

12. To Vallabhbhai Patel, 19 August 1950[1]

My dear Sardar Saheb,

Narendra Deva's secretary, Ajaya, whose home is in Gwalior just telephoned to me from Gwalior to say that my friends and prominent members of the Socialist Party, Shri S.M. Joshi and Shri Ganga Sharan Sinha of Patna were arrested yesterday at the Gwalior railway station. This news has greatly angered and distressed me. I cannot describe this act as anything else but madness.

Gangababu and Joshi are members of a control commission which the Madras Conference of the Socialist Party set up to deal with indiscipline and disputes within the Party. For some time past there has been trouble in the Gwalior and Madhya Bharat Party and I know that the tour programme of Joshi and Gangababu had been fixed up some weeks before. But even if it had not been so and if these friends were visiting Gwalior in connection with the recent disturbances there, there was no justification in dealing with them as if they were Movalis[2]. These friends are as responsible and patriotic as any other two individuals can be either in the services or in the ministries. It is possible that you yourself might be knowing them. I do hope that this outrage will be immediately set right.

In connection with the disturbances in Gwalior, may I suggest that an impartial judicial enquiry and not a departmental or official enquiry be held? That will go a long way in allaying public discontent.

I have been encouraged to write this letter in view of the cordial talk we had yesterday.

With kind regards and wishing you the best of health.

Very sincerely yours,
J.P.

[1]*J.P. Papers* (NMML).
[2]See Appendix 1 for Patel's reply to J.P.

13. To Jawaharlal Nehru, 21 August 1950[1]

Dear Bhai,

I shall be passing through Delhi on my return from Jaipur to Patna. I wonder if I could see you on the 24th, for a somewhat longish talk. I shall be arriving at Delhi on the 24th morning and leave the next day morning. So any time during the day or the night will suit me. As soon as I arrive I shall ring up Mathai[2] and find out.

[1]*Brahmanand Papers* (NMML).
[2]M.O. Mathai (1909-81); Special Assistant to Nehru till 1959.

Among the questions that I should like to discuss with you is one regarding the system of distributive voting.

As a second choice we are prepared to accept single-member constituencies, but where the Government itself is going to have plural-constituencies, it is very unfair to introduce the distributive system. As far as I am aware, every political party in the country, except the Congress about whose views I am not sure, is opposed to the distributive system. No matter what alternative system these parties may advocate, they are all united in opposing the distributive system. It would not be wise nor fair to use the overwhelming Congress majority to flout this united opinion of the Opposition.

Regarding the Labour Bills, as suggested by you, we had sent a memorandum to the Labour Ministry which has, through Shri Dharam Vir,[3] sent us its reactions. Asoka and I saw Shri Jagjivan Ram[4] last evening. It appears that certain changes are going to be made in the draft Bills, as also that, if I am not disclosing any secret, the Hon'ble Labour Minister[5] himself felt helpless in certain matters. Be that as it may, the agitation against the Bills shall continue till independent labour is satisfied that the obnoxious features of the Bills have been removed or that the Bills are going to be dropped.

I also wish to draw your attention to recurring police firings and train accidents. Every time such an incident takes place, non-Congress public opinion invariably demands judicial and public enquiries. Unfortunately your Government or the State Governments have so far steadfastly resisted these demands. It strikes me that this is not how a popular government should behave.

I hope you remember that after the Bihta train accident, the British instituted a public enquiry and the Award has a far-reaching effect on the Railways. Recently, train smashes far more serious than the Bihta one, have taken place, but except for Departmental enquiries, nothing more has been done and the plea of sabotage seems to have become a convenient handle for the Administration.

Likewise, there have been a distressing number of firing in the country, but the Government never has shown the courage to hold a judicial and public enquiry. All this is hurting the nation because harmful traditions are

[3]Dharam Vira (1906-2000); joined ICS in 1930, held various posts in U.P.; joined Government of India 1941; Joint Secretary to Cabinet 1947-50; Principal Private Secretary to Prime Minister, 1950-1; Ambassador to Czechoslovakia 1954-6; Secretary, Ministry of Rehabilitation 1956-62; Chief Commissioner Delhi 1963-4; Cabinet Secretary 1964-6; Governor of Punjab and Haryana 1966-7, West Bengal 1967-9 and Mysore 1969-71.

[4]Jagjivan Ram. For biographical note see *JPSW*, Vol. IV, p. 224.

[5]Refers to Jagjivan Ram.

being built up, discontentment is aggravated and a climate of bitterness is becoming all-pervasive.

More when we meet. With kind regards,

Affectionately yours,
J.P.

14. To Gopalaswami Ayyangar, 22 August 1950[1]

Dear Shri Ayyangar,

I am writing to you about an upper primary school at Dinapore run by the staff for their children.

The Baliga Upper Primary School was started on 2.12.1947 by the efforts of the staff, notably of Shri A.M.A.R. Fatmi, and named after Shri B.S.D. Baliga, Senior Superintendent, Way and Works.

The school was recognised by the Government of Bihar on 3rd April 1948.

The present position of the school is as follows:

(a) There are nine teachers, one Head Master and two chowkidars.
(b) There are 448 students of which 350 are the sons of railway employees, mostly of class IV.
(c) This is the only school for the primary education of the children of the railway employees.
(d) The school is run by a managing committee of which Shri B.S.D. Baliga, S.S.W., Dinapore, is the president and Shri A.M.A.R. Fatmi is the founder secretary. All other members are railway employees.

The school was being run mainly on tuition fees collected from the students. That the school has been run well should be apparent from the remarks of the Inspector of Schools, who concluded a long inspection note thus:

"Inspection of such schools is really a pleasure. It has been rightly established and well run. It primarily serves the interest of the menial staff of the railway employees and the managers deserve thanks. They have rightly taken up the cause of those who deserved to be looked after. The institution has been now run on smooth lines and its overwhelming strength has proved its necessity. The Railway authorities should now take it in its

[1]*J.P. Papers* (NMML).

own management. It will be a feeder to the high school as well."

Now, the State Government decided some time ago that primary education should be entirely free. In pursuance of that decision the Government instructed last April that no fees be collected from the students of the Baliga School.

This has placed the school in a most difficult position and unless some way out is found there will be no option but to close it down. That will be a great pity, for nearly 500 boys will be denied the opportunity of receiving even primary education.

The State Government, of course, while making primary education free, should have made provision for the running of at least the existing schools. But criticism of the Government will hardly help the school or the children concerned. I am therefore writing to request you to come to the rescue of this little institution and keep it going. The E.I. Railway runs a High School at Dinapore, but there is no primary school except a European Day School in which there are naturally a very few students. The Administration, I understand, spends Rs.600/- a month upon the European school. The other children far larger in number and of poorer parents should not suffer just because they belong to the Indian race! I am sure you will do the needful in this matter.

With kind regards,

Sincerely yours,

Jayaprakash

15. To H.M. Jagtiani, 23 August 1950[1]

Dear Shri Jagtiani,[2]

I am writing to you about Shri Panchkari Banerjee, Secretary of the Calcutta branch of the EIR Employees' Union. I know Shri Banerjee for the last several years as a devoted and competent trade unionist. I have also found him to be an able and honest person.

Shri Banerjee writes to me that for some reason or the other the Administration or, at any rate some of its officers have been trying to humiliate him and restrict his legitimate trade union activities. Now the whole policy of the Government with regard to the scope that its employees should be permitted for trade union activities is somewhat indefinite. Yet it has been a convention so far and it also seems to be the future intention of

[1] *J.P. Papers* (NMML).

[2] H.M. Jagtiani; General Manager, East Indian Railway, Calcutta.

the Government that those of its employees who hold executive posts in their unions should be given enough latitude to attend to their trade union work. In this connection, I should also draw your attention to the following remarks of the Central Pay Commission: "If the Government wish to encourage management (of union) by servicemen, they must see (1) that official work of public servants holding responsible office in the Unions and representing the union on the staff side shall be so arranged as to ensure that they are not called upon to carry too heavy a burden of official work. . . ."

The recent Labour Bills that have been introduced in Parliament lay the utmost possible emphasis on the desirability of Government employees managing their unions themselves. But that would be impossible if the employees were not given freedom and opportunity to work for their unions during office hours.

If my interpretation of Government policy is not incorrect, it seems to me to be wrong deliberately to shift Shri Panchkari Banerjee to a section where he will be constantly under the immediate and direct supervision of his officers and where members of the staff or his colleagues on the executive of the union cannot come to speak to him about their difficulties. As Secretary of the Branch Union, Shri Panchkari Banerjee should be given freedom and a light job so that he may be able to attend to his work as union official and contact members of the staff and the officers concerned.

I hope you will be good enough to look into this matter and prevent this petty and vindictive treatment of an accredited trade union official.

When I was at Delhi for the Working Committee meeting of the All India Railwaymen's Federation, I was told about the discharge of 12 workers of the Jamalpur workshop on the ground that they had been convicted by a Court to a term of imprisonment. I understand that the case against these workers was not at all of a criminal nature nor did it involve any moral turpitude, but had arisen out of a conflict between rival unions, the 12 workers concerned belonging to the EIR Employees Union. When I go to Patna I shall send you the details.

Yours sincerely,
Jayaprakash

16. To Hirday Nath Kunzru, 26 August 1950[1]

My dear Hridaya Nathji,[2]

I regret the delay in replying to your letter of August 9. It would have given me the greatest pleasure to attend the Pacific Relations Conference, but

[1] *J.P. Papers* (NMML).

[2] Hridaya Nath Kunzru; eminent liberal leader, at that time President, Indian Council of World affairs, New Delhi.

unfortunately I would be touring Andhra from September 23 to the end of October. This programme was fixed a long time ago, and it is not possible to alter it now. I hope therefore that you will excuse me for my inability to participate in this important Conference.

With kind regards,

Sincerely yours,
J.P.

17. To K.K. Menon, 27 August 1950[1]

Dear K.K.,

I thank you for your letters of August 17 and 24. I am sorry that my letter reached you late and that you could not go to Jaipur.

The National Union of Students have fixed their dates and I believe Jawaharlal is going to Bombay on the 15th to inaugurate the open session of the conference. In any case I shall be in Bombay on the 14th. I have to go to Poona for a day for the conference of the civilian employees of the Defence Service. S.M.[2] when I met him at Jaipur promised to fix the final date and inform me here. I had given him two dates from which to choose, 16th or 17th of September. For the Standing Committee you may fix either the 14th or one of the two dates that I have given to S.M. You may find out from him which of the two he is accepting for the Defence workers' meeting.

I am enclosing herewith a letter received from Kunwar Jagdish Prasad, with copies of resolutions of the U.P. Zamindars' Association.

At Delhi I spoke both to Jawaharlal and Ambedkar about the system of voting. Ambedkar is helpless and Jawaharlal did not seem to be at all interested. In fact, he did not seem to understand what the different systems actually were. His secretary, M.O. Mathai, told me that he is interested in the matter and probably he has been asked by Jawaharlal to collect the relevant material. I am writing to Shri Sukumar Sen and also to Rajen Babu. Public agitation and education of public opinion on this question should continue. Paranjpye's article did not appear in the press on this side. You may send out copies again to the Calcutta, Patna, U.P. and Delhi press with a covering letter to the editors concerned to give publicity to the article in view of the importance of the subject dealt with. I wrote a short article some days ago which the PTI accepted as a feature article and which, I understand, is going to be released by it on September 3.

Regarding delimitation, the National Executive decided at Jaipur to ask every provincial branch to have delimitation proposals prepared

[1] *J.P. Papers* (NMML).
[2] S.M.—refers to S.M. Joshi.

independently by the provincial branch itself and send them to the Chief Election Commissioner. I believe some branches are already at work. In Bihar some progress has been made and by the end of the month, perhaps, the work may be finished.

The instances of gerrymandering that you have received from Madhya Bharat and elsewhere, should be given publicity on behalf of the Secretariat of the Standing Committee. You may issue a joint press statement to that effect.

Regarding inviting a few Congressmen to the Standing Committee, I think no useful purpose would be served. What is more important is propaganda and educating of the public. That, I am afraid, is not being done adequately. You may try the *Times of India*, which might give better publicity to our views at least on this matter. If you directly contact Lala Feroz Chand,[3] you may find it more useful.

Yours sincerely,
J.P.

[3]Lala Feroz Chand (1899-1974); veteran journalist and freedom fighter, former editor of *Times of India*, Managing Editor of *Samachar Bharati*, closely associated with Lala Lajpat Rai; served as his Private Secretary.

18. Address at the Inaugural Session of the Nav Sanskriti Sangh, Varanasi, 27 August 1950[1]

The new Indian culture should be national and artistic in character and it should be the depiction of the life of the common man of the country. The builders of the new Indian culture would have to face various kinds of problems. There is no national church here like that in Great Britain and the village pandits have got great hold over the illiterate masses living in the Indian villages. People have got great faith in old dogmas. They are in the grip of famine and very badly divided. The country is a subcontinent comprising various races who speak different languages. Keeping these things in view, they have to build their culture in such a fashion that everybody may accept it ungrudgingly. The new culture should have a spirit of harmonising diverese elements into one.

[1]Adapted from report in *National Herald*, 28 August 1950.

19. Speech on the Food Situation in Bihar, Patna, 28 August 1950[1]

The Socialists would start picketing before grain shops in Patna shortly if it is found that stocks are held back for the purpose of hoarding and black-marketing by the dealers.

The food situation in Bihar has not become acute all of a sudden. The situation in Saharsa and Darbhanga particularly had been deteriorating alarmingly for some months and the Socialist Party had drawn attention to it long ago without any effect. The situation in Bihar has been allowed to deteriorate due to the complacency of the Bihar Government.

There are only three ways of solving the food problem. The social and economic structure must be changed, fresh cultivable waste land must be brought under cultivation and a land army must be raised for the purpose. Such measures had been undertaken with profit in other countries, but the authorities in this country have shown no inclination to derive benefit from such examples.

I want that in scarcity areas of Bihar at least one relief centre and one fair price shop should be opened in every circle consisting of about 15 villages. Efforts to render relief through the official machinery with the aid of the Congress only has led to corruption and favouritism and relief has not reached deserving people. If the State Government is sincere, it should set up all-party relief committees everywhere to supervise the relief operations.

The Government has arrested prominent Socialist workers in Daltongaj in Palamu district for having led demonstrations against black-marketeers and hoarders when food stocks suddenly vanished from the local markets. I regret that instead of punishing the hoarders and profiteers, Government has penalized the demonstrators. I warn the Government that the Socialists would not hesitate to fill the jails of the State if that becomes necessary for bringing hoarded food stocks into the market.

[1]Adapted from *Hindustan Times*, 29 August 1950.

20. 'Social Democracy in Free India', 28 August 1950[1]

The concept of social democracy developed in Western Europe largely as a result of the Labour and Socialist movements. When the overthrow of feudalism and establishment of political democracy brought disillusionment, attention was devoted to the social and economic aspects of democracy.

[1]Adapted from *Tribune*, 28 August 1950.

We in India are passing through a similar stage today. The overthrow of British Imperialism and the achievement of freedom have already brought deep disillusionment and disappointment. I have heard educated and sensible persons remark that British rule was better than what we have today. Likewise, in the Indian States it is common talk that the Princely rule was more desirable than rule by the popular ministries.

In India the foundations even of political democracy have not been firmly laid down. The 1950 Constitution is undoubtedly a major step in that direction. But that Constitution itself is defective in many parts and secondly it still remains largely on paper and no one can tell when it will come to be fully enforeced. Franchise, for instance, has become the constitutional right of every adult citizen in India, but the present Governments at the Centre and in the States do not represent the majority of the adult citizens of this country.

Further, the Constitution does not provide for the deliberate creation of social democracy. While, on the one hand, certain of its provisions seriously limit the unfoldment of political democracy such as the restrictions on civil liberties and extraordinary powers given to the Executive in the States and at the Centre, on the other hand, certain other provisions put serious obstacles in the path of social democracy such as the clauses relating to compensation for property taken over by the State.

Thus we have started with serious constitutional handicaps, if we have started at all, towards social democracy. The Nehru Government is, through its official pronouncements in Parliament, pledged more or less to preserve the existing social order. The constitutional impediments to the creation of a new society are not likely to be apparent till a Socialist Government is established and it comes to grips with the Constitution and the Judiciary which have been specially charged to protect property. When that occasion arrives it will be found necessary either drastically to alter the Constitution or scrap it altogether and convene a new Constituent Assembly to draft a more inspiring and progressive organic law.

Apart from the Constitution, there appear to be other powerful social forces in free India which stand in the way of social democracy. One of these forces is that of communalism. Another is represented by the caste system. Since the advent of freedom, communalism for one reason or another has been in the ascendance. The Congress which in the days of the freedom struggle was a powerful anti-communal force, has, in the states such as the Punjab and Bengal, become deeply infected with the virus of communalism. Communalism is an enemy of democracy, political or social, because it denies to other communities than the chosen one equal rights and privileges.

The caste system in India is the largest obstacle in the path of social democracy. Caste and class privileges are synonymous in our society. The present Government, for instance, is entirely in the hands of the few so-called higher castes: Brahmins, Kshatriyas, Vaishas, Kayasthas, Khatris, etc. Likewise in the economic sphere; princes, zamindars, jagirdars, industrialists, merchants, and the wealthy of the professions almost exclusively belong to these upper castes. The backward and depressed castes, the tribal peoples have no or little share in political or economic power and privilege even in free India. For the achievement of social democracy it is not only necessary to establish a legal equality among castes and creeds, but also to produce in reality a social system in which the disprivileged and dispossessed castes of today come to acquire through the preponderance of their numbers a preponderant position in the social and economic life of the nation. This, perhaps, would be the most difficult task that social democracy will face in this country; far more difficult than merely the abolition of zamindari or nationalisation of industry. For, it is likely that abolition of feudalism and capitalism may still leave effective economic power in the hands of the upper castes. In Bihar, for instance, abolition of zamindari, if and when it becomes a fact, is not going to affect very much the hierarchy of castes that obtains today. The Brahmins and the Bhumihars and Kshatriyas will still remain at the top and the Ahirs and Kurmis and the Harijans and Adivasis will remain where they are.

In other class societies of the world, the problem of social democracy is mainly economic; in other words the abolition of economic classes. In India the problem is two-fold: the abolition of economic classes as well as of social castes. In the words of Mahatma Gandhi the problem of social democracy in India is that of establishing a classless and casteless society.

Turning to the economic aspects of social democracy, namely that of abolition of economic classes, it is painful to find that since the achievement of freedom, the privileged classes have grown in strength rather than the contrary. This might cause surprise at first. The popular belief, perhaps, is that since the achievement of freedom, the reactionary forces have been on the run. However, quite the opposite is the truth. During the British days the reactionary economic forces, namely, the feudal lords and the capitalists had no strength of their own except what was lent to them by the foreign power. A section of the capitalists, of course, by aligning itself with the national movement, had acquired a certain prestige, but even that section was not a force by itself.

Since the establishment of Congress rule there has been a polarisation of economic interests and political power. Feudalism, represented by the princes and the zamindars, as also capitalism, have moved closer to be centre of power by their daily growing integration with the Congress and its leadership. It is true the princes have been divested largely of their powers. But at the same time the biggest among them have been integrated into the new scheme of power by being promoted to the position of Rajpramukhs and Maharajpramukhs and Uparajpramukhs. The others too, who had to surrender their power, realise that they owe their remaining privileges, wealth and position to the Congress. So the support, political and economic, of the Rajpramukhs and of the others, inspite of expectations to the contrary, is naturally thrown on the side of the Congress.

It is true again that the zamindari system has been or will be abolished, But as the elections to Congress Committees have shown, it is the zamindar class, and the new class of zamindars known as Bhumihars, who are going to be the main props of the Congress organization in the countryside. In the election of delegates to the Nasik Congress, many erstwhile anti-Congress and pro-British zamindars, noted for their oppression and tyranny, have been returned, defeating old and tried Congress workers.

Again, the capitalists, while they chafe at some of the restrictions imposed upon them and at the uncertainties about the economic policies of the Congress Governments, realise that their safety lies in the Congress alone. And therefore from the Birlas downwards they have rallied under the flag of the Congress.

The combination of a political organization such as the Congress, which happens to be also in power, with the forces of feudalism and capitalism constitutes a great danger not only to the growth of social democracy in this country but to democracy itself. This shift in the politics of the country is not apparent even to Congressmen themselves, for they have never been accustomed to understanding politics in terms of social and economic forces. Their understanding of politics has remained always on the personal level. They look to Nehru and Patel and feel assured that as long as they have leaders like them all must be well with the Congress. I am not speaking, of course, of those Congressmen who are not concerned with ideals and goals towards which they strive. Most Congressmen today are interested in the plums of office and the fruits of licences and permits, in personal power and aggrandizement, in sordid intrigue and in little else. These Congressmen make it easy for the sinister combination of which I have just spoken to be consolidated. Thus the Congress is fast becoming a citadel of reaction and the coming years will show that the main battle for social democracy will have to be fought between Socialism and the Congress. On the issue of that battle will depend the future of Social democracy in India.

21. Statement on Flood-affected and Famine-stricken Areas in North Bihar, Patna, 1 September 1950[1]

In about 50 villages in Saharsa district which I visited between August 23 and 30, the flood situation is critical and alarming. These villages comprise 100 to 1,200 families and of them only 4 to 40 families have either grains or money to maintain themselves and the rest of the families have nothing to fall back upon. Consequently starvation is stalking the whole area. Three months of continuous malnutrition and slow devitalisation have rendered a large number of labourers and kisans weak and incapable of doing hard work.

Many houses are collapsing due to unprecendented Kosi floods. The whole area presents a ghastly appearance. More or less this is the condition of the whole district. When such is the situation, people do not get private loans even though they are ready to sell their lands and ornaments. Labourers have no work.

Of all the villages visited by me, Government has given *takkavi* loans only to 4 villages of Bangaon Thana. Labourers and *bataidars* and even many deserving landowning persons have been denied loans. Five work centres were started in Bangaon Thana, seven in Sourbazar Thana and none in Dharhara Thana. To each centre a sum of Rs. 300/- was allotted which means one day's wages for 480 labourers at the rate of ten annas per worker per day. That meagre sum too is already exhausted. Therefore, the centres have been closed. Even a very small number of labourers who were employed are now without employment and are wandering about for work.

Only one seer and four chhatanks of wheat or gram is given per family per week from control shops. This is nothing but a drop in the ocean. Moreover, great delay and favouritism in distribution of grains and loans have further added to the sufferings of the people.

In fair price shops at Saharsa and Bariahi there is such a great rush that people have to struggle from morning till evening for one seer and four chhatanks of wheat. Even then many people go disappointed. Prices continue to rise. Rice is selling at Rs. 38/- or 40/- a maund, wheat at Rs. 32/-, maize at Rs. 38/-, Marua at Rs. 27/-, and Moong at Rs. 24/-. Even at such high prices grains are not easily available in hats, bazars and village shops.

On the strength of my personal reading of the situation I can say authoritatively that if Government do not send adequate relief and arrange proper distribution on a non-party basis immediately, hundreds will die of starvation in coming weeks. I have personally held a spot enquiry and found three starvation death reports correct. The names of these three are:

[1]Adapted from *Amrita Bazar Patrika*, 3 September 1950.

(1) Murli Mosamat, village Sislagmanpur, thana Bangaon; (2) Akli Mosamat, village Sarauni, thana Dharhara and (3) wife of Kusho Mahto, village Jiwachhpur, thana Saurbazar.

22. Statement on Bihar Government's Relief Measures in Famine and Flood-affected Areas of North Bihar, Patna, 15 September 1950[1]

I have just returned after fifteen gruelling days of touring in North Bihar. I travelled by train, car, jeep, bullock cart, country boat, on elephant back and on foot. The areas covered were the famine and flood affected parts of Monghyr, Saharsa, Purnea, Bhagalpur and Darbhanga districts.

Usually we travelled from morning to midnight. Twelve hours of elephant ride was not unusual and once we spent 15 continuous hours on elephant back.

We spent whole nights on boat and the longest single stretch of boat travel was of 29 hours in the Madhepur and Biraul thanas of Darbhanga. We visited scores of villages and looked into hundreds of homes and talked to thousands of people. Occasionally, I addressed public meetings, though the tour was not intended for speech-making. I had rather gone to make human contacts and see things and hear people.

The strenuous character of the tour left me no time to prepare a detailed report. I shall attempt in the next few days to place before the people a detailed report on the situation as I found it. At present, I will only give an overall picture of what I witnessed. The need to present this picture is all the greater in view of the urgency of the situation, and because of the hope—it may turn out to be a false hope—that the Government's attention might be drawn to the question and urgent steps might be taken to alleviate avoidable sufferings.

The State and Central Governments have persistently refused to recognise that there are famine conditions anywhere in Bihar.

I am convinced, however, that had the British been in power and the Congress in oppostion and had the situation been even half as serious as it actually is, the Bihar Congress would have rent the skies with the cry of famine and would have severely condemned the Government for not declaring a famine. But being in power the Congress is anxious to avoid the responsibility of such a declaration, with the result that suffering grows apace and the situation deteriorates with the passage of time.

The one uniform impression I gathered was that measures, so far adopted by Government, have been totally inadequate to meet the situation. I say

[1]Adapted from *Janata*, 24 September 1950.

this not with a desire to find fault, but in a spirit of helpfulness.

The present famine has been caused mainly by successive failure of crops. The story with minor variations is the same every where in the affected areas. At least three successive food crops had failed before the failure of the last *jethua* and *bhadai* maize crops, which precipitated the crisis. In some parts, money crops such as that of chillies had also failed in addition. In some other parts, crops had been failing for the last two or three years. In the Kosi affected areas, the terrific yearly devastations which have been piling up human misery and economic ruin for years, floods occurred on a vaster scale this year and at an abnormal time.

The result of this was serious impoverishment of the rural populations: complete depletion of food reserves and acute scarcity; stoppage of the normal agricultural operations, including those of borrowing and lending; and precipitous rise of food prices. These added up to the present famine. The consequent human suffering could have been mitigated had the State Government been alert and taken appropriate measures in advance.

Even today, if adequate steps are taken much suffering can be alleviated. But I am afraid, Government already feel that the worst is over and there is no further need for anxiety. Let me warn, however, that unless large scale relief and other economic and health measures are adopted, the famine will take a heavy toll of life.

The worst affected section of the population is of the landless labourers and among them those belonging to the Scheduled Castes and tribes. Desperately poor at all times, with no reserves and staying power, their condition today is pitiable indeed. Not one among them, I am sure, is able to have two meals a day even though the meals are of leaves and roots, crabs and snails. Most of them are able to eat only once in two days or even three. I saw whole hamlets of 'Musahars' and Harijans that were scenes of patent starvation.

In the villages that I visited, the landless labourers constitute from 40 to 80 per cent of the population. In the current season, and practically till the harvesting of the autumn paddy crop, i.e. till November, no employment will be available to these unfortunate people. In normal times, too, this period is one of difficulty for them. But in ordinary years when crops have not failed one after another, the peasants have food reserves and they keep the landless workers going on loans of grain which they realise later according to custom. This year, however, when the peasants themselves are faced with starvation, they can hardly help their labourers. Thus the life of millions of these physically debilitated and economically and socially oppressed people is slowly ebbing out.

The only salvation for them is provision by the state of adequate employment through large-scale public works. What the state and District

Boards together have so far done in this respect is not even one hundredth of what is necessary. The roads in North Bihar are the worst in the whole of India, and large areas have no roads whatever. Railway communications too, are sorely inadequate. If the Railway Ministry, the PWD and the District and Local Board combined their efforts and subordinated red-tape to the urgency of saving human lives, not only would the hungry and destitute find employment and therefore food, but also would North Bihar be saved from a terrible scourge. There are many other forms of public works which too might be taken up. The essence of the matter is speed and adequacy of the measures adopted.

As for the peasantry, that is, those who possess land, except for a very small proportion, not more than 10 per cent in any case, the rest have no reserves of grain or cash. Many of them have already been driven to sell or mortgage their lands and other properties. This class, too, finds it difficult to carry on without assistance. Their need is for loans and seeds for the next sowing.

The state Government have given loans no doubt in the past few weeks, but here, as elsewhere, the aid has fallen far short of requirements. Very small sums have been given and the number of beneficiaries is so far too small.

Nothing less than Rs. 50 per acre should be given and all the needy, without any discrimination, should receive the benefit. The *bataidars*, who do not possess any land but who constitute no less than 75 per cent of the cultivators in Purnea and Saharsa, should also be included in some manner in the loan distribution. Seeds—Kalai seeds are in immediate demand—should be supplied in time and not in accordance with the time schedule of red tape.

The cash benefits provided for labour and the cultivators would render little relief in the absence of fair price shops. And this is the third most urgent need that must be met again on an adequate scale. Food prices in the open market have risen and coarse rice is selling at Rs. 35 to 40 per maund. The most common and insistent demand that I met everywhere was for fair price shops. The number of shops opened so far is too small and the supplies actually available at them are even smaller.

The poor complained everywhere that there was discrimination at these shops and the better off sections of the population always used influence and other means to get priority. The only remedy for these irregularities is ration cards not only for 40 but 90 per cent of the village population in the affected areas.

In this connection, I might refer to the bungling in seizing hoards. I heard complaints, which deserve investigation, that there have been widespred partiality and corruption in seizing stocks. But, apart from that the whole purpose of this dramatic measure is defeated when the seized goods are allowed to rot for weeks under official lock and key while there is acute scarcity everywhere. The only result of this has been that the scarcity has become acuter, prices have shot up further and the traders have stopped bringing in more grain. Surely it is commonsense that the seizing of stocks should have been followed up immediately by a planned distribution. But there seems to be no fore-thinking or planning in official measures and one step is not co-ordinated with the rest.

It would be wrong to exclude the Kosi affected areas from the measures of relief on the ground that the problem there is nothing different from what it used to be in previous years. In those areas, too, people are faced with starvation and they require the same type of aid and relief as elsewhere. In addition, they require tube wells for drinking water and urgent medical aid. The people of these areas which are under water from six to twelve months in the year require to be rehabilitated elsewhere. But I shall say more about this in my fuller report. Here I should like to add this much, that till I actually saw with my eyes the extent of human suffering and devastation caused by the cruel Kosi, I had no idea of their magnitude.

I feel now that apart from economic considerations, from the human point of view alone the Kosi project should have received not top but first priority. Even from the economic point of view the prevention of the wastage and loss caused by the Kosi would alone mean a vast addition to the national wealth.

Finally, practically everywhere that I went, I heard complaints about partiality and corruption in the distribution of the benefits and relief given. Recently at a public meeting at Patna, I had suggested to the Chief Minister that he should call for the formation of non-partisan instead of the Congress dominated committees to secure cooperation with official agencies in the implementation of relief measures. My suggestion has gone unheeded so far. I repeat it here and wish to add that the refusal to do so would only mean that even in the face of a national calamity such as famine the Congress Party is not prepared to subordinate its partisan interests to the common good.

Finally, let me urge that if there is any field of activity apart from war, where military speed and efficiency are called for, it is that of fighting famine. But while there is so much talk of putting this or that on a war footing, there is no proof that any one is serious about it. I appeal, in the name of the hungry and starving, for expedition and seriousness in dealing with the lives of millions of our people that are in danger.

23. Address at the National Students Convention, Bombay, 15 September 1950[1]

The student movement in India had a brilliant record of suffering, sacrifice and achievement, but is marred by splits and splinter groups.

I do not think that there is any better person in the country than Pandit Nehru (who had inaugurated the Convention) to give a correct lead to the youth of the country. I fully endorse the Prime Minister's advice that the students can take part in politics as individuals. I agree with him that it is not possible nor advisable for students to keep away from politics. But I am in favaour of students first gaining knowledge and experience before venturing into poltics.

A lot of problems face the country for which we have a habit to blame Government, but we should not forget that we are also responsible for them. I suggest that the Union should work on the lines of similar unions in Britain where political parties have their own associations for students. I advise you not to consider your associations as trade unions in perpetual fight with college authorities.

During the past three years there has been a rapid deterioration in the tone of Indian public life with corruption growing unchecked. If we fail to check this, India will remain where she is today. I call upon the National Students' Union to impress upon its members the need to develop character and to imbibe the spirit of truth which Mahatma Gandhi lived to infuse in all of us.

I urge Government to provide more opportunities for students to work out their constructive programmes. At present the students have a despondent feeling that they have not been taken into confidence by the Government.

[1]Adapted from *Hindustan Times*, 16 September and *Tribune*, 17 September 1950.

24. Address to the Striking Mill Workers, Bombay, 17 September 1950[1]

My advice to you is to continue the strike indefinitely, till the bonus issue is satisfactorily settled. Go back to your homes, but not to work.

The Home Minister of Bombay, Mr. Morarji Desai,[2] is attempting to

[1]Adapted from *Bombay Chronicle*, 18 September 1950.

[2]Morarji Ranchhodji Desai (1896-1995); resigned his post of Deputy collector in 1930 and joined the Civil disobedience movement; imprisoned several times; Minister for Revenue, Agriculture and Forest, Bombay, 1937-9; Minister for Home and Revenue, Bombay, 1946-52; Chief Minister of Bombay, 1952-6; Union Minister of Commerce and Industry, 1956-8; Union Finance Minister, 1958-63; Chairman, Administrative Reforms Commission, Government of India, 1966-7; Deputy Prime Minister and Finance Minister, 1967-9; Prime Minister of India, 1977-9.

prevent the settlement of the dispute, although I have reliable information that the millowners are willing to pay the bonus. I ask the strikers to pay the Home Minister in his own coin by continuing the strike indefinitely, say even for six years, till their legitimate grievances are redressed.

I strongly refute the accusation that the textile strike is part of a political game played by the Socialist Party. I am of the opinion that it is the result of the strength and solidarity of the workers who have rallied round a powerful labour organization, namely, the Mill Mazdoor Sabha. Such charges are deliberately made to besmirch the fair name of the Socialist Party and to bolster up the Congress sponsored INTUC in which the workers have absolutely no confidence.

The textile strike[3] of Bombay has demonstrated in no unmistakable manner the strength and unity of the semi-starved and half-naked working class. The strike is of all-India importance as it has aroused the entire labour of the country, which is evidenced by the large-scale token strikes staged in its various parts.

The fact that the workers have held out for well over a month is itself a victory for them. My visit to the textile centres of the city has convinced me of the unity and solidarity in your ranks.

My advice to you is to continue the struggle in a peaceful manner. I warn you against enemies in your midst who are out to provoke you to violence against the police and the public with a view to discrediting your organization. I remind you that the police are also "mazdoors" like you and have to carry out the orders of their superiors. I further point out to you that the strike is directed against the capitalist millowners and not against the police.

We had much hopes from the Nehru Government, but the way in which this Government is functioning has given us only disappointment and frustration. The country faces today shortage of food, shelter, and water, and famine conditions are prevalent in many parts of India. The Government has succeeded in producing only a plethora of paper plans, which remain unimplemented. I warn that the country is already on the verge of stagnation and decay.

Finally I repeat my appeal to you to continue the strike till you are paid your bonus, which is legitimately due to you as part of your wages.

[3]See Appendix 2 for Nehru's reply to J.P. on Bombay textile workers strike.

25. Statement about an Appeal to the Prime Minister, Bombay, 20 September 1950[1]

I have personally appealed to Prime Minister Pandit Nehru to intervene in the textile strike in Bombay and bring about a settlement of the dispute.

I have also sent a letter to Pandit Nehru on Tuesday through a special messenger to Nasik (which the latter is visiting).

I feel that refusal to look into the matter would be an example of partisan attitude on the part of the Prime Minister. A strike of two lakhs of workers in any part of the country can not be a matter of local importance only.

As the strike affects the whole country as well as its foreign trade, I feel that it is wrong to treat it as a local affair. The Bombay Government is adopting a narrow, partisan view.

It is wrong, in my opinion, to substitute litigation for direct negotiations and collective bargaining between employers and employees.

The strike does not represent a political stunt on the part of the Socialist Party, but is the spontaneous outcome of the pent up feelings of the aggrieved workers.

[1]Adapted from *Bombay Chronicle*, 21 September 1950.

26. Address at the Bharatiya Nritya Kala Mandir, Patna, 20 September 1950[1]

I am here to vigorously plead for making art a dynamic vehicle for the cultural elevation of the masses.

I regret that Bihar is specially backward today in the realm of art. While in Bengal, Maharashtra, Tamilnad and Kerala, art in its various forms is accorded a high place in the social life of the people, in Bihar the people are generally indifferent to art and even look down upon some of its forms such as dancing. Art has become today circumscribed within the bounds of money and luxury. The poor masses have forgotten the glow that art imparted to the lives of their ancestors.

Art was born with life and would continue to inspire humanity, as long as man realises the importance of beauty and joy in his life. The time has come when art must inspire the masses to shake off their inertia, beautify their surroundings and evolve an impressive art of living. The people in Maharashtra, Kerala and other states know how to decorate their houses and live artistically. In Bihar, however, we have forgotten our traditional way of living.

[1]Adapted from *Searchlight*, 22 September 1950.

In this connection, I recall how Mahatma Gandhi and Pandit Madan Mohan Malaviya made their lives true symbols of art. I urge the citizens of Bihar to appreciate the value of art in human personality and its development and try to improve their cultural life in the true aesthetic sense.

Art can not flourish in the midst of dirty drains and squalid surroundings that we generally see in Patna. Where is the ancient glory of Kusumpur? Far away in the jungles of Chotanagpur, our Adibasi brethren and sisters are still continuing their artistic traditions of music and dancing, but we so-called civilised people have become today mechanical and devoid of aesthetic sense.

I appeal to the people of Bihar to help the rising institution of the Bharatiya Nritya Kala Mandir by generous contributions and enable Shri Hari Uppal, the Director of the Mandir, to realise his mission of rekindling the flame of art in our social life.

Unless art and life embrace each other and give birth to sparks of real beauty and joy, the life of the masses can not be improved and enlivened. Art has to descend from the palaces of the rich to the huts of the poor people living in villages. The intelligentsia of Bihar has to propagate the message of such art among the rural population and give a lead to the country in this direction.

I hope that the Kala Mandir would become a beacon-light of cultural renaissance in Bihar and the children who come out of this temple of art after their training would try to illumine the social life of the people.

27. Interview to the Press on Food Situation in Bihar, Patna, 21 September 1950[1]

It is not only the number of starvation deaths that should guide the Government in dealing with famine in Bihar.

The general economic situation arising out of successive crop failures, floods, high prices, hoarding and black-marketing should be properly assessed and steps taken to ease the situation.

In connection with the Food Minister, Sri K.M. Munshi's retort on food situation in Bihar, I would like to say that if a person like Sri Munshi relies on arithmetic of deaths, I am afraid famine will have taken a terrible toll of life before any serious steps could be taken. Mr. Munshi will do well to undertake a personal tour of the affected areas to find out the real situation.

Sri Munshi is only making himself ridiculous by issuing circulars and

[1]Adapted from *Searchlight*, 23 September 1950. This was J.P.'s reply to the Union Food Minister, Sri K.M. Munshi's statement issued at Bombay on 16 September 1950 on food situation in Bihar.

statements about Bihar far away from Delhi. I have no reason to exaggerate things. When after 15 days of strenuous touring in all affected areas, I issued a statement which should have received careful consideration of Sri Munshi instead of being rejected off hand. Sri Munshi has been insisting, in spite of the statement to the contrary by such high authority as the Chief Minister of Bihar, that only one beggar had died of starvation in the state. It will be remembered that the Chief Minister of Bihar had said that in one district of Purnea there had been starvation deaths.

Sri Munshi had asked me for a list of persons who had died of starvation. I had given him a list when I was at Delhi last. He has charged that my list included names of those who had died years ago. I am rather surprised at this and have asked Sri Munshi to give me details of investigation that he has made into the matter. This list that was given to me was prepared by the workers of the Socialist Party in the areas concerned. They had assured me that their list was correct.

28. To P.R. Das, 21 September 1950[1]

Dear Mr. Das,

I understand that you have been kind enough to agree to plead before the Supreme Court the case of the Jharia strike. We are all obliged to you for this. I further understand that the Court has agreed to fix any date in October suitable to you for hearing of the case. Mr. B.P. Sinha is going to see you in this connection and I hope you will be able to give him an early date in October.

Thanking you,

Yours sincerely,
J.P.

[1]*J.P. Papers* (NMML).

29. To Suraj Narayan Singh, 24 September 1950[1]

My dear Suraj Babu,[2]

Excuse me for writing in English which I am doing because it is easy to dictate. I had to leave Patna in a hurry and could not discuss with you several important matters, only three of which I was able to raise at the meeting of the Provincial Executive.

[1]*Brahmanand Papers* (NMML).
[2]Suraj Narayan Singh—for biographical note see *JPSW*, Vol. II, p. 222.

Another question to which I want you to give your serious attention is regarding what I had said at the Party Convention about demonstration against blackmarketing and picketting of blackmarketeers' shops. I am anxious that this movement should start from Patna. Picketting need not be the first step. We might begin with leafleting against blackmarketing and processions. After that picketting might be taken up, but before that an appeal should be issued for volunteers to picket. The volunteers should be trained and asked to remain peaceful in spite of all provocation.

Yet another question which I want you to take up in cooperation with the Party. City Party is the building up of a Meherally Youth Home in the Party's grounds of Aryakumar Road. I shall send you an appeal addressed to the youth of the city to give voluntary labour for the erection of the Home. But you must consider how the materials, namely, bricks, bamboos, tiles and timber could be procured. I shall send you an appeal for these materials also.

I sent through Benipuriji[3] Rs. 1400/- out of which he might have spent a small amount on his travelling. I had asked Benipuriji to tell you that you should give a part of the sum to Razi Saheb to keep the *Janata* going and to use the rest for the needs of the Provincial Party. I had also asked him to tell you to give Rs. 100/- out of the amount I sent with him to Shri Ram Bhajan Dutt[4] and a hundred or two as the case may be to Jogendrabhai. If I find the Andhra tour fruitful I shall take a loan from the Andhra fund and send you a little more money after a week or so.

I hope you are well,

Yours sincerely,
J.P.

[3]Rambriksh Benipuri—for biographical note see *JPSW*, Vol. I, p. 61.

[4]Ram Bhajan Dutt, one of the prominent members of the Socialist Party in Bihar.

30. To Ramdhari Singh Dinkar, 3 October 1950[1]

Dear Dinkarji,[2]

The other night I was highly impressed by listening to your recital of your poem on Karna.[3] However, I did not like the use in it of the word '*Virat*'

[1]*J.P. Papers* (NMML). Original in Hindi.

[2]Ramdhari Singh 'Dinkar' (1908-74); Renowned Hindi poet, Professor and Head of the Department, L.S. College, Muzaffarpur (Bihar) 1950-2; member Rajya Sabha 1952-64; Vice-Chancellor, Bhagalpur University, 1964-5. Recipient of Padma Bhushan, 1959, Sahitya Akadami Award, 1959 and Gyanpeeth Award, 1973; author of more than 50 books in prose and poetry.

[3]Karna; one of the heroic characters of the Indian classic, *Mahabharat*.

(implying Godhood), in spite of its being quite good from the point of view of poetry. Today I got some time, so I thought of conveying a few words to you.

You are our revolutionary poet. It is your duty to guide the society from darkness to light. Giving the position of God to man is the greatest among the crimes committed to humanity by the Hindu religion. I hold that until the Hindus move ahead from the childish worship of Ram, Krishna, the darkness of their mind cannot be removed and they cannot begin their journey on the path of cultural progress.

Krishna's character as a human being is not any less interesting or full of miracles that effort has to be made to make it attractive by introducing a ridiculous element like vision of God into it. For a poet of the age like you it is befitting to analyse Krishna, not as an incarnation of God, but as an extremely complex human being, endowed with all the virtues and defects of a human being and fully involved in the struggles of the society. Man can be respected as a man only; the effort to turn him into God is to destroy both and further deepen the mental darkness of the people.

Hope you are liking your new assignment and are happy.

I shall reach Patna by 10-12 November.

Yours affectionately,
Jayaprakash

31. To Tilakraj Chaddha, 18 October 1950[1]

My dear Tilakji,

I thank you for your letter of 9th Oct. I am glad you are out on bail. I read your letter to Dr. Gopichand[2] with great interest.

As regards my programme I want you to bear in mind the following points:

1. The programme should not be too heavy, because my health is not what it used to be before. Therefore you should not fix too many meetings during the day. I think three meetings a day should be enough.

2. In view of my experience in Andhra, I should like to make a few suggestions about the rest day. I should like to reach the place[3] selected for

[1]*J.P. Papers* (NMML).

[2]Gopichand Bhargava (1880-1966); joined Congress in 1921 and jailed several times; member Punjab Legislative Assembly 1937-40, 1946-51, 1957-64; Premier East Punjab, 1947-9; Finance Minister, 1959-64.

[3]Place of Stay unknown.

the rest on the night previous to the rest day. Also the place should be, as far as possible, quiet and isolated and there should be no public or private engagements on that day. As a matter of fact the rest day should be a kind of *agyatwas.*

3. please avoid, as far as possible, feasts and other similar "parties". During the nights we will not take any dinner, but only fruits and milk. Chillies, green or red, should be totally avoided and other spices should be mildly used.

4. Prabhavati, as you know, takes only milk and fruits on Mondays and Fridays and she is strict vegetarian and does not take even onion or garlick. I am of course non-vegetarian and so is Shanker.

5. Wherever available, I shall prefer to stay at Dak Bungalows rather than in private houses.

6. In fixing up the programme, please keep in mind the distances to be travelled and the time required for speaking and the ceremonies of reception, etc.

7. There will be three of us, myself, Prabhavati and Shanker and I am afraid the luggage with us will be rather heavy and would require special transportation arrangements.

8. Wherever possible, please arrange Party workers' meetings.

I hope to reach Delhi on the 20th of November. Some of you should meet me there. We shall start for the Punjab tour on the 21st night or the 22nd morning. Please send me a copy of the programme at the following address as soon as you can so that, if necessary, I might suggest changes.

With best wishes,

Yours sincerely,
J.P.

32. Address at a Public Meeting, Madras, 22 October 1950[1]

I call on the people of this country to build up the Socialist Party, if they seriously mean to solve the problems facing them.

I observe that the question placed before us by the Chairman, K.G. Sivaswami, is undoubtedly a most urgent one, not only for the people of Madras but also for the people of the whole of India. I am afraid that I can not give a direct answer to it. However, it is possible to make suggestions

[1]Adapted from *Hindu*, 23 October 1950.

as to what the Government of the day should do in order that the people might have enough to eat. But the suggestions placed before the Government by the various organizations do not seem to make any impression on it. The party in power seems to think that there is no one in the country to challenge it. It has bewildered me as to why, while there is so much of dissatisfaction and discontent in the country, the Congress party is successful at by-elections. Are the people of this country not capable of any kind of collective action? My reply to this question is that the people are not prepared to act, to do anything in order to solve their problems. All that they do is to complain and grumble. They can go on grumbling and complaining till Doomsday. Nothing will happen.

We had all hoped that when the Congress came to power it would be a people's Government. During the last four years, it has shown that it is not so. Profiteering, exploitation and inequality are being perpetuated and black-marketing and corruption growing. People seem to be interested only in making money. Even if the Congress Government remains in power for 40 years, I feel that people's problems would not be solved.

I, therefore, appeal to the people to prepare themselves for the forth-coming elections. Our fate is going to be decided at these elections. The Congress Party would do everything possible to win at the polls. But if the people are organized and alert, they can not be fooled.

The Socialist Party believes that none of the problems facing us can be solved with the present structure of society remaining intact. The Socialist Party believes that as long as the present structure of society is unchanged, there are going to be millions without enough food, clothing, shelter, etc. Only under a Socialist plan of agriculture and industry would it be possible for us to increase production. I admit that, even if there is a Socialist Government, it would not be possible immediately to increase production. It would take a little time. As production would take time, it is first of all necessary to give our attention to the problem of distribution. When the Socialist Party comes to power, it would abolish the Princely Order. The Princes will not go away of their own accord. In my view it would not be difficult to carry out the programme of nationalisation and distribution of land even through peaceful, democratic methods. While nationalising industries, there will be need for starting a new service for managing them. I am certain there is enough talent in our country to handle this task. I would be very happy if the Congress Government implements its own Agrarian Reforms Committee's report. I am sure it would not be implemented even for 20 years to come. Only the zamindari system has been abolished. But the villager remains where he was before the abolition of the zamindaris. Only the implementation of a programme of social change would enable them to solve the problems facing the country. I can not understand why anybody should take it for granted that the Congress would win at the next elections. The people should realise that the result is in their hands. If Congress comes to power again, its policies would continue to be the same as at present. For another five years there would be a steamroller of Congress reign, crushing all the aspirations of the people. Let the people choose what they want.

33. Address at the General Council of the All-India Railwaymen's Federation, Perambur, Madras, 23 October 1950[1]

It is for the first time after many years that the All-India Railwaymen's Federation is meeting in Madras and on behalf of the delegates assembled here I extend my cordial thanks to the M.S.M. Railway Employees' Union for being the host and making us all so welcome and comfortable.

We have gathered here to discuss many grave issues, One such issue, namely, the question of pay and allowance of the Running Staff, we have been discussing since yesterday in a special conference of the Running Staff. That conference has already taken a well-considered decision and I have no doubt that it will receive your fullest support and endorsement.

The second issue which affects all Railway employees, indeed all State employees, most vitally is that of the two Labour Bills, namely, the Labour Relations Bill and the Trade Unions Bill, already introduced in Parliament.

At a joint conference of unions of State Employees and other labour unions held at Delhi some time ago, it was decided to oppose these Bills tooth and nail by even calling a one-day General Strike, if necessary. You have to decide here your further policy in this regard.

The Government have paid no heed to the unanimous opposition of organized labour, and except for a very few changes all the obnoxious provisions of the Bills remain as they were. At the same time the Select Committees appointed by Parliament have not yet submitted their reports. It appears unlikely, in view of the absence of any opposition, that the Parliament would make any major amendments to the Bills. You have, therefore, to decide now in what manner Railwaymen should express their opposition to these Bills. I have no doubt that unless there is an effective demonstration of your oppostion, these Bills will not be dropped nor will the desired amendments be made.

The Congress Government seem to be determined to outlaw strikes, particularly by State employees. For, while the Labour Bills are still pending before Parliament, the Railway Ministry has proposed the introduction of a Model Strike Clause into the conditions pre-requisite for the recognition of unions of State employees. Among other things this Model Clause requires

[1]Adapted from *Janata*, 5 November 1950.

that 75 per cent of the members of the unions must participate in a strike ballot of whom three-fourths must vote in favour before a strike can be legally called.

Such a condition for railwaymen, who are spread over more than 4,740 railway stations and other establishments, and perform shift or travelling duties, is virtually to make a strike impossible. The Federation can in no event lend its approval to such a Model Strike Clause.

The case of employees of the integrated ex-State Railways is one of grave anxiety. According to a recent letter of the Railway Board these employees have not been given weightage for their earlier years of service. The weightage given to the employees of the Indian Government Railways has itself been found to be utterly unsatisfactory, but even this weightage has not been granted to the ex-State Railway employees. In an integrated system of Government Railways, it seems to be very unfair to treat different employees differently. The ex-State Railway employees should not be treated worse than similar employees of the Indian Government Railways.

As you are all aware, the period of the Joint Advisory Committee has been extended to another three months. It has been a matter of some satisfaction that in recent weeks the Committee has worked more expeditiously and got through a good deal of business. I am sure, had it been possible for the Committee to sit more regularly, its work would have been finished before the end of the original year sanctioned. As it is, I understand, the Committee sat only for 134 days since its creation and has by now disposed of about 300 issues.

The Government, however, have not passed their final orders on more than 50 per cent of the issues decided by the Committee. I hope the Committee will complete its work within the extended period of three months.

While it is possible to view differently the results of the Committee's labours, I have no doubt that some such machinery of a permanent nature is essential for the negotiation of hundreds of issues that must arise from day to day between the employer and the employees in an industry so vast as the Railways. The periodical meetings with the Ministry can never take the place of a permanent joint machinery for negotiations, such as the Joint Railway Advisory Committee.

I hope, therefore, that in finally determining the future of the JAC, the view of the Federation would be taken into account.

Regarding the suggestion of the Railway Ministry that joint meetings between the Federation and the Ministry be held along with the representatives of the rival federation organised by the Congress, you must express your clear and firm opinion. Speaking for myself, I cannot agree to any such procedure.

In the first place, the Railway Ministry have no justification whatever in giving any degree of recognition to any rival organizations that may be formed. The AIRF had been for the last 25 years the sole representative of railwaymen in this country and uptil the time the Congress Government was formed the AIRF was treated as such. The rival organization was obviously set up for political purposes, for the AIRF was entirely a non-political trade union embracing members of all political views. However, when the Government was faced with the claims of a rival organization, it should have prescribed some tests for ascertaining the comparative strength of the organizations in the field and, instead of encouraging rival unionism, it should have given recognition to the organization that was most representative.

Be that as it may, when the Federation goes to the Ministry to negotiate on any issue, it does not want other parties to intefere in any manner whatever. The negotiations must be conducted entirely between the Government and the Railwaymen's Federation. If the Government wants to negotiate with others, that is its own business, which we can only stop by proving to the Government that it is the Federation alone that can deliver the goods on behalf of Railwaymen.

Among many other issues that are before you, the most important one that causes perhaps the utmost anxiety is that of dearness allowance. It will be recalled that when in January 1949, the Central Government announced an increment of Rs. 10 in the cash dearness allowance as a result of successful strike ballots by railwaymen, postmen and others, the Government communique promised that the issue of dearness allowance would be examined every six months taking into account the change in prices.

Though it is nearly 22 months since that solemn promise was made, not once has this matter been reviewed by the Central Government, even though the Federation and other organizations of Central Government employees brought this matter repeatedly to the notice of the Government. The only conclusion to be drawn from this is that the Congress Government has no regard for its pledged word and that it is prepared to act only under the threat of direct action by its employees.

This is not a very healthy basis for employee-employer relationships. I am afraid, if we wish to force the Government to carry out the pledge given in the said communique, we must be prepared again to hold out an effective threat. The Government communique of January 1949 had hoped that prices would fall in the next few months. Instead of that prices have steadily risen. Let it be remembered that we are demanding nothing more than the implementation of the scales of dearness allowance recommended by the Central Pay Commission. In these circumstances I cannot imagine of any case stronger than the demand for a revision of the dearness allowance.

Finally, I should like to draw your attention to a rather neglected aspect of our activities. The function of a trade union movement does not end with collective bargaining, but also includes constructive activities in the interest of the union membership. The affiliated unions have not been giving as much attention to these activities as they should have. These activities include the opening of cooperative consumer stores, educational institutions, housing societies, etc. The Hon'ble Minister for Railways, gave me a definite assurance that his Department would give all possible help to the unions in carrying on such activities. Where difficulties may be experienced, due to the unsympathetic attitude of officialdom or of provincial governments, specific instances should be brought to my notice or to that of the General Secretary.

The Federation and the unions have also a part to play in the matter of checking corruption and waste and pilfering of railway property. The Working Committee had appointed a sub-committee to draw up a scheme to this end and I hope the committee would be able to submit the report. It would, of course, be considered as confidential.

The Working Committee had appointed another sub-committee to prepare a scheme for the final disposal of individual cases that cause so much headache to the unions and end in such unsatisfactory results. I hope such and other constructive activities would be taken up by the unions and other branches and difficulties will not discourage them.

These are grave issues, friends, and I hope that you will consider them with your usual wisdom and sense of responsibility.

34. Address at a Press Conference, Madras, 24 October 1950[1]

The Socialist Party would be setting up candidates for the ensuing general elections in as many constituencies as possible.

There is no other party except the Socialist Party which can challenge the might of the Congress on a national plane. I appeal to all those who are dissatisfied and disillusioned with the Congress Party and those who come from the ranks of the common people to rally round the flag of the Socialist Party.

Dissatisfaction with the present Government is widespread but this must find its expression in a constructive way. The only possible constructive expression is the creation of an alternative party to the Congress. If, in spite of the all-pervading dissatisfaction, the Congress is to come back to power it would only be on account of the absence of an alternative party. For the

[1]Adapted from *Tribune*, 25 October 1950.

success of democracy the two-party system is the most suitable one. Multiplicity of parties is as much destructive of democracy as a single party rule.

Although tentative dates have been announced, two primary requirements have yet to be fulfilled. Firstly, the electoral rolls have yet to be published and corrections therein made. Secondly, the work of delimitation of constituencies is yet to be completed. In most States, the work of delimitation has been conducted by the Congress party alone and this work has not been based on any well-defined principle but on the convenience of the party in power, or even of particular candidates and their communities. Where delimitation proposals have been published by the State Governments, the public have not been supplied with the data on the basis of which those proposals have been made so as to enable the public to critically examine them.

I may point out that although the Indian constitution has made a special provision for an independent machinery to be set up to ensure non-interference of the Government of the day in the conduct of elections, this machinery has not yet been built up. This machinery should be set up immediately not only at the Centre, but also in the States.

I would like to refer to the semi-official report published from New Delhi some time back purporting to give the substance of the new electoral law that has been drafted and circulated to the States. It appears from the report that the Government proposes to have a certain number of two-member constituencies where the system of voting is to be the distributive vote. Any one who has the least acquaintance with the subject knows that the distributive system of voting in a multi-member constituency is a dishonest device in the hands of the majority party to multiply its strength artificially and thus to perpetuate its majority. If in a two-member constituency, parties A and B have 51 and 49 per cent strength respectively, under the distributive system, party A will capture both the seats. This would mean that while 51 per cent of the voters will have two representatives, 49 per cent of the voters will go completely unrepresented.

Under a proper democratic system if there are two seats in a constituency, one each should go to both the parties A and B. At a conference of opposition parties, held a few months ago at Bombay, it was unanimously decided that whatever system of voting was finally adopted, under no condition the distributive system with multi-member constituencies should be adopted.

The report from New Delhi also said that the use of hired transport was to be banned for bringing voters to the polling-booths. I cannot imagine a more ridiculous provision than that. Banning of transport is necessary to prevent plutocracy from defeating democracy, but the very opposite would be the result of the Government's proposal. Parties of the common people can never hope to secure any but hired transport and that too in a very limited number. On the other hand, parties of the rich can command private vehicles on a liberal scale. Thus, a ban on hired transport alone would put a premium on wealth. I hope, therefore, that the use of all transport will be banned for conveying voters to the booths, except transport provided by the State for invalids.

Regarding foreign policy, the Socialist Party would go one step ahead of the present Government's policy of keeping away from the two power blocs. It would try to form a third bloc of countries composed of nations which do not identify themselves with either of the two Big Powers in the world to-day.

I am strongly in favour of an immediate solution of the Kashmir problem which is providing a great drain on national resources and a hindrance in the way of all national development. I am personally in favour of a solution even at the cost of partitioning Kashmir.

It would take some time for the election manifesto of the Socialist Party to be prepared and published, but the manifesto would be based on the national revival programme adopted recently by the Madras session of the party conference. If it came into power, the Socialist Party, would first reorganise the services and eliminate corruption.

The Socialist Party would not join hands with Hindu Mahasabha. Opposition to the Congress is not the main plank of the Socialist Party. It has its own ideals and programmes to give effect to.

I deprecate the slogan of "Dravidistan", and hope that the people of the South would keep away from such unpatriotic activities. I also condemn picketing of North Indian shops in furtherance of the Dravidistan movement. India is one, and the people of any part are free to go anywhere they like and carry on their legitimate activities. The problem in our country is not that of domination of one part by another, but of domination and exploitation of the toiling millions by the upper classes of society, whether of the North or South.

Finally, I would like to mention about the food situation in the country. The six ounces of ration given is inadequate and it must be raised to twelve ounces.

35. To K.K. Menon, 24 October 1950[1]

Dear K.K.,

I found from a report published on page 4 of the *Janata* of October 8, regarding the decision of the Standing Committee of the Conference

[1] *J.P. Papers* (NMML).

on Free and Fair Elections that a committee consisting of Purshottam Trikamdas, P.R. Lele[2] and the three secretaries was appointed to examine and report on the materials that should be incorporated in the proposed Representation of the People's Act and all matters ancillary thereto. It strikes me that this was a very important committee and I hope the report of the committee has already been prepared and sent to the parties concerned. It would be good if the report were released to the press also. If Asoka makes a special arrangement with the PTI, the report might get good publicity throughout the country. I hope that this matter will be expedited.

I thank you for the note that you have sent to me. I have found it very useful. I am writing in a hurry. I shall write again Later.

Affectionately yours,
J.P.

[2]P.R. Lele; an advocate of Bombay.

36. Statement regarding the Forthcoming General Elections, Madras, 24 October 1950[1]

1. It is a matter of gratification that Government have finally announced the dates for the forthcoming general elections. This ends the period of uncertainty and sets at rest the fear that was sedulously being cultivated in some disruptive quarters that elections were never going to be held from which the conclusion was drawn that violence was the only possible means for changing the Government.

Early elections must be welcome to all, but I hope the necessary preparations for a sound election will not be sacrificed in the interest of haste. The Congress' propensity for ordinance-making gives rise to the apprehension that unhealthy makeshifts might take the place of steady and natural development of the processes of democracy.

2. Though the final election dates have been announced, the two primary requirements have yet to be fulfilled. First; the electoral rolls have yet to be published and corrections therein to be made. I am afraid, the State Government have not made adequate arrangements to ensure that the rolls when published are properly checked up. To leave this difficult job to the electorate, particularly when the electorate is for the most part illiterate and backward, is to shirk responsibility. It was necessary for the Government to carry on a vigorous propaganda to make the people conscious of their franchise and to rouse their interest in their registration as voters.

[1]*J.P. Papers* (NMML).

3. Second, the work of delimitation of constituencies is yet to be completed. In most States the work of delimitation has been conduced by the Congress party alone, and, speaking generally, this work has not been based on any well-defined principles, but on the convenience of the party in power or even of particular candidates and their communities. Where delimitation proposals have been published by the State Governments, the public have not been supplied with the data on the basis of which the proposals could be critically examined. In the absence of figures of population of the smallest administrative areas, it is impossible to criticise concretely the actual delimitation of constituencies. These data in most cases have been denied to the public. I hope the necessary data would be published and sufficient time would be allowed for criticisms to be made.

4. The Indian Constitution makes special provision for an independent machinery to be set up to ensure non-interference of the Government of the day in the conduct of elections. This machinery is yet to be built up. In view of the fact that the elections are not more than five and a half months ahead, there should be no further delay in setting up this machinery not only at the Centre but also in the States. The Chief Election Commissioner, by himself, cannot be said to constitute an effective independent machinery. Nor is it possible to consider the election officers appointed in the States as being independent of the State Governments.

5. Some time ago a semi-official report was published from New Delhi purporting to give the substance of the new electoral law that had been drafted and circulated to the States. It appeared from that report that the Government proposed to have a certain number of two-member constituencies where the system of voting was to be the distributive vote. Any one who has the least acquaintance with the subject knows that the distributive system of voting in a multi-member constituency is a dishonest device in the hands of the majority party to multiply its strength artificially and thus to perpetuate its majority. If in a two-member constituency, parties A and B have 51 and 49 per cent strength respectively, under the distributive system, party A will capture both the seats. This would mean that while 51 per cent of the voters will have two representatives, 49 per cent of the voters will go completely unrepresented. Under a proper democratic system if there were two seats in such a constituency, one each should go to both the parties A and B. At a conference of opposition parties held a few months ago at Bombay, it was unanimously decided that whatever system of voting was finally adopted, under no conditions should the distributive system with multi-member constituencies should be adopted. But the Congress Party seems to have turned a deaf ear to the unanimous voice of all the opposition parties, including among them the Socialist Party, the Liberal Association, the Hindu Mahasabha, the Scheduled Castes' Federation, and others. There cannot be a better manifestation of totalitarianism.

6. The report from New Delhi also said that the use of hired transport was to be banned for bringing voters to the polling booths. I cannot imagine a more ridiculous provision than that. Banning of transport is necessary to prevent plutocracy from defeating democracy, but very opposite would be the result of the Government's proposal. Parties of the common people can never hope to secure any but hired transport, and that too in very limited numbers. On the other hand, parties of the rich can command private vehicles on a liberal scale. Thus, a ban on hired transport alone would put a premium on wealth. I hope therefore that the use of all transport will be banned for conveying voters to the booths except transport provided by the State for invalids.

7. The general elections being only five months away may I appeal to my countrymen to make up their minds now? It will be soon too late.

Dissatisfaction with the present Government is widespread. But this must find expression a constructive way. The only possible constructive expression is the creation of an alternative party to the Congress. If in spite of the all-pervading dissatisfaction, the Congress were to come back to power, it would only be for the absence of an alternative party. Speaking dispassionately there is no other party except the Socialist Party in India which can challenge the might of the Congress on a national plane. Local or communal parties or splinter groups can hardly achieve any results. For the success of democracy, the two-party system is the most suitable. Multiplicity of parties is as much destructive of democracy as a single-party rule. I therefore appeal to all those who are dissatisfied and disillusioned with the Congress party and who come from the ranks of the common people to rally round the flag of the Socialist Party.

With the elections being so near, it is necessary to allow fullest scope to all peaceful political parties for their propaganda. I have been surprised to know that in Madras city the beach or other open spaces are not allowed for political meetings, at any rate non-Congress meetings. I hope that this discrimination and serious handicap would be immediately removed. To hold elections without giving free scope for political propaganda, demonstrations and organizations, cannot be anything but a mockery.

I find that some people in this part of the country have raised the slogan of Dravidistan. . . . I hope this is not a serious slogan and that the good sense of the people of the South will keep them away from such unpatriotic activities. The slightest effort at thinking should convince anyone that while Dravidistan would be harmful to the national interest, it would be much more harmful, even suicidal, for the Dravid people themselves. In furtherance of this Dravidistan movement some North Indian shops have been picketed in the city by some of these misguided people. India is one and the people of any part are free to sojourn anywhere they like and carry on their legitimate activities. To talk of domination of one part over another is to raise fantams and distract attention from the main issues before the people. The problem in our country is not that of domination of one part by another, but of domination and exploitation of the toiling millions by the upper classes of society whether of the North or South.

The question of the communal GO seems to agitate the minds of a great many people in the South. I must say that it is the duty of the Sate to help the backward and particularly the depressed communities to catch up with the more advanced communities in the matter of education and economic progress. But communal reservation of seats in the educational institutions may not be the best way of achieving this purpose. Educational expansion, grant in scholarship perhaps would be more suitable methods. In this attempt at establishing social justice, it is the duty of the more advanced communities to offer their cooperation and to accept the necessary sacrifice. It is necessary to remember in this connection that caste domination has always been linked with class domination. Therefore injustice and oppression in this country cannot go except under socialism.

In the few days that I have been here, the seriousness of the food situation in the State has been borne in upon me. While I do not wish to say much about this problem, I cannot but point out that the ration of six ounces of rice is very inadequate and must at least be raised to 12 ounces. Also the rationed areas are restricted only to certain towns, whereas in a deficit province even the rural areas should be brought under the sphere of rationing. It appears to me that the entire handling of this problem of food is haphazard and unscientific. Procurement for instance seems to have no scientific basis. Procurement must be based on a study, village by village, of production and needs. It is also clear that no serious attempt has been made so far to check corruption, blackmarketing, hoarding, etc. Where there is so much suffering, under-nourishment and even starvation, the Government cannot be so complacent about corruption and blackmarketing. I am sure that if a vigorous attempt were made to clean up this business and drastic punishment were meted out, this scoruge, if not completely wiped out, would be brought considerably under control.

37. Address to the Members of the All-India Postmen and Lower Grade Staff Union, Madras, 25 October 1950[1]

I propose to severe my connections with all trade union organizations to concentrate on the general elections.

In the coming months, owing to the general elections my time will be

[1]Adapted from *Hindustan Times*, 26 October 1950.

occupied mostly with politics. I have many other things to do. But I can assure you that I shall continue to do all I can to help trade unions.

On the problems of postmen in general, such as abolition of the confirmation examination for postmen promoted as clerks, pay for the strike period and individual members' grievances final decisions would be taken at the ensuing conference of the All-India Postmen and Lower Grade Staff Union to be held at Amritsar in November.

I have been repeatedly assured by the Communications Minister that some formula would be devised soon to satisfy the Union's demands in those matters, but nothing has been done. Recently, I have again written to the Minister to take a decision relating to them.

An assurance has been given to me by no less a person than the Central Minister himself. So I feel that if this assurance is not carried out, I will have no other alternative but to take recourse to a moral weapon [i.e. a hunger strike]. Do not take any action in haste. You all know it and even the Central Government know it. When a peaceful and moderate man like me takes such an extreme course of action, I believe there will be no room for misunderstanding.

38. To S.M. Joshi, 27 October 1950[1]

Dear S.M.,[2]

Pratap[3] brought your letter of October 16th to me at Madras on the 20th. I am sorry for the delay in reply. I have read Mr. Wanchoo's[4] letter which you have sent to me. There is no reason why the Government of India could have noted our resolution with regret, because I had given Mr. H.M. Patel[5] a long enough notice. However, I agree with you that the Federation cannot co-operate with the Committee that has been set up by the Government. We must demand the same kind of committee as we have for the Railways. In the Railway Joint Advisory Committee, there are 4 representatives of the Railway Board and 4 of Railway Labour, and there is a

[1]*J.P. Papers* (NMML).

[2]Refers to S.M. Joshi. For biographical note see *JPSW*, Vol. IV, p. 186.

[3]Pratap Shah; a prominent Socialist worker of Bombay.

[4]Niranjan Nath Wanchoo (1910-79); joined ICS in 1934, joint Secretary Ministry of Defence and Controller General of Defence Production, 1948-57; Secretary Ministry of Finance, Department of Expenditure, 1958-61; Iron & Steel 1961-6; Industrial Development 1967-72; Member Planning Board, Government of M.P. 1972-3; Governor of Kerala, 1973-7.

[5]H.M. Patel; then Secretary, Ministry of Defence.

nominee of the Labour Department who is the Chairman. But he is not a Departmental-Secretary, but an independent person who has been many years an Industrial Judge. Among the labour representatives there are three representing our All-India Railwaymen's Federation and one representing the Congress Federation. In this manner, the Government have provided for both these Federations to be represented. In like manner, if the Defence Department wanted to give representation to labour, the fact that there were three labour federations should have created no difficulties for them whatever. I am sure the three labour federations could have very easily agreed among themselves as to the personnel of their representatives. Mr. Wanchoo seems to think that the representative of the Labour Department of the Government represents labour itself. Nothing can be more ridiculous than this. I advise you therefore to write to the Defence Secretary again suggesting that the committee set-up should be reconstituted, failing which the Federation will have no alternative but to implement the verdict of the strike ballot.

I regret I could not write to the Prime Minister. But I hope I will be able to do so in a day or two. I shall send you a copy of my letter.

I will be in Andhra till the 7th of November and shall reach Calcutta on the 9th where we shall stay till 12th night. I expect to be in Delhi on November 28th. If there is anything to be done there, please let me know. I will be in Patna from 13th to 17th November. I hope we shall meet on 22nd November at Nagpur at the National Executive.

I hope you are well.

Sincerely Yours,
J.P.

39. To Jawaharlal Nehru, 28 October 1950[1]

Dear Bhai,

May I write to you again about the system of voting and the nature of constituencies? When I met you last in New Delhi, you seemed to be too tired to give your attention to what I had to say and it also seemed that you did not consider the question of the system of voting to be of any great importance. From all reports that I have had and also from what I learnt from Dr. [B.R.] Ambedkar himself, it appears that it is the policy of your party and of your Government to form a certain number of 2-member constituencies. These constituencies may be in those parts where seats had to be reserved for the scheduled castes or tribes, or they may even be formed

[1] *J.P. Papers* (NMML).

arbitrarily just as the U.P. Government has proposed to do, where 2/3rds of total number of constituencies are to be proposed to be double-member. I further understand that the system of voting in these constituencies is going to be the distributive vote. As you are aware the distributive vote in multi-member constituencies simply multiplies in an arithmetical manner the strength of the majority party to the *utter* exclusion of all minorities. In multi-member constituencies with distributive voting, no matter how many seats there are, even a 51 per cent majority is bound to capture all the seats. There cannot be a more unfair electoral system than that of multi-member constituencies with distributive votes, and nothing can be more inimical to the growth of democracy. I am stressing this point, because I feel assured that your interest in democracy is not less than mine.

When I had convened a conference of opposition parties in Bombay, it was their unanimous opinion that no matter what system of voting was finally adopted by Parliament, in no case should it be the system of distributive vote in multi-member constituencies. Among the parties represented there were, in addition to my own party, the Hindu Mahasabha, the Scheduled Castes Federation, the Depressed Classes League, the Liberal Association and the Servants of India Society, and among the persons attending the Conference were such eminent men as Dr. R.P. Paranjapye, Mr. N.M. Joshi and Pandit Hridayanath Kunzru. Even though there is no opposition in Parliament, it will not be fair for you and your Government to disregard the unanimous opinion of all the combined opposition parties and of such eminent men. I hope therefore that whatever decision your Government ultimately takes in this matter, you will save the country from this system of distributive voting. Our demand of course is for 3-member constituencies with cumulative vote, but as a second choice we would be happy to have single-member constituencies all over. But in case your Government itself desires to have some plural constituencies, please do not couple them up with the distributive system of voting. I am afraid that due to overwork you have not been able to give your personal attention to many matters of importance to the country. But I do hope that you will find a little time to apply your mind to this problem.

In a day or two I shall be writing to you again about certain problems of the railwaymen and of the civilian employees of the Defence Department.

I hope you are well. With kind regards,

Affectionately yours,
J.P.

[2]See Appendix 4 for Nehru's reply to this letter, also see M.O. Mathai's letter to J.P. Appendix 6.

40. Statement Appealing to the Government to Help the Tibetan People to Maintain their Independence, Madras, 2 November 1950[1]

India being vitally interested in Tibetan affairs, we should do all that may be possible to enable the Tibetan people to maintain their independence and pursue their own way of life. If the Chinese Government does not wish to follow the ways of imperialism it must withdraw its forces from Tibet and the Tibetan people should be allowed to hold a plebiscite under the supervision of the United Nations to determine their future. It is remarkable to find that while the Communist powers have been making such a tremendous noise about world peace and peace pledges, it is they who, in the last few months, have disturbed the peace of the world, once in Korea and now in Tibet.

In connection with the so-called sovereignty of China over Tibet, I would like to say that sovereignty of one nation over another has no sanction whatever, except that of force. For any Communist Government to take shelter behind imperialist formulae, is only to adduce further proof that modern Communism is not different from imperialism.

After all, the vital question is whether the people of Tibet are prepared to accept the sovereignty of China. Whether India or Britain accepts it or not is completely irrelevant to the issue. Every one talks of this or that country acknowledging the sovereignty of China over Tibet, but nobody bothers to consider the wishes of the Tibetan people themselves.

The plea of the Chinese Government that Britain and America are intruding in Tibet is a plea which the Communists can use with equal facility anywhere they like. For instance, there is nothing to prevent a Communist Government from interfering in Indian affairs on the plea that India is an Anglo-American puppet. But can there anything be more fantastic?

[1]Adapted from *Hindu*, 3 November 1950.

41. To Jawaharlal Nehru, 10 November 1950[1]

Dear Bhai,

I thank you for your letter of November 1.[2] I hope you will excuse me if I say that the impression your letter gave me was that the question raised by me had received a very superficial attention. First of all, I am no believer in

[1]*J.P. Papers* (NMML).
[2]See Appendix 3 for the text of Nehru's letter.

P.R.[3] and there was no need to point out its defects to me. There was also no need to refer to the difficulties in the way of three-member constituencies and cumulative voting. I do not at all agree with the criticism made in your letter of this matter, but as that is beside the point, I shall not waste your time with it.

The issue raised by me was a very narrow one. If your Government decides to have single-member constituencies all over, I for one shall accept it as a second choice. But if some constituencies, no matter how small or large their number may be, are going to be two-member, I must oppose with all my strength any attempt to introduce the distributive system of voting into those constituencies.

You say in your letter that you do not understand why I should be apprehensive of "single-member constituencies plus some double-member." Let me explain. Firstly, I do not think that the word "some" needs to be lightly treated. According to the U.P. Government's proposals two-thirds of the constituencies in the State would be double-member. Secondly, even if the number of double-member constituencies is small, it would be a serious impediment to the working of democracy. It has been found that democracy works best in a two-party system, particularly when the two parties are more or less equally balanced. When parties are so balanced the results even in a few constituencies are enough to tilt the balance in favour of one or the other. If we have distributive voting in two-member constituencies, as I wrote to you in my last letter, the party having even a 51 per cent majority is bound to capture both the seats. This would mean a simple arithmetic multiplication of the strength of the majority party. This would be very unfair to the electorate. You say that elections are not decided by arithmetic means or mathematical conclusions. I never suggested any such thing though mathematical calculations have a great deal to do with elections. What I maintain is that the device of the distributive vote has no other but an arithmetic result. This is not vitiated by the number of candidates and the different pulls that there may be. I do urge you to treat this matter more seriously.

You also suggest in your letter that the cumulative system would be more complicated than the distributive one. I do not agree with this view. In a two-member constituency as far as the electorate is concerned, no matter how backward it may be, the distributive or the cumulative vote is equally simple or complicated.

In this connection, may I again remind you that while the opposition parties might differ in their preferences for different systems of voting, *they are united in their opposition to the distributive system*. I hope the

[3]Proportional Representation.

Congress party will give some weight to the combined opinion of all the parties except itself.

I do not know what to make of your reference to the difficulties of democracy in a large country such as ours. I hope that whatever else you might have had in your mind, it was not your intention to suggest that because of the vastness of the problem any less care should be given to the rearing up of a sound democratic edifice in this country. If the tragic failures of the Congress Governments in the past years have shown anything, it is the danger of a compromise with principles.

I did not fail to notice the note of irritation in your letter. I am really sorry for having given you so much trouble about this matter, but I hope you will excuse me in view of the importance I attach to it.

With kindest regards,

Yours affectionately,
J.P.

42. To M.O. Mathai, 11 November 1950[1]

Dear Mr. Mathai,

I hope you remember the talk we had when I met you last about the system of voting. You had told me then that you were studying the problem yourself and were collecting material from foreign countries. I find from my correspondence with Panditji that he has not made an effort to understand the problem. It is too late for any one to make a comparative study of different systems of voting in the world. The Government of India as well as the State Governments have already decided upon single-member constituencies with a simple majority vote. This is acceptable to us as a second choice. But a certain number of constituencies are going to be double-member and as Dr. Ambedkar told me, the Congress party wants to introduce the distributive system of voting in those constituencies. This I consider to be dangerous to democracy and unfair to political minorities. But I seem to have been unable to convince the Prime Minister of it.

I wonder if you can do anything in the matter. If there were single-member constituencies all over the country, I would have little objection. But if there are even a few double-member constituencies, the system of voting must be the cumulative or the restrictive one. I hope you will be able to do something to help us in this matter.

Yours sincerely,
J.P.

[1] *J.P. Papers* (NMML).

43. To Jawaharlal Nehru, 17 November 1950[1]

Dear Bhai,

I met the Koiralas before and after they went to Delhi. The story they told me after their return was incredible and literally heart-rending. So this is how you wish to treat a democratic revolution in a neighbouring state! Koirala is doing for his country what you did for yours, and you speak of putting him in bars and fetters! And all that because of some imaginary embarrassment that the Nepali revolution has caused you. Bhai, I write to you like this because of my love and admiration for you. I wonder if there is any one around you who tells you the truth and talks straight to you. You are destroying yourself. One by one you are denying your noble ideals. You are compromising, you are yielding. You are estranging your friends and stepping into the parlour of your enemies. All this is clearly visible to an outsider though it may not be to you. But for heaven's sake do not let Nepali freedom be assassinated by your hesitations and the bunglings of your advisers. You have all the trump cards—the king and the revolution on your side. Remember history depends upon your policy in this regard.

And please learn to discipline your temper.

And finally please do not be annoyed by the tone of this letter.[2] I required no courage to write it (for I seek nothing from you), but only honesty and sincerity to you.

With love,

Jayaprakash

[1]*J.P. Papers* (NMML).

[2]See Appendix 5 for Nehru's reply to J.P.

44. Presidential Address to EIR Employees' Union, Rosa (Shahjahanpur), 18 November 1950[1]

If the Central Government does not settle the outstanding issues between the Railway Board and the employees, a general strike on the railways would be inevitable.

Let us all hope that the Government will show the same wisdom and spirit of conciliation as they exhibited last year and the grave eventuality would be avoided. But let us also be prepared to meet it, if it does arise, with courage, unity and wisdom. We are meeting at a time when we are faced with serious difficulties, both internal and external. Since the amalgamation of the three unions into the present union, internal conflicts

[1]Adapted from *National Herald*, 19 November 1950.

had stood in the way of the development of the union. The amalgamated union has been and is the largest single trade union in this country and yet we have not been able to make the amount of progress that such a powerful union is expected to make. A few months ago the internal situation had become so difficult that it appeared that the great achievement of amalgamation itself was in danger. But finally the leaders of the union have able to sink their differences and preserve the integrity of the union and the unity and solidarity of the workers.

While in the past year, we had made substantial progress particularly through the efforts of the Joint Advisory Committee, our difficulties are surely not at an end and many outstanding issues have yet to be settled. The general council of Federation at its last meeting at Madras instructed the working committee of the AIRF to arrange for a strike ballot if the Railway Ministry did not respond satisfactorily to the major demands that still remained outstanding. Those demands have been brought under five heads by the general council which need to be emphasised as often as possible:

(1) Withdrawal or modification of the two labour bills; (2) Dearness allowance or relief on the basis of the Central Pay Commission recommendations; (3) Demands of the running staff as embodied in the resolution of the Running Staff Conference held by the All-India Railwaymen's Federation in Madras; (4) Settlement of other pending issues raised by the affiliated unions and the federation in respect of other staff, such as nationalistion of company-managed railways, proper weightage for service, confirmation of temporary staff, implementation of favourable recommendations of the Railway Joint Advisory Committee and Central Pay Commission, and cancellation of wrongful discharge and punishments; and (5) Weightage for past service in fixation of pay in the Central Pay Commission scales for Darjeeling, Himalayan Railwaymen and ex-Indian state railwaymen on the same basis and principles as are applied to the Indian Government railways and further required to be rationalised by railway employees so that for same service in same scale same pay may be ensured throughout India.

As for the demands formulated by the Running Staff Conference there are 21 such demands including (i) abolition of bottom scales now prescribed for drivers, shunters, firemen, motormen, guards, brakesmen and others; (ii) reduction of the three prescribed scales to two for drivers and guards; (iii) removal of the distinction between matric and non-matric literates; (iv) fixation of the rates of running allowances for different categories of staff members, together with a gurarantee of minimum running allowance equivalent to 75 per cent of basic pay; and (v) treatment of all running staff as class III employees without any exception.

In January 1949, the Government had promised that every six months the scales of dearness allowance would be revised. Even though 22 months have passed since then, the revision has not once been made, while prices have risen higher. Therefore in terms of Government's own announcement, it is the duty of the Government now to revise the scales of dearness allowance in accordance with the recommendations of the Central Pay Commission.

In addition to these all-India problems, they on the East Indian Railway are faced with some peculiar problems. One such is the non-implementation of the recommendations of the Joint Advisory Committtee, even after their acceptance by the Railway Board. Some instances of this are the upgrading of 25 per cent of the clerical staff, with regard to which orders had been passed by the Railway Board on November 9, 1949, weightage for length of service and fixation of scales for master craftsmen and highly .killed staff.

At their last meeting with the General Manager, an assurance had been given that the implementation of these decisions would be expedited as fast as possible. They were also told that there were many difficulties involved in the implementation and that the delay was not due to neglect.

While labour is never satisfied till the achievement of its final objective, namely, the establishment of socialism. Some of the discontentment among the railway staff seems to me to be totally unjustified. Before the appointment of the Central Pay Commission there were all kinds of grades and scales and it was one of the demands of labour and particularly of the AIRF that there should be standardisation of scales and grades. This task has to a considerable extent been achieved in the commission's report, but some sections of the staff still wish to perpetuate the old, myriad distinctions between worker and worker. I for one cannot support this viewpoint nor I believe can our union or the AIRF do so. I am sure we would like the differences between worker and worker to be narrowed down still further. I am also sure that in a workers state, these distinctions will be far less than they are today. While the drive of labour may not be towards complete equality of incomes, it surely is towards a more egalitarian distribution of wealth.

I may refer to the danger of sectional organizations that have appeared before us and that the strength of labour lies in subordination of sectional interests to the larger interests of the workers. If the larger interests are served the sectional interests are also bound to be furthered. No section of railwaymen by itself had the strength to fight against the administration of the Government of India. That is why I have been advocating a sort of combination of sectional organizations with large industrial unions.

I refer to the Central labour bills which, except for the INTUC, organized labour in this country has been unanimous in being opposed to. Under the provisions of those bills, railway employees of various categories like the supervisory personnel, watch and ward Staff at the head office and hospital staff would be denied the right to belong to their own common industrial organization. By recognising in this manner sectional unions, the proposed legislation is intended to disrupt the class unity of the workers. If these bills are passed, slowing down can be declared as an illegal action, disputes relating to wrongful removal from service and staff retrenchment would not be allowed to be referred to industrial tribunals and other settlement machinery. Works committees or staff councils would usurp the functions of trade unions and railwaymen and other industrial workers in nationalised undertakings would be deprived of their political rights, including the right to organise a party of labour. By these and other means the bills would destroy all independent trade unions and convert the workers into slaves of the state.

These are the problems before you. Your success in dealing with them will depend upon your success in building up your union. I hope at this conference, which is the first annual conference of the amalgamated union, you will be able to lay the foundations of unity and solidarity that will withstand all onslaughts of time and of the INTUC and the Government.

45. To U. Ba Sawe, 20 November 1950[1]

Dear Comrade U. Ba Sawe,[2]

I cannot thank you adequately enough for the help[3] that you were so good as to render to the cause of freedom. I hope that the struggle so brilliantly started with the resources that were mainly supplied by you would soon end in victory. It may be possible that more help of the same nature would be soon required and I hope in that case we will not be disappointed. I need hardly say that the people concerned and all of us will remain ever grateful for the help already rendered.

I hope you are well. With best wishes for the success of socialism in Burma and with kind regards for you.

Sincerely yours,
J.P.

[1] *J.P. Papers* (NMML).

[2] U. Ba Sawe; General Secretary, Burmese Socialist Party, Rangoon and Head of the Burmese Government.

[3] Refers to the supply of a plane-load of arms by the Socialist Government of Burma to the Nepali Congress then fighting for democracy in Nepal under the leadership of B.P. Koirala.

46. To Thakin Chit Maung, 20 November 1950[1]

Dear Com. Thakin Chit Maung,

I hasten to offer my heartfelt thanks for the generous way in which my request was treated and the help that was so kindly rendered. I am writing separately to Com. U. Ba Sawe also to convey my thanks. Let us all hope that the struggle for freedom so brilliantly started will soon end in success and the great citadel of reaction in Asia would be demolished.

With greetings to you,

Sincerely yours,
J.P.

[1]*J.P. Papers* (NMML).
[2]Thakin Chit Maung; Dy General Secretary, Burmese Socialist Party, Rangoon.

47. Statement regarding the Kashmir Problem, Nagpur, 22 November 1950[1]

The only visible and practicable solution left for the Kashmir question is the convening of a constituent assembly to settle finally the future of the state.

Once the assembly is elected by May next, as demanded by the Kashmir National Conference, and a decision taken, it should be binding upon the Government of India as well as the United Nations. There would then be no question of plebiscite and India should withdraw her case from the UN and refuse to take any part in any further deliberations which might not be of her seeking.

People in the Pakistan-held Kashmir should also be given the opportunity to elect their representatives to the proposed constituent assembly. But, if this can not be arranged for any reason, the future of that part of Kashmir should be left to be decided later on as one of the several matters in dispute between India and Pakistan.

[1]Adapted from *National Herald*, 23 November 1950.

48. Reference to Nepal, Pakistan and Kashmir at a Public Meeting, New Delhi, 26 November 1950[1]

The Government of India should recognise the unfettered right of the people of Nepal to establish a democratic Government in their country with King Tribhuvan Vir Bikram Shah Dev,[2] now in Delhi, as its constitutional head.

It is a matter of regret that the Government, by adopting a vacillating attitude, has made the Nepal issue more complicated. India must take an independent stand over the Nepal issue, and must not allow her attitude to be influenced by outside pressure from either Great Britain or any other power.

To-day a revolution is taking place in Nepal. The urge of the Nepalese people to free themselves from Ranashahi has taken the form of armed conflict. The Nepali Congress, leading the Nepalese people, never asked for any aid from the Indian Government. In consonance with the will of the people and the King of Nepal, whom they consider as their constitutional head, they want to democratise the State, and for that they only expect the Government of India to openly extend diplomatic support to the rightful King as against the Ranas.

I warn that other powers like Great Britain are interested in seeing that the Ranas continue to rule over the people of Nepal with the sword. The British Government has a big stake in Nepal, from where it gets tough, sturdy Gurkha soliders to work as mercenaries in its army, to be used for imperialistic purposes in Malaya and other places. A democratic government in Nepal would never allow its people to be used as mercenaries.

I appeal to the people to render full support to the Nepalese Congress in its fight against the despotic and tyrannical rule of the Ranas, irrespective of the decision the Indian Government takes in the matter.

The Rana regime can be ended in a very short time if the King of Nepal, now in Delhi, goes to the liberated areas of Nepal, and takes his rightful place as constitutional head of the Government.

[1]Adapted from *Tribune*, 27 November 1950.

[2]Tribhuvan Bir Bikram Shah Dev (1906-55); acceded to the Nepalese throne in 1911, lived virtually as a prisoner of the Rana Prime Minister; sought asylum in Indian Embassy, Kathmandu, 1950, visited India in 1950 and with help from Nehru brought about an agreement between the Rana Prime Minister and the leaders of Nepali Congress, who were then spearheading a powerful rebellion for the end of Rana rule and eastablishment of democratic government in Nepal with the King as a constitutional monarch, in early February 1951; returned to Nepal as a Constitutional monarch on 18 February 1951; went to Europe for medical treatment in 1953; delegated royal power to Prince Mahendra in 1955.

As far as the incarceration of the Khan Brothers[3] in Pakistan, it would not be wrong to say that it exposes the fascist nature of the Pakistani Government. There is no vestige of civil liberty in Pakistan where the Government is adopting fascist methods to crush all democratic opinion. We in India can only express our indignation at the incarceration of the Khan Brothers and other Khudai-Khidmatgars languishing in Pakistani jails. But we hope that this will arouse world opinion against the Pakistan authorities, and put an end to this state of affairs.

The state of civil liberties in India, is not as bad as in Pakistan, even though the Indian Government too has been restricting civil liberties, which can be said to smack of fascism in certain respects.

I welcome the Kashmir National Conference resolution, proposing the holding of elections in the state and setting up of a constituent assembly. The decisions of this assembly will be final and irrevocable, and will put an end to the present state of suspense and indecision regarding the future of Kashmir.

[3]Refers to Khan Abdul Ghaffar Khan and Dr. Khan Saheb.

49. To U. Ba Sawe, 4 December 1950[1]

Dear Com. U. Ba Sawe,

The letter of thanks which I had written for you[2] was not sent in time because, on second thoughts, I thought it was advisable not to use the post. Now since these friends[3] have again to go to Rangoon, I am sending both these letters with them. As I wrote in my previous letter, these friends are in need of more help from you and this time of a more substantial nature. The movement though brilliantly started will take some time to reach its conclusion. I believe these friends are in a position now to make payment, if necessary, for the help received. I trust they will not return disappointed.

I send you my best wishes and kind regards,

Very sincerely yours,
J.P.

[1]*J.P. Papers* (NMML).
[2]This refers to J.P.'s letter dated 20 November 1950.
[3]Some young leaders of the Nepali Congress.

50. To Thakin Chit Maung, 4 December 1950[1]

Dear Com. Thakin Chit Maung,

The accompanying letter[2] which I had written some days ago was not sent earlier because I did not think it advisable to use the post. These friends are going again for more help of the same kind. The movement had a brilliant start, but it will take some time before success is finally achieved. I believe the friends concerned are now in a position to pay, if necessary, for the help received. I am writing separately to Com. U. Ba Sawe regarding this matter. I hope you will be kind enough to help us out again.

With best wishes and kind regards,

Very sincerely yours,
J.P.

[1]*J.P. Papers* (NMML).
[2]Refer's to J.P.'s letter dated 28 November 1950.

51. To Awadhesh Nandan Sahay, 4 December 1950[1]

My dear Awadhesh Babu,

When I left Delhi for the Punjab I had asked a friend of mine, Mr. [Vaidyanath] Iyer, to send you a thousand rupees for the Bihar Party. I do not know if this money has been sent yet, but I am writing so that you may know for what purpose the money had been sent.

We are doing fairly well. This is my rest day at Simla. The Punjab tour has been very satisfactory so far. I hope you are well.

Affectionately yours,
J.P.

[1]*Brahmanand Papers* (NMML).

52. To M.O. Mathai, 4 December 1950[1]

Dear Mr. Mathai,

I thank you for your letter of Nov. 21. I was rather sorry to find you also writing as a bureaucrat or a Minister. I had hoped that since you had told me that you were studying the different systems of voting in different countries, you would be able to advise the people concerned dispassionately.

[1]*J.P. Papers* (NMML).

But you also seem to be echoing the opinion of others. To contend that in a two-member constituency, the cumulative system of voting would encourage communal politics is, to my mind, fantastic in the extreme, and so far no one seems to have answered the main criticism against the distributive system of voting, namely, that it is a dishonest device to artificially multiply the strength of the majority party and to deny any representation even to a 49 per cent minority in such a constituency. However, it does not seem possible to get justice from the Prime Minister regarding this matter and so I must leave the question where it is and not trouble you any more about it. I had hoped that the combined opinion of all the opposition parties on this matter would have more weight than it has been given by the Congress.

You write in your letter that my letters to the Prime Minister have been sent to the Chief Election Commissioner. While the Commissioner's opinion may be obtained, I hope it is realised that the question is outside his jurisdiction. At least that is what Mr. Sen had told me when I had met him in Bombay. He had said that as far as the system of voting was concerned, it was not within his jurisdiction to recommend any particular system to the President or the Parliament.

Hoping you are well,

Yours sincerely,
J.P.

53. To Jawaharlal Nehru, 8 December 1950[1]

Dear Bhai,

I thank you for your letter of Nov. 20. I am sorry that you found the tone of my last letter offensive. It was not meant to be so.

You accuse me of lack of understanding. I admit this possible failure, but I am afraid, the understanding shown on your side too has not been particularly realistic. Koiralas and their colleagues might have embarrassed you by some of their actions, but you should not forget that all these Nepali revolutionary leaders have been living for years in India and it is natural for them to act as if India was their home. Bishweshwar has lived for years in Patna and he took part in the Indian freedom movement just as if he were an Indian national. In using Indian territory during the current revolutionary struggle in Nepal, he and his friends were no doubt acting naturally and without inhibitions of any kind. If some of their actions were found to be embarrassing, there was enough liaison between the Government of India and them to enable the former to advise them in a friendly manner and in

[1] *J.P. Papers* (NMML).

due time. There was no reason for any one to fly into a temper and treat the revolutionary leaders as if they are criminals.

In understanding the actions of the Nepali Congress people it is also necessary to remember that on the borders of Bihar and Nepal there is a feeling among the people living on both sides of intimate kinship. Furthermore, during the 1942 struggle, hundreds of Indian revolutionaries crossed over to Nepal and took shelter there and even built bases for their revolutionary activities. Even the reactionary Ranas did not throw up a fit, as we seem to be doing, because their territory was being used for the purposes of Indian revolution. The Ranas, as you might know, resisted for a considerable period of time British pressure and arrested me only when the pressure was irresistible for them. India should never forget the help that the people of Nepal rendered during her last struggle for freedom. All these things, no doubt subconsciously, were working in the minds of Koiralas and their colleagues. An understanding of these factors would have perhaps enabled those in power in India today to take a more tolerant attitude towards the alleged misbehaviour of the Nepali Congress leaders.

As for the demands that Koirala had made on the Government of India, I do not take such a frightful view as you seem to have taken. In the present world it would have been rather natural for any group of revolutionaries anywhere to make such an demand on a friendly government, and I am sure no other government would have taken such a tragic and unfriendly view of the matter as you did. Bishweshwar was asked to put down on paper the specific kind of help that he wanted, which he did. If you did not wish to give him that help, which someone else in your position might well have given, you should have told him so politely. I do not think Bishweshwar committed a crime by hoping that the Government of India would so far deviate from the path of rectitude as to render unofficially the kind of help that he sought from it. I am sure in his position I would have not only asked the Indian Government to give me that help, but also would I have held that Government responsible for upholding reaction and defeating progress if it denied me that help. You have no doubt to take into consideration world opinion and such other important matters. Personally, I feel we do more harm to ourselves than otherwise by first taking tentative steps in a certain direction and than retreating in confusion by fear of 'world opinion'. However, it appears that there is nothing for us to do, but to agree to differ on this matter and leave the question at that.

I hope that in any case the present talks with the Ranas will not end in the complete suppression of the movement in Nepal.

With regards,

Affectionaly yours,
J.P.

54. To Rafi Ahmed Kidwai, 11 December 1950[1]

My dear Rafi Saheb,

There were many questions regarding postmen and lower grade staff which the All-India Postmen's and Lower Grade Staff Union had taken up with you and your Department. While on some questions favourable decisions were made, on many others either no decision has yet been taken or there has been an unfavourable decision. When Shri Dalvi and Shri Akhtar, with other representatives of the Union, had met you in August last, many of these issues were discussed, but with practically no result. My Union is soon to meet in an annual conference, and I should be obliged if I have the considered and final reply of the Government on those points. The following are some of the important points:

I. *Dearness Allowance*

In January 1949, the Central Government while announcing an increase of Rs. 10/- in the dearness allowance in a communique, had promised to review the issue of dearness allowance every six months in the light of movement in prices. It is over 23 months now since the Government made this promise, but not even once has this matter been reviewed although prices in the meantime have steadily moved up. This has naturally been agitating the minds of the staff and I hope Government would take immediate action to implement their own promise without any further delay.

II. *The Two Labour Bills*

As for the two Labour Bills that are now before the Parliament, independent labour throughout the country has expressed itself in unequivocal terms against them. It is the considered opinion of labour in general and of Government employees in particular, that some of the provisions of these Bills are so obnoxious as to render free trade union movement impossible. These Bills should therefore be withdrawn forthwith or at least altered drastically in the light of the criticism made at the Labour Conference held at Delhi in August last.

III. *Confirmation of Temporary Staff*

The usual procedure of confirming temporary posts is that they should be confirmed within a period of two years. But during the war all the posts

[1]*Brahmanand Papers* (NMML).

were kept as temporary. Two years ago the Government issued orders that 50 per cent of the temporary posts up to 1946 should be confirmed. Since then no further orders have been issued in this connection. The result is that there are still a large number of posts and staff, with many years of service, who are still treated as temporary. Though the temporary staff have been granted most of the benefits enjoyed by the permanent staff, still they are deprived of certain benefits, such as that of getting annual increments on due dates while on leave. Apart from benefits, the temporary staff always suffer from a feeling of insecurity and naturally there is accumulated resentment. The efficiency of the department also suffers by keeping the staff as temporary for a number of years.

I therefore urge that temporary staff should be confirmed without any further delay irrespective of (i) age limit; (ii) physical fitness; (iii) domicile; and (iv) literary qualifications.

IV. *Upgrading of Cities for Compensatary and House Rent Allowance*

The population of cities like Poona, Amritsar and some others have increased considerably since the Pay Commission had made their recommendations. The Union had raised this issue in its interview with you on 22.8.1950, and you had promised to consider the matter sympathetically. I shall be obliged if this matter is expedited.

V. *The Scales of Pay for P&T Staff in Merged States*

The scales of pay, allowances and conditions of service for the P&T Staff in the merged states should be in line with those obtaining in the Indian Union, with effect from 1st April 1950, as has been done in the case of the integrated railways.

VI. *Implementation of Recommendations of the P&T Expert Committee*

The position regarding this matter was that we were told that no recommendation of the Expert Committee would be implemented if it involved any extra expenditure in view of Government's difficult economic position. We hope the position has improved now. In any case, Governments themselves are responsible for the position in which they find themselves and therefore they should not use that as an excuse for not doing justice to their staff in accordance with their own expert committee.

VII. *Supply of Uniforms*

Two sets of uniforms, umbrellas, etc. should be supplied every year as before.

VIII. *Examination for Promotion to Clerical Cadre*

Government were kind enough to agree that 50 per cent of the vacancies in the clerical cadre would be reserved for postmen and lower grade staff. But this privilege has almost been nullified by the examination prescribed for promotion to the clerical grade, which is the same as that for outside candidates. The standard of these examinations is naturally too high, and some times the papers set (for instance at an examination held in the Punjab Circle on 30.7.1950) are of the BA or FA level. It is not possible for the departmental candidates to succeed at these examinations. If, therefore, the Government do really intend to fill up 50 per cent of the vacancies in the clerical grade with postmen, a separate examination, not so much in academic subjects as in practical knowledge necessary for the routine work of the clerical staff, should be prescribed along with the necessary text-books. I believe that an assurance that this would be done was given some time ago. May I hope that this vexed question which seems capable of easy solution, will now at last be settled.

IX. *Introduction of New Schemes and Reduction of Staff*

The Union should be consulted whenever the Government seek to introduce new schemes, such as mail motor service, affecting the transfer or reduction of staff. Even where they do not introduce new schemes, but only seek to reduce staff on the plea of less work, the Union should be consulted because it is often found that Government's method of assessing the workload is faulty.

During my tour of the Punjab I came accross many complaints from the staff. I am requesting the General Secretary of the Union, Shri Akhtar, to take up these matters with the Director General. I should like, however, to draw your attention to one particular complaint regarding housing. Just as in salaries, so in housing, the difference between high and low officials presents a painful contrast. At Simla, I visited the one-room quarters of the staff and was deeply distressed to see the same 8' x 8' room being used as a sleeping room, bath room, kitchen and store room. The least that should be done there is to provide a separate kitchen. This would be easily done by allotting one-and-a-half room to each official. Housing is perhaps the most neglected of all of labour's demands. It is time that some attention is paid to it now. I hope you will give it your sympathetic consideration.

I shall be thankful if I have your reply as soon as possible. I should also like to interview you with other representatives of the Union on the 18th or 19th December as it may suit you.

Hoping you are well,

Yours sincerely,
J.P.

55. To Asoka Mehta, 11 December 1950[1]

Dear Asoka,

I have your letter of December 6, regarding Aruna.[2] You may publish her correspondence with the Gujerat comrade in the Party Letter, but I am afraid, that will not be enough to deal with the situation that she has created. Whatever she is doing is a part, I am sure, of a deliberate plan. As for her views, there is nothing original or new about them as you see. They are the same naive and childish things that all our so called Marxists have always been peddling around. As for the method that she is following in trying deliberately to discredit the Party, we will have seriously to consider how to deal with it. What Prem[3] pointed out to me the other day might be a way out of the difficulty. Every member of the Party has to renew his membership every year. I am sure Aruna's membership has lapsed and I would be surprised if she had applied for membership again. In that case she automatically ceases to be a member of the Party. And if she does apply, as she well might, I do not see how she can honestly say that she subscribes to the programme and policy of the Party. No body is forcing her to join the Party which, according to her declared views, is anti-Marxist. It would be highly dishonest for her to try to enter such a party. The only purpose that she can have is to destroy the party. There are many "Marxist" parties in this country and she is free to choose from them or form her own Party. I have been thinking of saying something about her in the press. Press correspondents have often asked me about her, but so far I have evaded the question. If you think I should say something on the above lines, please write to me c/o. Shri Madanlal Sodhani,[4] Park View Road, Karol Bagh, Delhi. I might issue a statement from Delhi when I am there on the 18th of this month. I have asked Prem who has gone to Delhi on your instructions

[1]*Brahmanand Papers* (NMML).
[2]Refers to Aruna Asaf Ali.
[3]Refers to Prem Bhasin.
[4]Madanlal Sodhani. For biographical note see *JPSW*, Vol. IV, p. 222.

to speak to Aruna and find out just exactly what she is planning to do. I shall write to you again from Delhi after I have talked to Prem or possibly to Aruna.

Suren Dwivedi had written to Prem about Orissa subvention. If you could possibly do so, I should like you to continue the subvention. I hope in any case Suren Dwivedi's own personal allowance is being regularly remitted.

I hope you are well,

Affectionately yours,
Jayaprakash

56. Statement regarding Treatment of *Satyagrahis* in Saharsa District (Bihar), 12 December 1950[1]

It will be recalled, some weeks ago there was a satyagraha movement started by the Socialist Party in the district of Saharsa in order to compel the authorities to take the necessary steps to meet with the famine situation. A number of the satyagrahis were arrested, about forty of whom are in the Bhagalpur Camp Jail. I have just received information that all these prisoners are being treated as ordinary 'C' class criminals, and even the ordinary privileges available during the British raj, such as daily newspapers, are denied to them. Several of these prisoners had been given upper class treatment in the British days. While the socialist satyagrahis are not demanding distinction to be made between themselves, they are justified in demanding for all of them special treatment as political prisoners. It appears that when Shri Nirapada Mukherji, Parliamentary Secretary, had recently visited the jail he had promised speedy consideration of this matter. But so far nothing has been done. It is rather remarkable that this Government of erstwhile *satyagrahis* should now find no difference between ordinary criminals and those who seek imprisonment in the pursuit of a public cause. May I hope that the Bihar Government will give some attention to this matter?

[1] *J.P. Papers* (NMML).

57. To Rafi Ahmed Kidwai, 15 December 1950[1]

My dear Rafi Saheb,

In a letter written a few days ago, I had asked for an interview on the 18th or the 19th in connection with the All-India Postmen's Union. I regret that I shall have to leave Delhi on the 18th afternoon, so if it is possible for you to give me an hour's time before 3 p.m. on the 18th I should be obliged. If, however, this is not possible, I would be happy if you could meet us on the 26th of December at any time that may suit you. In fact for the Postmen's Union I should prefer the 26th December and on the 18th I should like to meet and discuss politics. I shall reach Delhi on the 17th night and shall contact Jainarainji[2] on the 17th night or 18th morning.

With kind regards,

Sincerely yours,

J.P.

[1]*Brahmanand Papers* (NMML).
[2]Private Secretary to Kidwai.

58. Statement on the Situation in Nepal, 27 December 1950[1]

The repeated comings and goings between Kathmandu and Delhi of agents of the usurper Rana regime might give the impression that the fate of Nepal is in the hands of the Government of India. Nothing can be farther from the truth. The fate of Nepal is in the hands of Nepali people and it is being decided right now by the course of the Nepali revolution which is one of the significant events in Asia. The policies of Government of India no doubt can influence, for good or evil, the course of events in Nepal. But in no circumstances should it be assumed at Delhi or anywhere else, that the ultimate decision in Nepal lies in the hands of anyone but the people themselves. Having said so, I should like to add that as an Indian who can never forget the debt that our freedom movement owes to the people of Nepal, I do fervently wish that our policies in relation to Nepal were guided by the highest principles and considerations of the good of the Nepali people. I therefore feel that when both when both the King and the people have jointly repudiated the Rana regime, our government has shown undue softness for that infamously reactionary Government. It also appears to me to be highly inconsistent to recognise on the one hand King Tribhuvan Bikram Shah and on the other hand to deal with Rana Mohan Shumsher as if he were the legally constituted Government of Nepal. I hope the

[1]*J.P. Papers* (NMML).

Government of India will not weaken on its stand of continuing to recognise King Tribhuvan and will soon terminate its parleys with the unconstitutional Prime Minister and will ask the King of Nepal to name a government with which we can continue our talks and eastablish diplomatic relations.

I should also like to add that while the proposal for convening a Constituent Assembly elected by adult franchise is a sound one, the suggestions made regarding the formation of an Interim Government are fraught with danger. If the future of democracy in Nepal is not to be put in jeopardy and the proposed Constituent Assembly is not to be reduced to a farce, no member of the Rana family should retain the office of the Prime Minister, which should go to a representative of the people. Nor should the proclamation regarding the contemplated reforms should be made by the Prime Minister who has no authority whatever, but by the King himself. I hope that our halting and dilatory policies with regard to Nepal would change and we would act swiftly and firmly in view of the worsening international situtation.

59. Interview to the United Press of India, on the situation in Nepal, Bombay, 1 January 1951[1]

The situation arising out of the insurrection in Nepal could not possibly weaken India's north-eastern frontier even in the face of Communist China's advance in Tibet.

The insurrection in Nepal is a people's insurrection, and as such they will resist any open aggression upon their country by any foreign power, after they are able to take power in their own hands in Nepal and shape the future of their country.

The real danger in the interim period, is that if the people of Nepal found that there is no relief from the Rana tyranny, they may seek help from the Communists across the frontier.

The insurrectionists in Nepal are now much stronger than they were before. For the time being it seems that things had quietened down, but now they have acquired more power for defending themselves and launching offensives against the Rana troops as well.

The Nepali insurrectionists have enough men and they do not need any volunteers from India, but arms and ammunitions which the Socialist Party can not supply them. The Socialist Party, however, has given their full moral support to the insurrectionists in Nepal.

[1]Adapted from *Tribune*, 2 January 1951.

60. To Suraj Narayan Singh, 21 January 1951[1]

My dear Surajbabu,[2]

I thank you for the letter that you sent through Pinakin.[3] I was very sorry for not being present at the General Council. I hope, however, that every thing went well and the meeting was a success.

Regarding Pinakin, I do not think that we should shunt him again to trade union work. It is best that he is given some work in the field of agricultural or industrial cooperation.

Since you were on tour, I have been corresponding with Hari Krishnaji[4] regarding my programme in Bihar. It had originally been arranged that I would be touring U.P. some time from the end of February to the end of March. I am happy to inform you that the U.P. tour has now been shifted to May-June. This means that I would be able to give a whole month to Bihar excluding the time that would be necessary for the Kisan Panchayat and the National Executive at Delhi. I expect I will go for a day to Lalgunj to attend the marriage of Jagannath Babu's[5] daughter. From there I will go to the Bhumi Sena Sammelan. After that I should like to go to my village for three days and then I have to go to Jamalpur for a day to attend the E.I. Railway Employees Union Conference. I shall know in a week the exact dates of Jamalpur conference and then I will write to Hari Krishnaji again so that my tour programme in Bihar may be fixed up. I suggest that out of the 30 days fifteen may be used for touring and I might be allowed to stay at Patna for 15 days so that I can do my writing work as well as I might have opportunity to meet and discuss with you all at some leisure. I should like to take interest in the Bhumi Sena Sammelan. The idea came to me when I had gone to Sitamarhi to see the work that Rambahadurlal[6] and his friends have done in that area. I felt that if a conference of all Bhumi Sena workers were held it would give a great fillip to the entire movement of mass constructive work in the villages. That work has great possibilities. When Benipuriji was in Bombay I discussed the question with him and I fixed up the dates for the conference to suit my programme. The dates fixed at Bombay were February 18, 19 and 20. I shall soon prepare a

[1]*Brahmanand Papers* (NMML).

[2]For biographical note on Suraj Narayan Singh, see *JPSW*, Vol. II, p. 222.

[3]Pinakin Patel; then a trade union leader belonging to the Socialist Party.

[4]Harikrishnaji; prominent socialist leader, and one of the secretaries of the Bihar Socialist Party at that time.

[5]Jagannath Singh; a Congressmen from Ballia (U.P.) imprisoned several times during the freedom movement; member of the U.P. Assembly, 1947 and 1952; later became member of the U.P. Legislative Council.

[6]Rambahadur Lal; a prominent Socialist worker in Sitamarhi (Bihar) engaged in village reconstruction work there.

programme for the conference and send you a copy. I want the Provincial Party and the Provincial Kisan Panchayat jointly to take up this work.

I hope you are well. With best wishes,

Affectionately yours,
J.P.

P.S. This letter was dictated in the train yesterday. We reached here [Madras] this morning and the doctor said that I would have to stay here for a month instead of three weeks. This means that I would not be able to reach Patna before February 25 or so. Accordingly, I am writing to Benipuriji to shift the dates of the Bhumi Sena Sammelan to Feb. 27, 28 and March 1. This change does not mean that I shall give any less time to Bihar. I shall still give a month from February 25, excluding the days necessary for the Kisan Panchayat (Meerut) conference and National Executive.

61. Statement on Government's Food Policy, Madras, 22 January 1951[1]

The decision of the Central and State Governments to abolish rural rationing in some areas and to reduce the quantum of rations by about 25 per cent in others, coupled with an increase in the price of rations of about 25 to 30 per cent is proof of the tragic failure of the Government's food policy and administration and will cause widespread suffering to working people.

Lack of uniformity in these decisions has resulted in discrimination between different areas as also between the workers themselves in the same area. As I am particularly concerned with employees of the Railways, Post & Telegraph and civilian employees of the Defence Department, I must voice their sufferings. These employees will suffer this discrimination in a marked degree. Not only will there be different conditions of obtaining food supplies, but there will also exist different standards in the quantum of rations. In those areas where an increase in the cost of rations by 25 per cent or more is decided upon the employees will suffer a further discrimination and disadvantage to that extent.

The Railway workers are particularly affected by Government's decisions. In addition to the above-mentioned disadvantage, those railway workers who receive their quantum of Dearness Allowance partly through the subsidized grainshop scheme will suffer a direct reduction in their Dearness Allowance because that is dependent upon the quantum of subsidized ration allowed them. The effort of standardizing the living

[1]*J.P. Papers* (NMML).

standards of the employees of Central Government undertakings all over India, which the Central Pay Commission had laboured so hard to bring about, is now thrown out of gear.

These decisions in regard to Government's Food Policy have come on the top of mounting discontent as a result of inadequate compensation for the high cost of living. Government have not only not honoured the recommendations of the CPC but also violated the undertaking it gave in February 1949 to bring down prices and review the position every six months.

Government must immediately revise this policy so as to enforce austerity standards uniformly in all areas, grant Dearness Allowance to fully compensate the increased cost of living and above all to restore the cut in the quantum of rations without which there will result a permanent deterioration in the workers' physical capacity to discharge their responsibility.

62. To H.M. Patel, 24 January 1951[1]

Dear Mr. Patel,

I came here two days ago for rest and massage treatment. Shri T.S. Ramanujam, President of the Madras Area Military Engineer Services Civilian Employees' Union, came to see me yesterday in connection with certain serious grievances of the workers and the Union at Avadi. He had also written to me previously about the matter.

The grievances seem to fall into two categories: first, transfer of union officials; and second, retrenchment, discharge and dismissal of staff.

Shri M.V. Krishnamoorthy, General Secretary of the Area Union has recently been ordered to be transferred to Vizagapatam. I understand from Shri Ramanujam that transfer of Union officials without any reason or justification is rather common in the South. The previous General Secretary of the Union, Shri A. Lakshminarayanan, as well as President of the Avadi branch of the Union, Shri P.J. George, had been transferred against which the Union had entered a protest. Shri B.L. Sharma previous President of the Avadi branch had also been transferred. Likewise the Secretaries of the Coimbatore and Tambaram branches were transferred.

The contention of the Union is not that union officials can never be transferred. But the Union does expect that its officials would be transferred only when absolutely necessary in the interest of the Service. If the Department looks upon recognised unions as friendly agencies, mutual

[1]*J.P. Papers* (NMML).

cooperation with which is of benefit both to the staff and the employer, it should be the particular anxiety of the Department to give every facility to the Union for efficient working. Frequent transfers of union officials obviously interfere with such efficient functioning and therefore to my mind it is not of any advantage even to the employer that such transfers should be effected.

Generally speaking there should be certain well-defined principles to regulate transfers. The Union's contention is that these principles are not applied, at any rate, to the transfers of its officials or active members. In this particular case of Shri Krishnamoorthy it does not appear even by the longest stretch of imagination that his transfer is essential in the interest of the service. There are other men even more senior and perhaps willing to go to Vizagapatam who could have been transferred in the place of the General Secretary of the Union. The Madras Area Union has taken a very serious view of this transfer and I cannot but endorse their attitude. I do therefore hope that if the workers are not to be provoked into unnecessary conflict, the transfer order will be cancelled.

I might add for your information that during our negotiations with the Railways, it has been more or less agreed that in the case of Union Officials there will be no routine transfers and in any case the president or the general secretary of the union concerned will be advised beforehand of any transfer orders for union officials that may be in contemplation. It strikes me that in the Defence Service a closer co-operation between the men and the Department is desirable and therefore the attitude of the Department towards recognized unions should be much more considerate, friendly and helpful.

Regarding retrenchment, I have seen your reply to Shri Ananthasayanam Ayyangar.[2] I recall very well the discussion that we had regarding the inclusion of the question of retrenchment in the terms of reference of the Kalyanwala Committee. You are quite right in saying that it was agreed that the Federation would send you a note on this question of retrenchment which would be considered by your Department after which the matter could be thrashed out across the table between representatives of the Federation and the Defence Department. I regret that the Federation has not yet sent you the said note. I am writing to my General Secretary, Shri S.M. Joshi in the matter today and I hope that within a week or ten days the note will be sent to you. Meanwhile I should like you to look personally into the cases of retrenchment, discharge and dismissal of which Shri Ayyangar wrote to you. I am happy to find that you have assured him that

[2]Ananthasayanam Ayyangar (1891-1978); participated in the freedom movement; Secretary, Congress Parliamentary Party, 1947; Deputy Speaker, first Lok Sabha, 1952-7; Speaker, Lok Sabha, 1958-62; Governor of Bihar, 1962-7.

the matter would be examined and any irregularities found would be corrected. I hope that this examination will not be unilateral because it is my experience that officialdom is the strongest trade union in the country, by which I mean that official enquiries into official acts are likely to end in official condonement. I therefore suggest that the Union also be given a chance in this enquiry to place its own point of view with regard to these retrenchments.

This might appear somewhat irrelevant but I can not but make a reference to it. Mr. Ramanujam tells me that the officers in this area have definitely given him the impression that the Madras Area Union has earned the deserved displeasure of the local officers if not of the Department itself by affiliating to a Federation which is presided over by such an objectionable person as my humble self. I have had two occasions in the past to visit Avadi and as it turned out after each of my visit a certain number of workers were discharged and it seems that the officer class gets no end of pleasure out of such patriotic acts and does not attempt to suppress its joy.

At my two interviews with you and your colleagues I certainly did not get the impression that the Department was wedded to any politics or that it was anxious to discriminate between two trade unions. I joined the Federation only a year and a half ago, but I feel that all through its career the Federation has given a good account of responsible trade unionism. I hope therefore that neither your Department nor your officers will ever use any discrimination whatever in their dealings with recognized unions, whoever their president or whatever their affiliations might be. It seems to me necessary that you should send out instructions to all your officers to maintain this attitude of impartiality. As you know there are certain trade unions in the country which are definitely favoured by the party in power and it may be that certain officers feel that if they openly show their partiality, the party in power, with which they are apt to confuse the Government, will make it worthwhile for them. If your Department does not hold this view, as I am sure it does not, it might be useful to disabuse the minds of those concerned. A general instruction requiring impartiality as between recognized unions might be sufficient for this purpose. When a similar question arose on the Railways, the Hon'ble Minister for Railways agreed to send out instructions enjoining impartiality in dealing with trade unions.

I am sorry for the length of the letter.

Yours sincerely,
Jayaprakash Narayan

63. To Vinayak Kulkarni, 24 January 1951[1]

My dear Vinayak,[2]

You remember that when we met Shri Patel and Shri Wanchoo[3] last at Delhi, it was agreed that on the question of retrenchment the Federation would prepare a comprehensive memorandum which would be considered by Defence Department after which a joint meeting between representatives of the Federation and the Defence Ministry would be able to thrash out the whole question. It appears from a reply of Shri Patel to Shir Ananthasayanam Ayyangar that the Federation has not yet sent him the memorandum. Will you kindly have this memorandum prepared immediately and send it to Shri Patel? I should also be obliged if you let me know what exactly is the position with regard to the Kalyanwala Committee. I take it that the three organizations could not agree on a single representative for membership of the Committee and it was decided that each of them will send its representative as an observer or advisor. What is the latest position in this regard? I am here for almost four weeks and I should be happy to hear from you as soon as possible.

I have written a letter to Shri Patel with regard to certain matters concerning Avadi.[4] I am enclosing a copy of my letter for your office.

Hoping you are well,

Sincerely yours,
Jayaprakash Narayan

[1]*J.P. Papers* (NMML).

[2]Vinayak Kulkarni; Organizing Secretary of the All-India Defence Services Civilian Employee's Federation.

[3]N.N. Wanchoo; then Joint Secretary, Ministry of Defence.

[4]For matters of Avadi Union see previous item, letter to H.M. Patel 24 January 1951.

64. To K.K. Menon, 25 January 1951[1]

Dear K.K.,[2]

You must have received a copy of Chakradhar's report on the Amalapuram election. One fact that stands out in that report is that the organization of the election offices was practically non-existent, as also that our election agents had practically no training or experience. It appears that we did

[1]*J.P. Papers* (NMML).

[2]For biographical note on K.K Menon, see *JPSW*, Vol. IV, p. 225.

enough propaganda though it was of not a very high quality. It strikes me that the Central Office would do well to prepare a short pamphlet giving detailed practical instructions as to organization of election offices and for the training of election workers. A mere circular letter will not serve the purpose. A concrete pamphlet, illustrated if necessary and translated into the provincial languages, would go very far. I hope you will give your thought to this and also consult Asoka in the matter. Perhaps Harris or some others who have practical experience of election work could produce such a pamphlet. Experience of rural elections would be more valuable than of elections in the urban areas. I do not know where you will be able to get people with such experience. In any case I hope this matter will receive the serious attention of the Central Office and the General Secretary.

This is the fourth day of my treatment and I am doing fairly well. The treatment is Navarrikiri[3] and Dr. Shankunni Menon[4] wants me to stay here for a month instead of three weeks. Unfortunately he does not allow me even to read much which is a great pity.

Hoping you are well,

Affectionately yours,
Jayaprakash Narayan

[3]A type of Ayurvedic treatment based on oil massage to strengthen body tissues.

[4]Dr. Shankunni Menon; a noted Ayurvedic physician from Kerala.

65. To M.R. Masani, 25 January 1951[1]

Dear Minoo,[2]

Your letter of Jan. 23. Of course you may quote from my letters to you in your foreword to Burnham's[3] book. I finished the book only last night. As doctors do not allow me to read much, I had it read to me by Shanker and Pratap. My regard for Burnham has been sustained by his latest effort. Having written the book primarily for Americans and even more so for the American Government, he has naturally neglected to deal with certain very important aspects of the world struggle against communism. For instance, if we in India were to rely entirely on American initiative to stem the tide of

[1]*J.P. Papers* (NMML).

[2]For biographical note on M.R. Masani, see *JPSW*, Vol. I, p. 66.

[3]James Burnham (1902-); an eminent writer who authored several books including *The Machiavellians* (1943), *The Struggle for the World* (1947), *The Coming Defeat of Communism* (1950), and *Containment of Liberation* (1953).

communism, we would meet with total failure. In India communism cannot be met with merely by anti-communism but only by a positive economic and political alternative. I see no such alternative to communism in India, but the Socialist Party. The Party may not be prepared to line up behind America in this world struggle, but it is the only alternative to communism in India. Wherever the issue has been joined with the Communists we have pushed them to the wall. I am afraid this aspect of the struggle has not received adequate attention in the *Coming Defeat of Communism*. I hope in the Asian edition, Sidney Hook[4] has been able to deal with this aspect. You will forgive my what may appear as a tall claim that while in Europe the Labour Party is the main political answer to communism, in Asia the Socialist Party is the only alternative. The Congress under Mahatma Gandhi might have been a far more effective alternative, but under Nehru it might be, in the words of Sardar Patel "a body of sappers and miners for world communism". Some of us in the Socialist Party have been very close to the Communists at one time and therefore as Burnham says, we understand better the nature of communism and the fight against it. However, I have digressed.

I remember you telling me of the some work prepared by Ram Swarup[5] on the Peasants and Soviet Communism. Is it possible to get a copy of that work? I will have to write an address for the Hind Kisan Panchayat and I shall be dealing with the question of communism and the peasantry. On arrival here, there has been a slight change in my programme. Originally I was supposed to stay here for three weeks, but now the Doctor says that I must take the treatment for a whole month. This would mean that the land army conference in Bihar would be held on Feb. 27, 28 and March 1, instead of February 18, 19 and 20. In a way this is better because it gives us some more time to prepare. I have not yet heard from Gokhale. I fear he has not returned from Nagpur yet.

Yours sincerely,
Jayaprakash Narayan

[4]Sidney Hook (1905-); Professor in the Department of Philosophy, Washington Square College, New York University; works include *An Understanding of Karl Marx* (1933), *Marx and the Marxists* (1955); *Political Power and Personal Freedom* (1959).

[5]Ram Swarup; a writer who wrote several books against Communism; namely *Communism and Peasantry* (n.d.), *Russain Imperialism: How to Stop it? Brain-Washing In Red China* (1955).

66. To M.L. Dantwala, 26 January 1951[1]

My dear Mohanlal,[2]

I hope you have received my previous letter. I am writing now about the Khoj Parishad. It seems to me that it would be a good occasion to call a meeting of the Council of Governors at the time of the National Executive at Delhi. The Council has not met for many months and I think it would be time by March for it to meet. If the dates suit you, you may consult Asoka and fix up a particular date and time and issue the necessary invitations.

At Jaipur it had been decided to get legal help to recast the memorandum and articles in order to simplify them and to make such other changes as were desired. I hope this would be done before the meeting. If you leave it to Suresh,[3] I am afraid, the work would never be finished. We have a large number of young lawyer friends and you may entrust the task to any one of them.

I am discussing with friends here the possibility of starting a branch of the Khoj Parishad. I shall write to you about it if I am able to make any progress in the matter.

Affectionately yours,
Jayaprakash Narayan

[1] *J.P. Papers* (NMML).
[2] For biographical note on M.L. Dantwala, see *JPSW*, Vol. III, p. 51.
[3] For biographical note on Suresh Desai, see *JPSW*, Vol. IV, p. 225.

67. 'A New Power Combination', 26 January 1951[1]

With prices rising steadily, with cuts in food rations, with cloth virtually disappearing from the open market in the largest cloth manufacturing centre in the country, with discontent and misery spreading far and wide, with war clouds gathering fast, the prospect on this fourth Independence Day is rather dismal. For three years and a half, the Government has muddled and staggered from failure to failure. There was no co-ordinated overall policy. In the welter of pressing tasks, the Government was unable to make up its mind about priorities. By turns different items were taken up, toyed with for a time, and then shelved. Food, inflation, industrial production each had its brief hour of attention. But nothing followed. There was no unified, integrated direction. There were only stray, pious wishes.

The Prime Minister, frightened by the gathering gloom on the home

[1] Adapted from *Bombay Chronicle*, 27 January 1951.

front, desperately seeks the limelight of the world stage and seems to enjoy the role of a world saviour just when he is unable to save his people from primitive hunger!

What is needed is an integrated policy and not hopping from one problem to another. Priorities must be fixed and steadfastly followed. The machinery of Administration must be overhauled and the dead hand of the past removed and corruption ruthlessly put down. The people's enthusiasm must be aroused and their active cooperation secured.

All this can be done only in a certain socio-political context. The Government have not been able to make up their mind as to the social direction in which they are to travel and the social and economic structure they are to build up. This is the root cause of the prevailing confusion in their policies.

After Sardar's death it is generally expected that Nehru will follow a more clear-cut policy. First of all, it is doubtful if Nehru has any clear idea as to what has to be done. His views, always vague, have become more so since he became Prime Minister. Secondly, to think of policy in terms of individuals is, to say the least, foolish. Nehru is not an individual but the leader of the Congress party. That party represents certain interests, which, by and large, are linked up with the status quo and might jeopardise its position and throw up other power groups. So, the inherent natural tendency of the Congress party is to preserve the existing framework of society.

This state of affairs encourages the vested interests in present society to infiltrate into the Congress. Thus there arises a combination of power-politics with the vested interests, which themselves are of two categories. In the first category are the interests of feudalism and capitalism. In the second, there are the interests of the higher bureaucracy. Thus the high-salaried civil servants, businessmen, the clever princes and landlords have joined hands with the power-politicians of the Congress to their mutual advantage.

Unless this combination is smashed not only at the Centre but also in the States, there can be no basic change in Nehru's policies or in the policies of the Congress government.

This combination can be broken only when another stronger power-combination is built up. When the latter is done, a peaceful struggle, such as a general election, or a violent struggle, can settle the issue.

Since the Sardar's death, there has been a great deal of wishful thinking. It is being commonly suggested that men of good-will should now come together and pull the country out of the present morass. In the face of the existing power-combination, no group of men of good-will can be effective. They will never be able even to make a start, much less any progress.

The social forces, that can be pitted against and defeat the present power-nexus are the workers, peasants, low-salaried employees and the middle classes generally. But of these a large part is, for historical reasons, still under the domination of the Congress party. The prevailing misery and discontent have helped considerably to loosen the old loyalties, but no new and firm loyalties have yet been created. To wean the masses away from the present power-nexus and to bind them firmly into another power pattern, the realization of which would smash the status quo and bring into being a new social order, is the main constructive task at the present moment. The Socialist party can today perform this revolutionary task in our society. The Communist Party and nearly all other leftist groups represent projections of foreign policy of the Soviet Union rather than any indigenous movement of social change. Their only hope of success lies in the victory of certain external forces, namely world communism. They have nothing to offer to the Indian people except the badge of Soviet conquest.

The only other constructive force in the country that relies on a new combination of social forces to break the present combination is the group of Gandhian constructive workers. But this group is not in the realm of political action; and for historical reasons, it still continues to lend its general support to the Congress party. If this group could take over the leadership of that section of the masses that still is loyal to the historical tradition of the Congress and then could combine with the Socialist Party, the present power-nexus could be broken up here and now. But while there is a good deal of mutual sympathy between the Gandhian constructive workers and the Socialist Party, there seems to be no possibility of a development such as I have visualized above. The leadership of the Congress party is bound to be in the hands of the group that has combined with the vested interests. Nehru, even supposing that he wants to break up that combination, must continue to be its prisoner.

68. To the Ambassador of USSR, 29 January 1951[1]

Your Excellency,

I beg to be excused for this trouble.

The Socialist Party and the Kisan Panchayat in my State, Bihar, are convening a conference of rural constructive workers and members of our voluntary "land army". This conference is likely to meet in the middle of March. On this occasion we are anxious to secure documentary films to show the life and work in the villages in Soviet Russia, and particularly on the collective farms. We shall be deeply obliged if we could secure a few

[1] *J.P. Papers* (NMML).

films of this nature. If there is a list of such films available, we might select a few from them. I shall be obliged for a reply at the above address.

With best regards,

Yours sincerely,
Jayaprakash Narayan

69. To the Ambassador of Yugoslavia, 29 January 1951[1]

Your Excellency,

I beg to be excused for giving this trouble.

The Socialist Party and the Kisan Panchayat in my State, Bihar, are convening a conference of rural constructive workers and members of our voluntary "land army". The conference will meet some time in the middle of March. We would be obliged to get some documentary films to show the work of village and rural reconstruction in new Yugoslavia for which we have great regard and respect. The films might show the life and work at a co-operative farm or other aspects of rural development. A representative of our Party had met the Yugoslav Consul General at Bombay who was good enough to promise all possible help in this connection, but he had advised us to write to Your Excellency also. I shall be obliged to have a reply at the above address.

With best regards,

Yours sincerely,
Jayaprakash Narayan

[1]*J.P. Papers* (NMML).

70. To B.G. Gokhale, 29 January 1951[1]

My dear Gokhale,[2]

I thank you for your letter and I am happy to know that your mother is better.

The Bhumi Sena Sammelan, which we now wish to call Gram Nava Nirmana Sammelan, will meet in the middle of March. The change in dates

[1]*J.P. Papers* (NMML).

[2]B.G. Gokhale; one of the prominent workers of the Socialist Party in Bombay; working at that time in the central office of the Party.

had to be made because my doctor here wants me to stay longer than the time he had originally fixed. I do not expect to reach Patna before the 27th of February and then we have the Kisan Panchayat meeting at Meerut and the National Executive. So I have written to the Bihar friends to shift the dates to the middle of March.

I have written today to the Russian and Yugoslav Ambassadors. Please inform the Yugoslav Consul of this.

Apart from selecting the films what we have to do further is to arrange to secure the mechanical apparatus. The USIS representative had told me that they have a portable projector at Calcutta which could be shipped to Sitamarhi. You have to inform the USIS people that this will have to be done. You might also tell them that I shall be in Calcutta about the 25th February and will get into touch with their people there. Please also finalize the arrangements with the Israel Consul. I shall write to you as and when any further advice has to be communicated. I hope you will also keep me in touch.

My treatment is progressing though my great disappointment is that the doctor has forbidden all mental and physical exertion. I am not even allowed to read except the daily newspapers though I can have others read to me. Please tell Asoka that I shall send him my Foreword in the next three or four days.

With best wishes,

Yours sincerely,
Jayaprakash Narayan

71. To Gopichand Bhargava, 29 January 1951[1]

My dear Dr. Gopichandji,[2]

I am very thankful to your letter of Jan. 6, which I am sorry to say I received only today, because the letter was following me all round the country. I am sending a copy of your letter to Tilakrajji Chaddha and I am asking him to communicate further with you on the question of ejectment of tenants.

I am thankful to you for release of the Satyagrahis and I hope that even the convicted prisoners would be released because their offence was

[1] *J.P. Papers* (NMML).

[2] Gopichand Bhargava (1889-1966); participated in the Non-Cooperation Movement, 1920-1; the Civil Disobedience Movement, 1930-1, and Quit Indian Movement, 1942; Chief Minister of Punjab, 1947-51, and Minister, 1957-64.

technical and the so-called violence of which they are supposed to be guilty was not indeed violence.

As regards the Kacha Pacca incident,[3] it is very difficult for me to say anything further in view of the fact that official versions of the story and the version of Sardar Sajjan Singh Margindpuri[4] are so contradictory. Having some experience, however, of official versions which are really based on the enquiry and fact-finding of officers of the State, I would be inclined to give more credence to the version of a person of the reputation of Sardar Sajjan Singh. I think our popular Ministers often go wrong when they rely entirely on the advice of their officers. In my last letter I had suggested that to put the matter beyond all doubt and to satisfy popular demand, a judicial enquiry might be instituted. The facts that are in your possession are those that were reported to you by your officers. It is the commonest thing in India for one officer to try to hush up or whitewash the action of his brother officers. The murder of the ASI in question certainly deserves our condemnation but there is the law to deal with such murders and I understand three persons have already been convicted by the Courts for this offence. While the police are justified in taking strong measures to find the culprit, they can never be justified is using inhuman methods or methods that are contrary to law. The simple question is whether certain persons in Kacha Pacca had been made to crawl on their bellies or not. If they had been, I am quite clear in my mind that the officers responsible for that inhuman incident must be taken to task. I do not think that our Law or Administration is based on the principle that the police have the right to deal as they like with people in their search of culprits.

What you write about the alleged false signatures obtained by Sardar Sajjan Singh has distressed me and I am writing to Tilakrajji for further information on the subject.

Thanking you once again for your letter and with kind regards.

Yours sincerely,
Jayaprakash Narayan

[3]In the Punjab, the tenants who were agitating against the ejections from their lands by the authorities felt harassed due to police atrocities and large scale arrests. At Kacha Pacca, in one such incident the mob alleged to have turned violent and killed one ASI on the spot. This was followed by brutal and inhuman police actions against innocent public, even though three persons had already been arrested and convicted.

[4]Sardar Sajjan Singh Margindpuri (1899-1990); founder-member of the Punjab Socialist Party, 1948; Chairman of the Punjab Praja Socialist Party, 1954-5.

72. To Tilakraj Chaddha, 29 January 1951[1]

My dear Tilakji,

Since I left Punjab I had often wanted to write to you, but somehow I kept on putting it off. I wanted to tell you of my very happy impressions of the Punjab tour and I also wanted to thank you for all the care and affection you bestowed upon me. Even though it is late, I am doing all this now and I wish to send you heartfelt thanks and deep appreciation for all that you did. It was not only the personal aspect of the tour that impressed me so much, but also its general efficiency and successful management. It was one of my best conducted, if not the best, tours.

I have received a letter from Dr. Gopi Chand, which though dated 6th Jan. reached here [Madras] only today. I am enclosing a copy herewith as also a copy of my reply. Will you kindly pursue the ejectment question with him further as also the other two questions if you like to do so. If you send me your comments on these matters I shall also write to Dr. Gopi Chand again.

I am here for a month's ayurvedic treatment. The treatment consists mainly of a kind of massage which weakens all the nerves of the whole body. After three weeks' massage of this type, there is massage of a different type which then strengthens the body. At present I have been forbidden to exert myself physically or mentally. I cannot even read anything except the newspapers. I hope after this treatment I will be able to do my work more vigorously.

Prabhavati is with me and she is also well. Ganga Babu has also come here to attend the meeting of the South Coordination Committee, for which Purshottam, Kamaladevi and Pratap had also come. Pratap will be here with me till I am in Madras. Purshottam and Kamaladevi have already left. Unfortunately our work in the South is not progressing so well, even though after my Andhra tour that province is faring better.

I hope both Ajit and you are well and so are the children.

Affectionately yours,
Jayaprakash Narayan

P.S.: Will you please let me have your comment on what Dr. Gopi Chand Bhargava says about Sardar Sajjan Singh obtaining false signatures.

[1] *J.P. Papers* (NMML).

73. To Harris Wofford, 30 January 1951[1]

Dear Harris,

I thank you for your nice and long letter. I am glad that you and Clare think so well of the Socialist Party and of our work. I hope we shall be able to justify this confidence.

I am afraid, there is no possibility whatever of my going to the States in the near future, indeed of my leaving India at all. I think Rammanohar should go, but you can best persuade him. I shall also press him to go. He is our international expert and it is right that he develops as wide contacts as possible.

I am glad you met my friend, Ozer. I should like to have his address if you know it. I am glad that Shanker has impressed you so well. I would be very happy if you could take him out of India for some time. It is for him to decide how best he should employ his time abroad. There is a tendency in our young men, they go out just to have a good time. But I believe Shanker is a more serious type and he might try to learn something.

I hope your law course is progressing well. With greetings to Clare and yourself.

Yours sincerely,
J.P.

[1]*J.P. Papers* (NMML).

[2]Harris Wofford; an American writer associated with the movement for World Government; had cordial relations with the Socialist leaders of India and especially with Rammanohar Lohia; wrote a book *India Afire* (1951), and jointly with Mrs. Clare Wofford, *Lohia and America Meet* (1951).

[3]Mrs. Clare Wofford, wife of Harris Wofford; a sympathizer of the Socialist Party; visited India in 1949 along with her husband and co-authored *India Afire* (1951).

[4]Shankar Shetty; Jayaprakash Narayan's Secretary for some time.

74. To Prafulla Chandra Ghosh, 1 February 1951[1]

My dear Prafullababu,[2]

A great deal has happened since we met last in Calcutta. I do not know how you have been reacting to these incidents.

After the death of Sardar Patel it was generally expected that Jawaharlalji would make some such effort as has now been made at the Ahmedabad

[1]*Brahmanand Papers* (NMML).

[2]For biographical note on Prafulla Chandra Ghosh, see *JPSW*, Vol. III, p. 187.

AICC.[3] I cannot again say what your reaction has been to this newest development. Speaking for myself, this appeal for unity seems to have no basis whatever. According to what was said and done at the AICC, it appears things will go on much the same way as in the past three and a half years and yet Congressmen are to unite and carry on together this worthless lead of confusion, corruption and do-nothing.

I have been very anxious all these months, since the formation of Krishak Mazdoor Praja Party to meet you. The resignations of Dr. Suresh Banerjee and Shri Devan Sen had made my desire to talk to you and to them stronger. But unfortunately I was touring in distant parts of the country. I, of course, have been meeting Kripalaniji and Rafi Saheb often.

Now I am taking massage treatment here [Madras] which will take another three weeks. I hope to reach Calcutta on the 23rd or 24th of Feb. I am looking forward to meeting you and your colleagues for a long chat then. I shall get in touch with you as soon as I reach Calcutta.

I hope you are well. With kind regards,

Yours sincerely,
Jayaprakash Narayan

[3]This refers to the Resolution on Unity of Action, adopted on 30 January 1951, by the AICC session at Ahmedabad, which among other things, suggested that efforts should be made to make the Congress organisation broad-based, and its doors open even to those who had left it.

75. Statement Denying Correspondence with Nehru on United Front, Madras, 8 February 1951[1]

I should make it clear that Prime Minister, Pandit Nehru, was not in correspondence with me on the question of forging a united front with a view to meeting the extraordinary economic and political situation facing the country, as envisaged in the unity resolution recently passed by the Congress. The report is completely unfounded and there is no correspondence between me and the Prime Minister on this question at all.

[1]Adapted from *National Herald*, 9 February 1951.

76. To Rafi Ahmed Kidwai, 8 February 1951[1]

My dear Rafi Saheb,

I am writing to you again about that old question of strike period pay. I had hoped to meet you in Delhi in December last, but you had gone "underground". I met Shri Khurshed Lal[2] who was very kind and we were able to settle satisfactorily many outstanding questions. When I raised the question of strike period pay, he naturally said that I had better discuss the matter with you. After you emerged from your period of rest, I thought of writing to you immediately, but I had to come here [Madras] for treatment and it was not possible to write earlier.

I understand that an official order has gone from the Department to the Union saying that Government have finally decided that nothing could be done about the question of strike period pay. I am afraid I do not find myself in a position to accept that decision and I am writing to you to reconsider the matter.

Let me first give you a brief history of the negotiations with respect to this demand. Let me start at the very beginning.

The strike covered a period of 23 days from 11th July 1946 to 2nd August 1946. In some cases the strike extended to 26 days as the last date for resuming duty was 7th August 1946. Negotiations for calling off the strike were held between the DGPT on the one hand and Shri V.G. Dalvi[3] on the other. When the latter desired that payment for the strike period be included in the terms of settlement, Shri Krishna Prasad[4] pointed out that he was empowered to discuss only the demands included in the strike notice and as the above demand was not one of them—as it obviously could not be—he was unable to discuss it. It was then suggested by Shri Mangaldas Pakvasa,[5] then President of the Bombay Legislative Council, who acted as a mediator in the negotiations, that the Union should not at that stage stretch that point too far and that there being a liklihood of immediate political changes, the question could be settled favourably by the National Government at a later stage. Sardar Vallabhbhai Patel was also consulted on this

[1]*J.P. Papers* (NMML).

[2]Khurshed Lal; a senior official in the Ministry of Communications.

[3]V.G. Dalvi; trade union leader; General Secretary, All-India Postmen and Lower Grade Staff Union.

[4]Shri Krishna Prasad (1894-1969); a member ICS, a senior official of the Ministry of Communications, Government of India for several years; appointed Director-General, Post & Telegraph, 1950.

[5]Mangaldas Machharam Pakvasa (1882-1968); President, Bombay Legislative Council, 1937-47; Governor of Madhya Pradesh, 1947-52; acting Governor, Bombay 1954-5; acting Governor of Mysore, 1959, 1960-1.

point by the Union leaders and he too endorsed Shri Pakvasa's view. When subsequently the Interim Government was formed the question was taken up with Shri N.V. Gadgil[6], who was a former President of the Union and was then the Chief Whip of the Congress party in the Central Legislative Assembly. Shri Gadgil and Shri Vadilal Lallubhai[7] advised that Government might not be agreeable to pay for the strike period on principle, but that it was possible to compensate the strikers immediately by giving them leave with pay for the duration of the strike. It was further suggested by them that the Union should pass a resolution to that effect and it would then be supported by the Congress party. Accordingly, a resolution was passed at a meeting of the Executive Council of the Union held at Calcutta in February 1947, and personally handed over to Shir N.V. Gadgil by Shri Dalvi. The issue, however, remained unsettled. (Parenthetically, let me add that this account of what happened at that early stage has been supplied to me by Shri Dalvi himself.)

When I took over the Presidentship of the Union [1947], there was great agitation about this and many other issues and the Union decided to take a strike ballot. After that I met you in Delhi with the representatives of the Union to find out if even an eleventh hour settlement was possible. The General Council of the Union had been called at the same time to take a final decision. At that interview several points were settled and several others were promised further consideration. Regarding this question of strike period pay I was assured that after three or four months the question would be favourably settled. In this connection you had told me of your success in settling a similar demand of the patrols of the Irrigation Department of the U.P. Government. You told me that the payment was made not as pay for the strike period, but as against leave earned. You assured me that some such formula could be evolved in this case also.

There was another point about which too a definite assurance was given, namely, the deductions that were being made in some centres from the extra dearness allowance of Rs. 10/- that was granted as a result of the strike ballot on the Railways and P&T Department in February 1949. Later I had an accident due to which I was not able to do anything further in the matter for some months. When after six or seven months the question was raised again, I was told that the Finance Department insisted that the deductions from the extra dearness allowance must be made in terms of some previous order, and further that it did not seem possible to do anything about the strike period pay. I again pressed those demands and finally wrote

[6]N.V. Gadgil (1896-1966); Member, Central Legislative Assembly, 1934-40; Constituent Assembly, 1947-50; Provisional Parliament, 1950-2; and Lok Sabha, 1952; Minister of Works, Mines and Power (GOI), 1947-52; Governor of Punjab, 1958-62.

[7]Vadilal Lallubhai; an important official in the Ministry of Communications.

to you and the Prime Minister saying that on these issues assurances had been given to me personally which I had conveyed to the General Council of my Union on the strength of which assurance, *inter alia*, the Union had decided to postpone the strike. Therefore, for me it was a moral question and if the demands were not satisfied I would have to undertake a fast. I had given a month's notice. Before the period was over, I had occasion to go to Delhi to meet the Railway Ministry as well as to attend the meeting of the Executive Council of the All-India Postmen's Union. At that time you were good enough to lunch with me at Sodhani's place. It was then that you told me that it had already been decided that no deductions from the extra dearness allowance would be made. Thus one of the two contested points had been settled.

As for the strike period pay, you told me that a satisfactory formula would soon be evolved. If you remember, I told you that I was going to the Executive Council meeting directly and asked if I might tell them that you had assured me of a satisfactory solution and if I might also tell the press. You readily agreed that I might do both. I acted accordingly and also decided to postpone my fast. After that there was a good deal of correspondence on the question between you and me, but finally nothing came of it. I might add, because from your point of view this is very important, that from the beginning you had made it clear to me that Government would never agree to pay directly for any strike period, but that the payment might be made in some other form such as against leave due. I make this clear because I am anxious that the issue is not sidetracked by merely denying that any assurance to pay for the strike period was ever given.

It is a matter of great regret that Government never agrees to do anything for labour except under pressure. If there had been no strike agitation, even the paltry increment of Rs. 10/- in dearness allowance would not have been granted. If I had not written to the Prime Minister that I felt compelled to undertake a fast, the Finance Ministry would not have agreed to make no cuts from the dearness allowance. I regret that after our talk at Sodhani's place I decided to postpone my fast, because, the pressure having been removed, the Government again felt that there was no need to do anything in the matter. It may appear queer, but I must say that on this point I have always felt a moral obligation, and if the Government is not prepared to carry out an assurance given by one of its Ministers, I would feel compelled to resume the course of action from which I had desisted for the time being.

I believe in the past two or three years that I have negotiated with the Government of India on behalf of its employees in several departments, I have not given cause to be considered unreasonable, hasty or unfair. I hope therefore that my stand on this issue will be viewed in a proper perspective. The point is a very small one and its settlement does not involve any large expenditure, nor any compromise of principle. The fear that once payment is made for leave, all employees would start forgoing their leave and demanding payment for it is fantastic. In the U.P. when you paid the patrols for the strike period in the shape of payment for leave earned, did it lead to a demand suddenly from all the employees of the U.P. Government of the nature now apprehended. I shall be obliged if this letter were treated urgently.

I do not wish to appear as serving a notice, but I do wish to make it clear that if within a month I failed to have a satisfactory reply, I should feel myself free to act as I thought fit. I hope to be in Delhi between the . . . and 9th of March and look forward to meeting you then.

I hope you benefited from your rest period.

Yours sincerely,
Jayaprakash Narayan

77. To J.C. Kumarappa, 9 February 1951[1]

Dear Professor Kumarappa,[2]

It is a long time since we met, and so much has happened since, that I have often felt the need of spending some time in Wardha to discuss matters with you. I do not know exactly when this will be possible, but I wonder if you will be there in the middle of April. If you are, I should like to meet you there about that time. I wish I could go to Wardha earlier, but that unfortunately does not seem possible.

I am writing this letter about a conference we are holding in Bihar from March 11 to 13. We have been doing some kind of constructive work in some villages of Bihar, particularly in the Sitamarhi area of Muzaffarpur district. We call it the voluntary land army (*bhumi* sena) movement. Some times it is called the gram-nava-nirmana movement. The activity mainly has consisted so far in organizing voluntary bands of villagers who working one hour daily (the slogan is 'ek ghanta desh ko') construct their village roads, excavate tanks, make bunds etc. In the areas where the work has been done, the people have responded enthusiastically. We want now to extend the activity and make it province-wide if possible. We also want to add to the constructive activities. To encourage both these processes, we are holding this conference. All the *bhumi-sainiks* from the neighbouring villages and ten workers from each district, doing or interested in constructive work will participate. No resolution will be passed at the

[1] *J.P. Papers* (NMML).

[2] For biographical note on J.C. Kumarappa, see *JPSW*, Vol. I, p. 126.

conference. After the opening of the conference, there will be several sittings each devoted to a single (or allied) problem and there will be talks delivered. The talks would be on such subjects as (i) principles of village reconstruction, (ii) land reform, (iii) improved farming—seed, compost and manure, irrigation implements, (iv) agricultural cooperation and cooperative farming, (v) village industries etc. These are illustrations. We have to choose a few simple subjects and secure competent persons to talk in simple language to the people. I wonder if you could help us in this. If we could get from Wardha two or three competent persons who could go to Bihar a few days in advance to help us in this mass constructive movement, we would be much obliged. We would bear the expenses. I should also appreciate very much any advice that you may want to give us. The idea is nebulous, because we have never before convened a conference of this type, but I do feel that if simple constructive activities could be taken up by the people, if we could move and inspire the masses to constructive work, the whole picture in the country would change. There will also be some recreation like *kushti* [wrestling] and some documentary films shown during the night.

I should add that the conference is of course organized by the Bihar Socialist Party and the Kisan Panchayat, though the purpose of the conference is not directly political. But there will be flags of the Socialist Party and our political slogans might be heard.

I hope you are well. With kind regards,

Yours sincerely,
Jayaprakash Narayan

78. To Vinoba Bhave, 10 February 1951[1]

Dear Vinobaji,
Sadar Pranam,

In the locality of Sitamarhi of the Bihar province, a Gram Nav Nirman Sammelan is being organized on 11-13 March under the sponsorship of the Socialist Party and the Kisan Panchayat. After having organized villages in that area, the work of constructing roads, building embankments, digging culverts, planting trees etc. is being done today in several villages for several months. The people of villages are doing all work themselves, each sparing one hour daily—their new slogan is "one hour to the country". Another slogan is: "we will build up new villages". Wherever this work took place, there seemed to be unprecedented enthusiasm among the people.

[1] *J.P. Papers* (NMML). Original in Hindi.

Now we want to make this work province-wide (in other provinces also some work has taken place here and there). Simultaneously we want that other activities of village construction should also start. For these two reasons the above-mentioned conference is being organized. We want that at least two brethren should come from Wardha for giving guidance. There will be no resolutions at the Conference. After the opening session, there will be sittings devoted to five different subjects. The subjects are: (1) Cooperation; (2) Sanitation, health, education; (3) Home and village industries; (4) Land reform and improved production; (5) Our country.

We desire that we should get some knowledgeable friends from Wardha to speak on these subjects and also to explain them. In this respect, I have already written to Prof. Kumarappa yesterday. In course of time, if this work progresses, I shall commit the impertinence of troubling you also. We shall meet the expenses of journey etc. of those friends who will come there.

Hoping you are well. Prabhavati is conveying you *Pranam*.

I have already made it clear that the conference is being organized by the Socialist Party and the Kisan Panchayat. Though there will be no direct political talks at the Conference, party flags will be there and some of our slogans can be heard.

Yours respectfully,
Jayaprakash Narayan

79. To Rammanohar Lohia, 12 February 1951[1]

My dear Rammanohar,

You probably know that we are convening a conference near Sitamarhi in the district of Muzaffarpur on March 11, 12 and 13, in order to give fillip to our constructive work. The conference has been named Gram Nava Nirmana Sammelan. There will be no resolution at the conference, but talks on different problems. There will also be recreation in the shape of *kushti* (wrestling) etc. and documentary films shown during nights. All the bhumi sainiks from the neighbouring villages and ten constructive workers or those interested in such work from the districts will participate in the conference which will be open to the public. Apart from the opening session, there will be five sittings devoted to the following five groups of subjects:

[1] *J.P. Papers* (NMML). JP sent identical letters to several others such as Mukut Bihari Lal, N.G. Goray, S.M. Joshi, Surendra Nath Dwivedi, Aryanayakam, Anna Saheb Sahasrabudhe, Pinakin Patel, etc.

1. Cooperation;
2. Sanitation, health and education;
3. Land reform and improved production;
4. Home and village industries;
5. Our country.

We would be very happy if you could attend the conference and speak on some of the subjects. All the local organizers and Benipuriji are very keen that you should attend. My keenness is no less. On my behalf and others I do request you to include this conference in your programme.

I am eager to hear from you about Burma. Looking forward to meeting you at Meerut.

Affectionately yours,
Jayaprakash Narayan

80. To Eric Britter, 14 February 1951[1]

My dear Britter,[2]

You remember that gruelling trip to Bihar that I had forced upon you and Mrs. Britter. You might be glad to know that we are convening a conference of constructive workers near Sitamarhi in the district of Muzaffarpur from March 11 to 13. All the *bhumi sainiks* (volunteers of the land army) from the neighbouring villages and ten constructive workers from each district of Bihar will be participating. The object of the conference is to give a fillip to this movement and some training to the workers. During the course of the conference there will also be a demonstration of some constructive activity. Some recreation in the nature of wrestling and other village sports and documentary films at night will be other features of the conference. I cannot say whether the Foreign Journalists Association and its members will be interested in this conference. But I do hereby extend to the Association and its members a very cordial invitation. The workers would like particularly to have you and Mrs. Britter. They are already acquainted with you and think so highly of you. I shall personally be very happy if you both could attend the conference with some other members of the

[1]*J.P. Papers* (NMML).

[2]Eric Britter (1906-77); correspondent of *The Times* (London) in several Asian countries; also its New York correspondent covering the United Nations Organization; President of the Foreign Journalists Association, New Delhi, in 1951.

Association. Apart from the opening session of the conference, there will be five other sessions devoted to the following five groups of subjects. . . .

I shall appreciate an early reply at the above address. With greeting to Mrs. Britter and you,

Yours sincerely,
Jayaprakash Narayan

81. To Gita Prasad Sinha, 15 February 1951[1]

My dear Gitaji,[2]

I have both your letters for which many thanks.

I am afraid the draft programme for the Deculi [Bihar] conference has been hastily prepared. Benipuriji had written to me that in addition to the opening session, there would be five more sessions devoted to the following five groups of subjects. . . .

The programme should state definitely when these subjects would be taken up. It is not enough to say: *Vishesh Adhiveshan* [Special Session] from such a time to such a time. For each group of subjects three hours at least would be necessary. It should also be kept in mind that no single session should last longer than three hours. This is the first improvement that has to be made in the programme—allot different sessions to different subjects.

Then please turn to the programme for the 11th March. There is a special session from 6 to 8 and then from 8.30 there is documentary film. I wonder when the people would take their meals. The shows might take at least an hour and a half. Would not 10 o'clock be too late for dinner? On the 12th of March, the programme says 2 p.m. to 5 p.m. inspection of work already done by the Bhumi Sena. Obviously only those from outside would be going for this inspection. What will the rest of the people do? I suggest therefore that on that day also there should be sports from 2 to 5. The same remarks as above about dinner time apply to this date also. Please ask Benipuriji to give more thought to preparation of the programme.

I have written to Vinobaji, Prof. Kumarappa and Shri Aryanayakam, all at Wardha. I have asked them to send two or three people or more to give prepared talks on some of the subjects. I have also written to Anna Saheb Sahasrabudhe and S.M. Joshi and to Sukumar Pagare in C.P., who has been doing good work in the co-operative movement. I have written to the Foreign

[1] *J.P. Papers* (NMML).

[2] Gita Prasad Sinha; a prominent socialist leader of Bihar.

Journalists' Association at Delhi to send their representatives if they are interested. Finally, I have written to Dr. Lohia and Prof. Mukut Bihari Lal. I have asked Anna Saheb Sahasrabudhe to preside over the session devoted to cooperation. I have asked Prof. Mukut Bihari Lal to take charge of the session devoted to 'Our Country'. I shall write him again to preside over the same.

Narendra Devaji's health is very poor and I do not want to put any further burden on him. Kamaladevi's presence will not be of much use, because she will not be able to talk in Hindi. I do not want this conference to be turned into a show where a number of leaders are invited and there is a lot of advertisement of their names. It is not the presence of leaders that is of value for this conference, but the quality of work that is done. I shall be writing to Shri Suren Dwivedy who may be of help to us at the conference, because in Orissa also they have done some work of this type.

I am writing to Benipuriji in Hindi today.

I hope to hear soon from you.

Yours sincerely,
Jayaprakash Narayan

82. Address at a Public Meeting on the Prospect of Socialists' Return to Congress, Madras, 18 February 1951[1]

There is not an iota of chance of Socialists going back to the Congress. Why there should be a clamour for unity soon after Sardar Patel's death? Of course, it may be to set their house in order, but as far as we are concerned, unity with today's Congress is impossible. How presumptuous it is for the Congress to ask all those who left the Congress to come back? Let the Prime Minister declare that the Government has accepted Socialism as their goal. Let the Government adopt certain policies to be implemented here and now, and then we will consider the question of going back to the Congress, not beaten but victorious.

We will not be satisfied with the oft-repeated unity slogans of the Prime Minister unless a real change in the Government's major policies has taken place.

The Congress had pledged to accept Rs. 500 as maximum salary. Today the highest salary under the Congress Government is Rs. 10,000 plus

[1]Adapted from *Hindustan Times*, and *National Herald*, 19 February 1951.

allowances. Let Mr. Nehru cut down that to Rs. 1,000 and then we will find a proof of the real change in their policy.

Impartial judicial inquiries should be conducted into the charges against Ministers and other high-ranking Government officials. The programme and policy of the Socialist party is intended to free society from all kinds of exploitation, while the Congress intends to maintain the status quo.

Many Congressmen who thought it was wrong for the Socialists to separate from the Congress are themselves drifting away. They now admit that the Socialists were right in getting away from the Congress fold, as they, too, are gradually losing faith in it.

Before the country was free, the Congress was a kind of national army and every freedom-loving man its soldier. After the achievement of freedom the Congress has become a conservative party. Mahatma Gandhi would have led the Congress and the masses along the right path in regard to the future set-up, and the Socialists would have remained within the Congress, if he had been alive.

83. Address at a Public Meeting on India's Foreign Policy, Madras, 22 February 1951[1]

Foreign policy has assumed great importance since we became free. It is good for any nation to be united on its foreign policy, just as America or the United Kingdom. The Socialist Party will be very happy if this country evolves a bi-partisan or non-partisan foreign policy. India should take a lead in placing before the United Nations a concrete plan for establishing world peace on the basis of a world community of people sharing the good things of life with one another.

The making of India's foreign policy is more or less a one man's job at present, though I do not mean to blame the Prime Minister for taking upon himself the responsibility. In the absence of a real opposition in Parliament, the evolution of a foreign policy is bound to be in the hands of a single party. And, in that party, the Prime Minister occupies a commanding position, and is considered an unchallenged expert on foreign affairs. I wonder whether a convention should not be started that, in view of the peculiar circumstances in which Parliament was elected or nominated, there should be consultation with others also who might not be members of Parliament. On our side, the Socialists are not only prepared, but anxious, to evolve a common foreign policy.

In determining the foreign policy of a country, the foremost factor is national interest, and next, the international objectives which the nation

[1]Adapted from *Hindu*, 22 February 1951.

may have in view. While different ideas may be put forward as to what constitutes our national interest, there is no doubt that economic development of the country is a national interest of prime importance, which should receive first priority in determining our foreign policy. Likewise, it may be possible to prepare a list of priorities by which national interest may be served. A nation in defining its foreign policy would be committing a grievous error if it concerns itself only with vague principles, however noble in themselves, and overlooks the demands of national interest.

As for the international objectives of a nation, these are determined by the character of the nation, its economy and outlook. These objectives may change with changes in the domestic scene. It is difficult to say, what the character of our national state or its economy is, because, things are now in the melting-pot. Since the attainment of freedom, so far as economic and social life is concerned, there has been little vital change except for the paltry legislation for abolition of the zamindari system, where it existed.

One can not say how long the status quo will continue. Today the foreign policy of India is one of friendliness with all and peace in the world. This is no doubt a noble idea. But it is one thing to aspire for peace and friendliness and quite another to maintain and preserve the same. As a matter of fact, it will be an act of self-delusion on the part of anyone to say that there is peace today, with undeclared wars going on and with the danger of their areas expanding any day. It is no longer a question of maintaining peace but rather of re-establishing peace. It is important to understand the nature of peace and the meaning attached to that word. Today words seem to have lost their meaning, since there are certain individuals talking of peace while really intending war, and others talking of liberation while actually intending enslavement of others.

Expansion or world domination, is a vital part of the Communist theory. In the expansion of communism, the Red Army will play the predominant part, which means communism will spread at the point of the Russian bayonet. This is, in fact, a new imperialism imposed from without, and not an internal change of capitalism into communism. If anyone believes that it will be possible to stop the spread of communism by a concession here and a concession there, he will be much mistaken. It requires a different approach. The Communist Party in India can not do anything by its own strength, but it becomes a danger when it goes to the Himalayas, Assam or Kashmir and attempts to link up with outside forces. Suppose with aid such linkage, the Party builds up a red pocket in India, and the boundaries of that pocket expand with outside help, what will be the position? It will not be a peasant's revolution, but will mean foreign domination and a new slavery for the country.

If there be an armaments race between nations for establishing peace, there can never be peace. That race will never stop and it will go on adding to the burdens of millions all over the world. But peace can be established in another way by Russia and America this very day. Russia could have established peace for ever when Germany fell in the last war and her prestige had reached its highest. Even to-day Russia can ensure the peace of the world by lifting the 'Iron Curtain', by assuring all peoples that they have nothing to fear from her, that it is for the peoples to decide their destiny by their own free will, and Russia should have no fifth columns, or subsidized press or literature anywhere in the world. There will then be no need of the atom bomb. But Russia will not follow this path, because it will not be communism!

Again, if today America decides to follow a policy different from what she has been pursuing, there may be peace. If today Russia appears to some as a liberator, it is because she offers a picture of a world community. If America were to offer another picture of world community, share with other nations whom she had helped to develop their economies, then not a single atom bomb will be needed to establish peace, and the entire psychology of the world will be changed, and peace becomes possible. Russia will be isolated and the totalitarian system will exist no longer.

But all this is a dream. It might be that the American people are willing to share their goods with others; but their bosses are not going to do the same. There is, therefore, no hope of America coming forward with such a message, nor is there any hope of Russia adopting such a policy. The world is weary of war. Another war can be avoided, not by atom bombs or hydrogen bombs, but by creating a new faith on which to base the reorganization of the world. Any country believing in peace should go down to these fundamentals. India should speak out to the world, to Asia and to other backward peoples, that if they like to live together in peace, it should be on this basis. Let not India's representatives merely act as mediators—they may even make themselves ridiculous by trying to mediate between two giants. The Socialist Party holds that the Indian Government should come forward as the leader of the Asian and African peoples and, as the land of Mahatma Gandhi, to enunciate a new doctrine of peace in the United Nations, face both America and Russia with a concrete plan for world peace based on a new world order. Ideas are always more powerful than arms. Let India go forward with the idea, and people will soon rally round it, providing a tremendous moral force behind it.

84. Statement on Bihar Government's Handling of Police Agitation, Patna, 1 March 1951[1]

The Bihar Government's mis-handling of the so-called police rebellion some four years ago might still be fresh in the public mind.[2] It might be recalled that Gandhiji himself had tried to intervene, but unfortunately the Provincial Government resisted his efforts at mediation. There followed a long tale of four years' persecution culminating in the triumphant acquittal of Shri Ramanand Tiwari, the police hero of 1942 and the leader of the awakened policemen. Tiwariji's acquittal on the charge of attempting to overthrow the State has completely vindicated the cause of the policemen. The Government has cut a rather sorry figure in this whole affair.

It was hoped that the Government had learnt from its experience and would follow a more enlightened and liberal policy in this regard. But I am afraid this Government is even more wooden than the British. On his release Shri Ramanand Tiwari immediately applied himself with his usual vigour, not only to the cause of the policemen, but also to the very laudable endeavour to raise their morale and to make them conscientious servants of the public. But unfortunately the Government's vendetta against Tiwariji continues and four persons including two students have been arrested for the offence of distributing a rather strikingly public-spirited appeal to policemen issued by him. By acting in this manner, the Government is only bringing itself into contempt in the eyes of the public and the policemen in particular. These men ought to be released forthwith, and instead of persecuting him the Government should use Tiwariji's undoubted influence and talents to good purpose in re-moulding the police force in the Province.

I should further like to suggest to the Government to reinstate the 900 or more policemen who had been discharged from service. The courts have not found them guilty of rebellion or of any conspiracy to overthrow the State. In these circumstances, it would be an act of statesmanship to reinstate these men whose loyalty to the country and the Government is beyond doubt. By this act the Government would create a great fund of good-will which will be of great value to the administration and the people and will create a new moral climate in the Police Force.

[1] *J.P. Papers* (NMML).

[2] For details of Police rebellion and J.P.'s statement see *JPSW*, Vol. IV, pp. 183-5.

85. Statement on the Breakdown of Negotiations between the All-India Railwaymen's Federation and the Railway Ministry, New Delhi, 11 March 1951[1]

The discussions between the Ministry of Railways and the All-India Railwaymen's Federation held on March 9 and 10 have proved to be abortive. The Working Committee of the Federation had been charged with the duty of negotiating a settlement on the basis of the demands of the General Council formulated in October last. The Railway Board took more than two months and a half to send a reply which completely rejected the demands of the Federation.

The principal demands of the Federation included the burning question of dearness allowance. The Federation was agreeable to relief being given partly in kind, as an anti-inflationary measure. The Ministry of Railways proposed that the railway grain-shops should close down supply of all commodities other than cereals and that they were prepared to arrange the sale of cereals at the rate of five annas per seer. The representatives of the Federation pointed out that this meant a loss of more than Rs. 100/- per annum to each of the concessional card holders and the relief given for the present rise in price level was not at all adequate and far below the recommendations of the Central Pay Commission. The Railway Ministry were, however, not prepared to grant any additional cash benefits.

The other demands of the Federation, included those relating to proper fixation of pay with weightage for service, problems of skilled, semi-skilled, running and other class three staff, confirmation of staff, restoration of pass privileges to ex-State Railways' employees, insecurity of service, and several issues not settled by the Joint Railway Advisory Committee.

The Federation had proposed that in view of the failure to reach a settlement, the issues should be settled by adjudication. The Railway Ministry refused to accept this proposal and the discussions ended abruptly without any agreement being reached on any important issue.

The Working Committee of the Federation is of the view that the situation is fraught with serious consequences in view of the failure of the Government in the matter of food policy and the failure of the Ministry of Railways to meet the reasonable demands of the federation. The Federation has, therefore, decided to summon the General Council to take further steps to defend the railway workers' interests. The All-India Railwaymen's Federation considers that the acid test of the Government's policy in the matter of industrial relations and disputes is their treatment of the Railwaymen's burning grievances. The Government's complacent attitude is responsible for precipitating a serious crisis in the railways.

[1]Adapted from *Tribune*, 12 March 1951.

86. Speech at Nava Nirmana Sammelan, Dekuli (Bihar), 12 March 1951[1]

This Conference was organized mainly with three objectives in view:

1. To find out how far you have progressed in this direction from the previous year to this day.
2. The people from other districts should come here, take inspiration from your work and start this work at their places also.
3. We wanted that your work be discussed all over the country. The work should begin in other provinces also on the basis of *Ek Ghanta Desh Ko* [one hour to the country]. In this connection we wanted also that you should decide what further steps you want to take. That is why we have invited people of other provinces, including leaders of constructive work in the country, specialists and friends from Wardha.

I beg your pardon because I could not be present here on time. I had to stay in Delhi on the 10th instant on account of work of the railway workers. Yesterday the pilot of the aeroplane refused to come here pointing to hazards on account of strong winds. Today I got the opportunity of listening to a friend from Wardha, Om Prakashji. What can I say about it, if the voice of Wardha, which he articulated before us, is the same that I know, the country is going to be immensely benefited. Anna Saheb is an old constructive worker of the Congress. All that he had said, has raised great hopes.

Today the condition of the country is peculiar. I have heard that impediments are placed in constructive work also because of political differences. Perhaps educated brethren of villages would have known it that a session of the Congress took place at Ahmedabad recently at which Pandit Nehru moved a resolution asking for cooperation of the people in the work of reconstruction of the country. Today I want to make this declaration on behalf of the Socialist Party and Comrades engaged in the work of the Gram Nava Nirman that we are prepared to give full cooperation in all such work of construction relating to the welfare of the country. Whether it be the question of Grow-More-Food or the work of irrigation, education and construction, we are prepared to give full cooperation. In the same way, we also certainly want that the Government should cooperate with this work of ours. I want that after this Conference the Government should send to these villages its specialists, who may point out the errors of villagers and help them in their work of construction. This is why we have invited the representatives of the Government also to this Conference.

Prior to the Conference, some friends told me that in the region where

[1] *J.P. Papers* (NMML). Original in Hindi.

the Conference was to take place there were starvation deaths: workers did not get food; they did not get wages; hence it would be better for me to convene a *Bhukkhar Sammelan* (a conference of the starving people); instead of *Nav Nirmana Sammelan* (a conference on new construction). This made me also despondent. But, ultimately I decided [to go ahead, thinking] that, after all, this Conference was being convened only to root out famine. Yesterday, the number of participants in the open session was not satisfactory. I feel sorry that when any big leader is to come, then you attend, but when the work of your welfare is being done, you do not participate in it with enthusiasm. You should think of the work regardless of the fame or defame of anybody. It is possible that you do not get pleasure in building roads, digging ponds and canals because you are hungry. But if you think carefully, you would find that in the event that in this area, in this district more and more such work is done, then there would not be any one who is hungry or naked, there would not be any necessity for any police, the mismanagement of today would become a dream for us. Today while the pond was being dug up, a member of land army said that when there was no foodgrain, what would an earning man eat? I said that all this was being done only to produce more foodgrains. He said that when he had no land, where would foodgrains be produced? I said that the land would be made available. He asked if the landlord would forsake the land. My heart received a great blow by this talk. I begun to think how our farmers are sitting, frustrated and sad.

The new village which we want to build will not be of the kind in which any man will have no land, no employment, no arrangement for medicine and education. There are several such issues which are within the domain of the Governments at Patna and Delhi. But these Governments will do something for you, only then when you get it done by them. May such a wave of awakening spread to the country's five and a half lakh villages that the Government can be compelled to make such a law that there should not continue to exist in the country a few multimillionaires on the one hand and millions of hungry people on the other. Neither Jayaprakash Narayan nor Nehru can do this work. This work can be accomplished by you alone.

When I went to a village for inspection, old mothers and sisters came to me thinking that I was some big officer who had come to distribute foodgrains. But there are no foodgrains in my pockets. The Socialist Party has no stock of foodgrains and money. We have no capability for providing employment to the people. We do not have government in our hands that we may do something for these helpless people.

Bihar was not visited by famine only this year. Last year famine-like situation arose in Saharsa, Purnea, Bhagalpur and also Monghyr. People had also died of hunger. Schemes, prepared to prevent starvation deaths, were submitted by the Socialist Party to District Magistrates. They were told that if arrangements of a special kind were made, then hungry people might get some relief. The most difficult problem affects the landless labourers who have no source of livelihood. The District Board and the Government could help them by opening more and more centres of work where they could subsist by virtue of their own hand work. At the same time the request had been made to the Government to open more and more ration shops so that their hard earned money should not go into the black market in course of purchasing foodgrain. There is no doubt that in this process some centres of work were started, some shops opened, but nothing was done to the proportion of the wide expanse of the spread of the scourge of famine. Efforts are made by the government to deny starvation deaths. In Purnea the people died after eating uneatable things like leaves but they were not counted among starvation deaths. Even though the Bihar Government acknowledge some starvation deaths, their number was reduced to one on reaching Delhi. The representatives of newspapers should go to the villages in order to know about the actual situation and not only upon the statements and talks of the Government in which the element of showing-off is considerable. The ministers of the Government even want to brush aside, do brush aside, the news of starvation, deaths by describing them as baseless talks of the socialists. They say that there had been some shortage of food grains and that had been made up.

Here the people said that clothes had disappeared. People are facing difficulties because of lack of clothes. It is the responsibility of the Government to bring clothes where found and to cover the bodies of the people. The Government should understand its duties clearly and perform them with regard to feeding the people and covering their bodies. You have a duty towards the work of construction. You are doing that and it is also your duty to complete it. Today the digging of the pond that was done is not meant for demonstration. You have to complete the remaining digging.

Comrade Rambahadur Lal is endeavouring to provide wages to workers with the help of local arrangements. He has declared that those who would work for digging ponds for five hours, would be given 5 seers of food grain. The Socialist Party is making some effort to find employment for workers and will also continue doing, but such effort is possible only within a definite and narrow limit.

Last year I toured the famine-affected areas and saw the condition of the people. In those areas the contractors had been given enough money to open centres of work, but only a little work was done in that respect; the rest of money remained in the pockets of the contractors. This happened also with regard to shops of cheap food grains. Some shops were opened somehow, but they depended on the Congress for their management etc.

The people complained that rations were given only to the henchmen of the managers. We complained against this to the Government and placed the suggestion of an all-party management before the Government. At places they included moneylenders and zamindars, who had been opposed to our nationalist movement during the British period, and said that they had included other people in it. We suggested the inclusion of Harijan brethren in those bodies. Possibly they may not open their mouth at the first few meetings, but they will have to open their mouth under the compulsion of circumstances and will be able to place their views before the committees. When I mentioned it to Rajendra Babu and Anugraha Babu, they endorsed its necessity, but no effort was made to put that into effect.

It is my firm belief that if any arrangement is not made speedily, the situation is going to deteriorate very badly. No harvesting of any crop is likely to take place within the next two-three months. The people belonging to *Bhumi Sena* wanted to grow foodgrains after cultivating fallow land in some districts. They referred their proposal to the SDO. The SDO said that the land was the property of the Zamindar and if he did not permit, nothing could be done. However, it is a hollow plea. In view of the present food situation the Government can issue an ordinance within 24 hours that the landless farmers and workers would have the right to cultivate such lands. It is a strange phenomenon that on the one hand the people are perishing in agony because of the scarcity of food grains and on the other millions of acres of land are lying fallow. I do not understand the Government's slogan of Grow-More-Food. The people of a village told that a river flowed beside their village. If a canal was dug there, then 5,000 *bighas* of land could be cultivated but the Government has rejected the proposal for digging a canal there. I am not an engineer, but I told that if the digging of the canal was possible, why not dig it with your own labour. They said that whatever could be done with physical labour, they were prepared to do, but besides that a gate would have be fitted into that; for that iron was needed, cement was needed, money was needed; where would these come from? Indeed it is a matter worth considering. If the Government actually wants the cooperation of the people and to take advantage of their imperishable store of labour power, it should extend at least this much cooperation I have instructed my local comrades that they should complete this work in association with the officials of the Government and the District Board. If a dam is built across the Baghmati river, then a great project of irrigation would be completed. It seems that the Government has been hit by paralysis; the whole administration has become slack. But I have not been hit by paralysis. The village is ours. Pandit Nehru will not come to our villages for building roads and doing sanitation work. If the road is built in the villages, doctor's cars can easily come to them and the danger of death from diseases would become remote. Trees should be planted both sides of the road so that wood for construction and fruits for eating could be made available. Today if Mahatmaji would have been alive and would have given the slogan of *Ek Ghanta Desh Ko* at his prayer meeting, then this slogan would have reverberated all over the country. The newspapers would have published it in bold letters. The capitalists have control over newspapers. Our voice is not able to spread. They do not attach importance to this work. Pandit Nehru has formed a committee to consider the problems of the country's development. He has said that there is an acute scarcity of capital in the country. For this reason the country's development work will be executed in six years by spending Rs. 200 crore per annum. It is true that we do not have capital in the form of money, but we have the largest capital in the form of labour. If our brethren and sisters work one hour for the country, for the villages, then the condition of the country, of the villages, would change, if the work of building roads is started simultaneously in five and a half lakh villages of the country, then roads can be built in every village of the country within a month. If 20 out of 35 crore people of the country work daily for an hour, then a capital of 300 crore would be produced within a year. A dam was recently built on the Durgawati river in the Sahabad district. The people belonging to the Socialist Party said to villagers, showing their wilting plants of crops, that the time for rains was over. However, there was a river nearby, if they wanted to save their crop, they could do so with a little effort on their part. The people of the village became prepared for it. At the cost of Rs. 400 the dam was built and the canal was dug. You will be surprised as well as happy to hear that the irrigation of 36,000 acres of land became possible through this. Prior to the building of this dam, when our Comrade, Badriji, went to meet the SDO for this purpose, the latter being startled by his red cap got him moved out of his Chamber. But the same SDO came to give money after the dam was built. I know that the entire fault in such matters is that of higher people, not of officers. Since the government belongs to the Congress, at the instance of Congressmen the people do not hesitate to indulge in unlawful acts out of fear or greed, whereas they feel nervous in giving cooperation to the opposition's lawful works. This situation is an indication of the country's misfortune.

It is not surprising that under such circumstances your mind is depressed, and your heart broken. Perhaps you are beginning to think that this spade, parade and red cap are things for exhibition. If it is so, then your heart will be broken for good. The Socialist Party does not want to take political advantage from the work of construction. This work is taking place for new construction of villages. The road is a public property. Neither the Socialist Party's road will be red nor the Congress' white. I heard that in a village the zamindar did not allow the digging of pond. [When someone who had enjoyed digging right before began this work again, he (The Zamindar) settled that pond with another person]. The zamindari system is a great impediment in the way of the new construction of villages. Your problems can not be solved without changing the present arrangement relating to land. In a village a person has hundreds of *bighas* of land and some have not even one inch; under this condition an all-round new construction of village is never possible. The work of construction will not be completed by building roads only. If there are 500 *bighas* of land in a village, then every person of that village should have a share in that land regardless, whether he is a worker or a zamindar. The poor farmer who has a small piece of land, lacks capital; how can he produce more? Prosperous farmers can arrange fertilizers, irrigation etc., but the number of such farmers will not be more than 10 per cent.

Sarju Babu said that the people of villages should have their own administration. Through the existing Panchayat laws villages cannot get benefit unless the Panchayat of villages becomes the owner of the land of villages. If farmers do not want to get their land managed through the Panchayat, they can be made to understand its advantages. The Government should give the village Panchayat a share of its revenue by which fertilizers, bricks, cements, etc. can be purchased or made for the management of the village. The sale of the produce of villages should be done through the Gram Panchayat-directed cooperative societies. The Proceeds-Collection Scheme should also be worked by the Panchayats. The life of the entire village should be permeated by the Panchayats. All the adults of the village should be members of the Gram Sabha and the executive should be formed by their own choice. The officers who look after the Panchayat or provide cooperation to it should be familiar with the life of villages. They should be honest and impartial workers and in this work the cooperation of all parties should be welcome. If the Government wants that there should be new constructions of villages, then it should repose its confidence in the public and, to some extent, it should also be prepared to run some risk.

You have strength in your hands. You should utilize it fully for your own benefit. You should build roads and plant trees on their sides, which may be used as fuels. You can make invaluable manure by saving cow-dung Sitting together in villages you should prepare schemes for irrigation, work for implementing them and secure the cooperation of the Government. There should be a ditch near every house for manure. This work can be done collectively also.

Our villages have become symbols of filth. We have been scattering the dirt of our house and body here and there inadvertently. We saw that our workers also sit here and there on the field with *Lota* (small water pot). In this condition what shall we teach the farmers in villages. The only proper course is that we should dig ditches and use them as latrines. Having seen dirt Mahatmaji often used to say that after seeing this, his patience based on non-violence sometimes broke down and he felt like, setting the people right by whipping them.

The work that I had expected from you could not be done. By now double the work of previous year should have been completed. This work should have been spread on all sides speedily like lightning. We want that in Bihar 50 per cent of the work of road-building should be completed in the next three months. The single worker of the village cannot complete it. This work can be done only on a cooperative basis. If even a few persons, devoted to such work both in theory and practice, can emerge, that would amount to a great miracle.

Now I want to present before you that picture of a village which is in my heart.

1. The land should be distributed again. The relationship between the owner and the worker should be based on equality. The owners of land should be those who cultivate it with their own hand. If it is not possible to give land to landless workers in their own village, they should be given land where land might be lying fallow, and that land should be cultivated by *Bhumi Sena.* The ideal villages should be settled by the Government on places of that sort and collective farming should be introduced. The people said that in the Purnea district one and a quarter lakh acres of land were lying fallow. The landless people can be constituted into *Bhumi Sena* and be sent to cultivate and settle on the land of that sort. In Purnea the people from outside have become owners of land ranging from 5 to 30-40 thousand *bighas.*

2. Differences among the castes should be abolished. This should not happen that some people putting on sacred thread would sit on chairs and some kicked away. In villages the people belonging to the so-called high caste suffer a blow on hearing this. They forget that all are the children of God. I warn the people belonging to high castes that if they are not watchful now, they will have to repent. The people belonging to lower castes also have souls. They have also hearts. They have pride. They are not animals.

3. Bapuji had endeavoured to spread village industries. The Congress governments should have put into effect what he said. But those who are working today in village industries are shedding tears of sadness. In Purnea where there are many rice and oil mills, the people said that their livelihood was destroyed because of these mills. But the government instead of providing encouragement to small industries, want to give still more encouragement to the latter without giving any thought to the problem of unemployment and livelihood of others.

4. The breed of animals should be good.
5. There should be full arrangement of education in villages.
6. All people in village should have clean houses of brick and clay.
7. There should be expansion of games, sports, music, dances, arts etc. The level of life of the village should rise from high to higher and from higher to the highest. There should be full opportunity and atmosphere for the growth and expansion of civilization.
8. The group of villages belonging to a particular area should be formed into units. Things should be so arranged that the main necessities of each unit should be met from the same area. All programmes should be conducted on the basis of cooperation. Our brethren of Wardha too want this and this is also the path of welfare for farmers. The condition of land can be improved by doing this. Leave aside the situation in other countries, even in China the produce is twice-thrice more than that in our country. Our land instead of improving has been deteriorating day by day.
9. The reconstruction of the village should be carried on in a well-planned manner. We should plan how much land should be set apart for planting of trees, how many and where wells, ponds or canals have to be dug, where and what sort of schools have to be established, what kind of management of hospitals should be etc., etc.

Do not forget that if you sit down feeling helpless and unconcerned, then you will go down day by day. In order to remain alive and live like human beings you have to undertake the distribution of land. If the Congress Government does not do it, you have to change it. Om Prakashji (a constructive worker from Wardha) in his speech said that we have constantly to go on insisting on truth. I also repeat it, and want to say this that today we are doing the work of youths, farmers, workers, women, writers, *Bhumi Sena,* culture etc.; if there is any objective behind all this, that is the discovery of the truth. We accept that as Socialists we are also engaged in search for truth, that truth after finding which the public can be made happy and prosperous, which can make the people well cultured and civilized, which can put an end to the exploitation and oppression in society.

In an era of democracy and in every country which follows the democratic system, there is necessity of political parties! The people cannot form the government of their choice without establishing organizations. We dislike party politics. We do not have to indulge in party politics, but the organization of parties becomes necessary also to discover the truth: every kind of organization, of farmers, of workers, of students, of libraries etc., etc.

We do not claim that if the government of the Socialist Party is formed, the rivers of milk and curd will flow and all inequality will be removed overnight. The reconstruction of villages, cities, industries will take time. We have the same ideas with regard to the work of reconstruction which

Gandhiji had. We have very few differences. We are not doctrinaire. Whatever little differences there are, we can remove them also by sitting together. Mahatmaji's true disciples have drawn up a plan on behalf of the Sarvodaya Sangha, I am satisfied with that. If Nehruji and Sri Babu endorse that, we shall be happy. That will only be socialism. Sarvodaya and Socialism are two words with one meaning. We and the Sarvodaya people believe that until the exploiting classes do not forsake their wealth or wealth is not taken away from them, neither Sarvodaya nor Socialism is possible till then.

We shall endeavour to spread to every village and every city of India the message of *Ek Ghanta Desh Ko* that you have given. Do not forget the suggestions that friends from Wardha, Poona and the Government Departments have given you. Have patience, do not be overwhelmed by grief. We shall not leave anything undone for getting assistance from the Government for famine-afflicted people.

87. To Asoka Mehta, 22 March 1951[1]

Dear Asoka,

After the change in the venue of the Cultural Congress I had almost decided not to attend, but both Minoo[2] and Vatsyayan[3] are so insistent. Furthermore I am myself rather keen on meeting Thomas[4] and Silone.[5] I shall be reaching Bombay from Calcutta on the 27th night by plane. The plane reaches there at 9.30 p.m. I have written to Minoo that I shall be staying with him. Some arrangements will have to be made for a car to fetch me from the airport. Will you kindly find out if Minoo himself would be able to do so; failing him will you kindly make some other arrangement? The Rungtas, I am sure, would be happy to send their car. Pratap or someone else might go to the air port with the car.

[1]*J.P. Papers* (NMML).

[2]M.R. Masani.

[3]Sachchidanand Hiranand Vatsyayan (1913-88); poet, writer and journalist; editor, *Vishal Bharat,* 1937-39, *Prateek* 1946-52, *Vak*, 1958-9, *Dinaman*, 1964-9, *Naya Prateek*, 1973-7, *Navbharat Times*, 1977-9; received Sahitya Akademi Award, 1962, and Bharatiya Jnanpith Award for poetry, 1979.

[4]Norman Thomos (1884-1968); Leader of the American Socialist Party; Socialist candidate for Presidentship of USA, 1928, 1936 and 1944; visited India, 1951.

[5]Ignazio Silone (1900-78); writer and thinker; member of Executive Committee of Italian Sociologist Party, 1941-7; member, Italian Constituent Assembly, 1946-8; President Italian PEN Club, 1945-59; Chairman Italian Committee for Cultural Freedom, 1945-59; Publications include, *Fascism: its origin and Growth* (1939); *The Seed Beneath the Snow* (1941); *The Fox and The Camellias* (1961).

I wonder if you have made any final decision about the Executive camp. I met Swami Bhagwan[6] at Sitamarhi and he thought that even during the rains, the U.P. Party could hold the camp at a suitable place. He suggested Saranath for the camp and Banaras for the General Council. I think his suggestion is worth considering. You may write to Genda Singh[7] in the matter. My offer for holding the camp at Ranchi, of course, stands. But I should be happy if the U.P. Party were not deprived of the opportunity.

More when we meet.

Affectionately yours,
Jayaprakash Narayan

[6]Swami Bhagwan; peasant leader from Punjab, Member of the National Executive of the Socialist Party.

[7]Genda Singh; General Secretary, Socialist Party, U.P.

88. To the Secretary, International Solidarity Commission (New York), 23 March 1951[1]

Dear Sir,

I wish to convey to the International Solidarity Commission my sincere thanks for the gift of 20 CARE food parcels donated to me by the Commission. The food contained in these parcels would be distributed by members of the Socialist Party in the food scarcity areas of the State of Bihar. The situation in a large part of the State verges on famine and is expected to worsen in the coming months. I have no doubt that this token gift would be greatly appreciated by the suffering people of this area.

I remain,

Yours very truly,
Jayaprakash Narayan

[1]*J.P. Papers* (NMML).

89. To Jawaharlal Nehru, 24 March 1951[1]

Dear Bhai,

I am enclosing herewith a copy of a letter that I wrote some time ago to Rafi Saheb.[2] I shall be happy if you kindly go through that letter. This question has dragged on for a very long time and I now feel there is no other course left to me but to undertake a fast in order to persuade Government to honour its promises. I am always opposed to the method of fasting applied to a trade union dispute. In the present case, however, the point at issue is the fulfilment of a promise that had been made by a Minister of the Central Government. In my letter to Rafi Saheb I have set out the whole history of this promise. When I met Rafi Saheb recently, he told me that he did not find it possible to do anything in the matter. I am therefore writing to you to know if there is anything that you can do. In case there is a negative answer from you, I shall regretfully have to take recourse to the action indicated above. I do hope that in spite of your being extremely busy, you will have the time at least to read my letter to Rafi Saheb with care. In the past there have been all kinds of subtleties indulged in by Government spokesmen in their statements on this question. I have tried to keep these subtleties in view in my letter to the Communications Minister. I hope, therefore, that the whole issue is not sidetracked by merely entering into a disputation as to what was said or meant by one party or the other. If the intention is to deal with this matter fairly and frankly, it will be found easy to settle. I am not used to heroics or melodrama and my intention to stake my life over such a simple issue should not be brushed aside as a stunt.[3]

I hope you are well. With regards and greetings of the season.

Affectionately yours,
Jayaprakash Narayan

[1] *Brahmanand Papers* (NMML).

[2] See letter to Rafi Ahmed Kidwai dated 8 February 1951, item no. 76.

[3] See Appendix 7 for Nehru's reply to J.P. dated 31 March 1951.

90. To the Prime Minister of India, 24 March 1951[1]

The Prime Minister,
Government of India,
New Delhi.

Dear Sir,

I wish to draw your attention to a very serious problem concerning employees of your Government. I have the good fortune to be connected with three trade union organizations of Central Government employees, namely, the All-India Railwaymen's Federation, the All-India Postmen & Lower Grade (including R.M.S.) Staff Union and the All-India Defence Services Employees' Federation. The most urgent and pressing problem facing these employees is that of the high cost of living. A system of dearness allowance was introduced some years back to deal with the changes in the cost of living, but instead of being an elastic system as it was originally conceived of, particularly by the Central Pay Commission, it has now come to acquire a rigidity which offers no relief whatever to the wage earners. You might recall that at the end of 1948 and the beginning of 1949, there was a big clamour by the men for increment in the dearness allowance and several organizations had decided upon a general strike. At that time the Central Government agreed to sanction an increment of Rs. 10/- in the dearness allowance. In the communique that was issued on behalf of the Government at that time, it was admitted that the increment was not adequate to the rise in prices, but it was stated that in the next few months prices would definitely be brought down and no further increment in dearness allowance would be necessary. But, as you know, prices have generally risen since January 1949, and yet all Government Departments with which I have been dealing have been persistently refusing all demands of labour for a higher dearness allowance. The situation has so far worsened by now that there is again talk of a general strike. The Railwaymen are meeting in their General Council on the 24th of April to decide this issue. The Postmen are also meeting on the 7th of April in their Annual Conference at which this will be the predominant question. Labour is, of course, conscious of the difficulties of Government, but labour expects that Government also should be conscious of its difficulties. I therefore, urge on behalf of over a million of the employees of your Government to give to this matter your earnest consideration. An immediate announcement on your behalf that the matter is under your personal consideration and that you are fully aware of

[1] *J.P. Papers* (NMML).

[2] Jawaharlal Nehru had delivered his speech on the budget in the Parliament on 14 March 1951.

the hardships which the rising cost of living is causing to the employees and that in spite of the unsatisfactory economic position, you will do something to alleviate those hardships would go a long way to calm the workers.

The keynote of your speech[2] on the Budget as of that of the Finance Minister was that the Budget was aimed at laying sound foundations of the national economy. It appears to me, however, that it is a very unsound principle of any kind of economy, to keep the employees in semi-starvation or to reduce their wages continually. Constantly rising prices together with an inelastic wage system cannot but result in a continual wage cut. Any Government which aims at economic soundness cannot build on the basis of such gross exploitation of its own employees. I hope, therefore, that this serious wrong is soon rectified failing which the Government should be prepared for large-scale labour unrest.

Yours sincerely,
Jayaprakash Narayan

91. Presidential Address to the Indian Congress for Cultural Freedom, Bombay, 28 March 1951[1]

Friends,

We have just listened to five powerful speeches from the distinguished guests from abroad and to the inaugural address of Mr. Munshi.[2] You can thus imagine the disadvantage under which I am labouring in making my concluding remarks as Chairman of this session. Yet, I beg you to bear with me for a few minutes as I do not propose to detain you long at this late hour.

From what has been said here this evening it would appear that the danger to cultural freedom stems only from totalitarianism. But there are other sources too of danger. The change in the venue of this conference is itself a pointer to other dangers. One who has been described here as the "greatest apostle of freedom" presides over the Government of this country and yet this Congress, devoted to the very cause of freedom, was found too subversive to be held in Delhi.[3] This shows that the danger is not only from totalitarianism but also from so-called democracy.

To the Indian delegates assembled here I should like particularly to point out how difficult is that task of achieving cultural freedom in our country.

[1]*J.P. Papers* (NMML); summary published in Indian dailies on 29 March 1951.

[2]K.M. Munshi; for biographical note, see *JPSW*, Vol. III, p. 31.

Tributes have been paid here to the cultural traditions of India and it has been stated that India has always believed in cultural freedom. This unfortunately is not my understanding of Indian history and culture. To the contrary, I believe Indian culture has been too often narrow, sectarian and oppressive. Any one who is acquainted today with the hierarchically stratified village society, with the untouchable on one end and the high-caste landlord on the other, will realize the immensity of the task that faces those who believe in cultural freedom. The caste system has been the bane of Indian society and it stands today as the greatest negation of this freedom.

Totalitarianism has been the main theme of the speeches heard this evening. I, as a representative of a movement which believes fervently in democracy, have no hesitation in asserting my uncompromising opposition to all varieties of totalitarianism, whether of the right, left or centre. But how shall we fight totalitarianism, particularly totalitarian communism? The movement to which I belong is doing more than any other body to educate the common people about the true nature of communism. Let me tell you of our experience.

In many parts of India and particularly in the part I come from, there is a great deal of scarcity. There is scarcity of food and of other daily necessities of life, such as cloth. And I don't know who tells the villagers and how, but many of them seem to believe that their salvation lies in communism. This depressed me a great deal and we are trying to remove this delusion. But this perhaps shows you the root of the problem.

The problem of cultural freedom is, to my mind, basically a problem of equality of opportunity. Conservatives, Socialists and Liberals have gathered together on this platform to assert their faith in cultural freedom. But I would remind them that without equality of opportunity they will never be able to establish cultural freedom. There are millions of people who do not have enough to eat and enough to cover themselves with, and whose children cannot go even to the primary schools. It seems comic to talk to them about cultural freedom. I am convinced that unless the distinguished delegates to this Congress addressed themselves to this task, they would not be able to achieve their objective.

We have been called upon by speakers here to join in the fight against communism; and we have heard the amusing story of the lamb, the shepherd and the wolf. (One of the speakers had alluded to the neutrality of the lamb when he was attacked by the wolf and the shepherd was trying to protect him.) That is just the trouble with the present world and with the fight

[3]The Government of India, in refusing to permit the Congress to be held in New Delhi, was perhaps guided by the impression that its parent organization, the International Congress for Cultural Freedom, was being manipulated by the US Central Intelligence Agency (CIA). When this was confirmed several years later, J.P. resigned from that body.

against totalitarianism. Why should the world, or rather the free world as it is called, be divided between the shepherds and the lambs. And what does the fight mean to the lambs. Let us concede that the lambs have been protected. What happens then? The shepherd comes one day with his shears and the lambs are shorn of their wool. And finally the shepherd appears with his knife, and who will then protect the lamb? In the circumstances you cannot blame the lamb if he does not enthuse over his protectors.

There is a great deal of talk today of the conflict between totalitarianism and freedom. During the last war too there was a great deal of talk of a similar conflict between fascism and democracy. Mr. Churchill had then invited the Indian people to take part in that war for democracy. The world knows the answer that the Indian people and Mahatma Gandhi gave to Mr. Churchill. India, he said then, as may still be remembered, that she could not fight for 'democracy' when she herself was enchained in slavery. And for that answer "democracy" did not hesitate to shut up Mahatma Gandhi in prison and turn the whole country into a concentration camp. Is the situation different today? Take Africa—the continent of the future. Over a hundred million Negores of Africa and millions of Arabs are being ruled today by the free nations of the world: Britain, France, Spain, Portugal. What does the fight against totalitarianism mean to these millions of people?

Let us suppose that by a great misfortune a third world war overtook us. If in this war, the leaders of the free world, the US and Britain, were to win, are we assured that the victors would treat the lambs justly. And will the lambs remain lambs, or be raised into shepherds? And what if Churchill were to return to power. We know what kind of a shepherd he has been. We do not like such shepherds. And what, if the present set-up were to change in the United states. If an individual cannot be trusted with too much power, can a nation be trusted with the power that would accrue from a world-conquest?

Therefore, let us not over simplify the world issue. The issue today is not only that of totalitarianism vs. democracy. Totalitarianism must be combated, but not only by anti-totalitarianism. The struggle against totalitarianism must have a positive content. If anti-totalitarianism means mere protection of the weak by the strong, this country is not interested in it. We have seen the result of the last anti-fascist war. If at the end of the impending anti-totalitarian war, the world picture remained essentially unchanged, i.e., of a world divided between the weak and the strong, the prosperous and the abjectly poor, the ruler and the ruled, the master race and the sub-human, the war would have been fought in vain. In such a world, one giant might usurp total power.

Therefore, if the war for democracy has any meaning it is necessary before the fight against the common enemy is launched, that we all sit together and create here and now the conditions that will guarantee freedom, justice, well-being and equality to all at the end of the conflict. For this purpose, the free nations of the world must merge themselves into a world community, in which the big nations willingly share their power, prosperity and knowledge with the small and backward and thus promote a true sense of equality and fraternity. If such were the picture of anit-totalitarianism and of the struggle for freedom, the peoples of all the continents would gather enthusiastically under its flag and Communism would collapse the next day. The message of such a world community of the free and equal would be like a proclamation of manumission to the people enslaved to totalitarianism.

92. To Jawaharlal Nehru, 6 April 1951[1]

My dear Bhai,

You might still remember the trouble that had arisen in Dalmianagar some two years back. The Bihar Government had functioned at that time with patent partiality and even after Basawan Sinha's thirty days' fast, the Government had not acted honourably. Industry, labour and the nation had all suffered just because the Congress party had placed partisanship above everything else.[2] I am afraid, a similar situation has arisen again.[3] I am sure that there would be no trouble whatever if the Government only followed its own laws and its officers and Ministers acted fairly and impartially. A strike which has already been declared illegal is impending, but it could be avoided if either the Employer or the Government shows the least desire to settle. If you think fit you may write to the Chief Minister to see that the situation is handled properly and fairly.

I am sorry to trouble you so often.

With best regards,

Affectionately yours,
Jayaprakash Narayan

[1] *J.P. Papers* (NMML).

[2] For Dalminagar episode see *JPSW*, Vol. V; item no. 106, dated 5 February 1949.

[3] Trouble in the Dalminagar factories was not over even after the strike formally ended in February 1949 and Basawan Sinha broke his fast on J.P.'s advice on the basis of certain assurances by the Bihar Government and the management which were not fulfilled. Prolonged tension, dissatisfaction and worsened economic conditions again led to a situation of strife at the beginning of 1951.

93. To Jawaharlal Nehru, 18 April 1951[1]

Dear Bhai,

I thank you for your letter.[2] Even at the risk of forfeiting what little affection you may still have for me, I should like once more to trouble you about the strike period pay of the Postmen.

First let me say that though it was always clear to us that your views with regard to this matter were rather strong, may I submit that your views are not particularly relevant. When the P & T Workers' delegation met you in December 1948 and returned disappointed and empty-handed, they felt compelled to resort to the ultimate weapon in their possession. Accordingly a strike ballot was held. The ballot was overwhelmingly in favour of strike. It was at this moment that the Communications Ministry (like the Railway Ministry) agreed to negotiate with the Union. It was during this negotiation that Mr. Kidwai gave me the assurance about the strike period pay. Your personal views or views as Prime Minister had no relevance to these negotiations. The Union was negotiating with the Ministry concerned in the hope that whatever agreement was arrived at with that Ministry, would be honoured and implemented by the Government as a whole. I hope therefore that you will not allow your personal views of your colleagues to interfere with the settlement of a labour dispute reached between the Department and the men concerned.

Secondly, you have suggested in your letter that only some vague statement was made by Mr. Kidwai and no definite assurance was given and you have accused me of taking advantage of the Minister's vague but kind-hearted promise to try to do something. I am not used to making mis-statements and if Mr. Kidwai were to state that he gave me no definite assurance, I would still have to go on a fast, but not to persuade your Government, to honour its word, but to recompense for my own incompetence and stupidity as a negotiator. The very essence of my case all along has been that a definite assurance was given which was repeated at a very critical moment and yet the Government has refused to carry out that assurance. Even if for argument's sake it is conceded that the assurance originally given at the time of the strike ballot was not very definite, there cannot be any doubt that when I had announced last year my intention to fast in this connection and when at that time I had met Mr. Kidwai, he had most definitely said that a satisfactory solution would soon be found of the problem and had even authorized me to make a press statement to that effect. Had Mr. Kidwai not been so definite at that time, I would never

[1]*J.P. Paper* (NMML).

[2]Refers to Nehru's letter dated 31 March 1951; for text see Appendix 8.

have agreed to postpone my fast then. I should like therefore to make it clear that I am not basing my case on any vague promise, but on a definite assurance and all I am asking you and your Government to do is to carry out that assurance. I cannot make my position any clearer. The rest lies in your hands.

I hope you are well. With best regards,

Affectionately yours,
Jayaprakash Narayan

P.S.: I have not yet had any reply to the formal letter written some time ago about dearness allowance. I am enclosing herewith a copy of that letter.

94. Statement on Food Situation in Bihar, Bombay, 24 April 1951[1]

So much has been said and written about the famine situation in Bihar that I need hardly emphasis its gravity at this time. I have just come from a tour of some of the northern and southern districts of Bihar. The State is traditionally divided into North and South Bihar. The impression so far has been that South Bihar is not immediately faced with famine. My tour, however, of the South of the State has convinced me that practically the entire State is facing starvation if immediate steps are not taken with war-time speed to relieve the situation.

For the last four years the food position in Bihar has been steadily deteriorating, partly due to natural calamities, but also due in a considerable measure to the failure of the Bihar Government to step up food production and to procure and administer distribution of food as well as to the complacency and light-hearted attitude of the Central Government, particularly of Mr. K.M. Munshi. Even today in a patently desperate situation the Director General of Food of the Central Government after a tour of the State has with unexampled irresponsibility declared that the position was not as bad as it was made out to be. One fears that unless thousands of innocent lives are lost, the Centre will not awaken to the reality of the situation. Under the existing circumstances it is only the Central Government which can rescue the people of Bihar from the jaws of death, but the allotments so far made by the Central Government to the State fall far short of adequacy. The next three or four months are going to be extremely serious because there is hardly any new crop that is expected. The late summer

[1]The Statement was made at a Press Conference at Bombay, 24 April 1951 and appeared in many newspapers on 25 April 1951, also in *Janata*, 29 April 1951.

maize crop is not in the least promising and in the *Adivasi*[2] areas the failure of the *mahuva* crop has destroyed the mainstay of the people for at least three months. Not only adequate quantities of grains will have to be supplied by the State through a proper system of rationing, but also the power to purchase will have to be created through loans, reliefs and public works. An efficient system of famine administration covering all these activities must be immediately created. The existing system of administration is too inadequate to cope with these heavy tasks.

[2]Tribal.

95. Address to Railway Workers, Bombay, 24 April 1951[1]

I gave an ultimatum to Prime Minister Nehru about a month ago[2] that more than one lakh workers on the railways and posts and telegraphs, and the civilian employees of the defence services would go on strike if their problems are not solved without much delay. But I have not yet received any reply from the Prime Minister.

The proposed railway strike will not affect the trains carrying food grains to Bihar and other starved areas and the workers will continue to run such trains.

I wrote the letter of ultimatum to the Prime Minister after the Ministries of Communications, Defence and Railway had in their reply to my demand for discussing the worker's demands, said that it was the duty of the Prime Minister to look into the matter.

As the President of the All-India Federation of Railwaymen, Posts and Telegraphs workers, defence services, and civilian employees, I, on behalf of them, drew (in my letter) attention of the Prime Minister to the spiral of rising prices and increasing deficit in the country which the Government had not been able to solve.

I had also written to Pandit Nehru, that only slogans of patriotism will not fill the stomach of the workers, and if the Prime Minister's characterization of this year's budget as built on the foundation of sound economic basis is true, it has been made sound by starving labour.

The soaring prices and the consequent diminishing value of the rupee have rendered the railway workers half-starved even after the Government conceded some of their demands two years ago. At that time, the Government strove to check the soaring prices but now they have given up this effort.

[1]Adapted from *National Herald*, 25 April 1951.

[2]J.P.'s letter to the Prime Minister dated 24 March 1951, item no. 89.

Two years have passed without any result after the joint advisory committee was appointed in 1949, and the workers can not wait any more.

If the railway workers decide to go on strike they will do so after due consideration. The proposed railway strike will not affect the trains carrying foodgrains to Bihar and other starved areas and the workers will continue to run such trains. They have to be peaceful in their strike and not to indulge in anarchy and subversive activities as there are forces in the country which want to create chaos by exploiting the starvation of the masses.

A strike by railwaymen will be a real service to the country because that may compel the Government to change their harmful policy and set them on the right path. Unless the workers surge themselves into action, the condition of the people will not change. The railway workers have to go to jail in thousands, if necessary, and to raise funds, organize volunteers and make united efforts to solve their problems.

The present Government have forfeited their right to be called a people's Government as they have not been able to perform their primary duty of properly feeding the people.

Strikes are no means of solving the fundamental problems of the people. The real solution lies in the setting up of a people's Government by replacing the present one. If the Congress returns to power in the general elections, there will be chaos in the country.

96. To the Chairman, Indian Mining Association, 1 May 1951[1]

Dear Sir,

I am writing in connection with the labour situation in Jharia. I had gone to Jharia on the 22nd of April and has desired to meet the representatives of certain European-managed mining companies in that area, but though on all previous occasions the European managers were good enough to meet me, this time they excused themselves on some pretext or the other. I was rather sorry that they did so, because I should have liked them to understand my point to view and that of the Socialist Party as far as it related to labour work in Jharia.

I take this opportunity to explain that point of view here, because I want your Association to determine its policies after understanding the position. Some months ago a number of persons, including among them B.P. Sinha, Imamul Haye Khan and Bhagwat Tripathi were expelled from the Socialist Party. The decision to take action against these persons was taken not only

[1] *J.P. Papers* (NMML).

with my concurrence but at my own initiative. The situation, as it subsequently developed, has been described by certain managements as a quarrel between two groups of labour workers, with which they must observe strict neutrality. First of all, it is necessary to understand that the efforts of a responsible political party to punish disloyalty and dishonesty are not just a quarrel between two groups. The Bihar Socialist Party took action against these persons because for over a period of at least three years it was found that (a) they were sabotaging all our efforts to put the labour movement in Jharia on a sound basis, (b) they were guilty of dishonesty in matters of money, and (c) they persisted in using methods of goondaism in the course of their trade union activities.

Some of the managements belonging to your Association might be aware that for a long time past the Socialist Party had tried to close down the small individual unions which had become the private zamindaris of some of the persons against whom action was taken and to create in their place a single union embracing all the units. It was thus that the Koyala Mazdoor Panchayat was born. After the formation of the Panchayat, B.P. Sinha and his friends were given clear instruction to dissolve the separate unions, or rather to merge them all into the Koyala Mazdoor Panchayat. For the last two years or more, none of the separate unions has really been in existence and there has been no enrolment of membership of these unions. The only membership enrolled was that of the Koyala Mazdoor Panchayat. Had B.P. Sinha and his friends been honest and loyal to their party, not one of the separate unions could have claimed any existence today.

After the Koyala Mazdoor Panchayat was formed, an attempt was made by me and my friend Shri Purshottam Trikamdas of Bombay to set up a high-level joint machinery for negotiation and settlement of disputes. I believe both the Indian and European managements had agreed to co-operate in forming this joint machinery. We, on our part, were anxious to set up such an agency, because we had repeatedly discovered that some of our workers when they were left to negotiate independently were not amenable to discipline nor were always honest in their transactions. Some of them even went to the length of practising blackmail. The facts concerning dishonesty in money matters that had come to my personal knowledge were of such a nature however that they could not be proved before any impartial body. The reason was that those who supplied the proofs did so privately. Even when the proofs were to our complete satisfaction, the parties concerned were not prepared to give us anything in writing or to appear before any investigating body. But the evidence of corruption went on accumulating and a stage was reached where we were not prepared to put up with the situation for a day longer. I was prepared, even at the cost of all our work and all our unions in Jharia being wiped away, to fight this corruption. But because the evidence was not capable of being produced even before the disciplinary bodies of the Party, the Executive Committee of the Bihar Provincial Party decided to ask the persons concerned to leave Jharia and to report to the Party Committees in their districts and to follow the instructions of these committees. This Party direction B.P. Sinha and his friends were not prepared to follow because it meant the end of their profitable career of labour leadership and a life of comfort and ease. Consequently they were expelled from the Party.

After that they have been fighting the Socialist Party and the Koyala Mazdoor Panchayat with every mean weapon that they know how to use. In this fight the managements, particularly of Lodna and Gazli Tand, have been giving them all possible support and help. The European managements in this country have usually maintained an enlightened labour policy and have been known for their partiality towards honesty and decency. But the attitude of the European managements with which we have to deal in Jharia after the expulsion of Sinha and others has caused me great surprise. I believe the managements concerned are merely trying to exploit the prevailing confusion to their own advantage. But such a policy is always short-sighted and never pays in the long run. The Socialist Party is not going to give any quarter to Sinha and his friends, and I do not believe that even with the combined efforts of the managements and the Ministry they would have any chance. At any rate, the labour movement run by the support of the State and management can never be a genuine movement of labour, nor deliver the goods on the latter's behalf.

B.P. Sinha continues to be a member of the various official committees. He was nominated to these committees only on the strength of his being a representative of the Socialist trade unions in Jharaia. Had he been an honest person he would have resigned from all these committees after his expulsion from the Party. But he continues to enjoy all these positions, as he finds them profitable.

In this connection, I should also like to inform you that the Bihar Khan Mazdoor Federation, as whose representative B.P. Sinha originally sat on the official Committees, was also liquidated way back in 1949, when the inaugural conference of the Bihar Hind Mazdoor Sabha had met at Kodarma. Shri Asoka Mehta and I were present at that conference and the resolution dissolving the Bihar Khan Mazdoor Federation and merging its powers and privileges with the Koyala Mazdoor Panchayat was drafted by me. But, as in other matters, Sinha was deceitful here too and he never informed the Government that the Bihar Khan Mazdoor Federation had been dissolved. We have apprised the Central Government of the position and have advised them that B.P. Sinha has no right to represent the Socialist labour movement in Jharia or the Koyala Mazdoor Panchayat and that the

Bihar Khan Mazdoor Federation had ceased to be nearly two years ago.

This, in brief, is the situation in Jharia as far as we are concerned. It is for your Association to determine its policy. I can only hope that the Indian Mining Association will prefer to deal with a responsible party and a consolidated labour union such as the Koyala Mazdoor Panchayat rather than with a group of dishonest careerists.

Yours truly,
Jayaprakash Narayan

97. To B.N. Rao, 1 May 1951[1]

Dear Shri Rao,[2]

I thank you for your letter of 11th April.[3] The maximum limit of a thousand rupees necessarily implies limitation of property also to that extent, i.e., to the extent of property that can yield a monthly income of a thousand a month. How these objectives can be achieved is a technical problem for our economists to solve. But the method will include abolition of zamindari, redistribution of land with maximum size of individual holdings fixed, nationalisation, taxation, control of profits, etc.

I am happy to find you taking interest in this problem.

Sincerely yours,
Jayaprakash Narayan

[1]*J.P. Papers* (NMML).

[2]B.N. Rao; an Economist, associated with the Institute of Politics and Economics, Hyderabad.

[3]B.N. Rao, in his letter, had expressed his disagreement with the Socialist Part's suggestion to fix Rs. 100/- p.m. as minimum and Rs. 1,000/- p.m. as maximum income if it came to power. Rao thought that amount of income insufficient till the maximum limit of property to be owned by an Individual was fixed.

98. To K.T.V. Sreedharan, 1 May 1951[1]

Dear Shri Sreedharan,[2]

Thank you for your letter of 9th April. I am happy to know that you are forming a Meherally Youth League at Colombo so as to further the ideals of democratic socialism. I am also happy to know that you wish to maintain

[1]*J.P. Papers* (NMML).

[2]K.T.V. Sreedharan; a young Socialist leader from Colombo University, who had organized Meherally Youth League in Colombo.

contact with the Indian Socialist Party and to promote its policies. I wish you all success in this noble task.

I send you my best wishes for the success of the inaugural function of the league in June next.

Yours sincerely,
Jayaprakash Narayan

99. To Jawaharlal Nehru, 16 May 1951[1]

Dear Bhai,

I thank you for your letter of April 21 concerning the postal strike period pay issue. It is a pity that I have not been able to have my point of view understood. My reference in my last letter to the irrelevance of your views has annoyed you, and I am afraid you have caught hold of words instead of understanding the other fellow's point of view. However, there does not seem anything further that I can do to make my position clearer.

I therefore most reluctantly wish to inform you that if the assurance that was given to me by the Honb'le Communications Minister with regard to the strike period pay issue is not fulfilled, or a definite undertaking is not given by Government to fulfil it, in a month's time I shall undertake an indefinite fast. If the Honb'le Minister informs you that no such assurance was ever given I should still undertake a fast, but limited then to 21 days, inorder to make amends for my carelessness in negotiating on behalf of labour and for the consequent delay in the settlement of this issue by labour's action.

I should add that the entire history of this issue and of the negotiations connected with it was given by me in my letter of Feb. 8 to the Hon'ble Communications Minister.[2]

You are faced with many national and international problems and I was reluctant to add to your worries, but I would be untrue to myself and to labour if I did not take this step.

Please reply[3] c/o Socialist Party, Aligarh.

With best regards,

Yours affectionately,
Jayaprakash

[1]*J.P Papers* (NMML).

[2]For Rafi Ahmed Kidwai's letter to J.P. see Appendix 10

[3]For Nehru's reply dated 18 May 1951, see Appendix 9.

100. To Takhatmal Jain, 26 May 1951[1]

Dear Takhatmalji,[2]

Most recently Pandit Baleshwar Dayalji, Shri Keshavchandraji[3] and member of District Kisan Panchayat, Shri Laksman Singhji have been externed from Ratlam. It appears to me to be a great injustice that a person is externed from his work place due to political reasons. I know these three friends. They are not criminal people but they are social workers. It is possible that their views and activities are not liked by the Government, but it cannot be a reason for their externment. I hope that you will give a thought to this injustice and remove it.

I also want to draw your attention to another question. There is a famine like condition in some areas of Madhya Bharat. But, still I have heard that in those areas also, even after the *Akshay Tritiya*, the collection of land revenue is continued and it is being carried on rigourously. I feel that this land revenue collection should now be stopped and simultaneously distribution of grains even if it is in form of loan should be done in the famine striken areas during the monsoons. This can later be returned by the farmers after harvesting. I hope that you will give due consideration to this question too and take necessary action.

Hope your are O.K.

Yours,
Jayaprakash

[1] *J.P. papers* (NMML).

[2] Takhatmal Jain (1895-1975); first non-official Minister for Rural Welfare and Local Self-Government of Gwalior, 1940-2; Finance Minister, Gwalior State, 1947-8; Madhya Bharat Chief Minister, 1950-2 and 1955-7; Minister for Commerce and Industries and Agriculture, M.P. Government, 1956-8; General Secretary AICC, 1958-60; Minister for Planning and Development, 1962-4; President of Madhya Pradesh Bharatiya Kranti Dal, 1969-70.

[3] Baleshwar Dayalji and Keshavchandraji were members of District Kisan Panchayat, Madhya Pradesh.

101. To Lakshmi Babu, 28 May 1951[1]

Dear Lakshmi Babu,[2]

I was in Hardoi [U.P.] yesterday. The Socialist Party there have gifted me

[1] *J.P. Papers* (NMML). Original in Hindi.

[2] Lakshmi Babu; a disciple of Gandhiji and a prominent leader of 'Charkha Sangh' (founded by Mahatama Gandhi) in Bihar.

100 maunds of grains for the famine affected areas of the country. I have decided to send 50 maunds grain to Bihar and 50 maunds to Madras. I have said to the secretary of the Socialist Party in Hardoi to send that grain to your relief committee. He will correspond with you in this regard. Kindly inform them how this grain should be sent. Hardoi is a surplus district of U.P.

Yours humbly,
Jayaprakash

102. To Jawaharlal Nehru, 29 May 1951[1]

Dear Bhai,

Your letter of May 9 regarding Dalmianagar reached only a couple of days ago.[2] I am thankful to you for the trouble you have taken in this matter. But may I point out that we have not moved an inch forward in regard to it. I wrote to you about the partisan attitude of the Bihar Government. You referred the matter to your Labour Ministry. They were lucky to have the Labour Secretary, Bihar, in Delhi to whom the matter was then referred, who very kindly supplied all the necessary information which, very kindly again, has now been communicated to me. This is, by the way, a fine instance of the way in which Governments, at least in this country, function.

I shall not, however, trouble you any further in this matter, because the Dalmianagar Management having made certain concessions to the workers, the strike has been stayed for the time being. I should only like to point out that the "facts of the case" as stated by the Labour Secretary, Bihar, are full of mis-statements. I am having a note prepared[3] on the subject which I shall send later for your information and the information of your Labour Ministry.

With regards,

Yours affectionately,
Jayaprakash Narayan

[1]*J.P. Papers* (NMML). See also J.P.'s letter to Nehru, 6 April 1951 in this volume.
[2]Nehru's letter to J.P. dated 9 May is not available.
[3]J.P.'s note on Dalmianagar not available.

103. Constitutional Amendments: A Denial of Democracy, Lucknow, 31 May 1951[1]

It is a great pity that a man like Pandit Nehru has to propose the amendments to the Constitution.[2] It is a great tragedy that in a single-party Parliament the ruling party should take advantage of its majority to tamper even with the Fundamental Rights. The very purpose of defining the Fundamental Rights in the Constitution is to place them beyond the interference of parliamentary majorities.

Pandit Nehru's repeated reference to the security of the State was itself, a pointer to a grave danger that has been created for the future of Indian democracy. Except those in power, no one else in the country seems to be aware of any threat to the security of the State and yet these crippling amendments are sought to be made in the name of this danger.

The restrictions, that are sought to be imposed on criticism of friendly nations are not only unwarranted but they will also prevent the growth of a sound foreign policy in the country.

The limitation on freedom of press is unjust and unwarranted. However, as long as newspaper production is a profit-making business, moneyed interests are bound to control the press. The only way to guarantee the freedom to press against monopolies is either to ban the publication of advertisements or recourse to measures to prevent business firms from publishing newspapers. The enactment of a legislation, permitting only non-profit-making public institutions to publish newspapers, is the best way to guarantee the freedom of press.

Amendments aimed at validating the Zamindari Abolition Acts are also defective in the sense that they are not based on any principle. Instead of these halting amendments, the Constitution should have been so changed as to empower the Government to acquire any private property in public interest with or without compensation. Unless such power is vested in the Government no social and economic legislation of a progressive nature will be possible apart from the present Zamindari Abolition Acts.

I am afraid that under the present Constitution nationalization of industry and other interests are practically impossible. It is necessary to remove these general impediments to progressive economic legislation.

[1] An interview to the United Press of India. Adapted from *National Herald*, 1 June 1951.

[2] The Constitution (First Amendment) Act 1951 was enacted to confer on the State the power to place restrictions on the freedom of expression in the interest of maintaining public order and friendly relations with foreign States.

104. To Sampurnanand, 9 June 1951[1]

Dear Sampurnanandji,[2]

In the course of my U.P. tour I had gone to Lakhimpur-Kheri also. There some discharged teachers of the Municipal Schools met me. It seems that five of them, who had participated along with many others in the strike of primary teachers in 1949, were not reinstated in their posts. They had later appealed for reinstatement, and while the Education Department DO (copy enclosed) regretted that the matter was entirely in the hands of the Chairman of the Municipality, it recommended that the cases of these teachers, particularly when all others had been reinstated, should be leniently dealt with. But unfortunately the Chairman had disregarded the advice of the Government, and the reasoning he has advanced for so acting is far from reasonable. He merely says, as you will find from the enclosed papers, that the behaviour, past and present, of the teachers concerned does not "appeal" to him. This is hardly reason enough to deprive five old men who have served the Municipality for so many years of their means of livelihood. Instead of showing leniency, the Chairman has been deliberately hard on these unfortunate persons.[3]

I wonder if you can do anything in the matter. These men have every right to be reinstated. I shall be very happy and feel grateful if justice is done to them.

I hope you are well. With regards,

Yours affectionately,
Jayaprakash

The names of the five teachers concerned:

1. Shri Devi Prasad, 2. Pandit Ramadhar, 3. Pandit Pyarelal, 4. Maulvi Maqbool Ahmed, 5. Munshi Gurucharan Lall.

[1]*J.P. Papers*, (NMML).

[2]For biographical note on Sampurnanand, see *J.P.S.W.*, Vol. I, p. 72.

[3]For Sampurnanand's reply on the question of reinstatement, see his letter dated 18 June 1951, Appendix 11.

105. 'Socialism and Gandhism', 10 June 1951[1]

I have often wished that my public speeches were not reported. I am not blaming the reporters or the newspapers. The fault must be mine. But the fact remains that I often find myself saying things in the newspapers that I never said to any audience. I also wish that newspapermen did not wait for the statutory fifteen years to learn Hindustani. . . . Speaking and reporting then might not be at such variance.

Certain reports of my recent Gujarat speeches have led to a great deal of confusion. I should like to clear up this confusion.

I have been reported to have said that I was in favour of dissolving the Socialist Party and joining the Congress if the latter accepted and implemented the Sarvodaya Plan. This statement, in isolation, conveys a very different impression from what my speeches as a whole gave to the audience that heard them.

The whole burden of my speeches in Gujarat was that there was nothing whatever to be hoped from the Congress now that it had turned into a conservative party of India and was serving only the vested interests. Further that under the impact of social forces the Congress was fast disintegrating and had already become incapable of holding the country together, which as popularly supposed was its main achievement and utility. I went further and said that those, who having lost hope in all else were now pinning their faith on an individual, were also bound to be disillusioned because that individual, Jawaharlal Nehru, too, had been shown by events to be incapable of taking any constructive forward step. I then explained that socialism and the Socialist Party were the only alternative. These arguments were developed at some length, because in my schoolmasterish fashion I am accustomed to elaborate, particularly when the audience happens to be large.

In view of this clear and categorical view that I placed before my audiences, there was no sense in throwing the whole argument into confusion again by raising the possibility of our rejoining the Congress under certain conditions. I am sure the audience nowhere carried away any such impression.

The reference to Sarvodaya which has given rise to so much confusion was made exactly with the view of reinforcing the argument that the Congress had fallen beyond redemption. I was dealing with the all too common attempt of Congressmen to exploit the name of Gandhiji, and I asserted, as I assert now, that there was not an iota of Gandhism in what the Congress and the Congress governments were doing today.

If the Congress believed in Gandhism, as it pretended to do, here was

[1]*Brahmanand Papers* (NMML). The article was published in *Janata*, 10 June 1951.

the Sarvodaya Plan, I said, which was prepared by the Gandhian constructive workers; let the Congress accept that Plan and proceed to implement it. If the Congress really did so, I would be prepared to advise the Socialist Party to rejoin the Congress.

What I intended to convey by this argument, and what the audience clearly understood, was that the Congress had forsaken Gandhism so completely that it was incapable of putting into force any Gandhian programme and policy.

The question might yet be asked why should a socialist offer to dissolve his party even if the Congress were actually to implement the Sarvodaya Plan. The question is worth examining. But the difficulty is that while the educated have some vague idea of socialism they know little of the Sarvodaya Plan. To most people Sarvodaya is some crankish creed which talks a good deal of non-violence and trusteeship, but is afraid to bring about any social change. To all serious minded persons, however, I would recommend a careful study of the Sarvodaya Plan. The Plan is no wishy washy sentimentalism, but a concrete programme of basic social revolution. Outside the conventional socialist circles, it is the first attempt to picture concretely a new social order. Socialists, particularly scientific socialists who must be objective and take into account facts instead of preconceived notions, must view these attempts with sympathy and try to understand and draw near to a group of persons than whom no more devoted servants of the people can be found. I am afraid even in the Socialist Party, which takes a scientific rather than a dogmatic view of theory, there is no sufficient awareness either of the importance of this group of workers or of the startlingly familiar conclusions to which they are arriving. Any one who cares to read the Sarvodaya Plan will find that it contains eighty per cent of the immediate programme of the Socialist Party, besides sharing the common ideal of a classless and castesless society.

It may be interesting to recall how the Sarvodaya Plan came into being. When Gandhiji was still alive, it had been decided in view of the rapidly deteriorating situation in the country and the prevailing confusion in government policy, that the constructive workers should meet at Wardha towards the end of February 1948 and prepare a programme embodying the Gandhian principles of national reconstruction to be placed before the country and the Government. Mahatmaji was himself to guide this meeting, but history willed otherwise. Later, however, the contemplated meeting was held and finally in December 1949 two hundred constructive workers met in Wardha and endorsed the programme which was published on 30th January 1950 as the Sarvodaya Plan.

This is not the place to describe the Plan in full, but let me set forth its basic points.

The ideal that the Plan sets out to achieve is that of a non-violent, non-exploitative cooperative society which shall not be based on caste or class and in which there shall be equal opportunity for all. The present competitive economy shall be replaced by a social economy based on co-operation.

Proprietorship in agricultural land shall vest in the tiller of the soil under regulations laid down by society. There shall be redistribution of land and no one shall have more land than three times the economic holding. The uneconomic holdings shall be pooled into co-operative farms. There shall be collective farming on waste lands brought under cultivation. Farmers carrying on cultivation on individual farms shall have to function through the village multi-purpose society. At present price levels, rupees hundred per month should be the lowest wage or income, and twenty times that amount, i.e. two thousand rupees per month, should be the highest wage or income.

The Plan divides industry into centralized and decentralized. To quote: 'Centralized industries should be owned by society and run by autonomous corporations or by co-operatives if possible.' Then the *Plan* makes the following striking statements: 'Such centralized industries should be socialized on payment of compensation calculated on the basis of the ceiling allowed under the scheme (i.e. Rs. 200/- per month) and which should be only a rehabilitation compensation.'

In the public owned centralized industries the employees will also be associated with the management. Foreign concerns should either go out of existence or pass under public ownership.

In de-centralized industries the instrument of production will be owned either individually or by corporations. The foreign trade of the country should be placed under the control of a public Corporation.

With regard to Banking and Insurance the minimum programme should be to organize mass saving and control of investments in the interest of agriculture and decentralized industries and ultimately to socialise Banks and Insurance companies to save the national economy from the vicious manipulations of high finance.

Regarding taxation our aims should be to evolve a finance system under which 50 per cent of the public revenues collected may be spent by the village panchayats. From the remaining 50 per cent the administration of the higher bodies should be financed.

This should give an idea of the nature of the Sarvodaya Plan. It would be worth anyone's while to study the entire plan. Whoever does so with an open mind would agree with me that if this Plan were implemented it would take us a very long way indeed towards Socialism.

The next step would then be easy. It may be asked what then is the need for a Socialist Party if the Sarvodaya Plan itself is sufficient? The answer to this too will be found by those who care to read the Plan. The authors of the Plan are not politicians and they have no political party of their own. As they say in their note, they have merely tried to place before the country a Gandhian programme of national reconstruction. But they are aware that they have no instrument through which to implement the Plan. No doubt they still hoped (i.e. in January 1950) to persuade the Congress to implement it. But that hope must have faded away by now; and there is no reason to suppose that if the Socialist Party gives promise to implement the Plan, the Gandhian constructive workers would refuse to cooperate. Indeed I have been feeling for some time as I wrote in the Independence Number of the *Janata* this year that the constructive workers and the Socialist Party must join hands to create a new social order. I wish members of the Socialist Party had the intellectual honesty to study objective facts and refuse to be swayed by prejudice. Let me hasten to add that Socialism is not just the Sarvodaya Plan. It is much more. But then there is no reason to suppose that the further content of socialism would be unacceptable to the constructive workers; or that the Sarvodaya Plan is the last word by them on the task of creating a new civilization.

A word now about Gandhism and Socialism. I have been reported as having said in Gujarat that Gandhism was socialism. I never made any such statement. I should, however, like to state now as emphatically as I can that socialism in this country would neglect Gandhism at its peril. The conventional attitude of the "scientific socialist" is to brush Gandhiji aside as a crankish old man who was so much out of date in this atomic age, who was medieval, reactionary and even an indirect apologist of the vested interests. The more sophisticated among them go forward and poke fun at his theory of trusteeship and sum him up as a class collaborationist. The trouble is that the so-called scientific socialist is seldom scientific. More often than not he is just a bigoted phrase-monger. Far from being reactionary, Gandhiji was a social revolutionary of an exceptionally original kind, and he has made contributions to social thought and the methodology of social change that constitute imperishable contributions to human progress and civilization.

The first aspect of Gandhism that must interest the socialist is its moral or ethical basis, its insistence on values.

Russian or Stalinist interpretation of socialist philosophy has reduced it to a crass machiavellian code of conduct utterly devoid of any sense of right or wrong, good or evil. The end justifies the means; and when the end is power—personal and group power—there is no limit to the depths to which the means will sink to secure the objective. The struggle for power in every communist state—struggle not against the old order but amongst communist power-seekers themselves—has led to a totalitarianism that bears little resemblance to that free and egalitarian society that was proclaimed by the father of socialism as the goal of the social revolution.

To the horrors of this unscrupulous, amoral political philosophy Gandhism offers a corrective that socialists would overlook only at the cost of the very substance of their creed. The values of individual and social life that socialism strives to achieve and make the basis of a new civilization also constitute the foundation stone of a Gandhian society.

It is true that philosophically Gandhism has a non-secular and religious or super-natural foundation, whereas socialist philosophy is wholly secular and natural or material. But translated in terms of the practices of life, the values are not different: social and economic equality (casteless and classless society), freedom from exploitation; fullest possible freedom and opportunity for self development; dignity of the human personality; co-operation; society's responsibility for the well-being of each and the responsibility of each towards society.

The second aspect of Gandhism that must attract every socialist is its undying contribution to revolutionary technology. Till before Gandhiji the only means that the suppressed and exploited had with which to fight against their oppressor were violent means. The peaceful means a of struggle were limited to agitation, and in the case of industrial labour, to strike and general strike. Beyond those limits the struggle was powerless to go. Violent means were not always available nor advisable. Therefore the struggle for social justice was unable to express itself adequately.

In Mahatma Gandhi's method of civil disobedience and satyagraha the suppressed and exploited have found a new technique that carries the struggle forward beyond the usual peaceful limits and gives full expression to the urge for social justice and social change.

A third aspect of Gandhism is the insistence on decentralization—economic and political. Ordinarily, in leftist circles this is characterized as antedeluvian. But all those socialists who do not equate their own power with a workers' democracy, who are aware of the disastrous consequences of centralization of economic and political power, must carefully and sympathetically consider this aspect of Gandhism. Economic decentralization does not necessarily mean the rejection of modern science and technology; though it does mean that the modern techniques of productions are neither used as a means of exploitation nor as a means of domination of man by man. The need of decentralized industry in a backward economy like India's, where production must be labour-intensive instead of capital-intensive further underlines the nearness of Gandhism thought on this matter with socialist reconstruction in India. Political decentralization neither means a weak State nor absence of planned life. The actual forms of economic and political decentralization suited to the needs of a socialist society have to be studied and evolved. In this task the Gandhian constructive workers have a vital role to play. I have selected just these three issues to illustrate my view that socialism will neglect Gandhism at its peril. There are many more problems of the social revolution and of social reconstruction on which Gandhism had some definite contribution to make.

And my plea is that it is the duty of every scientific socialist, as distinguished from the dogmatist, to understand Gandhism and assimilate as much of it as found desirable in order to establish socialism.

106. Statement on Lohia's Arrest, Patna, 16 June 1951[1]

The shocking news of Dr. Lohia's arrest in Mysore brings to light two of the darkest and sorest spots in the Congress regime. Liberty of the citizen, even of the best, seems to be worth not a moment's care. That a leader of such constructive genius as Dr. Lohia should under any circumstances be put under arrest ought to be a matter of deepest shame for any decent government. Dr. Lohia was to leave India before the end of this month to attend the international socialist conference in Europe. He was also to visit Yugoslavia on invitation, and the Foundation for World Government had invited him to visit the United States. His arrest will be a fitting response from the Congress Government to these invitations, and an eloquent commentary on Nehru democracy.

The other dark spot in the present regime is the deteriorating agrarian situation. Quick and drastic agrarian reform was a top priority in free India. But even after four years of Congress rule the most elementary step of according protection to tenants and crop-sharers has not been taken, and hundreds of thousands of these helpless cultivators have been ejected from their lands. In Mallenad in Mysore the landlords, most of whom happen to be absentee, are trying to eject the crop-sharers, who constitute ninety per cent of the cultivators, by legal trickery. Officialdom and the ruling party being as usual on the side of the landlords, the unfortunate crop-sharers had no chance against them. They were thus driven to resort to satyagraha. Thereupon, the Mysore Government let loose a reign of terror. A large number of the kisans were arrested together with leading members of the Mysore Socialist Party. There was a lathi-charge upon the prisoners. It was in response to the urgent appeals sent by the satyagrahis to Dr. Lohia that

[1] *J.P. Papers* (NMML). Summaries were published in various newspapers on 17 and 18 June and full text in *Janata* on 24 June 1951.

he went to Mysore, only to be locked up by the Government there.[2] His arrest is as much a vindication of the cause of the Mallenad tenants as condemnation of the Congress regime. Such misdeeds serve only one purpose: they bring the doom of the Congress nearer.

[2]In Kagodu village in Mysore a struggle between the share-croppers (peasants at will) and the landlord (being supported by the Government) led to large-scale ejections of old tenants from their lands. The peasants started *satyagraha* against the illegal ejections in April 1951 and approached the Government for redress. The Socialist Party, Mysore, joined the *satyagraha* on 16 May, when repressive measures were let loose upon the movement. Beatings, harassment, and large-scale arrests followed for about a month and the entire Executive Committee of the Mysore Socialist Party was sent to jail. Rammanohar Lohia, too, was put in prison on 15 June when he joined the satyagrahis in Mysore.

107. Statement on Dearness Allowance, 21 June 1951[1]

The present policy of Government with regard to dearness allowance is utterly devoid of any guiding principle. The Central Pay Commission had recommended a basic pay structure and scales of DA, determined according to certain well-defined principles. By their declaration of May 16, 1947 the Government of India accepted those recommendations and stated in regard to DA "that a review will be made every six months and as recommended by the Commission, any variation of 20 points in the cost of living index upwards or downwards will necessitate a change in the allowance" (quotation from Ministry of Finance Press Communique, January 1949).

Employees of the Central Government, among them railwaymen, are demanding no more than that Government should honour its pledge. Since May 1947, there has been not a single six-monthly revision of DA as recommended by the CPC and accepted by Government. Only after a great deal of agitation and two strike ballots on the railways there was a revision in February 1949, and again in June 1951, and a total increment of Rs. 15/- per month was painfully obtained, when at least three times of that amount was rightfully due to the workers.

As I have been able to understand Government's case, it is something like this:

Labour's demand for high DA as prices rise is justified, but Government cannot implement the CPC's recommendations and its own previous pledge because:

(a) of financial stringency

[1]*J.P. Papers* (NMML). The Statement was issued to the press on 21 June 1951, and a summary published in *Searchlight* and several other newspapers on the next day.

(b) progressive rise in workers' emoluments will aggravate inflationary trends

(c) railwaymen are already better paid than other employees.

Let me take these one by one.

(a) *Financial Stringency*

Financial stringency is likely to be a chronic feature of Government budgeting. It is implied in the programme of economic development. The Five Year Plan, in fact, provides for deficit budgeting over a period of years. If capital development is to be undertaken through Government finance, stringency will be a permanent feature of the economy. In a way, it is a result of State policy and does not necessarily reflect the strength or weakness of Government's finance.

Development programmes cannot be carried out by depressing the standard of living of the workers particularly when other sectors of society are not called upon to make similar sacrifices.

Further, I do not think a serious attempt has yet been made (a) to eliminate wasteful expenditure, (b) to control tax evasion.

(b) *Inflation*

A Government which has removed limitation of dividends, repealed the excess profits and the business profits tax, and has time and again raised prices of various commodities, cannot seriously put forward the inflation argument. The eight-point anti-inflation programme enunciated by Dr. Mathai is yet to be implemented. Unless and until an anti-inflation policy is made all-embracing and is strictly enforced, it is not fair to apply it to one sector alone.

But more important than all this is the consideration that no anti-inflationary policy can have any application where remunerations are below these necessary to maintain *minimum standards*. An anti-inflationary policy, if it is to be just, must begin where the incomes are inflated before coming down to attack minimum standards.

(c) The argument that railwaymen are *better paid* than others is regrettable. By this argument the Government sets the public against its own employees which no Government ought to do. Besides the argument is in part untrue and unsound. Untrue because in several industries workers are better off than railwaymen. Unsound, because acceptance of the principle that no class of workers should be paid more than what workers in other industries are getting, would lead to a disastrous result. Some industries will claim that they cannot pay more because they have no "capacity to pay". Those who have capacity will contend that they should not pay more than what others are paying. The net result would be that wages would always remain below the minimum level.

Let me add in conclusion that the workers have been patient and have waited for several years. They cannot wait indefinitely and they cannot be penalized for the failure of the Government to reduce prices. The Planning Commission does not expect prices to go down for many years yet; so it is time that the Government faced the question of DA squarely. *Ad hoc* increases as and when pressure from the workers begins to be uncomfortable cannot solve the problem. There must be a more principled approach. Otherwise, discontentment and agitation would remain permanent features of the trade union movement of Government employees.

108. Message on the Birth of Daily *Janata*, Patna, 22 June 1951[1]

When, years ago (1937), the (Hindi) weekly *Janata* had been born, it had offered a new direction to the political and literary life of the province of Bihar. Since then while facing different calamities, and sometimes being their victim, the weekly *Janata* continued to nourish this new life and remain the chief organ of the exploited and the oppressed. Today the daily *Janata* is being born. Our wish for years is going to be fulfilled. These days, bringing out a daily paper is like crossing the *Himalaya*. However, thanks to the enthusiasm and hard work of comrades this audacious effort is succeeding.

I am convinced that the people of Bihar and the neighbouring provinces will accept this paper as their own. *Janata* will assess the present administration with alertness; bring to light the problems and difficulties of the people; suggest from time to time measures for the building up of the country and the province; oppose and expose oppression, injustice, exploitation, theft and immorality; and will be the voice of the Dalit and exploited people of the society who are becoming dumb today because of neglect by the newspapers of the rich. *Janata* will strive for the building up of a New India which will not have hungry and naked people, exploitation and poverty, distinction between the ruler and the ruled or between the owner and the worker and in which all will work, and all get just remuneration for their labour. *Janata* will contribute towards the development of a new civilization, which will have only one community, the human community, and in which humaneness will receive the greatest respect; in which personal interest will not be the chief objective of life, rather every individual will serve the society and the society will be

[1]*J.P. Papers* (NMML). Original in Hindi.

responsible for each individual's development, including the education of every child, employment for every family, medical treatment of every ill person; in which man will become man.

On the occasion of the birth of this daily I convey my heart-felt good wishes to it and its editor, Rambriksha Benipuri.[2] Let the pen of this talented literature remove, by its brightness, the darkness which has been enveloping the national sky. Let 'Jai Janata' become meaningful.

[2]For biographical note on Rambriksha Benipuri, see *JPSW*, Vol. I, p. 61.

109. To the General Secretary, Insurance Employees Federation, 28 June 1951[1]

Dear friend,

I was glad to learn from your letter of the 24th June that Insurance employees from all over India are meeting in a conference in Bombay on the 30th June.

I find myself in complete sympathy with the memorandum you have kindly sent me, and I hope the conference will succeed in creating the central organization that is so badly needed. Only then would the insurance employees be able to fight successfully the employers and the Government.

I send my best wishes for the success of the conference and of the new central organization that is proposed to be set up.

Yours sincerely,
Jayaprakash Narayan

[1]*J.P. Papers* (NMML).

110. Statement on the Prisoners of the Kagodu Satyagraha, Ranchi, 3 July 1951[1]

I understand that nearly twenty prisoners of the Kagodu Satyagraha[2] are on hunger strike for the last six days as a protest against the vindictive and inhuman treatment to which they are being subjected. Even those facilities that political prisoners had under the foreign rule are denied to them. They are classed as ordinary criminals, food is bad and sanitary conditions are

[1]*J.P. Papers* (NMML).
[2]Kagodu Satyagraha; see item no. 106 fn. 2.

scandalous. Due to these conditions more than half the satyagrahis are under medical treatment and six have been admitted to hospital. The hunger-strikers are not demanding any special facilities but the normal treatment meted out to political prisoners. I hope the Mysore Government will stop the suffering of the satyagrahis without further delay and humanize their treatment of prisoners.

111. To M.L. Dantwala, 4 July 1951[1]

My dear Mohanlal,

Your letter regarding the Khoj Parishad rather depressed me. I think we should carry on even if there is not much co-operation from outside. I am sure Bombay City alone should be able to sustain such an institution intellectually. Even the limited work that the Parishad is doing is useful. When the matter was raised in the National Executive, every one of those who had read the bulletins said that it was a very useful publication. I think you will have more subscribers in the future.

How is Sree Narayan[2] whom I sent to you from Bihar doing? Please make him work hard so that he does not waste his time in Bombay. After he has finished his brochure on the food situation in Bihar you may give him some other definite work or he may work for the time being with K.K.[3] in the preparation of our election pamphlets. But in any case he should work directly under your guidance.

We have had a very nice time here and done a fair amount of work, mostly on the *Platform*.[4] I hope you will approve of the changes made in it. There is no change made in principle except with regard to the redistribution of land in the ryotwari areas. Had Lohia stayed here longer we might have discussed the foreign policy more fully and also prepared the agrarian policy.

I shall be happy to hear from you as often as possible. I hope you are well.

Affectionately yours,
Jayaprakash Narayan

[1]*J.P. Papers* (NMML).

[2]Sree Narayan Prasad; an educated young man, hailing from Bihar and then working in the Socialist Party office in Bombay.

[3]K.K.—refers to K.K. Menon.

[4]See Appendix 12 for the *Platform* of the Socialist Party.

112. To Vaidyanath Aiyyar, 4 July 1951[1]

Dear Mr. Aiyyar,

We have just completed a very successful camp of the National Executive and General Council. The main job that we have done here is preparation of the Party's *Platform*, a copy of which Asoka will send you.

I am writing this in connection with financial assistance to the Punjab Party. You were good enough some months back to give a thousand rupees per month for the Punjab. After that I had toured the Province and collected something like Rs. 30,000/-. That money is finished now and the Party is in need of a subvention as before from the Centre. The Punjab Party is one of our best Parties, if not the best, in organization, discipline and team work. We must do everything possible to help that Party. The jurisdiction of the Punjab Party extends to PEPSU also.

Some time ago you were contributing four to five hundred rupees a month to the Delhi Party which was stopped some months back. Asoka joins me in the proposal that you should add something to that amount and if possible contribute a thousand rupees per month to the Punjab Party for the next few months. If you cannot spare this amount, the amount that you were contributing to the Delhi Party might be diverted to the Punjab with such addition as you my find possible to make to it.

My friend, Prem Bhasin, Joint Secretary of the All India Party and the chief organizer of the recent *Janvani* Day Demonstration in Delhi will see you with this letter. Please do the utmost that is possible, in this connection.

I hope you are well. With regards for Mrs. Aiyyar and you.

Sincerely yours,
J.P.

[1]*J.P. Papers* (NMML).

113. To D.F. Karaka, 4 July 1951[1]

Dear D.F.,[2]

I am sorry for not replying to your letter earlier. We all liked very much the story that you made out of the tour. You were very kind and flattering indeed.

[1]*J.P. Papers* (NMML).

[2]Dosabhoy Framji Karaka (1911-74); Editor, *Current*, Bombay, 1949-69; earlier worked with *Bombay Chronicle*, 1938-48, first Indian to become President Oxford Union during his student days; publications include, *I go West*; *Out of Dust*; *Fabulous Mogul; Nehru—The Lotus Eater From Kashmir*.

I was somewhat frightened by the title of the story, but when I read its origin I felt somewhat relieved. You have made out a very interesting story and skilfully woven together all the little incidents. My wife was quite amused by your remarks regarding her attention to her *pooja* and charkha.

As soon as you send me your first set of questions I shall try to send you my answers.

Regarding the matter that you had raised, I had a talk with Asoka. When he returns to Bombay, he will get into touch with you.

The six days that we had you with us were very pleasant and we missed you very much after you left. My wife joins me in sending you our best wishes and regards.

Yours sincerely,
Jayaprakash Narayan

114. To Awadhesh Nandan Sahay, 4 July 1951[1]

My dear Awadhesh Babu,[2]

We were all very sorry that we neglected the *Janata* so much. But the fact was that after coming here [Ranchi] I was so steeped in work that I did not think of anything else. Ganga Babu[3] also was engrossed in the management of the Camp apart from the time that he was able to give to the Executive. I think there was also a mistake made from the very beginning. At Patna when we were leaving some one should have been definitely made responsible for preparing and sending despatches to the *Janata*. As it was, no one in particular was given a definite responsibility and perhaps each one of us felt that the other was doing something in the matter. Shishir[4] too when he came, and he came late, was given together with Karpuriji the job of translating the *Platform* and he was so much buried in it that he also forgot what you had told him. It was only when your first letter to Ganga Babu was received that we became conscious of our terrible negligence. Since then regular despatches have been sent to the *Janata.* Hamid also after his arrival worked hard in this respect.

[1]*J.P. Papers* (NMML).

[2]Awadhesh Nandan Sahay; For biographical note see item no. 51 in this volume.

[3]Ganga Babu; refers to Ganga Sharan Sinha.

[4]Shishir Kumar; he was at that time working with J.P.; later became one of the secretaries of the Bihar Socialist Party.

The *Platform* was to have been released from Calcutta today by Madhu Limaye. The PTI summary might have been received by this evening at the *Janata* office. I shall send you tomorrow with Shishir a corrected copy of the *Platform.* Only a couple of paragraphs on forests have to be added to the cyclostyled copy that is being sent. The additional part will be sent by Asoka from Bombay. I will be leaving for Kharagpur via Bakura tomorrow morning. I shall be in Calcutta on the 8th or 9th and shall find out whether we can get some more money. I shall also look into the advertisement business. I shall reach Patna on the 10th morning.

I hope you are well.

Affectionately yours,
Jayaprakash Narayan

115. Address at the Meeting of the General Council of All-India Railwaymen's Federation, Kharagpur (Calcutta), 6 July 1951[1]

There is no other alternative before the Council but to take the decision in favour of the strike. The manner in which the Railway Ministry and the Government of India have dealt with the situation and the lack of understanding in their dealing with labour and the railwaymen have compelled the Federation to resort to certain extreme measures. I would have been ready to avert the strike by peaceful settlement even at the cost of my popularity, had there been any avenue open.

The Prime Minister's appeal, not to go for strike cannot be considered anything else but political propaganda. If the Prime Minister has sincerely wanted to settle the issue amicably, he should have come forward with some concrete proposals and made a categorical declaration to that effect.

I hold the Government responsible for precipitating a situation which may create difficulty in the movement of food grains in case of railway strike. We have to convince the affected people of Bihar and Madras and also the people in general that it is not the Federation, but the Government who is responsible for their distress and miseries.

I appeal to all railwaymen to close their ranks and offer a common struggle, so that not a single wheel be moved after 6 a.m. on August 27 next.

[1]Adapted from *Statesman*, 7 July 1951.

116. Statement Explaining Railwaymen's Decision to Go on Strike, Calcutta, 8 July 1951[1]

It was an unanimous decision that railwaymen took yesterday to go on strike from the 27th of August. The appeal of the Prime Minister not only came too late but also held out no definite promise. The Prime Minister appealed that no precipitate action should be taken, but it was forgotten that thirty months have gone by since the postponement of the strike in 1949. During these weary two years and a half prices went on rising despite Government assurances to the contrary and long-drawn out negotiations were conducted through the Joint Advisory Committee and at Ministerial levels which failed to yield satisfactory results. Then a last minute effort was made by the Federation when it compressed the numerous demands of the men into two major ones, namely, (i) revision of dearness allowance scales in accordance with the present price index, and (ii) referring of the disputed points to arbitration. Both these demands were totally rejected by the Government. Later a tiny crumb was thrown to the workers in the shape of an extra Rs. 5/- of DA. It was after the failure of all these patient efforts to settle the dispute that the Federation finally decided to call a general strike. Had the Prime Minister realized the gravity of the situation earlier and taken concrete steps this decision might have been avoided. But a mere appeal even from such a high quarter at this stage could have no meaning nor produce the least effect. Even now if the Prime Minister is anxious to avoid the catastrophe the Federation has left the door open for negotiations. Mr. Nehru must be aware of our demands and it is for him to say the next word.

Some of Mr. Nehru's colleagues have tried assiduously to prejudice the public against the railwaymen by insinuating that the Federation had political motives. The Federation has some times been described as being Socialist-controlled. Nothing could be farther from truth. It is true that I happen to be the President of the Federation but the Socialist Party is in no manner responsible for the policies of the Federation. Any one who is in the least acquainted with the functioning of this largest single labour organization in this country knows that it is the workers themselves who run the Federation and make all its decisions. The Socialist Party has nothing to gain from a railway strike at this or any other time. The relations between the Federation and the Government might not have been so vitiated had not the Government been so obsessed by this political bogey.

An impression seems to have been created that the railwaymen are asking

[1] *J.P. Papers* (NMML). The statement was made at a press conference in Calcutta on 8 July 1951 and its summary published in daily newspapers the next day.

for a favoured treatment, when they already are in the enjoyment of privileges not available to other workers. This is a case of complete misunderstanding. All that the railwaymen are able through collective bargaining to secure for themselves is automatically available to all employees of the Central Government. In this manner the railwaymen are fighting not only their own battles, but also those of others. It just happens that the railwaymen are better organized and more advantageously situated for collective bargaining, but they claim no special privilege for themselves. It should also be understood that the scales of pay and allowances of the railway workers during the days of the private companies were lower in many cases than those of other employees. It was only after the Central Pay Commission that they were brought on the same level as of other Central Government employees. As compared with workers in private industry, railwaymen are hardly in a better position. In this very matter of dearness allowance, for instance, the textile workers in the Bombay State have a far higher scale than railwaymen have today or will have if their demands are fulfilled. The textile workers in Ahmedabad and Bombay get a Dearness Allowance of about Rs. 70/- per month whereas in the railways the scale is Rs. 35/-.

The Federation is conscious of the hardships that the general strike will inflict on the public, but the responsibility for this lies squarely on the shoulders of the Central Government. The Federation has done its best to avoid a strike. It was this same Federation that in 1949 after an equally successful strike ballot, had stayed its hands because the doors of negotiations were opened. No one who is acquainted with the record of twenty-six years of the All-India Railwaymen's Federation can accuse it of unreasonableness, lack of public spirit or precipitateness. The Federation hopes that in its struggle to maintain the standard of living of the working class the public would lend their sympathy and support.

117. To Gyan Chand, 11 July 1951[1]

My dear Gyanbhai,[2]

I was sorry that I was late that evening. We were delayed at the Railway Ministry longer than I had expected and then I had to attend the meeting of the Federation's Working Committee. By the time I reached Sodhaniji's place you had just left.

I will be in Delhi on the 14th and 15th of this month. I should like to see you on one of those days. I shall get into touch with you when I arrive in

[1] *J.P. Papers* (NMML).

[2] For biographical note on Gyan Chand, see Vol. V, p. 147.

Delhi. But I should like to tell you in advance about the points that I would want to discuss with you particularly.

Asoka has already sent you a copy of our Party's Draft *Platform*. The National Executive has made some changes which I shall show you when we meet.

In a couple of weeks the Bihar Party will be preparing its *Provincial Platform* and I should like to consult you about Provincial Finance. I should like you to think over the matter. Supposing the Socialist Party wins a majority in one of the States in India, what would be the new sources of revenue and how the entire provincial budget should be recast. You may take Bihar as an example. I had asked a young man who has passed his M.A. in economics recently to work on the question of salary revision. Fixing the Governor's salary at Rs. 950/- a month and the lowest at Rs. 100/-, he has worked out the entire salary pattern and he finds that in spite of scaling down at the top the salary bill of the Province would be raised by 50 per cent, from four crores to something like six crores a year. A Socialist State will have to spend a lot on social services. Where is the money to be found? We would also like to revise the entire structure of State Finances. I should like to discuss with you all these matters when I meet you next.

I hope you have sent to Asoka your reactions to the *All India Platform*.

I hope Anu bhabhi and you are well.

Yours affectionately,
Jayaprakash Narayan

118. To J.J. Singh, 11 July 1951[1]

My dear J.J.,[2]

I am very grateful to you for sending me press cuttings and other material to keep me in touch with American public opinion *vis-à-vis India*. As soon as our *Platform* is printed I shall have a copy of it sent to you. I cannot tell you how much all of us appreciate your fight in the USA for India, in spite of all manner of odds. Your work in connection with the food loan was magnificent.

I hope you are well.

Sincerely yours,
Jayaprakash Narayan

[1]*J.P. Papers* (NMML).

[2]J.J. Singh; President, India League of America. For details see *JPSW*, Vol. IV, p. 120.

119. To Sree Narayan Prasad, 11 July 1951[1]

My dear Sree,

You have not written to me since you went to Bombay. I am anxious to know what you are doing. I hope you have completed your brochure on Food in Bihar. I should like to know what you will take up after finishing this work. Bombay has many attractions and I hope that while you will amuse yourself, you will also put in some hard work. You will not get again such an opportunity as you have just now. But it entirely depends upon yourself as to what you will make of this opportunity. I expect you to write to me at least one letter a month giving me a report of what you have done in the previous month.

It is possible that you may be asked to work on the preparation of our election pamphlets. If that is so, I hope you will put your heart and soul into it. I am sure it will give you a good deal of experience and knowledge.

For the remaining part of this month, you may write to me at the above address.

I hope you are keeping good health.

Affectionately yours,
Jayaprakash Narayan

[1]*J.P. Papers* (NMML).

120. Reaction to Ordinance to Illegalise the Railway Strike, Patna, 12 July 1951[1]

The Ordinance promulgated by the President to illegalise the railway strike and to punish the strikers even with imprisonment exposes the true character of the Prime Minister's appeal to the railwaymen to desist from strike, issued at twelfth hour.

I cannot say for certain what will be the next step of the Federation. I have called an emergent meeting of the working committee of the Federation at Calcutta on July 21 and 22.

My natural reaction to any such repressive policy is that of determined resistance, but the AIRF is a trade union which has ordinarily to function within the framework of the law. I cannot say what it will choose to do in the present extraordinary situation. I can only say this that if ordinances are to rule our lives, this country will have no freedom whatever. The ordinance

[1]Adapted from *Searchlight*, 14 July 1951.

makes it clear that the Government has already made up its mind not to concede the demands of the workers. In that case there is no point in the Prime Minister's issuing his appeal. If the Government is anxious to stave off the railway strike, instead of an ordinance an invitation to negotiation should have been issued.

If the general council of the AIRF had before it at Kharagpur not an empty appeal but a definite call to negotiation, there would have been no need of taking the strike decision. But first an empty appeal was issued to prejudice the public and now this ordinance has been promulgated to cow down the poor workers.

This railway strike affair, incidentally, throws light on the Government of India's labour policy in regard to its own employees. It would be correct to say that the Government has no policy whatsoever, where the State is itself the employer.

Mr. Ayyangar's[2] last night's broadcast, particularly in reference to the food situation, shows that he has lost his balance. He is using language unworthy of a gentleman. He says that in the existing food situation to precipitate a railway strike would be a criminal abuse of the right to strike. It is strange that our ministers have suddenly become so solicitous about the starving people.

The railway strike is yet to come, but so many people have already died of starvation in many parts of the country. Who was responsible for those deaths?

[2]Gopalaswami Ayyangar; then Minister for Transport, Government of India.

121. Presidential Address at a Conference of the All-India Postmen and Lower Grade Staff Union, New Delhi, 14 July 1951[1]

There is no politics behind the strike decision of the AIRF It is the Government, which is deliberately pushing a simple labour dispute into the arena of politics.

The strike decision of the AIRF is part of normal trade union practice. But by promulgating a draconian ordinance the Nehru Government has thrown a challenge to the entire working class in India. Nay, the ordinance has gone further and challenged the civil liberties of the people.

The problem of transport of food and other supplies may be created in the event of strike, but the strike which in its very nature must be short and

[1]Adapted from *Tribune*, 15 July 1951.

swift will not appreciably add to the starvation already caused by the Government.

In any case, the railwaymen have given a long notice of seven weeks to Government during which period food and other essential supplies may be moved to the appropriate areas. Still we shall try, as far as possible, to assist the movement of food.

Regarding the reported concentration of Pakistani troops on our borders, I wish to make it perfectly clear that if there is any danger to our defence, railwaymen, in spite of all their grievances, will be the first to rally round the Government.

But the Government has not so far taken us into confidence and not even the slightest hint has been given to us of any such danger. If the Government were really aware of this danger, nothing could be more perverse than their handling of railway labour. Any way, from our side the door is still open for an amicable settlement of the strike decision. There can be no earthly objection to adjudication, and the setting up of a permanent machinery for the settlement of disputes. The dearness allowance question is not insoluble if Government rises above politics and suppresses its anxiety to save the face of its stooges in the labour movement.

Mr. Nehru scouts all talk of "isms". But there is one "ism" which from the very beginning has been the sheet-anchor of his policy, that is "crisisism". The crises were usually the Government's own creation; but after they were created, they were used as excuses for doing nothing and for not allowing others to do anything. Railwaymen waited for years. Semi-starvation cannot be accepted by them as their eternal destiny. When prices go on rising and wages remain inelastic, a situation must arise sooner or later when there will be an explosion. Workingmen will listen to appeals and false economic theorisings for some time, but not all the time.

The Transport Minister, Mr. Gopalaswami Ayyangar, is responsible for plunging the country into a serious labour upheaval. While Mr. Ayyangar has denied in his recent broadcast that there are any outstanding issues left to be settled between the AIRF and his Ministry, apart from the vital issue of dearness allowance there are hundreds of other issues which have not been settled at all or the Government's decision on which have been rejected by the Railwaymen's Federation.

An intolerable situation has been created by the Government's refusal to accept the railwaymen's demand for a permanent machinery for the settlement of disputes. The machinery the railwaymen demanded is to start from the shop level and go up to railway level and finally to ministerial level. If the procedure ultimately fails to settle any dispute, the machinery should provide for automatic adjudication or arbitration. The whole machinery, further, should be smooth and speedy in its working. The Railway Ministry turned down even this constructive demand. This is an intolerable situation.

There are four important issues facing the postmen and lower grade staff, namely, dearness allowance, 1946 strike period pay, implementation of the Expert Committee's report, and promotion and confirmation of postmen and lower grade staff.

The Expert Committee made some recommendations to the Government in 1948. Three years have passed, but the Government has taken no action on those recommendations. It is high time that all the recommendations are implemented.

The indifference of a certain section of the Press to opposition's views is painful. Many of my important statement regarding the railway-labour dispute did not get adequate publicity, whereas official statements, including the broadcast made by Mr. Ayyangar, were given wide publicity.

122. To M.R. Masani, 15 July 1951[1]

Dear Minoo,

I am writing to you in connection with the Chairmanship of the High Power Joint Consultative Board on Industry and Labour of which you are a member. I do not know if you have any one in view for this post. If you have an open mind, I should like to suggest the name of Ex-Justice, Amarendra Nath Sen, who has just retried from the Calcutta High Court after a full term of 13 years. Before that he was a District Judge for nearly 12 years and before that he was a Bar-at-Law. As a High Court Judge he was always known for his independence of judgement and for his ability and integrity. I understand the Board is meeting on July 18, in Bombay to elect its Chairman.

I hope you are well. With love.

Affectionately yours,
Jayaprakash Narayan

[1]*J.P. Papers* (NMML).

123. To Gulzari Lal Nanda, 15 July 1951[1]

My dear Nandaji,[2]

You may recall the talk we had together about not allowing the work of the Planning Commission and the National Plan to be exploited by the Congress Party for election purposes. You had given me an assurance that that would never happen. In fact you had told me that you were more anxious than I was to avoid such a fate for the Planning Commission. I am afraid, however, that from the very beginning the report of the Planning Commission and all its work were being used for party propaganda by the Congress. It has been suggested in the papers that the summary report of the Commission was hurried through so that it might be published before the meeting of the AICC. The papers have also suggested that the report was made the basis of the Congress Election Manifesto. I also read in the newspapers that you, as the Deputy Chairman, were yourself present at the Working Committee to explain the implications of the Plan. I do not know if there can be any crasser exploitation by the Congress of the Planning Commission. I do not know how the non-Congress members of the Planning Commission allowed all this to happen. I have so far said nothing about the report, but my whole attitude towards it has been changed as a result of this partisan association of the Planning Commission. You need not remind me that you as a Congressman naturally were expected to participate in the deliberations of the Working Committee of the AICC. You may be a Congressman, but you are also Deputy Chairman of the Planning Commission which you assured me was a non-political body and not a policy-making instrument for the Congress Party. I had always feared that the main plank in Pandit Nehru's platform would be the Planning Commission. My fear has now been wholly vindicated. This is a matter of deep regret.

I hope you are well.

Sincerely yours,
Jayaprakash Narayan

[1] *J.P. Papers* (NMML).

[2] Gulzari Lal Nanda (1898-1998); joined the Non-Cooperation Movement and was jailed in 1921. Secretary, Textile Labour Association, Ahmedabad, 1922-46; took part in the freedom movement and imprisoned in 1932 and 1942-4. Deputy Chairman, Planning Commission, 1950-1 and 1960-3; Minister for Planning, 1951-2, Irrigation and Power, 1952-7, Home Affairs, 1963-6, Railways, 1970-1, interim Prime Minister in 1964 and 1966. Awarded Bharat Ratna in 1997. Publications include: *Some Aspects of Khadi*; *History of Wage Adjustments in the Ahmedabad Textile Industry*; *Approach to the Second Five Year Plan*, etc.

124. To Asoka Mehta, 15 July 1951[1]

Dear Asoka,

Your promised letter regarding my interview with Dr. Ambedkar has not yet arrived. Therefore I have made no attempt to meet him. I do not even know whether he is here [Delhi]. Since it is getting late for us[2] I suggest the best thing to do is for you yourself to meet him somewhere. Before you meet him you should write to him and send him a copy of our *Platform* with the portion regarding the Scheduled Castes marked. You may also draw his attention to the corresponding part of the National Revival Programme.

The Railway Strike is getting more and more complicated. I feel the challenge thrown out by the Government by this draconic Ordinance must be faced. I wish to call a meeting of all the organizations of Central Government employees. Will you ask G.G. to send me at Calcutta the names and addresses of these organizations. My Calcutta address would be: c/o. Shri Prabhudayal Dabriwala, 90, B.K. Paul Avenue, Calcutta.

As soon as the *Platform* is printed, will you kindly send a copy to Vaidyanath Aiyyar.

I hope you are well.

Yours affectionately,
Jayaprakash Narayan

[1]*J.P. Papers* (NMML).

[2]The note of urgency here was apparently the result of the Socialist leaders' desire to have an electoral understanding or alliance with the All India Scheduled Castes Federation, led by Dr. B.R. Ambedker.

125. To Vaidyanath Aiyyar, 15 July 1951[1]

Dear Mr. Aiyyar,

This is to introduce to you Prof. Swarup Singh of the Hindu College, who is the Chairman of the Delhi Party. I think it is for the first time that the Delhi Party has been able to secure the services of such an able and fine person. Will you please give him all possible co-operation?

On advice from Asoka Prof. Swarup Singh is re-constituting the Delhi Executive and I hope after his efforts the Delhi Party would be better. In that case you may have to continue your monthly contribution to Delhi

[1]*J.P. Papers* (NMML).

also. But please do not stop doing anything for the Punjab. I am afraid, I am over-burdening you, but I hope you will not mind. Prof. Swarup Singh might also discuss with you about the Parliament seat. I have also written just now to Asoka about the matter. When Asoka comes next to Delhi he will talk over the matter with you.

With best regards,

Yours sincerely,
Jayaprakash Narayan

126. To Jawaharlal Nehru, 17 July 1951[1]

Dear Bhai,

I am writing in connection with the railway strike, but only in my personal capacity.

You may remember that on March 24, last I had written you that the question of dearness has been again seriously agitating the men and that you should issue some kind of a statement that the matter was receiving your attention and that something would be done to lighten the burden of prices. That time you did not think it was possible to do any thing and you rejected my suggestion. That was the time when the AIRF General Council was to meet in Bombay to consider the question. A statement or an appeal at that time might have been effective. The General Council duly met in Bombay and instructed the unions to take strike ballot. In the midst of the balloting your Government announced five rupees increment in DA., but 3 lakhs of railway workers who had opted more than two years ago for the grainshop concession were excluded. This, plus the utter inadequacy of the five rupees increment failed to produce any appreciable effect on the men. Meanwhile, the strike ballot proceeded, and in the end it was found that the vote was overwhelmingly in favour of strike. Then on the 12th hour exactly you issued an appeal which apart from pointing out the disastrous consequences of a railway strike held out no hope whatever. On the dearness question you clearly stated that you had already gone as far as possible. The General Council could not but give effect to the verdict of the ballot.

Then the President promulgated the infamous Ordinance. The Federation had kept the door open for negotiation and Mr. Ayyangar too had stated that he was prepared to walk through the open door. Then where was

[1]*Brahmanand Papers* (NMML). For Nehru's reply dated 18th July 1951 see Appendix 13.

the need for the Ordinance? If the intention was to intimidate the men, Government's understanding of the workers' psychology was hopelessly wrong. I assure you that the only result of the Ordinance has been stiffening of the workers' morale. The reaction of the other State employees is also bitter and hostile. You may recall that when the British were still here in 1946, there was a strike ballot on the railways and the matter had gone so far that even notice of strike had been served, but yet there was no Ordinance promulgated and the Railway Board negotiated a last-minute settlement.

The Ordinance, further, has given to this purely labour dispute an unnecessary political colour. Your colleagues in the Cabinet are in the habit of going about accusing me of political exploitation of labour. If they had been honest or had cared to find out the truth they would never have made this accusation. I have tried scrupulously to keep my politics out of the AIRF or the other unions of State employees of which I happen to be the president. Indeed I have been trying for some time past to get out of these unions. A year ago at the Annual Conference of the AIRF at Nagpur I refused to accept the presidentship of the organization, but had ultimately to yield to the unanimous pressure of the delegates.

And all along I have been exercising a restraining influence on the men. In 1949 it was largely due to my advice and Mr. Ayyangar's reasonableness that the general strike was postponed. But this time I do honestly feel that the workers have no alternative left but to strike.

I have no idea as to how you propose to handle this situation. The promulgation of the Ordinance indicates that contrary to public statements, the Government has no desire to settle this matter amicably. If that is so, it would be a great pity. Judging from the widespread discontentment among the men I have little doubt that the strike would be a success. It might conceivably be broken in the end, but not before a great deal of damage has been done to the country, and the suppression of the strike would leave wounds which might never be healed. To hope that things would be better after the workers had been taught a lesson, is not hope but despair. The real difficulty is that your Government has no labour policy whatever. By this I do not mean that your Labour Ministry has not prepared the drafts of two labour Bills which except for the Government's own labour movement has received universal condemnation. What I mean is that your Government has no well thought out policy with regard to its own employees. The Government is the biggest employer in this country and still, till now, there is no kind of regular machinery for settlement of labour disputes. You might know that one of the demands of the AIRF is for the setting up of a permanent machinery for negotiation and settlement starting from the shop level up to the railway and the Ministerial level. We are demanding further that this machinery should provide, in the case of issues not settled through joint negotiation, for adjudication. I cannot think of a more reasonable demand. But the Railway Ministry does not see its way to accept it. As a part of this demand we are asking for adjudication of all the present outstanding issues. The Railway Ministry's answer to this last point is that the Railway Joint Advisory Committee was itself a sort of arbitration board and accordingly the issues that have already been dealt with by the JAC cannot be referred to arbitration. Our answer to this is that the JAC was never meant to be an arbitration board. It was merely a joint committee of a quasi-permanent nature set up to deal with what were called anomalies. We had made no commitment that issues settled by the JAC would not be raised by us, as it would have been the case if the JAC had been an arbitration board.

The Ordinance that has been promulgated implies that the Government will never allow a strike in what it considers to be the essential services or industries. In that case there is more reason why the Government should agree to arbitration. If the road to strike is blocked, the workers must be given an alternative way for the solution of their problems. To illegalise strike and refuse arbitration particularly when the latter is so often declared to be the sheet-anchor of Congress labour policy, is the height of unreasonableness.

I should also like to draw your attention to another aspect of Government's labour policy or lack of it. In many industries and services, the Congress has set up INTUC unions. These are in the nature of old company unions and cannot last a day without official support. We have been demanding that this practice of setting up rival unions and then playing one against the other should be given up. And we have been suggesting a very simple solution, namely, of holding a plebiscite of the workers to decide which union commands a majority. The trouble in the railways is largely due to Mr. Santanam's partisanship for the INTUC Federation and Khandubhai's interference in affairs with which he should have had no concern. Even now I would suggest that the Railway Ministry would order a plebiscite and whichever organization secures majority vote should be treated by it as the sole bargaining agent and the only representative union. I hope some decision on this vexed problem would be taken.

As for dearness allowance, you must consider a further increment. The men have waited for years in the hope that prices would be reduced. They are not in a mood to wait any longer. Their hardships are real. Even private industries such as the textile industry in Ahmedabad and Bombay have given nearly twice as much dearness allowance as your Government does. Your Bangalore argument that the railwaymen were better off than others and therefore it would not be right to give them any more, rather surprised me. There are a good number of people including Ministers of Government who are better off than railwaymen. I wonder if they have any right by your logic to their present emoluments.

Lastly if the Government is really anxious to avert the strike, as Mr. Ayyangar told the Indian Chamber of Commerce at Bombay, the only sensible thing to do is to call the representatives of the Federation and talk it over across the table.

Before I close, may I refer to a personal matter? I understand that you wrote to a common friend that I was going about the country abusing you. I was rather shocked to hear this. I have been rather strongly criticizing you and your policy for the past few months, but it is far from me to abuse any one, least of all you. If you consider criticism to be abuse, that is another matter. I hold that you, by your person, are upholding, no doubt unwillingly and may be to a large extent unwittingly, conservatism if not reaction in this country.

I hope you are well. With regards,

Affectionately yours,
Jayaprakash Narayan

127. Statement on the Food Situation in Darbhanga District of Bihar, Darbhanga, 20 July 1951[1]

I had gone to the Rajnagar and Pandaul areas of Darbhanga district on a short fact finding visit. During the day and a half that I was there I visited the following villages: Rajnagar, Kasianwar, Isahpur, Lakshmipur, Chipchiri, Balwar, Maksuda, Dhopura, Pandaul and Sagarpur.

Before I went I had heard conflicting reports. The Prime Minister, Shri Nehru, after his recent visit to the district had stated that the situation, though once grave, was under control and so much grain had been shipped to the affected areas that there was no longer any danger of starvation. The Socialist Party of Darbhanga had a different story to tell.

It is agreed on all sides that the grain at present received has removed the scarcity, but the danger of starvation is no less. Socialist workers had pointed other dark pictures too. So, I went to find out. This is in brief what I saw and heard.

The supply of grain is indeed adequate for the moment, and almost every one seems to have received a ration card. But 50 per cent, at a conservative estimate, of the rural population have no earnings with which to buy anything. The public relief works had been started too late and due to the onset of rains most of them have now been stopped. For a month there will be some work for the landless labourers in the transplantation of paddy, and then harvesting of *bhadai* might offer partial employment. During this

[1] *J.P. Papers* (NMML). Published in *Searchlight* on 23 July 1951.

season too not all the labourers will be able to find work, for the Raj Darbhanga which has extensive *zirat* in this area is using considerable mechanical labour and is also leaving extensive fields uncultivated. Secondly, the cultivating tenants are largely unable to secure loan from the Government in order that they may finance their agricultural operations. The difficulty, delay, corruption and harassment that are attendant upon this business of obtaining loans was the chief and universal complaint of the cultivators in this area. I met peasants who said that for as many as three months they had been trying to obtain loan and had paid money in bribes, but to no effect. They gave me their names and the names of the officers whom they had paid money.

To return to the agricultural labourers, who are mostly of the depressed castes, their position, particularly of the womenfolk, is still pitiable in spite of all the grain in the shops. A month later after the seasonal employments cease, nothing will stand between them and starvation. I estimate that the number of those so affected in this district alone would not be less than ten lakhs. The next thirty or forty days will not take long to pass, and it is necessary that the Government prepared from now for the coming calamity. Even for the interim period, it would be wrong to rely entirely on the season's inadequate employment.

I understand that, according to rules, $2\frac{1}{2}$ per cent of the population in this area receive free relief. In actual fact the percentage is much lower. But from what I have seen the theoretical percentage too is very low. It should be raised at least to ten per cent. Furthermore, such employment as can be provided even now should be given. The delay and corruption in the distribution of loan must strongly be put down. I was appalled by the stories of open corruption that I heard. These human vultures who are trying to profit from famine and starvation of their fellow men should receive summary punishment. The evil plant of corruption has grown and foliated before the very eyes of this Government, but so far it has refused to deal it a single blow. I heard once a Central Minister complain that he had no power to discharge even a *chaprasi*, so how could corruption be put down. The Government shows great alertness and expedition when it comes to promulgating ordinances to suppress the liberties of the people or the struggle of the workers for a decent living. Can not an ordinance be issued empowering Government to put down corruption?

The problem of cloth struck me to be even more important at the present moment than that of food. One felt so miserable to see the women in such tattered clothes. Not one woman I saw had a whole *sari* on her. The men whose nakedness does not hurt so much were no less in tatters. About food it can at least be said that those who have the means can buy their rations. But cloth is just not available, or what is available cannot suffice for more than one per cent of the population. It is the immediate and imperative duty of the Government to arrange for the supply of cloth. The normal trade channels have failed. It is for Government itself to secure stocks, and supply directly to the people. But I am afraid quite a large portion of the population is too destitute to buy cloth even if it is available at reasonable price. The Government must arrange for free distribution of cloth to them. There is no other solution.

Travelling in this area, I became acutely conscious of the justice of the slogan of redistribution of land. Here is one of the richest men in the country, the Maharajdhiraj of Darbhanga, owning thousands upon thousands of acres of *zirat* lands, while thousands upon thousands of families are starving in the midst of the Raja's smiling fields on which they themselves and not the Maharajdhiraj labour. I cannot imagine any greater inequity. The poverty of this areas will never go unless the *zirat* lands of the Maharajdhiraj are distributed to the landless people. But only under socialism will that be possible.

While the main responsibility of rendering relief is upon the Government, the people too must come to the aid of their suffering countrymen. I therefore appeal to them to give what help they can to relieve this colossal human suffering. Cash and cloth are particularly needed. I appeal specially to the cloth mill-owners and the cloth merchants of the country. In Bihar a non-official relief body called, Bihar Sankat Sahayata Samiti, National Hall, Congress Maidan, Kadam Kuan, Patna, has been formed of which Shri Lakshmi Narayan of the Khadi Samiti is the President. All relief should be sent to him or in consultation with him.

128. Address at the Seventh Annual Conference of the West Bengal State Socialist Party, Calcutta, 21 July 1951[1]

The Party had a three-fold task before it: (1) to oppose and check the Congress administration, (2) to do constructive work, and (3) to establish democratic socialism.

The political situation in West Bengal is somber. There are in the state as many as 27 political parties to contest in the coming General Elections, not to speak of those who would appear as 'independents'. Unstable administration would be the consequence of any multi-party Government and the condition will be as in France today. It is, therefore, the duty of the citizens to choose the best of the candidates and the best of the political parties.

[1]Adapted from *Janata*, 5 August 1951.

Personally, I would prefer the existence of only two political parties in India: one for the "status quo" capitalism and inequality, and the other for the masses and for changing the social order.

I am opposed to the communal parties that want to divide Indians into communities or annex Pakistan by force. Communalism in Pakistan can not be answered by communalism in India. If there be war between India and Pakistan, it will not be a war between Hindus and Muslims but between India and Pakistan. We will surely resist if India is attacked by Pakistan. But communalism is one thing and confronting injustice is another. If I have to choose between the Congress and the Hindu Mahasabha, I shall surely pick up the former. I do not see eye to eye with those of the political parties whose only aim is to defeat the Congress in the General Elections. This may mean supporting men who are worse than Congressmen.

The various Leftist parties cannot unite, because there are fundamental differences among some of them. Take for instance the Communist Party. It believes that there can be no change in the social order without civil war, bloodshed and anarchy. It believes in totalitarianism, liquidation of its opponents and one-party system. A communist regime would mean perpetual slavery and domination of Moscow. Therefore, how can there be unity with the Communists, who are the enemies of India. Those of the Left parties that support the Communists are more reactionary than the Communists themselves.

The Socialist Party, believes, on the other hand, in changing the social order from capitalism to socialism peacefully.

Internationally, the world is today divided into two opposing camps: one of America and the other of Russia. The Socialist Party would support none of the two. It would not like that India be under the slavery of either, but we are enemies of neither. I would rather like to have one organization of all those countries that are neither in American bloc nor in the Russian bloc.

The Congress, has been breaking up and it has failed to solve any of the country's problems. Many good people have come away from the Congress and formed their own parties, such as the Kisan-Mazdoor-Praja Party of Acharya Kripalani or KPMP of Dr. Prafulla Chandra Ghosh.

I thought that those people broke away from the Congress due to some ideological differences. But now we are being told that they (of the KMPP or KPMP) had had no ideological or political differences with the Congress but that they had differed on the question of the implementation of Congress pledges and programme. What was the need for founding a separate political party in that case? It was only a change in personnel; for instance, replacing Dr. [B.C.] Roy by Dr. [P.C.] Ghosh in West Bengal.

On some occasions, I have tried to stretch the hand of cooperation to the political parties led by Acharya Kripalani and Dr. Prafulla Chandra Ghosh, but the latter felt that they could alone confront the Congress and that they might cooperate if they needed such cooperation. On my part, I am ready to cooperate. The leaders of the KMPP or KPMP can build up a new India, but they must have some new principles as the basis of their work.

The Socialist Party wants to change the present social order by peaceful means and on the basis of sanction given by the people. Socialism is the only way out in present-day India. I can not say that every problem will be solved the moment the Party comes to power. The establishment of socialism may take years. The Party has concretely indicated it in the *Platform* what it will do in the first five years if it is returned to power. The aim of the Party is to establish a regime of workers, peasants and the middle class people. If it fails, it will be up to the people to change the Government.

129. To Gulzari Lal Nanda, 30 July 1951[1]

My dear Nandaji,

I thank you for your letter of 22nd July. I am afraid, the Planning Commission's Report has already suffered a great deal from the manner of its association with the Congress Election Manifesto. However, I do feel happy to find that you and your colleagues in the Commission are determined to give to your labours a national character and to seek the co-opperation of all Indians. I have not yet said a word about the Plan and do not propose to do so till I have time to study it carefully. It is not quite clear to me what manner of co-operation we can give you as a Party, but I should like to assure you that unless the whole foundation of the Plan proves unsatisfactory to us, we would be prepared to give whatever cooperation is possible.

You know our conception of a Plan. A socialist plan would not merely deal with national resources and their development within the framework of the existing social order, but would form part of an overall plan of social and economic change so that in a number of years along with economic growth a Socialist society is re-constructed. I am afraid, your Plan suffers from this lack of social and economic objective. To plan production and to leave distribution unplanned is to my mind no planning. The question of distribution is as important in a plan as that of production. It is for this reason that the Socialist *Platform* advocates capital levy, a new structure of taxation and re-distribution of land. It has become fashionable in Delhi to

[1]*J.P. Papers* (NMML).

scout isms, the only result of which would be the perpetuation of the status-quo. As long as the present social structure lasts, development of either the private or the public sector will result in the same system of distribution. The nationalization of the Railways, for instance, has not abolished a capitalist wage structure in that sphere.

After I have gone through the Report I shall send you my further criticism.

With regards,

Sincerely yours,
Jayaprakash Narayan

130. To Asoka Mehta, 30 July 1951[1]

Dear Asoka,

I regret very much that I carried your letters in my file for so many days and was able to read them only today. In fact I did not know that there was any letter from you in the file.

I have sent you a wire today to say that it is not possible for me to go to Delhi to meet the Japanese Socialists whom it would have been a pleasure to meet. I am at this camp [at Daltonganj in Bihar] till the 1st. Then I go to Patna on the 2nd, Moghalsarai on the 3rd and Jubbalpore on the 4th evening. After that I have some railway engagements; then I reach Bombay on the 9th where also I have railway and postmen meetings.

Regarding my fast, I had not agreed to give it up and there was no need for me to make any public declaration about it except for the Special Conference of the All-India Postmen & Lower Grade Staff Union. At this special Conference it was my duty to give the delegates a report on the latest situation with regard to the demand for strike period pay. There was no way in which I could have avoided telling the men what had happened and there was no way also to keep what I said a secret from the public because the Special Conference was open to every one including the press. Even if I had called a private session of the conference, I am sure, some garbled version of my talk would have appeared in the press. I therefore thought that the best thing to do was to give written handout which I did. In any case I do not propose to do anything which would embarrass the Party.

More when we meet at Jubbalpore.

Affectionately yours,
Jayaprakash Narayan

[1] *J.P. Papers* (NMML).

131. To Jawaharlal Nehru, 4 August 1951[1]

Dear Bhai,

Your letter has greatly disappointed me. I hope when you are able to attend more closely to my last letter, the result would be more helpful.[2]

I was persuaded to write to you about the railway strike by two considerations. One, I had gathered the impression from your public pronouncements that you were anxious to find a way to settle the matter: I thought my letter would give you an opening. Two, friends had pressed me to write , assuring me that the gesture would promote an amicable settlement. Your last letter leaves me in doubt whether I and my friends were not mistaken.

You have reacted rather strongly to my suggestion that you might act as a mediator. Perhaps you took the word too literally. I wonder in what capacity you had issued your appeal to railwaymen. In that same capacity it was, and is, possible for you to take a hand in this affair. My reference to Truman only meant that the head of a government cannot sit quietly when a department fails to deal with a serious national emergency. Railways throughout the world are of vital importance irrespective of whether they are nationalised.

In your letter you have emphasised the nationalised character of the Indian Railways and have claimed certain privileges for the State as an employer. But when an industry is nationalised, do all the rights and privileges go to the State and have the workers no share in them? Whenever we raise an issue, we are told that the State cannot be treated on par with private employers. Have not the employees of the State, then, corresponding advantages over the employees in private industry? Nationalisation of industry has little meaning if the status of the workers in such industry does not change. It is this aspect of the matter that we have been trying for the past years to bring home to the Indian Government, but while every Minister talks of the claims of the State as an employer, no one thinks that the workers in a State industry have any special claims. In my last letter I have already dealt with these special claims.

I should like to protest against your remarks about Pakistan being encouraged by the prospect of a railway strike in India. If the Government of India has no faith in the loyalty and patriotism of its employees, I am sure the Pakistan Government has no illusions about them. The AIRF has already clearly stated its policy in this regard, which I reiterated in my last

[1] *J.N. Papers*: Files at Home (NMML).

[2] See Appendix 14 for Nehru's reply to J.P.

letter. You can stop the preperations for the strike by merely appealing to the men to postpone action in view of the Indo-Pakistan situation.

You have written that you were too busy to reply in detail. Could I have a detailed and definite reply to the points raised in this and the last letter at Bombay by the 9th of August? I shall be much obliged. My Bombay address would be:

c/o Socialist Party,
National House,
6, Tulloch Road,
Fort, Bombay.

I am sorry to take so much of your time when you are so desperately busy.

With regards,

Affectionately yours,
Jayaprakash

132. To Ajay Kumar, 6 August 1951[1]

My dear Ajayji,[2]

Acharyaji has written some brilliant articles recently analysing the differences between the Congress and the party programmes and policies. I hope these articles are being brought out in a pamphlet form. If not, please let me know because we would like to prepare a pamphlet out of them for publication by the Bihar Party. Have the articles that Acharyaji wrote regarding Arunaji been published as a pamphlet? If not, we would like to have the right to publish them too.

When I was in Lucknow last, Prof. D.P. Mukerjee was telling Acharyaji about certain new books which he was praising very highly. One of them was a translation of Rosa Luxemburg's works on Accumulation of Capital; another was a symposium and the third was, I believe, some work by Mannhiem.[3] Will you get the names and publishers of these books from

[1]*J.P. Papers* (NMML).

[2]Ajay Kumar (1922-); participated in Quit India Movement, 1942 and States' People's Movement, 1945-7, Secretary to Acharya Narendra Deva, 1947-56, edited *Sangharsh* for some time, Secretary Acharaya Narendra Deva Samajvadi Sansthan.

[3]Karl Mannhiem (1893-1947); Hungarian sociologist who settled in UK in 1933. He distinguished between ruling class ideologies and those of Utopian or revolutionary groups. He wrote *Ideology and Utopia* in 1929; *Man and Society* in 1940.

Mr. Mukerjee and let me know? You may reply at the Bombay Central Office address.

I hope you are well.

Yours sincerely,
Jayaprakash Narayan

133. Interview to Press Trust of India regarding Railway Strike, Bombay, 10 August 1951[1]

The very legitimate strike of the railwaymen is being hopelessly mixed up with questions of national security. I personally do not think that there will be war between India and Pakistan though the existing tension is undeniable.

But the Prime Minister and the Railway Minister have definitely expressed the view that if the Railwaymen's Federation proceed with its strikes, it would seriously endanger measures of national defence. Their appeal which was received only yesterday left no alternative to the Action Committee or the Federation but to defer strike till the danger of war is removed. The Federation had already at its Calcutta meeting categorically stated that it would offer its fullest cooperation of the Government in any emergency.

It should, however, be fully understood that the Federation has not retreated a step from its demand and that the strike has not been abandoned. When it decided to postpone the strike, it was as a matter of patriotic duty and showed that for the railwaymen the interest of the nation is always above their self-interest.

I hope that in the breathing space that both sides have now got it would be possible to settle amicably the long-standing disputes between railwaymen and the Government.

The case of the railwaymen is unanswerable. I hope that the Government would not proceed with its bill to outlaw strikes.

The ordinance promulgated by the President has received universal condemnation not only in India, but also outside. International labour organizations like the ICFTU and ITWF have pointed out to the Government of India that it is a denial of free trade unionism to illegalise a strike without providing for adjudication.

Had the Government of India agreed to the demand for adjudication there would have been no need for the Federation to take a strike ballot. In any case, the next step is with the Government. The workers have done their duty.

[1]Adapted from *Tribune*, 11 August 1951.

134. Address at a Mass Rally of Railway Workers regarding Postponement of Rail Strike, Bombay, 10 August 1951[1]

I would like to explain to the railway workers the decision of the Action Committee of the Federation arrived earlier in the day to defer the scheduled railway strike.

In spite of differences on other issues, the Prime Minister's stand on the Hindu-Muslim question, his uncompromising attitude towards communal organizations in the country and his firm handling of the present crisis created by Pakistan's threat of use of force, all these are matters of pride and admiration.

In view of the last-minute appeal from the Prime Minister to stall the strike as it would seriously jeopardise security measure in the country and bolster up Pakistan's *jehad* preparations indirectly, there is no other alternative in the present critical situation than to defer the strike.

It is not justifiable to say that the Federation has let down the railway workers with that decision; on the contrary, it has enhanced the strength and prestige of the organization and restored faith in the public that railwaymen are not a whit behind others in their devotion to the country. The Federation, the only representative organization of railway workers, has served and fought for their rights for the last 26 years. I can challenge anybody to prove that workers would have benefited more than what they had under my leadership of the Federation during the last four years. They should remember their success in the past, when on the question of retrenchment in 1946, and again on the issue of dearness allowance in 1950, the workers emerged victorious without even going on strike. Even recently an increase of Rs. 5 in DA was granted by the Government while the strike ballot was being taken. Though undoubtedly critics of the Federation would make capital out of the decision to postpone the strike, the record of the organization would effectively answer such propaganda. I received a letter stating that I should resign from the Federation as I have badly let down the workers. I am only too willing to hand over charge of this onerous responsibility, but the Federation, would not let me go. The railway workers have done their duty and it is up to the Government to do theirs. The recent ordinance banning strikes in essential services is outrageous. To deny adjudication to the workers in case of a dispute and at the same time take away the worker's fundamental right to strike can not be justified in any way. The workers should fight for the repeal of the black measure, which was unheard of even in the 100 years of British rule in this country. If

[1]Adapted from *Bombay Chronicle*, 11 August 1951.

railwaymen are to bow down before this naked and drawn sword of Mr. Nehru they will not be able to rise again even for two centuries.

The workers should utilize these two months to build up their strength to such an extent, that when the strike issue comes up again the Government have to accept their demands immediately.

135. To Asoka Mehta, 13 August 1951[1]

Dear Asoka,

I am sorry for the delay in sending you accounts of the U.P. tour.

Purse presentation during my last U.P. tour was rather unregulated. At some places, certain amounts were announced but only half the announced sums were paid. On enquiry, we were told the remaining portion was the districts' share and would be collected later, or had been spent already and so forth. At most places the amount announced was less than the amount presented. Thus, it is difficult to say how much the total collection came to. But the share of the Province amounted to Rs. 30,753/-. On the principle that 50 per cent of the collections went to the Province, the total collected amount must be taken as Rs. 61,506/-. It must however be understood that this is a theoretical sum, because while the Provincial share was in actual fact Rs. 30,753/-, the sum of the amounts left in or taken by the districts would not be of an equal amount.

However, of the Provincial quota of Rs. 30,753/-, I took Rs. 8,500/- as the Centre's share and another Rs. 4,000/- was sent to Calcutta in payment of a loan of the same amount taken by the U.P. Party some months back, and Rs.1,000/- were given to Ramendra Varma, leader of the Prantiya Raksha Dal rebels for their new organization, Lok Raksha Dal, leaving Rs.17,250/- with the Province.

Of the Rs. 8,500/- taken as the Centre's share the following items of expenditure have been incurred:

Rs. 3,000sent to the Central Office to be paid (against loan of Rs.10,000/-) to Joshi of Hyderabad.
2,500 sent in payment of loan of Rs.10,000/- to Manubhai Bhimani.
1,500 Paid to Ramnandan Mishra for Hind Kisan Panchayat
500 Paid to Bagaram Tulpule
250 Munshiji's son

[1] *J.P. Papers* (NMML).

650	Rajaram Shastri (as monthly help at Rs. 200/- per month).
100	Stationery, telegrams, etc. during the U.P. tour.
Rs. 8,500	

Yours sincerely,
Jayaprakash Narayan

P.S.: This loan was taken at the time of the U.P. bye-elections and sent to Narendradeva together with Rs.10,000/- from Central Party funds.

136. To the Editor, *Statesman*, 13 August 1951[1]

Dear Sir,

It is very regrettable that in a paper of your standing one should firstly be misquoted and then attacked. In your editorial of August 11, you write: "The strike has been . . . only postponed for two months, when, according to one account, the 'general political situation in the country' will be reviewed." Then you comment: "So, inspite of strenuous denials, it appears that politics had something to do with the strike—though perhaps only Indo-Pakistani 'politics' is meant."

I do not know what account your paper received, but in the resolution passed by the Action Committee there is no mention of taking stock of any political situation. Here are the words of the resolution: "Accordingly as a matter of patriotic duty this Committee resolves that the decision to serve notice of strike in terms of the Kharagpur resolution be kept in abeyance and the whole situation be reviewed after a period of two months." To invent an account in order to be able to condemn, is, to my mind, not fair journalism. Furthermore, for us Indians, railwaymen or others, the present strained Indo-Pakistan relations are not 'politics'.

Yours sincerely,
Jayaprakash Narayan

[1] *J.P. Papers* (NMML).

137. To C.D. Deshmukh, 18 August, 1951[1]

Dear Sir Chintaman,[2]

You were good enough in May-June last to speak to me and my colleagues in the All-India Railwaymen's Federation about Government's policy with regard to the question of dearness allowance. The Federation was unable to accept your view of the case and the decision to strike was duly taken. But, as you know, that decision has been kept in abeyance for two months due to the Indo-Pakistan situation. This gives time to all concerned to review the matter and settle the dispute if possible.

The issue of dearness is the foremost point in dispute and you, above every one else in the Government, are in a position to settle it. I do earnestly beg you to find a way to settlement. The workers' case is unanswerable, and if the Government has the will, it can find the way.

I am seeing Mr. Ayyangar today and handling him a brief note on the question of DA of which a copy is enclosed herewith.[3] I do not so much want a reply from you to this note as a solution of the problem. My talk with Mr. Ayyangar would be of an exploratory nature today and if the trend of it is satisfactory, we might meet again. That would then give you enough time to take counsel among yourselves and come to a conclusion before I meet Mr. Ayyangar again.

Yours sincerely,
Jayaprakash Narayan

[1]*J.P. Papers* (NMML).

[2]Chintaman Dwarkanath Deshmukh (1896-1982); joined ICS in 1918, served in various executive capacities in Central Provinces & Berar up to 1939; joint secretary, Government of India, 1939-41; Secretary to Central Board of Reserve Bank of India, 1941-3; Deputy Governor and Governor of Reserve Bank of India, 1943-50; Minister of Finance Govt. of India and member Planning Commission, 1950-6; Chairman University Grants Commission 1956-61; Vice-Chancellor University of Delhi, 1962-7; founder and Life President India International Centre.

[3]This was an exact reproduction of J.P. statement of Dearness Allowance issued on 21 June 1951 and printed in this volume under item no. 107.

138. 'Political Vacuum', 18 August 1951[1]

The rapid disintegration of the Congress is creating a political vacuum. That there should be a vacuum in the political life of the country is dangerous, for it will lead to chaos and anarchy. The vacuum must be filled up.

[1]*Tribune*, 18 August 1951, also published in *Indian News Chronicle* and some other papers.

There are in the main three groups of forces that are aspiring to do so. In one group are the forces of reaction; in the second those of democracy, social revolution and peace; in the third those of totalitarianism, civil war at home and war and world domination abroad.

The Congress, at its worst, is a conservative party and, being afraid to take any big step in any direction, hugs the status quo. But the status quo cannot be maintained. Change is inescapable. The question is, change in what direction? Backwards, forwards or sidewards?

There is one group of forces that is trying to take the country backwards, that is, towards fascism; towards feudal rule; towards a non-secular and communal state; towards national disintegration. Among these forces communalism—of the upper castes—is also ranged on the side of reaction and so are the forces of racial and tribal separatism.

These forces are slowly finding organized political expression, though a great deal of their strength lies hidden in non-political institutions and activities. The All India Jagirdars and Landlords Association, the Ram Rajya Parishad of Rajasthan, the Praja Party of U.P., the Bhartiya Jan Sangh, the Hindu Mahasabha, the Union of Rulers are some of the political expressions of these forces. Some of these may fuse together, and all will work to enthrone political and economic reaction in the country. The popular forces that are mixed up with these movements are there merely as a facade and are bound to drop off as success approaches nearer.

In the second group are the forces of democracy, of social revolution, and peace. Among them are the forces of democratic socialism and of Gandhism. Both these trends are secular and non-communal, even though the Gandhian philosophy is non-secular and deeply religious. But the super-naturalism of Gandhism is not sectarian but imbued with universalism, and so in the social field it plays a secular and progressive role.

Both these trends, again, stand for social revolution and not merely for social reform. They both aim to abolish feudalism and capitalism and establish a classless, casteless, non-exploitative, co-operative or in other words, socialist society. Both wish to preserve individual freedom and ensure the dignity of the human personality. Both wish to avoid civil war and use democratic means for the achievement of their aims.

Of these, the forces of Gandhism, since their break with the Congress, have no political expression. They find expression almost entirely through non-political constructive activity. The stray Gandhians who are in the political field are being hopelessly mixed up with the power-groups that have split away from the Congress. These individuals and groups are at the moment going through a process of political crystallisation.

The forces of democratic socialism are represented largely by the Socialist Party. There is, unfortunately, mutual suspicion today between the forces of democratic socialism and of Gandhism. This is largely due to lack of objectivity on both sides. The names of Marx and Gandhi often act as barriers; and the issue of violence—even theoretical violence—confuses all other issues. The philosophical differences obtrude themselves upon the considerations of political and economic problems. But, all this differences notwithstanding, the broad agreement on social and economic goals and the demands of practical work are bound to bring these forces ever nearer.

In the third group are the various "left" parties that believe in totalitarianism or party-dictatorship as a part of peoples' democracy that advocate civil war as the only means of accomplishing the social revolution, and further, that advocate international war by seeking to line up India behind Soviet Russia in the present struggle for world mastery.

Which of these groups of forces should fill up the political vacuum that is being created by the disintegration of the Congress? It is not difficult to see that all the three cannot join together in replacing the Congress. Reaction and revolution cannot join hands. Nor just replacing the Congress can be of any worth while objective. The Congress, if it has to be replaced, must be replaced with something better, healthier, more constructive. It should be obvious that the reactionary and fascist forces must not be allowed to grow. It should also be obvious that when the choice is between the Congress and these reactionary forces, it is the first that must be supported. There is a great deal of confusion with regard to the third group of forces. These claim to be, and are sometimes considered as, revolutionary and progressive. But they too are in a sense reactionary. If they do not take the country backward, they do not take it forward, but rather in a side direction that deviates so much from the goal of freedom and social and economic justice that it plunges civilization into a new darkness. Left deviation is as much a deviation from the right path as right deviation.

At the top of these forces is the Communist Party, and among them are various small, even infinitesimal parties. All these have once again raised the slogan of 'left' unity, and the average political Indian wonders why all the leftists do not merge together. If they did, he feels sure the combination would be powerful enough to fill up the vacuum and take the place of the Congress.

There is no doubt that a combination of all those who style themselves as left would be powerful. But such a combination presupposes common aims, a common course of action, a certain commonality of fundamental principles. It should be obvious that without these common bases, it would be impossible for different parties to work together.

Those who desire a left combination assume that such commonality does actually exist among the left parties. But this assumption has no foundation in fact. There are many important points of difference out of which I shall select three that are fundamental. Parties that differ on these basic issues cannot, in the very nature of things, work together at election or any other time.

The first is the question of aims. It is commonly presumed that all the left parties have a common aim, namely, the establishment of socialism or, in common parlance, a workers' and peasants' raj. Nothing can be farther from the truth. Socialism is a much abused word, and it is made to cover a multitude of sins, and while all the left parties talk of workers' and peasants' raj, they mean entirely different things.

To the Communist Party, for instance, and to all near Communists, peasants' and workers' 'raj' means nothing more than party dictatorship. If the Communist Party, by a great mischance, were to be elevated to power, all other parties would forfeit their right to exist, all opposition would be suppressed and the "peasants and workers" would themselves lose their very sovereign power to change the government, if they so choose. Today under Congress rule, if the people are unhappy and dissatisfied, they have the right and the opportunity to change that rule, and elect a new government. Under Communist rule no matter how unhappy and dissatisfied the people might be they would have no chance, except the slender chance of a violent overthrow, to change the government and elect another of their choice. A vote at the General Elections for the Communist Party is a vote for the people's slavery.

The Socialist Party aims at no such dictatorship. On the contrary, the Socialist Party aspires to establish a truely functioning political and economic democracy. Under a socialist government the opposition or rival political parties will not be suppressed except those that might practise violent means, and the people will not lose their sovereignty or forfeit their right, or be denied the opportunity to change the government. There is thus all the difference of the world between Communist and Socialist aims and the twain can never meet. Those who have some appreciation of the deep human tragedy that has been enacted in Europe in the name of peoples' democracy and the communist millennium know the significance of the distinction between totalitarian communism and democratic socialism. The two are different social goals, far apart from each other and approached by two entirely different paths.

Parties that differ so vitally in their very aims and their very conception of government, cannot work together at the job of electing a government.

The second vital issue that divides the left parties, particularly the Socialist and Communist parties, is that of the method of political action. The Socialist Party believes that given the framework of democratic political functioning, such as adult-franchise and assurance of fundamental democratic freedoms, it would be both possible and desirable to use the democratic or peaceful method for the establishment of a socialist government and eventually the creation of a socialist society. By the democratic method the Socialist Party does not merely understand parliamentary activity, but also the formation and development of class organizations of the working people, creation of mass consciousness and peaceful forms of mass struggle such as strike and satyagraha. The democratic method, as understood by us, also includes constructive activities such as building up of the co-operative movement; the "one-hour a day for the nation" movement; the mass constructive activities popularized during the last Janvani Day demonstrations, workers' education, etc.

The Communist Party has no faith in the democratic method. It believes that in every country and in every circumstance, the method of violent revolution alone can succeed. Apart from their propaganda value, elections have no meaning for this Party. Whatever be the policy that the CP might be following at a particular moment, their unalterable policy at all times and every where is to fan the flames of civil war. To seek to plunge the country into chaos and civil war under the present democratic conditions, (notwithstanding their limitations) is not to serve the cause of revolution but of reaction. There is danger of the people being misled by the CP's current slogans of democracy. It would be foolish to be taken in by this hypocritical propaganda. The Communists are trying now to behave as good boys, not because they have discarded their basic thesis of violence, but because they are anxious to utilize the opportunities offered by the General Election to widen their sphere of influence. Let no one forget, despite Communist professions to the contrary, that the method of violence, of murder and loot and arson, of civil war, remain the unalterable articles of the Communist creed.

Parties that differ again so vitally as to the methods to be used can hardly be expected to work together.

The third issue relates to international policy. Left parties and particularly again, the Socialist and Communist parties, are sharply divided on this vital question. The principal task of the Communist Party in India, as elsewhere, is to attempt to drag the country by whatever means possible into the Soviet Camp. Every other objective is subjected to this over-riding policy. Herein lies the most pernicious character of Communism. Communist parties the world over are mere projections of the Soviet State and endeavour to further Soviet policy in their respective spheres of work. This must necessarily be so, because according to communist theory Soviet Russia is the spearhead of the world revolution, and so it is the duty of all good Communists, who are supposed to be working for the world revolution, to follow implicitly every command of Moscow.

The Socialist Party rejects this spurious theory of world revolution. In the hands of the present rulers of Soviet Russia the theory of world revolution has been converted into the theory of world domination. If the CPL, for instance, were to succeed in its foreign policy, India would be reduced to the status of a Russian dependency. If Russia won the present struggle for world mastery, the entire world would come under her domination and

Russian hegemony and the Russian pattern of life would be imposed over the world.

Therefore, the Socialist Party, while harbouring no ill-will for Russia, will resist every attempt to make India a Russian satellite. Likewise, will the party oppose American domination and every attempt to drag India into the American Camp.

The Socialist Party believes in a new world of freedom, equality and peace. Such a world is guaranteed neither by Russia nor America. So the Party wishes to keep out of all entanglements with these powers. At the same time, realising that many countries and millions of peoples throughout the world share the ideals of this new world of freedom, equality and peace, and at the same time live in constant fear of being trampled upon by the two power-drunk giants, the Socialist Party desires to build a third camp of these countries and peoples so that a new vista of hope might open before mankind.

These are the three main issues that divide irreconcilably the left parties. On these issues there can be, nor should be any compromise.

The objective at the next elections cannot be merely to defeat the Congress but to educate the people and to place before them clear-cut policies from which they could choose. To confuse the people and to cover up vital issues in order to serve opportunist purposes is to betray the people. Our aim is not only to defeat the Congress but also to pursue certain ideals and to build a new India and a new world in accordance with those ideals.

The recent splits in the Congress and the formation of the Kisan Mazdoor Praja Party are of considerable political significance. Their significance, however, appears to be more negative than positive: negative in the sense that the disintegration of the Congress is carried further. But the repeated statements of the KMPP leaders that they have no particular ideology, nor any difference with Congress policy and programme has robbed this significant political development of much positive value. It was hoped that the forces that were splitting away from the Congress would swell the tide of democratic socialism, but I fear more and more that a parallel Congress is in the making. The KMPP will no doubt offer to the people an alternative at the general elections, but it will only be in the nature of an alternative personnel of leadership. That is disappointing, no doubt, but as long as the KMPP fights the Congress and insists on democracy and a clean administration, it represents a progressive force with which Socialists will find possible to co-operate.

Here, then, are the forces aspiring to fill up the vacuum being created by the disintegration of the Congress. Their number seems at present to be large and the electorate is likely to be confused by their very variety. But, as I have attempted to show, they can be classed into three main groups:

(i) the forces of reaction; (ii) the forces of democratic Socialism; (iii) the forces of totalitarian and extra-territorial Communism. The choice between these is not difficult. Which of these alternatives the people will choose, will determine not only the fate of India but of the entire continent.

139. To Jawaharlal Nehru, 24 August 1951[1]

Dear Bhai,

I am sending you herewith a copy of the note[2] on dearness allowance that I have sent to Shri Gopalaswami Ayyangar, Shri Deshmukh, Rajkumari[3] and Jagjivan Ramji. I hope this matter will receive your attention too.

Affectionately yours,
Jayaprakash Narayan

[1]*J.P. Papers* (NMML).
[2]For note on dearness allowance see ante, item no. 137.
[3]Rajkumari Amrit Kaur (1889-1964); closely associated with Mahatma Gandhi; founder member, All India Women's Conference; MP Lok Sabha, 1952-7; Union Minister of Health, 1947-57, with additional charge of communications, 1951-2; Member Rajya Sahba, 1957-8, and 1958-64; President World Health Assembly 1950, International Red Cross Conference, New Delhi, 1957; Founder Chairman, Indian Red Cross Society, 1950.

140. To Jagjivan Ram, 24 August 1951[1]

Dear Jagjivan Ramji,

I am sending you herewith a copy of the note[2] on dearness allowance about which I had spoken to you.

After seeing you the other day in Delhi, I met the Labour Secretary to the British High Commissioner. He told me that in all the national committees set up for the purpose of resolving differences between the Departments and their employees in England, the Ministry of Labour is always represented. I wonder if some such procedure cannot be adopted here.

I shall be in Delhi on the 29th of this month.

With regards,

Yours sincerely,
Jayaprakash Narayan

[1]*J.P. Papers* (NMML).
[2]For note on dearness allowance see *ante*, item no. 137.

141. To Rajkumari Amrit Kaur, 24 August 1951[1]

Dear Rajkumariji,

I received your message through Prabhavati. I may assure you that as long as peaceful avenues of settlement of disputes are available, labour will never take precipitate action. In this connection I should like to tell you that the talks we had with Rajbahadurji[2] were cordial and helpful and I hope it would be possible for us to settle the outstanding issues.

I am enclosing copy of a note[3] on dearness allowance that I have sent to Sir Chintaman Deshmukh and Shri Ayyangar. As head of the second largest employing department of the Central Government, I hope you will give it due consideration.

I hope you are well.

Yours sincerely,
Jayaprakash Narayan

[1]*J.P. Papers* (NMML).

[2]Raj Bahadur (1912-90); took part in Quit India Movement and suffered imprisonment; active in the states people's movement in Rajputana; Secretary Congress Parliamentary Party, 1951-2; MP Lok Sabha, 1952-66; Deputy Minister and Minister of State for Communications, Government of India, 1951-6, Shipping, 1962-3, Transport, 1964-6, Information & Broadcasting, 1966-7.

[3]For note on dearness allowance see *ante*, item no. 137.

142. To All Members of the National Executive, Socialist Party, 28 August 1951[1]

Dear Friend,

It is for the first time perhaps since the formation of the Congress Socialist Party that I find myself in such utter disagreement with the National Executive on a matter of vital policy. This is in connection with the question whether all the prominent workers of the Party should contest the forthcoming elections. It was my view at Ranchi that at least one such worker should be kept out. There were arguments for and against, and when the votes were counted there was a majority of one for the view that all the prominent workers—three names were specifically considered—should be asked to contest. As the voting was narrow, and Acharyaji was not present the General Secretary circularized to the absent members for their opinion. Asoka now informs me that Acharyaji has also favoured the majority view.

The matter is thus settled. But I should like to make another effort to persuade the Executive to change its decision.

[1]*J.P. Papers* (NMML).

To me this question is of vital importance to the growth of the Party and the future of democratic socialism. We in this country have been developing a theory and practice of socialism, that are in many vital respects different from those found elsewhere. One of the decisive items of difference is our view that state power and initiative are not the only means of building up a democratic socialist society but that popular initiative and day-to-day efforts are also essential; indeed, the latter are ultimately more important. If we really believed in this, parliamentary or governmental work should have had no more importance to us than fieldwork among the people. If both activities are of equal importance, why should all the important men be sent to the legislatures? To believe, further, that the same persons can do both parliamentary and extra-parliamentary work is to practise self-deception. Both these activities are of the highest importance and both would require time and devotion. While members of the legislatures (or of governments for that matter) can and should participate in extra-parliamentary work, their main task will be in the legislatures. If all the important men are sent to the legislatures, the task of building up the popular bases and sanctions of socialism (except as agitational appendages of parliamentary work) would be relegated to secondary importance; and no amount of theorising would convince even the Party's rank and file—let alone the public—that the contrary was the truth. Socialism would then have only two alternative courses of development: (a) liberalism, (b) party dictatorship. This would be particularly so because in this country (unlike Great Britain and Sweden) socialism lacks the popular bases of co-operative and trade union movements.

I feel therefore that the whole future of democratic socialism in this country would be jeopardized if the present decision of the National Executive with regard to this were to be implemented. I am acquainted with all the arguments that have been advanced in favour of the Executive's decision, including those of Acharyaji; nevertheless I press you to reconsider, because for me the above consideration outweighs all other arguments.

If you agree with me that all the prominent people should not be sent to the legislatures, the question would arise who should be kept out. I am not so presumptuous as to believe that I would be the most suitable person to be kept out, but I do fervently hope that the Executive would be pleased to leave me out, for, in the first place, I have no aptitude for parliamentary work, and secondly, I do earnestly wish to be allowed to do fieldwork. It is for you to judge what would be the best for the party. I would advise you to reply directly to the General Secretary, and the less delay the better.

Thanking you,

Sincerely yours,
Jayaprakash

143. To Gopalaswami Ayyangar, 7 September 1951[1]

Dear Shri Ayyangar,

I was to have sent you a wire in this connection. As a matter of fact, by some trick of the mind, I had the impression that this had already been done.

When I returned to Patna I learnt that the restrictions on meetings and leave had not been withdrawn till then. I was to speak at Dinapore on the 5th, and the DS had again laid down silly conditions as to what should be spoken. This is most irritating. The union people at Dinapore have been complaining for some time past against this affair. I feel now that their complaint is not without foundation. It seems necessary to restrain the misconceived enthusiasm of such officers. The way the General Manager (EIR) himself acted in counteracting our Union's activities in connection with the proposed strike betrayed his misconception of labour's rights. I hope railway officers will be persuaded to adopt a healthy attitude towards organized labour. At any rate, I hope the restrictions on meetings and leave would be immediately removed.

Yours sincerely,
Jayaprakash Narayan

[1]*J.P. Papers* (NMML).

144. To Lord Boyd Orr, 7 September 1951[1]

My dear Lord Boyd Orr,[2]

I do not know how to express my regrets for not having replied to your letter of 9th June in time. Being constantly on the move, I somehow managed to forget about your invitation.

I am very thankful to you and to your Committee for the invitation to attend the London Parliamentary Conference for World Government. It would have given me great pleasure to attend this conference, but I regret that it would not be possible for me to do so at this time. I send you, however, my best wishes and those of my colleagues in the Socialist Party for the

[1]*J.P. Papers* (NMML).

[2]John Boyd Orr (1880-1971); British physiologist; served Royal Army Medical Corps, 1914-18; Director, Rowett Research Institute on Animal Nutrition, 1945; Director-General, Food & Agricultural Organization 1945-8. Received Nobel Peace Prize 1949.

success of the London Conference. I am sure it would mark a step forward towards the goal which all of us cherish in common.

Yours very sincerely,
Jayaprakash Narayan

145. To J.B. Kripalani, 9 September 1951[1]

My dear Dada,

I am writing in connection with your Party's attitude towards the communists. Both the KMPP and the Socialist Party have announced their decision to cooperate with each other at the forthcoming general elections. But the SP has made it clear from the very beginning that it will not cooperate with the Communist Party and their fellow travellers. Our reasons were set forth by me in an article on Political Vacuum which was published some time ago in the *Indian News Chronicle*, among other papers. The policy of the KMPP in this regard does not seem to be clear. I believe there was a press announcement by you to the effect that the KMPP will not cooperate with the Communist Party. But even in the U.P. KMPP leaders have spoken, as in Lucknow and Meerut, along with the communists at public meetings. The situation is worse in Bengal. When I had discussed this matter with Dr. Suresh Banerjee he argued rather emphatically in favour of cooperating with the communists. I understand that the Bengal branch of the KMPP is going ahead with this policy. This would make impossible our cooperation with the KMPP in Bengal or at other places where a similar policy is being followed. I wonder if you could do any thing in this matter. I shall be obliged to have your reply at the following address:

8, Nangambakam High Road,
Cathedral Post, Madras.
With best regards,

Yours sincerely,
Jayaprakash Narayan

[1]*J.P. Papers* (NMML).

146. To Gopalaswami Ayyangar, 13 September 1951[1]

Dear Shri Ayyangar,

I am putting down my afterthoughts for what they are worth, on our Delhi talks, and some further suggestions.

When you had agreed to discuss the five questions raised by me in my letters to the Prime Minister, I had thought that you had reached a favourable conclusion with regard to them. As it happened, we could reach some kind of an agreement on only two of the five questions. I was hopeful when the talks started that you would also accept our plea that the AIRF should be accepted as the sole bargaining agent. It was clear that you were favourably inclined to our view, but yet the question was shelved. Had a favourable decision been taken on this question, it would have gone very far in creating cordial relations and resolving the present conflict. The question of workers' participation in management is under your consideration, and I hope at our next meeting we would be able to agree to some suitable formula regarding it.

I do not feel happy with the provisions we agreed upon regarding the procedure of dealing with disciplinary actions. I feel strongly that at the appellate stage these cases must be reviewed by an *impartial authority*. I have always held that the strongest trade union in this country is that of officers or bureaucrats. There is a tendency among them to stand by one another. When an action has been taken at a lower level by an officer, appellate authorities belonging to the same class, are likely to take a biased view. In actual practice this is what generally happens and staff do not get justice, and efficiency and good-will suffer. I request you therefore to reconsider this matter. I have no definite suggestions to make, but could you consider establishment of a zonal railway staff tribunal in each of the six zones? This tribunal could consist of one judge, with judicial experience, or one judge president and a nominee each of the Administration and the Union (concerned), selected from a panel previously supplied by the latter. If this idea is not acceptable, will you please think of some other manner by which an impartial authority might deal with disciplinary cases at the appellate stage.

With regard to the permanent negotiating machinery, there are several details which will have to be fixed up. I am having these details examined and shall write to you later about them.

As for the DA question, it appeared that we were up against a blank wall, even though there was no other issue in dispute that was more just. I

[1]*J.P. Papers* (NMML).

[2]See Appendix 15 for Shri Gopalaswami Ayyangar's reply dated 26 September 1951.

realize the difficulties of Government. Yet, I think some thing needs to be done. If it is decided, as you had indicated, to set up another Commission, its recommendations might not be published before January next. I wonder how long it would take for the recommendations to be implemented. It is Government's practice to "re-examine" issues after they have already been thoroughly examined by Government's own committees and commissions. In view of this long delay that is expected to intervene, is it not possible to sanction as interim allowance or adopt some other interm measure? Here are some suggestions for your consideration.

The staff that had opted for the grainshop was excluded from the benefit of the extra five rupees that were granted during the strike ballot. To my mind it was unfair to have excluded them, because they had exercised their option on the advice of Government and they had not been told at that time that for doing so they would be discriminated against when DA was revised again in the future. It is true that the grainshop concessions do constitute a partial protection against rise in prices, but only partial. Therefore, this staff too might be given proportionate benefit of the latest DA revisions.

May I make another suggestion which would not involve other Ministries and complicate your task? Since the railways still maintain the grainshops, I suggest that when prices rise beyond certain limits and the rise is maintained over a given period (say six months) the staff should be allowed to exercise fresh option. Even if you do not accept this suggestion as a general principle, could you sanction one more option to the staff in view of the present hardships? This plea is further strengthened when it is recalled that the staff had exercised their option in the background of a definite assurance given by Government that prices would soon be brought down. Now that the Government has failed so completely to carry out that assurance, it is only fair to give the men another option.

An alternative suggestion is that the grainshop relief may be extended to the rest of the staff in such a measure that the quantum of additional relief comes to Rs. 5/- per month per employee. This suggestion too will not involve the other Ministries or affect much the ways and means position.

With regard to the proposal of merging a part of the DA with basic pay, I am glad to say that the reaction of the staff is uniformly favourable. In fact, as I told you, this has been one of the demands of the men not only on the railways, but also in the P&T.

During my recent travels and talks with railway staff, I have been deeply impressed with the ubiquitous and insistent grievance, namely, weightage for service. I know that this question has been discussed so many times at the highest levels and there have been so many decisions taken on it. But I am sure that had the grievance not been real, I would not have heard so much about it wherever I went. I am afraid the Railway Board has a closed mind on this question, and perhaps Mr. Santhanam too. But I do very earnestly plead with you to see that a more sympathetic view is taken of this matter. Mr. Guruswami in his memorandum has given specific instances showing the injustice done to staff who had devoted their whole lives to the railways. This injustice ought to be rectified.

After Mr. Guruswami has discussed the issues with the Railway Board, I believe it would be necessary to have another meeting with you—perhaps in the second or third week of October. Would that time suit you?

I must apologize for the length of this letter.

With regards,

Yours sincerely,
Jayaprakash Narayan

147. Statement on Linguistic States, Cuddappah, 14 September 1951[1]

I support the formation of linguistic states subject only to viability of such states.

The 29-day old fast of Sitaramayya Ranuva[2] and others on the Andhra State issue is a matter of grave public concern. I cannot understand why the Government should have allowed such a serious situation to develop when Congress policy on linguistic provinces had been so clear.

When new provinces are to be created, there are bound to be disputes regarding the boundaries, financial settlement, and other matters. Where things cannot be adjusted by mutual agreement between the parties concerned arbitration is the universally accepted method for an amicable settlement of all disputes.

I appeal to the Prime Minister to take prompt action in the matter so that Swami Sitaram and others may be saved for further service to the people.

[1]Adapted from *Bombay Chronicle*, 15 September 1951.

[2]Sitaramayya Ranuva (1920-); joined Congress in 1939, offered individual *satyagraha* 1940-1, took part in Quit India Movement and suffered two years' imprisonment from December 1943 in Alipur Camp Jail; President District Youth Congress Committee 1946-9, President Panchayat Board, 1956-9, Member A.P. Legislative Council, 1958-64, Member APCC, 1967-71, elected to A.P. Legislative Assembly in 1972.

148. Outline of the Electoral Policy of the Socialist Party, Madras, 16 September 1951[1]

The main alliance on an all-India plane, with the Kisan Mazdoor Praja Party, has more or less been finalized with Mr. J.B. Kripalani. There is no question of any joint parliamentary board, or any such formal arrangement between the two parties, but only mutual adjustment at the State level to avoid triangular contests. Any disputes between them will be settled by the central parties. The basis for the alliance is democracy and clean administration which both the parties have accepted.

The Scheduled Castes Federation is another party with whom the Socialists are trying to enter into an agreement. The Harijans have been oppressed by other communities for long. So if they organize themselves and strive for their own uplift even on a caste or communal basis, I would consider it progressive. The Adibasis and their organization are also on a similar plane.

Two other parties with which the Socialist Party has working arrangements in West Bengal on a purely state level are the section of the Revolutionary Communist Party[2] led by Mr. Soumyendranath Tagore[3] and the Forward Bloc led by Srimati Leela Roy.[4] I presume that the present election alliances will be carried on into the field of parliamentary activity too after the election.

But I rule out any alliance with the Communists. The general principle governing the election alliances which we are entering into is that there should be some progressive elements in the policies of the allied parties.

The list of candidates will be finalized at the meeting of the Central

[1]Statement made at a Press Conference at Madras. Adapted from *Amrit Bazar Patrika*, 17 September 1951.

[2]Revolutionary Communist Party—For note see *JPSW*, Vol. III, p. 82.

[3]Soumyendranath Tagore (1901-74); political leader and author, founder of Revolutionary Communist Party of India, India's delegate to VI Communist International Congress 1928, imprisoned by Hitler in 1933, spent more than 8 years in jail in India under British; published 35 books in Bengali and English—*Biplavi Russia*, 1932; *Yatri* (autobiography), 1950; *Communism and Fetishism*, 1941; *Tactics and Strategy of Revolution*, 1948; *Gandhi* in French, 1944.

[4]Leela Roy (1900-70); Secretary, All Bengal Women's Suffrage Committee 1921; active in female education, founded Dipali High School, Nari Siksha Mandir and Siksha Bhavan in 1925; joined Sri Sangha, a revolutionary Society of Dacca and remained associated with it till 1937; edited a journal called the *Jayasree*; took active part in anti-salt tax movement in 1930; after 1937 became close associate of Subhas Chandra Bose, edited *Forward Bloc* weekly in 1940; arrested in 1942 and kept in detention up to 1946; General Secretary, West Bengal Forward Bloc, 1949; on the Bloc led by her merging with Praja Socialist Party in 1954, she became one of its national executive members and Chairman of the Bengal PSP in 1960; retired from active politics in 1962.

Election Board of the Party on October 15 and 16. The selection of the candidates will be done in a democratic way with the local committees being made responsible for pitching on the best man for each constituency.

149. To Prafulla Chandra Ghosh, 24 September 1951[1]

My dear Mr. Ghosh,

Mr. Sadiq Ali[2] told me at Madras about your reactions to my letter to Kripalaniji about the attitude of the KMPP towards the communists, particularly in Bengal . It seems that you told your Committee at Madras that I had met you often at Calcutta and that you had made it clear that you were not going to cooperate with the communists. I am afraid that is not the whole story. In my letter to Kripalaniji, I had mentioned a talk I had with Dr. Banerji who had, while agreeing with all that I said about the communists, quite frankly expressed the view that in order to defeat the Congress it would be necessary to cooperate with the communists. I was deeply disturbed by his attitude. The defeat of the Congress is certainly not our only goal. I would much rather see a Congressman win in a given constituency rather than a communist. Kripalaniji told me at Madras that he also felt exactly like that.

It seems that you told your Committee at Madras that all that you had decided to do in respect of the communists was that wherever they had a strong candidate and you had none, the seat would not be contested by the KMPP. I am afraid the position in Bengal is far different. In several districts, the KMPP has already fought local bodies' elections jointly with the communists. For the general elections, too, such a joint working has been in contemplation and all overtures that the SP made in Bengal for a similar understanding have so far been cold-shouldered.

You complained to Kripalaniji about my Calcutta Maidan speech in which I had criticized the KMPP. It is true that I did so. But has it occurred to you to ask why a person like me who had, and still has, the utmost of goodwill for the Praja Party felt compelled to criticize it? You will perhaps remember that much before you had even left the Congress, I had spoken in praise of you at several Calcutta meetings. Whenever I used to go to Calcutta I tried to find time to call upon you. When you were considering leaving the Congress, I had tried to persuade you not to form another party but to join the SP. When the KMPP was being inaugurated at Patna, where not a graceful

[1]*J.P. Papers* (NMML).

[2]Sadiq Ali (1910-2001); member Provisional Parliament, 1950-2; MP Rajya Sabha, 1958-64, 1964-70. General Secretary All India Congress Committee, 1938-48, 1958-62, 1966-7 and 1968. Governor, Maharashtra, 1977-80 and Tamil Nadu, 1980-2.

word had been said about the SP, I had, of my own accord, welcomed the KMPP and offered the cooperation of my party. After all this, if I felt compelled to criticize the KMPP at Calcutta, there must have been some reason: the reason was largely the unhelpful—even arrogant—attitude of the Bengal KMPP towards the SP and its policy towards the Communist Party. I had thought that after you friends left the Congress, the one party that you would cooperate with in Bengal—because of the ideological nearness and the ethical approach to politics—would be the Socialist Party. But our proffered hand was never accepted and all manner of difficulties were placed in the way. Being baulked and disappointed the SP entered into an alliance with Soumyendra Tagore and Leela Roy, thinking that it would quicken the pace and help to bring about a wider alliance. From our side no conditions were ever made for such an alliance except "no truck with the communists."

Kripalaniji said that he was going to Calcutta on the 30th. SP comrades will meet him and I hope his presence will be utilized by both sides to settle this vexed question of electoral agreement in Bengal between the KMPP and SP.

I hope you are well.

Yours sincerely,
Jayaprakash Narayan

150. To Prafulla Chandra Ghosh, 10 October 1951[1]

My dear Prafulla Babu,

I thank you for your letter of 1st October. It is a matter of great regret to me that you have finally decided to form an alliance with the Communist Party also. However, you know our policy with regard to the Communists and I hope there will be no further misunderstanding.

As regards the weakness of the Socialist Party in Bengal, you need not have reminded me of it as I need not remind you of the weakness of the KMPP in several States in this country. I had always feared that your attitude towards the Socialist Party in Bengal was determined by its weakness, but I had hoped that you might take a broader view of the matter. However, in view of your last letter and public reports of your decisions, there seems little that can be done at this stage. In any case you have my best wishes.

Yours sincerely,
Jayaprakash Narayan

[1]*J.P. Papers* (NMML).

151. To Gyan Chand, 11 October 1951[1]

My dear Gyanbhai,

The Parliamentary Committee of the Bihar Party met today and considered your letter. The position is something like this.

1. The Congress is setting up from the Pataliputra constituency Shri Baliram Bhagat[2] who comes from one of the backward communities and commands on that account considerable influence in the area. He is a sitting member of Parliament and there is nothing against him. As Congress candidates go, he is considered to be a fairly good candidate.

2. We are contesting all the six State Assembly seats that form part of the Pataliputra constituency. You know that the voting for both the Parliament and Assembly will be simultaneous. It is therefore felt that it would be difficult for the voters to cast their votes for one symbol in the Assembly ballot box and for a different symbol in the Parliamentary box. It is feared that this will create confusion among the workers which the Congress candidate might exploit and which would weaken our chances in the Assembly seats also. It was felt that if the Congress agreed not to set up any one against you, the situation would be ideal. But if the Congress did not agree to let you go uncontested, the Committee felt that the chances would be much better if you fought the election as a Party candidate rather than as an independent.

3. I wonder if you have yet got into touch with Jawaharlalji in this matter. However, I have put the position frankly before you and it is for you to decide. I should even advise you, if possible, to come down to Patna for a day. Any time between the 22nd and 24th would suit us.

I hope you enjoyed your visit to Pachmarhi and all of you have benefited from it.

Yours affectionately,
Jayaprakash Narayan

[1]*J.P. Papers* (NMML).

[2]Baliram Bhagat (1922-); participated in the Quit India Movement, 1942; member, Provisional Parliament, 1950-2; member, Lok Sabha, 1952-77, 1980-9; Deputy Minister, Finance, 1956-63; Minister of State, Planning, 1963-4; Planning and Finance, 1964-6; Finance, 1966-7; Defence 1967; External Affairs 1967-9; Cabinet Minister, Foreign Trade and Supply 1969; Foreign Trade 1969-70; Steel and Heavy Engineering 1970-1; Speaker, Lok Sabha 1976-7; Minister, External Affairs 1985-6; Governor, Himachal Pradesh 1993, Rajasthan 1993-8.

152. Speech at a Public Meeting, Calcutta, 14 October 1951[1]

The Socialists stand for the positive policy of replacing the present Congress rule by a better one. To unite merely to defeat the Congress in the ensuing general election is a negative policy.

No unity of positive value is possible with numerous left parties until they dissolve their respective identities and merge with one major party, that is the Socialist Party of India.

With differing policies and plans of action, left ranks will not be able to effect any lasting unity, which alone can provide positive replacement of the present rule.

The possibility of Socialist-Communist line-up in the election is categorically ruled out and the Socialists would have no truck with any other left parties, unless the latter completely merged with the Socialist Party.

The election, scheduled to take place early next year, would virtually be a battle between the Congress and the Socialist Party. All other parties aspiring to participate in the elections will completely be wiped out, leaving no trace whatsoever after the elections are over. Those parties have formed a united front to fight the elections with the sole object of defeating the Congress. But merely to defeat the Congress should not be the rallying point of united left action. Even if such left united front is returned to power, would it be able to work for a single day with their mutual differences undissolved?

In case this happens, people should be prepared for elections every three months. The idea of building up unity of a dozen parties with as many ideologies, policies and plans of action is therefore dismissed

I am disappointed at the West Bengal Congress list of candidates for the elections. If these are the persons Congress want to be elected, Bengal, instead of moving forward, would go as far back as five years from today. But nothing better can be expected of the Congress.

Unlike the Congress, Socialist candidates, selection will be done by the people. The Socialist process of selection will start from below and not above. That is why release of the List of Socialist candidates is being delayed.

[1]Adapted from *National Herald*, 15 October 1951.

153. Statement to Press on a Labour Dispute, Patna, 14 October 1951[1]

Some time ago the workers of the Ballabh Das Catering Establishment at Kiul, Jhajha, Mokameh Ghat, Gaya and Moghalsarai had gone on strike. The strike was the result of the accumulated grievances of the staff over a long period. The grievances were many. The workers were deprived even of elementary privileges of industrial labour. They were denied sick and casual leave; they had no provision of provident fund; no quarters to live in and an utterly inadequate dearness allowance. After the strike had continued for a number of days and the workers had undergone much suffering there having taken place and some 200 arrests, the matter was taken up by the reconciliation officer whose labours unfortunately failed to achieve any result. After the failure of the conciliation proceedings, the next step obviously was for the Government to refer the dispute to adjudication. I fail to understand why this has not yet been done.

I hope that in view of the seriousness of the dispute and the number of staff involved and the repression and suffering through which the workers have had to pass, the Government will not delay any further in referring the dispute to an adjudicator.

[1]Adapted from *Amrit Bazar Patrika*, 16 October 1951.

154. To Evelyn Reynolds, 30 October 1951[1]

Dear Evelyn,

It was wonderful to receive such a long and sweet letter[2] from you. And I assure you that not only didn't I look once at my watch, but read the letter twice over and enjoyed it thoroughly, particularly what you called your "flippant" remarks and the account of your personal doings. By the way, you mustn't wade through ice and snow again without sufficient protection for your feet.

Let me first thank you most dearly for the "Age of Longing" and the Tribune pamphlets, the photographs, and the French Revolution Souvenir, which I shall treasure not only for its historical connection.

I was not surprised to learn of the indifference of the Labour Party towards us "poor relations". May be now that Labour is out of power, it might take a more objective view and be in a mood to treat Asian socialists if not on a footing of equality, at least from a lower pedestal. I find myself greatly in

[1]*J.P. Papers* (NMML).

[2]See Appendix 16 for Evelyn Reynolds' letter to J.P. dated 1 October 1951.

sympathy with the Bevanite view (though I do not share its optimism about a negotiated settlement). I hope you have met by now the overawing Mrs. Bevan.[3] I would be interested to know the result of the encounter. I shall be obliged if you keep me in touch with developments in Britain. The understanding that one gets from personal contact is far more valuable than the one derived from press writings, and we seem to look at things very much from the same (or similar) angles. And need I tell you that, apart from the political reporting, I should like to hear from you as often as possible?

Shankar, my Secretary whom you may remember, has collected some material, mainly election literature, for you, which I am sending by separate cover. I shall send you the press cuttings you want as soon as I get them from Delhi. Shankar will keep mailing you whatever we might consider of interest to you. You will also get *Janata* regularly.

The "Shock treatment" here has been a fiasco, and no one expects any miracles. The Congress remains what it was before and there are very few Congress candidates set up who would answer to the description of "men of honesty and integrity". Nehru, painfully aware of the failure of his Government, is trying to divert attention from that failure and the serious domestic problems to the twin issues of secularism and foreign policy. The latter two are the main theme of his propaganda.

I was greatly amused by your remarks about the [Kisan Majdoor] Praja Party and the Acharya. The party is more than half dead and no one takes it very seriously now. I should say that is one contribution Nehru has made to the growth of Indian socialism: he has nearly killed the Praja party. What remains of it is merely a transitional group of Congress dissidents, who might well scatter in different directions after the General Elections.

We are getting into stride for the election campaign now. I inaugurated the campaign at Patna on the 23rd October. The response was heartening. Finance is going to be our main headache. The millionaires are naturally against us and the rich zamindars, nor can a socialist party be run with their money. Nor have the trade unions in this country any financial strength. So we are depending largely on mass collections. This is hard work and requires a large band of workers. But we are going ahead. In Bihar I inaugurated the mass drive for collections by going from door to door in the Patna bazar. I collected about 325 rupees in an hour. Collections started on that day all over the province. I was in Calcutta on the 28th and 29th last, and there also I inaugurated a similar drive. The popular response everywhere is very hopeful (except in Bengal where a multiplicity of left parties confuses the issue), but the Congress has far more money and a long functioning machinery. Congress resources and ours are roughly in the proportion of

[3]Mrs. Jennie Lee Bevan; wife of Aneurin Bevan; Labour Minister, England; a staunch left wing member of Labour Party; elected to Parliament in 1951.

25:1. In something like one-third of the country we have no organization worth the name yet. Moreover, official intimidation, particularly in backward areas (backward even from our standards) and among the minorities (chiefly Muslim), is going to play no small part. Press support for us is also negligible. However, we are trying to do our best. In any case, we shall utilize fully the election campaign to educate the masses, and to raise the socialist movement to a far higher level. The Indian political situation after the elections, no matter who wins, will never be the same.

The defeat of British Labour, though it was expected, has saddened us deeply. So much of the future of the world depends upon the success or failure of the British Labour Party. However, it was some satisfaction to find that the defeat was not a rout and Labour still enjoys such considerable support.

I am personally fairly well, though tired and stale. If the elections turn out well, I do intend to go abroad and Nottingham, or wherever you are, will surely be on my itinerary. But won't you come to observe the first elections of free India? In any case, you must come after the election and this time for a longer stay. By the way, I am not contesting myself. I feel that some one of us must remain out to look after the extra-parliamentary work of the Party.

I showed your letter to Asoka Mehta and other colleagues. They all asked me to convey to you their gratitude for your efforts on our behalf.

I shall be happy to hear from you as often as possible, and please do not mind if in the rush of the coming days I am not able to write as often as I would like.

Will you please give my greetings to your husband whom I look forward to meet. Mr. Sharan and all the other friends whom you remembered in your letter send you their regards and greetings. Prabhavati sends you her best wishes and thanks you for remembering her.

Wishing you the best,

Yours sincerely,
Jayprakash Narayan

155. To Justice William O. Douglas, 4 November 1951[1]

4 November 1951

Dear Justice Douglas,[2]
It was a great pleasure to hear from you. The short meeting with you was

[1]*J.P. Papers* (NMML).

[2]William Orville Douglas (1898-1980); Associate Justice Supreme Court of United States, Washington D.C. 1939-75. Publications include *Democracy and Finance*, 1940; *Beyond the High Himalayas*, 1952; *Russian Journey*, 1956, etc.

most exciting, and I am looking forward to our meeting again. It is encouraging to find that an American like you shares with us our dream of a new India and a new Asia.

I am hoping to make a trip to the USA after our General Elections—as I always say "if the results are favourable". If I do go to the States I shall certainly let you know in advance so that we could have some time together.

By separate cover I am sending you some of our election literature.

Very sincerely yours,
Jayaprakash Narayan

156. To Sadiq Ali, 4 November 1951[1]

My dear Sadiq Saheb,

I am very sorry for not replying to your letter of October 5,[2] earlier. Of course adjustment between two parties does mean give and take. It has never been the policy of the Socialist Party not to agree to make any change after a decision has once been taken regarding a particular seat. But it should also be understood that a change need not necessarily be made just because the Praja Party or any other party wishes it to be so.

As far as Shri Morarji Desai's seat is concerned, I am afraid, the Socialist Party will not agree to make any change whatever. I had told Shri Puratan Buch[3] to discuss this matter with Shri Asoka Mehta. I am sure Asoka must have given Puratanji the reasons why the Socialist Party could not agree to make any adjustment as far as this particular seat was concerned.

Yours sincerely,
Jayaprakash Narayan

[1] *J.P. Papers* (NMML).

[2] See Appendix 17 for Sadiq Ali's letter to J.P.

[3] Puratan Janmashankar Buch (1907-); Gujarati writer, Publications include *Gandhijina sannidhy-man*, 1946; *Apana Kasturba*, 1950; *Apana Javahar*, 1951; *Apana Sardar*, 1952 (all in Gujarati).

157. Statement to the Press regarding Grievances of the Policemen in Bihar, Patna, 4 November 1951[1]

The question of policemen and kindred services, such as that of jail warders, has been a rather vexed one in this State; and as in all other spheres, so here, the Congress Government by its mishandling has made it worse. Policemen and warders, suffering from many wrongs, have recently been agitating for certain specific demands which they communicated to the Government as early as August 31 last. The demands include revision of basic pay scales, adequate dearness allowance, revision of daily allowance scales, confirmation of temporary posts, adequate quarters and barracks, hospital facilities, provision for the education of their children, improvement in the treatment meted out to them by officers, recognition of the right of association, etc. There is nothing in these demands that is unreasonable and the Government should have by now settled the matter by negotiation. But nothing has so far been done. The result is resentment and dissatisfaction, affecting the morale of the services. While I generally endorse the case of these employees, I should like earnestly to counsel against any precipitate action. The present Government has neared the end of its term, and the policemen and their conferers must wait till after the elections. I hope Shri Ramanand Tiwari[2] who has so bravely and ably led the policemen and the warders will also endorse my counsel of patience.

[1]Adapted from *Searchlight*, 5 November 1951.

[2]Ramanand Tiwari (1909-80); began his career as an ordinary constable; acquired fame for his role during Quit India Movement (1942) when he led a strike by 700 policemen at Jamshedpur and was dismissed from service and put in prison (1942-6); Founder-President, Bihar Police & Jailmen's Association; imprisoned several times; member, Bihar Legislative Assembly, 1952-72; Minister for Home, Bihar Government, 1967 and 1971; actively participated in the JP movement suffered imprisonment; member, Lok Sabha 1977-9.

158. To Jawaharlal Nehru, 10 November 1951[1]

Dear Bhai,

You probably know that Dr. Gyan Chand wants to stand for Parliament. He has selected the Pataliputra constituency in Bihar. He was a Professor of Economics at the Patna College for 22 years and in that capacity has served the Province for those long years. I am sure, the people of Patna and Bihar would be happy to have him as one of their representatives in Parliament. Gyan Chand has decided to stand as an independent candidate. The Socialist

[1]*J.P. Papers* (NMML).

Party has assured him that it will not put up any candidate against him. I understand he had spoken to you some time ago about the possibility of the Congress party not contesting his seat. On your advice he has also spoken to Sribabu and Anugrahbabu, but it is doubtful whether the Bihar Congress leaders would rise above their petty group interests. If the Congress party agrees that a person like Gyan Chand should be a member of Parliament even as an independent, the decision has to be taken at the highest, top levels. I hope it will be possible for you to see that such a decision is taken.

Yours affectionately,
Jayaprakash Narayan

159. Statement to Press Trust of India regarding Rejection of Nomination Papers of Socialist Party Candidates, New Delhi, 11 November 1951[1]

I am really worried about the rejection of nomination papers very often on quite flimsy grounds. In Travancore and Cochin where my party expects to be returned in good numbers, as many as 11 nominations were rejected on technical grounds. Since India is embarking on an election for the first time on the basis of adult franchise and experimenting with democracy on a big scale, a certain latitude must be given to technical and formal lapses. A proposer and seconder is necessary for a candidate and his name must be on the roll of voters.

I have a report from the Punjab yesterday, that nomination papers of one of Socialist Party candidates was rejected because he had not given three symbols. After all, people sponsored by a political party would have the party symbol but yet the returning officer thought it fit to reject the nomination of that candidate. The election commissioner's press note issued day before yesterday stating that candidates, who have not given an alternative of three symbols would be condoned, was shown to the returning officer, but in spite of that the returning officer rejected the papers.

Then there was another incident where the name of a particular candidate was wrongly spelt. Even though the Election Commissioner assured that it must be easily rectified, the candidate concerned had to run from pillar to post for days to get the mistake corrected.

[1]Adapted from *Searchlight*, 12 November 1951.

160. Address at an Election Meeting, Madras, 14 November 1951[1]

The Socialist Party, if elected to power, will reduce the present wide gap between the rich and the poor by taxing the rich and imposing a capital levy. The capital levy will be 90 per cent in the case of those who have wealth of Rs. one crore and above.

My party will abolish landlordism and redistribute the land, making the tillers, owners of land. This will lead to increased agricultural production. The maximum holding will be restricted by legislation to 30 acres in the case of a joint family and twelve acres in the case of an individual. It will reduce the burden on land by giving facilities to people to engage themselves in new cottage industries. A land army will be formed.

In the industrial sphere, the party believes in the creation of only small-scale industries since we have neither large capital resources nor enough technical personnel to be able to develop industries on large-scale basis. At the same time, the Socialist Party will nationalize the existing basic industries. Nationalized undertaking will be run not as departments of government but by industrial corporations in which consumers, workers and government will be represented.

The country presents a picture of sadness, despair, discontentment and disillusionment. I ask the people not to be taken in, if the Congress raises the slogan in the elections that a vote for the Congress is a vote for Mahatma Gandhi.

The Communist Party of India has a long record of betrayal, and the reason for this is that it does not work with the interests of the country at heart. When the Communist Party takes a decision on any vital question, it is not a decision made in India but a decision made either in Moscow or somewhere else.

I fully endorse the foreign policy of Pandit Nehru. The Socialist Party, however, wants to go a step further. There are other countries who, like India, do not attach themselves to either the Anglo-American bloc or the Soviet bloc. Those countries, which live in constant fear of these two blocs, can be brought together.

[1]Adapted from *Tribune*, 16 November 1951.

161. To Hemant Sanyal, 20 November 1951[1]

Dear Mr. Sanyal,[2]

You know that I am President of the East Indian Railway Employees' Union. There is a serious question that has arisen as a result of the Administration applying the disciplinary rules for the staff to the trade union activities of employees who happen to be trade union officials. The General Secretary and the Joint General Secretary of the Union will see you in this matter. The Union is not in a position to pay the fees of such an eminent lawyer as you. I am therefore requesting you to be good enough to take up this case and do what you can as a matter of personal favour to me and to the labour movement. I shall be obliged.

I hope you are well.

Very sincerely yours,
J.P.

[1]*J.P. Papers* (NMML).
[2]Hemant Sanyal; one of the leading lawyers, Calcutta.

162. Telegram to Sheikh Mohammad Abdullah, 1 December 1951[1]

Amazed to learn of your impending visit to campaign for the Congress party. Other parties than the Congress have lent you full support. Kashmir has never been a party question. You are not a Congressman nor Kashmir National Conference a part of that organization. The Socialist Party out of consideration for you and the National Conference has refrained so far from forming a party branch in Kashmir. I advise you strongly to desist from identifying yourself with a single party. You will do incalculable harm to Kashmir thereby.

[1]*J.P. Papers* (NMML).

163. Explaining Socialist Party's Electoral Alliances, Cuttack, 6 December 1951[1]

The alliance with the Jharkhand Party[2] is not only an electoral alliance but a political alliance and I look forward to the time when the Jharkhand Party will merge with the Socialist Party. So far as the question of Jharkhand province is concerned, we have made it clear that the Socialist Party does not support the demand. However, the Party advocates regional autonomy and the creation of sub-areas within the different states of India for the tribal peoples so that they can manage their affairs themselves within the constitution of the country.

We are accused of compromising with communalism by allying with Jharkhand Party and the Scheduled Castes Federation. The Socialist Party does not regard these organizations as communal. We feel that if the castes and communities which have been suppressed and submerged raise themselves by forming their own organizations, it is a progressive development and a sign of social and economic revolt.

It is not generally known that the Congress tried its best to persuade Dr. B.R. Ambedkar and Mr. Jaipal Singh[3] to join hands with it, but those efforts failed. And now when Congressmen are charging us with communalism, it is something in the nature of grapes being sour.

The alliance with Dr. Ambedkar has nothing to do with the foreign policy of the Socialist Party which remains the same as Dr. Lohia has developed it. The same holds good with the party's policy towards Kashmir which is complete support to Sheikh Abdullah.

[1]Conversation with press representatives at Cuttack. Adapted from *Tribune*, 8 December 1951.

[2]Jharkhand Party: Demand for Jharkhand autonomy was raised by Adivasi Mahasabha in 1938; its name was changed to Jharkhand Party in 1950.

[3]Jaipal Singh (1903-70); President All India Adivasi Mahasabha since 1939-50; Founder-President, Jharkhand Party since 1950; member, Constituent Assembly and Provisional Parliament, 1946-52; member, Lok Sabha, 1952-70.

164. Address at an Election Meeting, Bombay, 9 December 1951[1]

The statement made by Mr. Nehru in his recent speech in Bombay that he, too is a Socialist but his method of achieving the Socialist objective differs from that of the Socialist Party. I beg to differ with this claim, as during the last four years of his regime he has set back the clock of the country's progress by as many as forty years.

[1]Adapted from *Bombay Chronicle*, 10 December 1951.

Mr. Nehru promised that he will reform the Congress once the elections are won, but he will do nothing of the sort, and I am sure that the same Congress will throw him out immediately after the elections are won. Whereas, I can promise a square deal for the middle and the working classes in a Socialist regime. I think this can be done by taking away all wealth from the rich and distributing it equally among all.

Socialism is the only remedy against the existing conditions in the country. The Socialist Party has pledged to establish a welfare State in which there will be a radical change in the very structure of society. There will be equal distribution of wealth, equal opportunity for all, and freedom from want and fear under the Socialist rule.

The immediate programme of the Socialist Party includes abolition of landlordism, redistribution of land, and nationalization of important industries. In this connection the five-year plan of the Congress is a farce which that organization will not be able to implement even within 25 years.

The four years' Congress rule has allowed the services to be demoralized and compelled them to become subservient to one-party rule. The Congress has done so much for retarding the progress of the country in its four years of control of the Country's administration that it will be nothing short of a disaster to put it back into power.

The Congress party today is a tottering organization and is so full of corruption, nepotism, jobbery and internecine squabbles that no body can save it. It can not be trusted with the charge of reorganizing our society, nor can it be expected to extend a square deal to the toiling masses, because people who control it are all capitalists, and now even the former maharajas.

Mr. Nehru is now taking back those Congressmen who had left the organization and joined reactionary parties. He is inviting back those whom he had called "opportunists", because it suits his purpose of winning the election. He is trying to get back even Mr. Gopichand Bhargava who was responsible for the most corrupt administration in the Punjab.

Unless our society goes through a rapid transformation the country will not be able to produce wealth nor can it achieve any economic self-sufficiency. We must understand that increased production can not be achieved by setting targets but by giving the tiller of the soil and the worker in the factory his due and freedom from fear and want. The Congress as a political organization is too old and being bereft of enthusiasm cannot achieve this. The Socialist Party alone can achieve this objective by rapidly transforming the society.

The Socialist Party's electoral alliance with the Scheduled Castes Federation is perfectly alright. The Congress feels sore about it because it can not obtain the support of the Harijans. It is not an opportunistic alliance as charged by the Congress. It is quite natural that these two parties have come together.

165. Address at an Election Meeting, Kanpur, 16 December 1951[1]

The economic problem of India can be solved only by the formation of small-scale industries to be run by industrial corporations started by the public. The big industries like shipping, iron and steel and mining should be nationalized.

The mushroom growth of a number of parties formed on religious, communal and sectarian basis on the eve of the elections is detrimental to the interest of the country. The main question before the public at present is to end corruption, remove food scarcity and raise the standard of living of the masses. Any organization which raises the cry of culture and religion, should realize that legislative assemblies are not the place where culture can be developed.

There are only two main political parties—the Congress and the Socialist Party—in the elections. This is the time for the public to consider that a new shape has to be given to society and the economy of the country.

During the last four years' rule of the Congress there is a general degradation all round. Corruption has become rampant and black-marketing has reached its zenith. Four years ago, when the Congress took over the administration, the people rejoiced and there was a feeling that a real people's government would be established, exploitation, poverty and scarcity would end and a new India would be built. But all these hopes have been dashed to the ground. The situation instead of improving has, in fact, deteriorated. Within four years of Congress rule, moral degradation has set in every sphere of life. That kind of degradation was unknown even during the rule of foreigners.

It is now time for the Government to be replaced with a better one. The people had seen the utter failure of the Congress of 1947 which had many good points. Nothing better can be expected from the Congress of 1951 which is weak and disintegrating owing to indiscipline, selfishness and corruption in its ranks. The claim of Pandit Nehru that the Congress alone can maintain unity and solve the problems of the country is absurd.

Pandit Nehru had given the assurance to reform the Congress when he assumed presidentship of the organization. He has failed to fulfil the promise and the same set of Congressmen who were responsible for the degradation in the Congress, have become Congress nominees in the elections. No reliance can be placed on his promise to reform the Congress after the elections.

[1]Adapted from *National Herald*, 17 December 1951.

Even Mahatma Gandhi had realized that he would not be able to bring about any improvement and therefore called for its dissolution after the achievement of independence. The only possibility of Congress being reformed lay in its being defeated in the elections. This setback will make Congress leaders realize their shortcomings and mistakes.

The question before the country is whether the present social and economic structure should exist or be fundamentally changed. Until the structure is changed, mere slogans like "grow more" or "produce more" can serve no purpose.

The economic policy of the Government cannot solve the problem of poverty. Establishment of small-scale industries to be run by industrial corporations can be of immense help in this regard. The Planning Commission had offered no solution to the problems of the country.

In his Orissa speech Pandit Nehru said about doing away with the privileges of the princes, but I would first like to know what Pandit Nehru has done to remove the disparity which exists in the salaries of the high Government officers and the low paid employees. The lowest salary of a Government employee is Rs. 30 and that of the highest Rs. 10,000. The Socialist Party, on assuming power, will resort to equitable distribution and fix the minimum salary at Rs. 100 and the maximum salary at Rs. 1,000.

It is incorrect to characterize the manifesto of the Socialist Party as "vague". The adjective can in fact be applied more correctly to the Congress manifesto.

The Communists keep on changing their policies from time to time. Their definition of freedom is very strange. According to them slavery to Russia is "freedom". The Communists claim that the country even today is a slave of the Anglo-American bloc, though India boldly diferred from America and Russia wherever she found them wrong.

The alliance of the Socialist Party with the Scheduled Castes Federation is for the uplift of the down-trodden. There is nothing wrong in this alliance. I do not agree that the Scheduled Castes Federation is a communal organization. The depressed classes have organized themselves to revolt against the social system which has kept them slaves for such a long time. Only those communities which organized themselves for the preservation of their privileges can be placed in the category of communal organizations. The down-trodden classes have a right to organize themselves against society. Even the Congress had tried to reach an agreement with the Scheduled Castes Federation but when it failed, "grapes became sour" Our alliance will prove a step forward towards social progress.

166. Address at an Election Meeting, Jalandhar (Punjab), 20 December 1951[1]

The great jubilation which the countrymen had on the advent of freedom has turned into despair, after experiencing four years of Congress rule and administration leading to poverty, starvation and rampant corruption. The Nehru regime has been a complete failure.

The system of controls has only benefited a few and enabled them to amass wealth while the country has become poorer. The voters should remove all the communal parties from the political field, as the mushroom growth of parties at the advent of elections is sure to create anarchy in the country. Only two parties should exist in our country one which represents the capitalists and is interested in maintaining status quo in favour of the present system and the other which stands for mazdoor and kisan raj and wants change and overhaul of the present system of Society. If representatives of many parties are returned to the legislature, no party will be able to set up a permanent ministry and our country will be faced with the same situation as has been witnessed in France.

The Jan Sangh is raising a slogan that culture is in danger. There is no instance of any country in the world where culture has been protected by force of law. If communal parties continue to have sway in the political field, the real issues like poverty, starvation and economic emancipation will be thrown into the background. The communal organizations are, therefore, a great danger to the country's well-being.

The Socialist Party is the only organization which stands for equitable distribution of wealth in the country and for a raj which would bring happiness and prosperity to all the people. The promises given by Pandit Nehru have turned into a mirage as he has failed to fulfil them. The net result of his rule has been complete disintegration of the Congress and moral degradation in the whole country.

Pandit Nehru is now touring all over the country and asking the people to vote for the Congress. But the Congress of 1951 is much worse than the Congress of 1947, and if the people vote the Congress to power, it would be most unfortunate for the country. What is the hindrance to Pandit Nehru purging the Congress now, and why does he want to delay this till the elections are over? Pandit Nehru said, "consolidation of freedom is necessary, before the country can be prepared for socialism". But it is a ridiculous type of socialism that he wants to establish by maintaining the status quo of capitalism and feudalism, with a handful of very wealthy men on the one hand and 99 per cent poverty-striken people on the other.

Not only the Congress has not been able to touch the fringe of the basic

[1]Adapted from *Tribune*, 21 December 1951.

problems of food, cloth and shelter and hold in check the spiral of ever-increasing inflation and black-marketing, but the fact remains that the Congress does not even place them before the people for their awareness and goes on misguiding them.

I denounce those parties which bring religion and culture into politics. A Punjabi speaking Province would not solve our problems which are essentially economic. Bengal has a Ministry and administration as also other provinces by their own respective people, but has that solved the problems. Your choice lies between the two parties, the Congress and the Socialist Party, the one conserving the existing social structure and the other promising equitable distribution of wealth. The future of our country depends on how you exercise your choice.

167. Address at an Election Meeting, Ambala, 21 December 1951[1]

Mr. Jawaharlal Nehru is the biggest stumbling block in the way of introducing socialism in this country, despite his oft-repeated claim from the Congress stage that he subscribes to socialism.

Pandit Nehru's declaration that he is a Socialist is a moral victory of the Socialist Party. It is basically incorrect to suggest that there is similarity between the Congress and Socialist programmes. These are poles asunder—the former is a party of capitalists aimed at perpetuating the hold of the moneyed people on the masses while the latter stands for the uplift of the down-trodden people.

The forthcoming elections will have a far-reaching significance not only for the coming five years but also for many years to follow. India is learning a lesson in democracy and the scores of parties which have sprung up in the country would prove a great hindrance in providing a stable and good government. Independent candidates in the elections are a further danger to a stable government, for every one of them would strive for Chief Ministership and Ministership and would make it impossible for any stable government to be formed.

I would like to ask the people not to follow the various political parties in the field blindly but to exercise their precious right of vote after full consideration.

In my opinion the two-party system, one in power and one in the opposition, is the best system in a democratic country. The real fight in the elections is between the Congress and the Socialist Party. The seasonal parties which have been set up only with the purpose of fighting elections

[1]Adapted from *Tribune*, 22 December 1951.

should be totally ignored in the interests of the public and the country.

I condemn the communal parties and the slogans of culture and civilization raised by the Bharatiya Jan Sangh. The Parliament or the legislatures are not the forums for discussing or formulating religions or cultures.

India to-day stands threatened not with any danger from Russia, China or America, but from the extreme poverty, starvation and the unequal distribution of wealth prevailing among her people .The only way to remove that danger is equal distribution of wealth and land, industrialization and eradication of capitalism and the jagirdari system.

The experience of the last four years of Congress Government in the country has shown that the Congress has miserably failed in bringing about any improvement in the lot of the people excepting the handful of capitalists and big jagirdars. The Grow-More-Food campaign has been a total failure. For agricultural production of the country has gone down instead of going up, the prices of commodities have grown abnormally high, the production of cloth has benefited only millowners and the poor and middle class people are left in a condition of utter helplessness and misery. Their plight has indeed gone from bad to worse. During the four years' Prime Ministership of Pandit Nehru capitalists have thrived freely, Congress Ministers and MLAs and their relatives have held monopolies; corruption has grown to a high pitch and black-marketing has become the order of the day.

There was a time when Congress was considered to be a hallmark of, ideological soundness, good work and sacrifice, but after the death of the Father of the Nation, Mahatma Gandhi, the intoxication of power has converted it into a body of highly degenerate, selfish and corrupt persons. Real Congressmen have gone out of it and those who have flouted its principles and ideals all their lives have become Congressmen overnight. If the people vote the Congress into power again, in the hope that it would do better in future, they would be sadly disillusioned. The Congress is beyond cure. Effective reforms in the country are possible only by defeating it in the elections and replacing it by the Socialist Party.

Punjabis should give no chance to the Congress to instal its ministry in the state. The Socialist Party would have floored Congress candidates in straight contests, but, unfortunately, the mushroom-like growth of parties, taking advantage of the disintegration of the Congress may not allow the Socialist Party to succeed.

The Socialist Party does not oppose a Punjabi-speaking province, but its demand at the time of election creates doubts about its genuineness.

I think that the dangers to the security of the country are poverty and communalism. I believe that communalism in the Punjab can be stamped out through the Socialist way of equal distribution of wealth and land, not through the methods of appeasement of communalists adopted by the Congress.

Pandit Nehru has promised during his recent public speeches that he would purge the Congress of its evils after elections, but he had given similar assurances while ousting Purshottamdas Tandon from the presidentship of the All-India Congress in 1950. Pandit Nehru's selection of Congress candidates for the elections has shattered all hopes of any change in the Congress organization. Those who have been given Congress tickets are singing the hymn of the organization while other Congressmen are opposing official Congress candidates. If the Congress can at all be cured of its evils, it would only be when it is given a crushing defeat and is made to feel that it has done something very wrong which has made the masses throw it out of power. Such a result of the elections would make Pandit Nehru appreciate where he and the Congress stand in the estimation of the people in the country.

While Pandit Nehru is repeatedly harping on the bugle of secularism, some Muslims recently told him that they had been threatened that in case they did not vote for the Congress, they would be sent to Pakistan. The curse of communalism can only be done away with by removing poverty and by equal distribution of wealth.

On the eve of elections, the Congress is propagating that they would fight against communalism, but afterwards the Congress would join hands with communalists.

The record of the Congress has been similar on the issue of corruption. Dr. Gopichand Bhargava's Ministry in the Punjab had not been removed not because of corruption, as claimed by the Congress, but because of internal differences among the Congressmen of the state. There are several other Ministries in India which are corrupt but the Congress has not raised even a little finger against them.

It is strange that Congressmen who had petty incomes before are not content even with thousands of rupees which they earn as Ministers today, but repeated demands of the Socialist Party for increase in the salaries of low-paid poor and middle class people have been turned down on the pretext of financial stringency. This shows the real nature of Congress rule. It will be disastrous if it is given another chance.

168. Statement on Jawaharlal Nehru's Criticism of the Socialist Party, Patna, 30 December 1951[1]

History will record Mr. Nehru as that curious Socialist who was in his time the greatest single impediment to Socialism in Asia. Pandit Nehru was opposed to Socialism for four years of his rule and pouring ridicule on all

[1]Adapted from *Tribune*, 1 January 1952.

talk of Socialism despite his present protestations from every platform of his Socialist faith.

He had the whole people behind him and a powerful revolutionary organization and the Government of the country. He could have done almost anything, but he failed and let go that historic opportunity. History has again knocked at Mr. Nehru's doors at these elections. But he has once again failed to answer the summons of the times. When the whole of Asia is hankering for change and deliverance from the tyranny and injustice of the old order, Mr. Nehru has stood up as pitiful champion of that same old rotten order and has become a road block to all change.

Mr. Nehru has become fearful of change. He says repeatedly that Socialism cannot be built in a day or by a miracle or by slogans. But no one in this country has ever suggested that it could be so. We have always been emphasizing that it will take time to build up Socialism.

Mr. Nehru has neither prepared the blue-print of a Socialist India nor in the last four years has laid its foundation nor is he going to do so in the next five years if he comes back to power. What then is the value of his reiterated faith in Socialism?

A Socialist must practise his faith but Mr. Nehru's practice is rejection of his oft-proclaimed faith. He argues in self-defence that the people of this country are not ready for Socialism. Thus did the British argue that India was not ready for freedom. It is amazing that Burma and Indonesia and so many other countries in Asia should be ready for Socialism. But unfortunate India alone should lag so far behind.

Mr. Nehru argues that the primary task today is to consolidate the freedom of the country and not to talk of Socialism. How can freedom be consolidated except by freeing the masses from exploitation and injustice? Our freedom today limps on a single leg because we have achieved only political freedom. Before it can stand firmly and march forward, economic freedom must be added to the first. In other words Socialist reconstruction is the only way to consolidate the freedom of the country.

169. To Jawaharlal Nehru, 16 January 1952[1]

Dear Bhai,

The other day I learnt in Calcutta that you were good enough to make a reference to me in one of your meetings there. I wish you had been better informed. It seems that you spoke with some feeling and wondered how I

[1]*Brahmanand Papers* (NMML).

[2]For Nehru's reply to this letter see Appendix 18.

would consider you so bad as to have said that in four years you had done more harm to the country than the British had in a hundred years. I had never said anything of this kind. What I had said and what I would still repeat was that: 'Moral degradation caused by four years of Congress rule in the country exceeds that of hundred years of British rule'(original in Hindi). I maintain this to be true. The British were cruel and unprincipled when it came to fighting the national movement. But in their normal administrative work they maintained certain high standards of honesty and integrity which are absent, generally speaking, in the Congress administration.

There are several other matters which I should like to take up with you in regard to your election campaign. But I must wait till the elections are over. The above was a personal matter so I have taken the liberty of writing about it even when you are still campaigning.

With regards,

Yours affectionately,
Jayaprakash

170. To Gopalaswami Ayyangar, 16 January 1952[1]

Dear Shri Ayyangar,

Since our last meeting I have been entirely in the dark as to what steps Government have taken to implement our agreement. I shall be obliged to know authoritatively from you. As soon as the elections are over, I shall have to call the General Council of the AIRF and place before it a report on the result of our negotiations. It is possible that the Railway Board has kept Shri Guruswami informed but he is in the throes of his election campaign, and I do not wish to disturb him. In any case, I am anxious to know from you as to what has been done or is being proposed to be done.

1. I was under the impression that a commission was soon to be appointed to go into the question of dearness allowance and the proposal to merge part of it with basic pay. Mr. Deshmukh was not in Delhi when we had met and I understood that as soon as he returned the Commission would be appointed in consultation with him. May I know where the matter stands now?

2. It was agreed that an enquiry would be made into the position of the pre-1931 staff so that on the basis of the facts ascertained, the matter might be amicably settled.

[1]*J.P. Papers* (NMML).

3. I should like to know if the negotiating machinery and appellate authority (for disciplinary cases) agreed upon has been set in motion. I have not read any news published about the appointment of the Permanent Rly. Staff Tribunal.

4. There were several other issues which had been discussed between the Board and Shri Guruswami. I should like to know if anything has been done regarding them.

5. Regarding that Moghalsarai affair, Tiwari tendered an apology to the General Manager, EIR as suggested. But I should like to have an assurance from you that criticism made by trade union officials at public meetings (apart from abuse and libellous charges) will not be made a basis for disciplinary action. At our meeting you had assured me that it was never the intention of the Administration to muzzle the staff or deny their right to ventilate publicly these grievances.

In a few months there will be new Government at Delhi and you are not coming back. I am therefore anxious to have the present dispute settled during your regime.

I hope you are well,
with regards,

Yours very sincerely,
Jayaprakash

P.S.: Please reply at my Patna address.

171. Address at an Election Meeting, Lucknow, 19 January 1952[1]

The salvation of the country lies in the defeat of the Congress as the ruling organization and success of the Socialist Party in the elections.

The Nehru Government during the last four years or more has failed to bring economic and social freedom to the country. The freedom of the country stands threatened from inside. The moral degradation which has set in the country under the Congress regime has surpassed even that under the British rule.

I am disappointed at the programme and ideology of the KMPP[2] and denouce its election tactics. The KMPP is an opportunist organization and is making unholy alliances with all sorts of people. I condemn the

[1]Adapted from *National Herald*, 20 January 1952.

[2]Kisan Mazdoor Praja Party; founded at Patna on 16 June 1951 by J.B. Kripalani, T. Prakasam, P.C. Ghosh, K. Kellappan and others. Kripalani was elected its first President.

Communists and the communal organizations like the Jan Sangh and the Ram Rajya Parishad.[3]

The Nehru Government has brought about no change for the better during the regime. By voting for the Congress, you will be perpetuating the present conditions of poverty, unemployment, exploitation, black-marketing and profiteering for another five years. Now is the time to act and take a wise decision for the future. The next five years' reign of the Congress Government will be even worse than that of the last five years.

Mr. Nehru has been going about the country canvassing support for the Congress and making to the electorate extravagant promises. On the food front, Pandit Nehru has suffered the biggest defeat in so far as imports of foodgrains from abroad are concerned. Moreover, he has failed to bring about unity in the ranks of the Congress and purge it of undesirable elements.

I appeal to the people to vote for the Socialist Party. You are not going to decide the fate of any individual candidate by voting in the elections; it is going to be a question of your personal victory or defeat. So far as independent candidates are concerned, they are without any organization or the backing of any political party. As such, they are solitary figures who cannot make their voices heard in the legislature. Do not, therefore throw away your precious votes on such candidates because they are not capable of serving your interests in any way. So far as the Congress is concerned, what has it done for the people during the period it has been in office? The people are suffering untold hardships and the middle classes are politically becoming extinct. The rich are becoming richer and the poor poorer. There is appalling disparity in the salaries of low-paid government employees and the high-ups. Corruption, black-marketing, nepotism and profiteering are rampant on a wide scale throughout the country.

The problem of poverty can be solved only by a fair and equitable distribution of wealth and redistribution of land. The Congress is only concentrating on increased production of food and wealth to the exclusion of fair distribution. During the last four years there had been no increase in production of either food or industrial goods.

Pandit Nehru claims to be a socialist, but he has so far done nothing to take the country towards socialism since he became the Prime Minister. The Socialist programme envisages socialised and planned industry, full employment, social equality, land army for food production, maximum income of Rs. 1,000 and minimum income of Rs. 100, right to recall legislators and cultural and educational facilities for minorities.

[3]Ram Rajya Parishad; founded in 1947 by Swami Karpatri (1907-82), religious leader and vedic scholar. The Party opposed cow-slaughter and Hindu Code Bill.

172. To Jawaharlal Nehru, 12 February 1952[1]

Dear Bhai,[2]

Some days ago I had written to you about certain remarks you had made at Calcutta meeting. I hope you received that letter.

Now that the elections are over I should like to take up with you another serious matter in the hope that it would receive your dispassionate attention. You are perhaps aware that the main line of attack of the Communist Party upon us was that we were American agents. Congressmen too had joined in this propaganda. In certain constituencies in Bihar, the Congress slogan was:

"Three agents of America
Mehta, Lohia, Jayaprakash" (original in Hindi)

But it is not about this that I am writing to you. The Communist press has been persistently alleging that Lohia brought thousands of dollars (the figure varies) from America for the Socialist Party's election campaign. Again it is not Communist lies about which I am complaining to you. But I understand that when challenged the communists have replied that it is not they but the Indian Embassy in Washington that is responsible for the story. [B.G.] Gokhale of the Foreign Bureau of the Socialist Party has received a letter from Harris Wofford (of the World Government movement), who was responsible for Lohia's trip to the USA, to say that it is persistently rumoured by sources connected with the Indian Embassy that Lohia was paid money by the USA for the funds of the Socialist Party. This is a serious matter. Lohia and the Indian Embassy didn't get on well with each other, but that was no reason for the latter to carry on such a vile whispering campaign. Friends here had to put together small sums of money in order to enable Lohia to go abroad, and even while he was in the USA a SOS had come for a small sum. The Socialist Party may be objectionable in the eyes of the Indian Embassy in America, but that is no reason why it should villify its leader. I understand that Aruna also has been going around saying that the story of Lohia getting money from the USA has the authority of the Indian Embassy. When there is so much smoke there must be fire somewhere. Will you please look into the matter? The Socialist Party may be thoroughly bad in your eyes, but I hope you do not believe that we have all started accepting bribes from foreign sources.

Another complaint that I have to make this time about yourself—is concerning your Patna speech. I was told that while recounting the sins of

[1]*J.P. Papers* (NMML).
[2]For Nehru's reply to this letter see Appendix 19.

the Socialist Party you had said that "these people have entered into a pact even with the Jan Sangh". I did not expect such an utter misrepresentation from you. I have no knowledge of any pact with the Jan Sangh, nor does Narendra Deva, Lohia or Asoka have any knowledge of it. If you had in mind any individual case in which a Socialist candidate had entered into an alliance with the Jan Sangh, I cannot say anything with certainty. But in that case, if you are interested, I would send you details of alliances between Congress candidates and Jan Sangh. And there are other pacts that the Congress party makes. Asoka wrote to you the other day of a Congress pact in Bombay with the fourth party (no less communal than the Jan Sangh), but you had no knowledge of such a local affair.

I hope you are well. With kind regards,

Yours affectionately,
Jayaprakash

173. Speech on Election Results, Patna, 14 February 1952[1]

The first thing which I would like to say on this occasion is that the electorate gave a good display of their spirit of democracy in the first general election of the Indian Republic. The Chief Election Commissioner of India, Mr. Sukumar Sen, deserves hearty congratulations for conducting the elections in a most peaceful and constitutional manner. It was the greatest experiment in Asia from the point of view of the vast number of electorate. Mr. Sukumar Sen spared no pains in making the elections free and fair.

But in spite of the election rules there were certain defects that were perceptible to all. The ink marks on the thumb of the voter did not prove indelible. The boxes could be opened even without interfering with the seals. There were many officers who were unaware of the election rules and they had no training in election matters.

The zamindars committed various acts of high-handedness in the elections and they are still victimising those who voted for the Socialist candidates. Voters were intercepted and prevented from casting their votes for the Socialists. Able candidates were defeated in many cases and various ill-famed people were elected.

By securing only 32 per cent of the votes in Bihar the Congress won 241 seats in the Bihar Legislative Assembly. The total votes polled in favour of the Congress candidates amounted to about 36 lakhs. The Socialists captured 23 seats by securing 17 per cent of the votes. Over 16 lakh votes

[1]Adapted from *Searchlight*, 15 February 1952; *National Hearld*, 16 February 1952; and *Amrit Bazar Patrika*, 20 February 1952.

were cast for the Socialists as a whole. The total of votes polled in the elections came to about 95 lakhs.

The independent candidates did much damage to the cause of the Socialists and so did the Kisan Mazdoor Praja Party. Only 12 independents were elected and the Kisan Mazdoor Praja Party got only one seat. I urge the KMPP to join the Socialist Party. It got one seat because of Shri Mahamaya Prasad Sinha[2] against whom the Socialist Party had not set up any candidate. Had it done so, Shri Sinha would also have been defeated. Casteism also harmed the Socialist candidates very much. The independents numbering 650 made the Congress victorious. With 32 per cent votes the Congress got 241 and with the rest of 68 per cent other parties and individuals captured only 89 seats. This illustrates the glaring defect of the electoral system based on the single-member constituency.

In many places the Socialists have lost by a very narrow margin. The Socialist Party would file election petitions against a number of successful candidates. Though the Socialist Party did not fare well in the elections, it was not a loser. It got 23 seats and in addition to this it got the opportunity of carrying the message of socialism far and wide in Bihar.

The election results show that the Socialist Party is a big party, next only to the Congress. In fact it is the only rival of the Congress. I reject the claim about the importance of the Communist Party. In this election the Communists secured about 60 lakh votes in the whole country while the votes polled in favour of the Socialists came to about one crore. The Communist Party is much inferior to the Socialist Party in strength and dignity in this country.

As I mentioned earlier, the Socialists lost so many seats because of single-member constituencies. The Socialist Party had demanded proportional representation in the election but this was rejected by the Congress. Had there been the system of proportional representation the Socialist would have captured 60 seats and the Congress 125 in Bihar.

After the publication of the election results some friends have suggested that the Socialist Party and the Communist Party should work together. The Socialist Party would be prepared to join hands with the Communist Party of India if they act independently of Russia in India. I have no enmity with Russia or China. I hold them in respect. But I refuse to be dictated to by them. Besides, the Communist Party of India has never been sincere in

[2]Mahamaya Prasad Sinha (1910-87); gave up studies at Banaras Hindu University; joined Salt Satyagraha and Civil Disobedience Movement; nominated first dictator of Satyagraha Movement in Saran 1930; jailed several times during freedom movement; resigned from Congress in 1951, founder member of KMPP; elected leader of Samyukt Vidhayak Dal 1967; Chief Minister Bihar 1967-8; MP, Lok Sabha 1977-9.

their talks about unity and common front. The unity they want is something like the embrace of Dhritarashtra to crush Bhima. They want only to break up the other parties and to take advantage of the resultant disruption.

Everywhere, except Yugoslavia, wherever the Communists had the upper hand they were dictated to by Russia. Such dictation the Socialist Party can never accept. The history of the last 25 years shows that the Communist Party of India had changed its policy again and again to suit the convenience of Russia. For instance, when Mahatma Gandhi raised the slogan of "Quit India", they dubbed him as a fascist agent and co-operated with the British rulers.

A whispering campaign has been launched by the Communists that I am an agent of America and that the Socialist Party is subsidised by American dollars. If they sincerely believe their own canard, I fail to understand why they are anxious for the co-operation of the Socialist Party.

The ideals for which the Communists are working are entirely contrary to those of the Socialist Party. While we want to establish a democratic socialist society in this country, the aim of the Communists is the establishment of their own party's dictatorship. The people of the country must clearly choose between the two.

The other small left parties who talk of left consolidation do not fully understand the nature of the problem. What is needed is a new approach to the problem of left unity. The time had passed when different parties maintaining their separate identities could form a consolidation and achieve unity. Such consolidation in the past did not last long. The only way to achieve unity is for the various parties believing in socialism to merge together. Those who believe in Communist dictatorship should straightaway join the Communist Party instead of maintaining their separate existence. On the other hand, those who believe in the democratic way of life should merge into the Socialist Party or join together to form another party.

I am sure that after the next five years the Congress is not going to be voted back to power. The choice before the people then would be the Communist Party or the Socialist Party. And the people must make up their minds whom to return to power.

174. Speech on Election Results, New Delhi, 22 February 1952[1]

I attribute the success of the Congress and debacle of Socialist Party in the elections to the utter ignorance of the electorate. From the election results which had been contrary to expectations, it was crystal clear that a large number of voters did not exercise their franchise with discernment.

I predict that in states like Madras, Travancore-Cochin, Rajasthan and PEPSU, where the Congress had failed to secure absolute majority, there would be neither stable Congress ministries nor coalition governments. The only alternative would be fresh elections.

Though the Congress has secured resounding victories in the elections, it does not mean that it is a party having a considerable mass appeal. The very fact that only 40 per cent of total votes polled were cast in favour of the Congress has confirmed the belief that the Congress influence is fast declining, and it is doubtful whether it would be able to rule the country for the next five years.

The Socialist Party plans to launch an intensive satyagraha campaign throughout the country if the party in power fails to remove the difficulties of the people. In our opinion satyagraha is the only powerful weapon to combat injustice and oppression.

I disapprove the idea of independent candidates contesting the elections. Such candidates were, to a great extent, responsible for the splitting up of the anti-Congress votes, thus causing heavy reverses to the parties with constructive programmes. I hope that the people would learn a lesson from the present election results that the candidates representing no one except themselves have no place in a democratic set-up.

[1]Adapted from *National Herald*, 23 February 1952.

175. Speech on Election Results, Madras, 24 February 1952[1]

Co-operation with the Communist Party will be an embrace of death. There can be no question of the Socialist Party forming any kind of coalition or alliance with the Congress or the Communist Parties. The Socialist Party would function in the legislature as a democratic opposition. Whatever Government is formed by whichever party, we will judge that Government on its merit.

The Socialist Party has fundamental differences with both the Congress

[1]Adapted from *Tribune*, 26 February 1952.

and the Communist parties. The Congress fought the elections to maintain its programme of 'status quo' which is contradictory to the Socialist Party's programme. The most objectionable feature of the Communist Party is its extra-territorial patriotism, which is a very serious matter.

The first conclusion that anybody can draw from the elections is that the people voted against the Congress as it failed to secure the majority of votes polled.

The Congress successes in certain states were mainly due to Mr. Nehru's promise that he would clean up the organization after the elections. I know from personal experience that a large number of people in the country were carried away by that promise. The time has come for Mr. Nehru to fulfil this promise.

It would not be very long for the people to realise that neither Mr. Nehru nor anyone else can clean up this organization. The Congress will go down lower and lower with its internal factions and disputes. The disintegration of the Congress will become an accomplished fact in the next few years.

Some people refer to Mr. Nehru's statement that he too is a Socialist. I do not know how Mr. Nehru is going to create a Socialist India by promoting the development of capitalism. Since he became President of the Congress first, I have been hearing about his Socialism. I have not witnessed so far any Socialist measure undertaken either by Mr. Nehru or by his colleagues in any of the States since they came to power.

The Socialist Party's expectations about elections were rather high. The number of seats we have won are much less than expected. We have polled over one crore votes while Congress polled only about five crore votes in this country. This is a great achievement for a party which has been functioning independently only for the last four years.

176. To Gopalaswami Ayyangar, 28 March 1952[1]

Dear Mr. Ayyanger,

A few days ago I wrote you a letter regarding the sweepers of Allahabad. So far I have received no reply. I hope the matter is under your active consideration.

I am writing this in connection with the formation of the North Eastern Railway. The enclosed Memorandum, prepared by my union (EIR Employees' Union) sets forth in some detail our case. Upon study of the materials before me I have no doubt that certain decisions in regard to the NER have been taken not on grounds of economy, efficiency, rationalization

[1] *J.P. Papers* (NMML).

or of the national interest in general, but merely to satisfy certain political and provincial interests. You know that the AIRF had welcomed the idea of regrouping of the Indian railways. But we had put forward certain governing principles, which were generally acceptable to your Ministry. In accordance with this understanding, we had been assured that organized Labour would be taken into confidence and consulted at every important stage. But when the original scheme of the Railway Board was so drastically altered, there was no reference to labour, nor, I believe, to any other of the parties concerned. On behalf of labour I must protest against this unilateral decision.

Yours sincerely,
Jayaprakash

177. Statement regarding Shifting of the North Eastern Railway Headquarters from Calcutta to Gorakhpur, Patna, 28 March 1952[1]

The proposal to station the headquarters of this railway at Gorakhpur instead of Calcutta would mean eventually mass transfer of staff, fresh expenditure on a huge scale and serious inconvenience and harm to trade and industry. Calcutta is an industrial and commercial nerve centre and the difficulties that industry and commerce would have to face in dealing with a railway with headquarters so remote would not be easily surmountable. Not only would trade and industry suffer but also the railway itself. The decision to locate the North Eastern Railway headquarters at Gorakhpur has been taken against all previous proposals and assurances and is based not on technical, economic or rational but entirely on political and provincial considerations. It would be ruinous to the nation if provincial interests are allowed to override the national good. From the point of view of the railway staff, the Gorakhpur headquarters would mean, in spite of current assurances to the contrary, large-scale transfers, uprooting and breaking up of families and homes.

The All-India Railwaymen's Federation had welcomed the proposal for the regrouping of the Indian Railways in the interest of rationalization and national economy. There were, however, certain governing principles which were put forward by the Federation and which were generally accepted by the Railway Ministry. It was, for instance, suggested that organized labour should be taken into confidence and consulted at every important stage, and that the interests of the staff should always be taken into consideration

[1]Adapted from *The Searchlight*, 29 March 1952.

and given due weight. But for some inexplicable reason these principles have been entirely disregarded in the case of the proposed North Eastern Railway. The original picture of this railway as drawn by the Railway Board has completely been mutilated and altered by the Central Advisory Committee and neither considerations of operational efficiency, national defence, economy, service to trade and industry nor the interests of the staff have been taken into account. Nor was the Federation or its affiliated unions that are directly concerned, consulted before the drastic changes were hurriedly made at the final stage by a poorly attended Central Advisory Committee. The indiscriminate cutting up of the EIR, particularly the truncating of the Allahabad division, is bound seriously to affect operational efficiency and convert Moghalsarai which is the most focal point in the entire railway system of the country into a congested bottle-neck.

In view of all these considerations I earnestly urge the Hon'ble Railway Minister to stay action in regard to this matter, and either to revert to the original scheme of the Railway Board or to have the new scheme examined by an expert committee.

178. To Ramanandan Mishra, 12 April 1952[1]

Dear Ramanandan Babu,

I received your letter.[2] I have nothing to say after knowing your views about me. Please do whatever you think proper.

Yours,
Jayaprakash

[1] *J.P. Papers* (NMML). Original in Hindi.
[2] See Appendix 20.

179. To Asoka Mehta, 21 April 1952[1]

Dear Asoka,

I came here [Calcutta] on the 17th and was to go from here to Dehra Doon, Delhi and then to Bombay. But unfortunately I fell ill and am still in bed—pain in the ear and fever. There is no fever today and the pain too has

[1] *Brahmanand Papers* (NMML).

subsided. If doctors permit I shall leave for Bombay on the 23rd by the BNR mail reaching there on the 25th.

At Patna I had received your wire about the chairmanship of the special conference, to which I had replied suggesting that you request Lohia instead to preside. I hope you received that telegram and Lohia has agreed.

Regarding our stand on the Presidential election issue, I think we have no alternative but to support K.T. Shah. If we don't, apart from everything else, there will be a great setback to our efforts to bring the non-CP leftists near us. Tridib Chaudhury,[2] Soumyen Tagore,[3] Meghnad Saha[4]—all of whom I met here and at Patna—are anxious that we support Shah. We will alienate them all if we don't, and in return we shall get nothing.

More when we meet,

Yours affectionately,
Jayaprakash

P.S: Apart from the HMS and Cultural Congress programmes please see that no public engagement is fixed for me in advance. I shall have to rest more than work.

[2] Tridib Kumar Chaudhury (1911-97); played a prominent role in the organization of Revolutionary Socialist Party in 1940; elected to Lok Sabha from Beherampur Constituency from 1952 onwards for six terms; was put up as a joint candidate by several parties to contest presidentship of Indian Republic in 1974, but lost.

[3] Soumyendranath Tagore—For biographical note on Soumyendranath Tagore see item no. 148, fn. 3 in this volume.

[4] Meghnad Saha (1893-1991); eminent scholar of Physics; President Indian Science Congress 1934; President National Institute of Science 1937-8; Member National Planning Committee of Indian National Congress, 1938; President Royal Asiatic Society of Bengal 1945; President Postgraduate Studies in Science, Calcutta University 1947; member University Commission, Govt. of India 1948-9.

180. To K.K. Menon, 21 April 1952[1]

Dear K.K.,

I came here [Calcutta] on the 17th and since the next morning I am lying ill—pain in the ear & fever. Both symptoms have dispeared now and I hope to be able to leave for Bombay on the 23rd April by the BNR mail (via Nagpur) reaching there on the 25th.

[1] *Brahmanand Papers* (NMML).

I received P.T.'s[2] wire at Patna. Before leaving I shall send you a wire so that some one can meet me at the station.

Sometime ago you had sent me a communique asking my opinion about the Presidential election. I feel that we have no alternative but to support K.T. Shah. Tridib Chaudhury, whom I met at Patna, and Soumyen Tagore and Meghnad Shah, whom I met here are all very keen that we support Shah. If we don't we will alienate them all and get nothing in return. Besides, in spite of what Jawaharlal might say Rajen Babu is a Party candidate. I am writing to Asoka also to the same effect.

I hope you are all well.

Affectionately,
Jayaprakash

P.S.: I hope there will be no crowd at the station.

[2] P.T. stands for Purushottam Trikamdas.

181. Statement about Firing on Gorakhpur Railway Workers, Bombay, 26 April 1952[1]

I demand a judicial inquiry into the firing on Gorakhpur railway workers, which resulted in two deaths. While I appeal to the strikers and other railwaymen to be disciplined I also call upon the Government to punish those responsible for the firing. From press reports the firing seems to have been wholly unwarranted.

Since assuming power the Congress administration has shown scant regard for human life. The Congress probably feels that people have endorsed their policy of treating human life so lightly and for facing brick-bats with bullets. It is for the people to make the Congress learn the simple civilized lesson that mass massacre is not the only way of controlling an unruly crowd and that a policeman's life is no more precious than that of an ordinary citizen.

If the people of this country are to breathe the air of freedom, the present gun and lathi rule must be replaced with something more humane and civilized. The Gorakhpur firing deserves severe condemnation and those responsible should be punished.

[1] Adapted from *National Herald*, 28 April 1952.

182. Speech at a Public Meeting, Bombay, 30 April 1952[1]

I urge the people to start a countrywide agitation against the rise in food grain prices in order to force the hands of Government in the matter. If need be, we should offer 'satyagraha' and court arrest if Government remains adamant.

The Socialist Party should prepare the people for this struggle by offering volunteers in hundreds. If Gandhiji were alive today, I feel sure that he would have supported any movement to fight injustice, from without or within, against the people.

I strongly denounce the Government policy of taking away land from the small farmer for tillage by big zamindars. On the one hand Acharya Vinoba Bhave, a true disciple of the Mahatma, is roaming over the country for Bhoomidan so that every farmer would have a plot of land to himself, Government by its policy are reversing the process.

The day is not distant, when Acharya Bhave and Socialist Party would join hands to unite the millions of small peasant-farmers in the country to fight against the Government policy, which is responsible for growing unemployment.

I ask the people not to ignore the prospect of the next five years of Congress rule even though they are likely to forget the lesson of the past five years. You may recall Mr. Nehru's pre-election promise to clean up the Congress, to fight corruption and to eradicate poverty. Where is the purification? Where is the much-promised reformation of the Congress? The same old Pradesh Committees continue and the same old cabinet formations are to be seen.

If the experience of the past five years be any indication, I see a gloomy future for the country under the Congress rule. I ask the people not to sit with folded hands, but organize themselves into a 'Sangathan' and force the Government to give up their wrong policies.

To the small traders and petty merchants and the service men of the middle classes, I suggest the setting up of consumer's cooperative societies and health societies for combating the black-market and alleviating their grievances. The present policy of the Government of setting up big industries has acutely aggravated the problem of unemployment.

[1] Adapted from *Bombay Chronicle*, 1 May 1952.

183. Speech on May Day, Bombay, 1 May 1952[1]

The state of the trade union movement in the country is far from satisfactory. The working class is not the force it could and should be in the economic, political and social life of the country. This weakness of organized labour is due to the baneful influence of political parties which has resulted in multiplicity of rival unions, to the recent labour legislation and lastly to workers' apathy to trade unionization. The whole structure of trade unionism would have to be changed if the apathy of the workers has to be eliminated.

It is necessary to make the workers union-minded through collective agreement and suitable legislation. In this direction a beginning can be made in private industry and the labour class itself can be educated. I deplore that the Indian labour is politically so backward as to re-establish a conservative party in power. It is a matter for deep reflection on this May Day for all the working men and women of this country.

The other causes of labour weakness are that Government has been partial in its labour policy. The favoured treatment given to the INTUC has lured away the ranks of labour from other independent labour organizations. I warn the misled parties not to sacrifice their independence for immediate and transitory gains. The labour laws have entangled labour in the coils of litigation, delays and futility.

I appeal to the United Trade Union Congress and even the INTUC to sink their political differences and present a joint front for the progress of the working class.

Communism is a new threat to labour. If anybody is responsible for breaking up the unity of the workers of the world, it is the Communists. I ask the workers to do a little introspection on this day on the state of labour in the country and try to remove its weakness so that labour might have its rightful voice in the political, social and economic affairs of the country.

[1] Adapted from *Bombay Chronicle*, 2 May 1952.

184. Intervention in the Debate on General Secretary's Report (by Asoka Mehta) at the Pachmarhi Convention, 24 May 1952[1]

Normally I would not have intervened in this debate. I decided to speak because of certain things which have been said here.

[1] *Report of the Special Convention of the Socialist Party held at Pachmarhi*, Madhya Pradesh, 23-7 May 1952, pp. 23-7.

I am intervening more in self-explanation than in reply to the criticism of the General Secretary's Report.

Whenever a battle is lost the responsibility for the defeat is always squarely that of the general. I admit that the party suffered defeat though not to the extent some of you have imagined. The leadership of the Party must take full responsibility for that defeat. But if you will excuse me for a personal note, the responsibility is more mine than of my colleagues, and I have come forward to make that admission. During the past few years I have been, for good or ill, mainly responsible for the development of Party policy and programme. It is for me, therefore, to take full responsibility for what happened at the elections. And it is to me, more than to any one else, that your criticism and censure should be directed.

It is natural that defeat should create lack of confidence in the leadership. But if this feeling were to be extended to the Party itself or to its fundamental principles, it would be disastrous. It is not so much the defeat, but the reaction to it, in the ranks of the Party, that is worrying me. I observed during this debate a feeling among the Party ranks that our policies were responsible for our electoral defeat. I was pained at this reaction and I tried to explore and re-examine and locate the errors in policy. But I did not find any such error. There was nothing wrong with the policy or programme of the Party.

It has been suggested by some of you that the defeat could have been avoided if we had not deviated from our revolutionary path and had launched nationwide struggles. There was no such deviation, and there were any number of local struggles. No other party fought so zealously for the people. True, there was no 'nationwide' struggle launched. But when could such a struggle have been launched and how? At Kanpur we did think in terms of a nationwide struggle—a struggle for freedom. Had not the Congress accepted partition, I have no doubt this struggle would have been inevitable, and the party would have been in the forefront. But partition became a fact, and the terrible riots followed. Was a struggle possible then? Then Gandhiji was assassinated, and soon after we left the Congress. Don't forget, that was only four years ago. Our main and primary task was to build up the Party; open branches in every province, get workers, enroll members, extend the organization to the districts and lower down, propagate the message of the Party, start journals and periodicals, collect money for all this and many other activities. There were not many of us to do this, and they were breathlessly busy in carrying out this fundamental work. A nationwide struggle was not possible till the Party organization itself had become nationwide. Either we were wrong in trying to build up a nationwide organization, or you must understand that it was not possible to start a nationwide struggle before at least the foundation had been laid of a national organization.

I should remind you again that wherever possible local struggles were launched. The work done by Rammanohar in this connection is before you. He has been our guide to action. He jumped into struggles when occasion arose. He courted arrest a number of times. Asoka also did not idle. Remember that glorious textile strike of Bombay. So you will see that regional and partial struggles were not neglected. You have to go from strength to strength. Before a national struggle is launched strength and resources have to be built up; people have to be mobilized and enthused; public opinion has to be created and a struggle psychology has to be built up. These things take time. Nationwide struggles were visualized. It was felt that we may get an opportunity to do so after the general elections.

Some of you feel that I should have personally led a struggle. I could have; but you had burdened me with other responsibilities and tasks. The organizational responsibility was on me. There were the nationwide tours, the fund collections. I could not do everything at the same time.

I can understand if you argue that we could have gone in for a different policy and strategy. Instead of undertaking extensive organizational work we could have decided not to expand but concentrate on selected areas and could have launched well-conducted local struggles. But such a policy of intensive organizational and struggle activities would not have given us the necessary national status and face. Imagine what would have been the position in the South today had such a policy been followed. Till 1947 we had practically no organization in the South. We started almost from scratch. If we have secured a few seats in the South, if there are Party branches in all the states, it is because some of us went to the South frequently and spent time and collected money. We could have remained in our respective provinces, Rammanohar in U.P. and I in Bihar. Those States would have gained, but the Party would have been practically non-existent in the South.

The Party had to choose between intensive and extensive work, and I think, the choise made of extensive work, was correct.

What about the future then? We will make progress, I have no manner of doubt about it. But let us not be under any illusion that we will achieve some revolutionary change in two or three years. A true revolutionary should be capable of patience and should work diligently and regularly even when the fruit is no where in sight.

There has been much discussion here about the causes of our defeat. Asoka has given his assessment of the past. Some of you have your own reason to give. While these reasons are valid in their own ways, I approach the question in a different way. I think that the real reason of our defeat is within us. Let us not blame our resources and organizational weakness. I believe that if we were better individually, then even with the limited resources in men, money and organization, we could have done better. The very first thing I did after the election results were out was to examine myself before finding fault elsewhere. Let each one of us do an honest self-searching. How much time and energy were we devoting to Party work? How truthful and honest were we in our work? How selfless? Were we free from groupism? Did we train ourselves well and study Party literature and other necessary literature necessary for our work? Do we observe discipline? If we are 'whole-timers' do we give at least eight hours every day to Party work? Is there system in our work, and do we try to avoid waste? It is the character of the Party worker that makes the Party more than theses and doctrines. Self criticism is not criticism of others, such as the General Secretary, but criticism, first of all, of oneself. If everyone of you undertook such criticism, you would realize that you could have *been* and *done* better, and had everyone of you done better, the Party as a whole would have done far better.

Many of you live in an unreal world. You do not read Party literature. It has been my experience that a large majority of our workers have not even read the Policy Statement. You run after current ideas and thought, as a result of which there has been a terrible barrenness in the realm of thinking. The tendency is strong to run away from fundamental thinking, from new ideas, fresh approaches and new thoughts. Do not be scared by freshness. Objective conditions have changed. New situations have arisen. Can we learn and understand the objective conditions and new situations if we shun fundamental thinking and freshness of mind?

Let me conclude now. Let me sum up in one sentence the cause of our failure at the elections. We failed because we had not put in enough work. Work is not merely waging the class-struggle. There is constructive work which we had sadly neglected. There are many other kinds of work. Let us do our work, our appointed tasks, honestly, diligently and devotedly. We can leave the future then to take care of itself. Can anyone suspect that the future will be anything but the most glorious?

185. Speech on the Chairman's Address (by Rammanohar Lohia), at the Pachmarhi Convention, 24 May 1952[1]

Comrades! Let me first remove a few misunderstandings. It might appear to you to be a strange procedure that the Chairman's Address should be subjected to discussion. But this procedure has been deliberately adopted. The General Secretary had proposed to the Chairman that he should deal in his Address with the doctrinal problems of the Movement and discuss the

[1]*Report of the Special Convention of the Socialist Party held at Pachmarhi*, Madhya Pradesh, 23-7 May 1952, pp. 27-34.

[2]For the text of Lohia's address see Appendix 21

political line for the future. The Address then could become a basis for discussion at the Conference. You will all agree, I am sure, that Rammanohar has done an outstanding job of it.

There is another misunderstanding under which some of you are labouring. You fear that you are going to be committed to vital doctrinal formulations without being given sufficient time to discuss them. There should be no such fear. The Chairman's Address is the basis for discussion. After it has been discussed here, it will be re-written, if necessary, in the light of the discussion, and published as a pamphlet and serialized in Party organs. Party units and members will then discuss it further, after which the document would be placed before the General Council for final acceptance. This was the procedure adopted at Kanpur with regard to the Policy Statement. Thus you will see that no attempt is being made to force you or to rush you.

Let me now turn to the Address.

Through his Address Lohia has placed before the Party an integrated doctrine. His is a new approach and not a deviation as some of you have alleged. It will be entirely wrong to say that the Party is being made to face something which is quite different from whatever we have understood so far to mean democratic socialism. As I have said, Lohia has achieved an integration of socialist thinking. Integration is not merely bringing together of scattered ideas, but it is an act of creation. In this sense Lohia's thesis is new and not new. It is not new in that it has carried forward the tradition of our doctrinal development, gathered the loose trends of thought. It is new in the sense that he has woven a pattern out of these trends, and created a body of socialist thought whose limbs are not borrowed from different sources but grow out of fundamental roots of thinking and form parts of an organized whole.

Let us trace back the evolution of the Party's ideology. When in 1934 the Party was founded, we called ourselves a Marxist Party. What did we understand by Marxism then? What did Marxism mean to Socialists the world over? Those were the days when all Socialists drew inspiration from the Russian Revolution and the efforts of the Bolshevik Party to build socialism. Generally speaking, Marxism was till then very largely identified, at least for us, with all that Soviet Russia stood for. Even then, it should not be forgotten, our policies were not identical with those of the Communist Party of India, which was connected with the Communist International and followed Russia unquestioningly. There were two vital differences, among others, between us. Though we were admirers of Russia, it never occurred to us that we should be guided by her in our policies. The other point of difference was that we believed that as Socialists we must take full part in the freedom movement and, for that purpose, work through the Indian

National Congress. The Communists at that time were out of the Congress and vigorously opposed to it.

Slowly, however, as new experiences, national and international, started accumulating, question marks appeared on our horizons. Our experiences of the communist movement in India was a great lesson and an eye-opener. We went out of our way, as you will remember, and admitted the Communists into our Party in the fond hope that we shall thereby achieve socialist unity. That experiment of four and half years taught us unforgettable lessons. They taught us about the utter unscrupulousness of the Communists and their lying and deceit. Above all, we learnt that they had no faith in unity with any party whatever, that they are a branch of the Communist International, which at all events must maintain a separate branch in every country. We learnt further that as tools of the Communist International they were not free agents but acted as directed from Moscow.

I have said that we started as ardent admirers of Soviet Russia. But the first shock came with the first great purge in 1936. In that and the second purge that followed, practically all the Old Guard of the Bolshevik Party, the men who had made the Revolution, were liquidated. There was obviously something vitally wrong in Russia. Then came other shocks, the biggest being Stalin's pact with Hitler just before the war in 1939. Then the war started and Stalin divided up Poland with Hitler. Later Hitler attacked Russia. The attitude of the Communists, all over the world, towards the war went through interesting somersaults.

We discovered that the Communist Party of Russia was prepared to go to any length, was prepared to compromise its ideals, for the sake of Russian nationalism, while the Communist Party of India was advised to sacrifice India's national interest for the national interests of Soviet Russia. Further material on the internal situation in Russia became available in ever-growing mass and the character of her totalitarian polity and economy became clearer and clearer.

All these experiences and information slowly changed our minds. The question marks increased in size. We became aware that the differences between us and the Communists were much more fundamental than those thought of earlier.

When we met after the war at Kanpur in 1947 the need was felt to restate our fundamentals. The totalitarian distortions of socialism in Russia had made it necessary that we define the ideals—the true socialism—for which we were working. Thus it was that we defined our goal as democratic socialism and asserted that socialism could not exist without democracy. Since then we have been trying to clarify our picture of democratic socialism, its methodology, its technique, its philosophy. Practice and experience raised further questions. Further answers were sought. At every annual conference thereafter something was added to the picture, to the evolution of our ideology and clarification of doctrinal issues.

Let me deal here with the question whether we are or not Marxists or whether Lohia's doctrine is consistent with Marxism. Personally, I feel that we should not cut ourselves off from the Marxian tradition. Traditionalism has both advantages and disadvantages, but if it does not enslave the mind, it lends ballast and strength and provides working hypotheses. But there is one danger in the controversy about Marxism and non-Marxism—the controversy is apt to get lost in words and formulas and the content and the substance are forgotten. Moreover, Marxism, in practice, has often meant all manner of contradictory ideas, and persons thirsting for the blood of one another are insisting on calling themselves Marxists. Under these conditions, the controversy and the label tend to lose all meaning.

In this evolution of the Party's policy and method Lohia's Address is a major contribution; it is at once original and yet crystallizes and consolidates much that has gone before. Some of the issues posed by him were raised before also. These were debated in the past six years but in a vague way. Lohia has in his Address taken a great stride forward by systematizing much of this ferment; his Address is a beautiful summation of the efforts of the past few years. The Policy Statement, as we all have felt, is incomplete at a number of places. It does not deal with the ideological considerations that arise in the struggle for socialism. Lohia's formulations will help us to re-state our Policy Statement in a manner that will remove these lacunae.

I do not propose to discuss everything that he has said or the manner in which he has stated it. I am in complete agreement with what he has said, though the manner of putting it may differ. Please remember that like others we cannot live on ready-made doctrines and canned ideas. Our ideology has to emerge out of our experience; its constants must remain, but its variables will keep changing.

I have always believed myself to be a Marxist and I approach Lohia's Address as a Marxist. Frankly, even then I have no difficulty in accepting what he has said. Marxism is not a dogma. It is a scientific method of studying changes in society and bringing about social change, and as long as we preserve this scientific attitude, we will always have the courage to face new facts. Since the death of Marx so many new problems have come up, new situations have arisen that their answers are not available readymade in Marx. A Marxist, however, is never afraid of facing new situations as and when they arise. He is never afraid of saying that for such and such a problem Marx offers no solution and therefore let us find out an appropriate solution after a careful analysis and study of the objective conditions. I believe that is what Lohia has done.

Sheela Perera has said earlier that the Russian Revolution should continue to inspire the toilers of the world. It was because of this revolution that, she argues, the Russian State got a glorious and progressive economic base but unfortunately Stalinist bureaucracy has raised a vile fabric on this foundation. Her analysis is fundamentally wrong. In Russia today there is not only heavy concentration of political power but also of economic power. It is not that the Stalinist dictatorship is merely political, its grip in economic life is equally pervasive. What solution has she for this problem? She wants to destroy one dictatorship; but what happens to the other? Lohia has offered a correct characterization of the communist system. Was a more searching and thought provoking attempt ever made before?

He has also explained the full significance of decentralization through the four pillar State and has brought within the same focus the question of labour intensive versus capital intensive production. These issues were raised before, but a co-ordinated answer is available today.

Marx had said that socialism is born in the womb of capitalism and the capitalist chain breaks at the strongest link of its development. What sort of capitalism was before Marx then? What is the nature of capitalism in our country today? Marx never visualized it, because the present state of capitalist development belongs to the post-Marx period. It is said that a chain of historical events leads to socialism. Surely you are not going to wait till the fateful, final event occurs. That is not what Marx meant.

When we are faced with new situations, unique problems, fresh approaches and original thinking become necessary. At least that is what I have learnt from Marxism. But some of you who swear by the name of Marx are perturbed when that is done and immediately a cry is raised that Marxism is being rejected. Science grows through a ceaseless quest and through adding on of new things. Marxism is not a static thought. It does not shun improvements and fresh approaches. Marxian thought is also capable of interpretation and development. Lenin did it. Stalin could do it. But if some one of us does it we are told that we are abandoning Marxism! I therefore sometimes feel that we should give up Marxism.

I submit that the Socialist Party is the only Marxist party in India. We have not only correctly understood Marxism but have applied it also correctly. Even then it is not necessary to declare every time that we are Marxist. Our objective is clear. Just as we recognize the over-arching significance of social values so also our means are well demarcated. In each country circumstances and objective conditions are different. The real thing is to understand and correctly analyse these conditions and apply our findings scientifically. But when people do this it will be wrong to ask them whether they are applying Marxism or not. Such a question is irrelevant because with such an attitude you are not inclined to judge issues objectively, and when you fail to judge issues objectively, you fail to judge ideas placed before you on their merit. You get involved in endless argumentations, quotations and interpretations. That is not Marxism.

This futile controversy of who is a Marxist or who is not leads to an attitude which makes us believe that we are better Marxists than others. And thus we come across a strange situation wherein two Marxists not only make mutually contradictory statements but sometimes even get at each other's throats.

Marx was not faced with the realities of today. The economic situation in two-thirds of the world is a challenge which Marx never faced. He could not think for all times to come. Neither had he a solution for every kind of situation. Lohia has correctly explained this new situation and suggested a methodology, technique and economic and political organizations needed to meet the challenge.

He has explained what socialism is and what it ought to be. You cannot build up an adequate doctrinal foundation for socialism by borrowing supposed economic democracy from communism and political democracy from capitalism. He is right in his indictment that socialism has so far failed to secure a doctrinal foundation of consistent logic. He has invited our attention to the necessity of achieving harmony of economic and general aims. Our Policy Statement is incomplete in this respect. Will it not be worthwhile to remove this inadequacy?

Some people claim that the Soviet State has a progressive economic base, only the Stalinist dictatorship is parasitic. This is a wrong characterization. The economic organization of the Soviet State is the real basis of its dictatorship. Application of Marxism to the Russian situation led three Russian leaders to three different formulations of economic policy. Bukharin had his own theory, Trotsky had another while Stalin had his own ideas. Ultimately, Stalin's views prevailed. The political organization of the Russian State emerged out of its economic organization. You cannot therefore separate the economic foundation of Soviet Russia from its political structure.

Lohia has correctly pointed out the irrelevance of both the capitalist and the communist systems to the situation in two-thirds of the world. He offers decentralization of economic and political power as a solution.

There are two other fundamental ideas of Lohia to which I wish to draw your attention. His formulations with regard to immediacy in struggle and organization, immediacy in science and planning, immediacy in democracy and power are brilliant in conception and fundamental in thought and approach.

This theory of immediacy leads us to the question of means and ends. Methodology is intimately connected with ideology. Out of the doctrine and ideology flow both organization and method. If we are inspired by such a high aim like creation of a classless society or even a higher aim of stateless society, the methods we adopt for its realization must also be pure. As Lohia has put it each act should contain its own justification. It must not justify a present lie by future truth, an immediate bureaucratization by remote democracy, a present sacrifice of national freedom by a remote One World. It should not reject the notion of absolute morality. If we adopt foul means for the achievement of a glorious end, we must face the shipwreck of our hopes.

Lohia has put before us a well-rounded doctrinal foundation for the Party. The task is not yet complete. But a beginning has been made. Let us not forget that Marxist philosophy is incomplete, it will ever remain incomplete, for scientific thought ever grows and with every addition it becomes richer in content. Lenin had once said that Marxism is a confluence of three streams of ideas: Marx took classical economics from England, revolutionary socialism from France and philosophy from Germany and achieved a synthesis of his own. Out of this synthesis he later developed his theories, which came to be known as the fundamentals of Marxism: dialectical materialism, class struggle and surplus value. As Marx had to achieve a synthesis, so have the Indian Socialists. Why should we not combine the Marxian thought with the thought and practice of Mahatma Gandhi and achieve a synthesis of our own?

Lohia has given facts and figures to prove the impossibility and inapplicability of mass production technique to India. To his technique of decentralization also must be applied the test of immediacy. We cannot take decisions about what will be done a hundred years hence. We are concerned with the immediate future. We should think and plan for a generation or two.

186. Speech Summing up the Discussion on the Political Line at the Pachmarhi Convention, 25 May 1952[1]

There has been very little discussion on the political line. Everyone was concerned with the doctrine. Some comrades have reminded the leaders that they expect the Convention to lay down a positive policy and a new approach which would enthuse the Party rank and file and give a new message of hope to the people, while some others have wondered why the ideological issues have been raised at this time. And yet you have debated the doctrine and said nothing about the political line.

[1]*Report of the Special Convention of the Socialist Party held at Pachmarhi*, Madhya Pradesh, 23-7 May 1952, pp. 59-65.

The political line flows out of the doctrine. Critics want to know what the Socialist Party stands for. They claim that it is easy to understand what the Congress or the Communist Parties want, what their ideology is, and what they stand for. Do you not want to tell the people in unequivocal terms what your policy and your ideology is? If you do not have a clear and unambiguous picture of socialism before you, what can you tell the people? You must first understand what you stand for and then explain it to the people. Otherwise the same old talk of the 'middle path' will continue.

I am in complete agreement with the political line formulated by Lohia. He has correctly characterized the Communist Party and the Congress as also communism and capitalism. We must avoid the danger of being confused either with the Congress or with the Communists and bring out the real differences. That is the importance of having our own distinctive doctrine and approach.

The political line formulated by Lohia is not something entirely new. Get rid of this complex that in this Convention you are being made to face wholly new things.

Our first concern should be to have our distinctive approach and build up our own strength. That does not depend only on organization. We have always said that we must go among the people, associate ourselves with their joys and sufferings, combat the injustices from which they suffer and create and build within them the necessary will and strength to fight for liberty and justice. Our constructive activities should have a vitalizing approach. These must bring relief to the people, and while releasing the creative energies of the people we must create in them an increasing awareness for social change. All this has been said before. But how much of it have we done? How many of you have said that we were defeated in the elections because we neglected constructive activities.

If we want that the Party should grow, its influence should increase and that it should become an effective instrument of social change, we must create within the existing society manifestations and evidence of the new society we want to build up. Struggles alone cannot achieve this. Who can deny the revolutionary content of the slogan 'one hour to the nation'? Who can deny the revolutionary role the spade can play? The fact that these revolutionary slogans failed to catch the imagination of the people is entirely our fault. The message of the spade can spread only if we take to it. People will give one hour to the nation if we take it up as a continuing activity.

Do we lack faith in constructive activity? Do we not consider them revolutionary activities? We cannot have struggles every day. If we take to combative activities only, the question is what happens next when we have exhausted our strength. Constructive activities and struggles must be so intertwined and mutually complementary that one strengthens the other. Mahatma Gandhi was the greatest technologist of revolution. His was a continuous programme of construction and struggles. He had struck a creative equilibrium between constructive and combative activities. Continuing constructive activity builds up the strength to resist evil and injustices and opens up almost unlimited reservoirs of strength. Struggles in their turn, when they come, sharpen social awareness, and help to give decisive orientations to the minds and lives of men.

In this connection I draw your attention to Lohia's idea of socialist ashrams. Let every member of the National Executive take to this activity or select his locality, and try to build up a model of our ideas. If we had done this before, it would not have been less effective than struggles.

If all our comrades give their active consideration to this aspect of constructive activity, and take to it as a continuing function, sloth will disappear, faith will be restored and strengthened. We must also enter the field of activity thoroughly equipped ideologically and with a clear grasp of the doctrine.

Lohia has kindled a burning desire in every heart, the desire to resist and fight injustice wherever it occurs. Let this fire spread. It does not matter even if our organization breaks up while we are resisting and fighting injustices. There has to be diligent action and intelligent approach. Public opinion must be built up, people's awareness to injustice and will to resist it must be given a shape and, in the meantime, the wrong-doer should be given a chance to correct himself. If all other means of correcting injustice fail the way of struggle is there, and we should not hesitate to go that way. We must then throw ourselves headlong into it.

There has been a lot of talk about revision of the Policy Statement. Some have complained that an unnecessary effort is being made to add 'peaceful' to democratic means. Others want to remove the ambiguity in the Policy Statement. I think all this unnecessary. The confusion is not due to the Policy Statement about means. Neither is there confused thinking. 'Under the existing circumstances, only the democratic means would be the correct means to follow' is a forthright statement and is in keeping with the historic need of the times and is a complete statement. Lohia has referred to spontaneous violence. I fervently hope that it will never come to pass.

Some of you have asked Lohia if we can fight dictatorship with non-violence. I think it should be possible. But the possibility apart, this is a hypothetical question.

The ideas expressed by Lohia about satyagraha and class struggle should dispel all doubts. Injustice is to be resisted and fought. The menace of communism is also to be fought. Prove it to the people that it is not the communist way of murder and loot and degradation of human personality but the socialist way which would bring about a revolution.

The Socialists do not have to wait till the capture of power. To be able to create a force in the society which can transform it, power or no power, is the test of socialist action.

Do not wait for instructions from the centre to resist injustice. As in constructive activity, so in struggles, there should be decentralization of initiative. It is eagerness to do it and awareness of the situation which alone can take us forward on the road we have chosen. We must build up a big force today. That is one of our tasks. There are forces outside the Socialist Party whom we must attract towards us. The Socialist Party must work for the integration of all progressive forces of revolution. This work we could not do before for various reasons. Today, in the new situation, efforts for it must be renewed. It is out of ignorance and unawareness that people are attracted by the Communist slogan of integration of anti-Congress forces. That is not the need of the hour. Once before the Party had invited fraternal parties and forces, linked together by deep rooted allegiance to nationalism, devotion to the liberties and rights of the people, and burning anxiety for social change, to come together and build up the vital leadership that the people need to fight and end the reactionary rule of the Congress. We must even appeal to the radicals inside the Congress Party to leave it and help us in this task. We must convince them about the futility of appealing to the Socialist Party to return to the Congress, and must convince them that their place is in the Socialist Party.

We must also show enough maturity and try to understand the Sarvodaya movement. The Sarvodayavadis today find themselves in the same state of affairs as the Congress. They are a society of men with different approaches and often with conflicting affiliations. Some among them are attracted towards communism, some continue to treat the Congress party as their political platform, while quite a few feel that they are very much near us—ideologically. This latter group of Sarvodayavadis also desire to co-operate with the Socialist Party. We too should agree to get together. Why should all such forces whose ideological motivation are the same and who agree on certain fundamental approaches get at each other's throat?

Vinoba Bhave has started his movement for redistribution of land. He calls it *Bhoodan Yajna*. What does he want? What does he propose to achieve? Critics say: 'His methods cannot solve the land problem. Vinoba is begging for land. He is essentially a class collaborationist. His *Bhoodan Yajna* is an effort at class conciliation. It will blunt our instrument of revolution if we co-operate with him.' Let me assure you that to ask for 'Dan' is not the same thing as begging. We must try to understand Vinoba Bhave's efforts and not ridicule them. It is another matter whether his efforts can solve the land problem or not. One thing is certain. He is mobilizing public opinion in favour of land redistribution. He is focusing the attention of the people and government on this problem. He is even thinking of launching a nation-wide satyagraha movement at the end of two years if the Government fails to redistribute land. Do not run away with the idea that he does not realize the limitations of 'change of heart'. Who are the people that are responding to his appeal? His efforts have such an appeal that even the poorest of the peasants owing just a meagre 3-4 acres of land are giving away a substantial portion of their holdings. Is his not a revolutionary appeal? Vinoba Bhave is the spark of the revolutionary force of Gandhism. If this spark and the Socialist Party can combine, it can shake up the whole country and start a big conflagration against injustice. Such a dynamic combination of forces cannot be achieved by combining with the signboard parties.

Then there are the communal parties. With such parties who are given to politics by religion we can have no truck and our policy of uncompromising opposition to them must be pursued vigorously. But towards the frustrated youth of the Rashtriya Swayamsevak Sangh we may well have a sympathetic attitude. The young boys and girls who belong to the RSS are all drawn from the lower middle classes. They are a disciplined lot. If in this hour of their frustration and disillusionment the Socialist Party can hold forth an effective alternative to them it may be possible to win over the best of them. Neither the RSS nor the Jan Sangh has any future and their ideals no more inspire the youth who belong to their fold. Let us not treat these young men as untouchables.

Then there are such other parties whose policies are influenced by two predominant impulses. There are those among them who consider themselves as better Communists than the Communist Party, while there are those others who are motivated by the impulse of loyalty to national freedom. The attitude of the latter towards democracy is not the same as ours, while most of them have an urge for communistic dictatorship.

But with regard to these lefts parties it will be of interest to observe a strange phenomenon which has overtaken them. You will note that each one of them—The Revolutionary Communist Party, the Peasants & Workers Party, the Revolutionary Socialist Party, the Forward Bloc—is split up into two because the two impulses alternate.

There are a few among these leftists who are near us. We should draw closer to these and work in cooperation with them.

The next group of parties are those who combine both radical and conservative tendencies, such as the Scheduled Castes Federation, the Kisan Mazdoor Praja Party and the Jharkhand Party. We must take these parties along with us. The backward and the exploited people are living in isolation today. Through our alliance with Scheduled Castes Federation we have an opportunity to work with them and pull down this wall of isolation. We must work for the political integration of these elements with us.

In the Madras resolution our policy with regard to these forces and the left parties has been clearly laid down. If we must remedy the fragmentation of our political life, the policy of consolidation of such elements and forces who are loyal to national freedom and democracy and who stand for social change must be pursued for achieving a massive force of radicalism and socialism. This should not only be our political line but a movement. We must also throw our doors open to such of the left parties as fulfil the three conditions.

The leftist parties which had moved very near the Communists and had walked into their trap of United Front are today moving away from them. The Communist policy of fronts today stands thoroughly exposed. While the left parties are moving away from the Communists our attitude towards them must be governed by two considerations. We must follow a policy of breaking them away from the Communists and bringing them as near to us a possible. We must work for this political consolidation. The situation in Bengal today needs an effective execution of this policy. Before elections we had achieved consolidation with Forward Bloc (Subhasist) and the Revolutionary Communist Party (Soumyen Tagore). At the same time let us take in those who want to merge with us.

The Kisan Mazdoor Praja Party is another story. Before elections we tried to have an electoral understanding with them. But their attitude was unhelpful. They consider themselves the only inheritors of Gandhiji's ideas of a Sarvodaya Society. Yet during the elections they entered into an alliance with the Communists. Kripalaniji had no experience of the Communist embrace of death. I hope they have realized their mistake. There are indications today that they want to end their honeymoon with the Communists. Purshottam Trikamdas who was recently in Delhi has done excellent work in this connection. Because of his efforts and those of Rammanohar, there is a possibility of the formation of a bloc with the KMPP in the Parliament. Whatever our past experience, this bloc should be achieved. Kripalaniji is even thinking in terms of a merger with us.

Such a policy towards the KMPP will help our efforts for political consolidation in Bengal. Dr. P.C. Ghosh has often declared that Gandhism is non-violent socialism. If he is earnest about it, he would realize that he is nearer to us than to the Communist and the separate existence of the Socialist Party and the KMPP becomes a political overlapping. This overlapping must end. After all what future has the KMPP? Their place is in the Socialist Party.

This should be our political line. This political line, if honestly pursued, will lead to a great movement for the consolidation of national life. We must address ourselves to this task. I am placing this political line before you for your approval.

187. To Jawaharlal Nehru, 25 May 1952[1]

Dear Bhai,[2]

I thank you for your letter regarding Jaggia. I hope you have talked to Nandaji about him and that it would be possible for you to do something for him.

I have yet to reply to two of your earlier letters. I do not mind telling you that the tone of those letters had so discouraged me that I thought no purpose would be served by continuing further the correspondence. But, in one of your later letters, you were good enough to ask me to see you when I went to Delhi next. As it happens I shall be in Delhi on the 29th of this month, but unfortunately only for a few hours. If you have time on that day I should like to meet you. I shall reach Delhi by the Grand Trunk Express and leave by the Delhi Express the same night.

Since there is this possibility of meeting you I should like to say something in reply to your earlier letters so that when we meet there would be some background of understanding.

I was happy to know from your letter of February 14 that the Ambassador of the time[3] had assured you that there was no truth in the allegation that the Indian Embassy at Washington was the source of the rumour that Lohia had brought with him American dollars for the Socialist Party. While it is difficult for me not to accept the then Ambassador's statement, I should like to draw your attention to the following:

In a letter of November 5, 1951, Harris Wofford wrote to Lohia: "I hear that you had to deny receiving 1,00,000 dollars. Sorry you had to deny it. We heard that tale even here probably from its source. An Embassy friend (your Embassy) told us authoritatively that, although I did not know it, the embassy had been informed by the USFBI that you got 1,00,000 dollars. Someone must have slipped it to you in your sleep or you did better in Los Angels—or was it Imperial Valley up in the plane? As if the FBI would send its reports to the Indian Embassy."

He wrote again to Lohia: "They want to try to find some way to cloud you. After the million dollars in America story (which we were told by the Embassy), the latest is that you are a notorious reactionary, as proved by

[1] *J.N. Papers*: Files at Home (NMML).

[2] See Appendix 22 for Nehru's reply to J.P.

[3] Vijaya Lakshmi Pandit.

the fact that you own a great Rickshaw Corporation! Which hits at your first principles."

You made a reference in your letter to some statements of Mr. Norman Thomas when he was visiting this country, It was interesting to find you taking so much pains to trace (if not to justify) through press cuttings from the *Janata*, *The News Chronicle*, etc., the origin of the propaganda about which I had complained to you. Personally, I do not see why it is wrong for a socialist to say that international socialism should come to the help of the socialist movement in a particular country. That, however, may be a debatable point. But, what I fail to understand is how such a statement can be the ground for people in this country or elsewhere to allege that the Socialist Party had actually accepted American money. You write that Thomas's statement was not contradicted. I am not sure about the propriety of a contradiction in such a case, but I hope you know that it was made absolutely clear to Thomas that the Socialist Party would not consider accepting any such aid.

Later, when Julius Braunthal, Secretary of the Socialist International, broached the question in a communication to our Foreign Affairs Committee, Lohia replied *interalia*:

> We have not so far understood the purpose of the fund. Your circular no. 1/52 of January 3rd indicates that the fund may be used for political purposes. I should like to point out with all humility that the Asian Socialist parties may not like the Socialist International to set up a fund to aid their political activities. Our Party's view on such a fund is very clear. In the past a few Socialist Parties from the West had offered to send us monetary help even for such activities as elections, which we had declined.
>
> I should therefore like to suggest to the Bureau and the Council of the S.I. that they may raise the fund but should earmark it to aid constructive activities like labour schools, cooperative activities of the trade unions and peasant organisations, scholarships to socialist youth and students who may like to go abroad to receive training, and for such other ad-hoc purposes like famine relief, flood relief etc.
>
> If the Socialist International would create such a non-political fund, our party would also cooperate in this effort.

You had also referred to Lohia's behaviour towards the Indian Embassy, which you have described as a 'pattern of courtesy'. I do not know anything about protocol but I have been advised by competent people that Lohia's stand was correct and that the Indian Embassy was guilty of discourtesy. Harris Wofford who was one of the sponsors of Lohia's American trip has brought out a booklet *Lohia and America Meet*, of which I am having a copy sent to you with certain passage marked. (I hope you will glance through the rest of the booklet too.) On pages 30-31, Wofford has dealt with the courtesies involved. I am also enclosing a copy of Lohia's letter to me which he had written upon reading your letter.

In your letter of February 7, you wrote about your having been "deeply pained at the numerous and continuous personal references made about me by the leaders of the Socialist Party." I am sorry that you have been so pained, but I wonder if you are aware of quite a different view of the matter, held even in Congress circles. For instance, there was a post-election article by Sampurnanandji in which he made a reference to 'the Socialists' soft corner for Shri Nehru from whom they had received nothing but kicks. There is also that somewhat sticky label of "Nehru's B Team" that has been attached to the Socialist Party. Further, the fact that the Socialist Party had the consideration not to set up a candidate against you also has some significance in this regard. I am not suggesting that had the Socialist Party contested your seat it would have made much difference to the results. But it was a political gesture, the meaning of which seems to have been completely missed by you and the Congress party.

To me, however, it is not so important who denounced whom. Individuals are of no great significance. What pained *me* was what you did to socialism. I wonder whether you have paused to consider the harm you have done to the cause in which you profess such faith. It is remarkable that on the one side you went on declaring yourself as a socialist and, on the other, opposing and ridiculing socialism. You have on occasions criticised all extant forms of socialist thought and practice, but I have searched in vain in your recent writings and speeches for your own picture of socialism. Don't you think you owe it to the people to tell them what according to you is true socialism? If you continue to call yourself a socialist without making any effort to give form to your faith, much less to practise it, are you not, to put it mildly, misleading the people?

At Delhi, I would be available at 8258.

As ever,
Jayaprakash

188. Speech moving the resolution on Political Line at the Pachmarhi Convention, 26 May 1952[1]

A number of comrades want to include communal parties in para 1. The idea of para 1 is to focus the attention on the artificial polarization. The communal parties are nowhere in the picture. Therefore nothing more can be added to para 1.

I however agree that a mention should be made of the communal parties and our policy towards them. With your permission I propose that to para 9, the following be added towards the end: *with regard to another group of parties that base themselves on communalism, the Convention reaffirms its policy of uncomprising opposition.*

I am also accepting V.D.N. Sahai's amendment which reads: *from para* 7, *line* 1, *delete the word 'reveal' and substitute it by 'fully exposed'*.

These amendments were accepted and the statement as amended was carried.

Statement on Political Line

1. This special Convention of the Socialist Party affirms that the Party shall not confuse its identity by coalitions or fronts with the Congress and Communist parties and directs its members so to behave that its features become sharply distinguishable and the message of socialism is clearly heard.
2. The essential duty of the Socialist Party is continually to refine itself as the instrument of socialism. Fear of isolation or escape from this duty must not be permitted to give rise to the diversionary wish for unprincipled alliances.
3. The Party must make comprehensive constructive work a continuing mode of its action. Out of such constructive work centres will arise its organization and volunteer bands and around them must be woven its network of study and training centres. Every member of the Party should participate actively in the community life.
4. The injustice and misery of present society must become for us constant spurs to action. Units and members of the Party must not wait for calls from above in order to resist injustice and misery. Such satyagraha or struggle should become the natural reaction of a socialist to injustice, when constitutional methods have exhausted themselves.
5. Through accomplishment of reconstruction and resistance to injustice,

[1]*Report of the Special Convention of the Socialist Party held at Pachmarhi*, Madhya Pradesh, 23-7 May 1952, pp. 79-80.

the Party will become the organizer of the people's will. Distress and threats of famine are growing and the years ahead under a government of a minority vote and without policy are full of sorrow. To the extent that the Party becomes an organizer of the people's will, situations of such deep sorrow shall not occur and, if they do, the Party will be in a position to overcome them through the practice of a nationwide struggle.

6. While the Party's chief duty is to refine itself, it cannot overlook the fragmentation of political life resulting from the general elections. It is responsible to the Indian people for putting an end to this fragmentation consistent with the claims of national integrity and of social change.
7. Desirous of pursuing a policy that will *fully expose* the Congress party as a party of conservatism and capitalism and consolidate the Socialist Party as a party of radicalism and socialism, the Convention appeals to radicals inside the Congress party not to waste their energies over empty wails for the return of the Socialist Party but to help the Socialist Party in the fruition of this policy.
8. The Convention realizing as it does the urge for social change that actuates the Sarvodaya Movement appeals to it to respond to the Socialist Party's desire for closer co-operation between the two.
9. Of the other parties that exist in the country, some belong particularly to the group whose radicalism is mixed with conservatism and others to the group whose loyalty to national freedom and democracy is not completely overcome by extra-territorial affiliations or the urge for Communistic dictatorship. With both the groups the Socialist Party is anxious to draw closer and work in co-operation in the hope that through such efforts common identity of purpose and policy will emerge and opportunities created for achieving a consolidated party of radicalism and socialism. *With regard to another group of parties that base themselves on communalism, the Convention reaffirms its policy of uncompromising opposition.*
10. This Convention directs the Socialists to work for the realization of this policy. It appeals to other parties, and intellectuals and the youth in particular to take part in this great movement for the consolidation of national life and social change and building up of the Socialist Party as a party of radicalism and socialism. The Indian people, in this manner, will be forging the instrument that will enable them to move forward to a life without poverty and fear and vibrant with contented activity.

189. To Baleshwar Dayaluji, 21 June 1952[1]

Dear Baleshwar Dayaluji,

Received your letter and telegram, your telegram just now and letter yesterday. God knows what do you think of me. I have no magical powers. I have been observing constantly that wherever there is a problem, you start sending me telegrams and letters, urging me to issue statements; go on tour and write letters to ministers. Everyone has his own capacity and I do not think that my statements can solve the problem. After all we all belong to an opposition group. Why the rulers will pay so much attention to our suggestions. As far as possible, I tried to meet your demands. This time when all the programme was already settled I went on tour on your suggestion. I had hoped to get myself relieved from this duty. Now, you are asking me to write a letter to the President. What purpose my letter will serve? At Pachmarhi I had requested you and other colleagues to discuss the matter with Purushottamji and write to him at Indore, so that he may discuss the matter with Chief Minister and convince him thoroughly. But none of you had discussed with Purushottamji. Do you think that I am the only person to write to the Government repeatedly? I may be excused to do this job and I want all of you not to depend on me for such matters. If the Government of Madhya Bharat is not prepared to take suitable action in a deteriorating situation, you may, if you wish, launch a peaceful movement to fight for your cause.

Kindly do not trouble me with this matter during the fast.[2]

Yours,
Jayaprakash

[1]*Brahmanand Papers* (NMML). Original in Hindi.

[2]This refers to the fast for three weeks to be started by J.P. at Dr. Dinshaw Mehta Nature Cure Clinic, Poona, on June 23. For the background and purpose of the fast see the next item.

190. To Rajendra Prasad, Poona, 22 June 1952[1]

Dear Babuji,

Please find below a short statement on my fast for your information.

Yours sincerely,
Jayaprakash

[1]*Rajendra Prasad Papers* (NAI); identical letters were sent to several other persons.

To my Friends and Doctors,

1. This fast is not against anybody, nor for any thing outside of myself.
2. It may be recalled that the decision to fast had originated over a year ago from certain unsuccessful negotiations I had carried on with Mr. Rafi Ahmed Kidwai, the then Communications Minister, regarding payment of strike period wages to postmen and lower grade staff.
3. But to-day the fast has nothing to do (except for his historical connection) with those negotiations, nor with the Central Government, nor with Mr. Kidwai.
4. The fast is (a) in the nature of a self-correction, and (b) in fulfilment of vow.
5. During my negotiations with Mr. Kidwai, I found I was guilty of carelessness and negligence. This was not in connection with a personal affair, but in the course of public work; and it affected a large number of men.
6. The vow to fast was taken at that time to atone for the mistake. To-day that particular mistake serves only an illustrative purpose and I venture to hope that the fast will fit me better to discharge my duties in the future.
7. The fact that I have not been able to carry out my vow till now has pained me. I cannot delay it any longer, and I hope I shall have the blessings even of those friends who have not approved of the fast.
8. The fast will commence on the morning of June 23 and will last for three weeks, subjects only to the limitation that I have no wish to die in its course.
9. During the fast I shall take only water with Soda-bi-carb and common salt.
10. The fast being an entirely personal affair, I do not want any publicity, agitation or any sympathetic public manifestation in connection with it.
11. The postmen, particularly, should not feel that they have any responsibility in the matter, and should not indulge in any agitation on my account.

Jayaprakash Narayan

191. To Asoka Mehta, 9 July 1952[1]

Dear Asoka,

I am enclosing my letter to Prafulla Babu.[2] I do not have his address here, so you will have to have it posted from Bombay. Please have copies made, one of which you may send to Kripalaniji.

The other day I forgot to speak to you about another point which struck me after reading Kripalani's letter. He has referred to Shibbanlal Saxena[3] expounding the KMPP's labour policy, but it is strange that they have forgotten the policy hitherto followed by them. Even after leaving the Congress they have continued to function in the INTUC which is affiliated to ICFTU. How, then, does the question to international affiliation arise now? Please bring this matter also to Kripalaniji's notice. You should, of course, also enlighten him on the true character of it.

I am well, but for the pulse. There is no cause for anxiety.

Yours,
Jayaprakash

[1]*Brahmanand Papers* (NMML).
[2]See the next item.
[2]Shibban Lal Saxena (1907-85); one of the founders of KMPP in 1951; a veteran freedom fighter; earlier occupied several important positions in the Congress organization in U.P.

192. To Prafulla Chandra Ghosh, 9 July, 1952[1]

My dear Prafulla Babu,

Kripalaniji has written to Asoka about the discussion of the KMPP Executive. I regret very much that the United Democratic Front in Madras is proving a stumbling block, but I hope that when we have come so far we shall be able, with patience on both sides, to complete the journey.

In his letter Kripalaniji has said, *inter alia*, that I had told you that I have no objection even after a merger of the KMPP and the SP to the former continuing its alliance with the CP in Madras. I am sorry that I gave you any such impression. What I probably told you was that if our two parties come to an all-India alliance (as distinct from a merger) we could reconcile ourselves during the transitional period with the KMPP-CP alliance in the Madras State. But it seems to me to be utterly fantastic for this alliance to continue even after the KMPP and SP have merged to form a single party.

[1]*Brahmanand Papers* (NMML).

However, in spite of all these difficulties I continue to be optimistic and if there is good will and sincere desire to come together, I am sure we shall succeed.

My fast is progressing well and today is the seventeenth day. The symptoms of acidosis are under control, thanks to Dr. Dinshaw's eliminatory and other treatment.

I am able to drink as much water as advised.

I hope you are keeping well.

With kind regards,

Yours sincerely,
Jayaprakash

193. To Jawaharlal Nehru, 10 July 1952[1]

Dear Bhai,

I was very happy to receive your letter. All these days I had been missing this word of love and cheer from you.

You write of embarrassment. You need have felt no embarrassment at all because I am not fasting against you, your Government or any of your colleagues.

The fast has progressed well so far, and I hope that with the good wishes of all of you and under Dinshaw's expert care the remaining three days will also pass without trouble.

With love and regards for you.

Yours affectionately,
Jayaprakash

[1]*Brahmanand Papers* (NMML).
[2] For the text of Nehru's letter see Appendix 23.

194. Press Note, 15 July 1952[1]

I was pained to find that during my fast[2] a bitter controversy was raised inside and outside Parliament as to whether Government or myself was wrong in the matter of the postmen's strike period pay. The fast should have made the controversy unnecessary. For my part, I had unreservedly accepted Mr. Kidwai's word and my own mistake. Among other things, it

[1]*J.P. Papers* (NMML).
[2]The fast began on 23 June and ended on 13 July 1952.

was to atone for that mistake that I had undertaken the fast. Therefore, it was not right to blame Mr. Kidwai any more. The blame was mine. I hope, therefore, that the unseemly and unprofitable controversy would now cease. Both the Prime Minister and the new Communications Minister, in their statements in Parliament, have reopened the door to a fresh effort at settlement. Let us all explore this new opportunity. I am sure that if there is a will, a solution would be found, and I feel sure that Mr. Kidwai himself would come forward to help. I further hope that the Prime Minister and the Finance Minister, who has a big say in the matter, would also be helpful. I regret that I would not be able to carry on the impending negotiations in person, but Mr. Dalvi[3] and Lala Achint Ram[4] will, I am sure, ably plead the postmen's case. According to the Union's decision, notice of strike was to be served on the Government on July 14. I have advised the Union not to do so, because it is not right to do so when a new possibility of amicable settlement has arisen.

Jayaprakash Narayan

[3]For biographical note on V.G. Dalvi see *JPSW*, Vol.V, p. 104.

[4]Lala Achint Ram (1898-1961); imprisoned for participating in Congress movements 1930-2, 1939, 1940, 1942-5; member Working Committee and General Secretary Punjab PCC; member AICC; Vice-President All-India Postmen & Lower Grade Staff Union; Member Provisional Parliament 1950-2; elected to first Lok Sabha 1952-7.

195. Appeal to the All-India Postmen and Lower Grade Staff Union not to Serve Strike Notice on the Government, Poona, 15 July 1952[1]

The statements of the Prime Minister and the Communications Minister in Parliament have reopened the door for fresh efforts at the settlement of the dispute and it would be improper to serve the strike notice before fresh negotiations are completed.

Let us all explore this new opportunity, I feel sure that if there is a will a solution would be found. Mr. Kidwai himself would come forward to help. I further hope that the Prime Minister and the Finance Minister, who have a big say in the matter, would also be helpful. I shall not be able to carry on the negotiations in person, but Mr. V.G. Dalvi, general secretary of the union and Mr. Achint Ram, vice president of the union, will plead the postmen's case.

I regret that the alleged promise of Mr. Kidwai to pay the strike period wages to postal workers should have caused a bitter controversy inside and outside Parliament.

[1]Adapted from *National Herald*, 16 July 1952.

I have unreservedly accepted Mr. Kidwai's word and my own mistake. And it is to atone for the mistake, among other things, that I had undertaken the fast. Therefore, it is not right to blame Mr. Kidwai any more. The blame is mine.

I would not be able to serve on the DA Committee, partly due to reasons of health and partly due to other reasons. I regret that the Government should have taken such a considerable time in appointing the committee particularly when I was assured by Mr. N.G. Ayyangar in October last, that such a committee would be formed at an early date.

The present terms of reference of the committee are very much restricted and the scope of the committee should be enlarged. In a letter to Mr. C.D. Deshmukh, the Union Finance Minister, I have suggested that the committee should at least determine if the present scales of dearness allowance paid to Government employees are adequate and are consistent with the present cost of living. Many Government employees' unions are not satisfied with the present scales and feel that they are much below the minimum necessitated by the cost of living index.

The Gadgil Committee was formed to evolve an alternative plan since the Government considered that the pay commission's recommendations were not applicable in this matter. I have not received any reply from the Finance Minister.

196. To Pyarelal, 16 July 1952[1]

My dear Pyarelalji,[2]

I am very grateful to you for your statement and advice and guidance. I have seen your statement in the Harijan. I am enclosing herewith a copy of the statement[3] that I released yesterday to the press. I hope it meets with your approval. You may make such use of it as you desire.[4] Panditji has written me two rather nice letters and I hope some good might come even for some others out of this fast. As for myself, it has done me a great deal of good.

Hoping you are well,

Yours sincerely,
Jayaprakash

[1] *J.P. Papers* (NMML).
[2] For biographical note on Pyarelal, see *JPSW*, Vol. III, p. 261.
[3] See item 194 in this volume.
[4] See Appendix 25 for Pyarelal's reply to this letter.

197. 'The Fast', 20 July 1952[1]

Fasting, particularly as a means of self-culture, has had no place in socialist philosophy or practice. I, therefore, owe a word of explanation to the Party.

The fast developed, even as the fasting days went by, more and more into a self-purificatory sacrifice, and each day brought new inner strength and some times an unanticipated experience. I was chary at the beginning of claiming to do anything by way of self-purification. So full of faults and vices one found oneself, that it seemed presumptuous to speak, publicly at any rate, of self-purification. But I was guided and prompted in this by Rao Saheb and Achyut Patwardhan and Dr. Dinshaw Mehta. I am grateful to them for the guidance and encouragement.

All this will sound odd in socialist circles, and all manner of eye-brows will be raised. Nevertheless, I should not like to detract a word from what I have said.

Traditionally, socialism has relied on institutional changes for curing the evils of modern society. We have in our movement, however, realized that institutional changes are not enough and that the individual man, the root of society, must also be cured. That is why we have latterly been laying more and more emphasis on values and the right means. I am afraid, however, that the awareness of this vital principle has not gone deep enough and we have not applied it fully to our individual selves. The detachment, the self-control, the conquest over desires that are necessary for us, are absent in us in ample measure. If we have to serve socialism and create a new society and a new man (which is more important) we must make ourselves worthy instruments. Then only shall we succeed. Success does not mean, as in Stalinist Communism, only conquest and maintenance of power. Success means the realization and establishment in actuality of the noble ideals of socialism. If those who set out to achieve noble ends are unworthy and ignoble, what guarantee can there be that those ends will ever be achieved? Conceivably, right socialist institutions, when created, might shape man and society, but who will shape those who undertake to shape those institutions? Obviously, they themselves and none others. Was it not asked long ago wherewith will the salt be salted if it loseth its flavour?

Let me say then that this fast has been to me a cleansing experience. I claim no more than that, and I think it could not have done any harm to the Party. Nor do I wish to suggest that every colleague in the Party should

[1]*Janata*, Vol. VII (No. I), 20 July 1952, p. 1.

take to fasting to purify his self. But I shall say this that whatever method one chooses, everyone of us must constantly endeavour to make himself worthy of the noble ideals which we all seek to serve.

Jayaprakash Narayan

198. To Rohit Dave, 22 July 1952[1]

Dear Rohit,

I congratulate you upon the first issue of the *Janata*. It looks neat and dignified.

Here are some suggestions for your consideration:

1. Just as every good menu has a piece-de- resistance, so every issue of the *Janata* should have a main article—studied, high-browed and certainly not journalistic in any way. It need not be written by the Editor every time. You, Asoka, K.K., Dantwala, Sabavala,[2] some of us and other friends may be allotted the job from week to week. The *Janata*[3] piece-de-resistance may be on a topic of the week, on a question of theory or an international question, on literature (political, economic or otherwise), on Govt. policy, or any other subject under the sun. The only requirement is that it should be high class, scientific and studied.
2. The proof-reading should be improved and printer's devils set right.
3. Party activities should not be trumpeted loudly but dressed in sober, restrained language.
4. There should be a good weekly letter from Delhi covering both Parliament and Govt.

Enclosed you will find a note on Nepal for the Notes and Comments section. It should not bear my name or initials.

Hoping you are well.

Yours sincerely,
J.P.

[1]*J.P. Papers* (NMML).

[2]Sharokh Ardeshir Sabavala (1918-); had a long and distinguished career in business and journalism in Bombay and was a sympathiser of the Socialist Party.

[3]*Janata*, 3 August 1952.

199. A Note on Nepal, Poona, 22 July 1952[1]

Since our comments last week the situation in Nepal has further deteriorated. The Nepali Congress Working Committee and the Congress President, Shri Bishweshwar Prasad Koirala, have shown extraordinary ineptitude in dealing with a delicate and grave situation, which in a large measure is the result of their own mishandling.

The Nepali Congress, in relation to the public affairs of Nepal, is not just one political party among several others. It is, or at least was, a revolutionary popular body that by a revolutionary act brought to an end the feudal autocracy and established the first popular government that Nepal had ever seen in its long history. As such, it is the responsibility of the Congress (a) to give to Nepal a stable government which is the prime necessity; (b) to prepare the ground for the establishment of a real democratic government elected by the people in accordance with the fundamental law made by a popular Constituent Assembly; (c) in the interim period to keep law and order, maintain a rule of law and effect such economic reforms as may be urgently necessary.

It is a tragic fact that in the discharge of these elementary responsibilities the Nepali Congress has woefully failed. The causes of its failure are many, but the most important among them is the spirit of personal rivalry, with the consequent struggle for power, among the leaders of the Congress. That this struggle for power sometimes is sought to be cloaked with ideological robes does not change its fundamental character.

The essence of the present political crisis in Nepal seems to be that in the opinion of the Working Committee of the Nepali Congress Shri Matrika Prasad Koirala, the Prime Minister, has fallen under certain evil influences which have gained the upper hand in his Cabinet and have been responsible for his many bunglings and deeds of misadministration. Accordingly, the Working Committee proceeded to choose a new Cabinet for the Prime Minister. No person with the least self-respect would have agreed to such interference and Shri M.P. Koirala naturally refused to be dictated to. Thereupon the Working Committee, knowing full well that its directive was going to be rejected, expelled Shri Matrika Prasad who, let it not be forgotten, was the first popular Prime Minister of that country.

In this manner the Working Committee reduced itself (along with the Congress), as also the office of the popular Prime Minister (along with democracy as such), to a laughing stock. No doubt, the Working Committee took this bold step to impress the people and the world with its own importance and power. But, unfortunately, the result has been just the

[1]Enclosure to item 198; published in *Janata*, 3 August 1952, without mentioning J.P. as its author, as described by the letter (see item 198).

opposite, and democracy has received a severe setback almost at its very start.

Let it freely be admitted that Shri M.P. Koirala's Government has not been much of a success; let it also be admitted that all members of his Cabinet are not exactly milk pure. But, firstly, anyone in Shri Matrika Prasad's place, with incessant intrigue going on behind his back, would not have shown much better results; and secondly, the limitations of the human material in Nepal's political life should not be overlooked. We are sure that, were the Working Committee itself to become the Government, the new Cabinet would not be free from 'evil influences,' not very much different from those that plague the present Ministry.

The question of the proper relationship between the Government and the Party has been at all times and places a rather vexed one. Where the party in question is wholly a parliamentary body or where a dictatorship rules, the question is simple of solution. But in a democratic context, where the party has, too, an extra-parliamentary existence and function, the question bristles with all manner of practical difficulties. No doubt the party has the final word, but in actual working democratic functioning is not possible if the parliamentary wing of the party and its leadership are not left with a very wide field of initiative and, in matters of details of administration, complete autonomy.

In Nepal, there being no elected legislature, there is no parliamentary wing of the Congress, but there is the Advisory Council, recently constituted, which is meant to do for a parliament. This Council has been completely kept in the background throughout the present dispute. This is not healthy for democratic growth.

Furthermore, if the Working Committee of the Nepali Congress disapproved of the policies or deeds of the present Government, it should have kept personalities out and not attempted to force a ready-made Cabinet on the Prime Minister, but concentrated on the matters of policy in question, so that the dispute could have been kept above personal intrigues and rivalries and the people educated about the issues involved. In that case, the Prime Minister would have found it difficult to reject the advice or directives of the Working Committee. As it is, by trying to force a Cabinet of its choice on the Prime Minister, the Working Committee has set up a bad precedent, undermined its own authority and that of the Prime Minister, brought the dispute down to a personal level, and finally strengthened immeasurably the hands of the King—a development of the utmost danger to Nepali democracy.

Luckily, it does not seem even now to be too late; and we urge strongly, in a spirit of friendship and helpfulness, that the ugly dispute be ended. The only basis of settlement to our mind is to leave the Government in the hands of Shri M.P. Koirala, to leave him a free hand to choose his Ministers, to lay down broad policies for the Government to follow, to make the Advisory Council function as a sort of interim Parliament, to strengthen and widen the organization of the Nepali Congress and to prepare for the Constituent Assembly. Any other course would result not only in the disintegration of the Nepali Congress, but also in the strengthening of the King and other feudal elements, on the one hand, and the prophets of anarchy and civil war, on the other. The leaders of the Congress, of both sides, are at present engaged in legal and constitutional quibbling, but these will never save them. They must rise over these petty acts of party warfare and act in solidarity to save themselves and their country.

200. To the Provincial Secretaries and other Members of the Committee on Land Distribution, Poona, 22 July, 1952[1]

Dear,

In accordance with the resolution of the National Executive[2] I have pleasure in appointing you a member of the Central Committee on Land Distribution.

The first meeting of this committee will be held on August 20 at Poona.[3] You are requested to attend. You should reach Poona either on the 19th evening or early on the 20th morning.

In view of the fact that the work of this committee is of great importance, I do hope that you will not fail to attend the Poona meeting.

In the meanwhile, I should like you to acquaint yourself with the nature of the problem of distribution of land in your State and to gather the necessary information and figures. Information about cultivable waste land should also be gathered under this head. In the same connection, you should also gather all relevant information regarding ejectment of tenants.

Thirdly, you should get in touch with the Sarvodaya Samaj in your state and acquaint yourself with their organization and activities concerning the Bhoodan Movement and Vinobaji's likely visit to the state.

Fourthly, I would urge you to discuss the problem of Land Distribution with the State Committee or any special Committee that might have been set up in your state and bring with you the concrete proposals that might be formulated.

[1]*J.P. Papers* (NMML).

[2]J.P. had been appointed Chairman of the Central Committee on Land Distribution and authorized to appoint its members.

[3]The meeting was later preponed to 19 August.

I would expect you to place before the Central Committee on August 20 a *brief, factual* and *written* report on the above four points.

Please intimate time and date of your arrival to the Secretary, Socialist Party, Poona.

Sincerely yours,
Jayaprakash Narayan

201. To Jawaharlal Nehru, 25 July 1952[1]

My dear Bhai,

I am very sorry for not replying yet to your letter of the 12th,[2] which gave me great happiness and peace of mind.

Thanks to Dinshaw's care, I was able to stand the fast better than I had expected. I am slowly recovering now and am carefully following the regimen laid down. Dinshaw wants me to stay here till December, so that he can cure my gastric ailments and the sciatica. As I hardly had any physical and mental rest in the past six years, I feel tempted to accept his advice. But I have not yet made up my mind. I shall do so after watching the progress of the treatment for some weeks.

As soon as I am well and leave Poona, I shall keep my promise and come up to Delhi to stay for some days, so that I could have more time with you.

I cannot say how grateful I am to you for having that postmen issue settled at last in such a satisfactory manner. I am writing to Jagjiwan Babu also to thank him.

May I take the liberty of writing to you about Rao Patwardhan (P.H. Patwardhan, 'Sitaram', Prabhat Road, Kachrewadi, Poona)[3]. You have often complained of lack of men. ('Where are the damned men?' I have heard you exclaim sometimes.) Now, here is a first rate man—both in ability and character. And no national use is being made of him. He has, of course, retired from active politics, and apart from editing the late Sane Guruji's 'Sadhana' is doing practically nothing. Had he cared to remain in politics and use the common methods, he would have been at the top in Maharashtra, indeed in Bombay. But he chose to withdraw. Let there be no misunderstanding. He has not (nor Achyut nor anyone else) even remotely ever suggested that I should write to you about him, nor has he ever spoken

[1]*Brahmanand Papers* (NMML).

[2]See Appendix 24 for the text of Jawaharlal Nehru's letter dated 12 July 1952.

[3]P.H. Patwardhan alias Rao Sahib (1903-69); leader of Maharashtra Provincial Congress; imprisoned 1930, 1936, 1939 and 1942; after Independence he left politics and joined Vinoba Bhave's Bhoodan Movement.

of his not being used. Rather, he always speaks of you with affection and, what seems to me, unbounded admiration. He does not know that I am writing anything about him to you; nor can I say how he would react if you were to call him to a worthy post. But, I do feel that if his services can be obtained, the country and your administration would be the richer for it.

Begging to be excused for this long letter and with love.[4]

Yours as ever,
Jayaprakash

[4]See Appendix 28 for Nehru's reply dated 28 July 1952.

202. To B.P. Koirala, 26 July 1952[1]

Dear Bisheshwarji,

Your telegram had reached in time, I had sent one more telegram in reply. Received your letter yesterday. Many thanks.

Kindly pardon me, but I am very worried about the Nepali Congress and Nepal. In this way no one among you will be able to do anything. There is a great responsibility on the Nepali Congress, but the responsibility is not being carried out properly.

When Matrika Babu met me in Calcutta he had stated clearly that first he would be removed from the post of the President of Congress party then there would be an effort to remove him from the Government. At that time you had said that no one had even imagined that. But now that exactly is happening regardless of the reason which may be advanced for it. There is nothing new in what you have written in the letter and telegram. And if you forgive me, I shall say that even if you had been in place of Matrika Babu similar things would have been said, though the persons saying those things would, of course, have been different. All those acquainted with the circumstances would agree that in view of the difficulties and the persons with whom one is compelled to work, no one can do any magic.

What should be the relationship between the party and the government is a complex question. No government can function because of the way your executive is interfering in the formation of the Ministry. Whoever is endowed with even a bit of self-respect, would not put up with this type of intervention in order to remain Prime Minister even for two minutes. If you

[1]*J.P. Papers* (NMML). Original in Hindi.

[2]See Appendix 26 for B.P. Koirala's reply to J.P.

[3]For the text of B.P. Koirala's telegram see Appendix 27 and also see Appendices 29, 31-4 and 37 for Koirala's, Mrs. Koirala's and Devendra Prasad Singh's letters to J.P.

had been the Prime Minister, you too would never have tolerated this type of interference.

You have written in the telegram and the letter that this Ministry has been bungling etc. and the Government is not working. However, these defects are likely to be reduced as a result of the policy the Congress party has adopted. Congress should not have gone into the personalities—keep this one and throw away that one—but should have concentrated on criticism of policies. Then the Nepalese people and the outside world both would have understood what the question was. As of now, all this conflict looks like a quarrel for personal power. I have read in the newspapers that your executive had opined that the agreement/compromise that had been worked out between the old president and the new president of the party was a private affair and had no relationship with the Congress party. If this news is true, I am amazed how even after the passing of this resolution, you continued to be president of the Congress party.

I have no intention to interfere in your affairs. I have dared to offer my advice to you only due to affection for you. And, of course, I am a well wisher of Nepal.

Hope you and Sushila are happy.

Yours affectionately,
Jayaprakash

203. To Pyarelal, 28 July 1952[1]

My dear Pyarelalji,

I thank you for your letter and all that you did for the fast.

I generally agree with what you say about workers' demand for payment for the days of strike, but I would make some reservations. Sometimes, rather more times than not, the workers are compelled by the obstinacy or cupidity of the employers to resort to strike. In such cases the workers would be justified in demanding payment for the strike period. Some labour legislations also recognize this right of the workers and there have been some industrial awards conceding this right.

I am progressing fairly well and have been put on buttermilk diet for the whole day getting vegetable soup and boiled vegetables and egg custard at night. I will be here for two or three months more.

I hope you are well.

With regards,

Affectionately yours,
Jayaprakash

[1]*J.P. Papers* (NMML).

J.P. during fast at Nature Cure Clinic, Pune (1952).

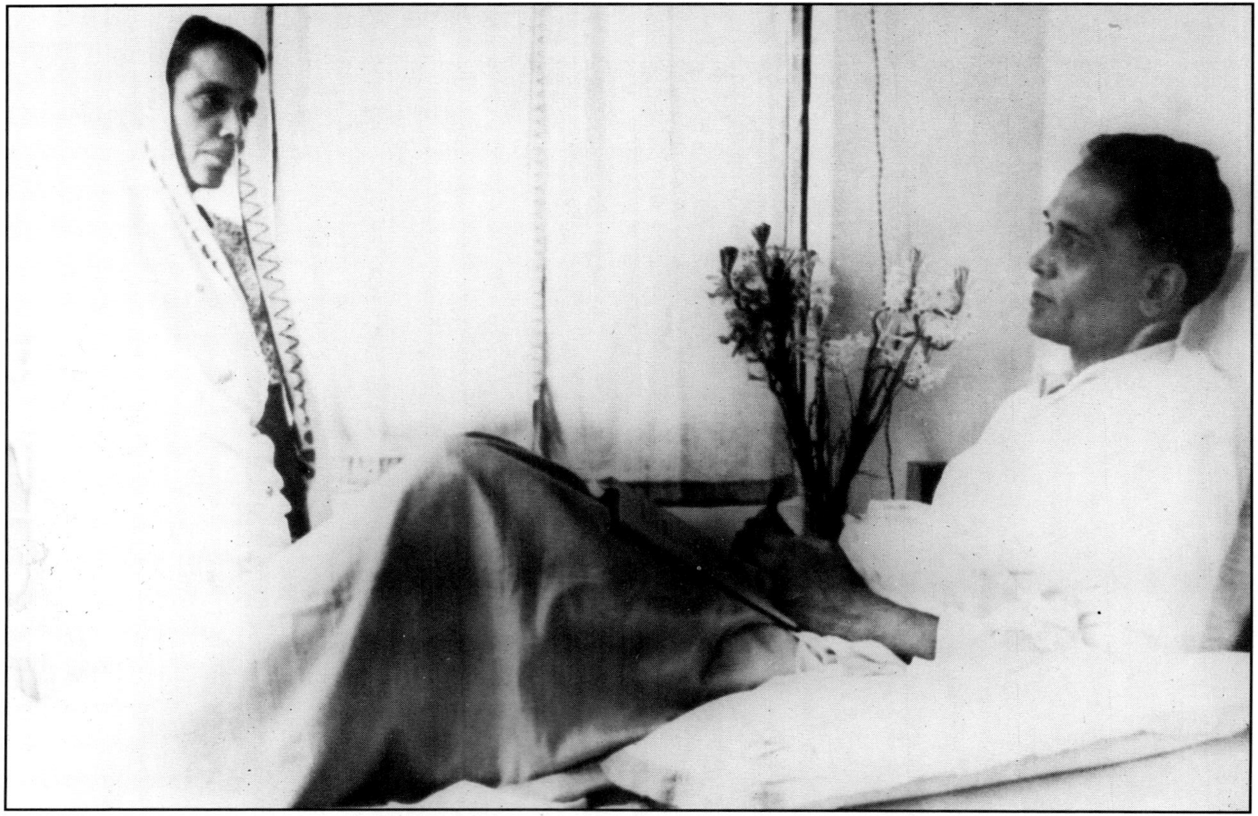

J.P. during fast at Nature Cure Clinic, Pune, with Prabhavati looking on (1952).

J.P. with Prabhavati, Kamaladevi Chattopadhyaya, Asoka Mehta and others (1952).

J.P. with Prabhavati and prominent Socialist workers in the Punjab (1953).

J.P. with prominent Socialist workers in Gujarat (1953).

J.P. with Prabhavati (1953).

J.P. with Vinobha Bhave (1953).

Calcutta
21.4.52

Dear Asoka,

I came here on the 17th & was to go from here to Dehra Doon, Delhi and then to Bombay. But unfortunately I fell ill and am still in bed – pain in the ear and fever. There is no fever today and the pain too has subsided. If doctors permit I shall leave for Bombay on the 23rd by the BNR Mail reaching there on the 25th.

At Patna I had received your wire about the chairmanship of the special conference, to which I had replied suggesting that you request Lohia in stead to preside. I hope you received that telegram and Lohia has agreed.

Regarding our stand on the Presidential election issue, I think we have no alternative but to support K T Shah. If we don't, apart from every thing else, there will be a great set-back to our efforts to bring the non-CP leftists near us. Tridib Chowdhary, Soumyen Tagore, Meghnad Saha – all of whom I met here and at Patna – are anxious that we support Shah. We will alienate them all if we don't, and in return we shall get nothing.

More when we meet.

yours affectionately,
Jayaprakash

P.S.
Apart from the HMS and Cultural Congress programmes please see that no public engagement is fixed for me in advance. I shall have to rest more than work.
J.P.

Facsimile of J.P.'s letter to Asoka Mehta.

204. To Peter Alvares, 1 August 1952[1]

Dear Peter,

Your letter. Why, of course, bring out a number of the *Janata* with those artices on the problem of land redistribution which you suggest. Shankar Raoji has left today for a fifteen days' walking tour of Maharashtra, so it will be difficult to get an article on Vinobaji's Bhoodan Movement. I shall have the article prepared here and sent to the *Janata*. When should it reach at the latest? If possible, I too shall send you something, but don't bank on it.

Was the Nepal note too late? Asoka who was here today did not know anything about it.

More when you come here on the 6th.

Yours affectionately,
Jayaprakash

[1]*J.P. Papers* (NMML).

205. To the Members of the Central Land Redistribution Committee, 2 August 1952[1]

Dear Comrade,

This is to inform you that the venue of the meeting of the Central Land Distribution Committee (of which you are a member) has been changed from Poona to *Banaras*. The date of the meeting will be as notified earlier, *August 19, 1952*.

You are requested to reach *Banaras* either on the 18th evening or early on the19th morning.

May I remind you that you have to place before the Committee a *brief, factual and written report* on the points mentioned in my previous letter, as also answers to the questionnaire.[2]

Please intimate exact date and time of your arrival to Acharya Narendra Deva, Banaras Hindu University, Banaras.

Sincerely yours,
Jayaprakash

Copy to:
1. Acharya Narendra Deva;
2. Asoka Mehta.

[1]*J.P. Papers* (NMML).
[2]For the text of the questionnaire see Appendix 30.

206. To Rajendra Prasad, 4 August 1952[1]

Revered Babuji,

Many thanks for your letter. I could not reply to you earlier because Dr. Dinshaw had gone to Bombay. I consulted him after his return. He is firmly of the view that I should not leave Poona during September. His treatment, he says, must continue for a period of six months. I am not in a position to say if I shall be able to stay here so long, but I do want to give a fair trial to this treatment. Under these circumstances, I cannot avail of the tempting opportunity to be for some time with you in Simla and it is a matter which has caused me deep regret. Dr. Dinshaw has also written to you about these matters. I am gradually improving and gaining some strength. My weight also is increasing at the rate of half a pound per day. Nothing, however, can be said at present about my stomach ailments and the pain in my waist.

Hoping you to be all well.

With profound regards,

Yours,
Jayaprakash

[1]*Dr. Rajendra Prasad Papers* (NAI).

207. 'Aphrodisiacs *vs*. Real Vitality, Plain-speaking to the Comrades', 10 August 1952[1]

The shock of the General Election had thrown most of us out of the ruts of our customary thought and action. There was heart and head searching all round and many brave resolutions were made. The general verdict was that we must dig in, localize and intensify our work, aim at depth, and so on. But what scanty reports are available go to show that the lessons of the elections are nearly forgotten and that we have fallen into the old ruts again.

True, some of us might yet mouth the new lessons, but it seems that there is no real conviction behind them. This is sad state of affairs. An experience such as that of a general election does not come every day; and if we fail to learn by one experience, the likelihood is that we will never learn.

In recent months I have noticed the growth of a hankering in the Party for loud agitation; for stunts; for always being in the news; for keeping the initiative. Satyagraha is becoming almost our second nature, and sometimes we seek to reduce it to an absurdity. Luckily, the satyagraha of locking in

[1]*J.P. Papers* (NMML).

Congress ministers in their offices proposed by a certain unit of the Party did not materialize. But it shows to what ridiculous lengths we are prepared to go in search of quick-acting drugs to build up our strength. But real vitality will never come by these spurious tonics. We must be prepared to sweat and labour patiently and to build brick by brick from the very bottom. We must shed our anxiety to be always in the public eye, to steal a march over everybody else in demonstrativeness and flamboyance, to compete in the race for initiative.

Comrades might ask in impatience; what would I have them do then? In my humble opinion, the Party's first slogan should be—back to the village. This might appear as an anti-climax to many. After the challenging opening remarks I was expected to say something new and striking. But that is just my point. Let us give up this quest for the new and striking; let us become pedestrian and plodding for a while. Back to the village may be an old slogan, yet, I am confident, that if we seriously set out to put it into practice, such a flood of strength and vitality would surge into the Party that socialism would soon become irresistible. The fate of all the political parties, indeed, the very future of the country, is in the lap of the villages.

I do not wish to suggest that we should wind up our shop in the towns and cities. But there are far too many of us in the urban centres. I have intimate knowledge of Bihar; and I make bold to say that in Patna, as well as in the district towns, there are far too many comrades concentrated. There is not enough work for all of us in the towns and, for more of us than less, work consists in visiting one another, gathering in some place to gossip endlessly and just idle away. Therefore, the more of us went back to the village, the better for the Party and socialism. And when I say more of us I do not exclude the leading members. Rather, I most emphatically recommend that they should be the first to go. And I would recommend further that it would be better if we go back to our own village (that is, those of us who have a village) and make it the centre of our activity.

Constructive work has always formed the tail end of our programme and every one of us, in recounting to Party workers all the various activities which they must carry out, has taken care not to omit it. But the matter has not advanced beyond that. After the General Election there was a tendency to lay greater emphasis then before on this type of work. But there seems to be no evidence that in actual practice there has been any change in our attitude towards the constructive programme. I feel that if the socialist movement has to strike deep roots and become stable and powerful it would be only in proportion to the amount and quality of our constructive work. Therefore, along with the back to the village programme I would like to emphasise the importance and need of the constructive programme not only for the village, but also for the urban areas. Let all the top leaders of the

Party in the country and the states take up this activity and convert it from the tail end to the front piece of the Party's programme.

I hope in subsequent notes to deal more fully with the constructive and rural programmes.

208. Address to the Rashtra Seva Dal Volunteers, Poona, 20 August 1952[1]

The honest and hard labour is the sheet-anchor of India's prosperity and I call upon every Indian to realize that there is no alternative to it in the task of national reconstruction.

The foreign aid from whatever quarter it comes, is of dubious quality, and dependence on it can only amount to alien bondage from which India has just emerged free. Among the few countries in the world, only America can afford such help as Russian help is restricted by the needs of the Russian people themselves. Under the circumstances India's manpower is the only resource of the country's prosperity.

If every Indian national devotes one hour daily for nation-building activities constructive work worth Rs. 300 crores annually can be turned out.

The community development projects undertaken by the Government of India are guinea pigs with a certain experimental value. But guinea pigs by themselves are no answer to the problem of rural uplift. In the face of over six lakhs villages, which need reconstruction, the projects would benefit only those who already possess lands, but not the landless masses. I am of the opinion that an equitable redistribution of land should have preceded such projects.

I compliment Acharya Vinoba Bhave for his land-gift mission. It is the duty of the Congress Government to secure equitable redistribution of land, if necessary, by means of legislation.

Government's action in this regard would have instilled confidence into the people in regard to its intentions. People at present suffer from a lack of faith in their Government and in consequence of it the Government has been deprived of the willing co-operation of the people in the work of national reconstruction.

[1] Adapted from *Tribune*, 1 September 1952.

209. Statement on the Merger of the Socialist Party and Kisan Mazdoor Praja Party, Poona, 28 August 1952[1]

The Praja Socialist Party, which has been formed by the merger of the Socialist and Kisan Mazdoor Praja Parties, is a new political force of considerable strength in the country.

The leaders of both parties deserve to be congratulated on their statesman-like decision to bring about the merger.

There is a major need to consolidate the opposition to the ruling party, whose huge majorities in the legislatures threaten to reduce democracy to a farce.

The accomplishment of an economic revolution is the next step after the achievement of political freedom in India. Experience of the past few years has, however, shown that the Congress has failed in its tasks, and holds out no hope of fulfilling them. I believe that the emergence of the Praja Socialist Party gives an assurance of the fulfilment of the economic revolution in this country by peaceful and democratic means.

I hope it would be possible later to bring other political parties into the new combination.

Socialism cannot progress merely by the support of the working class. If Socialism is to succeed, the peasants and landless must be won over. Our Socialism must necessarily be an agrarian Socialism. Redistribution of land, welfare of workers, efforts to increase productivity should be the immediate programmes with which to approach the villages.

[1] Adapted from *Statesman*, 30 August 1952.

210. To V.V. Giri, 29 August 1952[1]

My dear Mr. Giri,[2]

You must have received my telegram yesterday about the strike of civilian employees of the Defence Department here. I am enclosing a note prepared by Mr. S.M. Joshi, General Secretary of the All India Defence Services Civilian Employees' Federation. In one of the units, namely, the Central Armoured Fighting Vehicle Depot, the strike already began this morning. Out of some 2400 employees only 89, mostly clerks, are reported to have gone on duty. The strike will gradually spread to other establishments. The Defence Department, with which Mr. S.M. Joshi has been in long

[1] *J.P. Papers* (NMML).

[2] V.V. Giri was the Labour Minister, Government of India.

correspondence, has so far failed to amicably settle the dispute. If you could intervene in the matter, not only of the interests of the workers but also of the Defence Department itself and of the country at large will be served. I hope it will be possible for you to do something in the matter. Had Shri Gopalaswami Ayyangar been here I would have written to him also.

I hope you are well.

Yours sincerely,
J.P.

211. Statement on the Political Situation in Nepal, Poona, 7 September 1952[1]

It is with great reluctance that one has to speak about the affairs of another country. But not only are the people of India anxious about the prosperity and happiness of Nepal, but also developments in that country have a vital influence over us. It is, therefore, with deep regret that I find King Tribhuvan acting in a manner that is bound no only to affect the institution of Kingship in his country but also to add fuel to the fires that are burning.

It is true that the Nepali Congress and the ex-Premier, Mr. M.P. Koirala, did not exactly cover themselves with glory in the recent political crisis. But that is no reason for King Tribhuvan to add to their errors and deepen the crisis. His decision to dissolve the Advisory Council is, to say the least, most unwise. No one can claim that his present handpicked ministers have any representative capacity. On the other hand, the Advisory Council did represent, as far as possible in the present circumstances, the largest will of the people.

If King Tribhuvan desires to keep up any pretence of ruling with the consent of the people, he must convene the Advisory Council and appoint ministers who command the confidence of that body. If consideration of prestige should prevent him from calling to life a body that he has just dissolved, he has no alternative but to call the Nepali Congress to form Government.

He must honour the spirit of the interim constitution that he himself promulgated. Further, King Tribhuvan would be well-advised to prepare as soon as possible for the election of a Constituent Assembly.

[1] Adapted from *National Herald*, 8 September 1952.

212. Statement on the Strike in the Kirkee Central Armoured Fighting Vehicle Depot, Poona, 7 September 1952[1]

The issues involved in the present strike of the civilian employees of the Defence establishments in Poona are not insoluble. All that is required is a little goodwill and earnestness on the part of the Government.

The strike of 2,400 workers of the Kirkee Central Armoured Fighting Vehicle Depot since August 29, is the first strike to have been allowed to continue for such a long period in the history of strikes in the Defence establishments in India. Other establishments in Dehu and Kirkee will go on strike from tomorrow, involving ultimately about 34,000 workers. Such a serious labour trouble has not arisen suddenly but is the result of the failure of negotiations conducted over a period of years.

The issues involved in the present dispute are mainly three: (1) gradation of Poona as 'B' area, for the purpose of granting of house rent and city compensatory allowances, (2) the early release of the Kalyanwala Committee's Report, and (3) the question of retrenchment which is a source of perpetual worry of the Defence workers.

The demand for the gradation for Poona as 'B' area was placed before the Government about four years back. Which the Government had often said that it was under consideration, it has now replied that the demand cannot be conceded because Poona City, excluding the two cantonments of Kirkee and the camp, do not have a population of over 50,000. The exclusion of these cantonments where there is a large civilian population is only a convenient trick to deprive the workers of their rightful dues and thus effect a little saving in Government expenditure at their cost. It should be noted that this demand concerned not only the workers now on strike, but all Central Government employees such as those of Defence Accounts, Observatory, Postal Services, Railways, etc.

The Kalyanwala Committee was instituted in September 1950 and was required to complete its work by the end of that year. The way the committee had functioned showed that the Government did not take this matter seriously. Several times communiques were issued fixing dates for publication of the report, but it has not yet seen the light of day. The numerous anomalies created by wrong implementation of the recommendations of the Pay Commission, have played havoc with the Defence employees and it is their fond hope that the Kalyanwala Committee would rescue them from injustice and financial loss.

Regarding the issue of retrenchment the Federation had proposed to the Government on several occasions alternatives to retrenchment, but none of them had found favour with them. It would be embarrassing to the

[1]Adapted from *Statesman*, 8 September 1952.

Government, if the facts of the retrenchment of the 213 workers of the Central Armoured Fighting Vehicle Depot are given publicity, but if an impartial tribunal is instituted, the Federation can prove that the retrenchment is neither in the interest of economy nor in the interest of the State.

213. 'KMPP and UDF', 7 September 1952[1]

I would like to say a few words about the United Democratic Front in Madras in the context of the Socialist Party-KMPP merger. I had no intention of saying anything about this controversial matter before the joint meeting called at Bombay on the 26th of this month. But I am afraid that my silence may be misunderstood and create difficulties in the smooth working of the merger.

The Socialist Party's policy with regard to cooperation with the Communists has never been ambiguous and throughout the merger negotiations, our position regarding the Madras UDF has been clear. The commitments which the KMPP had made with the Communists when the UDF was formed were no doubt always taken into consideration and there was never a desire to face the Madras KMPP with a fait accompli. We always felt, as I do feel now, that a leader of the standing of Mr. Prakasam would himself resolve the difficulty and not ask us to take an illogical position.

The UDF was formed in the hope of forming a government in Madras when the Congress in spite of being the single largest party, was shirking the responsibility and unwilling to form a coalition with any one. This circumstance has completely changed now, and the emphasis in Madras, as elsewhere in the country, has shifted from the legislature to the constituencies outside.

The Madras KMPP should think in terms of winning the next election, which would surely be held in Madras earlier than elsewhere, rather than of scoring parliamentary points in the legislature. In this the UDF will be of no use because we will have to fight the Communists as much as the Congress.

In any case, it would be a fantastic situation in which the Praja Socialist Party would be fighting the Communists everywhere and a wing of it would be co-operating with them in the Madras legislature. No good could come out of such a make-shift policy. Either KMPP-SP merger is looked at in the larger perspective, and a consistent policy is followed, or the merger would defeat itself from the very start. If the merger is desirable in the higher interest, sacrifice will have to be made.

[1] Article in *Janata*.

214. To Narendra Deva, 7 September 1952[1]

Dear Narendra Devaji,

Thank you for your letter. Asoka has sent the copy of your letter today. When Asoka was here there was a discussion about the talks held at Banaras. I am unable to understand what should I write to you. I am sad at heart. Had I known your reaction earlier, the issue of merger would not have arisen. But we committed a mistake in taking such a drastic step in your absence. We may give any name to our discussion, but it is a fact that our minds work in the same manner and whatever Asoka, Lohia and myself collectively decide it generally meets your agreement. Working together for so many years a mutural confidence had developed but now it appears that it was baseless. We fail to understand what should be done in the present circumstances. Again and again it occurs to us that it would have been better, had we not involved ourselves in the merger issue. What can be done now?

Any how you must come to Bombay for General Council and Joint Meeting. A learned and impartial colleague like Prof. Mukut Bihari Lal is also against this merger. This increases our anxiety. But he has to be convinced and you can do it. It would be a big burden on you. I hope you to be well. Mahavir Babu[2] is suffering from Jaundice. A proper diagnosis has been possible after a month. I am getting well. Prabhavati is also well.

Please accept our respects.

Yours,
Jayaprakash

P.S.: Keep Sri Niwas Shastri[3] in your mind. I shall definitely attend Bombay meetings.

[1]*Brahmanand Papers* (NMML).

[2]M.P. Sinha; one of the prominent members of the Socialist Party in U.P.; closely associated with J.P.

[3]A prominent member of the trade union wing of the Socialist Party.

215. To Asoka Mehta, 8 September 1952[1]

Dear Asoka,

Here are the copies of the letters to Kripalaniji, Sadiq Ali, and Narendra-devaji. I hope I have not committed any further *faux pas*.

[1]*Brahmanand Papers* (NMML).

Please send to Lohia copies of my press statement (the one that has caused so much annoyance to him) and of my letter to Sadiq Ali.

I shall be writing tonight to Prakasam and Vishwanatham,[2] but as I do not know their address, I'll send the letters to the Central Office for posting. Incidentally, you will also be able to see them before they are mailed. If you happen to want alternations to be made, please send them back with your suggestions.

Ladhu rang up to explain what actually was agreed about the UDF at Lucknow; but if I was not able to understand the situation after hours of talk with him and you, a telephone talk could hardly enlighten me further.

Yours sincerely,
Jayaprakash

[2]Tenneti Viswanatham (1896-); he taught at Gujarat Vidyapeeth, 1921-4; President Vishakhapatanam DCC; 1925, Minister under C. Rajagopalachari, Madras Government, 1937; played a leading role in founding Praja Party, 1950; resigned from Madras Legislative Assembly, 1952.

216. Address at the Rotary Club, Poona, 8 September 1952[1]

Small and medium-scale production must be the industrial norm for an economically backward country, like India, and it should be the responsibility of the State to create conditions conducive to the development of small-scale industries.

Joint farming, subsidizing cottage industries for the rural population, and repairs of our broken irrigation works and bunds in the rural areas are the only answer to the Indian agricultural problem and not the pilot schemes, like the community projects.

Economic reconstruction of a backward country brings immediately to the mind the picture of industrialization, and scientific agriculture, and the mind turns to the big industrial States for inspiration and guidance. But for us neither capitalist America nor Communist Russia can be a model.

Any rational scheme of economic reconstruction, must take into account our vast population, correspondingly large unemployment and low per capita productivity. The scope of mechanization in agriculture, and large-scale industrialization in the American or Russian sense is practically nil in India.

A reconstruction of the mode of cultivation from individual farming to joint farming is the urgent need for salvaging agricultural production in

[1] Adapted from *Tribune*, 9 September 1952.

India. The Government is not unaware of these considerations, but nothing has been done to give effect to this economic policy. It is not a matter of lack of consideration, it is matter of corruption in high places.

In the last five years a great deal of stress has been laid on the costly plants, like the Sindri Fertilizer Factory, while cottage and small-scale industries have languished on account of the faulty commercial and industrial policies of the Government.

Any Government aware of the basic principles of economic reconstruction in the existing conditions would have hastened not only to give the much-needed protection to the handloom industry, but also to do everything possible to give it encouragement and aid. I support the view expressed by Mr. Rajagopalachari that the cotton textile mills should be barred from producing dhotis and saris which are the principal productions of the handloom factories. There is lack of public enthusiasm for government schemes. Such enthusiasm can be created only by concrete evidence of a new deal for them.

I would draw the attention of the people of India to the tremendous possibilities of the release of human energy in India.

The Five-Year-Plan does not basically alter in any way the present policy of the Government. Equitable distribution of wealth is the most important aspect of economic reconstruction and there can be no two opinions on it just because it is part of a socialist ideology.

217. To J.B. Kripalani, 8 September 1952[1]

My dear Dada,[2]

I am enclosing a copy of my letter to Sadiq Ali[3] Saheb. I am extremely sorry that I am the cause of so much misunderstanding. It will always be my endeavour to support and strengthen the edifice that you and Asoka have built. And now I shall hold my tongue, no matter what the provocation—though it does not mean that my views about the UDF have changed.[4]

[1]*Brahmanand Papers* (NMML).

[2]Dada: Refers to J.B. Kripalani.

[3]See item no. 219.

[4]See Appendix 36 for J.B. Kripalani's reply dated 12 September 1952.

It was very kind of you to have taken the trouble of coming down to Poona to see me.

I am progressing well and Prabha too is well.

With Kindest regards,

Yours sincerely,
Jayaprakash

218. To Madhu Limaye, 8 September 1952[1]

Dear Madhu,

I probably sounded curt on the telephone. I am very sorry. Both you and Asoka had told me at length what had happened at Lucknow. Kripalaniji's talk at the press conference and Sadiq Ali's letter have greatly confused me. Asoka's letter to Sadiq Ali did not remove my confusion as far as the nature of the agreement regarding the future of the UDF is concerned. A telephone talk under these conditions was hardly likely to help me. Perhaps you were all afraid that in my reply to Sadiq Ali I might say something that would complicate matters further. I think I have done no such thing. You can judge for yourself by reading the copy of the letter that I am sending to Asoka.

I am again very sorry for sounding so curt on the telephone.

Yours affectionately,
Jayaprakash

[1]*Brahmanand Papers* (NMML).

219. To Sadiq Ali, 8 September 1952[1]

My dear Sadiq Ali Saheb,

Asoka has sent me a copy of your letter. I am deeply hurt at your tone and temper, and feel extremely sorry that my statement has caused so much misunderstanding. I would, however, beg you to read my statement with sympathy and friendliness.

Let me explain how I came to make the statement. To begin with, I had no desire to say any thing about this matter. When Kripalaniji very kindly came to see me here we had arranged a press conference for him. I was not

[1]*Brahmanand Papers* (NMML).

very happy with the categorical manner in which he spoke of the future of the Madras UDF. But I did not say any thing to him because I understood that he was anxious not to offend Mr. Prakasam. Nor had it occurred to me then to make any public statement. But after that for two or three days I read statements made by Madras KMPP and Communist leaders emphatically saying that the UDF would not at all be affected by the merger, even though Mr. Prakasam had earlier made the statesman like reply, 'Wait and watch' to a question put to him about the matter. Then there was a Madras despatch published in the *Free Press* [Journal] directly raising the question, bringing my name into it and putting me a query. When these things happened, I thought my position, as well as that of the SP, on the question was likely to be misunderstood if I kept quiet. I would even then have kept quiet had I not been given to understand that (a) Kripalaniji himself was not keen on the continuance of the UDF, provided he was able to carry Mr. Prakasam with him, (b) it was agreed that SP members were free to express themselves against the UDF.

Now, let us turn to the statement itself. First, I have stated that the position of the SP on the question was never ambiguous; second, the KMPP commitment in Madras was always taken into consideration; third, there was never a desire to face the Madras KMPP with a *fait accompli*; lastly, I had said that we always felt, as I do feel now, that a leader of the standing of Mr. Prakasam would himself resolve the difficulty and not ask us to take an illogical position. These were the effectual parts of the statement. I wonder what objection can be taken to them.

The rest of the statement contained an argument why to my mind the UDF was outdated now and should be dissolved. Surely, one can argue with one another even after the merger. If the UDF is ultimately to go, some of us have to do this, without bitterness or hostility and in the manner of persons belonging to the same fold.

From your letter to Asoka it seemed that you thought when Asoka came here after Kripalaniji had left we discussed the statement and it was issued with Asoka's approval. I am sorry that you should imagine all this conspiracy. Kripalaniji came here on Sunday the 31st August, Asoka came on Monday the 1st September and left the next morning. I had not the least idea of making any statement then. As you will probably find from the papers, the statement was issued on the 4th September after, as I have said above, the Madras friends and Communists had spoken. Asoka, like every body else, must have seen the statement in the papers the next morning, i.e. September 5. Whatever the fault, it was entirely mine and please do not drag Asoka into it.[2]

[2]See Appendix 35 for the text of Sadiq Ali's reply dated 10 September 1952.

I would again plead for sympathy and friendliness in judging one another. Hoping you are well,

Yours sincerely,
Jayaprakash

P.S.: I am enclosing copy of my statement[3] for ready reference. Don't let my statement come in the way of holding the joint conference please.

[3]Refers to J.P.'s statement issued on 4 September 1952 and published in the *Hindu* and other papers the next day. It is not included in this volume as J.P.'s letter to Sadiq Ali dated 8 September 1952 contains a good summary.

220. To Madhu Limaye, 9 September 1952[1]

Dear Madhu,

Your letter this morning. I have already apologized for being so curt on the telephone. However, I am happy to receive your letter and to know that my statement did serve some purpose.

No, it was not Lohia's[2] letter that had put me in such a bad mood. No doubt his words had hurt me, but I had got over it when I remembered how good he was at heart. His outbursts have no effect at all on his real feelings for his friends. Then, he had probably not seen my full statement.

It is not worth speaking about now, but when we meet I'll tell you why I was in such a 'mood'. And for heaven's sake don't make it a rule not ever to telephone me again.

Some of the statements of the KMPP leaders that you have sent me I had already seen. Asoka might do well to send them to Kripalaniji—not in a querulous manner like Sadiq Ali, but just to draw his attention to them.

Yours affectionately,
Jayaprakash

P.S.: Your reference to the message that I had sent through Goray[3] has not added to my mental peace. I don't know what Goray said, or I would not blame him for whatever he might have said. When there is so much misunderstanding all around and matters are of such delicacy, a little variation in the stress of words might do unimaginable havoc. However, let me put down briefly what I had told Goray:

[1]*Brahmanand Papers* (NMML).
[2]Lohia's letter mentioned here could not be traced.
[3]Goray: Refers to N.G. Goray.

1. The merger has pros and cons. Balancing them I am of opinion that it is a desirable thing and we should have it.
2. But if at the Executive there is a violent difference of opinion and it is apprehended that a large section in the Party would be opposed.
3. And if Acharyaji cannot be reconciled to it.
4. Then we should not proceed with it.
5. In that case insurmountable hurdles could be created [avoided?] at the negotiations and the merger could be prevented perhaps without much bitterness.

This was not a picture of a divided soul, as far as I am able to understand myself.

[Yours sincerely,]
Jayaprakash

221. To Asoka Mehta, 14 September 1952[1]

Dear Asoka,

I am enclosing copies of Kripalaniji's and Sadiq Ali's replies. I am afraid I have not been able to propitiate them. I am happy, however, to learn from your latest letter that Mr. Prakasam and Mr. Viswanatham are now in a better mood. I feel encouraged to write to them.

Regarding Narendra's[2] complaint, you were right in telling him that nothing could be done immediately. He should wait till after the merger. In the meanwhile, it would be better if you called for reports from the present office bearers [in Bengal] Adhir Banerjee,[3] Sakti and others.

Regarding inviting the Subhasist Forward Block, you might consult Kripalaniji or Sadiq Ali and then decide. There are both advantages and disadvantages in inviting them. But if we are assured of their sound stand on the CPI it may be useful to have them at the conference. Ruiker, of course, I know and if he alone were to represent his party, his presence would be an unmixed disadvantage. But if Dr. Atin Bose[4] and Leela Roy[5] were also to attend, it might be useful. If I remember alright, Kripalaniji

[1]*Brahmanand Papers* (NMML).

[2]Narendra, an activist of the Socialist Party; in West Bengal.

[3]Adhir Banerjee (1908-68); participated in the Quit India Movement, 1942; joined journalism as Assistant Editor of *Hindustan Standard*, 1946; founder of Journalists Trade Union, became its President twice; actively associated with Socialist Party in West Bengal.

[4]Atindra Nath Bose (1909-61); belonged to Forward Bloc (Subhasist), West Bengal; Member West Bengal Legislative Assembly, 1952-7; Member Rajya Sabha, 1958-61.

[5]Leela Roy—For biographical note on Leela Roy see item no. 148, n. 4 *ante*.

when he was here, was of the view that we should proceed one step at a time. However, you may consult him afresh.

I admire the way you are carrying on in the midst of your ever-increasing headaches.

Yours sincerely,
Jayaprakash

P.S.: About the Subhasist F.B. you might also consult Prafulla Babu if you have not done so already.

Jayaprakash

222. To Gopalaswami Ayyangar, 15 September 1952

Dear Mr. Ayyangar,

I have sent you a telegram today to grant an interview to Vinayak Kulkarni, Organizing Secretary of the All India Defence Services Civilian Employee's Federation of which I happen to be the President and Mr. S.M. Joshi is the General Secretary. I am still in the clinic and Joshi is on sick bed. Therefore, Kulkarni has to deputize for us. I would have written to you earlier but you were in Europe. You know a strike is going on in the Defence establishments at Kirkee and Dehu in which some 34,000 workers are involved by now. When Mr. H.M. Patel had come down, the Federation representatives had discussed with him and Mr. Kulkarni has gone to New Delhi to continue the talks further. It is a pity that even though the issues involved are capable of every solution, such a situation has been allowed to develop.

The issues involved in the present strike are mainly three:

1. the issue of retrenchment;
2. that of Poona being declared a 'B' area; and
3. the publication of the Kalyanwala Committee's report. Kulkarni will explain to you the workers' case regarding all these three points. Briefly they are as follows:

The Federation is not opposed to retrenchment in principle. But it desires that (a) there should be prior consultation with the Union; (b) some method should be found, such as economic holidays, to make provision for the continued employment of surplus staff; and (c) to compensate staff that must be retrenched.

[1]*J.P. Papers* (NMML).

As far as the issue of 'B' area is concerned the workers have a very strong case. Poona has grown to be a large city, and the cantonments of Poona and Kirkee are today just as organic parts of the city as the rest of the municipal areas. With the inclusion of the two cantonment areas, the population of Poona would be 6 lakhs, and it would be very well qualified to be 'B' class city.

As far as the Kalyanwala Committee's report is concerned, it is a sad story. When the Committee was appointed, over two years ago, it was instructed to report in three months. But the report is still to see the light of the day.

These are the issues which, with good will on both sides, are not incapable of solution or adjustment. I hope that with you at the head of the Defence Ministry there will be no difficulty in settling the issues. I believe, the 'B' area question is a matter which concerns the Home Ministry. I have accordingly written to Dr. Katju. I have also written to my friend Mr. V.V. Giri, in the hope that he would be able to help.

I hope you are well.

With very kind regards,

Yours sincerely,
J.P.

223. To Madhu Limaye, 17 September 1952[1]

Dear Madhu,

Your circular letter about the meetings for the 22nd and 23rd. Though Dr. Dinshah has not yet returned, I do hope I would be able to be present at these meetings. I am, however, preparing no drafts. It is better that those of us who are able to meet the KMPP leaders oftener and thus know their mind better, prepare the documents.

About the UDF[2] I have now a clearer understanding of our position at the negotiations. It seems we definitely did not make dissolution of the UDF a precondition for merger; it also seems that it was definitely not agreed that the UDF would automatically be dissolved after the merger. In this case, it would be best to keep the merger issue [UDF issue?] out of the joint conference, and to leave it to time and Mr. Prakasam to solve.

[1]*Brahmanand Papers* (NMML).

[2]United Democratic Front in Madras in which the KMPP and the Communists were participants.

I asked Profulla Babu about the Subhasist Forward Bloc. He also was of the view that while we should welcome its merger with us, it should not be invited to the Bombay meeting.

From the papers it seems that Asoka has gone to Banaras. I hope there is nothing serious. Or is the news incorrect?

Yours sincerely,
Jayaprakash

224. To Jawaharlal Nehru, 5 October 1952[1]

Dear Bhai,

It was very kind of you to send your love and good wishes for my birthday. Age and youth have little to do with each other and those beyond 60 may feel younger than others younger in age. Any way, I do not find it pleasant to think that one has reached fifty and left the best years of one's life behind.

I came here for the merger talks and have stayed behind for certain medical investigations, after which I shall return to Poona for at least another month. I am feeling better.

I see that you appeared as the rain god to the South Indians!

With Love,

Yours affectionately,
Jayaprakash

[1]*J.N. Papers*: Files at home (NMML).
[2]See Appendix 38 for Nehru's letter, dated 23 September 1952.

225. To J.C. Kumarappa, 7 October 1952[1]

My dear Prof. Kumarappa,[2]

I am very sorry for this delay in replying to your letter of 20th September. I should have liked very much to participate in the Arthik Samata Mandal Camp, but I have not yet been discharged from the Clinic and do not expect to be so for some time yet. I came here in connection with the SP-KMPP merger talks and have stayed on for some medical investigations. I expect to return to Poona in a few days.

As I told you when you had so kindly come to Poona, I am wholeheartedly with the Arthik Samata Mandal in its aims and objects. I do feel, however,

[1]*J.P. Papers* (NMML).
[2]For biographical note on J.C. Kumarappa, see *JPSW*, Vol. I, p. 126.

that as far as action is concerned, if it is to be effective, it must embrace as many people as possible. For that reason I was not very happy at the divisions in the Wardha Gandhian Group to whom the country looks for guidance. When you yourselves begin to act through splinter groups, nothing but confusion would be the result. I think it would be but fair to give the Sarva Seva Sangh a chance and also all our co-operation. I understood from Shri Nargolkar that the representatives of the Arthik Samata Mandal who had met Vinobaji at Banaras agreed that the Mandal could work in terms of the Sarva Seva Sangh programme.

Before returning from Poona to Patna I intend to visit Wardha and spend some time with you. Will you kindly let me know your programme for November.

With regards,

Yours sincerely,

J.P.

226. 'The Merger' 7 October 1952[1]

Commenting upon the SP-KMPP merger Asoka Mehta wrote last week: 'I am more than happy, I am excited'. Well may all of us feel excited, for the merger is an event of great importance, pregnant with great possibilities. It is now up to us—the membership of both the parties—to grasp the full import of this event and develop the hidden possibilities. Healthy, constructive, withal revolutionary, politics will suffer a setback from which it will never recover if we allow this merger to fail.

After the piercing experience of the general election we were all in sobered mood. It was driven home to us that unless there was political consolidation and parties that shared common ideals and followed common methods came together, the way would be open for the forces of reaction, on the one hand and those of chaos, on the other, to lead the country to ruination and worse.

Accordingly, at its first post-election meeting, held at Madras, the National Executive declared political consolidation to be the urgent need of the hour. Since then efforts to this end have been proceeding. The Pachmarhi Conference again made this the central point of its resolution on political line. Asoka Mehta has traced this development in the last week's *Janata*, and there is no need for me to repeat it here.

In view of this development it is surprising to receive complaints from Party members about the undemocratic behaviour of the Executive. There

[1]*J.P. Papers* (NMML), published in *Janata*, 7 October 1952.

are perhaps two explanations for this peculiar situation. First, members do not care to acquaint themselves with Party decisions and to read Party journals, bulletins, circulars, etc. Second, they do not understand the implications of the policies they themselves advocate.

Any one who is acquainted with the of evolution of Party policy in regard to political consolidation, would agree that the merger decision has been taken in a proper democratic manner. There is no higher body in the Party than the all-India conference of delegates; and when the conference itself lays down a policy, what can be more democratic. If the members did not understand the implications of the political line adopted at Pachmarhi, the fault is not that of the Executive. That there was no ambiguity in our minds, and that the merger idea was not an after-thought is clear from the fact that some of us went straight to Delhi from Pachmarhi to place the proposal before the KMPP.

It is being said what whereas the KMPP was democratic is calling a meeting to discuss the merger, the SP leadership in failing to do so acted undemocratically. It is forgotten that before we made the merger proposal the policy was decided at the Party conference. On the other hand, the KMPP could consider it only after the proposal was placed before it. As for the ratification of the merger, I understand the general Secretary is calling the General Council at Bombay.

It may be objected that the Pachmarhi political line did not envisage a merger with the KMPP. To this all that I can say is that we obviously do not understand in the same way the words that we use.

Questions have been raised if the KMPP believes in Marxism. I beg comrades not to allow Marxism to become another religion and get lost in forms to the detriment of the substance. This issue was well discussed at Pachmarhi, and Lohia's memorable reply should have made it unnecessary to raise it again. Let us not forget that Marxism has many warring interpretations—not only at different times and places but also in the same situation—and varied and contradictory applications. Further, history (including Indian history) is witness to the fact that those who persisted in describing themselves Marxists went woefully wrong and committed historic blunders, while those who were content to do without the label (though eager always to learn from Marx) were proved by events to have been in the right and to have followed the truly revolutionary path. All this should bring sobriety to those who are proud to call themselves Marxists, unless the appellation means no more than an effort to shine in the glory of a great name.

Therefore, let us not get excited over, who is and who is not a Marxist. By all means let those who consider themselves Marxists continue to do so. But let them not flaunt their nomenclature, feel superior to the others and make themselves into a Brahmanic caste. That certainly will be a negation of Marxism. Let not Marxism, conceived as a narrow doctrine, become a barrier to the meeting of revolutionary forces. Let it, to the contrary, become a clarion call to unity.

The merger is a challenge to the Marxists. If Marxism is a superior revolutionary doctrine, it should help them in demonstrating their superiority in action, in initiative, in leadership. I am sure the non-Marxists would then be happy to follow them, because they are not enamoured of names but of results.

The important point therefore, is not who calls himself a Marxian or a Gandhian or something else, but to what extent is there agreement between the two parties and all of us. As Asoka Mehta pointed out last week by quoting from the terms of both the Delhi and Lucknow agreements, then is a very large area of agreement both on basic and immediate questions of policy and programme. I am sure the forthcoming joint meeting at Bombay would reveal further agreement. When that is so, it would be disloyalty and disservice to the people not to join our forces.

(Next week I shall consider certain other aspects which to my mind are far more important than the above.)

J.P.

227. To Gopalaswami Ayyangar, 8 October 1952[1]

Dear Mr. Ayyangar,

I thank you for your letter and I hope you will excuse me for the delay in replying. . . . I feel very depressed at the manner in which the employing departments of the Government deal with their labour problems, even though the Ministers in-charge are the best of men. I have found from my personal experience of the last five years that nothing is done in time or with grace and every attempt is made to delay decisions as far as possible and when at last decisions are taken there is again delay in implementing them. Taking the issues that were involved in the Poona strike, it is remarkable that, even though everyone of them was under the consideration of the Defence Department for at least two years, the workers got nothing more, even after undergoing the suffering and sacrifice of 21 days' strike, than promises of further consideration. The Defence Department at least was expected to work with greater expedition. My only satisfaction is that now you have personally been seized of the whole situation and I hope things will move

[1]*Sri Jayaprakash Narayan Sixty First Birthday Celebration, Commemoration Volume*, S. Vijay Laxmi, ed., Madras, 1963, pp. 164-5.

quicker now. This is the first time, at least in my experience, that labour matters have been taken up by the Defence Minister. Not only I but the workers in general feel that now their case will not go by default.

I had come here for the merger talks and have stayed on for certain medical investigations. I shall be returning to Poona in a few days where I expect to stay till the first week of November. I am generally better but the specific complaints still persist. I am concerned to read in the papers that you were indisposed. I hope you are fully recovered now.

With kinds regards,

Yours sincerely,
Jayaprakash Narayan

228. To Gen. Mohan Singh, 8 October 1952[1]

My dear Gen. Mohan Singh,[2]

Thank you for your letter of September 26.

When Sheel Bhadraji[3] came to Poona we had a very frank and cordial talk. As I had told him then, we would always be very happy to have a united front in action with the All India Forward Bloc. He had also assured me that the Forward Bloc would be equally happy to cooperate with us. I was pleased to find the same sentiments in your statement of which you were good enough to send me a copy.

I am afraid my health will not permit me to go to Delhi for some time yet, but the Chairman of our Party, Acharya Kripalani, is there and I am sure he would be very happy to meet you. I had shown your letter to him and he said that I should write to you to see him at Delhi whenever it may be convenient to you. I hope it will be possible for you to go to Delhi in the near future.

I shall be returning to the Poona Clinic in a few days where I expect to stay till the first week of November. I am better but not free from my complaints.

I hope you are well. With regards,

Yours sincerely,
J.P.

[1]*J.P. Papers* (NMML).

[2]For biographical note on General Mohan Singh see *JPSW*, Vol. IV, p. 62.

[3]Sheel Bhadra Yajee (1916-); member Rajya Sabha, 1957-72. General Secretary/President Forward Bloc Bihar; Chairman/Secretary General, All India United Left Front, 1947-9.

229. 'Incentives for Goodness', 12 October 1952

In days gone by men tried to be good, impelled by some higher moral force in which they believed; and goodness meant such things as truthfulness, honesty, kindness, chastity, unselfishness. Men felt that it was the highest moral duty to try to be good. Whether they succeeded in their trial, or whether they tried at all, was a different matter. The important point is that society provided every individual with the motive to be good: it was the command of religion, of God; it was necessary for one's highest growth for self-realization; it brought peace and supreme happiness; it brought salvation and freedom from births and deaths.

In present society, with the hold of religion gone, faith in God shaken, moral values discarded as dead-weights of the dark ages of history; in short with materialism enthroned in men's hearts, are there any incentives to goodness left? Indeed, has the question any relevance at all to present facts, problems and ideals of human society?

I hold emphatically that no other question is more relevant to us today.

In spite of what may be broadly described as the materialist climate of present society, men everywhere are engaged, in their different ways, in creating a heaven upon earth, in remaking, perfecting human society. These efforts, even the most idealistic and ambitious, such as communism of its original conception, seem, however, to be shipwrecking on one obdurate rock—human baseness. It is clearer today than ever that social reconstruction is impossible without human reconstruction. Society cannot be good unless individual men are good, and particularly those men who form the elite of society.

Here then is the crux of the modern problem. Men wish to create, if not an ideal, at least a good society. Modern science and technology make that task far easier than ever before. But men lack the tools with which to make themselves. And the ideas are forgotten, and they begin to fight for power, position, spoils, bringing down the whole edifice of the new society.

Therefore, the problem of human goodness is of supreme moment today. The individual asks today why should he be good. There is no God, no soul, no morality, no life hereafter, no cycle of birth and death. He is merely an organization of matter, fortuitously brought into being, and destined soon to dissolve into the infinite ocean of matter. He sees all round him evil, corruption, profiteering, lying deception, cruelty, power politics, violence. He asks naturally why he should be virtuous. Our social norms of today and the materialist philosophy which rules the affairs of men answer back: he need not. The cleverer he is, the more gifted, the more courageously

[1] Article in *Janata*, 12 October 1952.

he practices the new amorality; and in the coils of this amorality the dreams and aspirations of humankind become warped and twisted.

For many years I have worshipped at the shrine of the goddess—dialectical materialism—which seemed to me intellectually more satisfying than any other philosophy. But while the main quest of philosophy remains unsatisfied, it has become patent to me that materialism of any sort robs man of the means to become truly human. In a material civilization man has no rational incentive to be good. It may be that in the kingdom of dialectical materialism, fear makes men conform, and the Party takes the place of God. But when the God himself turns vicious, to be vicious becomes an universal code.

I feel convinced, therefore that man must go beyond the material to find the incentives to goodness. As a corollary, I feel further that the task of social reconstruction cannot succeed under the inspiration of a materialist philosophy.

It may be asked if any social conditioning is at all necessary for men to acquire goodness. Is not man essentially good? Are not most men in every society decent.

Yes and no.

Man is a socio-organic being: he is partly the product of nature and partly that of society. What man is by nature cannot be said with certainty. Indeed, the very concepts of good and bad are supernatural or super-organic. There is nothing good or bad in nature. Human nature, apart from the instincts of self and race preservation, is most likely of a neutral character which acquires moral tones in accordance to social conditioning.

It is true that in every society most men are decent and good. These men go through life without being called upon to make any vital moral judgements. Their routine of life runs within narrow circles, and custom and tradition answer for them the questions concerning right and wrong.

But firstly, these harmless, decent men are apt under social stimuli to turn suddenly wild and vicious. Decent Hindus and Muslims, living peaceably together, didn't hesitate, as we know to our cost, to fly at each other's throats when the social passions were aroused.

Secondly, what is vital for the character of society, and for the direction of its growth, is not so much the character of the inert mass as that of the elite. It is the philosophy and action of this group of the select that determine the destinies of men. To the extent the elite become godless or amoral, to that extent evil overtakes the human race.

Let me hasten to remove a possible misunderstanding. I do not mean to suggest that all those who profess a philosophy of materialism are vicious nor that all non-materialists are good. But what I do assert is that there is no logic in materialism for the individual to endeavour deliberately to acquire and practice goodness. On the other hand, those who go beyond matter will find it difficult to justify [being] non-good.

Non-materialism—I am using this negative phrase because I have no particular school in mind—by rejecting matter as the ultimate reality, immediately elevates the individual to a moral plane, and urges him, without reference to any objective outside of himself, to endeavour to realize his own true nature and fulfil the purpose of his being. This endeavour becomes the powerful motive force that drives him in its natural course to the good and the true. It will be seen as an important corollary of this that only when materialism is transcended does individual man come into his own and become an end in himself.

230. To M.P.N. Singh, 13 October 1952[1]

My dear Maheshwar Babu,[2]

Your letter of the 21st Sept. and also your note of the 5th Oct. to Ojhaji.[3]

I am sorry to know about your health. I hope that you will take care of it and will soon be well.

I think you are taking an unduly pessimistic view of the affairs of the Bihar Party. In the circumstances in which the young comrades who are running the Party are placed, they are, I think, doing very creditably. You knew the reasons for my withdrawal from Bihar Party politics. As long as those reasons remain I shall be unable to change my decision. This, however, does not mean I shall not come back to Bihar or do any work in that state. In fact I am looking forward to doing a lot of work there in connection with land redistribution and also village reconstruction.

I am relying a great deal on your help.

As regards American aid, while I do not like the present policy of the Government of India, I do not think I would take such an alarmist view as you. However, we can discuss the matter when we meet.

I am better now and am expecting to leave by the first week of November. I do not think I will be here till the middle of November. I would write to you again about my definite programme. Most probably it would be possible for us to meet before you leave for Delhi.

With best wishes,

Yours sincerely,
Jayaprakash

[1] *J.P. Papers* (NMML).

[2] Maheshwar Prasad Narain Sinha (1896-); Member Bihar Legislative Council between 1920 and 1952; member Rajya Sabha, 1952-6.

[3] Ram Janam Ojha; one of the prominent leaders of the Praja Socialist Party in Bihar.

231. To J.B. Kripalani, 15 October 1952[1]

My dear Dada,

Mr. Golwalkar,[2] Sarsanghchalak of the RSS, has written to me asking for support to the movement for prohibition of cow slaughter. Personally I feel that those who eat beef should not be prevented by law from doing so. But I do not wish to reply to Shri Golvalkar without consulting you. I think he must have written to you also because his letter seems to be a kind of a circular letter sent to many persons. Will you please advise me what I should write to him.

With regards,

Yours sincerely,
J.P.

[1] *J.P. Papers* (NMML).

[2] Madhu Sudashiv Golwalkar (1906-73); Chief Organizer of the Rashtriya Swayamsevak Sangh (RSS); joined Banaras Hindu University as Professor in 1930; met K.B. Hedgewar at BHU; joined Rama Krishna Mission Sargachhi in 1936; After the death of Hedgewar in 1940, he was appointed the head of RSS.

232. Tribute to Bhan Tendulkar, 22 October 1952[1]

It was only the other day that I saw Bhan Saheb Tendulkar, and his quiet, even sombre, face still seems to breathe life before my mind's eye. He did not appear to be in the best of health, but no one could have suspected then that the end was so near. I now learn that he had long been ailing, but with his characteristic disdain for personal well-being, had gone on working without respite, literally wasting himself inch by inch in the service of the people. In our public life there would be few to compare with Bhan in utter selflessness and devotion to duty. His devotion to his fellow-workers was no less marked, and though he found little time to give to his own family, he was like a father to all the young men whom his personality so strongly attracted.

In Bhan Tendulkar's death the Praja Socialist Party in Maharashtra has suffered a loss which it would be impossible to repair. The district of Ratnagiri particularly the common people of that fantastic land of beauty, poverty, talent and promise, have lost their sincerest friend and servant.

As it would be remembered, one of the last things that Bhan did was to issue an appeal for funds. The best that the people of Ratnagiri can do, in

[1] *J.P. Papers* (NMML).

token of their love for one who literally laid down his life for them, is to subscribe generously to this fund.

Let Bhan Tendulkar remain for us, his co-workers, an ever burning source of light and inspiration.

[Yours Sincerely,]
Jayaprakash

233. To the State Secretaries, Praja Socialist Party, 28 October 1952[1]

To
The State Secretary,[2]
Praja Socialist Party,
....

Dear friend,

The ex-Socialist Party had set up a Central Committee on land redistribution. state committees and 'in-charges' had also been set up. After the merger of the parties and the formation of the Praja Socialist Party it is desirable that adjustments are made in these arrangements. I, therefore, suggest that this matter be considered and the necessary changes be suggested.

1. The Central Committee was made up of representatives of the National Executive *plus* one or two members from each state. Selection of representatives of the new National executive on the Central Committee may be left to the Calcutta meeting. But you are invited to suggest one or two names (the same as before or new) to represent your state on the Central Committee. The person or persons suggested should be such as would be in a position to devote most, if not all, of their time to the work of land redistribution, including the Bhoodan Movement. The persons must also be of high standing and integrity.
2. The State Committees must be reconstituted by you or by the Party State Executive. The 'in-charge' for the State would be appointed by the Naitonal Executive. *Ordinarily*, the State representatives on the Central Committee (for land redistribution) would be the State 'in-charge'.
3. District 'in-charge' should be appointed by the State 'in-charge' in consultation with the State Committee (for land redistribution.)

Instructions regarding the future plan of work in this regard will be issued

[1]*J.P. Papers* (NMML).

after the Calcutta meeting of the National Executive. In the meanwhile, the organizational re-adjustments should be made, and the problem may be studied and relevant material collected.

Yours sincerely,
J.P.

234. To C.G.K. Reddy, 10 November 1952[1]

My dear C.G.K.,[2]

Asoka had sent me a few days ago a copy of your long letter to him. I cannot tell you how distressed I was to read it. I had not expected that a person of your maturity and balance of mind would come to such conclusions without even discussing the matters concerned with his colleagues. In your letter you have again and again expressed your regard for us, and even your faith in us, which is indeed is flattering; but nevertheless you consider us all such utter fools as have surrendered all along the line and with whom it is no use wasting any breath. Asoka in his letter had suggested that you come up to Bombay, and to Poona on the way. But I don't know what was your reaction. Now that I am leaving Poona shortly (on the 15th) and there seems to be no chance of meeting you in the near future, I am writing you this letter.

First of all, I request you earnestly not to make up your mind without discussing everything with us.

In the meanwhile, let me say that you have entirely misunderstood many of the decisions taken at Bombay. Let me illustrate. You seem to read a lot into the deletion of the words in the membership pledge which affirmed that the member did not believe in caste. When the question was raised in the Executive, I myself supported the deletion, not because I was keen to surrender to Kripalaniji, but because the clause was a dead letter. We go out to enroll a mass membership and set up targets of lakhs, and expect the persons signing our pledge to abjure caste. It is a kind of falsehood or self-deception that we practise. Caste certainly will not go in this manner. By all means let us fight caste, but not by make-believe. If we keep the clause, we must honestly enforce it. How many members would we have then? Gandhiji also fought caste and his was the greatest influence in this field, but he did not seek to fight it through formal declarations, or membership forms.

You are also reading too much into the decision that no satyagraha can

[1]*J.P. Papers* (NMML).

[2]C. Gopalakrishnamoorthy Reddy (1921-); one of the prominent leaders of the Socialist Party in Karnataka; Member Rajya Sabha, 1952-4.

be launched without the permission of the centre. This was a necessary check to the foolish, ill-advised, so-called *satyagrahas* that are some times started by our comrades, who after starting them run to the centre for help or try frantically to find some face-saving escape from their 'struggle'. To require that the Centre's permission be taken does not take away the initiative of the lower organs of the Party. They are still free to take all the initiative they are capable of. When the National Executive is not in session, the Chairman or the General Secretary has been authorized to take action: so no one can plead that delay would be harmful to the interests of the *satyagraha* he is contemplating. There may be rare, exceptional circumstances in which immediate action may be called for: these may be treated as exceptions to the rule.

The further condition that *satyagraha* can be started only when other methods have failed is the essence of *satyagraha*, and no one who does not understand it has any right to launch or participate in a *satyagraha*.

To think that on account of these conditions the Party has become a mere parliamentary party, or that Acharya Kripalani and the other leaders of the ex-KMPP are interested only in elections, is totally to misunderstand. Kripalani, Ghosh, Prakasam, Kelappan[3] are old fighters who still have the spirit to reject exalted positions and a soft life for the sake of principles. You may be interested to know that Mr. Prakasam had come to the Bombay Conference searching for a 'plan of action'. You complain that except for a bare enunciation of policy, the Bombay Conference gave no programme. I do not know what is meant by a programme; heaven knows there is already so much to do; however, you can't expect everything at once. There were so many worries at Bomaby, that it was not possible to go beyond discussing the immediate organizational adjustments that were necessary. At the forthcoming Calcutta meeting, we hope to go further, but if you are expecting a spectacular announcement of a magic programme, I am afraid you are in for some disappointment. Nevertheless, let me assure you that we are still far from becoming a constitutionalist body of the type that you fear.

You have other doubts, but it will take too long to write about them. I must wait for an opportunity of a personal talk, that is, if you care to give me such an opportunity.

Let me add that I appreciate that you have a real difficulty in Mysore. But, there is no reason to believe that Kripalaniji and his colleagues of the ex-KMPP will deliberately, and out of partisanship, shelter persons about whose unworthiness there is patent proof. Also, there is no reason to believe

[3] K. Kelappan (1890-1971); A veteran freedom fighter and Congress leader, based in Kerala; participated in all Congress led movements from 1922 to 1942 and consequently spent many years in jail; in 1951 he joined KMPP and in 1952 elected to Lok Sabha; became involved in Sarvodaya activities in 1957 and continued this work till his death.

that those who seek to defend the reactionary feudal order will have much chance in the PSP. But you must be patient and give us time. It is not reasonable to expect that just at the moment of merger each side should have sat down to screen the membership of the other.

I do not know where you got the idea that Suchetaji was made leader of the Parliamentary Party. She is, as before, the leader of the Party in the House of the People; and Acharyaji, as before is the permanent chairman of the Parliamentary Party.

You know the place you have in the Party and the high regard in which all of us hold you. I cannot conceive of the Mysore Party, without you, and you have already raised high the Party's prestige in Parliament. Please do not undo what you have done. You are young and have a great future. Do reconsider the whole matter.

I am leaving Poona on the 15th and hope to reach Patna by the 25th November.

With best wishes,

Your sincerely,
J.P.

235. To Jawaharlal Nehru, 13 November 1952[1]

Dear Bhai,

Prabha and I send you our warmest love and our very best wishes. May you live long to complete your work and see your dreams for India fulfilled. Millions of your countrymen are very distressed to see you wearing yourself out at such terrific pace. Couldn't you spare yourself a little so that you could serve longer and achieve more? The prayer of millions of hearts is with you.

As ever,
Jayaprakash

[1]*Brahmanand Papers* (NMML).

236. Replies to Questions Posed at the Praja Socialist Party's Monthly Camp, Bombay, 16 November 1952[1]

Question: Does your decision to withdraw from trade union movement and settle for constructive work in a village, reflect your mood to retire from active political work?

[1]Adapted from *Janata*, 23 and 30 November 1952.

Jayaprakash Narayan: My decision to withdraw from trade union movement and settle for work in a village is not at all motivated by any desire to withdraw from active political work. On the other hand, I have taken this decision with a view to make my political work more effective and productive.

Soon after the general elections some of us met informally at Acharya Narendra Deva's place at Banaras and at that time all of us arrived at the same conclusion after prolonged discussions that functionaries of the party at different levels, including the prominent spokesmen of the Party, will have to change their mode of political functioning. Instead of doing extensive political work we have to work intensively, selecting specific spheres and regions for our activity.

Unfortunately, we were not able to imbibe this new outlook of functioning and we continued functioning in the same old framework. I had observed that many of our trained and well equipped full-time workers were concentrated in towns and cities, and so I had appealed to our comrades that they should devote their time for work in villages. Little notice was taken of this appeal.

I, therefore, thought that I should myself settle down for work in a village so that I may help in changing the outlook of our workers towards Party work in this new direction. Today I am convinced, more than ever before, that the village must become the pivot of our political functioning if our movement is to be genuinely democratic. If we exclude from the orbit of our political functioning vast multitude of our people in the villages, we would fail in our effort to usher in Democratic Socialism.

There was a time when we were under the deception of our slogan that industrial labour is the vanguard of revolution. History has exploded this myth. In our nation's struggle for freedom the peasant in the village has played a heroic role. He still continues to be a significant factor in our struggle for socialism.

We can overlook him only at the peril of our own movement. Unless we understand the dynamics of the village life by identifying ourselves with village folk through our work, we will not be able to percolate our movement to the lowest strata of our society.

My concentration on village work will prevent me from going round the country to collect purses for the party. But in a way even this will do some good to our organization. Our local functionaries of the Party will redouble their efforts to improve the finances, and local initiative will be developed in this mater. If by adhering to some village for work I succeed in changing the outlook of our comrades on Party work, in the long run, the productive capacity of the Party machine will also go up.

Since my announcement to settle for work in villages all sorts of rumours have been in the air. Some have circulated the whispering news that I was not very happy over the merger of KMPP and the Socialist Party and actually I have lost interest in active politics.

There cannot be anything farther from the truth than this whispering campaign. Ever since the Pachmarhi Conference I have been pleading for steps leading towards the merger of the two parties. At the meeting of the General Council of the Socialist Party I made it abundantly clear that any vacillation in moving towards a merger at that stage would make ourselves the laughing stock of history.

It is unfortunate that to my actions and pronouncements are attributed such strange motives. I can assure the Party comrades with full confidence that by concentrating on villages I will increase the output of my political work in the long run.

Q: In your recent article 'Incentives to Goodness' you have expressed your view-point that materialist philosophy fails to provide a person with incentives to goodness. Is this attitude of your mind consistent with the rational outlook of our party?

J.P.: The views expressed in the article 'Incentives to Goodness' are my personal views. Our party may or may not accept them. As far as I am concerned the views I have expressed in the article are the culmination of rethinking which started long back.

At the Annual Conference of the Socialist Party in 1948, I had raised through my report the highly controversial issue of 'ends and means'. I strongly pleaded at the Conference that fair ends cannot be achieved through unfair and unscrupulous means. Unfair instruments undermine the strength of the person who aspires to reach the fair end.

If I remember right, the views expressed by me then were by and large accepted by the Party members. My recent views are the culmination of the process of rethinking which started at the Nasik Convention. There was a time when I felt that the philosophy of materialism could satisfy my intellectual quest in life, and so, for years I worshipped at the shrine of materialism but now, after fresh thinking I have come to the conclusion that such quest can be solved not by mere intellectual pursuits but by living experiences in life.

One question before me was, what is the incentive to goodness in our life? I failed to find any such incentive in materialism. My mind is, however, quite open on this matter, and I will not refuse to be convinced in the opposite direction. My statement that materialism fails to provide incentive to goodness should not, however, be misunderstood to mean that all materialists lack goodness and all spiritualists are good.

I only contend that to be good intrinsically one has to go beyond the material. No doubt certain values of our life are conditioned and determined by environment, but at the same time there are certain basic values which are absolute and eternal. There is something like absolute good the pursuit of which can give us contentment in our life.

Recently, I had an opportunity to have discussions with some Yugoslav friends. I asked them the same question. What incentives to goodness are offered by the Marxist philosophy which considers all the values of life as relative. I asked them the question that if relativism is accepted in every sphere of our life, will it not mean a free hand for unscrupulousness? Suppose in Yugoslavia there arises a problem as to who should hold the reigns of power after Marshall Tito, and there is a conflict between various power cliques. What can prevent these power groups from using any unscrupulous means to achieve power suppressing by other groups? Each group believing in relativism of values will feel that to attain the ultimate goal which that group considers to be good, other groups should be suppressed ruthlessly. 'Ends justify the means'—will be the rational interpretation of their unscrupulous acts.

All will pose to be good Marxists, and will pursue the path that they choose. When such problems are analysed with an open mind, materialism is found to be inadequate to provide incentive to goodness and one has to think in terms of non-materialism. This, however, does not mean that I embrace mysticism or spiritualism.

Q: Has the Praja Socialist Party any ideology? Do you think that the ideology of the Socialist Party is diluted due to its merger with the KMPP?

J.P.: I firmly believe that the Praja Socialist Party has a definite ideology. By ideology I do not mean any system of thought that includes metaphysics and philosophy. It only connotes an integrated set of principles and programme that guide the actions of a movement and depicts a clear picture of a society we strive to create through this movement. In this restricted sense of the term ideology, what are the main ingredients of the ideology of the Praja Socialist Party?

- Conception of a Democratic Socialist Society free from social, political and economic exploitation.
- Nationalization of that sector of industry where capital tends to accumulate.
- Decentralization and devolution of economic and political power.
- Redistribution of land amongst the tillers and co-operative farming.
- Adoption of peaceful and democratic means to establish a democratic socialist society.

These ingredients of our ideology give us an integrated picture of a social order we are struggling to create.

There are some critics of the Party, who have been alleging that the ideology of the Socialist Party is diluted after its merger with the KMPP. As an evidence of this process of dilution they state that whereas the former Socialist Party envisaged the possibility of insurrection in the event of the breakdown of democracy, the Praja Socialist Party has left no room for such a possibility.

Apparently the statement appears to be correct, but if we consider the practical implications of this problem we will have to agree that the issue of insurrection *vs.* peaceful and democratic methods is fast becoming a purely academic issue. No one, who takes a realistic view of the present conditions in our country envisages any possibility of insurrection to accomplish social change.

If at all the situation changes radically and beyond our expectations and violence becomes inevitable, I do not think that the spokesmen of the former KMPP will think in any way differently from those of the former Socialist Party.

Acharya Kripalani in his characteristic humour had thrown light on this issue of violence and non-violence. He was asked as to how he would behave if someone misbehaves with his sister, when he is accompanying her for a walk. Quick came the answer: 'Before my head begins to think, my foot will act as if with a reflex action.' This humorous reply is rich with meaning. Even in politics his attitude would not be very much different. Let us not make a fetish of the issue of insurrection.

There was a time when we emphatically asserted that we cannot get complete independence for India by peaceful methods. History has falsified our stand, and we saw that through the strength of our peaceful struggles and the pressure of international situation we could attain our independence. We should, therefore, refuse to be dogmatic on this issue. Refusal to be dogmatic does not mean dilution of our ideology.

Some of the critics of the merger have said that the Socialist Party was formerly a challenger of the Gandhian ideology, and hence the merger of the Socialist Party with the KMPP is, according to them, tantamount to rejection of our opposition to the Gandhian ideology.

Some of the articles that have appeared in the press after the merger also give the impression that the Socialist Party has changed its ideology entirely and has accepted the 'Gandhian Philosophy', which has been the sheet-anchor of the KMPP.

One does not know whether there is anything like an integrated Gandhian philosophy. At least Gandhiji never claimed to have evolved any new philosophy. He repeatedly said that he was propounding ideas which had been preached for centuries.

But even assuming that such a philosophy exists, it would be historically incorrect to state that either the Socialist ideology alone has drifted towards Gandhism or that Gandhian ideology alone has moved towards socialism. What happened in reality was that both the Socialist and the Gandhian schools moved towards each other under the impact of a challenging situation.

Let us see as to what are the changes that have taken place in the Gandhian school. The Gandhian school can be considered to be composed of three elements:

1. Gandhiji himself.
2. Gandhian political workers who worked in the Congress.
3. Gandhian constructive workers.

Let us see how Gandhiji responded to the changing conditions in the country. There was a time when Gandhiji propounded the idea of Dominion Status. This ideal was considered by the radical elements in the country as a reformist one.

Under changed conditions the same Gandhiji who formerly pleaded for Dominion Status gave the clarion call of 'Quit India' and exhorted the people to 'Do or Die' in the final struggle for freedom. Those of us who had criticized Gandhiji for his reformist thinking earlier were deeply moved by this radical orientation of Gandhiji's mind.

There was a time when Gandhiji assured the Zamindars that Zamindari would not be abolished provided the Zamindars acted as the trustees of the landless peasants.

Gandhiji had to change this attitude at a later stage. During his talks with Mr. Louis Fischer, Gandhiji expressed his view that in Free India kisans would take possession of the land and the Zamindari system would be abolished without any compensation. At a still later stage, he prescribed for the kisans the weapon of Satyagraha and peaceful resistance to put an end to injustice perpetrated on them.

Thus Gandhiji did move far away from some of his earlier ideas.

The second element of Gandhian school consists of men like Acharya Kripalani, Rajendra Prasad and others, who were political functionaries in the Congress. Men like Acharya Kripalani from this group revolted against the leadership of the Congress, which according to them, had proved to be ineffective in solving the urgent problems facing the common man in the country after the attainment of freedom. This group splintered away from the Congress and formed the KMPP.

If these elements were opportunists as is alleged in certain interested quarters, they would not have parted company with the Congress, but would have sought, instead, seats of authority and power, which were not beyond their reach.

Thus the change among some of the members of this Gandhian group of political workers is reflected in their decision, delayed but at the same time bold, to sever their connections with the Congress.

The third group of Gandhians, namely the constructive workers, also acquired a new orientation. Before the advent of freedom, these Gandhian constructive workers were carrying on their constructive activities in a detached manner, unconcerned with the problems of social and economic transformation of society.

In the post-freedom era the enthusiasm and the confidence of these constructive workers was revived by Acharya Vinoba Bhave who started the movement of Bhoodan Yajna and gave a new lease of life and abiding faith to the constructive workers. He has created amongst the constructive workers a social urge to build a society of free and equal citizens.

The transformation in the outlook of the Gandhian workers has brought them closer to the forces of Democratic Socialism.

Thus all the three elements of the Gandhian school were moving away from their old ideas and conceptions and were gravitating towards Socialism.

Parallel developments took place in the Socialist Party also. Through the experiences of history the Socialist Party realized that in our struggle for Socialism the technique of peaceful resistance evolved by Gandhiji during our struggle for national Independence must be adopted.

With the ghastly spectacle of the growth of totalitarianism with its Leviathan State on a world scale we realized that decentralization and devolution of economic and political power must be accepted as the essential tenet of Democratic Socialism. At the Pachmarhi Convention Dr. Lohia elaborated the conception of decentralization based on the small machine technology.

These developments in both the streams of thought brought the KMPP and the Socialist Party closer to each other, leading ultimately to the merger of both into one massive party of radicalism and socialism.

The merger has not resulted in the dilution of any ideology. But two streams or ideas moving towards each other have given rise to a confluence of ideology. The inevitable has happened.

237. Address at Youth Assembly, Bombay, 18 November 1952[1]

I pledge to take up the spade and work in a village to build there a 'replica of the socialism' of my dreams.

I have decided from now on to set myself to constructive work. This new phase of my life would begin in my own village, Sitab Diara, in Bihar.

I ask the youths of the country to conduct a self-screening and find out to what extent they are useful in a constructive way to society. If every man and woman in the country feels the responsibility of Pandit Jawaharlal Nehru, the lot of every member of the society would be much better than what it is today.

I also advise the Youth Assembly to keep away from politics and devote itself entirely to constructive tasks. In the past, all youth movements were turned into political platforms. I, however, hope that the Youth Assembly would be different and give a correct lead to the youth of the nation.

[1] Adapted from *National Herald*, 19 November 1952.

238. To Ibrahim Nathoo, 21 November 1952[1]

Dear Mr. Nathoo,[2]

It was a great pleasure meeting you that morning at Bombay. You were good enough then to invite me to East Africa, and you may remember that I had told you that I was, in fact, already contemplating such a visit. Now, the plan has been finalized and I expect to leave by the end of January, '53. In the meanwhile I am sending my friend and colleague, Shri Pratap Shah, in advance to meet friends and make contacts. I have asked Pratap to meet you particularly and I shall be grateful for any help given to him in his work.

Looking forward to meeting you,

Yours Sincerely,
J.P.

[1]*J.P. Papers* (NMML).

[2]Ibrahim Nathoo was a member of the Kenya Legislative Council, Nairobi, East Africa.

239. To A.B. Pant, 21 November 1952[1]

My dear Appa Saheb,[2]

I am very sorry that I have taken so long to reply to your letter, even though I thought so often to write.

Satyadeva Shastri had taken that letter from me some two years back, but he did not go at that time. When he actually left for East Africa I did not know. In fact, I had no idea that he was there till your letter came. Had I known when he was going, I would have taken care to advise you about him. I am sorry to say that he does not enjoy our confidence any more; in fact, he was expelled from the Party about a year ago. However, the mischief has now been done.

You may remember my proposal to visit East Africa. I was unfortunately not free to leave till now. But I find that I can go by the end of January '53. But in the meanwhile conditions there have become disturbed and I do not know if it would serve any purpose if I go early next year. Pratap Shah is scheduled to sail on the 9th December. But we would be entirely guided by your advice. Will you kindly write as soon as you can?

I had spent five months at the Poona Clinic. Poona was lovely. The rest and the treatment have done me a great deal of good. I was also very happy to spend so much time with Rao Saheb and Achyut. Rameshwar Rao also came twice and we had long chats. Now, I have to plunge into work again. But, if I can help it, I am not going to run about and lecture any more. I want to settle down and do some constructive work.

We talked a lot about you with Rameshwar and I cannot tell you how proud we are of you.

With best wishes,

Yours very sincerely,
Jayaprakash

[1] *J.P. Papers* (NMML).

[2] Apa B. Pant (1912-92); Prime Minister of Aundh State, 1944-8; Member AICC, 1948; Indian High Commissioner in British East Africa, 1948-54; Counsel General to Belgian Congo and Ruanda-Urundi and Commissioner to Central Africa and Nyasaland 1950; OSD External Affairs Ministry 1954-5; Political Officer in Sikkim and Bhutan 1959-61; Ambassador to Indonesia, 1961-4; Norway, 1964-6; UAR, 1966-9; High Commissioner to UK, 1969-72; Ambassador to Italy, 1972-6.

240. The Ideological Problems of Socialism, Rangoon, 7 January 1953[1]

I should like to start by saying that socialism is ninety per cent practice and ten per cent theory. I am afraid socialists are often inclined to forget this rather simple axiom. If we always remember that after all the test of theory is in practice, there would not be in the socialist movement so much controversy, so much hair-splitting. Practice and theory must obviously be interrelated. If we look at the ideological problems of socialism from this point of view, we will also have to examine the practical tasks which are facing he socialists throughout the world. The field is too wide to be covered in a short address. I shall, therefore, confine myself to a few problems which have arisen out of certain practical, objective situations.

I propose to deal only with five such problems, the first of which is the problem of socialist a axioms. I have placed this problem in the first place, because I am convinced that unless a solution is found to it, all our attempts at socialist reconsruction of society are bound to fail. The problem has arisen in many ways, but let me point out only two sources from which it has appeared. We have before us the very vast experiment of socialist building in the USSR It was assumed, I believe, by the architects of socialism in Russia that if they proceeded with certain changes in the society, in the social environment, in the foundation of the social structure and in the structure itself, it would be possible for them to build up the socialist society of which they had dreamed for years and for which they had struggled through perhaps an equal number of years. But while we find that the economic basis of socialist society has been laid down—industry has been nationalized, agriculture has been collectivized, the motive of private profit has been removed from the economic system—the social structure or superstructure that has been built up on this foundation does not answer to the description of socialism. I doubt whether there would be any delegate or any comrade here who would describe the society in Soviet Russia as a socialist society. He would perhaps describe it more as state capitalism than socialism.

Now, there must be certain reasons why all these things happen. If you go back to the ideological formulations of Marx, if you go back to dialectical or historical materialism, as it is called, for an answer, I am afraid you will be disappointed. The means of production are supposed to govern the

[1]Address by Jayaprakash Narayan while initiating discussion on the Ideological Problems of Socialism at the first Asian Socialist Conference at Rangoon, on 7 January 1953. The Conference was held on 6-9 January 1953. The present text is reproduced from Bimal Prasad, ed., *A Revolutionary's Quest: Selected Writings of Jayapraksh Narayan*, New Delhi, 1980, pp. 158-72.

relations of production, and the changes in the means of production are supposed to govern the changes in the relations of production. You have, as far as the productive technique is concerned, a highly-indusrialized technique based on electricity and large machines. You have mechanization of agriculture. You have a technique, which looked at purely from the technical point of view, is not different from the technique of production found in the USA; but whereas that technique in the USA gives you a capitalist society, in Soviet Russia it gives you an entirely different system. Therefore, you will have to go deeper into the problem.

Let me also at this stage point out that as far as the old ideological formulations are concerned, somehow their development has been arrested. The interpretation of history which was started by Marx, I am afraid, has more or less stayed at the stage where Marx had brought it. It was hoped that after a socialist government had been established in such a large county as Russia, we would have further development of the science of socialism, of its philosophy, of its historical interpretation and so on, but we find that in Russia instead of interpreting history, they are busy distorting history: and if you start distorting history, you cannot interpret history. If you begin to deny facts, historical facts, if you shut your eyes to events that have taken place, there cannot be any scientific interpretation. However, this was by way of digression.

Going back to Russia, we find that after the achievement of power there began a very bitter struggle for power inside the ruling party itself. That struggle for power knew absolutely no bounds. Every means was used in that game of power. We have found a repetition of the same process in other countries which have come under the domination of Stalinist communism. We had for instance the recent trials in Czechoslovakia and the execution of Slansky[2] and the rest of them. Now, here you are faced with a very serious problem. A party comes to power. It starts with very noble ideals. It aims at the creation, ultimately, of a society in which even the State has ceased to exist; there are no classes, there is no money, no wages—that is the ultimate picture of communist society which the Communist Party of Soviet Russia always had before it. But in the achievement of the objective they failed dismally. And you may have found that they are now claiming in Soviet Russia to have more or less completed the socialist stage of their task. They claim that they are now beginning with the building up of a communist society, that is, a society in which there will not be institutions, social and economic, which I have just referred to.

[2]Rudolf Slansky was one of the leading figures in the Communist Party of Czechoslovakia. Along with several other such leaders he was executed in 1952 on the charge of being a Zionist agent.

Every socialist party throughout the world must be constantly aware of this serious problem of the demoralization of the party and the corruption of the ideals in the midst of this struggle for power, and answers will have to be found for this very serious problem. I am afraid that the commonly-accepted philosophy of Marxism, a philosophy accepted by many socialists, including the Stalinist, is based on amoralism, a philosophy that does not take into account the question of good or evil, a philosophy that regards this question as relative and relative to such an extent that these considerations can completely be disregarded, if the immediate purpose were to be served in that manner. There is another source from which this problem arises and that is a universal source, that is, the weakness of human nature, the weakness of individual man everywhere, his ambition, his selfishness, his stupidity, his hate, his fear. Now, if you are engaged only in shaping the environment in which the individual man lives—the social, economic and political environment—and if you are neglecting the individual, I am sure you will find that all these elements that go to constitute the nature of man as he is today will vitiate all your efforts, all your attempts at social reconstruction.

We have in history attempts made to improve the individual by forgetting the environment in which the individual lives. For instance, we had Buddha. Looking at the problem of human misery and arriving at the conclusion that human misery can be traced to human desire, he developed a system of self-culture, a system for the culture of the individual, for the making, moulding and shaping of individual human nature so that he may be free from misery by controlling his passion, his desire. That was a very noble effort, but it was, if you forgive me for so saying, a one-sided effort. Today many socialists are again making the mistake of making another one-sided effort, namely, that of changing society alone and forgetting the individual. When Lord Buddha said that misery came from desire, he did not consider the misery that was the product of social institutions, of soçial environment. Supposing there are two babies born in this world, one in a very poor home, the other in a very wealthy home. The miseries of these two human personalities would not depend merely on their own nature, but also on their social circumstances. Similarly today, as I have already told you, if we merely create a socialist environment and leave the question of the individual alone, we will again find that it is a very partial effort at consructing a new social order, because the same individual will be functioning in that social environment and, if he is not a disciplined individual, if he is not an individual who is in tune with the aims of that society, who has not been trained, who has not learned to subdue and subjugate his personal desires and ambitions to the social good, we will find that the experiment of social engineering would miscarry.

I therefore place this before you as one of the fundamental problems of the socialist movement today. We are seeing before us experiments that are being shipwrecked on the question of amoralism. Therefore I hope you will agree with me that whatever be our conception of the path to socialism, whatever be our interpretation of theories, we in the socialist movement must subscribe to certain values, values which we will not consider relative in the sense that we could sacrifice them in order to achieve an immediate end. The communist started with this noble idea of a new society, a classless, stateless society, a society of free and equal individuals, but he believed that no matter what he did today, no matter what were the means that he employed today, as long as he was successful he would ultimately arrive at these goals. So we see that his objective is noble but instead of progressing towards it he has been going astray. He has taken a different path which will never take him to the goal of communism, and therefore, if I may refer to a very brilliant thesis of my friend Dr. Rammanohar Lohia, we should in our movement apply what he calls the test of immediacy, that is, we must see that what we are doing immediately squares up with what we intend to do in the ultimate stage. If our present action is in consonance with the ideals that we have before us, there is no reason to doubt where we would ultimately land ourselves. For there is some rational ground for assuming that if our present action squares up with the noble ideals that we have before us, then ultimately it is bound to take us there. If on the other hand we indulge in activities which contradict these ideals, these values, on which the new society will ultimately be based, there is no rational ground for supposing that we will by some dialectical contrivance ultimately arrive at that goal. Therefore, friends, I should emphasise that the socialist movement along with its like to economic and political and social programmes must also have a programme which includes this question of values.

II

I should now turn to the next problem which I wish to place before you, that is the problem of creating a proper political framework for the development of a socialist society. Here, I am afraid, we are still groping. various experiments have been made. If you go back to the classics of socialism, you will not get much light, because neither Marx nor Engels, nor Kautsky nor Lenin described in detail the political characteristics of a socialist society. Marx and Engels, as you know, were mostly concerned wth analysing the capitalist society and finding out the dynamics of that society which would help the socialists to create out of capitalism a socialist society. Now as far as the political expressions of socialism are concerned, the first, one that, historically speaking, arose was the Russian political system. The Russian political system, as you know, has gone through a long process of evolution. Some of us believe that if the original concept of the political structure had been adhered to then, possibly Russia would not have socialism or communism, but it would also not have landed itself in the morass in which it finds itself today. We have today there a structure which is a one-party dictatorship. At the same time we have there a party which has a restricted membership, which goes periodically through purges, a party in which democracy does not seem to exist any longer; and in this one-party dictatorship we have a completely bureaucratic State, which cannot in any way be described as a workers' State, as a people's State. Obviously for the socialist movement of the world the Russian picture of political organization would be found wanting and unacceptable. We would have to devise a defferent structure.

We have in certain Western countries such as Sweden or Finland, socialist governments trying to build up a socialist society. This task in these countries is being fulfilled within the framework of formal parliamentary democracy. It is possible in such countries, as happened in Great Britain, for instance, that the socialist party should come to power for a number of years and then again lose that power as result of the popular vote. To many socialists in Asia, and I have heard it being discussed in socialist circles, this would be a failure of socialism. Obviously those who consider this to be a failure of socialism believe that once a socialist party comes to power, every attempt should be made by that party by whatever means possible not to let that power slip out of its hands. Well, obviously that cannot happen whithin the confines of formal political democracy; there socialist reconstruction will have to take chances. It may be that in course of time socialism comes to be so entrenched in the hearts of the people that the socialist party is perpetually in power and has got unrivalled opportunities for socialist reconstruction. Then in that country the question would arise whether the political structure that was evolved through the age of bourgeois liberalism should be preserved or there should be drastic changes made. I believe it is felt in this country also that representative government is not enough, that it is necessary in the political sphere as well as in the economic sphere to give power of self-government to the people at large. I think socialists in the West too are becoming aware of the problem of decentralization of political power, so that the people themselves may participate in the management of their affairs. It is not enough for a socialist parliament through a socialist cabinet to rule over a country, it must be supplemented by the people's participation at the lower levels of the administration also. Socialism today has to give the answer to the question whether even in those countries which have a tradition of democratic, representative government, the political structure of socialist society should be the same as it is now. Would it be enough if the economy of the country has been socialized? Would it be enough if a socialist party has come to power, if all these conditions have been fulfilled ? Would we be satisfied or would we have to go forward and evolve a technique of political living and government in consonance with the ideals of socialism?

We have another example of a socialist political system that is in the process of evolution. It is very rapidly evolving and it is difficult for anyone to say at any period of time whether he is up-to-date with the developments that are taking place. I refer you to Yugoslavia. Yugoslavia is a country which till recently was ruled by the Communist Party. Yugoslavia too was and to a very large extent is today a one-party state. But the Yugoslav Communists are anxious to bring to an end as speedily as possible this one-party rule; and I hope you are aware of some of the most unorthodox steps that these communists of Yugoslavia have taken. When I say unorthodox I have in mind the orthodoxy that is preached and practised in Moscow. Somehow or other they claim to be the true interpreters of Marxism-Leninism which some of us, I am sure, would question. It is an axiom with all of us that socialism cannot exist without decocracy, nor democracy be complete without socialism. The Yugoslav communists are aware of this axiom of socialism which, I may say, is also the axiom of Marxism as I understand it. Being aware of this axiom the Yugoslav Communist Party has decided that it is or the people themselves to rule over themselves through People's Committees, Workers' Councils, and the representative institutions of the peasants. It should be these that should come forward and take the responsibility of administering the country, and therefore they are bringing to the forefront what was known as people's front and which they have now renamed as the Socialist Alliance of the Working People of Yugoslavia. The Yugoslav friends believe that in a society in which socialism has universally been accepted as the goal, the responsibility of ruling should be given to the people. They believe that a multi-party system does not answer to the needs of socialist politics, and that the problem is to create a new political framework for socialist society. According to them once the goal of socialism has been popularly accepted, there is no need even for one party, much less many parties. Instead of a multi-party State, they are driving at a no-party State. That is a problem which all of us must seriously consider, namely, creation of a no-party State. That is why they have converted the Communist Party of Yugoslavia into the League of Communists which is going to perform the functions of political education, and all education in general, civic education included. I am sure they are going to give their attention to the education of the individual also. I do not know what will be the outcome of this development, but it is a very interesting development. If the State is to melt away, to wither away, the party must also wither away. The aims of the party should become so broadcast, so popularized, so universally accepted that the party becomes superflous.

Now, I have my reservations about this development. It seems to me that if in a particular society at a particular period of time certain aims are universally accepted, it does not mean that there should necessarily be a single party in existence for instance, in the age of liberalism, in the age in which capitalism was performing a revolutionary function and playing a progressive role in Europe, the ideals of free enterprise and of individual liberty as conceived by liberal capitalism were commonly accepted by the people; nevertheless we had in these countries different parties owing allegiance to capitalism and still functioning in opposition to one another. The Conservative Party of Great Britain and the Liberal Party of Great Britain have accepted the foundations of capitalist society and still there are two parties. In America you have the Democratic Party and the Republican Party. Bother believe in free enterprise. Both accept the ideals of capitalist society and yet you have these two different parties. So I am not quite sure that when socialism comes to be generally accepted by most of the people whether there should be or there would be only a single party in existence. Socialists themselves might differ as to how to carry on their tasks from day to day and these differences might lead to the formation of different socialist parties. Therefore I am not quite convinced that at least at this stage it would be possible to do away with the multiplicity of parties. Some of us may not be very happy at the multiplication of socialism and multiplicity of parties in the world, but we have to adjust ourselves to the needs of the situation. It seems to me that the Yugoslav Communists are trying to create a democracy within a one-party dictatorship and therefore, perhaps, it is possible for them to go forward in the manner in which they are doing. But if we were functioning under democratic conditions and through the vote of the people a socialist party comes to power it cannot wish all the parties off the map, as it were. It will have to reckon with them if it does not wish to give up its faith in democracy, its faith in socialism itself.

If we believe that socialism is for the good of the people, if we believe that only under socialism will the people come into their own, then there should be no reason for us to deny democracy, because only through democracy can we go to the people. If we come to power democratically it does not seem possible for us to do away with the multiplicity of parties and the multi-party system might remain a feature of socialist society. How permanent a feature, it is not possible for me to say now, but in the foreseeable future, I am quite sure, that in a democratic socialist set-up other parties, even other socialist parties, are bound to exist. The socialist parties might act concertedly up to a point, but they may have their differences also. Now, whether there is this no-party structure, or whether there is a multi-party structure, that fundamental problem of the self-government of the people is always before you. All of us are apt to talk about the common man, but when we think of socialist reconstruction we think of ourselves. When we come to power we will do this, that and other things, and we will do it, if necessary, by force. But if we were to give the common people a place that is rightfully theirs in the political system, I am quite sure that we will have to evolve a decentralized State. I need not go into all the details of this question, but I should like you to keep it in view as the only possible means of translating socialism into people's rule at the lowest level.

III

The third problem is an allied problem, and that is the problem of the economic structure that would be necessary for a socialist society. Now according to Marxism, as you go to examine the superstructure step by step, you begin with the means of production and relations of production, the latter determining the economic structure. If in Russia we do not have socialism but some kind of state capitalism, there must be something vitally wrong with the economic structure also. All of us know what is wrong with the economic system there. Cenralization, bureaucratization, lack of industrial democracy, lack of workers' participation in the management of industry, in short, lack of popular control over the economic processes. We are apt to take over these ideals from Russia, the economic pattern that exists in Russia, in the hope of avoiding the defects that have grown out of it in Russia and grafting on it a democratic, decentralized political superstructure. Now one of the most important items of the economic programme of socialism is nationalization of industries. Well, the industries in Soviet Russia have been nationalized, but they have not produced socialism; they have produced something else. Therefore there must be something wrong in this system of nationalization, in this system of the management of nationalized industries. I do not know if in all the Asian countries the transport system has been nationalized, but speaking for India let me give you one example. In India our railways are a nationalized concern. They are not owned by private companies but by the State. We have a Railway Board which administers the railways and the railway administration is responsible to parliament. Now, supposing in India all the orther industries or big industries were nationalized and we had the same kind of administrative structure to run these industries as we have for the railway, then, even after complete nationalization, there will be no socialism. There would be bureaucratism, there would be exploitation, there would be no equal distribution of surplus value, as is the case with the railway system in India. The only difference between privately-managed railways and these state-managed railways is that whereas in the former there used to be a management borad responsible to the shareholders, here you have a management board officered by the bureaucracy and responsible to the Central Government. The railwaymen have no voice from the bottom up to the level of the Railway Board. They have no voice in the running of the railways. The wage structure is an entirely capitalist structure where the difference between the lowest wage and the highest wage is so great that we cannot imagine that difference being excelled even in a capitalist system. Now, we know that in Russia in the economic sphere these defects to exist. Neither the consumer nor the producer has a hand in the management and control of industry and in the distribution of profits. It is the bureaucracy, the hierarchy of the party, of industry, of the army, of collectivized agriculture that decides this question. Therefore, we in the socialist movement must think concretely of steps that will eliminate bureaucratism and centralism, give to the producer and to the consumer a hand in the management, and also ensure that the fruits of labour are equitably distributed. We will have to give our attention to this problem.

I believe that one solution of this problem would be the dispersal of the ownership at different levels, instead of concentrated ownership in the hands of the central government—dispersed ownership at various levels down to the cooperative, down to the village organization or municipal corporation. That would be one way of ensuring that too much economic power is not concentrated in too few hands, and we do not have an economic dictatorship along with the political dictatorship. We in Asia must also be conscious of our other limitations and in the light of those limitations approach this problem of economic structure. In most countries of Asia we have very meagre capital resources. The rate of capital formation is very slow because productivity is very low, even though the rate of consumption is low. The level of consumption is very low although the rate of saving is insignificant. Now, if we were to build up our economy under a dictatorship, it would be possible for that dictatorshipto extract as much surplus value as possible from the producer, from the primary producer. Take the peasants, for instance. For industrialization you require raw materials and food grains. Now whatever is available of these is not enough, because they have also to serve the individual needs of the primary producers, as well as the needs of socilist reconstruction. Now supposing we have a dictatorship, under that dictatorship it may be possible or the State to expropriate the produce of the peasant and let him starve. It would be possible to engineer a famine and blame the starvation on the famine; and with your censorship and your propaganda you can always make it out that it is not a State-made famine, but it is due to the nefarious activities of the foreign agent and various other circumstances, and in this manner, if over a period of time you went to on forcing the people to deny themseves, to deny their present needs, you could possibly industrialize at a rapid rate and on a large scale. If you function democratically and if you rely on the votes of the peasantry, on the votes of the workers, it will not be possible for you to go beyond certain limits in trying to force the savings necessary for economic development. Therefore, the structure of the socialist economy in most of the Asian countries is necessarily going to be a dispersed structure, a structure based not on concentrated, mass-producing manufacture but on dispersed, decentralized manufacture beginning with the homes of the producers and extending to small townships, etc. That again gives you a guarantee that economic power will not be concentrated in the hands of a small number of people, that you will be saved from economic dictatorship. Decentralization would more or less arise out of the limitations of the situation in which you find yourselves.

In connection with this problem of economic structure we will have also to take into account the relationship of socialism to the worker, to the peasant, to the trade unions and the peasant unions and so on. In Russia the unions of the workers, as you know, are merely to perform the function of what the Americans have called 'papboys', that is, to goad the people to produce more, to work harder. Now we have to consider, in a socialist society, the relationship of the party, of the State to the peasants and to the workers. We have in Asia trade union movements of sorts largely manned at the managerial level and at the level of leadership by middle class people. In that sense it is not a genuine trade union movement which draws up leaders from its ranks and grows up as a result of the efforts of that leadership. The relaionship of such trade unions to political parties is a very vexed question throughout Asia. There are many trade unions and there are many socialist parties or leftist parties or Marxist parties, and there is a race between them for the soul of the workers. But I should like to emphasise, as one of the fundamental ideological problems of socialism, at least in the East, that if we rely here on the working class and on the trade union movement to the same extent to which socialists in the West do, we will find that we will never be able to establish socialism. In the East it is not possible to establish socialism only with the support of the working class. It will become possible only if we have the support of the peasantry. If you wish to have the support of the peasntry, naturally you must satisfy their elemental urges. You have to give them land by abolishing feudalism and redistributing the land holdings. Now if you go about redistributing the land, what you do is to create a new class of proprietary owners, peasant proprietors. These millions of peasant proprietors are your constituencies, the constituencies of the socialist movement in the East. You must get their support in whatever you are trying to do; wthether it is an armed insurrection you are engineering or whether it is an election you are fighting, you must have the support of this peasant mass. If we understand this fully, then our conception of the economic organization of socialist society is bound to be drastically different from what it is elsewhere.

Many socialists, I am afraid, talk to the peasants with their tongue in the cheek. They think the peasant is a fool and we would cheat him, in the first instance, by giving him land and thus get his support, and after we have got his support we will deal with him properly and put him in his right place, expropriate him again and bring him into our collective farms. I shall very humbly beg to submit that if we follow that course of action, whatever we may be able to achieve, we will not achieve socialism. It may be a new pattern of dictatorship, but it will certainly not be socialism. Therefore you have to take the peasant with his small holding, living in his village, very emotionally attached to that plot of land which belongs to him, and yet make him socialist and create a socialist society in which he plays his part. I do not know the rural community in the rest of Asia, but in India we have villages, hundreds and thousands of villages. I believe that in a country like India the objective should be to pool their holdings, so that we might have, insead of collectivization or nationalization what I should call villagization of land: an economic structure which seems to me to be ideally suited to the rural community and in which the ownership of the land is transferred to the village community, not to an abstract entity known as the State or the nation, but to the concrete entity with which the peasant is acquainted and of which he is a part. Collectivization in Soviet Russia has become a tool in the hands of the bureaucracy for exploiting the peasnts. I am sure that you are aware that the rulers of Russia were not satisfied even with this weapon that they have in their hands of ruling over the peasantry through the collectivized farm, and therefore a proposal was made which has presently been given up but may be revived again, a proposal to create what was called *aggregare*, agricultural cities into which collectivized farms—five, six or a dozen of them—were to be amalgamated and the population of the villages were to be shifted to a town, so that the intimate human and personal relationship that exists in a village might cease and the impersonal relationship of a town come to take its place, so that it could become easy for the party bureaucrat to rule over the peasants who become workers of the *aggregare* or agricultural factories, if you wish to oall them so. That is the course of development that naturally comes out of the Russian system.

IV

Having dealt with the economic structure that we need to fashion in order to sustain a decentralized political system, I shall now refer to two other problems and close my remarks. The technique of struggle is also a part of the socialist ideology and there is a great deal of controversy in the ranks of socialism on this question. I hope that all of you will agree that if we are going to establish a democratic society, we should follow the democratic means, of course, if those means are available to us. But democratic means are not always available. They are not available in dictatorships. They are not available in a country where there is a civil war going on. However, if democratic opportunities do exist, it should be our concern to see that we function democratically. We have at the back of our mind, many of us, a lurking suspicion that democratic methods might take us forward to a certain extent, but at the last stage violence will be necessary, that without violence the socialist revolution would not be complete. Friends I wish most earnestly to impress upon you the wrong assumptions on which this belief, that in the ultimate stage violence would be necessary, is founded. For the Western socialists this is an axiomatic truth, but in Asia where we have been used to feudalism, imperialism, civil war, the idea that it is possible through democratic means to establish socialism appears to be a reformist proposition. When I speak of democratic methods, let me make it clear that I am not speaking only of parliamentary methods, of constitutional methods! I am also thinking in terms of vital, large, mass movements, mass action of a non-violent character, unconstitutional but at the same time peaceful. If we are working with the sanction of the people behind us, if we have achieved contact with the hearts of the people, if we have got their backing, there is no reason why it should not be possible for us to move the masses into such peaceful activity.

For instance, there is the problem of redistribution of land. The problem can be solved in three ways: by the socialist party coming to power and legislating in that behalf; by a violent action by the peasantry or by the landless workers for the occupation of the land, that may or may not succeed; by a peaceful mass action by the peasantry for the occupation of those lands. Where the socialists are in power, the other two questions do not arise; but where they are not in power and where they have the opportunity to function democratically, where there are civil liberties, where there is scope for organization and propaganda, there, if we are able to move hundreds and thousands of landless people and make them peacefully squat on the lands which are owned by landlords but which are tilled by the landless labourers and which should rightfully belong to them and thereby offer resistance to the powers that be, no matter whether there are arrests, baton charges and shootings, then there is reason to believe that no power would be able to overcome that force. Even violent action will not succeed unless it is a real mass action. The action of fully-armed insurgents will not help the landless people in forcibly occupying the lands. There also has to be a mass movement which will end up in the revolutionary capture of power by the socialists. Now this technique of peaceful action was experimented upon in India by Mahatma Gandhi in the course of our national struggle. And it proved successful. I for one am convinced, that under proper conditions and under proper leadership, this technique can succeed in the matter of land and social change also. Therefore, I do commend this technique of peaceful struggle against the State, the capitalists and other exploiters as a method, of achieving socialism.

I should like to refer here to a very interesting movement that has been started in India recentrly. When the Socialist Party in India thought of redistribution of land, we thought of it in terms of a movement which I have just now explained to you. But now has come forward a great Indian, the foremost follower of Mahatma Gandhi, called Vinoba Bhave. His is an entirely new technique. He said, 'Yes, land must be redistributed, land must belong to the tiller, landlordism must go. But let us do this by the method of love.' Now, this is not an Evangelist platform. I am aware that I am speaking from a socialist platform, but still I feel that this method is vital enough. Vinoba Bhave started going from village to village on foot and asking those who had land to give part of it for the benefit of those who did not. Just as simple as that; in fact so simple that it sounds nonsensical, foolish, but it seems to be working. We are all human beings, the landlord is a human being, the capitalistis a human being; there is something in all of us to which this man is appealing and there is a good response: hundreds and thousands of acres of land have already been given to him. When he started this movement he was alone, assisted by a handful of Ashramites, inmates of the Ashram of Mahatma Gandhi. But now there are thousands of people who work with him. Many in the Indian Socialist Party are working under him, going from village to village, asking people to give away land for the benefit of the landless people, making a moral appeal to them, saying that no one should have exclusive rights in land. For land is not created by man. Everyone who lives by land should have a share in it. As a result of this campaign a climate has been created practically in the whole country in favour of redistribution of land. Even those who were at one time opposed to this idea are coming round. They have begun to advocate redistribution of land as the immediate programme after which all other development projects can come or should come.

Now, I do not know why socialists in the world should close their eyes to a phenomenon of this kind, to this new approach to economic problems. As a matter of facts, I was very reluctant to come here, because I was in the midst of this land-gift movement, Bhoodan Movement. I was also going from village to village and I intend, as soon as I return from Rangoon, to go back to this work in the state where Bhave is at present conducting this movement. Everyone who has land, big landlords, small landlords, everyone is now convinced that he will not be very long in possession of all the land that he owns today. Everyone is convinced that this movement has created a new climate, a new atmosphere. Those who do not have land, will have land given to them. The test of immediacy of which 1 spoke to you in a different context is somehow proving very useful here. And so in the next movement when we start an action of this nature people will be attracted because they get immediate benefits. Whatever happens, happens immediately; you collect land, you collect 10,000 acres of land, 50,000 acres of land, 10,00,000 acres of land; you collect here and now and redistribute to them. True, there are millions of people who are to be given land and by merely giving it to a few thousand people you do not solve the problem; but a hope is generated in the hearts of the people that something is going to be done here and now, that we shall have our rights fulfilled. That is the tremendous advantage in this type of movement. Even if you have a peaceful resistançe movement for the occupation of land, it might end in absolute failure. Not an inch of land may come under the occupation of the squatters if the resistance is beaten down. But here that question does not arise and even if we have ultimately to go forward to that stage, the atmosphere, the consciousness, the hope and even the organization required for getting response of that kind is thereby created. I do not know if a similar technique can be evolved in other spheres for the redistribution of capitalist wealth, for the peaceful transformation of the caitalist system. This technique did not come out of my head, but I had humility enough to accept it when I saw it work. Therefore, friends, I would submit that in the sphere of technique, as in other spheres, the last word has not been said. We are all going through the stage of experimentation and it is worthwhile that we experiment in this sphere of technique also.

V

Yet another question that confronts the scocialist movement is the question of relationships between socialist countries. Marx will not help us here nor will Lenin help us here, except in the sense of giving us a general direction. Here also we have to go back to Soviet Russia. We find that when a number of communist States came into existence, the relationship of these States to Soviet Russia was not much different from the relationship of the metropolitan States to their colonial empire. The relation of Soviet Russia with Poland or Hungary or the Baltic States which have ceased to exist, or Yugoslavia, was not based on the principle of equality and mutual aid. You are all aware of the main issue on which the break between Yugoslavia and Soviet Russia came about. It was this issue of what the relationship between Yugoslavia and Soviet Russia should be. 'Are we equals,' asked the Yugoslavs, 'are we going to cooperate on the basis of equality? Or is

Yugoslavia going to become an economic colony? Are the resources of Yugoslavia going to be used for the development of the Russian economy at the cost of the Yugoslav economy?' I think that the Yugoslav Communist Party has made a great contribution to scocialist ideology by bringing this problem to the forefront and emphatically stating this principle of equality between socialist States. There are not enough socialist States established today for us to concretely discuss the issue but theoretically the issue has to be discussed, and I am sure that all of us will agree that no matter what the difference be in the development of the socialist countries, the relationship among them must be that of equality, of mutual aid.

As a matter of fact, if there is any tilting of the balance it should be in favour of backward and weaker countries and not in favour of the stronger and more developed ones as is unfortunately the case with the Communist bloc. If there is a highly developed country which has become socialist it should be its responsibility to remove the unbalance that exists in the world today. There are a few, as someone used the phrase, super-developed countries, some well-developed countries, some backward countries, and just as it is the task of socialism in a given country to equalize opportunities within, to redistribute the wealth that has been produced, and the power, economic and political, that has been concentrated in the hands of a small class, likewise, in the international sphere, it should be the task of socialism to remove this discrepancy, to help, through some kind of world development pool, world development organization, to raise the level of the backward countries. The domestic task should be extended to the foreign sphere. What we are trying to do in our own country we should try to do on the international level. This undoubtedly is a very difficult task. I have found that in our own country there are certain states which are, in the matter of food, surplus states, and some deficit. We have found it very difficult to persuade the surplus states to part with some of their food so that the deficit states might be able to feed themselves adequately. Even within a country this kind of provincial and regional selfishness exists, much more so on the international plane; but if we were to keep this in mind and at least accept this as a basis and make an honest attempt to implement it, I am quite sure that the socialist movement which is represented here will give a new direction to the world socialist movement.

241. To Jawaharlal Nehru, 10 January 1953[1]

Dear Bhai,

You probably know that a delegation of the representatives of the International Union of Socialist Youth has come to this country. Its tour of India and certain other South Asian countries has been sponsored by the UNESCO. The delegation is headed by Peter Strasser, who is President of the IUSY and member of the Austrian Parliament from the Eastern Zone of Austria, and consists of four other members, one each from Sweden, Holland, Israel and Australia. The sixth member of the delegation from the Gold Coast is on the way.

The delegation would be in Delhi from the 21st to the 23rd and would like very much to meet you. I am writing to Suchetaji to fix up an interview for them. I hope you will be kind enough to agree. I should like to add that the delegates have a concrete proposal to make to you and the Government of India which, I hope, will meet with your approval.

Hoping you are well and with kind regards,

Affectionately yours,
J.P.

[1]*J.P. Papers* (NMML).

242. To S. Guruswamy, 5 February 1953[1]

Dear Comrade Guruswamy,[2]

I am on my way from Delhi to Patna. When I was at Delhi, I met Shri Harihar Nath Shastri[3] and Shri Khandu Bhai Desai[4] and discussed the merger of the two federations. I am glad to inform you that they agreed to (a) an out-right amalgamation of the two organizations at the Federation level, and (b) amalgamation of the unions within a year. It was agreed amongst the three of us that Harihar Nath should be President of the amalgamated body and you should be General Secretary. It was further agreed that in order to settle the details of the amalgamation the two working committees should meet sometime in the middle of March—the exact date to be fixed later in consultation with you and other friends.

[1]*J.P. Papers* (NMML).
[2]For biographical note see *JPSW*, Vol. V, p. 101
[3]For biographical note see *JPSW*, Vol. I, p. 62.
[4]For biographical note see *JPSW*, Vol. V, p. 114

I hope all this meets with your approval. I shall be glad to have a line in reply. What are the final dates of the Mysore Conference? I am afraid, I would not be able to attend.

Please reply at my Patna address.

Yours sincerely,
Jayaprakash

243. To Jawaharlal Nehru, 6 February 1953[1]

Dear Bhai,

This is, in a manner, in continuation of our talks. Throughout the talks the underlying assumption was that there was general agreement between us over objectives & principles of national reconstruction. This indeed was so, and were it only a question of cooperation between you and me, that should have been enough. But when two parties have to cooperate there must be a clear and more explicit understanding and declaration of common objectives & principles. This should be necessary in order to avoid future misunderstandings and conflicts, as also to provide guidance and directive to both sides. This appears to me to be still the more necessary when I turn from your views and sympathies to those of other Congressmen and particularly of the state governments. Therefore, I shall try in the next few days to send you a statement of broad policies for your consideration.

On my way to Patna I broke journey at Banaras to meet Narendra Deva. His first reaction was unfavourable. He did not think that in spite of your personal views there was any sincere desire in Congress ranks for our cooperation. Secondly, he was very firmly of the view that unless there was an explicit common basis of agreement, in terms of a common programme and policy, it was not possible to offer cooperation. This is a reasonable view and strengthens what I have written above. Narendra Deva would soon be in Delhi and you would no doubt discuss the matter with him.

With affectionate regards,

Affectionately yours,
Jayaprakash

[1]*J.P. Papers* (NMML).

244. To Jawaharlal Nehru, 4 March 1953[1]

Dear Bhai,

I could not send you the draft programme without consulting my colleagues. It is now enclosed with this letter.[2]

Let me make a few introductory remarks.

I meet you after long periods and get the impression that you are not in touch with what we have been doing or saying or thinking. The last few times that I met you, I heard you repeat some points practically in the same language. For instance, your remarks about nationalization. I am afraid we are, in your mind, doctrinaire socialists who insist on sticking to outworn formulas. But had you cared to know better the evolution of thinking in our movement, you would not have found the need for impressing upon us the empirical and changing processes of socialist reconstruction.

I assure you our approach to socialism is not doctrinaire, hide-bound or conservative. But I must make one point clear. No matter how empirical and experimental may be our approach, the goals of values of socialism are unalterably fixed before us. Whether we give it or not the name of any issue, we all desire without the shadow of any doubt to create a new society in which there is no exploitation, in which there is economic and social equality, in which there is freedom of well-being for all. Further, these goals, for us or for that matter for any socialist, are not to be achieved in a distant future but in the soonest possible time.

You had written once to me, when you were perhaps a little rattled, that while you thought that socialism was not the monopoly of any group, you were not, in any case, a 'formal' socialist. You perhaps meant that you did not subscribe to any particular theory of socialism. But you could not have meant to say that you did not accept the aims and values of socialism. Those values and aims give direction and create a sense of urgency which, you will agree, have been lacking in your policies. A great deal can be said for caution and fearing to create too many upsets, but in the balance, if one has a definite political philosophy, one must act and move boldly towards one's goals. The move must be rapid and drastic at the beginning, when a new departure has to be made, than in the middle or at the end of the process. The move, further, must be such that the mass of people are able to appreciate and understand and realize that they are on the move. Some times a right move may be made, but at such levels and points that it is beyond the understanding of the man in the street.

[1]*J.P. Papers* (NMML). See Appendix 42 for Nehru's reply dated 17 March 1953.
[2]See the next item.

I should like also to place before you another ideological consideration. We have all been deeply influenced by Gandhiji. I do not mind saying that I have been re-discovering him lately and re-understanding him. I believe he was one of the most vital thinkers of the modern age. I am sure there is a great deal that governments and parties and peoples have to learn from him today and also tomorrow. I am sure, had he lived, he would have evolved further, as he ceaselessly did, and we would have had today a clear picture of the method he would have followed to achieve the goals that we jointly share. I do not find Gandhiji's dynamism and incessant quest toward his ultimate values except in Vinoba, who has produced a remarkably Gandhian method for the solution of the country's biggest problem—the land problem. I feel sure that the Gandhians and the socialists, dropping their respective jargons, must work together. I have said all this only to emphasize that I do not find in your policies any, or marked, awareness of these considerations. When the policies of the Govt. of India make a concession to Gandhi, well, it is just a concession.

Let me place a third consideration before you. China and India are the two countries in Asia to which all Asia and Africa are looking. If India fails to present anything but a pale picture of a welfare state (which phrase I do not particularly like; Gandhiji's and Vinoba's Sarvodaya is a far better phrase), I am afraid the appeal of China would become irresistible, and that would affect the lives of millions and change the course of history disastrously.

May I also point out that you seem to have been unduly impressed with the chits that foreigners have given your Government. I would not rate those chits too high. Often those foreigners do not share our common objectives. Often they come expecting to see a backward people just learning to manage their affairs, and when they find the Parliament, the Central Secretariat, the DVC, the polished English—well, they are just charmed. Whereas we have our own ambitions and wish to start where both the East and West have ended up and build a society in advance to theirs (not in material wealth). Our measuring rods must necessarily be different from those of the foreign visitors, and we must pass a severe judgement on ourselves.

With this as a background let me turn to the question before us. The proposal that you made to me was a bold and unusual one, because the Congress party stood in no need of a coalition either at the Centre or in most of the States. But you rose above partisan considerations and took a statesmanlike step. What you proposed was to my mind, not a parliamentary coalition in the accepted sense of the term; but a joint effort to build a new India. We are not a power in the legislatures, but we do claim to have a following in the country and a cadre which in some respects is superior to that of the Congress—a cadre which has some training and a distinct political philosophy, which in itself is a valuable thing.

I think it is the common people's wish that their leaders, irrespective of parties, should join hands to serve them and make their lot better. If a joint effort were made by us, great hopes would be aroused, and in the event of a failure, i.e. in the event of the people finding out that in spite of the joint effort their lot remained unchanged—the frustration would be so complete that nothing could save the country from eventual chaos and disintegration. The task of national integration of which you spoke the other day cannot be accomplished under static conditions. If we moved forward in new directions of social and economic change, the forces of integration would be vastly strengthened. The emotional and psychological climate that would be created should prove to be a powerful binding force.

Therefore a great deal would depend on how you conceived your own move in asking for our cooperation. If it means only this that a few of us are to be added to your cabinet and some of the state cabinets to strengthen the Government and your hands in carrying out your present policies, the attempt would not be worth making. But if it means launching upon a bold joint venture of national reconstruction, it might well have been a historic move. You do not have unlimited time and it is now that you must act.

It is in this perspective that the draft programme was prepared. It is not too ambitious a programme, and it can be carried out in the next four years if all of us make a determined effort.

First, we have suggested that certain constitutional reforms must be made. I for one was never able to understand how you permitted yourself to approve of such a drab and conservative Constitution. However while drastic changes may be made in it later, there are some amendments which should be made immediately if the social and economic revolution that has to be brought is at all to progress.

Second, the whole system of administration must be overhauled. While every one agrees with this, nothing or next to nothing is being done about it. The reform must be drastic and must affect all levels. We should also make up our mind as to what kind of political system we want. Centralization of political power and authority would be disastrous. We must deliberately work for devolution of powers and decentralization of authority.

Everyone likewise talks of corruption. An effective machinery must be created to deal with this monster.

Likewise with legal reform. The present law and legal procedure are too complicated, dilatory and costly. There is practically no justice for the common man today. The lower law courts have become a breeding and training ground for lying, deceit, forgery, perjury and worse.

I do not suggest that we have cut-and-dried solutions for all these things or that our solutions are the best. But we must make a determined effort at the highest levels to cure these ills.

You will find that we have suggested nationalization in two spheres: (a) banking and insurance, (b) mining. You had told me that while you considered it unnecessary to nationalize everything, the State must occupy the strategic points in the economy. We consider that one of the most strategic points is banking and insurance. Asoka told me that Mr. Deshmukh himself was thinking somewhat on these lines.

As regard mining, the case for its nationalization is unanswerable. The usual arguments against nationalization do not apply here. The mines are already national property. Maladministration in the grant of leases and licences and the wasteful operation of the small operators have brought about a chaotic condition, leading to destruction of mineral resources. British companies still hold a key position in respect of important minerals. The Coal Board, I understand, is virtually in the hand of Britishers. Exports of strategic and industrial minerals earns for us about 70 crores per year. By substituting finished or partially finished goods this sum can be multiplied several fold and will lead to direct development of major industries. River valley projects that lie in the mineral zones should be given responsibility of developing mineral industries. The minerals, power and river valley development must be grouped together.

Let me take this opportunity to make a few remarks about what you said about the general question of nationalization. You were of the view that it would do no harm if some industries were left in private hands, provided the mainsprings of economic policy and power were in the hands of the State and they were made to subserve the public good. I agree. But at present the main springs are in the hands of private enterprise and it is the State that subserves the interest of the former. This situation has to be reversed.

You had also spoken of the foolishness of buying junk and paying compensation. I agree. But if we have to buy junk why must we pay for it at any other rate than that of junk. There are also industries in which the capital invested has already been returned, such as the sugar industry. There is no reason for paying compensation in such cases. I think this whole question of nationalization must be fully examined and not disposed of by a few arguments such as you gave.

To my mind equally important with nationalization is the question of management of nationalized industries and State enterprises. The tendency of the State, in other words, of the ministers and officers, is to concentrate all power in their hands in the name of efficiency. This cannot but be destructive of the values of socialism. The bureaucracy is not interested in those values, and nationalization might merely end up in State capitalism, which is a horrible prospect. I should add that even from the point of view of production and efficiency, bureaucratization of industry would be disastrous. Efficiency and production would both rise if the workers were made willing and equal partners in the enterprise.

This leads to the question of labour organization. You may be surprised that we have included such a question in the draft programme. But we have done so because we believe that without a united, responsible, democratic and effective trade union movement, industrial re-construction of the type we envisage is impossible. We believe further that in our country such a movement can be built up only on the basis of what is called the Union Shop, i.e. one union in one industry, compulsory union membership for all employees, democratic functioning of the unions.

In the industrial development of the country small industries will play a predominant part. While everyone admits it, no adequate policy or plan is forthcoming. The 5-Year Plan is very inadequate in this respect. Unless the fields of small and large industry are demarcated and the former are protected from the competition of the latter, the talk of small industries would remain just a talk.

I need hardly emphasize the case for State trading in strategic and important lines.

Our goal of economic equality must not remain a distant goal. We must here and now move towards it. Our land policy would to a very large extent establish equality in the countryside. But the inequalities in other spheres are even greater. A beginning there also must be made. And it must first of all be made in the sphere of Government. Everyone talks of austerity but, New Delhi is the last place in India where one can seek austerity.

There is no need to explain every item in the programme. I shall lastly mention the urgent need for integrated and far-reaching agrarian reform. This to my mind is the most urgent reform that is needed, and all our efforts must be bent toward its accomplishment.

This in brief is my conception of the purposes and possibilities of our cooperation. If it be not also yours, I should respectfully urge that the whole idea be dropped. There would not be much harm done at this stage, and there would not be any misunderstanding or bitterness on our side. As there has been much public speculation over this subject, you might state at an appropriate occasion that you had certain talks with us regarding co-operation, but the talks did not reveal a common approach to the country's problems and so they were discontinued.

I was in Delhi on the 1st and 2nd because Kripalaniji had sent us for consultations. I did not think it would have served any purpose if I had tried to meet you hurriedly at that time. So, as I had told you when we had met last, I shall be in Delhi again to meet you from March 15 to 19. I shall be staying with Sodhani again at 5 Park View Road, Karol Bagh, Tel. 8258.

I hope you will excuse me for inflicting this long letter upon you.
With love,

Affectionately,
Jayaprakash

245. Draft Programme for Cooperation between Congress and PSP, enclosed with the Letter to Nehru, 4 March 1953[1]

Constitutional Amendments

1. Amendments to the Constitution
   (a) to remove obstacles in the way of social change;
   (b) to abolish guarantees to Princes, Civil Servants, etc.;
   (c) to ablish second chambers.

Administrative Reforms

2. (a) Administrative reforms at all levels, including decentralization of political power and administrative authority;
   (b) reform of law and legal procedure;
   (c) summary and effective machinery to deal with corruption.
3. (a) Redrawing the administrave map of India on the basis of linguistic, economic and administrative considerations. Appointment of a Commission by the Parliament to work out the details on the basis of the above mentioned principles;
   (b) Redution of administrative costs by having regional (multi-state) Governors, High Courts, and other top level Tribunals and Public Service Commissions.

Redistribution of Land

4. (a) Redistribution of land to remove economic inequality and exploitation; preference to be given in all such schemes to landless labour and poor peasants;
   (b) Immediate stoppage of all eviction;
   (c) Suitable legislation to prevent fragmentation and bring about consolidation of holdings;
   (d) Abolition of the remaining forms of landlordism;
   (e) Rural economy to be transformed into a cooperative economy

[1] *Socialism, Sarvodaya and Democracy*, ed. Bimal Prasad, Bombay, 1964, pp. 85-7.

through compulsory multi-purpose societies;

(f) State assistance in providing credit and other facilities to agriculture; such assistance to be given through multi-purpose societies;

(g) The State, as far as possible, to deal not with individual peasants but through a group of them organised in a cooperative or panchayat. This should include collection of land-revenue, a part of which to remain with the village as organised in the multi-pupose society or panchayat.

5. Reclamation of wasteland and settlement of landless labour on them through village collectives. No wastelands to be allotted for capitalist farming.

Nationalisation, Cooperatives and Trade Unions

6. Nationalisation of Banks and Insurance Companies;
7. Progressive development of State Trading;
8. Selected number of plants in different industries to be owned and run by the State or Cooperatives or autonomous corporations or workers' councils. Fostering organisations of technicians and managers to provide expert advice and administrative personnel for State enterprises;
9. Unified trade union movement organised on the basis of the *union shop*. This will enable the unions to become socially responsible agencies;
10. Nationalisation of coal and other mines producing important minerals;
11. Association of workers in the management of State enterprises.

Small-scale Industries

12. Demarcation of spheres of large and small-scale industries, and establishing, encouraging and protecting small-scale industries.

Economic Equality

13. As a first step towards achieving economic equality in the country higher salaries and emoluments in Government services shall be scaled down.

Swadeshi

14. The spirit of Swadeshi to be promoted and made to pervade all walks of life.

246. Address to Students at the Youth Conference, Chandil (Bihar), 8 March 1953[1]

I do not know why I have been asked to speak to you, young people, about your future work and organization. Because I am myself just trying to grasp the principles of Sarvodaya just now, I am under no illusion that I have the right to deliver any message to you. Though I have got connections with the youth of the country and have given some thoughts to their organization, still I now find myself at the cross-roads.

Now-a-days, generally speaking, my experience is that the students of the colleges and high schools are attracted towards either socialism or communism or communalism or movements based on communal ideologies of the Rashtriya Swayamsevak Sangh or towards the Dravidian Youth League of South India etc. I have seen this happen in my youth during the years 1921-22. At that time the Gandhian tempest raged over the country and the youth were all swept off their feet. But now-a-days the youth are of opinion that the ways of Gandhiji are old-fashioned. They say that Gandhiji's ways cannot appeal to them in this age of the atom bomb, and of revolutionary Russia and China. Perhaps the youth assembled here think differently and have been influenced by Sarvodaya.

I would prefer not to say anything regarding the leaders of communism and communalism, but I would have my say regarding Socialism. I have been asked whether I have been able to reconcile Sarvodaya with Socialism in my own mind. This question arises before those of the socialist persuasion, as for instance, the students.

If you understand the aims of Socialism, forgetting its theories for the moment, and bestow some serious thought on its aims alone, it would not be difficult for you to understand how we can very easily make both Sarvodaya and Socialism meet together. What we desire is the establishment of a society in which there will be no exploitation, there will be perfect equality and each individual will have equal opportunities for development. So the question of attaining these ends, and realizing these aims arises. We have seen that wherever attempts were made to achieve these aims through violent means, these aims were not realized, exploitation was not removed, equality was not established and the individual did not gain full opportunities for development.

Wherever a new order was brought about through a violent revolution we see an entirely new thing taking shape. Very often what we desire is to destroy the present established order of things and imagine that thereby we are bringing in the new order. The socialists think that no sooner we destroy

[1]Adapted from *Sarvodaya*, July 1953, Vol. 3, No. 1.

capitalism, the new order will get established. But in this they are mistaken. Socialism is not a negative thing. Take for instance nationalization which is a plank of Socialism. Nationalization alone will not bring in the Socialistic order. We have seen this in our own country and in other countries as well. Leave alone the case of Russia; our Railways today belong to all, they are no longer the possession of a company, but they are property of the entire nation. But if we are to say that the Railway administration is free form exploitation we would be mistaken. True, there is no capitalism now; but neither is there Socialism. What is ruling there is bureaucracy. Similarly, if we say that by nationalizing the other industries we will be ushering in Socialism we would only be deceiving ourselves. How then are we to get at the reality? How then to proceed further? We are now faced with this question. But Sarvodaya has already taken long strides in the direction in which we are proceeding, in which our thinking is taking us. Therefore if we are true socialists, we would be true followers of Sarvodaya as well.

We say that every individual has got the right to take part in the governance of the country. Answering a query as to how true democracy can be established, Vinoba has declared that it is essential to establish village government. And if we are true socialists we should also proclaim our faith in village autonomy. Thus are the two streams of thought meeting together. While some people make fun of my attendance at this conference, my participation in it and my admiration for Vinobaji, there are others who say, 'So you have come round at last!' But the time has come now for all of us to think truthfully, deeply and courageously. Any true socialist who strives day and night for realizing his aims, will find himself in the same position that I find myself in today.

Let us keep apart Gandhiji and Vinobaji. All the other leaders belong to a different category. There was a time when none was able to say how to proceed and where. The common people were then under the expectation that the close followers of Gandhiji would show the way to transform society which Gandhiji would of course have done, had he been alive. But after his exit, the entire prospect was one of utter darkness. My own impression is, had not Vinobaji launched the Bhoodan Yajna campaign we would have forgotten Gandhiji and forgotten Sarvodaya; we would have lost faith in what Gandhiji had said and done and the path of Sarvodaya would have been blocked. Vinobaji has infused new life into Sarvodya by placing the Bhoodan Yajna programme before us. Otherwise the constructive workers would have continued ploughing their lonely furrows. This would have certainly benefited the country to some extent, but the hope of the common man that the followers of Gandhiji would take steps for the transformation of the country would have been shattered and an armed revolution would have ensued with entirely different consequences. Therefore we should take to this method in order to achieve the aims we cherish. Let us, forgetting our self-importance and the prestige of the party, get down to work.

I place all these things before the students purposely, because they are all faced with the same question and they are in a dilemma. It seems to them that we are going astray. We should very sincerely keep our aims before our eyes and achieve them. The aims we have are not our sole monopoly; they are claimed by others also; but our means are different. So said Shankarrao Deoji just now and he is right. If the aim is to establish a society which will be free from exploitation and if that is achieved through violent means the aim will still remain unrealized. Violence sets in motion new forms of exploitation. Exploitation signifies the denial to one of his rights. We cannot expect the complete removal of exploitation. Even today the level of our own life is far higher than that of our brethren; so it cannot be denied that we have exploited them. You are today engaged in your studies; much money is being spent on you. Such expense cannot be incurred by the poor over the education of their children. So a part of the responsibility for the exploitation rests on you. Perhaps to hope for the complete removal of exploitation is to hope for the impossible. But we should pursue that ideal and have our limits defined. Even in Russia differences do exist; the high-paid drawing forty times as much as the low-paid. The level of life lived by the officials is very high; so exploitation is far from being extinct there. Because they gained power through violence, by the same means they decide the share of the fruits of labour that should go to each. The society which is truly free from exploitation can be created only through non-violence. Hence I have no objection in replacing the name of Socialism by the name Sarvodaya.

I have been questioned regarding trusteeship. When Gandhiji went to U.P. in 1935, the Zamindars of the place met him and asked him what their fate would be under the rule of the Congress Socialist party which had just then been formed. Gandhiji replied: 'I cannot prophesy what will happen when the Socialists would have gained dominance over the Congress; but I will not be a party to your extinction so long as you conduct yourselves as trustees of your lands.'

I was really put out when I heard this and told my colleagues that Gandhiji was telling this to those very zamindars who were committing so many atrocities on the poor. He wanted them to become trustees and assured them that he would not allow their removal. The meaning of all this is, neither are they going to become trustees nor would Gandhiji allow their destruction. We believed in those days that this ideal of trusteeship would remain only on paper; it would never be acted upon. But today I am seeing in Gaya, where a *bigha* of land is worth between two to six thousand rupees, people have given their lands. Some 48 thousands acres have been given away. Regarding Gandhiji's pet theories, Kishorlal Bhai once wrote: 'We are mistaken in thinking that the ideals he is expounding are never going to be practised. It appears to us that Gandhiji may exhort the wealthy to become trustees; but (if the wealthy were not wise) they are not going to do any such thing. The social set-up and its poverty will continue as they are. But if we view Gandhiji in this light, we will be committing a big blunder'. Were he alive today he would himself have taken up the work that Vinoba has undertaken. What is more probable is he would have done it much earlier and his manner of doing it would have been more attractive. Gandhiji was saying that we welcome those who would behave as trustees; if they will not we will prepare the poor and ask them not to cooperate in self-exploitation. Thus will we prepare both. Similarly in the Bhoodan Yajna both the donor and the beneficiary are being prepared. To the extent that Bhoodan Yajna gets popularized, the exploited in the villages will be awakened and they would begin to think of opposing exploitation through non-violent means. So if we simply brush aside the trusteeship idea on the plea that nobody is going to act up to it, we would be committing a great blunder. After all, do not even the socialists think of conflicts and class-wars? The working people are not armed with pistols or bombs; when they think in terms of general strikes, which according to their belief, will make the castle of capitalism topple down, a certain amount of violence is unavoidable in the process.

When I see the young people today I am reminded of those days when I was studying in the Patna College. At that time Maulana Abul Kalam Azad had come to Patna and I heard his non-cooperation speech. His speech made us all leave our college. The revolution that took place in the mind of the youth then was not due to any other cause in the same measure as to Gandhiji's movement. A similar revolution is in the offing today. I have not till now heard a speech comparable with the one that Vinoba delivered yesterday. He presented the matter before us as he viewed it from the philosophical stand-point. Whoever has grasped its significance is sure to have his life transformed. I am having some contact with the youth and their present condition makes me depressed. They have enthusiasm, but it appears to me that they are lacking in faith, concentration and mental depth.

If the seeds of Sarvodaya have been planted in your mind, you will become free from these defects and remember your duty by the performance of which you yourselves and the society to which you belong will be equally benefited. Vinoba has said that even if you are not to join the Bhoodan Movement, you should leave your colleges. It is impossible for a scholar of his stature to become an enemy of learning. Why then did he say this? Because the kind of education that is being given today is beneficial neither to the student nor to the society nor again to the country. Such is the present condition. So no effort should be spared towards the realization of our duty to the maximum extent.

We are living in stirring times comparable to 1921. Revolution is afoot. Let us play our due parts in it. Let us prepare ourselves for it. I want you all to give up your studies; go and wander about in the villages and make what contributions you can, to the Bhoodan Movement and try to make this revolution a success.

Why hesitate to leave college for a year? I have seen in America many students studying for a term and working during the next for earning the means for further studies. I had then become a convert to communism and having decided on a trip to Russia I had left college and was in search of a job which would fetch me enough to make the trip. But those were days of depression and unemployment was on the increase. I wandered continuously, was prepared for any odd job, but I could not secure any. Then I fell ill, incurred some debt in consequence, but cleared it all later by working. On looking back from this distance it does not appear to me that I lost anything by losing a year at the college. I have never felt that what I learnt in fields and factories was inferior or negligible instruction. The experiences that I gained there could never have been had in college. Similarly the education you will receive from the villages can never be got from schools and colleges. And I believe that if your parents are concerned about your future, about the development of your personality they will of their own accord say—'All right, my dear boy, go and work for a year.' It is expected of everyone that he dedicates himself to Bhoodan Yajna for a year. People are giving away their lands and let us give our time and energy. Vinoba says what a revolution it would be, a revolution that would set an example to the whole world if we succeeded in solving the big problem of land through a truly democratic method! If we succeed in solving the big problem of land in a big province like Bihar within a year, it will have far-reaching consequences. So we invite you all to join hands in this revolution and hope and trust that the youth of the country will not fail to take to this road.

247. To Jawaharlal Nehru, 18 March 1953[1]

Dear Bhai,

I am sorry to trouble you again. It is about publishing my letter. Already newspaper reports and leaders are trying to misrepresent me and throw the blame on me. I am sending you a sheet of cuttings. You will see how vicious is the *Hindustan Times* editorial. This is just the beginning. The best way to

[1] *J.P. Papers* (NMML).

answer my detractors and others who are to follow is to release my letter. I am not thinking in terms of apportioning any blame. And it is far from my mind to throw the blame on you. But I do not want to be misunderstood. And I want the public to understand the issues involved, otherwise there would be complete cynicism and public indifference whenever this question is raised in the future.

You have almost an unlimited opportunity of expressing yourself publicly. My opportunities are limited. Moreover, I have no stomach anymore for statementing. For months I have not said a word about any thing except *Bhoodan*. The press is generally hostile to me and my party. There is a pro-Congress press, and a pro-Communist press. There is a [Jan] Sangh press. But there is hardly any Socialist press. We have neither power, nor funds, nor the big club, nor do we shout much.

I might reply to the critics separately. But it would be difficult in that manner to express my integrated point of view in regard to this matter. Moreover I do not fancy joining in a controversy with leader-writers and special-correspondents.

For a long time past you have been speaking off and on of cooperation. The public have been under the impression that the socialists have been difficult and non-cooperative. I am anxious that it should not be made to appear that our unreasonableness has again stood in the way. I want the country to understand how I, at least, have viewed this question.

In my letter there is nothing which can cause embarrassment to you.

This morning when I read out the letter to our M.P.s, there was a unanimous wish that the letter be published. Even such a sober and senior person like Mr. Kelappan wanted me to get your permission.

We have often corresponded with each other and some times, with regard to public matters. Up till now I had never asked for anything that I wrote you to be published. This is the first occasion when I am making such a request. I hope you will agree. Please also let me know if I should also release your reply too.

I shall be obliged to have your reply by noon tomorrow. I am leaving tomorrow night for Bombay.

Yours affectionately,
J.P.

248. Press Statement on Talks with Nehru, New Delhi, 18 March 1953[1]

For a long time past Jawaharlalji had been wanting me to meet him. For a variety of reasons many months passed before I could do this. I met him in the first days of February last and we discussed a wide range of domestic and foreign questions, including the Asian Socialist Conference. Our talks disclosed a wide area of agreement. In the course of these discussions the Prime Minister expressed a desire for our cooperation, which, he made clear, included cooperation both at governmental and popular levels. The question of the merger of Congress and the PSP was never raised.

Personally I felt, as I feel now, that given a sincere desire on both sides and a common approach to the tasks facing us, it was in the national interest that a joint effort were made, particularly in the present transitional and formative period. Accordingly, I agreed to meet him again in the middle of March after consulting my colleagues. Later he met Acharya Kripalani and Acharya Narendra Deva.

The Prime Minister's proposal was considered at an informal meeting of some important members of the PSP at the beginning of March. At this meeting a programme was prepared to be sent to him as the basis for mutual discussion. A few days later I sent him this programme with an explanatory letter.

On the 16th March I met the Prime Minister again for further discussion. At this occasion he felt that while we were justified from our point of view in putting forth a minimum programme for the next few years, it was not going to be useful to tie each other down to any specific commitments. I felt, on the other hand, that without a common basis of work, the experiment in cooperation, particularly at governmental levels, was bound to result in mutual conflicts, ineffectiveness and failure. Individuals might work together on the basis of mutual personal understanding. But it seemed to me that political parties could not do so unless there was some mutually agreed programme. In the context of this difference in approach the question of coopération at all levels that the Prime Minister had raised was dropped.

I should like to add that it must be a matter of regret for every one that there has been so much speculation in the press about this matter. In the absence of authentic information speculation perhaps was inevitable, but the realization of how misinformed these speculations were will, I hope, teach us all to deal with public questions with greater restraint.

[1]*Brahmanand Papers* (NMML). See Appendix 43 for Nehru's Press Statement.

249. Clarifications at Press Conference regarding Talks with Nehru, New Delhi, 18 March 1953[1]

I sent a programme to the Prime Minister, Mr. Nehru, which was not acceptable to him as he thought it was not going to be useful to tie each other down to any specific commitments. I, on my part, felt that without a common basis of work, the experiment in cooperation, particularly at Governmental levels, is bound to result in mutual conflicts, ineffectiveness and failure.

Today no single party can build up this country. There must be close cooperation between all democratic and progressive forces in the country. A sense of urgency which is necessary is absent. Things do not move, both in respect of speed and direction and I believe a joint working would arouse new enthusiasm in the country.

I hope to release to the press the programme which I have forwarded to the Prime Minister, my covering letter as well as Mr. Nehru's reply[2] tomorrow after securing Mr. Nehru's permission to release them.

In my meetings with Mr. Nehru I did not discuss the merits of the programme nor was it placed before him in the sense of take it or leave it.

That was only meant to be a basis for cooperation. There was nothing in the programme which a person like Mr. Nehru would not agree to. My anxiety is that we must create in this country a sense of urgency and such a sense can be created by only placing before the people something concrete, something which can be achieved within a specified time. I do not believe that enunciation of general principles would meet the need of the hour.

The next four years are the most critical period and every year now would be equal to a decade in normal times.

The breakdown of the present talks does not mean that there is to be complete non-cooperation. There are certain spheres, such as anti-communalism and certain other constructive activities, in which the PSP would lend its cooperation to the Government. In regard to the 5-year plan as well there are certain aspects where cooperation is possible.

The programme I had sent to the Prime Minister was not discussed in any detail. The first question which arose was of approach to the problem. It was not a personal approach. Nowhere in the world would it be possible for two political parties to come together on the basis of mutual understanding between two leaders. There must be some other common basis. So my party considered the Prime Minister's invitation for co-operation both at governmental and popular levels. A programme was drawn up and forwarded to the Prime Minister.

[1]Adapted from *Bombay Chronicle*, 19 March 1953.

[2]See Appendix 44 for Nehru's reply.

There was a wide measure of agreement between myself and the Prime Minister, but on the question of approach we differed.

The main problem which seemed to worry the Prime Minister was the problem of national integration and the problem of reconstruction. Mr. Nehru considered it desirable to tackle the job jointly with the PSP.

From our point of view, the vagueness of policy of the Government is a major failing.

The PSP thought and suggested that we should come to some sort of agreement on a common programme which can not be a programme for all time to come, but one which can cover the next three or four years.

I emphasize that a joint effort is very necessary but I deprecate suggestions that the talks were motivated by any desire to share offices. It is true that the PSP is not in sufficient numbers in the Legislatures in the country but all the same, it has a following of nearly 140 lakhs of people who voted for the party in the last general elections.

I think that the country can and should move faster and take greater risks which is not the case today.

For the present, the talks have ended and I am planning to resume my work in connection with the Bhoodan Movement.

250. Address at a Rally of Peasants, Patna, 6 April 1953[1]

I greet the peasants for their spectacular demonstration and urge re-distribution of land, reduction in canal tax and other taxes and increase in prices of sugarcane and jute. The two and a quarter mile long procession and the meeting of the thousands of kisans bear testimony to the volume of public opinion favouring radical changes in the corrupt and decaying social and economic structure. The demonstration has done its bit by conveying to the Government the popular demands. The people are all powerful and if and when they are determined to achieve their social and economic objectives nothing on this earth can resist them. The future of free India depends on how the land system is rationalized and how lands are equitably distributed among the landless. In this process human energy would be released when the good earth would be harnessed, irrigated and nursed for adequate production. With unjust and corrupt land tenure system no social or economic progress is possible.

The question of redistribution of land is not being taken up seriously by the Government today. But I am sure that with the growing consciousness among the people at large and pressure of public opinion Government will have to yield to the demands of the time. The first draft of the five-year

[1]Adapted from *Amrit Bazar Patrika*, 8 April 1953.

plan opposed the theory of land redistribution but subsequently the Planning Commission, the Government of India and the Congress had to accept the policy of land redistribution. Power and authority lie ultimately with the people. I want people to realize the unlimited authority vested in them and utilize it for their social and economic emancipation.

The emergence of Acharya Vinoba Bhave was a historical necessity to undo the economic and social wrongs done to the people. As Gandhiji had undone the political wrongs on people, Vinobaji would do the same in the social and economic sphere. I want one crore landless people in Bihar to realize the implications of Vinobaji's mission. Vinobaji has said that land is the property of the whole community living in a village and all had equal share in it. Mother earth sustains children irrespective of colour, creed or caste. It is anti-social to rob community lands for individual pleasure and prosperity.

I ask particularly the Praja Socialist Party workers to go round every village and every home in Bihar with the message of Sant Vinova Bhave. The rich have to be told to part with their surplus lands to landless. In case the rich do not do so, a day will come they will have to leave their hearths and homes under moral pressure of the community. The first phase of economic revolution would be thus over, without any bloodshed or coercion.

I appeal to the college students to suspend their studies for one year and donate their time and energy to the cause of Bhoodan Yajna. Some price has to be paid for great causes. One year in the noble cause of economic and social revolution is no big sacrifice in comparison with the untold sacrifices undergone by thousands of youths in the cause of political emancipation. The one and only slogan which should echo and re-echo the stillness of summer sky throughout Bihar is 'give land to the landless'.

Bhoodan Yajna is an uphill task but without its completion no progress is possible. No country can advance with piecemeal legislation; it may not yield any result whatsoever. For creating a new world based on the Socialist ideal, a big psychological change is necessary.

Out of four crores of population in Bihar one fourth are the landless people who have to be rehabilitated. Without their being attached to the soil they cannot be expected to nurse the soil and grow corns for the consumption of others. They will regard any effort to harness them on land as forced labour. Hence in the name of justice and because of necessity, land has to be immediately redistributed. I hope that before the rains set in, the villagers will be made conscious of their obligations to the landless so that a situation is created in which land may be redistributed even without requisite legislation. Without legislative sanction miracles had happened and miracles would again happen if people stand united to wrest their demands by non-violent and peaceful means. I or my Party have no magic wand to mitigate the sufferings of the people. The ultimate power and authority for doing this is vested in the people themselves. So the people should forge unity and march ahead with the programme as enunciated above. The people's power was illustrated when the voluntary gifts of 50,000 acres of land were secured in Gaya district by the joint efforts of Congress, Praja Socialists, Sarvodaya Samaj and others. I predict that in an amazingly short period all surplus land would be redistributed in Bihar.

The peasants in districts of Shahabad, Patna, Gaya, Champaran and Darbhanga are in considerable distress. I want the people of those areas to deepen the agitation against increase in canal rates. In case the required reduction is not made, a no-canal-tax campaign should be launched. This weapon of non-violent non-cooperation would force the hands of the administration to redress the grievances of the people. I want the peasants and the workers to go to all villages and preach the message of Bhoodan Yajna and deepen the agitation to secure their just demands.

251. To Asoka Mehta, 10 April 1953[1]

Dear Asoka,

I have your letter of the 3rd April which I received on the 6th April in Patna a few hours before I left for Calcutta.

I am somewhat amazed at Acharya Kripalani's reactions and your sharing of them. You have taken an exception to the U.P. Committee passing a resolution[2] on the subject of possible coalition between our party and the Congress party and publishing it. I don't know what the position would have been if the National Executive and the conference had decided on coalition. But even then I should have thought that some freedom of action would be available to the dissenting view just as the same freedom should be available to the pro-coalitionist in the event of the National Executive and the conference deciding against coalition. In the present fluid position when no policy has been decided upon, it is astounding that anybody should take exception to the Provincial or even lower committees and individuals recommending certain polices and resolving on them. It cannot be anybody's desire to turn our various committees into rubber stamps and rob them of all capacity for initiative and even thinking. We must make a serious effort to learn to operate democratically even when expressions of opinion by various committees, particularly when the issue is yet undecided, differ and are published. I don't have to tell you that silence on the part of the

[1] *J.P. Papers* (NMML).
[2] For text of the resolution see Appendix 45.

anti-coalitionists facilitates the sliding of the party into a coalitionist attitude. Such a sliding is being encouraged by the daily press.

I will recount what happened at the National Executive. The account made it quite clear that they entirely disagreed with the pro-coalitionists' attitudes and various reasons attached to them. In the first place the Congress Party and Communist Party was objected to both as a matter of basic doctrine and as fraught with manifold consequences of the future of the party. The negotiations with the Congress party and documents relating to them have given rise to the belief that the Praja Socialist Party prefers the Congress party to the Communist Party on the ground that the former is democratic and nationalist and also perhaps progressive. This belief is not only contrary to the beliefs of the party but if worked upon will reduce the party to an ineffective existence or dissolve it into the Congress party without materially altering the latter. To combat this belief is as much your charge as mine. In the second place, the impression seems also to have gained ground that with the Congress party accepting the 14-point programme, there would be no further obstacles left in the way of coalition. This again is an erroneous belief on two grounds. It may well be that the party would consider it a better course to assist from outside in the execution of items in the 14-point programme by the Congress party and Government. The agency which executes it is at least as important as the items themselves of a programme. Various schemes of nationalization have aroused popular disapproval because of faulty execution.

Further more, the programme itself needs to be more properly defined and concretized so that the people may know what they have to expect should they return the Praja Socialist Party to power and also may be able to distinguish the party from all other parties in the land. You may remember that at the end of discussion when you were authorized by the Chairman to communicate to the press that the matter was dropped, you had asked if the programme had also lapsed, the Chairman replied in the affirmative saying that the programme had been framed for a specific occasion.

We had made it quite clear that the party was casting away all its anchors and losing patience. In such a situation if the U.P. Party resolves on a definite line, that should be welcome. I stand with the resolution and, although I was not present at the meetings of Executive in question, I am responsible for it more than any other individual. I understand that 17 out of 18 members present in that Executive had expressed themselves in agreement with the resolution and only one had disagreed. This is much better than the proposition laid down by the Chairman at the National Executive that he would have accepted pro-coalitionist formula if only one or two persons had been opposed to it.

Of the various items noted against the U.P. Party and the *Sangharsh*, I am really sorry that certain harsh passages should have slipped through into the articles. I and other colleagues have requested the editor to keep a stricter eye on the materials published. But what of the coalitionist *materials*. I would remind you of the sinister message published throughout the country on the eve of the last lap of the negotiations and also of the fact that anonymous politics are antidemocratic politics. At the same time instruments of publicity have been utilized for creating a coalitionist atmosphere and that will perhaps continue to be done if the ruling power so desires it. Such a use need not necessarily be made by party members. Furthermore, party members desirous of cooperation with the Congress party both before the negotiations and afterwards have given expression to sentiments that strengthen the coalitionist atmosphere and condition the party members' minds. I may only remind you that even after the meeting of the National Executive there have been several remarks by you and others that although the matter has been dropped the door is still open and any initiative undertaken by the Congress party will be fully reciprocated and one speech went so far as to say that anybody could take the initiative. I do not have to tell you that this is an invitation to the Prime Minister to undertake a fresh initiative. Was this the mood of the National Executive?

I want you and the Chairman not to minimize the strength of feeling both for and against that the issue of coalition has always aroused. When minority socialism decides to get into the Government of the day, it splits. At least that has been the experience so far. In such an extremely difficult situation, we will have to do our best. I do not imitate the language of the Chairman's letter to you, partly because it was a personal communication. I think it an act of charity not to go into people's motives and I try to practise this, though not always with success.

Acharya Kripalani is under some misapprehension that we had assured him that we would keep quiet. He should not imagine any such assurances. In fact, the reverse is true, for I had insisted right up to the end of the National Executive that the debate on the issue must continue. If that were not so, why should you all three at the private meeting next day have faced me with the choice to keep quiet or assume responsibility. I was unable to accept it. You had then modified the choice to mean keeping quiet during the negotiations and when I asked how was one to know that the Chairman would make an announcement to that purpose. Surely negotiations have not yet begun nor has the Chairman made any such announcement and, in any case, I was to think over even this restricted choice. Let us therefore not try to bully one another.

I would like to offer some suggestions as to how to overcome the distressing situation. I would request you to accept my resignation from the National Executive. Even if you or the Chairman may not be able to accept it straight away, you may announce it. I am not creating a precedent that all members of the National Executive of the Praja Socialist Party must hold homogenous views. But in view of the fact that we are only making beginnings in democracy, it may be wholesome for me to get out of the Executive. It will somewhat clear up the atmosphere and deny my activities at least some aspect of authority and also remove certain natural irritations. I am doing this, for as you well know, more than any other U.P. member on the National Executive I am the link between it and the U.P. Party and Acharya Narendra Deva should not be held responsible except in a general way. You may then appoint someone who would keep a better link between the Executive and the U.P. Party. You may also call a special meeting of the U.P. Party executive where this person or some of you may be present. I do not think it would be fair or proper for you to mix up this issue of the coalition with the question of resignation or of confidence or no confidence.

Another way out would be to announce that until the annual conference of the party meets and decides upon policies that may permit negotiations, no formal talks regarding coalition with the Congress party will be undertaken. This announcement should also request provincial and other committees not to publish any resolutions on the subject. I do not have to tell you how informal and exploratory talks may slide into formal negotiations.

I would like you to accept my resignation even if you favour my second suggestion. The situation in Andhra is somewhat anomalous. I may remind you, lest there should be further misunderstandings on the subject, that I had made my position clear at the National Executive. I had stood for the principle of toleration and no participation, and I had adopted an abstentionist or non-obstructionist attitude with regard to the resolution ultimately adopted.[3]

Furthermore, I have to tour Rajasthan and Saurashtra. You know how I had told Saurashtra people to be absolutely clear that I was an anti-coalitionist and their insistence on my tour should be viewed in this background. It would cause further irritations for an anti-coalitionist like me to tour those two provinces in an official capacity. I will naturally go where I like in a private capacity but this is another matter. Will you please cancel these tours and inform me accordingly?

The best way would be to drop the idea of coalition altogether. Mr. [C.D.] Deshmukh's speech coupling socialism and communism is not the last one. Let us by our thinking and action show that we are determined to decouple ourselves both from the Congress party and the Communists Party.

Many members of the party expect that what happened during the negotiations would at least be used in order to establish the distinct identity

[3]That resolution empowered T. Prakasam, the leader of PSP in the Andhra Assembly to take all steps necessary, including a coalition with the Congress, in order to form a ministry in the newly formed state.

of the party and its programme as against the Congress party. The fact that this is not being done gives rise to the suspicion that the desire for co-operation with the Congress party is so keen as to override realities. I am not doing so for fear that I may also be mistaken for a coalitionist in the event of the Congress party accepting a minimum programme. I need not tell you how you thought that Mr. Deshmukh had accepted nationalization of banks and insurance, while he has now declared that he does not. At the same time, Mr. Nehru has made it clear in his letter that his offer of co-operation also on governmental level came only when he was asked to define more precisely what he had only vaguely wished. These are only instances.

There are a lot too many contradictions in the pro-coalitionist position. Are party members able or are they not; it won't do to decry their ability when the question of striving for socialism in opposition is at issue and to count upon it when the question of socialist participation in the Government is considered. Are the activities of the Government and the character of laws of some consequence or not; it won't do to pooh-pooh all spheres of people's action except the governmental when participation in Government is advocated and to emphasize both at the personal and the people's level when the question of apportioning blame for existing distress is considered. Let us also not encourage our people in the dangerous and obscurantist belief that all good people must come together, for and after all who is good and for what are they to come together. The Chairman[4] has talked of being able to stand alone. I wish he had not talked this language to men who have in their activities for socialism known how to suffer calumny from congressmen, communists, communalists and all round. Even at the meeting of the National Executive I had twice tried to draw attention to his remarks that he wished for an alliance either with the Congress party or with the Communists and the communalists in order to form an effective opposition. Instead of challenging people like me who have no taste nor talent for internal opposition, let us of the Praja Socialist Party all stand together and alone as a challenge to the other mischievous elements in the country. I have in recent weeks been sometimes a victim of weariness—for it is not you folks who are alone—but I have had to overcome it. The Praja Socialist Party needs to settle down to some course of action. Do not unsettle it too often. A few individuals on the top may be able to retain their faith in the midst of continual turns and twists. The party cannot. If we have to pass through a period of ebb in the nation's and the party's fortunes, let us do so with patience. No party ever served the nation unless it was willing to risk popular disapproval in furtherance of necessary change. I would like you all to consider this as an appeal rather than a lecture to meet with a counter-lecture.

[4] Refers to J.B. Kripalani.

In the course of our work, we have all accumulated prejudices and time alone would show whether you folks are wrong or men like me or both of us in our separate ways. At the moment, policies and prejudices have got mixed up. Should you decide in favour of reconstructing the nation through the Praja Socialist Party in opposition and no indecisiveness about it, I should like to take leave from active politics for a year and even more. I might even go out of the country. It is a healthy practice with the Japanese, or so I think, for someone to withdraw even after differences are overcome and a definite policy emerges. I do not believe that anyone of you can now contemplate any other definite policy except to build up the party on the basis of equal irrelevance of the Congress and Communists. In fact, one of the reasons why I went to the Patna demonstration[5] was the information Prem Bhasin gave me that Jayaprakash Narayan [Narendra Deva?] had told him he would discourage any future initiative by Mr. Nehru. I was however unable to discover whether the last series of negotiations had alone ended or a new series were also unlikely to begin. I wish the party were somehow told this and its health would definitely improve. I am having copies of this letter sent to the persons whom you sent your letter and to Prem [Bhasin] who was to accompany me to Rajasthan. Please let me know early about Rajasthan and Saurashtra. I would also like you all to adopt an anti-coalitionist attitude and yet to announce my resignation from the National Executive, for our mutual prejudices would require sometime to wear out.

Yours sincerely,
J.P.

[5] It refers to Patna procession consisting of about 15,000 persons and led by leaders of PSP including Jayaprakash Narayan and Rammanohar Lohia on 6 April 1953, to the gates of the Bihar Assembly in order to submit a six-point charter of demands on behalf of the peasants to the Chief Minister.

252. To Jawaharlal Nehru, 6 May 1953[1]

Dear Bhai,

I saw in the papers before I left Bombay that the Congress had decided not to contest Kripalaniji's seat.[2] I am very thankful. But may I say that the whole grace of the gesture was ruined by Balwantraiji's statement that a PSP leader had requested that Kripalaniji be allowed to go uncontested.

[1] *J.P. Papers* (NMML).
[2] See Appendix 46 for the text of Nehru's reply.

My first impulse on reading the statement was to say that in that case, and if that was how the Congress felt, it was better that the Congress candidate was not withdrawn. But on second thoughts I decided to keep quiet. It is quite likely that some PSP leader had made the alleged request, but was it necessary to exploit it in this manner? When I had brought up the matter at our last meeting, my idea was only to bring it to your notice that we were going to put up Kripalaniji. And I had wondered what the policy of the Congress was going to be and had left it at that. You naturally had kept quiet.

There is another matter about which I wish to write. It is about the impending Vindhya by-elections. If an Ordinance or Act of Parliament sets at naught the decisions of the Election Commission, it would not be right to my view. Both the rule of law and the Election Commission would be brought into derision. It is better to go through the dozen or so bye-elections than to take recourse to what would the described as a subterfuge to protect partisan interests. For the future the law may be amended if it is found to be defective, but what has been found to be unlawful under the existing law should not be regularized by ordinance or otherwise. I am writing this not as a member of an opposition party, but as a friend and disinterested citizen.

I am on my way to Telangana in Hyderabad for Bhoodan work. The train is very shaky, so I have to apologize for the rather shaky hand.

With regards,

Affectionately,
Jayaprakash

253. Address to Bhoodan Workers, Surat, 16 May 1953[1]

The present party system of administration is bad in that the democratic views of the panchayats in villages do not mould the country's policy, but the centre's whip directs the policies of panchayats.

The path of Indian politics could have been directed on a different track when the Constitution was being made. But our Constitution itself was built on a basis of a party policy. The Constitution is an imitation of the West. Under the circumstances, I have not got the answer as to which path we should take. But I am exercising my mind on this point.

But there is no alternative unless the entire country is prepared to shed the party system of administration, or unless a new constitution is framed and all the parties are dissolved. Today this road may not be possible. The parties are not prepared to dissolve themselves. So we have to continue the present system for a time. But I definitely feel that there is something wrong

[1] Adapted from *National Herald*, 17 May 1953.

with the party system of administration. It will be good if all the parties join hands on programmes of welfare of the people. For this purpose, Gandhiji suggested the Lok Sevak Sangh. If Gandhiji had been consulted, the present Constitution would not have been given to the people.

254. Address at a Public Meeting regarding Bhoodan Yajna, Secunderabad, 17 May 1953[1]

The main question we are facing today is on what principles we should build our new society and on what foundation we should build our new India. Gandhiji had defined *Poorna Swarajya* as *Ram Rajya* and *Sarvodaya*.

The aim of the Socialist Party is also to build a society on justice and equality. But the question is what method we should adopt in bringing about the change. One answer invariably suggested to this question is that the Government should enact laws and bring about the change. There are others who are not prepared to wait till the Government took any steps in this direction. They resort to violence, snatch away lands from the landlords and distribute it among the landless. This is the programme followed by the Communist Party.

In Telengana within two and a half years, the Communists had only distributed 32,000 acres of land, after destroying crores of rupees worth of property. When such acts were being committed, no Government would remain a silent spectator. Naturally, the Government sent the army and put down the Communists. The net result was that, in the rule of violence, only the mightiest prevailed.

It was significant that another movement started from the same Nalgonda district, which had been the scene of violent activities of the Communists, and this sought to bring about the desired change in the set-up of the society through peaceful means. That movement was the Bhoodan Yajna. The notion of giving donations was not new. In other countries also people donated wealth for public institutions. But here the donations were secured from the rich and the landlords with a view to ending the capitalistic structure of Indian society. Within two years over 50,000 acres of land have been collected in the State without any bloodshed. Over 12 lakhs acres have been collected throughout the country. The Bhoodan Yajna movement is creating a new atmosphere of fraternity and brotherhood. This is revolution indeed. Revolution did not come overnight even in Russia. It came gradually. The method adopted to bring about the revolution was violent. Even today, in Russia, a poor man neither owns wealth nor has liberty.

I call upon everyone to contribute his mite towards the furtherance of

[1] Adapted from *Hindustan Times*, 18 May 1953.

the Bhoodan Yajna Movement. Bhoodan Yajna is a constructive work and is above party politics. All parties should unitedly work to prove this.

The Communists also believe in the party system, but they have only one-party rule. That is totalitarianism, which is bad. Mr. M.N. Roy suggested administration through the Soviets. When the Russian revolution was on, people imagined the soviet meant panchayat. The panchayat should hold the reins of administration. The administration should be based on the panchayat, but toady the party is controlling everything from the top. The party is having absolute power. That is not panchayati raj. Panchayati raj does not mean that Delhi should issue the directive and the village panchayats should follow the line, but the panchayat should mould Delhi's policy. Gandhiji's panchayat raj would have been this.

Bhoodan Movement should be pursued without any party politics. Then there will be a new outlook created. Perhaps, the present system of politics will go and a new system, devoid of parties, may emerge.

Wherever we talk with landholders regarding Bhoodan Yajna; we have to talk to the landless too, because the latter have become weak-minded as a result of continued suffering and frustration. They must realize that Bhoodan is not begging, but an assertion of their right on the land. If the landless realize their right and if they know that they should own land, then a huge mass power will flow out. It is certain that the Bhoodan Movement will open the flood-gates of such latent power. Vinobaji has told land-lords that on behalf of '*Daridranarayans*', he was asking them for their just rights. Do not be carried away by the word 'dan'. *Dan* only meant equal distribution.

The demonstrations in Patna were not in connection with Bhoodan. Like the Congress, the PSP is also working in the political field. We say that laws should be made on the basis of people's opinion. Once people's opinion is ready, a law should be made. Vinobaji also says that. He is not an enemy of the law, but law-making is not his business. What other work has a political party except moulding people's opinion.

Many ask Vinobaji: why not make laws for the redistribution of land? People may ask me: Why don't you force Mr. Nehru to make laws? It is true that such laws should be made, but without the people's support a law is not worth the paper on which it is written. So it appears to me that so long as Bhoodan does not succeed, it is no use making laws. In Bihar, the Bhoodan movement is taking big strides. In the Bihar Assembly, the Praja-Socialists have been pleading for a law for redistribution of land. To give support for this Bill, we wanted to demonstrate the demand of the people. Hence the demonstration in Patna.

Vinobaji has told the Bhoodan workers: You should not only bring landlords to me but bring the landless too. Let the landlords near me see the demand and the suffering of the landless, so they could realize that they should donate land. It is essential that the landlords should hear the cry of the landless. So I do not consider it wrong to demonstrate. The work of demonstration is, of course, for the political parties to undertake. It is not meant for the Bhoodan workers.

The Bhoodan workers may feel that many rich landlords do not donate land. They may be worried as to how to bring moral pressure on them. Is it correct to bring such pressure on them? I feel there is no occasion for such moral pressure. The Bhoodan slogan itself is giving a new stimulus. In Bihar, the landless said they would not cooperate if the landlords do not donate land to the Bhoodan Yajna. Even this may not be necessary.

Bhoodan is not simply getting donations, but it means proper redistribution and cultivation. The work of determining who is the poorest in the village should be done by the landless.

Thus the landless have a big part to play in the Bhoodan Yajna.

255. Statement on Kirpalani's contest in a Parliamentary Bye-election, Patna, 7 June 1953[1]

A most extraordinary situation has been created with regard to the parliamentary bye-election in the Bhagalpur-cum-Purnea constituency. In the first place, it is regrettable that it has not been realized that in spite of the fact that the Congress withdrew its candidate for the general seat, Kripalaniji's election is not a nominal affair. In a double-seated constituency the contest for the general seat is not confined only to non-Harijan candidates. Therefore, let it be clearly understood that Kripalaniji's election is being as keenly contested, if not more so, as it would have been if one of the Congress candidates had not been withdrawn.

In the second place, it is yet more regrettable that the Congress has adopted a very unfair tactic. Congress leaders, from the Chief Minister downwards, have been only asking the voters to cast both the ballot papers into the one and only Congress box. This they are doing not in the interest of their Harijan candidate for whom only one of the votes would be counted, in any case, but to stab Kripalaniji in the back. The extraordinary thing is that at the same time the same Congress leaders take every opportunity to advertise their great generosity in withdrawing their candidate for the general seat so as to facilitate Kripalaniji's election to Parliament. This is an extraordinary double game.

It is said that when the Congress withdrew one of its candidates, the PSP should also have reciprocated by withdrawing its Harijan candidate. I am sure the Congress Working Committee's decision was not in the nature of

[1]Adapted from *Searchlight*, 8 June 1953.

such a bargain. Nor would the PSP ever agree to a bargain for seats with the Congress. As I understood it, the Congress candidate was withdrawn because of the sentiment, commonly current even in Congress ranks, that Kripalaniji should not be opposed. If that was so, Congressmen themselves should have advised the voters to cast one of their votes for Kripalaniji, thus reducing the contest to one between the Harijan candidates of the PSP and the Congress. But as it is, Bihar Congressmen, led by the Chief Minister himself, have strained every nerve to defeat Kripalaniji, going to the extent of advocating double voting. If this was the intention of the Congress, it would have been far more honourable not to have withdrawn its candidate.

Apart from the ethics of double-voting in the present contest, one may ask if it was constitutionally appropriate for the Chief Minister of a State to openly ask the people to do what the Law and the Rules specifically prohibit. Section 63 of the People's Representation Act and Rule 25 of the Election Rules, as also the instructions issued by the Election Commission to the Returning Officers, clearly indicate that in a double-member constituency both ballot papers should not be inserted in the same box. Section 63 of Representation of the Peoples Act reads thus: 'In Plural member constituencies, other than a Council constituency, every elector shall give not more than one vote to any one candidate.' Rule 25 says: 'not more than one ballot paper shall be put by an elector into one ballot box.' The Instruction to Presiding Officers reads: 'In a two member constituency whether for Assembly or for Parliament the voter will get two ballot papers. The peon on duty on opening of the compartments should in such cases warn every elector as he goes in that he or she should insert each of the ballot papers in a different box and must not insert both the ballot papers in the same box'. These are clear and definite provisions and requirements of the Law. Yet no less a person than the Chief Minister of Bihar has asked the electors to do exactly what the Law and Rules clearly say must never be done. The law was asked to be defied just because the Congress had somehow to win an election. I wonder what would happen to this country when our rulers themselves go about preaching defiance of the law of the land.

But the Congress went even further. Pressure seems to have been put upon the Returning Officer to change the original instruction quoted above. The altered instruction reads thus 'Presiding Officers should not volunteer any advice to any voter as to how ballot papers should be used. If any voter asks for any advice he or she should be asked to do as he or she likes'. It will be seen that this is entirely contrary to the rule laid down in the Election Rules. It is amazing that a Returning Officer should prove to be so lacking in the ordinary sense of responsibility as to be brow-beaten by the Congress into acting in such an arbitrary and illegal manner. Happily as it appears in the newspaper reports, on protest from Mrs. Sucheta Kripalani, the Election Commission has corrected the mischief.

All this undermines the confidence of the people in the capacity of the present Government to conduct elections in a fair and honest manner. More important than victory at elections are principles and ideals of conduct, and if the latter are preserved, the country gains no matter which party loses.

256. To K.N. Katju, 10 June 1953[1]

My dear Dr. Katju,

I hope you will excuse me for giving you this trouble.

You know that certain tribal areas of Rajasthan, Gujarat and Madhya Bharat (which form a large contiguous trail) have been suffering from scarcity conditions for the past three years. You yourself have toured some of the areas. This is the third year of their suffering and Government too have declared them to be scarcity areas this year. This prolonged scarcity has left the people—mostly Adivasis—with practically no purchasing power. The sowing season, on the other hand, has arrived and they need seeds. The three or four months of the rainy season are the leanest months for the cultivators. So they also have to have food to sustain them. But they are not in a position either to buy the seeds or the food grains that they so desperately need. Under these circumstances, they cannot but fall a prey to the money-lenders. It seems urgent and proper that the Government save them from such a ruinous eventuality. I am writing that the people be allowed loan of grains and seeds from the Government shops on condition that the loan would be retuned in kind by Diwali, when the *kharif* crop is harvested. The people are agreed to do this and we can give you a full assurance that this promise will be fulfilled. I shall be obliged if you will be good enough to give your urgent consideration to this matter and accept my request.

I hope you are well.

Yours sincerely,
J.P.

[1] *J.P. Papers* (NMML).

257. Intervention in the Debate on General Secretary's Report, Betul, 16 June 1953[1]

Friends, if I have chosen this moment to address you, it is not because I wanted to reply to the debate on the General Secretary's Report,[2] but because I wished to listen to you all before I spoke.

As I sat back and listened to the speeches, I realized that the entire criticism was directed against me. The debate so far has centred round my talks with Mr. Nehru. When the National Executive met at Bombay in the last week of March, Asoka had asked me about the procedure of this Convention. I had suggested to him that since the cooperation talks were between me and Mr. Nehru, it would be appropriate if I reported to the Convention and the Convention debated my report.

It was much after I left Bombay that I received a copy of Asoka's Report. By raising the issue in the shape of a bold theory Asoka has acted as a shield for me. But except for one or two speakers, every one has avoided discussion of his theory and made my talks with Jawaharlalji the main target of attack. So, I shall leave Asoka's thesis alone and deal with the issues raised.

You all know the circumstances under which I met Mr. Nehru. Our correspondence on the talks we had is before you. You will recollect that in his letter Mr. Nehru had informed me that in view of the divergence in our approaches, the idea of all-level cooperation between us was dropped.

At Bombay and subsequently elsewhere also I had made it clear to many of you that the talks had ended and, according to my estimate, Mr. Nehru was not likely to make any further moves, not at least till after the next general elections. After the talks I had also made up my mind, seeing the difference of opinion amongst ourselves, not to pursue the matter further even if Mr. Nehru made a fresh offer.

That was my view even during the talks. After my first series of meetings with Mr. Nehru I had talks with Acharya Narendra Deva. Both he and Dr. Lohia were against the type of cooperation which Mr. Nehru was seeking. Subsequently, when Narendra Devaji met Mr. Nehru he had discouraged him. I had therefore thought then that the cooperation suggested by Mr. Nehru was not worth trying and would not succeed if colleagues like Narendra Devaji and Lohia were against it. I wrote to Kripalaniji accordingly and suggested that the talks be discontinued. In the meantime Kripalaniji had also met Mr. Nehru. Kripalaniji had felt after the meeting that nothing was going to come out of Mr. Nehru's move. He, however, felt that some

[1] *Report of the Special Convention of the Praja Socialist Party*, Betul (M.P.), 14-18 June 1953, pp. 59-73.

[2] See Appendix 47 for the text of Asoka Mehta's Report as General Secretary.

of us should meet informally at Delhi to consider the whole issue.

Accordingly, the Prime Minister's proposal was considered at an informal meeting of some important members of the Party. I had suggested at the meeting that the proposal be placed before the National Executive. But the Chairman felt, and rightly so, that since the issues were not clear no useful purpose would be served by calling a meeting of the National Executive. The Delhi meeting decided not to abandon the talks but to pursue them. Some friends had also felt that since nothing was likely to come out of the talks, the talks should be terminated in such a way as to avoid bitterness and the onus of the breakdown.

However, as far as I am concerned, I have made up my mind. If a proposal were again to be made I would tell Jawaharlalji that the time was not ripe for such an experiment.

Such joint efforts between two parties who are sharply divided from within on the issue would be ineffective and would fail. Some of you have asked for a guarantee. As far as I am concerned, I have no hesitation in giving such a guarantee. Even while I still hold that, given the necessary goodwill and agreement, the joint effort I was visualizing is desirable and appears to be the only way to face and solve the tremendous problems of economic development and national integration facing the country today, I will have no further talks with Mr. Nehru on the question.

It is however another matter that the issues may crop up in different and smaller contexts as in Andhra or may be Hyderabad and Travancore-Cochin. But even in such cases, I will not take any initiative. My suggestions however are always available.

Some of you have complained that the Andhra Executive has been bypassed by leaving the final decision in Mr. Prakasam's hands. That is not so. The Andhra Executive will function as before. When the agreement was reached between the Congress and the PSP in Andhra, the State Executive had full way. With regard to further steps too, the Executive is free to advise Mr. Prakasam. One important aspect of the matter is being overlooked. You should remember that the final decision would never have been left to the Andhra Executive. That would normally be taken by the National Executive. It is this final power that the National Executive has vested in Mr. Prakasam. It has not divested the State Executive of any authority.

Let us remember the facts about Andhra. The Andhra State is new-born. Indeed, it is in the process of creation. Its consummation is as much the responsibility of the Congress party as it is of the PSP. In order to give a stable government to Andhra, the Congress party in Andhra has been approaching us for cooperation. As the supreme authority the National Executive could have taken decisions itself. But the situation is changing constantly and it is not possible for the Executive to follow all its twists and turns. Mr. Prakasam is on the spot, commands overwhelming support of the people and also enjoys the full confidence of the National Executive. So the latter delegated to him its powers of final decision. It will be wrong for anyone to assume that Mr. Prakasam is committed to a coalition. One of the two courses is open to the Party in Andhra. The Praja Socialist Legislature Party may help the Congress party to form the government and support it without joining the Government. Or, it may decide to share governmental responsibility.

Which of the two courses should be followed now depends upon Mr. Prakasam. If the people of Andhra and their political parties overwhelmingly desire that Mr. Prakasam should shoulder the responsibility to run the new State, I, for one, would not want to bind him down to a particular policy. All that I would urge upon him is that, coalition or no coalition, the Party must demand early general elections in Andhra.

Now about the general policy of cooperation. My attitude on this question is very clear. If some one seeks my cooperation I will never deny it to him provided however there is agreement on the purpose of the cooperation and the work that is to be done together. It was thus that I had approached Jawaharlalji's offer. I do not see how such an attitude blurs the features of the Party. It is my claim that my talks with Jawaharlalji have done good to the Party. As a result of these talks, I claim, the features of the Party have been further sharpened. They helped to remove the confusion that there is not much difference between us and the Congress. The 14-point programme we had given to Mr. Nehru was not a full-fledged socialist programme. We had put forth a minimum programme for the next few years. The people have now come to know that even such a minimum programme is not acceptable to the Congress. Is that not clarification of our stand and sharpening of our features.

Some have spoken as if the Congress was dying for our cooperation. Make no mistake about it. The Congress is as much afraid of blurring its features as some of you are. Congressmen feel much the same way as you do in the matter.

But within the two parties there are enough people who not only appreciate but agree with my approach. If such people ever get together, given the necessary goodwill, I have no manner of doubt that they can achieve a great deal.

Much has been said about the theory of equi-distance. It has been said that we have abandoned the political line of the Party. I do not see how that has happened. People have talked of the Pachmarhi thesis of the Party. Quite apart from whether or not that political line is automatically the policy of the Praja Scoialist Party, I submit that my interpretation of the Pachmarhi thesis of equi-distance does not happen to be the same as yours. The old Socialist Party had affirmed at Pachmarhi that it shall not confuse its identity by coalition or fronts with the Congress and Communist parties. It had called upon its members to so behave that its features become sharply distinguishable. That is good as far as it goes. But consider a situation in which a political party has moved nearer to our position. What do we do then? Shall we be so dogmatic then as to move away from it as it moves nearer us in order to keep the distance constant?

Please remember that politics is dynamic and distance in politics is never static. If a political party moves near enough to us it should be our endeavour to bring it still nearer. If, for example, tomorrow the Communist Party of India declares that it will no more be controlled by the Cominform, that it has abandoned its extra-territorial loyalties and that it will never adjust its internal policies to the needs of the Soviet Union's foreign policy, I would say that the Communist Party had moved away from its original stand and towards us. Under such circumstances I would be perfectly willing to consider the possibilities of cooperation between the Communist Party and the PSP.

There are in the Congress today a large number of good people. Much ridicule has been heaped on me for saying that good people should come together. Lohia argues that goodness alone is not enough for people to get together and work. I agree.[3] When I say good people I am also concerned with their thoughts and approach to problems.

C.G.K. Reddy seems to imagine that Panditji's motive in making that offer of all-level cooperation to us was diabolical. It will be very unfair to imagine so. The proposal that he made to me was bold and unusual. The Congress party stands in no need of a coalition. Still he wanted our co-operation in and out of government in the interest of nation-building. But his approach, to my mind, was wrong. His conception was of an uninhibited cooperation between individuals. That would have been disastrous.

S.K. Saxena has asserted that it was merely an accident that the proposal came from Mr. Nehru. He claims from his assessment of the working of our minds that the proposals could have emanated from us as well.

In January last, when I was at Rangoon, such thoughts as I have expressed in my letter to Mr. Nehru had occurred to me. I had mentioned them to Asoka. I did not hide them. Subsequently, at a meeting of our delegates I had freely spoken out my mind. I had then said that the tremendous problems of national integration and economic reconstruction in India could not be faced and solved by any one party alone. There is a stagnation in the country. The Government, in the Centre as well as in the states, have miserably

[3]See Appendix 48 for Lohia's speech in course of debate on the General Secretary's Report to the Betul Conference.

failed. Their policies are wrong and therefore the sufferings of the people continue. I had also made a mention of Mr. Nehru's letter to me seeking the Party's cooperation to fight the growing menace of communalism. I had further said that it should be possible for the Party to join hands with the Congress to fight the disruptive forces. My ideas then were still vague. I had vaguely felt that, given a sincere desire on both sides and a common approach to the tasks facing the country, it would be in national interest for the Congress party and the PSP to cooperate on wider issues, particularly in the present transitional and formative period.

I have no desire to spread confusion in the Party and split its mind. I do not wish to carry on propaganda in favour of cooperation. If I were not a member of the Party I would have moved round the country; met the Congress leaders and leaders of others parties and tried to convert them to my point of view.

Let me make it clear that my views have not changed. But I do not wish to continue a controversy about an unreal issue.

It has been argued that those of us who have been in favour of programmatic cooperation with the governmental party have lost faith in the people's will and initiative. We are being charged that we are abandoning people's solutions in favour of governmental solutions. It will be wrong to argue thus.

If the Congress had accepted the 14-point programme there would have been cooperation no doubt. But that would not have meant that people's initiative or mass sanctions would have become unnecessary. Even then it would have been necessary for the Party to be very much with the people to lead their agitations, to organize their effective will, to give a point to their enthusiasm, in order that the implementation of the programme would be guaranteed. That would have further developed people's initiative and support. Lohia wants the creation of public opinion and popular will first. But I believe that if there is programmatic cooperation it would be possible to develop the opinion and the will.

Again, some apprehend that in the event of Congress-PSP cooperation, the monopoly of opposition would be with the Communist Party. That may be so. But if our cooperation leads to something being done, for instance, if land is re-distributed, if administration improves and corruption goes, if cooperatives are built up, if other items of the 14-point programme are carried out, what would be the value of the Communist opposition?

Some of you have argued that the Congress party can implement the 14-point programme by itself and without our cooperation if it really agrees with that programme. That is a naive way of thinking.

I understand the dynamics of politics in a different way. If the Congress party had accepted our programme and the joint efforts had been launched, things would have happened, and the whole nation would have moved forward. The Congress party did not accept the programme. But things have not remained static. The whole episode has set people thinking. Jawaharlalji had to write to the members of the Working Committee and the Chief Ministers asking them how much of the programme could be implemented. A certain amount of pressure of public opinion and events has worked. As this pressure increases, as the public opinion becomes more pointed, things should happen. To say that if the Congress party has the will and desire to do things you want them to do, it will do them, cooperation or no cooperation, is not to understand the dynamics of politics.

Lohia has argued that mere acceptance of a programme is not enough. What about the agency to execute it? The necessary public opinion to back it? In the absence of adequate agency and public opinion, he argues, the programmatic cooperation, the joint effort, must fail. May be he is right. But I submit the experiment was worth trying. I feel that, given a sincere desire on both sides and a common approach to the tasks facing us, there was every hope that the experiment would have succeeded.

Take, for instance, the 14-point programme. If it is argued that the people will be behind this programme only if they have voted for us, I would not agree. The fact that we lost the election does not mean that the people were not for all those things that the 14-point programme contains. We would be right in assuming that the people are overwhelmingly in favour of that programme.

Question has been raised about the possible failure of the joint effort. Suppose, it is argued, the Congress party creates difficulties and obstructs implementation of the programme. In that case, we would come out of the Government, go to the people and tell them the truth. The people, I am sure, would understand and be with us. But C.G.K. Reddy would ask: 'Then, why enact this drama at all. Only so that the Congress is exposed? Is not the Congress fully exposed already?' No. You are thinking only of the converted. But there are vast numbers of others who have yet to be converted. The failure of the joint effort due to Congress sabotage is bound to exert a powerful influence on these sections of the people.

I do not know why you are afraid of taking risks. The situation in India is such that the Party will have to become bold enough and try new approaches. I should like you to think about it. Consider the situation in India dispassionately. Approach the problems boldly. You may not agree with me. You may reject my solution. But why should you refuse to think?

And now about yet another matter which is agitating your minds. The trade union workers would be meeting on the 19th to discuss the trade union policy of the Party. But here certain questions have been raised. A few days back the Working Committees of the All-India Railwaymen's Federation and the Indian National Railway Workers Federation decided to merge their organizations together into a new, united Federation. Some of you have considered it as a step leading to the merger of the Party with the Congress. This is imagination run riot.

I do not know why our comrades refuse to take facts into consideration. The All-India Railwaymen's Federation is an independent organization. It has nothing to do with even the Hind Mazdoor Sabha, much less the Praja Socialist Party. I was its President for the last six years. A large number of our comrades are leading a number of railway unions. But none of us has functioned in a partisan manner within the AIRF.

The merger of the AIRF and the INRWF has been a persistent demand of the railwaymen themselves. It was not my move. Several non-party workers of various unions of the AIRF wrote to me and pressed me, before I left the Federation to move in the matter. It was then that I met the leaders of INRWF. In spite of its long-standing, the AIRF was not making headway. The INRWF might have been a mistake, but it was there. It functioned as a rival to the AIRF. And the Administration and the Government took advantage of the split in the ranks of the workers.

Even the INRWF is facing an impasse today, in spite of the fact that it had been sponsored by the Government party. The leaders of the INRWF have had bitter experience of the Railway Administration. In spite of the Government support they are finding it impossible to function and deliver the goods. They have realized their mistake. During the last one or two years, whenever I had occasion to meet Shri Khandubhai Desai or Shri Hariharnath Shastri, I found a district change in their attitude. They have begun to approach the trade union movement much the same way as we do. That is a welcome change.

Recently, in March, the Working Committees of the two Federations met together. A merger agreement was drawn up. An Ad Hoc Working Committee was formed. But when the Working Committee of the AIRF met separately those who had persistently wanted the merger voted against ratification of the merger agreement. Why? It was all over the personnel of the Ad Hoc Working Committee. I cannot understand such attitude.

Opposition to a move sometimes becomes so irrational that things are read in it beyond what it actually implies. I do not see how, if the merger of the two Federations is to the liking of the Railwaymen and in the larger interests of the trade union movement and its future, it can harm the Party. The merger was even construed to mean merger of the Party with the Congress. Some even suggested that the Communist unions also should not be excluded.

I can understand your opposition to a programmatic cooperation with the Congress. But I do not see why you should oppose any move which would help to build up a united, free, democratic trade union movement. The working class today is split up. As long as the trade union movement remains truncated it cannot grow. Surely it is our duty to bring together such trade union organizations as believe and are prepared to work for a free, democratic trade union movement in this country. There are today four trade union organizations, the Hind Mazdoor Sabha, the Indian National Trade Union Congress, the All-India Trade Union Congress, and the United Trade Union Congress. I do not see any reason why, in the best interests of trade union movements, the HMS, the INTUC and even the UTUC should not come together in a single organization. The INTUC today has learnt through experience. They have realized that it is derogatory to the trade union movement to subserve to the policies and requirements of the party in power. Today they are as much desirous of building up a trade union movement free from the control of Government, employers and political parties, as you are. They have realized that their Bareilly resolution calling upon the INTUC constituents to vote Congress was wrong. They have learnt from experience and are prepared today to join hands with you to build up a united, free, democratic, trade union movement in India. Why should we reject their hand of cooperation?

I am however against the inclusion of AITUC. They do not accept the principles of a free and democratic trade union movement. But the INTUC does accept it. May be, the UTUC too will do the same.

And now I should like to say something about certain of my thoughts, which seem to have disturbed you most. What I have said about the party system seems to have unduly alarmed some of you. I had no hesitation in indulging in such loud thinking. I have come to believe that the party system will not be conducive to national integration. It is an unsatisfactory system and is incapable of providing an adequate framework for the democratic requirements of the masses. As a result talent gets divided, national effort gets split and it leads to the imposition of a majority view.

The Western system of party democracy has not proved to be a conspicuous success.

I should say that I have no alternative to offer for the party system. But I clearly see its drawbacks and inadequacies. We will have to do serious thinking and find out an alternative.

I was happy when I found that the idea of lifting the village panchayats out of the competitive field of party politics was generally welcomed by you. May be, our experiment in this field will yield experience which may show us the way.

You may ask why, when I have no alternative to the party system, do I talk about it. I talk because I want people to think seriously about the problem. Should we have a constitution for the country which would not make it possible for any one to organize political parties, or that they would have no utility? We talk of villagisation, decentralization of economic and political power. It is necessary to devise a political system compatible with all these ideas.

I have never said that because the party system is defective, the PSP should be dissolved. As long as there are parties, the PSP must remain and grow; and personally I am its member, because of all the parties in existence it alone gives me utmost satisfaction.

But I should have the freedom to think aloud on the issue. It is a quest and I want you to join me in it.

Let me now turn to the Bhoodan Movement. The experiences I have gained through active participation in that movement has helped me a lot in my thought processes.

Some of you have doubts and misgivings about the movement. I had hoped that the Party would take to this movement seriously and plunge into it. But you don't seem to be inclined that way.

We have often talked of organizing the effective will of the people and of giving a point and shape to their yearning and sufferings. I submit that the Bhoodan Movement is a magnificent effort in that direction. You do not seem to have realized the tremendous potentialities of the movement, the effective public opinion it is creating for land redistribution, sharing of wealth and economic equality. There is a hunger for land in the country. A handful few have lands far in excess of their requirements, while there are millions who have no land and yet depend upon it. The Bhoodan Movement of Vinoba has given a point and shape to people's hunger for land, to their yearning for equality. Vinoba has moved the hearts of even the poorest of the peasants who today give to him not their mite but sometimes even their entire possession.

But we sit back and raise doubts. Will it solve the problem of land redistribution? Why take from the poor? Is change of heart possible. Is it a revolutionary and progressive movement? Is Vinoba in favour or against *satyagraha* for land?

It seems to be an old habit. During the fight for freedom, the CSP and the other Marxist parties used to sit back in much the same way and criticize Gandhiji and find fault with his methods. But when Gandhiji acted and called the people to action, we had no alternative but to follow him. We were driven like dry leaves in the storm. All Marxists, whether Communists, Royists or Congress Socialists, all the time picked holes in Gandhiji's ideology and methodology and patted themselves on the superiority of their own ideology; but when it came to action, none of them was able with his superior ideology to create a mass movement bigger than or anywhere near what Gandhiji was able every time to conjure up. Marxism had taught them that Gandhiji's methods, instead of sharpening class struggle, were blunting them. We held to the thesis that only a sharpening and intensification of the class struggle would help to overthrow British imperialism. I was myself a staunch critic of Gandhiji. In my book *Why Socialism* I devoted a whole chapter to the theory of trusteeship as propounded by Gandhiji. I had ridiculed it then. But today I realize I was wrong. I see in the Bhoodan Movement thousands of people parting with land freely. They are thus acting as trustees, they are returning the land to those whom society had deprived of their rights. I have just said that, in spite of our doubts and airs of ideological superiority, we were driven like leaves in Gandhiji's storm. I believe a storm is brewing again, and once again we are going to be blown about like shrivelled leaves.

Even the Communists will have to bow to the storm.

Some ridicule Bhoodan as glorified charity or almsgiving. Charity is degrading. But Vinoba is not asking for charity. He is demanding a realization of rights. *Dan* means to him, as to Sankaracharya, equitable distribution. The Bhoodan Movement is to Vinoba an experiment in non-violent economic revolution. Vinoba discovered Bhoodan in Telengana. You know what had happened in Telengana. The Communists claim they had distributed lands there. How and at what cost? Two and a half years of Communist violence had resulted in at least in 3,000 murders and the destruction of property worth more than six crores of rupees. Even at that high cost the Communists, according to their own claim, were not able to capture more than 30,000 acres of land.

Vinoba went to Hyderabad to heal the wounds of Telengana. I do not find today Gandhiji dynamism and incessant quest towards his ultimate values except in Vinoba. He stopped all activities, closed down his Ashram and started treading the dusty village roads. He has produced a remarkable method for the solution of the country's biggest problem—the land problem. In two years he has collected one and a half million acres of land. For Uttar Pradesh his target is ten million acres by the end of 1957. He has already collected half a million acres there. But Ram Chandra Shukla complains that most of the land he received is extremely poor and sandy. I doubt it. But suppose it is. Tomorrow Vinoba will get better lands because the movement will continue till the landless are satisfied. For Bihar his target is three and a half million acres by April 1954. He has collected already over half a million acres. And all this without shedding a single drop of blood. Instead of murder and loot, there has been an appeal to the better nature of man, an uplifting process. People's yearnings have been given a point and an expression, a powerful public opinion for land redistribution and economic equality has been created. You may choose to sit back and raise your doubts. But the thing is happening before your eyes.

I referred earlier to Gandhiji's theory of trusteeship. I believe we have in Bhoodan a bold application of that theory. That theory, as I understand it, has two aspects. To the owner of wealth and the exploiter it says: 'The wealth you have is not yours. It belongs really to society and you hold it as a trust. Therefore, keep only what you require and return the rest to society.'

In the beginning it was Vinoba's feeble voice of conviction which was dinning it into the ears of the wealthy. Today it is a whole army of workers which is echoing it all around. And we find the landowners coming forward and surrendering at least a part of their trust.

But that is only one part of the theory. Question is raised what would happen if the rich did not respond adequately to the appeal of trusteeship. It is generally believed that Gandhiji had no remedy for that. But he had an effective remedy. And that was non-cooperation. Gandhiji said that the exploited cooperated in their exploitation with their exploiters. If the latter refused to do justice to the exploited, he would prepare them for non-cooperation. And when that happened, the whole social order based on exploitation would come tumbling down.

In Bhoodan we find both these processes at work. On the one hand, the landed class is responding to the moral appeal, and gifts are being made. Indeed, there are areas today where more persons are ready to give than those where are ready to take. There is a great dearth of workers. This is one side of the movement. On the other side, we find a new consciousness dawning upon the landless people. In the first place, the landless are coming to realize that they have as much right in the land as the landlords, that land belongs to the community, that every one who works upon it must have a share in it. Secondly, when they find that in their village some landowners have gifted lands for them and some have not, they naturally ask themselves why should they work in the fields of those who have not given them their right. Thus, even without having ever heard of Gandhiji's theory of non-cooperation, the idea of non-co-operating with those who refuse to donate lands takes root in their minds. In this manner a powerful social force is being created that can be used when necessary in the second phase of the non-violent economic revolution.

The question of legislation is often raised. Vinoba is not against legislation. But he is impatient and does not want to wait till there is legislation. He says he is clearing the road for legislation. There must be public opinion created before a law can be made. He is creating opinion for redistribution of land. Legislation is bound to come. It would come sooner if the message of Bhoodan spreads to every village, and it will be better.

In a number of places Vinoba was asked by socialists if he was against *satyagraha* for land. His reply was that the question was wrong. Bhoodan too was *satyagraha.* It is his firm belief that he can bring about a change of heart by persuasion which too is a process of *satyagraha*. He would appeal, he would explain, he would warn. He does not, however, exclude what is ordinarily known as *satyagraha*, i.e. peaceful struggle.

Doubt has been raised if it will be possible for the Bhoodan Movement to collect enough land. It is my belief that it will be possible provided adequate number of workers are available. It is not true that men of status alone can get gifts of land. I know of cases where even unknown workers have been able to collect land.

But even if it is assumed that sufficient land cannot be collected, one should not neglect the dynamics of the movement. A tremendous public opinion is being created in favour of land distribution and eventually for that force of non-cooperation, of which I spoke earlier.

Sometimes it is asked why Vinoba accepts lands even from the poor. A poor peasant parts with his land willingly because he knows that another poor person will receive it. When the poor give for the poor, a new solidarity grows among them. Vinoba says the poor, by joining the movements, become his non-violent army of revolution.

It should be remembered that re-distribution of land is only the first step. Our work does not end with it. Those who will be receiving lands will have to be provided with agricultural implements. This is a tremendous undertaking. To this end Vinoba has started another gift-movement: *sampatti dan*. He and his co-workers are collecting ploughs, bullocks, seeds and gifts of wells, pumps, etc. Then there are problems of consolidation of plots, pooling of farming resources. All these problems the Bhoodan intends to tackle. Indeed, where several workers are available, these problems are being already tackled. A large army of workers is required for this task of reconstruction. Will, you answer this call of the times?

Ram Chandra Shukla has talked of priorities. I am not against priorities. I am not asking you to abandon your day-to-day work among the kisans. I am not asking you to shut your eyes to ejectments and other injustices. But remember that if you take up Bhoodan work all your other work in the countryside will become easier and smoother.

Finally, let me draw your attention to a remarkable development. Out of this Bhoodan Movement is emerging the final picture of our village society. In a few villages in Bihar and Uttar Pradesh, all the landowners have gifted *all* their lands. In this manner the entire village community has become the owner of all the village lands. I have called this *gramikaran*. To me village ownership of land is the final stage of the economic evolution of rural society. Here you have a glimpse into the vast creative and constructive possibilities of the Bhoodan Movement. Let me add just this much. If the Bhoodan succeeds, not only will the problem of inequality in the possession of land be solved, but it will release and bring into play such moral and social forces that the whole problem of economic inequality and exploitation will find its solution.

Thank you.

258. Statement on His Resignation from the National Executive of the PSP, Betul, 18 June 1953[1]

I am sorry, Sir. I owe an explanation to the Convention for this lapse.[2]

Yesterday, Lohia had said that those who are dissatisfied with the policy of the leaders should realize that such a state of affairs cannot continue for long. They should come forward and accept the responsibility of running the Party.

Those of you who are opposed to cooperation with the Congress should really come forward and take up organizational responsibilities. A majority of the delegates here are against our policy. Under such circumstances, it becomes necessary that there should be a change. We should step aside.

I am not saying all this with a view to coerce you into accepting my policy. I am not trying to create any crisis. I honestly believe that under the present circumstances I should step aside. Not only myself but all those who have been responsible for the execution of certain recent policies. But I can speak only for myself. I assure you I can work even in a minority of one.

I was primarily responsible for what has happened so far. I am tendering my resignation from the National Executive.

I realize that the opponents of our Party should not get an opportunity to attack us. Some way will have to be found out. The majority view must prevail. A new National Executive and office-bearers should be elected. But whatever is to be done should be in such a way that our opponents will not profit by it.

Party work must go on. I will faithfully follow the majority. Everyone has his limitations. The present office-bearers should not be forced to continue.

I will be at the disposal of the new Executive and General Secretary much the same way as before. If they so desire I will have no hesitation in joining the new Executive also.

But friends, a smooth way out must be found. Please realize the situation. That is all I have to say.

[1] *Report of the Special Convention of the Praja Socialist Party*, Betul (M.P.), 14-18 June 1953, pp. 73-4.

[2] This is with reference to the fact, brought to the notice of the Chairman of the Special Convention of the Praja Socialist Party (Betul, 1953) by M. Harris that J.P. had mentioned his resignation at a meeting of the delegates from South India and asked them to communicate the news to other delegates, but many in the convention were till then not aware of it.

259. To Rafi Ahmed Kidwai, 19 June 1953[1]

My dear Rafi Saheb,

I hope you will excuse me for giving you this trouble.

You know that certain tribal areas of Rajasthan, Gujarat and Bombay (which form a large contiguous trail) have been suffering from scarcity conditions for the past three years. This is the third year of their suffering and Government too have declared them to be scarcity areas this year. This prolonged scarcity has left the people—mostly all adivasis—with practically no purchasing power. The sowing season, on the other hand, has arrived and they need seeds. The three or four months of the rainy season are the leanest months for the cultivators. So they also have to have food to sustain them. But they are not in a position either to buy the seeds or the food grains that they so desperately need. Under these circumstances, they cannot but fall a prey to the moneylenders. It seems urgent and proper that the Government save them from such a ruinous eventuality. I am writing that the people be allowed loan of grains and seeds from the Government shops on condition that the loan would be returned in kind by Diwali when the *kharif* crop is harvested. The people are agreed to do this and we can give you a full assurance that this promise will be fulfilled. I shall be obliged if you will be good enough to give your urgent consideration to this matter and accept my request.

I hope you are well.

Yours sincerely,
J.P.

[1]*J.P. Papers* (NMML).

260. Bhoodan to a Party-less Democracy, Surat, 24 June 1953[1]

I visualize the day when there would be a non-party administration in the country—perhaps in every country in the world. Perhaps this may be the political outcome of the Bhoodan Movement, if the movement succeeds. Vinoba Bhave is also thinking on this basis.

In a world of warring 'isms' Vinoba Bhave's Bhoodan Movement has worked a miracle and has brought together various parties. Perhaps it is a mistake to always imagine that in a democracy there must be a ruling party and an opposition party. There should be some other way. I cannot exactly tell you to-day what this other system could be. But this is a problem which everyone should think about.

I do not mean that there should be a one party administration in the country. This will be suicidal. What I mean is that there should be no party at all. The constitution could be run without any party. Perhaps when the maps of our villages are redrawn after the successful completion of the Bhoodan Movement, this may be possible.

There are many parties having an all-India leadership. They do propaganda and set up their own candidates in elections. People have to select from amongst them. This is not a sound system of democracy. People may not be able this way to select the best candidate.

In five and half lakh villages, the people can meet and elect those they consider their best servants. There should be no canvassing. People will select the Panchayats everywhere. All the Panchayats together will select a Taluka Panchayat. The Taluka Panchayats will elect a District Panchayat and thus the State and Central Governments.

Mahatma Gandhi thought were also on these lines. But that does not seem to be possible under the present economic and social conditions. Presently there is the conflict between the rich and the poor and the exploited and exploiter. When the Bhoodan Movement is successfully completed this may be possible. Even after independence the work of establishing a new social system remains incomplete. The Communists feel that that they can solve the problem of redistribution of land and wealth through their own method. However, their violent ways in Telengana did not bring about the good result envisaged.

It was at that time when the people were looking to an alternative, Vinobaji placed his programme. First the idea of Bhoodan was laughed at while some said that the method will take 500 years to solve the land problem. Now it is conceded by one and all that the Bhoodan Movement could bring about a revolution. Thus we have got within two years fifteen lakh acres of land.

The Bhoodan method is better than making a law for redistribution of land. In Hyderabad there is a Land Distribution Act in the offing. While the law-makers claim that they would get eight or ten lakh acres once the Act is implemented, the landowners do not expect that the State would get even three or four lakh acres.

Vinoba Bhave has fixed a quota of 44 lakh acres for Hyderabad State. Provided there are enough workers, it would be definitely possible to get these lands today. It is not because people do not want to give but there are not enough workers to explain and demand from the landowners that more land should be donated to the Bhoodan Movement.

The Bhoodan Movement means land redistribution without crores of rupees being paid as compensation. Mahatma Gandhi once told Louis Fischer (American Journalist) that the zamindari problem would be tackled but without any compensation, because there is no money with the poor kisans to pay as compensation.

There is no question of ceiling in Bhoodan Movement because the landowners are asked to keep what is essential for them and give away the rest. Hence more land will be available.

To feel that the movement will not succeed is to accept defeat even before the start. The important factor is that the Bhoodan Movement has not only created an atmosphere wherein the landowners have got an opportunity to understand the significance of the movement and donate their holdings, but it has awakened the workers on the land. The workers are getting united and when called upon will peacefully non-cooperate with those who continue to hold land and exploit them. I am not going to hold a threat to the landowners of a Non-Cooperation Movement; the atmosphere at present is such that the landowner, even the smallest, should realize that he holds his land in trust.

In Russia and China where violent methods had been tried, I can not say that everything has been good. I do not say that in Russia and China the Government is in the hands of the common people. A few people who run the army and police have power. Of course there has been redistribution of land. But exploitation has not stopped. I cannot say what will be the future of China. In Russia, 35 years after revolution exploitation is still there. There is a new class, the bureaucracy, consisting of officers and those who run the party and the defence forces. This class enjoys 80 or 100 times more facilities than the ordinary worker. The leaders of this class fight among themselves and purge each other. But they hold the power. In the absence of an alternative. The world is looking this way. If the Bhoodan Movement succeeds, the world will have a new way before it.

261. No rift in the Praja Socialist Party, Ahmedabad, 30 June 1953[1]

There is no danger of rift in the leadership of Praja Socialist Party. What happened at the Betul convention was not any struggle for power among the Praja Socialist leaders. There were differences of opinion among the leaders which were subjected to oversimplification by some of the Party members and the press.

There will be differences of opinion among the leaders of any democratic party and that happened in the Praja Socialist Party. The differences should not have been seen from a superficial attitude but with deep thinking about the problem of the development of a backward economy. The real question is not of coalition with the ruling Party, but that of rapid development of a backward country with a democratic and secular governmental set-up.

[1]Address at public meeting; adapted from *The Pioneer*, 1 July 1953.

There are two ways of accomplishing the work of development, one is the way of the dictatorship of one party which secured savings for the capital formation by force and labour of the people by any 'inhuman means'; the other is the way of parliamentary democracy where one party rules and other four or five parties oppose it. The former way was adopted in the Soviet Union, while the second was the way of western democracies.

But history has not given as much time to India for the development of her backward economy as it gave to the western democracies. What they did in ten years, we shall have to do in one year. And in this condition a system in which one Party rules and others oppose should be modified according to the realities of our country.

There is no question of the merger of the parties, but of agreeing to a minimum programme of development of our country by all those parties which are democratic, patriotic and secular without any allegiance to foreign power, as is the case with Communist Party, and once the minimum programme is agreed to by the parties, all parties should work with singleness of purpose for the fulfilment of that minimum programme. If this way is adopted, the climate of the country will be changed and fresh energies would be released for the rapid development of the country.

It was unfortunate for our country that such a minimum programme was not agreed to by the democratic parties. It is not necessary that all the parties should agree to that programme, but the overwhelming majority of our people should be behind such a programme. Prime Minister Nehru does not want to bind himself to the minimum programme but wants a general agreement.

Many leaders of the Socialist Party as well as the Congress party do not think that there should be any cooperation between Congress and the Praja-Socialists. So the time is not ripe for any further talk of cooperation between Congress and the Praja Socialists. And it would not be so in near future.

I appeal to the Socialists to take to the Bhoodan Movement enthusiastically for it is an unprecedented, revolutionary movement.

262. *Satyagraha* at the Last Stage of the Bhoodan Movement, Ahmedabad, 2 July 1953[1]

I ask the Bhoodan workers to prepare themselves for 'satyagraha' in the last stage of the Bhoodan Movement. A stage will come in the Bhoodan Movement when a section of landowners will not part with their land. At that time, the Bhoodan workers shall have to organize non-cooperation

[1]Address to Gujarat Bhoodan Workers; adapted from *Tribune*, 3 July 1953.

with such landowners and the landless peasants will refuse to work for the landlords.

If the poor get so much strength that they decide not to be exploited, the whole system of exploitation will crumble down as Gandhiji asserted throughout his life. But that strength will not come till all the sections of our people participate in the Bhoodan Movement and bring non-violent pressure on those who do not cooperate with the movement for the equitable redistribution of land.

Before taking to non-cooperation or *satyagraha*, the Bhoodan Movement should be conducted on the present lines till 'extremely powerful public opinion' is created and the landless peasants feel that land is not a gift to them but is their right. For this purpose, the land should be accepted from poor peasants also and the message of Bhoodan should reach every family in every village. This mass propaganda and mass awakening of peasants cannot be accomplished by taking land merely from the few rich landlords.

It would not be proper to launch *satyagraha* till full opportunities are given to landlords to part with their land through the Bhoodan Movement. The atmosphere for the equitable land distribution can only be created if all Bhoodan workers plunge into the movement just as they did during the satyagraha movements of Mahatma Gandhi for the liberation of our country.

Vinobaji has decided that the Bhoodan Movement must solve the land problem of our country by the end of 1957 and till then no activity or work should get priority over it. What the Bhoodan Movement needs is workers to take land gifts from the donors who are ready to part with their land.

I warn those Bhoodan workers who are simply interested to fulfil the quota of their taluka or district, the Bhoodan Movement is not a movement only for land collection but for that of regeneration of our villages. The Bhoodan workers must be absolutely clear about the mission and goal of the movement, namely, the establishment of Gram Raj according to the Sarvodaya principles of Mahatma Gandhi.

The purest form of socialism is the Sarvodaya of Gandhiji. Marx and Lenin predicted that, after the establishment of Socialism, a Communist society would emerge in which there would not be any form of exploitation and, therefore, the State would wither away. Gandhiji's Sarvodaya society is the ideal Communist society which Marx had dreamt of. The present Soviet Russian society has nothing to do with the Socialist society of Marx's conception.

What is common between the community projects which rely on foreign aid and Mahatma Gandhi's concept of Sarvodaya which is based on self-reliance? Gandhiji's ideas of the regeneration of our country are diametrically opposite to the policies and actions of the present Government.

The present constitution is a 'hotch-potch' made out of the constitutions of America and many other Western countries. Our country should frame such a constitution as would enable us to use the energies of all parties for the rapid development of our backward economy.

263. Statement on the Death of Syama Prasad Mookerjee, Lucknow, 7 July 1953[1]

I regret deeply that the Prime Minister,[2] in his reply to Shri Atulya Ghosh,[3] as reported in the press this morning, has stated so categorically that there was no negligence shown by the Kashmir Government in the care of the late Dr. Syama Prasad Mookerjee. I cannot say what facts have been placed before the Prime Minister. But the facts as I know them lead to an entirely different conclusion.

I was at Calcutta only 3 days ago, when I took the opportunity of calling on Dr. Mookerjee's family to offer my condolences and my homage to the departed leader. It was on this occasion that Mr. Justice Rama Prasad Mookerjee told me the whole story, as he, a distinguished jurist, had been able to piece together. The story left no doubt in my mind that the Kashmir authorities were not only negligent but criminally negligent in looking after Syama Prasad Babu's health. I feel sure that the life of this great Indian could have been saved by better care.

It seems to me that after such a national tragedy the least that the Indian Government could do was to institute a proper and impartial enquiry into the whole affair. In the meanwhile it does not seem proper for the Prime Minister to pronounce judgement on such a controversial subject and to attempt to whitewash the guilt of those who seem to deserve severe punishment.

I have no intention to say anything about this matter. But I am afraid that the expression of the Prime Minister's opinion may lead to a grave injustice and I think it is necessary to challenge it publicly.

[1]Adapted from *Amrit Bazar Patrika*, 8 July 1953.

[2]See Appendix 49 for Nehru's letter to J.P. regarding this statement.

[3]A prominent Congress leader of West Bengal.

264. 'The Challenge to Democracy', Delhi, 22 July 1953[1]

Democracy has had a long and chequered career. Its origin perhaps was in the natural urge in man towards self-rule. That is why from primitive times

[1]Text of a talk broadcast by the All India Radio on 22 July 1953; published in Bimal Prasad, ed., *Socialism, Sarvodaya and Democracy: Selected Works of Jayaprakash Narayan*, Bombay, 1964, pp. 175-8.

man has attempted to establish different types of self-government. But there are other human urges which have interfered with this urge to self-rule and so the existence of democracy has always been precarious and its evolution slow and fitful.

While there is a natural urge in man towards freedom, he seems to desire this freedom for himself rather than for his fellow-men. There also seems to be a selfish urge in man which leads him to acquire wealth and power and position for himself. This sets in force a movement counter to democracy. Thus there is a perpetual conflict between the forces of democracy and those opposed to them. This conflict will perhaps continue till human nature becomes so refined that man comes to value the freedom of his fellowmen as much as his own.

Modern democracy grew up in Western Europe and, while its development enlarged human freedom in the countries of its birth, economic inequality, exploitation, unemployment and imperialism always dogged its forward steps. In Western Europe the problem of economic democracy yet remains to be solved. And as far as imperialism is concerned, we are yet witnessing the strange spectacle of democrats of the imperialist countries suppressing and trying to destroy the democrats of the dependencies. Thus man after 200 years of democracy in the West is faced with the challenge of capitalism and imperialism. That challenge has to be squarely met if Western democracy has to become a real democracy.

Asian society is backward economically and socially and feudalism is typical of the social order in Asia. The tasks of democracy are naturally far greater in Asia than in the West. No doubt, it is possible for us to take advantage of the lessons of Western democracy and we may start at the point which the West has reached after 200 years of democratic experimentation. But that will not make our task very much easier. We may copy the present forms of Western democracy and skip all that painful process of slow evolution, but nevertheless in substance we would remain as backward as we are.

Substance creates form, but not form substance. The challenge to democracy in Asia comes most from this backwardness. And here totalitarianism comes forward as an attractive alternative. Totalitarianism claims not only to establish economic democracy by abolishing at one stroke feudalism and capitalism, but it also promises to develop rapidly the backward economy of Asia. Nor can it be denied that the achievements of totalitarianism in these respects are not inconsiderable. Therefore, the appeal of totalitarianism is real.

If democracy is to survive in Asia, it must prove its superiority in solving the problems of economic inequality and exploitation as well as those of economic development. In our country while we have copied the form of Western democracy, we have not shown yet that Indian democracy is capable of handling these problems with speed and efficiency. The prospect of democracy in Asia becomes gloomier when it is realized that even in the West where democracy has had a long innings the problem of economic inequality and exploitation has yet to be solved. I have no doubt that the Indian people if given a choice between democracy and dictatorship would choose the former because the Indian culture has always respected the individual and his freedom.

But no people no matter how strong their faith in freedom and democracy will accept for long, particularly in these revolutionary times, the social system in which hunger and misery are the lot of the many, and wealth and happiness the fortune of the few. This will be still more difficult when the people will have before them the attractive alternative presented by Communist totalitarianism. Therefore, it is the urgent duty of all those who believe in the values of democracy to work for an immediate transformation of the present social order.

Democracy in Europe was able to keep in check the forces of social revolution because industrial growth and imperialism enabled it to raise the standard of living of the common people. Democracy in Asia has no such opportunity and therefore it cannot afford to imitate the ways of West in this matter. Economic development and raising the standard of living would be a slow process in Asia. In the meanwhile, the forces making towards equality in the abolition of exploitation cannot be denied their full impression.

Therefore in Asia the priorities will have to be reversed as compared with Europe. There economic development and prosperity took place first and then after 150 years the process towards economic equality was set in motion. In Asia, it is the latter process which must come first; otherwise democracy would never be able to stand up to the forces of totalitarianism.

As far as I have been able to understand, those who are in power in this country today are trying to do just the opposite and want to imitate the European development. All the emphasis today is on production. The question of distribution receives only a passing reference. I see in this the germs of the destruction of democracy. This, as I see it, is the challenge in our country. Unless this challenge is squarely met, it is certain that democracy would perish.

Let me add that if this challenge is to be met, and the foundations of economic democracy are to be laid here and now, the present shape of our political democracy will have to be transformed. There is no pattern in the world today of economic democracy which we would be able to copy. From the village upwards to New Delhi, and from bullock-farming to the major industries, forms of self-government will have to be evolved which will form essential parts of our democracy.

Economic democracy cannot be a function of the services, even that of a specially created economic civil service. The producers, agricultural and industrial, manual and intellectual, must play the main part in this democracy.

This is not the occasion to dilate further on this topic. I have drawn attention to it now merely to indicate the scope of the answer that needs be given to the challenge of democracy.

In concluding I do fervently hope that those who serve the nation will have the courage to face honestly this challenge of the age.

265. Three Stages of the Bhoodan Movement, Bombay, 4 August 1953[1]

The success of the Bhoodan Movement would establish the efficacy of the technique of love and persuasion in solving national and even racial conflicts.

That technique can be applied with benefit to the industrial and commercial sectors and perhaps, would also show a way for resolving conflicts that result in wars.

History has given us a chance to show to the world peaceful methods of solving problems and if we fail, I do not know whether we will be able to solve them.

I emphasize the superiority of peaceful over violent methods for the solution of issues. The Bhoodan workers have collected so far 19,00,000 acres of land since the movement was started in 1951 as against 30,000 acres claimed by the communists—but only 7,000 according to Hyderabad Government—in Telangana in their two-and-half years' efforts and that was, despite the atrocities, of the communists and the international prestige Communism has attained due to the success of the Chinese revolution.

Acharya Vinoba Bhave has been able to do more in less time by mere persuasion and without murdering anybody and, on the contrary, uplifting both the giver and the taker. He has created a climate which militates against injustice and inequality. The value of land is about 19 crores of rupees, but the actual gains would be very difficult to evaluate.

This is just the beginning. We have a long way to go, and I have every hope that India will show the world the path of non-violent, social and economic revolution just as it showed the way of non-violent political revolution.

I think three possible situations may arise as the Bhoodan Movement progresses:

[1]Speech at a meeting of Democratic Research Service, Bombay, 4 August 1953. Adapted from *National Herald*, 6 August 1953.

1. That the movement may be able to achieve its target of five crore acres of land.
2. That there may be state legislation for the redistribution of land. There are already attempts being made in some states in that direction. The Government may be persuaded to move as and when the movement grows in stature.
3. In case of failure of the movement and legislation to achieve the objective, the third possibility is to launch a non-violent, Non-Cooperation Movement.

266. To Jawaharlal Nehru, 8 August 1953[1]

Dear Bhai,

I am writing again about Burnpur. I am sorry to learn that even though the workers have made a gesture and production is going up, no serious attempt has been made to find a principled or more permanent solution of the problem there. As I wrote to you earlier, the whole issue at Burnpur is one of domestic adjustments within the Congress party. Basically there is no dispute between labour and management or between labour and Government. The dispute is between two groups of INTUC (i.e. Congress) workers. Mr. John is the President of the Union but there is no doubt that the vast majority of the workers is opposed to him. If the INTUC is working according to any principle of democratic trade unionism, Mr. John should not have any objection to a fair election. I have no doubt that, if a fair election were held and the workers were given full freedom to choose the office-bearers of their Union, industrial peace and goodwill would be established at the place.

It is sad to notice that both the country and the industry should be put to such heavy losses only because of a domestic dispute within the INTUC or the ruling party. That is why I wrote to you that you should act in this matter not so much as Prime Minister but as President of the Congress. Let me add that I do not think that Khandubhai or other leaders of the INTUC, or the Congressmen concerned, could give you disinterested advice.

I am eclosing copy of the telegram I received yesterday from Shri Chhotelal Vyas, President of the Action Committee at Burnpur as well as of the Jamshedpur Congress Committee.

Affectionately yours,
Jayaprakash

[1]*Nehru Papers*: Files at Home (NMML).
[2]See Appendix 50 for Nehru's reply.

267. Need for More Power to the Local Bodies, Poona, 12 August 1953[1]

If democracy is to succeed in India, decentralization of power both at the Centre and the states and giving of more power to Gram Panchayats, municipalities and other local bodies, is absolutely essential. If the present pattern of government continues, the people would lose faith in democracy as they have very little power to control the Government.

According to the present Constitution once in every five years the people are called upon to elect representatives that a party chooses and thereafter are forced to go back to their shells.

Sometimes a situation arises that the representatives are not acceptable to the people, but the people have no alternative but to vote for the same men. This makes the people feel that they are not truly represented in the legislature. I, therefore, suggest that selection of representatives to the legislatures should be done by the people and not by political parties. There is a great difference between a Government controlled by a party and a Government by the people.

If such a procedure, however, is not possible at the present moment, the political parties should not participate at least in the elections to Gram Panchayats, Municipalities and other local bodies. The representatives at such elections should be elected by the people as the ultimate aim of every representative is to serve the cause of the people and the city concerned.

In foreign countries and particularly in Europe the Mayor of a city has absolute powers in as much as he has the responsibility of maintaining law and order. I regret that the framers of the Indian Constitution should not have thought it fit to give more powers to local bodies.

I also suggest that the election of a Mayor should be done by the people of a city concerned instead of by the representatives of a party who may find themselves in a majority, in order to make democracy more effective. I call it direct democracy.

I am in favour of the holding of an All-India Municipal Conference where many important issues arising between municipal bodies and the Government can be discussed.

[1]Speech at a civic reception by the Municipal Corporation of Poona; adpated from *Tribune*, 14 August 1953.

268. The Dynamics of the Bhoodan Movement, Madras, 15 August 1953[1]

Gandhiji had brought about a political revolution through non-violent means. To many who had the privilege of watching Gandhiji's experiment at close quarters it was generally expected that a similar technique could be used for a social and economic revolution. Vinoba Bhave is to-day showing us how that can be made possible. One characteristic of a revolution is that a change takes place in the first instance and then those who come to power bring forward legislation which puts the seal of legal approval of the State on those changes brought about by mass initiative. Vinoba Bhave is trying to bring about an equitable distribution of land among the landless workers through the initiative of the people.

There is no reason to believe that India would not be able to have a successful non-violent economic and social revolution. Redistribution of land, is only the first step in this non-violent revolution, the question of land being the most important thing which affects a large section of the people of the country. This question has been taken up first in the hope that if this problem is solved, the other problems will be easy of solution. A climate would have been created, a psychological revolution would have taken place which would make it possible for other economic and social problems being tackled in the same manner if the problem which affects five hundred thousand villages of this country is solved. Therefore, it is not a question merely of getting a few hundred acres of land, but one of starting on a new path which would end in Sarvodaya, the creation of a new civilization and a new society in which there is no exploitation.

The communist activities in Telangana, aimed at violent economic change, had achieved nothing. Such attempts are bound to fail. If there was an attempt to establish by violence social and economic justice that attempt would be met by the superior violence of the State.

I am sure, situated as the people are in this country, no violent attempt on their part is likely to succeed. And if it succeeds, it will not be the masses who will come into their own, but it will be those who by the end of the revolution have come to possess the most effective means of coercion. A society free from oppression and exploitation and based on love and co-operation can not be established without faith in the essential goodness of man. Vinoba Bhave started the Bhoodan Movement with faith in the essential goodness of man and, therefore, in this sense, the Bhoodan Movement symbolises not merely an economic and social revolution, but also a moral revolution. The communists are idealistic people and they aim at the equitable distribution of land. But they are using means which are bound to

[1]Speech at a public meeting in Madras; adapted from *Hindu*, 18 August 1953.

defeat the end. They can not establish justice and create a new society based on justice by any methods which temporarily reduce the human being to the level of a brute.

I am myself one of those who had doubts about the Bhoodan Movement. I felt at one time that it would take five hundred years to solve the problem of redistribution of land by that method. But I was converted by what Vinoba Bhave has achieved. Vinoba Bhave, through his Non-Violent Movement, has now nineteen lakh acres of land given as gifts and has also created a humanizing climate.

We should organize this movement efficiently, approach landlords and ask for gifts. We have collected a little over nineteen thousand acres in Tamil Nadu. Our target for the whole of India is five crores of acres and for Tamil Nadu one and-a-half lakhs of acres. This is one-sixth of the total acreage of cultivable lands in the country and in Tamil Nadu respectively. I hope that we would be able to reach the target by 1957. To those who are pessimistic, I would like to say that if the Bhoodan Movement happens to fail, there is the next step which Gandhiji has taught us. We would apply the same technique which Gandhiji applied in the national struggle for freedom. The next step would be non-cooperation. What Vinoba Bhave is doing to-day is merely an application of Gandhiji's theory of trusteeship to the land problem. A psychological revolution has now taken place. It is double-edged in the sense that those who have lands are being persuaded to believe that the land does not belong to them but belongs to the community or society and should be used for the social good. It is a means of livelihood and not a commodity for buying and selling. A landlord should have for himself an extent of land which is necessary for his family. On the other hand, the landless are told that they are not getting the lands as gifts or charity. It is denied to them by society and that is a social injustice which is now sought to be removed. The non-violent technique is being applied to-day to the land problem. Tomorrow it might be applied to industries and commerce. Because the land problem is the biggest, it has been taken first. If that problem is solved, the other problems would be easy of solution.

269. Statement Supporting the Pardi Satyagraha, Madras, 31 August 1953[1]

I endorse fully Asoka Mehta's decision to offer *satyagraha* in the Pardi Taluka of Surat district. It is not widely known what has been happening in the last five years in this area. Thousands of acres of land on which food

[1]*Brahmanand Papers* (NMML).

crops were once raised have been allowed by the landowners to lapse either into wastelands or grass lands. More than 60 per cent lands in the taluka belong to the Scheduled Tribes, who have been living in conditions of great poverty. Substantial parts of the land in the taluka are owned by a handful of big landowners who have not hesitated to eject tenants, bypass tenancy legislation and divert land for cultivation of grass, which probably yields them higher profit but results in depriving the kisan of land and opportunities to work and earn his livelihood. During this period several attempts were made by the Praja Socialist Party and the Kisan Panchayat to settle the matter amicably. All such efforts having failed, the decision to offer satyagraha was taken.

The Gujarat Bhoodan Samiti has been persuading landowners concerned to donate their lands for the landless people. But so far it has not achieved much success. The satyagraha to be started by the Praja Socialist Party and the Kisan Panchayat under Asoka Mehta's leadership does not in any manner conflict or run counter to the aims and methods of the Bhoodan Movement.

270. To Rajkumari Amrit Kaur, 31 August 1953[1]

My dear Rajkumari,[2]

You may remember that when I had met you last you had promised to call Dr. Dinshah Mehta[3] to Delhi after your return from Europe. It is quite some time now that you came back but, as far as I know, you have not yet written to Dinshah. If you have not changed your mind about the matter, and if you really are interested in doing something for naturopathy, I would request you to call Dinshah as soon as possible for a serious talk. You need not call him just because I am pressing you to do so. I am sure Dinshah also would endorse my view.

I hope you are well. With regards from me and Prabhavati,

Yours sincerely,
J.P.

[1] *J.P. Papers* (NMML).

[2] Then Minister of Health, Government of India.

[3] Dinshah Mehta; an expert naturopath of Pune who had treated J.P. in his Nature Cure Clinic.

271. To Jawaharlal Nehru, 6 September 1953[1]

My Dear Bhai,

I saw your letter of Septemper[2] when I returned to Patna on the 4th morning. I have no desire to carry on any argument with you. It is clear that we look at the recent Bihar incidents from different points of view. However, I do admit freely that I may have been in the wrong.

I wish only to make two points clear.

(a) Brahman casteism is not so prominent or effective in Bihar politics. It is Bhumihar Casteism that is as active, if not more, than Kayasth or Rajput Casteism. All throughout the recent disturbances many people including those in high places, were not so much concerned with what was right or wrong, true or untrue, as with the fortunes of the "Bhumihar raj".

(b) Lest it should be thought that I did nothing but denounce the Police, may I point out that I too did my bit to restore peace and order and that wherever praise was due I freely gave it. At Gaya I, with Prabhavati, visited the house of the Deputy Superintendent of Police (a Bengali gentleman), who inspite of serious injuries had kept his head cool, and met him and his family. And at a largely attended public meeting in the same town—Gaya—I commonded that officer's behaviour as well as the good sense and energy of the District Magistrate, Mr. Abraham. It may have been a pure accident, but it was noticed by many persons that red-turbaned Policemen re-appeared on the streets the next morning. At other places too, such as Patna and Nawadah, I kept in close touch with the officer-in-charge. I was and am all praise for the then Commissioner, Patna Division, but I am afraid I Cann't say very much for the other officers.

With regards,

Yours affectionately,
Jayaprakash

[1]Brahmanand Papers (NMML).

272. Pardi Satyagraha, in relation to the Bhoodan Movement, Patna, 8 September 1953[1]

The Pardi Satyagraha recently launched in the district of Surat under Shri Asoka Mehta's leadership has raised a number of questions. I have been particularly asked to clarify the position insofar as it relates to the Bhoodan Movement.

[1]*J.P. Papers* (NMML).

The Praja Socialist Party, it is true, has expressed its full support to Acharya Vinobaji's unique movement. But that should not be taken to mean that the Party has put into cold storage all its other activities. In this particular instance, the Party felt, and quite rightly, that it must take up the cause of the tenants and agricultural labourers, both of whom were suffering at the hands of the landlords. It should be noted that the majority of the tenants and labourers is made up of *adivasis* whose exploitation and poverty are well known.

For the past some years, the landlords of the area have been engaged in a two-fold process. They have, on the one hand, been wrongfully evicting their tenants and, on the other, converting their lands which were under food crops into grasslands, thus throwing out of employment thousands of agricultural labourers. Cultivation of grass, though it fetches the landlords a good income, requires very little labour.

Before the launching of the *satyagraha*, as far as I know, every attempt was made to settle the matter by negotiation. The Bombay Government was also approached. But, while the Government showed sympathy for the people, it was perhaps powerless to help immediately. On the other hand, the people had waited long patiently and the situation, instead of improving, had deteriorated steadily. They could not wait indefinitely and see their lands and their livelihood taken away. They had to seek some immediate way of relief. A final request was made to the Bombay Government to appoint an enquiry commission. When even that was refused, *satyagraha* was the only alternative left to the people. The Chief Minister of Bombay has been pleased to call it *duragraha*. Giving the dog a bad name and hanging it is an old game. But by abusing others the Bombay Government cannot hope to solve a serious problem.

Be that as it may, whether *satyagraha* or *duragraha*, the important thing is that the tenants and labourers of Pardi taluka are fighting in a peaceful manner for a cause that is just.

Is it consistent with Bhoodan, it has been asked. For my part, I cannot see any inconsistency in it. Vinobaji has always made it clear that no tenant should allow himself to be evicted from land that is justly his. No doubt his resistance should be peaceful and moral, but he should never submit to injustice. The difficulty is that under the present social set-up no solitary tenant can resist a landlord no matter how just his case might be. Furthermore, what is conceded as right for an individual cannot be wrong for a combination of individuals. Nor does the right become wrong when a political party comes forward to help. Of course, there is always the question of political exploitation of the common people. I am wholly opposed to such exploitation but unfortunately when partisanship guides our judgement, even the sincerest effort of a party to help the suffering people may be run down as political exploitation.

The question is further asked whether Bhoodan itself will not solve the problem of evictions and landlessness. I am sure that it will. But it will take time to convert all the landlords. Many have already been converted. Others are sure to follow. But when a tenant is ejected or a labourer's livelihood is taken away in the immediate present, it can be small consolation for him to be told that in the course of a few years his rights will be restored to him and that till then he must patiently see his children starve. Obviously, an immediate remedy must be found. Bhoodan might in some cases bring immediate relief to the victims by persuading the landlords concerned to rectify their wrong; but in other cases Bhoodan might fail to do this. In the present case the Bhoodan Movement has had no chance on little convert the landlords of Pardi taluka. It will no doubt eventually succeed in doing so. But in the meanwhile, what are the suffering people to do? Hope for the future will not fill bellies. The sufferers in the present case waited patiently for years, tried to negotiate with the landlords, petitioned the Government. But when nothing availed, they were compelled, for sheer self-preservation, to launch their *satyagraha*. No fair-minded person can condemn their action.

I hope the Pardi *satyagrahis* will not deviate from truth and non-violence, whatever the provocation from the landlords, the police and mischief-makers.

273. Statement on Flood Situation in Bihar, Delhi, 10 September 1953[1]

Bihar has been unfortunate in having a series of drought and floods for the past some years. But this year's floods have been unprecedented even for Bihar. There is a danger of the devastation being minimized, because Bihar's name has come to be associated in the minds of the public with floods and other natural calamities. But it would be a costly mistake to treat this year's floods in Bihar as the usual annual event. Two factors, namely, excessive and continuous rain in the plains of North Bihar and simultaneous and record rising of all the rivers combined to keep submerged for weeks whole districts and the entire Tirhut division. The *bhadai* crop has been entirely destroyed and the winter paddy crop very nearly so. The extent of the damage has been calculated by the Bihar Government to be over 21 crores of rupees. This was an early calculation before full reports of the devastation were available, and the Bihar Government has pointed out in its report that the final estimate of the damage is feared to be much higher. The reports that I have received myself enable me unhesitatingly to support the Bihar

[1]*J.P. Papers* (NMML).

Government's assessment of the damage. The total loss may well be above [Rs.] 30 crores.

It would be impossible for the Bihar Government to deal with a catastrophe of this dimension. The Central Government must come generously to the rescue of the unfortunate people of Bihar. Millions of lives are involved. Nor is the suffering of the people going to be short-lived. Because, destruction of the crops means that for months to come there will be no food and little employment. Hundreds of thousands will have to be provided with new shelters. There will be disease afflicting men and beasts. The loss of purchasing power will create an enormous vacuum and will make the task of rehabilitation of the shattered economy costly and urgent. Economic rehabilitation, and not merely relief, should be the Government's goal. I shall go further and insist the human suffering and material loss of the present dimensions should jolt us all out of our ruts and forces us to look beyond the immediate task. Relief, even rehabilitation, would be only a stop-gap. This catastrophe should persuade the Central and State Governments to take up immediately and seriously the whole problem of flood control, so that these disasters are stopped from occurring. I am sure the total cost of this preventive measure would be less than the total cost of recurring relief expenditure. The saving in the cost of human suffering would, of course, be incalculable.

It seems fair to me that a part of the burden of these calamites, which are not confined to Bihar alone—Andhra being an equal sufferer this year—should be borne by the international organization when nations are not ready to share in human distress and sorrow? The world will not become one by merely talking endlessly of peace and war. This is an occasion when the moral resources of international organization are put to the test.

274. To M.N. Roy, 12 September 1953[1]

Dear Mr. Roy,

I have been wanting for a long time to come up to Dehra Dun to discuss with you the question of non-party politics. You have done more thinking on this subject than anyone else in this country.

I hope to be able to reach Dehra Dun for this purpose on the 15th morning. I will have to leave the same evening for Delhi, but there will be a whole day in which I could have as much of your time as you might be good enough to give me.

[1]*J.P. Papers* (NMML).

I do not like the news of my visit to get abroad in the town or people will give me no peace. I shall be staying with my nephew B.K. Sinha at the Doon School. If there is any change in this programme I shall inform you telegraphically.

I hope you are well. With regards,

Yours sincerely,
J.P.

275. To Bhimsen Sachar, 23 September 1953[1]

Dear Mr. Sachar,[2]

I am writing to you in connection with the tenants of the Nawab of Mamdot. I am sure you are acquainted with their case. In fact you had pleaded their case in a letter dated 28-12-1949 which you wrote to Dr. Gopichand Bhargava, who was then Chief Minister. I am enclosing a copy of your letter. It appears Dr. Bhargava's Government did not take any steps in the matter.

When I was up in the Punjab in connection with Bhoodan work recently the representatives of the tenants had come to see me. I gathered from them that the tenants were on the point of being evicted from lands which one of them have been tilling for 80 years. I am sure this injustice can be prevented. I shall feel obliged if you will personally look into this matter and do what is needful.

I hope you are well. With regards,

Yours sincerely,
J.P.

[1]*J.P. Papers* (NMML).
[2]Then Chief Minister, East Punjab.

276. Press Statement regarding Flood Situation in Darbhanga and Muzaffarpur, Muzaffarpur, 23 September 1953[1]

It is not necessary any longer to emphasize the immensity of the present floods nor the colossal damage caused by them. The Commissioner of the Tirhut Division only the other day placed the latest data before the public.

In a recent statement I had drawn the attention of the Central and State Governments to the necessity of taking immediate steps to give permanent, instead of annual, relief to the people of Bihar from this scourge of recurring floods. I understand that, among other things, the lack of detailed knowledge

[1]*J.P. Papers* (NMML).

about the behaviour of the waterways of North Bihar over any length of time stands in the way of undertaking any comprehensive scheme of flood control and irrigation. I should have thought therefore that the present floods have given the Government a fine opportunity to study the phenomenon of floods in this part of the country and to collect detailed data. I think it is not too late even now for such a study, and I suggest both to the Central and state Governments to send immediately a body of experts for the necessary study. I suggest further that in this task the experts should not treat the opinions of the village people with contempt. During my tour I was impressed greatly by the judgement of the village folk.

This leads me to another observation which I was able to make during my tour. I found that in some areas at least, the flood was not nature-made but man-made. In the Satmal area, for instance, Warisnagar thana, quite a number of villages were inundated because the Katalia-Kochil drain was dug in a thoughtless manner and the advice and protestations of the villagers were disregarded. In certain other areas also I found a similar situation in which large numbers of people suffered because of the planless manner in which bunds and channels etc. had been constructed.

It is the unanimous opinion of people whom I met that the commissioner of Tirhut Division, who unfortunately has just gone on leave, had shown commendable initiative and drive in dealing with the problems created by these unprecedented floods. I also heard praise for local officials, though in some cases, I am sorry to say, I also heard serious complaints. But the resources that have been placed at the disposal of the local officials for rendering relief and aid to the stricken people are far short of the needs. The section of the people that is worst affected is the landless labour class. During this entire flood period rations have not been supplied, either free or on work-basis, more than thrice: in some villages not more than twice, in some only once. I found the people prepared to work but there was not sufficient work for them.

In the matter of distribution of *takkavi* and agricultural loans the position is even less satisfactory. Government should instruct its officials to cut out all red tape and make the distribution of loans as simple and expeditious as possible. If loans are not given in time, not only the rural middle class, which is not less numerous and hard-hit than the labourers, will suffer greatly, but also the cultivation of the *rabi* crop will suffer, adding to the misery of the whole population.

I also heard complaints of favouritism in the granting of loans. I was told that people of influence, who were not in need, were granted loans which they reloaned to the needy people, while the latter were not able to get any help from the Government. This is a serious matter which the authorities should do their best to stop immediately.

I did not hear of the outbreak of any epidemics yet, but I also found that there was no adequate preparedness to meet any such outbreaks. As the flood waters recede it is feared that malaria and cholera and dysentery would break out. If adequate steps are not taken to check them, it will be too late to do anything once the epidemic starts.

In the areas I visited the sugarcane crop had been badly damaged. This being an important money crop, the cultivators are going to be severely hit. I therefore think it would be fair to revise the price of sugar cane.

I also heard complaints of partisanship in the administration of relief. I did not find these complaints in areas where flood committees of a composite character had been formed representing the main political parties. No one should be allowed to utilize natural calamities and the miseries of the people for partisan ends. This can be prevented only if composite committees are formed to assist the authorities in administering relief.

Finally, I wish to place before the people of North Bihar an humble suggestion. Man, in order to survive, must learn from his adversities. So, the people of North Bihar should draw a lesson from the present calamity. Every year this calamity, on a big or a small scale, affects us. Should we continue to suffer in the present helpless manner? Should we wait endlessly for the Government to save us from this scourge? If the people have to survive, they must answer 'no'. It is time that the people acted themselves. There is no power greater than the power of the people. It is this power that has to be created to deal with this great natural calamity. In the First Five-Year Plan there is no scheme to save North Bihar from floods or to convert its rivers from the scourge that they are to a blessing, which they can surely become. There is need for a coordinated plan of river training and irrigation works, drainage and bunding. I suggest that instead of waiting for the Government to act, the people of North Bihar should themselves decide to draw up a people's plan for this gigantic undertaking. I suggest as a first stage of this popular planning that every village should draw up a plan for protecting itself from floods and for the utilization of nearby waterways for irrigation. This village-level planning should create the necessary mass enthusiasm and sense of responsibility. The planning of the people would mean their preparedness to contribute in cash and labour towards the fulfilment of the plan. After this preliminary stage of popular planning, higher stages, involving expert knowledge, would follow.

I am sure that if such popular movements are built up throughout North Bihar and if every village is roused and the necessary interest and enthusiasm created, the Central Government could soon be persuaded to come forward to participate in the implementation of the plan.

This movement for a people's plan would naturally be a non-party movement. I invite all the parties, including the Congress, and the people generally to consider my humble suggestion.

277. To Jawaharlal Nehru, 10 October 1953[1]

Dear Bhai,

I see that the unsolicited advice that I had ventured to offer has had unceremonious reception. I read your statement regarding Mr. Prakasam.[2] It made me sad to find you arguing in such a partisan manner. You are apparently functioning on the basis that the Congress party alone can save this country and build it up. I cannot believe that you are not aware of the depths to which the Congress party has fallen. Your efforts to raise it up have not so far been a conspicuous success. If not as a Congressman, at least as an Indian patriot and statesman, you should see that an alternative to the Congress must slowly be created. Unless you think that the Communist Party is an alternative, you should not go out of your way to injure the development of the PSP. The stronger this party grows the better would be the chances of the Congress itself being improved. However, you are the captain of the ship and it is for you to set your course.

I might appear to be motivated in making these submissions by party considerations, but let me assure you nothing is farther from my mind today than partisan interests. If the party system is retained, I am sure that the development of Indian politics must be somewhat on the lines I have indicated above and that you must take a hand in this development in spite of your close association with the Congress party.

I am enclosing a cutting from a local newspaper.[3] I cannot describe to

[1]*Jawaharlal Nehru Papers* (NMML).

[2] This obviously refers to Nehru's speech at a meeting of Congress workers of the newly-born state of Andhra Pradesh at Kurnool on 1 October 1953. Here he had revealed that he had asked T. Prakasam, an old leader of the Congress who had recently joined the Praja Socialist Party and won a seat in Assembly on that Party's ticket, to become the Chief Minister of Andhra Pradesh; and at the same time advised him to join the Congress. Nehru's reasoning was that Prakasam 'would have to function as the Chief Minister through an organized party or a group and the only organized group that could support his government' was the Congress. See *Selected Works of Jawaharlal Nehru*, Vol. 24, New Series, ed. S. Gopal, New Delhi, 1999, p. 270.

[3] The press-cutting enclosed by J.P. reported the refusal of the PSP leaders, who had been arrested for their role in the Pardi Satyagraha to give their finger-prints to the prison-authorities, J.P. felt distressed by the fact that political prisoners in free India were subjected to such treatment—something never done to them under the British regime. On the receipt of J.P.'s letter, Nehru wrote to Morarji Desai, then Chief Minister of Bombay, drawing his attention to J.P.'s letter and asking him to do the needful. This led the Congress Government in Bombay to immediately drop the move to obtain finger-prints from the PSP leaders and workers.

you the feeling of anger and distress that this news has aroused in my heart. If all values have not changed just because British rule has been substituted by Congress rule, you too should share my feelings. If I am not mistaken in this assumption I hope you will do the needful in the matter. There are limits beyond which even Shri Morarji Desai cannot go.

With regards,

Yours affectionately,
Jayaprakash

P.S. You need not trouble to answer this letter.

278. Statement on Flood Affected Areas of North Bihar, Patna, 14 October 1953[1]

Some days ago I had placed the impressions of my tour of the Darbhanga and Muzaffarpur districts before the public as also certain suggestions. After that I had occasion again to visit the Katra and Paru thanas of Muzaffarpur and the greater part of Saran district. This subsequent tour confirmed my previous impressions. The two most affected classes are the landless labourers and the urban middle class. The measures taken so far for rendering relief have fallen far short of the needs. I heard of at least two villages in the Siswan and Raghunathpur thanas of Saran where no relief whatever had yet been distributed. There were some villages where rations were distributed only once during the whole period of the floods and in no village rations were given more than twice. The misery of the people of Saran particularly can be realized when it is remembered that that unfortunate district had four recurring inundations. Villages after villages in that district had been surrounded by water not for weeks but months. Consequently, damage to dwellings has been the severest in the Saran district.

The Government and the officials should not be miserly with gratuitous relief because the people have no alternative to starvation unless they are supplied rations. Wherever it is possible to give work to the people, relief should of course be given through work. But I am afraid these are areas where it will not be possible to provide any work for some time yet. There gratuitous relief should on no account be stopped.

As for the middle class, they would not be able to restart their life unless adequate loans were made available as expeditiously as possible. Both the adequacy of the loan and the time factor need to be emphasized. So far, the loans granted in the areas I visited were far too inadequate. In this connection

[1]*J.P. Papers* (NMML). Printed in summary form in several daily papers on 15 and 16 October 1953.

I also suggest that realization of all dues and taxes should be suspended for the present and there should be remission in rents.

I had appealed in my previous statement for a revision of cane prices, particularly for the growers in the flood-affected areas. While reiterating that appeal I should like further to appeal to the sugar mills in these areas to advance immediate loans to the cane-growers in addition to their seasonal *dadani* payments. This will help the cultivators considerably to tide over their present difficulties.

Not only man but also beast is faced with extreme necessity. I found that not enough attention had been paid to the problem of fodder. The cattle wealth of the province has already been greatly impoverished, and, if adequate provision is not made for cattle feed this year, the loss in death and debilitation would indeed be grievous and difficult to make up later.

There is a feature of the present situation that cannot but cause anxiety. At the time of such natural calamities on previous occasions there were always generous people in the community who came forward to help their less fortunate brethren. But in the present case the springs of charity and fellow-feeling seem to have dried up and everyone feels that it is the job only of the Government to come to the rescue of the suffering people. I am sure there are people in the villages as well as in such towns as Chapra, Muzaffarpur, etc., however small their number, who are in a position to give at least some relief to their fellow-men. But so far there has been little response from them.

Not only the well-to-do of the affected areas are apathetic and inclined to leave everything to the Government but so also are the people elsewhere in the country, including the charitable bodies. Even such bodies as the Marwari Relief Society and the Ramakrishna Mission have not considered the present calamity severe enough to deserve their sympathy. Perhaps the absence of appeals from the leaders of Bihar has also helped in creating the feeling that the situation is not so grave. And lack of adequate publicity has also contributed to the same feeling. Even a regular reader of the Bihar press would not get the impression that there was such colossal human suffering all around. The press here seems to have no initiative of its own and is not interested in finding out facts for itself. It is merely content to publish official statements and the statements of public men. If the newspapers pooled their resources, they could sent out quite and number of high-level reporters whose stories could be pieced together and published widely.

As the flood waters recede and dry up malaria and other diseases are bound to spread. While the Government has made arrangements to deal with the situation it is necessary that aid should come from other sources also. Medicines, and doctors are scarce and costly everywhere in the rural areas. I appeal therefore to the charitable institutions, such as the Marwari Relief Society, the Ramakrishna Mission, etc., for the supply of medicines, and doctors. I appeal also to the doctors all over the country, particularly the young medical graduates, to volunteer their services.

Winter will soon be upon us and there are hundreds of thousands of poor families who have no clothes or blankets. Their houses also have either fallen or made uninhabitable. In such a situation, unless clothes, particularly warm clothes and blankets, are distributed on a large scale, the suffering will be great and deaths from pneumonia and the like will be many. Therefore, I appeal also for these to my generous countrymen and to the charitable bodies particularly.

Regarding the distribution of relief, I suggest that wherever there are no properly constituted gram panchayats, non-official elected panchayats should be set up and the officers and relief workers should be guided in distributing relief by their advice.

While dealing with the present distress is of immediate importance, the problem of preventing the recurrence of such distress is far more important. This problem is of a two-fold nature: one of flood control and the other of irrigation. The calamity in the shape of floods can be converted into a blessing in the form of irrigation. Flood control and irrigation are interconnected and inter-dependent.

I had pointed out in my previous statement that the recent floods had offered a fine opportunity for a comprehensive topographical study of the entire North Bihar so that a coordinated and integrated plan of drainage, storage, channelling and bunding could be prepared. Accordingly, I had suggested that a team of high-level engineers should be sent to make such a study. I think it is not even now too late to do so. I find that people are talking in terms of Kosi and Gandak dams. These are all useful proposals but unless the whole area is properly mapped out and an integrated and interconnected system of irrigation and flood control is worked out I do not think we would be able to cope with the problem.

I had found during my tour that railway embankments and roads also played a considerable part in aggravating the flood situation. When these roads and railways were built no regard was paid to the problem of floods and drainage. In any comprehensive scheme these also must be integrated. I found further that some of the minor irrigation works were also responsible for aggravating the situation. Minor irrigation works are of course essential and all emphasis should be placed upon them, but they must be taken up as a part of an integrated scheme and must be properly planned. Hitherto, political influence and patronage have largely guided their development.

Finally, I once again suggest to the State and Central Governments to set up immediately a high-level engineering body to make a comprehensive topographical study with a view both to flood control and irrigation. The body should be charged to submit its report within a specified period of time. Construction could them start with popular cooperation in accordance with the general plan. I am not suggesting that the whole plan should be implemented at once, for that would be impossible. But the parts can be taken up in view of the whole, so that maladjustments do not arise and cause more harm than good.

279. To Sachin Dutta, 31 October 1953[1]

My dear Sachin Babu,[2]

I came here for a day to visit some of the flood affected areas. I was to come earlier but due to other engagements could not do so. Today I visited Di Ilahi, Shobhan, Khirma Pathra and Pacharhi. At all these places people from the surrounding villages had also gathered.

All these areas have some problems in common and some that are peculiar to each. The common problem is that of flood control through minor schemes of either bunding or channelling or works of similar nature. The problem of the landless people is also common to all.

At Di Ilahi there was a peculiar problem in that two young men of the village had been arrested in connection with a demonstration. As it is too late in the night and I feel tired I shall not go into the details of all these matters in this letter. My friends Shri Karpoori Thakur and Shri Brahmadev Thakur, who will see you with this letter, will give you all the facts.

I hope that you will be kind enough to give your personal attention to these matters and do all that is possible to relieve the suffering of these people. My friends may also tell you about the people's plan, of which I spoke to the villagers. If there is adequate response from them, special efforts should be made to do something for flood control in their areas.

If I had time I would have been very happy to meet you personally. I do not think we have met since you joined the administrative service.

I hope you are well.

Yours sincerely,
J.P.

[1]*J.P. Papers* (NMML).

[2]Sachin Dutta, a member of the Indian Administrative Service, was at the time District Magistrate of Darbhanga in Bihar.

280. Bhoodan, the First Step towards a Total Revolution, Mokamah, 14 November 1953[1]

Bhoodan is not a programme of merely collecting and distributing land. It is rather the first step towards a total revolution, social, political and economic. It stands for a society which would strive for the good of all and in which everybody would be happy. In such a society there would be no distinction of high and low. Justice and equality would form its distinguishing features and exploitation in any form would be completely eliminated. Power and authority would vest with the people in the true sense, and they would regulate and administer their own affairs. Central authority would be sought to be extinguished and, if it continued to exist, the sphere and extent of its operation would be minimized. The village will have all the authority and jurisdiction required. There will be perfect democracy based upon individual freedom and the individual will be the architect of his own government. This arrangement will be extended upwards to district and provincial tiers of administration with progressively diminishing authority. The central authority, so long as it exists, would be like a danger chain in a railway train. Passengers do not always have their attention fixed on this chain but would seek its help and support when required. In sum, there would be complete decentralization in the field of administration.

The question is how will such a society be established? This can be done through an economic reconstruction which will ensure the fruit of labour to the workers, which is possible only when there is decentralization in the economic field, when the system of production is organized on the basis of village industries and the large-scale industries that will have to be essentially retained, will be socially owned and managed by workers.

Bhoodan is closely connected with Sarvodaya. Today our society abounds with personas who are mad after their own interest. In Sarvodaya, however, one has to be solicitous of others' interest. Man's nature will have to be changed. Values of life will have to be re-valued. For if the individual does not change, even if exploitation is put out once it will appear again. This is a high ideal no doubt, but it is capable of being attained. And we have to make a beginning somewhere. Bhoodan to my mind is the process whereby we can reach this goal. The land problem is a problem that affects crores of our people and therefore, the Bhoodan Movement can make a direct appeal to the masses.

Through Bhoodan, Vinobaji wants to inculcate the idea of equality in our people. He wants to impress on them that all wealth belongs to society and not to individuals. It is easiest to do it by Bhoodan. When you state the

[1]Speech at the Bhoodan Workers Training Camp, Mokamah (Patna), *Vigil*, 21 November 1953.

same principle with reference to the industries or plants and factories, the owners are likely to think and argue that they have produced these things by their own diligence, industry and ingenuity. But one may not argue like that in respect of land, for man has not made it. Land is the gift of God. An old adage says that all land belongs to Gopal. So in the divine dispensation land rightly belongs to him who works on it. This is also in keeping with our ancient cultural traditions. In ancient times land belonged to the village community and the village panchayat distributed the same to the village people every 20 or 25 years, in accordance with the number of members in a family. This was dictated by the principle that nobody should have more land than he required. This applies equally to other forms of wealth as well, since nobody produces wealth singly by his own effort. Wealth is produced by the collective effort of society. For example, the cloth produced in a textile mill is the result not only of the effort of the mill-owner but also that of various other agents, from the cotton-grower to the mill-hand. How then does wealth accumulate with an individual? That is just like water, which does not accumulate on plain surface, but gets stored wherever it finds a ditch or sunken space. Likewise, there are hollow places in the present social structure where wealth accumulates. Therefore Vinobaji has now taken up the work of wealth-gift also. He wants sacrifice to be associated with our way of life. This also implies that we should keep with us no more than what we require. The question is who will adjudge this need? The individual himself, says Vinobaji. And we can do so. The needs of different persons vary, no doubt. But they vary like the stature of men, within a limited margin. If the difference in the acreage of lands held by different persons varies from 5 to 10 acres, it would not matter and similarly, of wealth. But when the disparity is out of all proportions, it becomes unconscionable and has got to be removed.

But this task cannot be accomplished by violence which, though it might change the present society, would not bring in the kind of transformation we aim at. Violence will not establish the rule of justice and equality in society. It will become the rule of a select coterie who will perpetuate their iron grip on the people. Violence ensures the victory of the party that is more skilled in its use. We all know that the Indian masses have neither the skill nor the weapons of violence and hence they are bound to lose against those who will be better equipped, in this respect. It is also argued that we could arm the people. Lenin had declared 36 years ago that he would arm the people in Russia. But it is common knowledge as to where the people of Russia stand today. In fact, it is not possible to arm the people en masse in this atomic age, when enormous and rapid improvements are effected in the weapons of warfare. Today we have not to choose between two alternatives. There is one and only one way, that of non-violence. Violence is definitely a bar against equality. In Russia even after 36 years, power is held by a handful of persons. We in India will have a similar experience if we follow the same way. Sarvodaya cannot countenance such a contingency. Indeed Sarvodaya does not want even to have political parties. It wants to shape and develop our body-politic on a pattern in which the existence of parties will be ruled out.

Besides, violence kills humanity. It has taken lakhs of years for man to rise from the condition of a brute to the present state. Surely, we do not want to relegate mankind again to the same state of brute creation. In this context, we should remember that even violence is of two kinds, organized violence and violence of the individual. Organized violence operates in accordance with certain rules of conduct. But there is no such thing in individual violence. It is totally unrestrained. Man becomes brute. We must understand that violence is opposed to the very grain of our culture which stands for peace. But at the same time we cannot lose sight of the fact that there is violence in our present social set-up itself. In fact, our society is based on violence which, in its turn, will induce another element of violence as it own reaction. This has got to be checked by cutting at the very root of the cause.

It is argued that revolutions are not made by persuading people to accept them. But the Bhoodan is being conducted in the belief that man is amenable to change. That is so, because all of us are essentially one, fragments of the same Supreme Being. When dust spreads over a glass mirror it loses its brightness and assumes a dusty look. But when the dust is removed, its brightness is restored again. Similarly man is overlaid with the dust of passions and habits and ways, of life. That dust has got to be removed by constant endeavour. Complete change of heart is an ideal condition and man progresses towards it only by degrees. To what extent, the change will come after each step depends on many factors. But the change does come

If persuasion does fail to convert the owners of property, one has to think of non-cooperation, that is, non-cooperation with injustice and inequity. Gandhiji believed that injustice was possible in society only with the co-operation of the wronged party. If this cooperation is withdrawn it will then crumble. We in India have seen how this technique worked in the case of the British rulers. We won our freedom with minimum of bloodshed and violence as compared to many other countries which strove for national liberation. But after independence, we have not known how to apply Gandhiji's teachings and technique to the task of reconstruction. Now we are able to form some sort of an idea in the wake of Vinobaji's movement. If the landless labourer withdraws his cooperation from the big landowner then the latter will have to yield. But then such a fight will be not a class struggle of the Communist variety but a moral fight for the vindication of right over wrong. But I do not mean to say that workers should go to the villages and start satyagraha forthwith. That will injure the cause of Bhoodan. We must understand that a man to be a *satyagrahi* has first to qualify himself by working on right lines. He has no right to launch *satyagraha* without that. But I believe that if we work with faith and confidence and in the proper spirit, the need for *satyagraha* will not arise.

Some people talk of legislation and ask, why not make a law to redistribute land quickly? This, they believe, will obviate the need for all the bother of Bhoodan. Such of them ought to bear in mind that by mere legislation we cannot change the present way of life of the people nor effect any fundamental social change, Law cannot come into effect without public opinion. As Gandhiji used to say, 'Legislation without conversion is a dead letter.' Do we not see the fate of the Sarda Act and the provisions in the Constitution on untouchability? I am afraid that, if we rely solely on legislation to achieve land redistribution, the powerful and well-to-do persons would make it impossible for weak, landless people to take possession of lands despite all enabling legislations. This explains why we should not look up to our legislatures as our only saviours and be sitting idle meanwhile.

An important thing to bear in mind is that in this work there is no place for political bias or motive. Workers of various political parties that are engaged in the Bhoodan campaign might often think as to how best they can strengthen their party interests through it. But they should cast off such considerations and work in a non-partisan spirit if the movement is to succeed. Parties are after all means to an end. If the object of a party is to establish a good society and the same is being achieved through Bhoodan, then why should anybody worry about his party? He should rather be happy that others are extending their cooperation in a work that is dear to him. If a worker is not imbued with this spirit, he should rather let this work alone. There is another point also. Vinobaji is putting forward the conception of a political set-up free from the operation of party system. Western thought, particularly Socialism, holds that parties are necessary to bring about a revolution, as parties represent different sectional interests in society. Vinobaji is, however, making an experiment in the direction of establishing a party-free society. We in India are wanting not to fight village elections on a party basis. And what is right for a village is also right for a nation.

It is the call of duty that all of us should plunge heart and soul in Bhoodan work. Duty is of two kinds, daily duty and that which devolves on one during emergency. Bhoodan represents the latter type of duty. Vinobaji has asked even constructive workers in charge of various important activities to reduce their normal activity and take up Bhoodan work, because this is the supreme need of hour.

281. To Badri Vishal Pitti, 27 November, 1953[1]

My dear Badri Vishalji,

I am going to Bombay in the middle of December and expect to be there from the 13th to the 25th December. I am going there mainly to collect funds for the Party, especially for the Travancore-Cochin general elections. You have many contacts in Bombay and we have never been able to take advantage of them. Will it be possible for you to meet me at Bombay during that time? I shall be obliged if you can come.

I hope you are well.

Yours sincerely,
Jayaprakash

[1]*Badri Vishal Pitti Papers* (NMML).

282. Need for a closer Study of Gandhism, Bombay, 19 December 1953[1]

It is well known that there are three ideological trends within the PSP today. One is that of the old Socialist Party, the other of Gandhism from the KMPP, and the third of Netaji from the Forward Bloc. Since the organizational merger of the three parties, there has been a process of interchange of ideas. But a complete synthesis is yet to come. I believe that this synthesis, which is very essential, is possible only on the basis of Gandhism.

The old Socialist Party had started, it will be remembered, under a strong influence of Leninist Marxism. But it had slowly travelled towards Gandhism. It did so when it gave up its faith in dictatorship, even as a transitional phase; when it asserted that socialism could not exist without democracy; when it came to believe that decentralization of economic and political power was essential for democracy; when it decided that good ends, could not be achieved through evil means; when it accepted, at least in words, *satyagraha* as a revolutionary weapon.

The KMPP was Gandhian, at least its outstanding leaders such as Kripalaniji, Dr. P.C. Ghosh, Shri Kelappan were and are ideologically devout Gandhians.

Netaji had rejected Marxian materialism, and stood for the spiritual values of life which he wanted to make the foundation of the new social order. It was true that he was not averse to violence in certain contexts. But I have no doubt that he would have been the first to reject violence in the context

[1]*Vigil*, 26 December 1953.

of social and human reconstruction in a free India. Use of violence in such a context would have been destructive of the very spiritual values for which he stood.

In view of this situation a synthesis on the basis of Gandhism should be a natural development.

I am sure that some think that to mix up Gandhism and socialism is a sign of ideological confusion. I wish that these friends did some fresh thinking. Both Socialism and communism are faced with failure. Communism, where it is victorious, has ended up in state capitalism and dictatorship—the very anti-thesis of Communism. Socialism, in Western Europe at any rate, has lost its pristine idealism and become only a parliamentary or legalistic creed. Thus, both the methods of violence and of parliamentary action have failed. Gandhism, to my mind, offers the third alternative: that of revolution by non-violent mass action.

We have a fine illustration of this in Vinoba's Bhoodan Movement. He eschews violence, but does not pin his faith on legislation. He wants to bring about redistribution of land by the action of the people. The law will come later to formalize what the people have already done. The common criticism of Bhoodan is that by 'begging' for land the question can not be solved and that therefore land must be distributed by law. The joke is that this is supposed to be a revolutionary view. It is little realized that a revolution cannot be made by law. A real revolution is a revolution in the values of life. No law can effect a transvaluation of values. The transvalution can be reflected in law once it has taken place in the life of the people. For this reason, Vinoba, a true Gandhian, is not concerned with legislation. He wants the people themselves to redistribute the land. For this he and his co-workers are going about trying to change the minds and hearts of men. Law cannot change minds or hearts. The question is raised about the time that such a revolution would take. The Gandhian revolution for national freedom did not take much time as compared with other national revolutions. The success Vinobaji has already achieved is unique in history. And 1957, the date-line by which he wants to complete the task of redistribution, is not far away.

I am afraid most people in the PSP are inclined to follow the Western method of establishing socialism by law. That is why there is so much concern with political action and the struggle for power. Most of us think that it is only when we capture power that we shall be able to build up Socialism by legislation and state power. If we persist in this legislative concept of social revolution, I have no doubt we are going to suffer the same disillusionment as socialists in the West. Gandhism does not concentrate on the capture of power, or depend on the power of the State, but it goes direct to the people and helps them to effect the revolution in their lives and consequently revolution in the life of the community. Support from the State power would be assured once the power of the people has been created.

It should be clear that in this manner the Gandhian technique necessarily goes beyond the confines of party and class because it aims at converting, or 'revolutionizing' if you please, members of all parties and classes. Socialism wishes to advance by setting class against class, Gandhism by cutting across classes. Socialism wishes to destroy classes by making one class victorious over the other—which seems to be somewhat illogical. Gandhism wishes to abolish classes by so bringing the classes together that there are no class distinctions left.

Socialism ultimately aims at creating a casteless society, but it wishes to make the state all-powerful by making the social revolution itself dependent upon state action. Gandhism, too, like Socialism, aims at a Stateless society. But on that account it proceeds more consistently by making the social process as little dependent upon the State as possible. The creation of the Stateless society begins here and now, and is not relegated to a remote and imaginary period in the future. It is, therefore, a more truly revolutionary process that is more likely to reach the goal than the other processes.

For these reasons, I should like to plead here for a closer study and understanding of Gandhism and the Gandhian technique. '*Satyagraha*', for instance, has become a fashion in socialist circles. But if *satyagraha* has to lead us to the free and fair and good society, and not deteriorate into partisan welfare, we must understand it better. It should be realized that any peaceful action is not *satyagraha*. *Satyagraha* is based on faith in the possibility of change of heart. A particular *satyagrahi* may fail in changing his opponent's heart but that is not failure of the faith. It is only his personal failure. In this manner *satyagraha* cannot be a partisan or a class struggle. Its appeal is to all parties and classes. It may not be possible for a *satyagrahi* to reach the ideal. But the important thing is that he should understand the ideal and work sincerely towards it. I am sure that if Socialists approached this weapon in this spirit they would become irresistible.

The other day, in receiving Asoka Mehta, I spoke at some length about Pardi. I do not want to repeat what I said there. But I do wish to point out again that the *satyagraha* has established beyond doubt (a) that there is need for an enquiry as demanded by the *satyagrahis*, and (b) that the *adivasis* must be provided with the means of employment and livelihood. This can be done only by giving them land. I do not think that there is any contradiction between growing food and growing fodder. The two can well be reconciled. I am also sure that the interests of the landlords, if they were only a little cooperative and farsighted, could be protected. This is not the place to make a concrete suggestion, but I am sure a way could be found out if all the parties concerned, including the Bombay Government, approached the problem with mutual goodwill and the desire to find a solution.

283. Pak-US Pact: Anti-Peace and anti-India, Bombay, 19 December 1953[1]

The proposed military pact between Pakistan and the United States is a matter of such grave importance that one cannot let it pass without comment. The whole of Asia is rightly exercised over it. Only since recently has Asia been emerging from European domination and ceasing to be arena of world power politics. The older European imperialisms have been on the run. But Communist and American imperialisms have been making serious inroads either by actual acts of war or by diplomatic and economic action. The Pak-US Pact is a major victory of American imperialism, to offset which the Communist side will naturally move its own pawns on the Asian chess-board. Thus, in the name of peace, Asia will further be dragged into the arena of war. No country in Asia has anything to gain from war and, therefore, there was growing slowly a no-war, or third camp, area in Asia. The growth and consolidation of this area is, to my mind, the only guarantee of peace not only for Asia but for the world. This growth is possible only if the Asian countries refuse to act as hyenas for either of the two snarling lions of the world.

Pakistan by entering into this dangerous pact has not only weakened its sovereignty but also dragged its people deliberately into the war zone and converted them into prospective cannon-fodder. Unfortunately, the people of Pakistan, do not seem to be aware of all this.

By this pact America has deliberately committed an unfriendly act against India. No other single act of the American Government had helped to turn the people of India against them as this military pact. That does not mean that India is panicky or is going to be deflected from its path. It only means that the struggle to build up India is going to be harder.

Hindu-Muslim differences were exploited by the British for their imperial interests. Indo-Pakistani differences are in a like manner being exploited by interested imperial powers on both sides that such advantage should be taken of our domestic quarrel. India and Pakistan are related by history and geography, by culture and religion. The two must live as brothers. The present disputes should be settled without delay and it is important that there should be a principled settlement and not a diplomatic game of chess. The main principle governing a settlement, to my mind, should be that no one should be forced to stay where he does not like to be. Unless both

[1]Concluding portion of the inaugural address at the 1st Annual Conference of PSP.

countries make a clean breast of it and give up horse-trading, they would both become, among other things, victims of the evil designs of others.

284. To Jugatram Dave, 26 December 1953[1]

Respected Jugatram Bhai,[2]

I received your kind letter[3] on the day I was leaving Patna for Bombay. I am obliged to you and Maharaj[4] both for the reply. I am also obliged to you for your guidance and instruction. You are an elder, and to guide is your right. I do not see any reason for taking umbrage at it.

I accept that in the first part of my letter there was anger. Non-violence is a penance, and by accepting it intellectually all faults of the inner self do not disappear. I try to put restraint on my mind. Perhaps I may succeed with the blessings of you people. In this connection I would like to submit—not for minimizing my faults but for securing forgiveness of you people—two points. One, other devotees of non-violence, who were much senior to me, had also not been able to overcome their faults. For instance, there was no lack of anger in Sardar [Patel]. Two, the circumstances of Pardi were such that in spite of having a cool temperament, I could not control anger. I found all those who are there engaged in maligning and criticizing Asoka Mehta, or the Socialist Party or the *satyagrahis*. No one criticized the owners. To what extent they indulged in falsehood would be known if you take the trouble of reading the full judgement of the Pardi Magistrate. But Morarji Bhai, honourable editor of *Harijan*, Gujarat Congress Committee all condemned the *satyagrahis* and took the side of the owners. All raised only the questions whether the *satyagraha* was proper *satyagraha* or *duragraha*, whether it was consistent with Bhoodan Yajna or inconsistent, *whether Vinobaji had approved it or not, etc*. No one took pains to think as to what would be the solution of the problem that Asoka Mehta had raised and how it could be reached. Having made Bhoodan Yajna an excuse, all

[1]*J.P. Papers* (NMML). Original in Hindi.

[2] Jugatram Dave (1892-1985); one of the most prominent Sarvodaya leaders of Gujarat; assisted Swami Anand in the publication of *Navajivan* and *Young India* and during Swami's imprisonment in 1922-4 shouldered responsibility of these two papers; worked as Secretary to Mahatma Gandhi during the illness of Mahadev Desai; took active part in Civil Disobedience and Quit India Movements and courted arrest in 1930, 1932 and 1942; after independence he devoted himself to propagate Sarvodaya.

[3]Not available

[4]Ravi Shankar Maharaj (1884-1986); became a devout follower of Mahatma Gandhi in 1916; imprisoned several times; one of the most prominent leaders of the Sarvodya Movement, particularly in Gujarat; a supporter of the J.P. Movement (1974-5).

responsibilities were imposed on that. If Vinoba had not started Bhoodan Yajna how would that have been solved? Again, I saw that when Asoka and other *satyagrahis* were pressed to make thumb-impressions in the prison and before the magistrate, nobody spoke anything. The owners gave false evidence, even then no one spoke anything. On the contrary, the Gujarat Congress Committee set its seal—without making an enquiry—on their falsehood that grain was never produced at the place where grass grows today. The socialists were accused of seeking advantage for their party through this *satyagraha*. But the other party also worked keeping its party interests in view from beginning to end. It did not attract any attention from impartial persons. If seeing all this, I got angry that should have been excusable to some extent.

I agree with you that Ishwar Bhai[5] etc. should have placed this issue before the Gujarat Bhoodan Samiti. I had advised Ishwar. Bhai and subsequently Asoka Mehta also to do so. I had also accepted this mistake in my letter to Maharaj.

I also accept it that the meaning of non-violence is not only external peace. Rather, peace should be in the heart, and there should be love for the other side. If the socialists have sown the poison of hatred and internal enmity in the Pardi area, they have done something wrong and have deviated from the path of non-violence. I shall surely draw their attention towards it and endeavour to set them right in this respect. You have rightly written that I have got a good opportunity to teach my comrades lessons in non-violence. Certainly, I shall not let this opportunity slip from my hand.

But here I would like to once again make a submission. I do not agree that spreading hatred beneath the surface and behaving peacefully on the surface are even worse than open violence. Those people who have at least agreed to maintain external peace, have taken a step in the right direction. The task of bringing to them success for non-violence was and is as much yours as mine. But I am observing from the beginning that no such effort was made by you people. If Maharaj had met Asoka etc. in the prison at my advice and had sought to persuade them affectionately, he could have won them over. How valuable that would have been for non-violence? But to do so was not thought proper even at my suggestion.

In this connection I would like to submit three facts.

[5]Ishwarlal Chhotubhai Desai (1907-); organized Student Movement Baroda 1927; participated in Gujarat Youth Conference 1929; Civil Disobedience Movement 1930 imprisoned 1930, 1932-4; started Nawjawan Sangh in Surat 1932; joined CSP 1934, member AICC 1937; offered individual satyagraha 1941; member national executive of PSP 1953-4; took part in Bhoodan Movement 1954; Goa Liberation Movement 1955; arrested 1955, released 1956; MLA Gujarat Assembly 1962-5; Editor *Chetna*.

1. In the copy of Maharaj's speech that you have sent me, it has been mentioned that some *satyagrahis* had come on their release from the prison and there was no anger or hatred of any kind in their hearts. If the socialists had spread poison secretly, some portion of it would have surely been in those who returned from the prison.
2. If the socialists had propagated internal violence, then that violence would have appeared somewhere. Is it possible that fire would be spread under the surface and there would not be any indication of that.
3. It seems to me that the feeling of hatred or enmity which has been found in the people is the consequence of the owners' injustice and deceitful behaviour. That the socialists have deliberately done so is not acceptable to me. That day I had talked over this subject before Mohan Bhai[6] with Asoka and Ishwar Bhai. Both said emphatically that the socialists never propagated the feeling of violence. It was decided that Ishwar Bhai would talk with Maharaj about this matter.

I regret that I differ from the owners' right to the land that you have written about. I indeed believe that the owners of Pardi have no right to the land. They may retain such land as is required to maintain their lives, but to keep an inch more than that is an injustice and depriving others' of their rights. I also believe that it is the duty of the Bhoodan workers to affectionately bring home to them this truth. It is the right of the landless people, who have a claim to that land, to demand its possession. I believe that one of the main objectives of the Bhoodan Movement is to create such awakening and power among the landless throughout the whole country. I shall say this much further, that I shall not blame them if the landless take possession of the land in a peaceful manner in order to get their just entitlement. I shall only help them if I can. If the workers of the Bhoodan Yajna do not cooperate with me in this, that would be my misfortune.

You have written that in the society injustice is taking place every day, but one has to bear with it and, getting to its root, seek to treat it. This is all right in principle. But there are occasions when some unusual injustices have to be confronted. At the time of uprooting the British Raj also such occasions arose when some injustices had to be opposed. It was not thought then that when the foreign rule ended all its injustices would end; so sporadic injustices should not be opposed. If such a thing had happened, many small *satyagrahas* which were fought, would not have been fought and the Bardoli *satyagraha* would not also have taken place.

Now only one submission has to be made in reply. It seems to me that the followers of non-violence are proceeding on the assumption that history

[6]Mohan Bhai; one of the prominent Sarvodaya leaders of Gujarat.

is to provide them with the opportunity to continue their experiment for eternity. But I would like to say with respect that if the question of social oppression, injustice or exploitation is not solved speedily, then all non-violence will be drowned in the flood of violence. We have been asking the poor to give us an opportunity until 1957, but it does not appear to me that the followers of non-violence have been working with the perspective that they are to solve the question of land through non-violence or manpower. I am indeed seeing in the whole country that there is an extreme sluggishness among the followers of non-violence. Many of them have become part of the Government and they think that they will build a non-violent society by their orders. Other people are engaged in a number of activities and they do the work of the Bhoodan in a leisurely way. Under these circumstances there is going to be a joke in 1957, the reaction to which will be terrible.

I have to submit another matter, with extreme humility: generally I find a lack of force in the followers of non-violence. They are gravely mistaken if they think that the type of constructive work they have been doing will result in a social revolution or creation of a new society. The constructive work that has taken place in Vedsi [Gujarat] is extremely valuable, but it is not possible that a non-violent revolution will take place merely by its expansion. If the constructive work continues in this manner only, a violent revolution is bound to take place in the country. The Bhoodan Yajna, Sampattidan Yajna (offering of wealth) etc. are of course, such a process that non-violent revolution can take place soon, and that a sufficient people's power can be created by which a new society can be formed. But I am getting the feeling after having toured the whole country that the great devotees of non-violence are indifferent to this. Bhoodan had been born in the violent land of Telangana. If the result of Pardi is such that we become aware of the dimensions of the problem, then the imprisonment of hundreds of brothers and sisters would be crowned with success.

In this letter I have written with the feeling that you have given me affection, so I should pour out my heart before you. I hope you will forgive my insolence.

Humbly,
Jayaprakash Narayan

285. Significance of the Bhoodan Movement, Speech at Patna, 3 January 1954[1]

Three years and ten months ago Bhoodan Movement was launched by Vinobaji at Telangana and got his first donation of land on April 18 that

[1] Adapted from *Searchlight*, 4 January 1954.

year. He had not yet addressed any public meeting in this town and the people here might not be acquainted with the basic principles of Bhoodan.

Bhoodan does not stand merely for giving land to landless. Its ultimate objective is to bring about changes in the modern society by virtue of an all-round revolution—political, social and economic. It stands for the formation of a new society, a new man.

Mahatma Gandhi endeavoured to bring into being a society based on the principles of Sarvodaya. In such a society every body would be happy and contented. All would be equal and exploitation would disappear. Gandhiji dreamt of a casteless and classless society.

The objective of Vinobaji in taking up the question of land distribution is to spread Gandhiji's dynamic ideas among the people. Ideas are very forceful and effective and possess the potentiality of effecting changes in the minds of masses. Buddha, Christ, Mohammad, Marx and Gandhiji changed society through the dynamism of their ideas. Man is distinguished from cattle because of ideas.

The basic principle on which the Bhoodan Movement is based is that land does not belong to individuals but to society. God is the owner of all land. An individual must not possess land more than he needs. If he does so, he is a thief.

It is incorrect to say that the rich are the owner of their wealth. They came to possess their wealth through the cooperation of several other individuals. They do not produce the wealth out of nothing, but take the help of human labour in amassing their riches. Therefore all wealth really belongs to society.

Vinobaji, being a great Sanskrit scholar, holds that asking for Bhoodan is not to be treated as an act of begging. According to him "dan" means equal distribution. Back to the Vedic age is his slogan. In that age all land belonged to the village community and it was distributed among the tillers alone. The ego of being owner of land and wealth, therefore, must be forsaken by every body. According to Vinobaji, man is a debtor of society. He is not the owner, but the trustee of his possessions.

The question is as to how much an individual should keep for himself. Gandhiji had given a very convincing answer. To decide the quantum of his possession he must look at the economic conditions of the people around him. The people are hungry and naked. This being so he has no right to live in a better condition. He must have some earthly possessions to satisfy his natural requirements only. Equality never means absolute equality. There would remain some sort of inequality, but it must be within reasonable bounds.

There have been violent revolutions in Russia and China. The future of China is a matter of controversy. But in Russia where revolution took place

36 years ago, the establishment of Kisan-Mazdoor Raj has not yet been effected. The people at large are not consulted on the question as to who should possess land. This is done by a handful of persons at the top.

In India we can agitate against Pandit Nehru and contest his election with safety but in Russia lives of opponents of dictators are always in danger. Recently Beria[2] and others were executed by shooting for their acts of opposing Malenkov.[3]

India is a land of peace. Since ancient times it has carried the torch of peace to distant lands. Today there are some people who think that peace is a sign of cowardice. This notion is completely wrong. Peace is the dearest thing and the world today is hungry for it. The world is looking to India for the message of peace. The Bhoodan Movement would make the human race look to a new direction, the direction of peace.

There are some who want that land distribution should be effected through legislation. But the object of Bhoodan is not the mere distribution of land. Its aim is to bring about a social revolution which can not be realised through law. Legislations for the eradication of various social evils still exist, but all of them have proved ineffective.

If once the idea of parting from surplus of wealth enters the minds of people, there would be no need of legislations. When Ramchandra Reddy,[4] could part from his surplus wealth by making the first donation of land to Vinobaji in Telangana, there is no reason why others would not follow suit.

[2] Lavrenti Pavlovich Beria (1899-1953); Russian Communist politician, one time regarded as a possible successor to Stalin; Minister of Internal Affairs of the Soviet Union and Head of the Secret Police (NKVD) 1938-53; expelled from the Soviet Communist Party in July 1953, removed from his office, found guilty of treason and shot dead.

[3] Georgi Maximillanovich Malenkov (1902-88); Member of Communist Party of Soviet Union 1920; Member Central Committee of Communist Party 1939; Member Committee of State Defence 1941; Member Committee of Economic Rehabilitation of Liberated Districts 1943; Deputy Chairman, Council of Ministers 1946; Chairman Council of Ministers of Soviet Union 1953-5; Minister of Electric Power Stations 1955-7.

[4] V. Ramachandra Reddy—A big landlord of Pochampalli in Warangal district of Andhra Pradesh. He was first to donate 100 acres of land to Vinoba Bhave in the Bhoodan Movement.

286. To V.G. Dalvi, 10 January 1954[1]

Dear Mr. Dalvi,

I am very sorry that I could not meet you in Bombay. When I recovered from my illness, I learnt that you had already left the city.

I am glad to know that the conference of our Union [All-India Postmen

[1] *J.P. Papers* (NMML).

and Lower Grade Staff Union] is being held at Calcutta on 16, 17 and 18 January. I regret that it would not be possible for me to attend the conference, but I do send my best wishes for its success.

I feel that the labour movement in the country has reached a stage where it is not possible for the trade unions to advance much further in respect of wages or emoluments. I feel strongly that if labour is to advance further, which it should undoubtedly do, the trade unions must be prepared to take responsibility for increased production. I think that if organized labour were to show that it is capable of persuading the workers to take greater interest in production, not only the strength of labour organizations would grow by leaps and bounds, but there will also be a steady rise in the standard of living of the workers. I feel therefore that the labour movement has come to a crossing of the ways. If it does not choose the right turning it would be impossible for it to raise itself out of the doldrum in which it finds itself today. I am aware that what I am saying would not be very popular among the ranks of labour, but as a friend and servant of labour I consider it my duty to tender this unpleasant advice.

Let me in the end wish a long life to the All-India Postmen and Lower Grade Staff Union.

I hope you are well,

Yours sincerely,
J.P.

287. Press Interview Clarifying his Stand on Labour Movement, Patna, 18 January 1954[1]

I do not think that trade unionism is a one way traffic and that all that the workers have to do is to make demands on the management. Producation, whether under a system of private enterprise or of social ownership, is a two-way traffic. I have no doubt that if our trade unions realise this and take interest in the problem of production, they would be able to serve the interests of the workers far better, apart from the service they would render to the nation.

I do not wish to enter into a controversy. The view I have expressed is so self-evident that there should be no difference of opinion about it. It is far from my intention to suggest that there should be no further improvement in the standard of living of the working class.

But I do definitely feel that a stage has been reached in which little improvement is possible unless the trade union movement is prepared to

[1]Press interview with PTI on the occasion of Silver Jublee Conference of the All-India Postmen and Lower Grade Staff Union, Patna. Adapted from *Tribune*, 19 January 1954.

cooperate in improving efficiency and standard of production. Apart from considerations of national interest, it is in the interest of the workers themselves to understand this simple fact. Those who are acquainted with the history of world trade unionism should find no difficulty in understanding it. I am not aware of any country in which the trade union movement has acquired decisive strength and succeeded in raising the standard of living of the workers without taking any responsibility for fostering production.

288. Address at a Kisan Rally to Fight Non-violently the Enhancement of Water Rates, Arrah [Bihar], 26 January 1954[1]

The whole country was united against the British Government under the leadership of Gandhiji and Congress. But the same is not the case today. It is not an easy task to remove the shortcomings of our own Government. However, Gandhiji had showed us the path. We should prepare ourselves to fight for our legitimate rights non-violently. Violence will not help us in achieving the desired end. We do not want that one Indian should cut the throat of another.

If you find that the enhancement of the water rates is unjustified, you should boldly refuse to pay it. But meetings and processions only will not suffice and you will have to prepare yourselves for any sacrifice that you may be required to make. I ask you to organize an action Committee in every village to carry out your struggle. People are all mighty and no government can dare take any step against their wishes. If it does, it would be a matter of shame for it. I feel happy to see people becoming more and more conscious and hope that there will not be much difficulty in finding a way out.

Those who seek to justify the action of the Government in enhancing the water rates on one ground or another do not sound convincing to me. I am not opposed to the imposition of taxes or also any reasonable increment in them but the Government should not think of making money out of canals and railways which should be maintained even at a loss in the interest of the public. Moreover the Government do not suffer any loss today from these departments. If they have to finance their numerous development schemes they should do it otherwise and not by increasing the burden of taxes on the poor masses. It is also pleaded that the prices of grains having increased, the kisans have earned a lot. This may be true, but it is also true that the kisans have to pay increase prices for other commodities they have to purchase for their use. Their standard has not improved in any way. And

[1]Adapted from *Searchlight*, 29 January 1954.

even if some big cultivators have become rich during the past few years, why should all the poor kisans be made to suffer?

289. Statement on the Death of M.N. Roy, Madhubani [Bihar], 29 January 1954[1]

In the death of Mr. M.N. Roy, India has lost one of her great sons.[2] No one in modern India had such a long revolutionary life, so full of drama and adventure. In the international Communist movement he had held the highest position in the oriental section, and was the closest Asian associate of the great Lenin. When that movement began to degenerate into imperialistic expansionism Mr. Roy had the rare courage, at the risk of his brilliant career and even his life, to oppose it at the highest levels. On his return to India he had to suffer a long imprisonment. In recent years he had retired from active politics, but had been doing path-breaking thinking. Not only India, but the world society needed his intellectual leadership at this moment.

[1]Adapted from *Searchlight*, 30 January 1954.
[2]See Appendix 52 for Ellen Roy's reply dated 17 February 1954.

290. To J.B. Kripalani, 7 March 1954[1]

My dear Dada,

I am sorry that I am not going to Madras for the Executive. I feel however that I should send you my own opinion on the Travancore-Cochin question. This opinion naturally will be based on newspaper accounts of the situation in the State.

I might begin by saying that when our election policy in Travancore-Cochin was discussed at the Delhi Executive I had told Shri Thanu Pillai that even though we agreed to an electoral arrangement with the Communists, I personally would not approve of a coalition with them in the event of successful results. I hold the same view now. I do not think that our Party should join the coalition with the Communists. At the same time, I do not think it would be right or wise to permit and tolerate a Congress Government in that State in the present circumstances. This creates a dilemma, the solution of which seems to me to be to permit the UFL[2] to form a ministry and give it conditional support. The conditions should not be difficult to lay down. I recognise that this policy is only a make-shift

[1]*J.P. Papers* (NMML).
[2]UFL—United Front of Leftists.

one and I am sure that the Party must think afresh from a long range point of view over its tactical political line. But there is time yet for it.

The electoral policy for Travancore-Cochin that we adopted at Delhi has borne fruit in that it has strengthened the Party in that State, but the advantage that we have gained should be properly utilised. Otherwise, we might end up in disaster. A policy of self abnegation, I am sure, will strengthen us further in Travancore-Cochin, and, at the same time, we might exercise a determining influence over the UFL Government[3] if it is formed. Many possibilities are open after that which it is difficult to be certain of at present. If events take the same course after the formation of the UFL Government as I at least visualise, the Party will find itself in a decisively improved position in the State after six months when we may again take stock of the situation and determine our policy accordingly.

This, in brief, is my view for what it is worth.

I hope you will excuse me for my absence.

With regards,

Yours affectionately,
Jayaprakash

[3] Travancore-Cochin Legislative Assembly had 117 seats. Election was held for twenty constituencies on 15 February 1954 and for the rest on 26 February 1954.

Congress won 45 seats, Communists 23, PSP 19, RSP 9, Tamil Nadu Congress 12 and independents 9. Sixty legislators supported Pattom Thanu Pillai and he became Chief Minister.

291. Appeal for People's Cooperation with the Forthcoming Sarvodaya Samaj Sammelan at Bodh Gaya, Patna, 16 March 1954[1]

In the present day social set-up the rise of one involves the decline of another. This is the cause of all conflicts. Mahatma Gandhi wanted to establish a social order wherein the uplift of one would imply the uplift of all. The Sarvodaya Samaj was brought into being in 1943 to give practical shape to this immortal idea of Gandhiji. Its membership is open to anybody who accepts the principles of truth and non-violence and tries to live up to them. Every year the members of Sarvodaya Samaj meet in *sammelan* for discussion and exchange of ideas. This year the *sammelan* will be held from April 18 to 20 at Bodh Gaya which is a place of international repute and pilgrimage. The Rajnath grove by the side of the river Phalgu has been

[1] Adapted from *Searchlight*, 18 March 1954. The appeal was issued by Jayaprakash Narayan along with some other prominent leaders.

selected as the venue of this *sammelan* at which Sant Vinobaji will also be present.

There is something in the atmosphere of Bodh Gaya which serves as a source of inspiration and confidence to make a solemn resolve. That is why at this sacred place Vinobaji felt an inspiration to make a resolve to solve the land problem of Gaya district. That being so, it was difficult to find a place more suitable than Bodh Gaya for the venue of the forthcoming *sammelan*. A meeting of the citizens of Gaya and other districts of Bihar was held on March 8 and 9 at Gaya in which a reception committee and its various sub-committees were formed. It is estimated that the *sammelan* will involve an expenditure of about 50 thousand rupees. An amount of about 20,000 is expected to be received as boarding and lodging charges from members. The rest will have to be met by donations in the province.

We earnestly appeal to the public of Bihar in general and Gaya district in particular to accord their best help and cooperation in this *sammelan*. Help can be given the shape of money, food grains and other materials, and personal services. Any remittances may kindly be sent to Sjt. Radhakrishna Bajaj,[2] Treasurer Reception Committee (Sarvodaya Samaj Sammelan) Station Dharamshala, Gaya.

We hope and trust the people of Bihar and particularly of Gaya will extend their helping hand in this sacred work.

[2] Radhakrishna Bajaj (1905-2001); participated in Non-Cooperation Movement, 1920-2; sales manager, Maharashtra 'Charkha Sangh', 1928-32; took active part in Civil Disobedience Movement and courted arrest in 1932; Secretary, 'Goseva Sangh' 1941; again went to jail in 1942; managing trustee, 'Sarva Seva Sangh', 1948; Incharge Publications of 'Sarva Seva Sangh' in 1955 and 1969; Member, 'Mahila Ashram' and 'Seva Mandal', Wardha; Remained associated with the Gandhian institutions throughout his life.

292. To Pattom Thanu Pillai, 23 March 1954[1]

Dear Mr. Thanu Pillai,

I am very sorry for not being able to be present at Madras. However, events have taken a rather cheering course and I do congratulate you on your success. I am sure that under your leadership the State Government would be able to tackle successfully many problems of Travancore-Cochin and the people of the State would be lifted out of the fog of frustration and disappointment. You have my best wishes in your great adventure.

I hope you are well.

Sincerely yours,
Jayaprakash Narayan

[1] *J.P. Papers* (NMML).

293. To K.K. Menon, 23 March 1954[1]

My dear K.K.,

I was extremely happy to have your letter of March 18. I was really sorry for not being able to go to Madras, but I don't think it matters very much. I quite share your enthusiasm for Pattom[2] and the great opportunity that the PSP has been offered in Travancore-Cochin. I do not, however, like to make Pattom feel that unless half a dozen of us keep him guiding all the time he might go off the rails. Madhu[3] has written to me to go to Kanya Kumari for my health and incidentally to see Pattom on the way in order to give him my advice. I have also seen Asoka's letter to Pattom in which much guidance has been given to the old gentleman. If I were Pattom I would surely resent all this prodding. So as far as I am concerned, I was going to leave him alone. But after reading your letter I have decided to write to him a personal letter of good wishes. I would be happy to see the RSP cooperating with Pattom but that, alas, does not seem to be possible immediately.

My health is not too good and of all things I have caught diabetes. I am committed to my present engagements till the end of April, after which I wish to go to Poona, preferably to Singhgarh, for a month. If my present plans remain unaltered I expect to reach Bombay on the 30 April when I am looking forward to meeting you.

Affectionately yours,
J.P.

[1]*Brahmanand Papers* (NMML).
[2]Pattom: Stands for Pattom Thanu Pillai.
[3]Madhu: Stands for Madhu Limaye.

294. To Kantibhai Mehta, 1 April 1954[1]

My dear Kantibhai,[2]

I hope you will excuse me for this personal letter even though we are not personally acquainted. A few weeks ago when I was in Delhi I had met Shri Khandubhai Desai in connection with Lodna affairs and he had talked about you. I am encouraged to write by what Khandubhai had told me about you. I seek your cooperation in solving the Lodna dispute and saving nearly 3,000 workers and their families from starvation and injustice.

[1]*J.P. Papers* (NMML).
[2]Kantibhai Mehta; a trade union leader of Koyala Mazdoor Panchayat at Lodna belonging to the INTUC.

I am sure that you are acquainted with all the details of the situation. I do not think that there is any room for partisanship or any kind of trade union rivalry in this matter. B.P. Sinha, whom I consider to be one of the most corrupt men in the entire trade union movement, is acting more as the management's tool than as a labour leader. I think justice requires that all genuine trade unions unite to have the workers concerned reinstated in their jobs. You know that the strike was not of the Koyala Mazdoor Panchayat's making. But just because the workers took a hasty step, that is no reason why they and their children should be deprived of their bread. Further, I understand that there is some Supreme Court decision to the effect that even for an illegal strike the workers cannot be discharged from service.

I have written to Khandubhai also in this matter and have sought his help. As a matter of fact I had suggested to Khandubhai when I had met him last that the mines should be the next industry in which an attempt should be made to merge the INTUC and HMS unions. I hope you will also consider this question.

I am sorry to give you this trouble.

Yours sincerely,
J.P.

295. To S.C. Joshi, 1 April 1954[1]

Dear Mr. Joshi,[2]

You know the situation that has developed in the Lodna Collieries. Mr. Reyasat Karim, accompanied by another friend from Jharia, came to see me today. The management seems to be determined to keep out the workers who had struck. The local officers of your department seem to be powerless to help. This is a very regrettable situation. Are Government and the present Labour laws so ineffective? I am sure there must be a way out. B.P. Sinha's union, which unfortunately is affiliated to the INTUC, seems to be not a union of workers but of blacklegs. I am writing to Khandubhai to ask if the INTUC approves of such a despicable labour policy. I am also writing to Mr. Giri.[3] Will you please advise him to take a firm hand in settling this dispute?

Our union was advised by the Regional Labour Commissioner to have the matter referred to the Tribunal, but tribunals are notoriously slow in their functioning. If the workers have to be saved from starvation and also restored to their jobs some more effective step would be necessary. I am

[1] *J.P. Papers* (NMML).

[2] S.C. Joshi; Chief Labour Commissioner, Government of India, New Delhi.

[3] Refers to V.V. Giri; then Labour Minister, Government of India. For biographical note see *JPSW*, Vol. I, p. 113.

sure you can find a way out and advise Mr. Giri accordingly.

You know that this strike was not of our choice. But if the workers took a hasty step, that is no reason why they should be victimised in this fashion. The Lodna management seems to treat everyone, including the Government, with utter contempt. I wonder if they should be allowed to get away like this. I do earnestly hope that you will be able to help the workers out of their predicament. I am sorry to give you this trouble.

I hope you are well.

Sincerely yours,
J.P.

296. To Khandubhai Desai, 1 April 1954[1]

My dear Khandubhai,

Since I met you at Delhi the situation in the Lodna Collieries has deteriorated further. I shall not go into the details because I am sure you are in touch with the situation. As you know, the Koyala Mazdoor Panchayat, acting on the advice of Mr. S.C. Joshi, persuaded the workers to go back to their work. The management however, backed by B.P. Sinha, has refused to take them back. Nearly 3,000 workers and their families are faced with starvation. B.P. Sinha's union, which unfortunately is affiliated to the INTUC, is acting more like a blacklegs' union than as a workers' union. I do not know what attitude Shri Kanti Mehta has taken in this matter. I am writing to him also today. I seek your help in saving the workers concerned. I may add that when Mr. Joshi advised the Koyala Mazdoor Panchayat to ask the strikers to go back to work he had said, on the strength of a Supreme Court judgement, that even for an illegal strike the workers could not be discharged from service.

Regarding Mahesh Desai,[2] I wrote a letter to Sri Babu, our Chief Minister, as advised by you. I received a non-committal reply from him to the effect that he would look into the papers of the case. In the meanwhile Mahesh Desai has been disallowed bail. It is feared that the District Judge also will refuse to give him bail. One does not know what view the High Court will take.

I am sorry to give you this trouble.

With regards,

Sincerely yours,
J.P.

[1]*J.P. Papers* (NMML).

[2]Mahesh Desai; an active member of Praja Socialist Party from Bombay, was at that time active in the Trade Union Movement in Dhanbad (Bihar).

297. To V.V. Giri, 1 April 1954[1]

My Dear Mr. Giri,

I am writing to you about the dispute in the Lodna Collieries in Jharia. I shall not take your time by writing in detail about it because your Chief Labour Commissioner, Mr. S.C. Joshi, is fully seized of the situation. The management is taking a very perverse view and the recognised union, which is utterly unrepresentative and is headed by one of the most corrupt men in the entire trade union movement, is in the pockets of the management. The result is that the workers are faced with starvation and loss of their employment.

I request you to take a firm hand in this matter and save the workers and the bread of their children. As Mr. Joshi will tell you, the management has so far taken a defiant attitude towards the Government. The Government must take urgent steps not only to have justice done to the workers but also to uphold the law and its prestige. Something urgent must be done. I am sorry to give you this trouble.

With kind regards,

Sincerely yours,
J.P.

[1] *J.P. Papers* (NMML).

298. To Rammanohar Lohia, 2 April 1954[1]

Dear Rammanohar,

It was a great pleasure receiving your letter.[2] I had received news about your health from Benipuriji.[3] I was worried and am still worried. Effort should be made to take care of it. You don't do as much as required in this respect. This is not good for the country.

My health has certainly worsened recently to some extent. These were already some old diseases, but now diabetes has appeared. Hope it will go soon.

I am surprised after going through your proposal.[4] For one thing, you are uselessly talking about (neglecting) your duty. You are performing your work very well, as you alone can do. Secondly, knowing my views at this

[1] *J.P. Papers* (NMML). Original in Hindi.
[2] For the text of Lohia's letter to J.P. see Appendix 53.
[3] Rambriksh Benipuri.
[4] The proposal was that J.P. should assume the leadership of the Praja Socialist Party.

time, you should not have made this proposal. Neither did I ever had the capacity to shake the country nor do I have it now. I also do not give much importance to shaking the country in this way.

Besides, I am myself shaken. It is a matter of regret that whatever I think most appropriate at present for socialism and for the country is viewed by you as shaking. At Patna, I had told you that I had an idea of opening a training centre, where persons working in the legislatures could be trained and where some legislative experiments might be made. From now on I have to devote myself single-mindedly to this work. It is my view that those engaged in this training programme should not themselves take part in any kind of election. Accordingly, I too will have to remain only a four-*anna* member of the Party. After completing some essential work after the Sarvodaya Conference (going to be held in April 1954) I am planning to go to Singhgarh for one month. I shall return to Bihar after that.

Hope you will look after your health.

Prabha says *pranam*.

Affectionately yours,
Jayaprakash

299. To Rajkumari Amrit Kaur, 6 April 1954[1]

My dear Rajkumariji,

You may remember that several months ago I had written to you about Dinshah Mehta's plan to establish a Nature Cure Institute. After that you were good enough to invite him to Delhi for a talk. It seemed then that the Government of India were going to help him and there was some correspondence with the Defence Department about the Purandhar Fort near Poona. Subsequently I had occasion to write to you to expedite things if possible. You were good enough to reply, and in your letter you had made what I thought were casual remarks about the difference in Dinshah's ideas of nature cure and Bapu's. I had thought that when Dinshah was up at Delhi these questions had been thrashed out and it was not for me to reply to that point or that further progress depended on my reply to it. Government could have got these points clarified by Dinshah and satisfied itself. I might say that when I had met Dinshah afterwards and showed him your letter, he had told me that he was sure he could satisfy you on that point. But he did not have any direct communication from you or from anyone on your behalf regarding the matter. In the meanwhile, many months have passed without anything having been done. May I humbly say that if Government have

[1] *J.P. Papers* (NMML).

any serious intention of doing anything in this matter, these and other relevant questions should be thrashed out between Dinshah and the persons concerned.

Finally, I cannot help adding that I wish the Government of India were as keen about Bapu's ideas about other things as it seems to be about his idea of nature cure. This is not to suggest that Dinshah is not equally anxious about Bapu's ideas.

With regards,

Yours sincerely,
J.P.

300. To B.R.T. Greer, 6 April 1954[1]

Dear Mr. Greer,[2]

I am writing to you in connection with the affairs of the Lodna Collieries (including Bagdigi Collieries and the Lodna Tar and Coke Plant). I do not have the pleasure of knowing you personally but I hope on that account you will not disregard what I have to say in this letter.

I am assuming that you are anxious to see the end of the continuous labour dispute and trouble in your company's undertakings in Lodna and Bagdigi. I suggest that the main reason for these recurring troubles is that your local management refuses to deal with the real representatives of the workers. As you know, the management has been dealing with a union which is led by Mr. B.P. Sinha and his friends. This union, it has been repeatedly shown, does not command the confidence of the workers who seem to have much greater faith in the Koyala Mazdoor Panchayat. The result is almost constant conflict between the management and the workers. I think you will agree with me that it is a very mistaken policy on the part of the management to try to bypass workers organizations by bolstering up company unions. The Koyala Mazdoor Panchayat, in whose interest I am personally interested, is a responsible body with which any management can deal on a fair and decent footing.

I am afraid Lodna has not seen the last of its troubles, and no amount of repression has ever been found to crush a genuine labour movement. Thousands of workers in Lodna and Bagdigi are being faced with starvation because your local management refuses to take them back to duty, even though there is a recent Supreme Court Judgement to the effect that even for an illegal strike workers cannot be discharged.

[1] *J.P. Papers* (NMML).

[2] B.R.T. Geer; Director, Messrs Turner Morrison Co., Calcutta.

I am writing to you to suggest that you should take a personal interest in this question because from all accounts the General Manager in Lodna is for some reason hands in glove with B.P. Sinha and his crowd and would rather let the company suffer a loss than agree to drop them. If anyone challenges my statement that B.P. Sinha's union is not representative and the workers regard the Koyala Mazdoor Panchayat as their real union a plebiscite can easily decide the matter, provided blacklegs are not allowed to vote.

I hope this letter will receive your serious consideration.

Yours sincerely,
Jayaprakash Narayan

301. Announcement of *Jeevandan*, Bodh Gaya, 19 April 1954[1]

History will not allow much time to non-violent revolution to succeed. If Vinoba's Movement does not produce quick results, forces of violent revolution would sweep over the land. I announce here today that I would dedicate the rest of my life to the cause of Sarvodaya and Bhoodan Movements. I also call upon others to come forward and give their lifetime for the success of the non-violent, social revolution.[2]

I am speaking today with a heavy heart. My devotion to the Bhoodan Movement and my understanding of the philosophy of Bhoodan have caused some migivings among certain sectors of my friends who are looking askance at my present thoughts.

With the experience of Bhoodan work I am today fully convinced that this movement would not only solve the land problem, but would also change the entire pattern of life. Such a social revolution can never be achieved through legislation. Laws are ineffective so long as they are not backed by mass sanction. Besides there is a general tendency to bypass the law. In such a setting how can one expect that legislative bodies would succeed in changing the present social order.

If social revolution does not take place soon, violence would be rampant in the land and the present order would automatically be thrown overboard. But if the present undesirable structure of society is demolished through violence, the result will be much worse.

[1] Address at Sarvodaya Samaj Sammelan; adapted from *Searchlight*, 21 April 1954.

[2] Vinoba Bhave, the founder of the Bhoodan Movement and the chief source of inspiration to all Gandhian workers, marked the solemnity of this event by writing a note to J.P., rededicating his own life also to the movement.

The political parties in Bihar are not participating in Bhoodan wholeheartedly although they are pledged to it. The Congress and Praja Socialist Parties have vast resources of workers. Yet the quota of collection fixed for Gaya could not be completed. It is an index of the lukewarm interest taken by these parties in this movement. Even now if they take to work in right earnest the whole target set out for Bihar can be achieved within a year.

The workers of the Congress and the Praja Socialist Party very often complain against one another. Evidently the workers of these parties are carrying their political proclivities into the Bhoodan Movement. It is most unfortunate that they do not deviate from their party lines even in this work. As a result of these tendencies even the land donors wait for leaders of particular parties to approach them.

I also stress that as I work for Bhoodan my faith in its immense possibilities for social change is growing every day.

I do not contemplate resignation from my party, but what I say does mean that I shall withdraw from what is ordinarily known as politics. I have some immediate political engagements which I am duty bound to fulfil. After that I want to devote my entire life to constructive work and the task of non-violent reconstruction of man and society to which the Bhoodan Movement is committed.

APPENDICES

APPENDIX 1

From Vallabhbhai Patel, 19 August 1950[1]

My dear Jayaprakash,

Thank you for your letter of the 19th August 1950 regarding the arrest of Shri [S.M.] Joshi of Poona and Shri Ganga Sharan Sinha of Patna yesterday at Gwalior.

These arrests were brought to my notice a little while ago, before the receipt of your letter. It appears that the local authorities, who are naturally quite nervous in the present situation in Gwalior, apprehended that the arrival of these two persons might accentuate the situation in Gwalior which, as you know, is already considerably disturbed. Some Socialists among the students are reported to be responsible, along with extremist elements like Communists and reactionary Mahasabhites, for the disturbances that have taken place. Nevertheless, things are showing some tendency to settling down and the local authorities thought that the arrival of these two persons might upset the whole atmosphere. They, therefore, decided that these two persons should be externed, but I understand that they refused to abide by this order. When the facts were reported to me, I asked [V.P.] Menon to have these persons released. Menon may have sent instructions to the Gwalior authorities already. However, they would be released some time today.

Regarding the Gwalior disturbances, I think what is necessary in the first place is to ascertain facts. In order to have these facts ascertained as impartially as possible, I decided to send an officer from the Home Ministry, who is independent and an outsider, to conduct enquiries. If, on the result of his enquiries, I find that there is a case for further judicial enquiry, I shall not hesitate to have one held. For the time being, it seems to me that the need of the moment is to establish peace and security and normal conditions as soon as possible. To ascertain and redress the students' legitimate grievances, a Committee has already been announced, but somehow the agitation is still continuing, in spite of the fact that the Students' Action Committee had, in their negotations with Menon, agreed to call off the strike. As I told you yesterday, the alliance of Socialist elements amongst the students with Communists and Mahasabhites in this case is rather distressing. I do not know how you look at this, but my own feeling is that it would, in the long run, be in the interests of Socialists not to have any

[1] *J.P. Papers* (NMML).

truck with these elements. Otherwise, I am sure their own cause would be damaged.

With best wishes,

Yours sincerely,
Vallabhbhai Patel

APPENDIX 2

From Jawaharlal Nehru, 22 September 1950[1]

My dear Jayaprakash,

I received your letter of September 19 at Nasik.

Whatever the merits of the Bombay textile strike, I think you will agree with me that it would have been quite improper for me to intervene in the way that was suggested. Any other way would have been difficult; but that particular way was completely out of the question. I was asked to attend a public meeting of strikers. Even if the meeting had been allowed by the Government or the Police, surely, I could not have attended a meeting of the strikers when such a conflict was going on. At the most, I might have met some representative who could have given me his version of the facts.

I quite appreciate that it is no small matter for two hundred thousand workers to be on strike in an industry of importance. It is not a local matter and not only the strikers, but the whole industry and the country are suffering because of it. Nevertheless, it is not clear to me how I can jump in and take a part in this business. Whatever the motives might have been, the strike raises very important questions of principle. Are we to put aside all ideas of approaching such conflicts through tribunals and the like and leave a decision of the issue to repeated conflicts? A strike is a legitimate weapon, but, surely, even a legitimate weapon can be misused. This particular matter is being considered in some tribunals. It is not a question of legalism being made a fetish. There is another side to it that the laws we frame have no importance and can be set aside at any moment. If that is so, then there can be no ordered approach to this problem or any problem. I can understand the strikers in a moment of excitement or frustration taking any action which is not strictly legal. We should not be hard on them. But to encourage them to do so is surely to encourage something which must result in confusion and chaos.

How can a Prime Minister jump into the fray and ignore the laws he is supposed to uphold?

[1]*J.N. Papers*: Files at Home (NMML).

I have no doubt that some employers misbehave and have misbehaved, not only in Bombay, but elsewhere. Is it wise to employ tactics which put them in the right and thus cover up their misbehaviour?

I am not referring here to the merits of the dispute about which I cannot form a final opinion without enquiring. But there are certain basic factors which seem to me to override the particular merits.

I understand that Rao Sahib and Asoka Mehta are likely to see me this evening. I should gladly meet them if they come.

Yours affectionately,
Jawaharlal Nehru

APPENDIX 3

From Rafi Ahmed Kidwai, 30 October 1950[1]

Dear Jayaprakashji,

I had received your letter sometimes back. As you were on tour I did not send an immediate reply.

I feel a little embarrassed at your interpretation of our talks about the pay of the strike period. Again and again it has been declared by the Prime Minister and the Deputy Prime Minister and myself that no pay will be paid for the period of strike. It is true that in our discussions I promised to explore the possibility of a formula that may convert the punishment in other form than the forfeiture of the pay. I found it difficult to find a way out. There were inherent difficulties in the issue. These difficulties were enhanced when it began to be whispered that we have "conspired to evolve a formula that would compensate the strikers for the loss of the pay."

I wonder if you have realized what reaction such an interpretation of our discussion would have. This makes it difficult to make a frank discussion even in private when that is interpreted as commitment. Whatever action you take, I hope it will not be based on those private discussions.

I am anxious to meet you to discuss all that has happened in the field of politics in the course of the last few months. I hope to be here on 21st of the next month to meet you.

Yours sincerely,
Rafi

[1]*J.P. Papers* (NMML).

APPENDIX 4

From Jawaharlal Nehru, 1 November 1950[1]

My dear Jayaprakash,

Thank you for your letter of October 28th. The matter has not been finally decided yet, but a good deal of thought has been given to it. Because you mentioned it to me, I have also thought about it and discussed it.

May I say right at the outset that I am a firm believer in a strong opposition. I do not think good work is done in Parliament or elsewhere without adequate criticism.

But I do not see how your proposal makes any great difference to this. I could understand a complete system of proportional representation by a single transferable vote and plural constituencies. That is physically impossible as it is very intricate. We could not possibly do it even if we wanted to. Please keep in mind the tremendous difficulties of organizing an election where about 160-180 million voters are concerned. It is a colossal task. If we introduced P.R. that would make it absolutely impossible, both from the organizational point of view and that of the voter who will not understand its intricacies.

Countries that have had proposed P.R. have usually had unstable governments and hence there has been a great repulsion against it. I know you are not advocating P.R. but anyhow I am mentioning it.

The simplest way of dealing with this or any election is to have single-member constituencies. That was our original idea and that appears to be more or less the intention still. The only difficulty that comes in is in regard to scheduled castes and tribes and for that purpose it becomes necessary to have some two-member constituencies. This will affect a number of seats but far greater number will remain single-member. This arrangement was not thought of in connection with what might be called political minorities.

Three-member constituencies were considered by us and the difficulties in their way were prodigious: the area and the number of voters involved.

If this approach is agreed to, then the question of cumulative voting would only apply to scheduled castes seats. It might have some advantage but, on the whole, I think the disadvantages would outweigh these advantages. It would tend to keep up in some way the separation of scheduled castes which we wish to avoid as far as possible.

I do not know why you should be apprehensive of a single-member constituencies plus some double-member. The election is on such a vast scale with thousands of constituencies that no one can predict the result. What we are up against are the failures of democracy when we enter into

[1] *J.P. Papers* (NMML).

these large regions. Democracy originally was thought of in smaller terms and was presumably effective. I just do not know what our elections will lead us or the country to, but the simpler they are the better.

You seem to think that elections are decided by arithmetical means or by some mathematical conclusions. Surely this does not happen, when there are numerous candidates pulling in different directions. As a matter of fact it will be difficult for any party even to find all these candidates.

Yours affectionately,
Jawaharlal Nehru

APPENDIX 5

From Jawaharlal Nehru, 20 November 1950[1]

My dear Jayaprakash,

Your letter of the 17th has just reached me. I am not annoyed by its tone, but I am distressed at the lack of understanding that you have shown and I am more than distressed by the astonishing stupidity of some of the things that the leaders of the Nepali Congress have been responsible for. I can understand their making mistakes in a difficult situation, but to make mistakes which might well ruin their cause and which no person with a grain of intelligence should have done, is almost inexcusable. If they are dealing with an insurrection, they should behave as persons generally do who are engaged in this task.

I quite agree with you that the opportunity of securing freedom for Nepal has come and that the trump cards are there. When I see this opportunity being almost lost and every kind of bungling being done by amateur politicians, who know nothing about politics and less about insurrection, I have a right to be upset. It is not enough for a person to have good motives when he is in a responsible position. Young Koirala may be an excellent person, but his conception of what should be done and how is primitive in the extreme. The kind of demands he made on me staggered me.

Nothing can stop a revolution in Nepal, except the folly of those who are supporting it. The revolution is, I believe, an indigenous one and a large number of the people of Nepal sympathise with it. Most people in India also sympathise with it. Widespread propaganda is being carried on by our opponents abroad to show that this is just an example of India imperialism and that we have engineered all this. This obviously can do a great deal of harm to the whole movement. We cannot ignore external forces at work

[1]*J.N. Papers* (NMML).

against us. What Koirala suggested would have put an end to the idea of an indigenous movement and made it just an adventure of the Indian Government.

That is just what I am afraid of. Adventurist tactics in politics or warfare seldom succeed. Daring does succeed and risk may be taken, but adventurism is infantile.

Yours affectionately,
Jawaharlal

APPENDIX 6

From M.O. Mathai, 21 November 1950[1]

My dear Jayaprakashji,

I have your letter.

The Prime Minister referred your two letters addressed to him to the Chief Election Commissioner, who has carefully considered the points you have raised. I am sorry you have presumed that the Prime Minister did not give serious consideration to your communications.

The Uttar Pardesh Legislative Assembly consists of 430 seats. The *tentative* proposals of the U.P. Government are to create 143 two-member constituencies of which 90 will be constituencies in which a seat is to be reserved for the Scheduled Castes and the remaining 53 constituencies without any reservation. These 53 double-member constituencies are intended by the U.P. Government to ensure the return of some Muslims, if possible.

The Government of India decided in October last that the delimitation of constituencies is to proceed on the basis of single-member constituencies with such number of two-member constituencies as might be necessary for the reservation of seats for the Scheduled Castes and the Scheduled Tribes. The Chief Election Commissioner is proceeding on the basis that we will have only such number of two-member constituencies as are necessary for the reservation of seats for the Scheduled Castes and Scheduled Tribes.

As far as I know, the Prime Minister is entirely opposed to any two-member constituencies except where a seat is reserved for the Scheduled Castes or Tribes. The Chief Election Commissioner is informing the Uttar Pradesh Government accordingly.

The main point in your second letter is that you are opposed to distributive

[1]*J.P. Papers* (NMML).

voting even in the very limited number of two-member constituencies which it is proposed to create for the purpose of reservation of seats for Scheduled Castes and Scheduled Tribes, and you favour cumulative system of voting. The Chief Election Commissioner is definitely of the view that the cumulative system of voting will result in efforts to bring about communal representation in the legislatures which is against the spirit of the Constitution and, therefore, should be avoided.

Having carefully considered the points you have raised, neither the Chief Election Commissioner nor the Prime Minister agree with your contention in regard to the system of voting in the limited number of two-member constituencies. In any event, the question of cumulative or distributive voting will have to be finally decided by Parliament.

You will, no doubt, treat this letter as a purely personal one.

Yours sincerely,
(M.O. Mathai)

APPENDIX 7

From Jawaharlal Nehru, 31 March 1951[1]

My dear Jayaprakash,

I have received your letter of March 24th. I have carefully read it as well as the letter you wrote to Rafi Ahmed Kidwai dated February 8th, copy of which you have sent me.

I must confess to a feeling of distress and a complete inability to understand the view-point you have urged. I have not been directly connected with this matter of strike period pay. But it has come up before me on numerous occasions. Indeed, even before we came into Government, I was interested in the strike and I visited at least one strike centre and met the striking postmen. I think this was in Banaras, though I am not sure. I am mentioning this to indicate that I have been in touch with this matter right from the beginning, that is July 1946. I was not directly concerned with the negotiations at any period. But, because of my interest in the mater, I kept in touch. Right from the very beginning, it seemed to me that the demand for strike period pay was not justified. It was an abnormal demand and such demands, so far as I know, have been very rarely made. Therefore, at every stage where I came in, I indicated that the demand was not justifiable. That was the opinion of the then Members of Government as well as of all those who have had to deal with it later. I shall not go into the reasons for

[1] *Brahmanand Papers* (NMML).

this, as they have been placed before you on many previous occasions. On one occasion, you will remember coming to see me with some of the leaders of the Postmen's Union. Even then I explained this to you, I think, quite frankly and clearly. There has not been at any time in my mind or, to my knowledge, in anyone else's mind, any doubt about this point.

You refer to some statement being made by Rafi Ahmed Kidwai to the effect that some other way might be found, such as treating the period as leave period. It is quite possible that some such statement was made in the course of a conversation to you, as Rafi Ahmed was no doubt anxious to please you and find a way out. You also refer to various other statements made by Shri Mangaldas Pakvasa, Sardar Patel and Shri N.V. Gadgil. All these statements, according to your own account, were vague suggestions which might be explored. Oddly enough, our very desire to go as far as possible to meet your wishes has been turned round and is now used against us. At no time was there anything that could be construed as an assurance, much less a decision.

We have considered this matter on many occasions and we have felt honestly convinced that any direct or indirect way of paying strike period pay would not only be unjustified in itself but would have other rather serious consequences. I should have thought that you would appreciate the very earnest attempts we have made in this matter to meet you as far as possible and that you would understand, if you did not wholly agree, the reasons for our decisions. I am therefore all the more surprised and distressed at what you have written.

You call this a moral issue for yourself. It would be equally possible for me to say that is a moral issue for others concerned. Certainly it is a moral issue, in such a matter, to hold up the possibility of a fast to compel acceptance of something which has been so earnestly examined and rejected. I do not wish to speak as a member of Government, but I can hardly conceive of any Government being carried on, if its decisions were made in this way. You refer to a previous incident when you made a like suggestion in another matter. I remember that incident. We examined it very carefully and, largely on the merits, we decided more or less in accordance with your wishes. I am free to confess that decision was partly influenced at least by the fact that you felt strongly about it. Nevertheless the decision was chiefly on the merits. In the present case I see no merits at all and wrong consequences. I just do not see how we can upset a policy and a line of action which we have consistently adopted for over four years, more especially as I am convinced that that policy was a right one. If I went against my own positive judgement in this matter under these circumstances, I feel that I would be definitely guilty of a lack of integrity.

Much has happened during the last four years and both nationally and internationally we live in times of deep crisis. It may be, in your opinion, that we are ourselves partly responsible for the situation that we have to face. That does not lessen the crisis or the problems that confront us. We have to view everything, therefore, from this point of view. Whatever we might have decided three or four years ago, even if we chose to do so then, is far more difficult from every point of view now. If then we decided against something, much more must we adhere to that decision today. Anything else, it seems to me, would be a complete abandonment of our own judgement and responsibility.

I hope you will give serious thought to what I have written. I have not written this as Prime Minister, but as an old colleague of yours who has had and still has great affection for you.

Yours affectionately,
Jawaharlal Nehru

APPENDIX 8

From Jawaharlal Nehru, 21 April 1951[1]

My dear Jayaprakash,

I have your letter of April 18th.

As my views are not relevant, we can leave them out of consideration.

During all these discussions in the course of the last two years or so, frequent references have made to me. At no time did I gather that any kind of an assurance, except an assurance that the matter would be explored thoroughly to find a way out, was given. It may be that there was a misunderstanding in your mind. The least I could expect is that you should accept our word for it.

I am sorry I cannot understand on any principle where a fast comes in.

Regarding your letter of March 24th, all I can do is to refer it to the Ministries concerned. I entirely agree with you that labour is experiencing difficulties. I would very much like to alleviate them, if I had the power and the resources to do so. Unfortunately my capacity is limited.

Do you wish me to make an announcement now which might create false hopes and then give rise to misunderstanding such as in the case of the strike pay for the postmen?

I function to the best of my ability and capacity. I can do no more.

Yours affectionately,
Jawaharlal

[1]*Brahmanand Papers* (NMML).

APPENDIX 9

From Jawaharlal Nehru, 18 May 1951[1]

My dear Jayaprakash,

I have received your letter of the 16th May.

There is no question of my being annoyed. I have, I hope, passed that stage. But I think it is true, what you say, that I am completely unable to understand your point of view in this matter, as presumably you have been unable to understand my point of view. I have carefully gone through the correspondence with you on this subject naturally with a desire to understand and meet your viewpoint as far as I could. I have failed to do so.

I am sending a copy of your letter to Rafi Ahmed Kidwai.

Yours affectionately,
Jawaharlal

[1] *J.P. Papers* (NMML).

APPENDIX 10

From Rafi Ahmed Kidwai, 2 June 1951[1]

My dear Jayaprakashji,

Jawaharlalji had sent me a copy of your letter dated 16th May. Later on I also received a copy of the letter from you.

More than once we have discussed this question. I have tried to explain to you what I had undertaken to do in our meeting in February 1949. All I had promised was to explore the possibility of evolving a formula which may enable us to treat this strike period as leave with pay of those strikers whose leave was due. That there was no definite undertaking is borne out by what you wrote to me on 24.9.1949. In that letter you wrote "If you remember you had told me that you might be able to do something in that matter after three months or so." Further on, you had written "I had reported your assurance to the General Council and naturally the men were all expecting that after three months were over something in that direction would be done."

I have looked into the minutes of our meeting on 11th and 12th February, 1949. I find the following note in that minute "Pay for the strike period of

[1] *J.P. Papers* (NMML).

July-August 1948. H.M. would be prepared to discuss this question after three months."

As promised I got the matter looked into. It was not found practical to treat the strike period as leave with pay for:

Firstly it was very difficult to ascertain the period for which the leave was due of all the employees on strike.

Secondly a large proportion of the strikers were temporary employees and no leave was due to them. Even if it were possible to accept this suggestion it would have benefited a very small proportion of the employees.

I had, therefore, reluctantly to drop the proposal.

I am sorry if what I had promised to consider in February, 1949 was accepted by you as a definite undertaking. This misunderstanding, it seems, was the basis of your assurance to the employees that their demand has been met. I am sorry for the misunderstanding. The representatives of the Unions have been seeing me off and on and I do not think anyone who had direct talks with me is under any misapprehension. Everyone of them knows my attitude to the question of strike period. They also know what I had meant when I promised to explore the possibility of treating this period as leave period. I am sure the Secretary of your Union, Mr. Dalvi, will bear me out.

I am sure you have got the personal letters I wrote to you soon after the interview about this issue. Your decision to fast is very embarrassing. I would again urge you to reconsider the question.

Yours sincerely,
Rafi Ahmed

APPENDIX 11

From Sampurnanand, 18 June 1951[1]

Dear Jayaprakashji,

I am in receipt of your letter dated 9th instant. As you know, Municipal Boards are entirely autonomous as regards the employment and re-employment of teachers except in a very few cases in which a provision for appeal to the Government exists. The cases of these teachers and a few others who acted like them have been specially complicated by the fact that the strike in which they participated had nothing to do with Municipal

[1] *J.P. Papers* (NMML).

Boards. It was a dispute between District Boards and the teachers in their employ. There was no reason why municipal teachers should have gone out of their way to take part in this strike. Beyond telling the Boards that they are free to employ these men if they so choose a step which we have already taken the Government can do nothing in the matter.

I was concerned to learn from the papers that you have had a bad heart attack. It is not for me to advise you to go slow with your political work but I think I can claim the privilege of an old friend to ask you not to jeopardise your health. You will believe me that even some of those who differ from you in the political stand, look upon you as an asset to the nation.

Yours affectionately,
Sampurnanand

APPENDIX 12

We Build for Socialism: *The Platform* of the Socialist Party, 4 July 1951[1]

After four years of freedom, on the eve of the first General Elections, the Indian people, wiser by experience, are looking forward with hope and expectation to the course of history that they are called upon to shape.

For two hundred years India remained under the domination of a foreign power, and those were the years of economic ruin and social stagnation. While free nations progressed and prospered, while economic opportunities grew and social freedom unfolded in communities enjoying freedom, in India under British rule, economic decay deepened from year to year and social inequities gained in rigidity and weight. Manufactures declined, agriculture was impoverished, employment shrunk and wealth was sucked up by a small fraction in the country and by the rulers overseas. The ancient inequities in India were deliberately perpetuated by the alien power to bolster up privileged classes, dependent upon the goodwill of the rulers for the preservation of their special advantages. Economic and social life became lopsided.

When the Indian people fought for freedom, it was not merely out of the desire to put an end to foreign domination but to release the freedom impulse to race through every sphere of life. When the peasant and the worker, the unemployed and the underprivileged, rallied round the banner of freedom, with enthusiasm and devotion, he had before him a vision of a new India

[1]Adopted by the National General Council of the Socialist Party, Ranchi, 4 July 1951.

wherein the removal of the British from the land was linked with the opening of avenues of opportunities and turning of the sod of social transformation. It was this hope of new life, of new voyages and new achievements, that stirred our people to deeds of matchless heroism.

Barren Record

The events of the past four years have blighted these hopes and crushed the green shoots of spontaneous efforts. The frustration and apathy in the land can be traced directly to the widening disparity between expectations and meagre achievements.

In the four years of freedom, peasants' hunger for land remains unappeased, the workers' yearning for a new status in industry remains unrealized, production falls, employment shrinks and prices soar. Food rations dwindle and the spectre of famine stalks the land. Every essential of life, such as cloth, continues to be in short supply, and men's quest for shelter has proved elusive. The mounting prices further depress the already low standard of life of persons with fixed income; insecurity grows. The technician, the small industrialist, the worker, the shopkeeper, the clerk, the teacher, finds himself as forgotten as before. Springs of popular enthusiasm have dried up and the Government have been compelled to fall back upon the antiquated social order and its established proprieties. The locusts of despair have ravaged the harvest of freedom.

The Socialist Party believes that freedom can become meaningful to our people only when its pulsating impulse is permitted to flow through every limb of society. Freedom to the vast majority of people must mean not merely rice and roof, but those economic and social changes that can evoke the ardour and enthusiasm needed to reconstruct this ancient land. The efforts at economic amelioration have failed because of the Congress Government's stubborn allegiance to privileged interests: vested rights remain inviolate, while the needs and desires of the people wilt and wither. The vast disparities in economic rewards not merely persist but under the impact of war and post-war economy have widened, making the rich richer, and the rest poorer. The fiscal and financial policies of the Congress Government have added to the age-old burdens on the bent backs of the people.

The measures for social emancipation have been likewise timid and superficial. Certain disabilities of the scheduled castes have been legally proscribed, but the economic and social suppression of the scheduled castes and scheduled tribes remains as before. Not merely landlordism flourishes, but rural serfdom persists. The shackles of centuries remain rivetted.

The sterile moves towards the abolition of zamindari, the oscillations between control and decontrol, the growing regression in taxation, the re-emergence of the traditional hegemony of the employers over employees, merely underline the Congress Government's fear of fundamental change in the socio-economic structure of the land. This hesitation and fear have resulted in the erosion of all reforming zeal in the Congress. In four years of power the Congress has been metamorphosed into a Conservative Party.

The apologists of the Congress claim credit for the achievements and put the blame for the failures on the inimical circumstances, internal and external. The disruptive aftermath of war, the tragic consequences of partition, the insecurity in the world all round are problems not peculiar to India. Other lands have been plagued with similar difficulties, but in many of them bold governments gifted with vision have grappled with difficulties and have tunnelled their way to the sun-lit heights of achievements. The failure of the Congress is self-invited.

Could the Socialists have managed the affairs of the country better during the years of turmoil and privation? Our answer is unhesitatingly in the affirmative.

But this is of the past. Let us look to the future.

Structural Changes

The Socialist Party believes that the continuing national deterioration of the past four years of freedom can be checked and the upward journey towards progress and prosperity begun; that the answers to the immediate problems of food, clothing and shelter can be found; and that a new India of free and equal and happy citizens can be created. But the fulfilment of these tasks would require boldness, vision, determination. The Socialist Party desires the people to understand that no piecemeal solution of their problems is possible; and that even their essential needs cannot be adequately fulfilled unless basic structural changes are made in the social and economic organization. We wish further earnestly to warn the people against promises of plenty to be realized without the surgery of social revolution. Let every one understand that as long as the existing social order, based on exploitation, inequality and privilege lasts, poverty cannot be banished, nor the productive energies of the nation fully mobilised, nor that psychological climate created in which nations are made. The proposals herein advanced are to be viewed and understood in this context.

Food and Agrarian Reforms

The most pressing national problem is that of food. The solution of this problem is linked up with the reorganization of our entire agrarian economy and of the village. In this sphere, more than any other, short-range schemes must form part of a well-planned, far-reaching, coordinated agrarian reform and development.

There has been no awareness of this over-riding principle in the food policy of the Congress Government. Indeed there has been no policy at all, but merely a number of haphazard schemes and day-to-day improvisation. All along, the mistake was made of identifying the food problem with that of making up the deficit; whereas, the essence of the problem was, and is, how to make the best use of, and produce the utmost from, our land. The ill-conceived plans of the Government mostly failed, at great cost to the country, and haphazard imports proved to be the only means of salvation for the people. In the past four years five hundred crores were spent on imports and not more than fifty on irrigation works intended to yield immediate results. While millions of acres of waste lands remained untouched, appeals were issued to grow food in flower pots and on house-tops! Grand river-training schemes were planned without regard to the needs, resources and future development of the country. The necessary agrarian reforms were only toyed with. Technological problems remained mere topics for learned discourse. Usury was attempted to be controlled without providing for other means of credit. Confusion reigned in the sphere of price fixation and controls. Procurement and distribution became monuments of administrative ineptitude.

The Socialist Party will approach these problems from many sides: technological, administrative, that of agrarian reform.

Land Volunteers and Food Army

The yield per acre of the land must be raised and waste lands brought under cultivation. To do the first, bands of land volunteers (*bhumi sevak*) will be raised in the village to dig wells, tanks, compost pits, drain water-logged areas, construct bunds, fences, etc. The State would assist these voluntary *bhumi sevaks* with training and necessary equipment. They will become the spearhead of technological innovations. To reclaim waste lands, the extent of which is estimated to be over 130 million acres, the State will raise and equip a Food Army (*Anna Sena*) from the landless and poor of the village. This Army will drain marshes, dig canals, cut jungles and also be the main coloniser of the lands so reclaimed. In the Land Volunteer Corps and the Food Army, the rural youth will find hope and adventure, work and comradeship. Together they will promote cooperation and social education and create the village of the future. The agrarian reforms herein advocated will provide the psychological motive force needed to enthuse and drive the youth to this grand creative effort.

Planning for Food

Crop planning, coordinated price fixation, integrated controls, procurement through village panchayats, distribution through fair price shops and co-operatives, will further induce production of food and other primary commodities.

Redistribution of Land

Abolition of zamindari can be no more than the first step in agrarian reform, affecting only one-third of the country. Even this first step, as taken by the Congress, has been false and halting. Because of their anxiety to respect property rights and claims, the Congress Governments have provided for compensation to zamindars. This has made the abolition of zamindari almost meaningless in practice. Financially the proposition is ruinous. Even in equity the zamindars have no right to huge unearned incomes, the title to which is dubious. The Socialists therefore propose to abolish zamindari without compensation, but providing for rehabilitation grant to the petty zamindars.

Abolition of zamindari will not fully solve the problem of land, nor establish social justice in the village, nor create the necessary incentive for production and creative effort, as far as millions of cultivators who have no secured rights in their tillage are concerned. So all cultivators will be guaranteed security of tenure and protection against ejectment.

In the zamindari areas, even after abolition of zamindari, there will be wide disparities in proprietorship of land. There will be a handful of peasant proprietors who will possess hundreds and thousands of acres. There will be medium and poor peasants and landless crop-sharers and tenants-at-will. In the ryotwari areas also, the same picture would prevail. The Socialist Party, intent on establishing social justice and working towards economic equality and anxious to release the pent-up energies of millions of our primary producers, will redistribute land so as to achieve these ends. No peasant family will be allowed to possess land more than three times the size of an economic holding, or roughly 30 acres of land of average productivity, and no one who does not personally participate in the processes of cultivation would be allowed to possess land. The land will belong to the tiller and intermediaries between him and the State will be abolished.

Proprietors of land possessing more than 30 acres will receive for lands over that limit, but only up to a maximum holding of 100 acres, an annuity for ten years calculated on the basis of fair rent. Efforts would be made to ensure as soon as possible that no cultivating family has less than an economic holding, that is, an area of land that would afford a reasonable standard of living. Redistribution of land will be accompanied with consolidation of fragmented holdings.

Cooperation

In spite of the reforms above advocated, many of the holdings will remain uneconomic. The productivity of such holdings will remain low because the tiller cannot afford the means of improvement. By offering inducements and incentives of assistance, the peasants with such holdings will be invited to form cooperatives. Pooling of resources and implements may precede pooling of lands.

Peasants with economic and larger holdings too will be encouraged to form multi-purpose cooperatives for marketing, irrigation, and the supply of better seeds, manure, etc., and, as far as possible, also for joint farming. Cooperation would be the key-note of the entire village economy. Thereby, both the productivity of land and peasant incomes would rise.

Collective farms will be organized on lands reclaimed through State efforts and the Food Army. Here landless labourers will find work and home and land.

Agricultural Labour

The problem of agricultural labour is mainly the problem of under-employment. Attempts will be made to raise double crops wherever possible through irrigation and other aids. This would partially reduce the seasonal character of agricultural employment. Processing industries like cotton ginning and pressing and oil extraction will provide fresh avenues of employment. Villages will not be just agricultural communities. Rural industries and decentralised processes even of large-scale industries will be located in villages. Certain manufacturing lines may be reserved for rural artisans where large-scale industries will not be allowed to compete. Public works like building and maintenance of roads and construction of minor irrigation will provide work to agricultural labourers. Their home-steads will be protected by law.

Constant efforts will be made to so reorganize the economy and social relations as to bring the income of the agricultural worker to the National Minimum Wage.

Organization of agricultural labour will be encouraged and their rights and interests will be protected by law.

Agrestic Serfdom

A still more actue problem is that of serfdom. Mere legislation or agreement among parties, though important, are not enough. These serfs will be freed from their burden of debt, which is usually the cause of their serfdom, and given independent means of livelihood. Among other things, they will be settled on the lands taken over according to the above programme of abolition of zamindari and absentee landlordism. Maintenance of even a vestige of serfdom will be made a penal offence.

State and Agriculture

The State will have to help the tiller in solving many of the difficulties that face him today. These would include provision of better manure, seeds implements, better marketing facilities, cheaper finance, technical assistance and research centres. The State will do this through cooperative banks, grain banks, warehouses, model farms and, above all, by the administrative reorganization discussed below.

The State will be responsible for reclamation of cultivable waste lands, prevention of soil erosion and development of irrigation. Here, Land Volunteers and the Food Army will play a vital role, canalising individual efforts into communal endeavour.

The State will be responsible for the maintenance of price parities between agriculture and industry so as to prevent exploitation of rural areas by urban interests.

Rights in Land

All this will spell a profound revolution in the concept of ownership of land. The determination of the size of holding will entail restriction on the right of alienation. The abolition of landlordism would mean curtailment of the right of subletting. Crop-planning would restrict the right to sow any crop one likes. Organized marketing would curtail the right of disposal of produce. But these curtailments, far from depressing the peasant, would help pull him out of his existing morass of difficulties, because the concept of rights of ownership will include the community's responsibility to the tiller. No longer will the peasant plough his lonely furrow; the chaff of theoretical advantages—rarely enjoyed by the tiller—will go, but the grain of practical benefits will grow.

Administrative Measures

The entire State machinery will have to be overhauled if the State is to discharge the new functions effectively. Today, agricultural problems are looked after by various departments of the Government under different Ministries. Naturally, there is very little coordination in their functioning. This only bewilders the peasant instead of helping him. Again, if the State were to function in a democratic way, it is imperative that as large a number of peasants as possible are associated with the administrative machinery. This necessitates the reorganization of agricultural administration on the basis of the four-pillar State. The principle behind this concept is that the commonality of the State is to be so organized and sovereign power so diffused that each little community in it lives the way of life it chooses. It will mean that the village panchayats will have pivotal place in the new set-up. Above the panchayats there will be three layers of administrative bodies: Regional, State, Union.

Village Panchayats

The panchayats will be elected on the basis of universal suffrage by a village or a group of villages.

They will tabulate the resources of the villages and assess their productive potential. They will prepare a crop plan for their village and send it to the higher organs of the Planning Commission. Through constant references pro and forth, a thorough exchange of information and ideas between the different echelons of planning, the plan will be finalised. Once the schedule is fixed the village panchayat will see that the targets are realized. They may demand necessary facilities for the purpose from the Land Commission. The village panchayats will fix appropriate rewards for those who exceed the targets fixed. They will be responsible for the collection of State revenue and other dues, and procurement of agricultural produce, the quota of which will be fixed by the Land Commission after consulting the village panchayats. The peasant will be dealt with directly and individually by the village panchayat; all outside contacts will be through the panchayat alone.

It would be the duty and privilege of village panchayats to represent the community in all matters affecting village polity and economy. They would be the main local agency for execution of various programmes of the Government affecting vitally the welfare of villagers, and would represent the Government in all activities in the village. They must have control over village sites, charitable and other communal properties.

Besides these *representative functions* they can also perform *regulation functions* such as supervision of elementary schools, encouraging sports and other extra curricular activities, looking after the village dispensary and maternity and child welfare centre, ensuring non-pollution of drinking water, removal of encroachments and keeping roads clean. Lastly, they may perform such *service functions* as rural welfare work and promotion of cultural activities.

The village panchayat is thus the tap-root of the wide branching tree of freedom.

Regional Land Commission

Over the village panchayats there would be Regional Land Commissions. They will coordinate the crop plans and agricultural resources in their region. They will be in charge of agricultural banking and would control and co-ordinate all rural credit institutions in their area. They will also be responsible for running model farms for the help and guidance of the villagers. They would arrange for technical help to the villagers as demanded by the village panchayats. This commission will be composed of representatives of village panchayats, cooperative agencies, the State Government, and agricultural experts.

State Land Commission

Over the Regional Commissions there will be a State Land Commission in each State. This will be in charge of planning, development and management of the rural economy and will look after such problems as land revenue, irrigation, agriculture, cottage industry, cooperative—both credit and multi-purpose crop-planning on provincial level and allied problems.

The Commission will be an autonomous statutory body. It will be composed of the representatives of Regional Commissions, cooperative agencies, the State Government and agricultural experts.

Union Land Commission

The Union Land Commission will be in charge of such items as agricultural planning on all-India basis, movement of crops, multipurpose development projects including river training and flood control. It will fix quotas for export and import of agricultural produce, import of agricultural equipments, will regulate in a general way the price of agricultural produce and allot scarce resources like chemical fertilisers.

Model Farms

Model farms will be maintained at Government expense. They will work as minor research and demonstration centres. Agricultural schools may be attached to some of these centres, as also museums. They will also serve as centres of medical relief-mobile medical vans radiating from them to the surrounding area. The model farm will not merely be an example, a lone star in the night, but a teacher that leads and inspires, a friend that understands and helps. Wherever possible, these farms will also supply pure water and electricity to the surrounding area.

New Village

When land is distributed among the tillers, when every tiller is an owner of land and every owner tills for livelihood, when landless labourers secure justice and rehabilitation, a new relationship will spring up in the village.

Administrative changes, wherein a pivotal position is assigned to democratically functioning village panchayats, will abolish the distance that has separated and estranged the peasant from Authority. The community of free and equal men will then be in a mood to labour cooperatively to better the village. Work will cease to be irksome toil and become the proud badge of active citizenship. The sap of self-assurance will flow again through the tree of life.

Forests

Forests are very important from the point of view of the development of our economy. They supply valuable materials, prevent erosion of land and help the rainfall. During the war, deforestation had assumed alarming proportions. The policy now needs to be changed. Afforestation should therefore have a high priority in the development schemes.

The existing forest laws create great inconvenience to the villagers in the forest area. They have practically to work under the dictation of the Forest Department. Their wages are very low and the contractors exploit these poor foresters. These laws should therefore be changed. And the villagers in the Forest Area should be given the maximum share of the benefit of forest produce. Their cooperation should be encouraged and model villages should be developed in these areas.

Industry

Once agriculture is properly organized through distribution of lands and on the basis of the village as a unit forming part of the lager planned economy, the demand for industrial goods will increase many-fold. Even today, industry is not in a position to satisfy the demands of the people. Production figures are almost at a standstill. Big industry has a variety of arguments to explain away this dereliction of duty to the community. The threat of nationalisation was the first obstacle listed in their long series of woes. Government beat a hasty retreat. Then came the cry of recalcitrant labour. It was proved that by and large industrial labour had performed its task loyally. The man-hours lost due to strikes continuously decreased and yet production did not show an upward trend. Then came the plea of lack of incentives. Tax structures were revised to suit their demands. Controls were relaxed. The transport system was improved. And yet production figures refused to rise. The cry for essential commodities continued in the market unabated. Now has come the lack of capital to be saved in industrial sector. The value of rupee is the Hamlet in the tragedy. Cornering of raw materials by the United States is shown as responsible for the incapacity of big industry to deliver their goods. It is a safe bet that even if all the demands of the Big

Business were satisfied production will remain as it is. The next big step in the development of our productive powers can only come through the capacity of taking big risks, the capacity for organization on a grand scale. Big industry, controlled by a handful of Managing Agents lording over our economy and industry as barons of old, is incapable of all this.

We have therefore to turn our face back from Big Business and turn it towards the technician, the scientist, the workers, the small entrepreneur, better able to deliver goods than the captains of industry who cling more to the anchors of security and profit than the sail of adventure.

This requires that industry should be divided into three sectors (a) the nationalised sector (b) the medium-scale private secotor and (c) the small-scale cooperative sector.

Socialisation

The community will have to take the responsibility of running certain industries on themselves, for a variety of reasons.

Lack of adequate capital is the chief problem of industry. Private savings have failed to supply the necessary capital. We have therefore to depend on institutional savings for our requirements. Credit institutions thus form the main source of capital accumulation and whosoever controls these determine the pattern of economic development. Similarly, insurance is helpful in ensuring saving and consequent capital formation. All these institutions therefore must be nationalised.

Textiles, sugar and cement form the bulk of the goods demanded by the common man. There is no immediate possibility of large-scale extension in these industries. The existing units have to be modernised as far as possible and run on the most efficient lines, serving the needs of the people. Private enterprise, as recurrent muddles in production and prices testify, has failed signally. The industries therefore have to be taken charge of by the community.

There is a fair amount of agreement on the necessity for nationalisation of key industries like iron and steel, electric power and heavy chemicals.

Mines and plantations are mostly in foreign hands and the necessity for exploiting these for the good of the country demands that they should be taken over by the community. They also provide some of the staples of export and as such need to be in the hands of the community.

To achieve coordinated development of transport, light railways will be nationalised. As highway motor transport forms an ancillary to railways, it will have to be State-owned and managed.

Finance is deemed to be the main obstacle in schemes of nationalisation. But measures of capital levy, suggested later, will make our task comparatively easy. They will tansfer to the State substantial share in the ownership of industries and real property. In these cases compensation will only be book entries. The small investor, protected from the operation of capital levy, will receive full compensation for his investments through fixed interest-bearing Government Bonds.

Private Sector

The rest of the industry can be left to small entrepreneurs who have shown great capacity for organization and taken risks even in these uncertain times. If the State provides them with additional capital needed, technical know-how and other requisite facilities, they can be of great use to the community in the development of our economy. The sphere of private initiative and enterprise, though limited, will be well defined and freed from erratic interference. The small entrepreneur will be free to experiment, explore and expand. He will be helped by the State, and not frustrated at every turn, as he is today by the barons of industry and finance.

The small-scale industry must receive devoted attention of the State. In a country rich in manpower and short of capital, small-scale industires must occupy a place of pride. The Government will not merely reserve certain lines of manufacture for them, not only give protection and help, but develop, through the mobilisation of world's best talents, a technique of production suited to small manufacture. New tools, simple yet productive, will be fabricated and the technological level will be slowly raised to avoid dislocation and ensure steady enrichment. This will also reduce the strain and augment the output of labour. The small-scale manufacturers will not only look after some of the essential needs of the community, but will satisfy the hunger for beauty and respect the sturdy independence of our race. The quest of the spirit may continue undisturbed by the side of silkworm and the loom, as in the days of Kabir.

Organization of Industry

Organization is the next important problem. We will have to devise patterns appropriate to the tasks assigned to industry. We will also have to determine at what level—Union, State or lower—the different concerns and services will be owned and managed.

Nationalised industry can best be run by public corporations, autonomous as far as the detailed policy is concerned but subject to the overall control of the State in general matters of policy. For every industry in different regions there shall be separate corporations competing with each other in trying out new processes and varieties of output. This will help to ensure all the advantages of large-scale production, while the danger of monopoly, centralisation and bureaucratisation will be avoided. Production will not be wholly at the mercy of unpredictable market forces and yet the consumers will be recording their choice. It will lead to greater efficiency, experimenting with new ideas and continuous development of technology. The technicians, supervisers and organizers will come into their own. Their talents will find full scope and will suitably be rewarded through increase in emoluments, promotions and State honours.

Municipal enterprises will be another mode of managing the nationalised sector. All local public utility services like electricity, water, gas, theatres, will be under the control of local bodies.

The private sector will have to be completely reorganized and a new concept of ownership developed. The State will help this sector through credit facilities, better technical advice and service, better tools and machinery and better processed raw materials.

The State will however exercise control through rules regarding location of industry; through licensing whereby certain conditions of working of industry will be prescribed and through capital control. Capital control will operate only in cases of concerns above three lakhs. Any entrepreneur wishing to try new experiments shall be permitted to do so provided his experiments do not cost him, and through him the community, more than three lakhs, and he does not draw upon the stock of scarce resources without the permission of the appropriate authorities.

Producers' Cooperatives

The State will encourage producers' cooperatives both in the private and the small scale sector. This will be useful in solving to a certain extent the problems created by inadequate capital, abundant manpower and low productivity. The cooperatives will help in raising productivity by the introduction of small machines without displacing labour. The State will assist them by providing special credit and marketing facilities, development of suitable technology, training of organizational and technical personnel and providing education for a cooperative life.

Workers' Control

The workers' place in the community will be revolutionised. They will be treated as honoured partners in a great enterprise. They will be taken into confidence regarding the conduct of the industry. Not only information will be shared and experience pooled but every facility given to the worker and the technician to receive training, to improve his abilities and add to his knowledge.

In the nationalised sector they will have representation on Corporations, and, through works councils and production committees, workers' co-operation will be enlisted in the planning of the enterprise. Production over target, collectively or individually, will mean economic rewards and social esteem.

In private sectors, as far as proprietary establishments are concerned, workers' control will consist in *double audit*, i.e. a system in which two auditors will be appointed, one by management, the other by workers. Workers will thus be able to know the exact financial position of the concern. They will also have the right of safeguarding their interests through trade union action. The management of such concerns will remain the responsibility of the proprietors.

As for the enterprise run by a joint stock company, workers' participation in management will be compulsory. This is on the principle that workers are as much concerned in the property of the enterprise as shareholders and if shareholders are delegating their responsibility to a board of diectors the workers must have representation on the same. The managing agency system will of course be abolished. Company Law will be suitably amended to protect the rights of shareholders and workers.

Social Security

Even after endowing workers with a share in the managment some insecurity may remain even under a planned and controlled economy. Rationalisation need not necessarily mean unemployment if the industry is in an expanding phase. Yet frictional unemployment cannot be avoided. Sickness and old age are bound to create hardship to the unsecured worker. The dividend of the worker will remain low till the bowl is made larger through increased productivity and ladling out of a larger share is made possible. All these make it incumbent upon the State to assume the responsibility of social security.

Those injured while on duty will be paid adequate compensation which would make necessary medical aid possible and enable him to maintain himself. Sickness insurance and maternity benefit likewise must be sufficient both for medical care and for maintenance. Similarly, the worker with years of hard labour behind him must be freed from anxieties in his old age. Old age pension will have to be granted to him for the purpose. Frictional and other unemployment has to be provided for by unemployment insurance.

As for the finances required, workmen's compensation will be a charge on industry. It is a part of the foreseeable risk which all industry must bear. Unemployment due to changeover or nationalisation has to be proved for either by industry or by the State.

Sickness insurance, maternity benefit and old age pension funds will be contributed to by the State, the employer and the worker.

Free Trade Unionism

The Socialist Party is anxious to give workers a share in the management of industry. That responsibility can be undertaken by the workers, their voice can gain full strength, only when every worker is a union member. The Socialist Party therefore advocates *union-shop*—every worker a union member. No worker may weaken the organization by remaining out of it. The unions will be organized National Industry-wise, with locals in every industrial establishment and branches in every region. Legal safeguards will be provided to preserve fullest internal democracy.

The unions will be wholly autonomous, responsible to their members alone. The unions will be organs of collective bargaining and they will be associated with organization of social security, of technical and general education of workers, of planning production and of participating in management. Workers' right to strike will remain inviolate.

Development of Industry

It will be the duty of the State to plan for the development of industry: A Planning Commission representing all interests concerned will have to work continuously for this gigantic task. But such a centralised machinery will neither be efficient nor desirable for controlling the destiny of 350 million people scattered over a vast area. It will therefore be necessary to build up the planning machinery from bottom upwards.

At the bottom we have village panchayats, public corporation, local bodies, cooperatives and the associations of small manufacturers and wrokers and of handicraftsmen, state trading corporations and associations of traders. Each of these bodies will prepare inventories of the resources at their command, assess productive capacity of these resources, list added facilities needed for extra productivity and the goods that they expect to get for their produce. These will be scrutinised and reconciled by the Planning Commissions at the State level. These plans will then be submitted to the Union Planning Commission for final approval and necessary action. The primary bodies enumerated above will be responsible to carry out the assignments given to them once the Plan is finalised.

State Facilities for Enterprise

When the State takes all these powers in its hand it must in its turn undertake the responsibility of finding facilities for different sectors of industry:

constitution of working parties and development councils, establishing and aiding fundamental research in the universities and State-aided institutions, training of scientists and technicians, organizing research in applied sciences and human relations, establishment of the Institute of Management and Production Efficiency Service, the Council of Industrial Designs, will be among the contributions of the State. Small manufactures can be helped by providing the manufacturers with buildings, general purpose machinery, industrial power on rent and even finance in suitable cases. The handicrafts can be helped by reserving certain lines exclusively for them; by encouraging research, by establishing workshops and training centres and by providing marketing facilities.

State intiative will thus break the stalemate in industry. The commanding heights will be occupied by State enterprise, but the rest of the terrain will be left free to individual initiative and enterprise. There too the fostering aid of the State will be available. What is not nationalised will be nurtured with State aid.

Trade

EXTERNAL

Organization of trade is one of the pressing problems facing the country. Black-marketing, hoarding and speculation are rampant today, exerting inflationary pressure on prices. Almost all the savings go into trade and hoarding, creating artificial scarcity. Essential commodities are exported and luxury goods are imported to bloat the profits of Big Business. Indian manufacture is acquiring a questionable reputation of never conforming to specifications. All this will have to be changed. All the requirements of nationalised sector of industry like capital goods and industrial raw materials will be imported by the State. Similarly, all the products of nationalised industry will be exported by the State. Scarce capital goods and industrial raw materials will be imported by the State and allotted to different industries. Export of important raw materials like jute and cotton will be through the State. Foreign capital will be imported solely by the Government.

For this purpose a State Trading Corporation with autonomous powers, subject to the overall control of the Government on general policy, will be set up. This Corporation will have to define priorities for import and direction of export.

The rest of the lines in trade will be in private hands. State control, here, will consist of exchange control, stipulation of standards and specifications and reserving a part of production for internal consumption.

The State in its turn will help the trade by establishing warehouses and supplying trade intelligence.

INTERNAL

As for internal trade, all requirements of nationalised industry will be procured through State Trading Agencies. Similarly the wholesable distribution of the products of nationalised industry will be through State Agencies.

Village produce will be disposed of through multipurpose cooperatives. They will also buy the requirements of the village on wholesale basis from urban areas.

The rest of the trade will be in private hands.

Retail trade in scarce essential goods will be through State Agencies.

Consumers' Control

It may be asked if it is desirable to concentrate so much power in the hands of the State when the performance of our State in this field is disappointing resulting only in hardships to the people.

The question is legitimate and the answer simple. The controls envisaged in this scheme are fundamentally different from the controls that are exercised today.

Present controls are partial and therefore ineffective. They concentrate power in the hands of bureaucracy without reposing corresponding responsibility. Corruption and bribery are not seriously dealt with. Consumers are nowhere associated with the control machinery.

The controls as envisaged by us are well-integrated. They start right from raw material and captial goods and go on till the wares are in the hands of the consumers. At every stage democratic check is provided. Workers and consumers will be associated at every stage of production and distribution.

In nationalised sector consumers can be associated with the corporation in advisory or representative capacity. Distribution of its product will be through State Trading Corporations where again the consumers can be associated. This will make consumers' choice effective. Multipurpose cooperatives will be in charge of wholesale trade in rural areas. In the private sector the State has the right to take over any concern which is not run efficiently.

Housing

Housing presents a serious problem both in rural and urban areas.

In rural areas, the reorganization of agriculture, described earlier, will help to build new houses of rammed earth and other material locally available.

In urban areas, the shortage of living accommodation will be overcome by providing facilities to Local Bodies to build houses for lower income groups. Cooperative housing societies, enjoying facilities of credit and capital from the State, will be encouraged. Not merely house-rent but the price of house sites will be controlled. To overcome over-crowding in cities priority will be given to temporary houses that can be built from local materials with local or even voluntary labour.

Public Finance

Nearly a tenth of our National Income of Rs. 8,700 crores goes into the public exchequer as revenues of the Union and State Governments. The Congress Raj has accentuated the tendency of increasing the Union revenues at the expense of State revenues, the proportion of the two having changed, in the past few years, from 43: 57 to 59: 41. This change fosters centralisation and strengthens bureaucracy. Likewise, there has been a tendency for indirect taxes to grow in the past few years and the ratio of direct to indirect taxes has falled from 34: 56 to 32: 58. This development makes taxation regressive and adds burdens on the poor in preference to the rich. Bulk of the revenues are used for maintenance of law and order, only a fraction is used for developing the economy and furthering the welfare of the people.

The Socialist Party, with its adherence to functional democracy and the four-pillar State, favours the re-organization of public finance so as to leave increasing resources with organs of administration closet to the people. Measures of economic equality, including capital levy, and nationalistion of a significant sector of economy, will basically change the character of public finance. Public expenditure will seek more to augment production and irrigate national economy than merely maintain law and order. Expenditure that augments wealth and furthers welfare robs taxation of its irksomeness.

Economic Equality

In a poor country like India whose abundance mainly lies in her man-power, production can grow only through the devoted cooperation of the people. Here, more than elsewhere, labour is the source of wealth.

The stagnation of centuries has built up in India groups and classes of men enjoying great privileges and thus accentuating inequalities. The contrast between dire poverty of the many and resplendent luxury of the few has escaped no observer.

Under the Congress Government this contrast has remained as glaring as before.

The hereditary privileges of the princes have been reduced up to a point, but the munificent *saliyanas* given to them, the failure to sequester their vast "personal" fortunes and the institution of the new order of Rajpramukhs and Uparajpramukhs have retained with the princes substantial privileges.

The Socialist Party consideres such hereditary privileges to be inconsistent with the democratic way of life chosen by the free people of India and it would therefore permit princes to function only as ordinary citizens; their *saliyanas* must lapse forthwith to the State, their incursion in administration as Rajpramukhs and Uparajpramukhs must end. Their private fortunes would be dealt with like the fortunes of other citizens, that is subject to the laws of the land.

The abolition of zamindari in all forms and the redistribution of lands would put an end to the fortunes of hereditary landowners and abolish inequalities in the countryside.

The two recognized means of narrowing inequalities are: (1) measures of public finance that reduce through graduated income-tax, super-tax, excess profits tax, capital gains tax and death duties, the expendable margin of large incomes and divert the difference to the State exchequer and (2) expenditure by the State on social services that improve the economic and social stauts of persons of small means.

Both these measures will be used by the Socialist Party to bring all incomes within the range of the floor of Rs. 100/- a month and the ceiling of Rs. 1,000/- a month. As production grows and nation's wealth expands the floor and the ceiling will rise.

These measures affect only income. Persons with inherited wealth can circumvent them by "living on their capital". Conspicuous consumption would continue, extra amenities would be received not by those who earn big incomes but by those who enjoy, through the accident of birth, large *unearned* incomes. A premium on unearned income is patently unjust.

To correct the above state of affairs, a capital levy will be necessary. Such a levy, affecting a few, would effectively curtail privilege and ensure economic equality.

The capital levy may be instituted on the following basis:

On property up to	Rs. 5,00,000 no levy
On the next	Rs. 5,00,000 levy of 20 p.c.
On the next	Rs. 15,00,000 levy of 50 p.c.
On the next	Rs. 75,00,000 levy of 80 p.c.
On property above	Rs. 1,00,00,000 levy of 90 p.c.

Once the tall and tapering peaks of property are removed, social topography will assume acceptable form. Social progress will then flow from a healthy economy uncursed by the corruption and corrosion of gross inequalities.

Social Mobility

Castes have stratified Indian society. There are groups of men who enjoy hereditary privileges and there are castes that are hereditarily under-privileged and suppressed. Freedom must mean the tearing down of these tradition barriers, it must mean free mobility for talent.

The Socialist Party offers the following programme of social mobility:

The cultivable waste lands and reclaimed lands will be made available to the scheduled castes and scheduled tribes for settlement. As owners of land they will be clothed with new social esteem.

Adequate communications will be built to link tribal areas with the rest of the country. This will facilitate the free mobility of the tribal people.

A vast programme of education costing Rs. 100 crores over a period of ten years, providing educational opportunities to the scheduled castes and tribes, will help to remove the cultural and educational lag between the advanced and backward castes. It will also remove the barriers confining them to hereditary occupations.

In public services place will be reserved for scheduled castes and tribes, at least in proportion to their population.

Wherever the tribes live in a distinct region, administrative autonomy will be given to it and efforts will be made to preserve the democratic pattern of their life and fit it into the wider national life.

The reorganization of society on cooperative basis through villages panchayats, industrial corporations and consumers' associations will narrow the social distance between man and man. These organizations will be expected to discover talents in their ranks and give them facilities for development. Talent, wherever found, will be nurtured by the State and given opportunities of advancement commensurate with its aptitude and experience.

The State by ensuring economic development and providing social security, the panchayats, trade unions and cooperatives by providing community life, will render obsolete the few socially significant functions of castes. An expanding society is a non-exclusive society.

The prevailing standard and values based on man's birth and his bank balance will yield place, under Socialist reorganization, to new norms and ideals. Work will become a badge of pride, idleness a crime. Men will be judged and esteemed for their aptitudes and achievements and not for inherited blood or wealth. In a free and equal society, organized democratically, private vices will cease to be public virtues.

Women

Any reorganization of society that seeks to release the social urges of its various sections must take into consideration the social and economic disabilities affecting women. Old concepts and customs have relegated women to a dependent and secondary place in society. This should go and they must have a status of equality and independence.

No arrangement of economic equality can be complete without a recognition of the economic worth of her work in the home and outside. The outmoded and unjustified idea that the housewife makes no economic contribution to the wealth of the nation will be combated. As a wage-earner she will be assured of an equal status, and guaranteed equal pay for equal work.

Her physical handicaps that impose certain restraints on her freedom will be compensated for by a programme of reservation of places in professions, such as teaching and nursing.

A civil code granting equal rights to women will be framed. Special educational facilities will be provided for women in the shape of scholarships and hostel accommodation. In brief, women will be assured a life which is wider in scope, fuller in opportunity and rich in content.

Minorities

The Socialist Party wishes to forge, not in theory but in living reality, an all-governing national unity.

At the same time, the Socialist Party recognizes the need of treating with consideration the culture, traditions and special interests of the minorities. It guarantees full protection to each minority in respect of its language, script and culture and assures that no law or regulation shall be passed which in any way would militate against this guarantee. No minority, whether based on religion, community or language, shall be discriminated against in any matter. All minorities will be allowed equal and full participation in all spheres of social, economic and political life. Minorities will have the right freely to profess and practise their religion and organize educational institutions and cultural associations for the study of religion and promotion of their language, script and literature. In places where a minority forms a considerable proportion of the population, the State shall provide facilities for imparting basic education to their children through their language, and for learning their language and literature up to the secondary stage. But the children of minorities will have to study the national language as well as the official language of the State concerned so that they might play their creative role as citizens.

The Socialist Party hopes that the minorities on their part will come forward and participate fully in the life of the nation and work creatively to establish the new civilisation herein envisaged, which alone offers a lasting solution of the problem of minorities.

Refugee Rehabilitation

The Government have failed to heal the wounds of partition. Millions of refugees from Pakistan who could have been absorbed in the life of the country and turned into useful citizens contributing to increasing production have been seized with bitterness and frustration. Even five years after partition they have yet to find their moorings in the national life.

The Government have no vision nor a purposeful scheme to settle these displaced persons in their new environment. As in other spheres, a hand-to-mouth policy to meet the immediate urgency followed by complacency marks the action of the Government in this field too. They leave this tide of human suffering to disperse by itself.

The Socialist Party would give the first priority to the problem and meet it in the following manner. As soon as a displaced person declares his intention to settle permanently in India, he will be granted the Indian citizenship. While temporary relief would be extended to him, he will have to opt for a calling in which the Government will help him to settle himself. The agriculturist will be settled through cooperative land reclamation schemes and on fallow lands in rural areas. The middle class, including artisans, will be settled in self-sufficient cooperative colonies near large towns and cities on the Faridabad model. Smaller colonies of this type will be started also in rural areas, especially near prosperous villages. As far as possible, families coming from the same locality in Pakistan will be settled nearer together so that their pattern of social life may not be rudely shattered. In the new colonies, however, there will be no rentier class nor exploiting class. Labour, skill and craftsmanship developed with State aid will turn the frustration and despair of the displaced persons into a new faith and hope.

While the principle of rehabilitation compensation will apply to these displaced persons, an effort will be made to come to a permanent arrangement with Pakistan on the wider question of property left behind by refugees in both the countries. A Joint Commission working in the two countries, with facilities for a joint checking staff, would help to solve this difficult problem.

Changes in the Constitution

The fabric of economic equality and social mobility cannot be raised on the framework of the present Constitution of India. Not only it presents many an obstacle to fundamental reforms, but fails to reflect, in crucial matters, the wishes of the people.

Even the nationalist aspirations of the Indian people have not been fully realized under the Constitution. India remains a member of a Commonwealth that tolerates racial inequality and denies access to Asian multitudes to the empty spaces in the Commonwealth countries. The Socialist Party therefore favours the withdrawal of India from the Commonwealth. That alone can complete our quest for freedom.

The social aspirations of the people are baulked and frustrated by the Constitution even more pointedly. The safeguards provided to the right of property facilitate the maintenance of present inequities and make any egalitarian advance wellnigh impossible. To ensure progress, these barricades raised to protect property rights will have to be razed down and the people's right to use State powers to establish equitable and juster social relationships will have to be asserted. This would include the power to take away property with rehabilitation grant only, if such taking over by the State is found necessary for social progress.

While the right to property, enjoyed by a microscopic minority of people, is fenced off from all encroachments, the universal rights to liberty are hemmed in from all sides. The fundamental freedoms of the people—of speech, press, assembly, association and above all freedom from arbitrary arrest and detention—cannot be allowed to depend on the whims and wishes of the authorities. A positive and absolute content given to these rights alone can assure minorities—political an religious—that they are free to live according to their own rights and even free to propagate their views so long as they remain loyal to the State which guarantees these rights. The Socialist Party would therefore repeal all repressive laws and make the fundamental rights as real and complete as possible.

The Right To Work has so far remained a pious wish. Its neglect involves not merely individual but social loss. Through work alone a person participates in the stream of community life and emerges as a citizen creatively associated in the building up of a new nation. The Socialist Party would assure the Right To Work and thus banish the haunting fear of unemployment, starvation and want.

The Constitution has likewise failed to create a truly democratic structure for the new Indian State. The absence of linguistic provinces denies millions of men opportunity to participate in the affairs of the State. The Socialist Party favours re-arrangement of the States on linguistic basis, consistently of course with geographical contiguity and economic viability. The new boundaries will be determined by a Boundary Commission. All States, thus brought into being, will enjoy equal status.

The Socialist Party will endow the electorate with the Right of Recall to make the will of the people consistently sovereign.

Social Welfare

Directives to the State included in the Constitution leave much to be desired. They sketch the outlines and skip over the content. Education, health and social security have to be conceived in more dynamic terms.

Literacy and elements of social education would be made universal. Primary education would be free and general. The village panchayats, local bodies, cooperatives, the various autonomous corporations of trade and industry, trade unions, teachers' guilds will be among the associations that will scout talent and help to provide opportunities for fullest training. Technial education will become the key thread round which the web of economic expansion—agricultural, industrial and handicraft—would be woven. Defence Services, Territorial Forces, Local Militia and Food Army will be additional schools of general and social education. Stipends and scholarships provided by the State as well as other bodies listed above would enable all deserving students to receive the education they desire. The flower of the nation need no longer blush unseen in the desert air of neglect and penury.

Public health will likewise be organized through cooperative efforts of the people. Mobile dispensaries will bring medical assistance to remote corners. Re-planning of administration and economy in the villages will help to transform the nature of these ancient yet not unoften dilapidated communities and make the task of organizing health services easier. A National Health Programme will be worked out to embrace widening sections of the working people.

Most of the corporations of trade and industry will be able to organize schemes for social security. Government employees and industrial workers will be provided for through contributory and other forms of social security. Cooperatives and village panchayats, with the help and guidance of the State, will work out, slowly but steadily, the details of social security for the millions of people they organize and serve.

While all the burdens of life cannot be lifted at a stroke, Socialist India would put an end to man's isolation and to much of his corrosive anxieties. Gymnasia, sports, music, drama and folk festivals will add colour and rhythm of life.

The vast effort at creation, the removal of ancient barriers of inequity, the surge of community life, will impart a new meaning to men's lives. No longer will the strings of their harps be scattered, they will recover their tension and be vibrant with new melodies.

Reforms in Administration

The new concept of State demand radical alterations in the character of the administration. It will have to be rid of the overtones of bureaucratism, red-tapism and indifference to public opinion given to it by the foreign rulers, and of the new weaknesses of inefficiency and corruption brought to it by Congress Government.

The reorganization of economy, discussed before, which would narrow inequalities, accelerate social change and decentralise political and economic power, will also, through the new positions assigned to village panchayats, nationalised industrial and trade corporations, cooperatives and trade unions, markedly modify administration and give it intimate contact with the people. In many spheres the people would be administering their affairs directly.

The following reforms would further simplify the administration:

Many of the legal rights of the poorer sections go by default because the administration of justice is very expensive and tortuous. Justice will therefore be made cheap and speedy. Courts of law will go nearer to the people. Fact-finding and punitive functions will be separated.

The best cure of bureaucratism is the association of public opinion at each level of the executive in advisory capacity. If the advice is rejected by the official concerned, the reason thereof will have to be given to the immediate superior.

Heads of departments will hold periodic meetings of the staff to review the work of the office and suggest ways and means of bettering efficiency and for cutting out of red-tape. These reports would be forwarded to the headquarters. The staff meetings would help to discover talents in the ranks, to whom opportunities will be offered for special training and the exercise of initiative.

In the Legislature, Standing Committees in charge of different subjects would be constituted. They would take public evidence on any topic of importance, interrogate officials and non-officials and help to resolve differences of opinion between advisory committees and officials.

Efficiency in administration will be maintained by fixing targets and the introduction of efficiency audit for officer. These will determine promotion or demotion.

Bribery and favouritism will be dealt with by establishing an Anti-Corruption Authority. This Authority can be moved by any person. When so moved, of its own accord, it can ivestigate any case and have access to all papers and information. It can examine Government officials and summon witnesses. If the crime is proved, in case it is a minor offence the Authority will deal with it summarily. In case of major offences, the Authority will be the prosecution and will be responsible to bring the offenders to book in special courts statutorily provided.

Peace through Freedom and Equality

The Congress Government claims to follow an independent foreign policy. But it neverthelss keeps on oscillating from one power bloc to the other. At the same time, economic and social disorganisation has been creating within the country growing adherents of the rival blocs. Four years of frustration have led sections of our people, no matter how small, to look to Moscow or Washington for deliverance and development. Taking advantage of this position, both the blocs are trying to entrench themselves in the country.

Further, the failure of the Government of India to put forward a positive world policy as an alternative to the policies of the American and Russian blocs has robbed our so-called "independent" foreign policy of all meaning, and belied the hopes that the emergence of free India had aroused among the peoples of Asia and Africa.

The foreign policy of a free but feudal-cum-capitalist India, with its extremes of poverty and wealth, its social injustices, its status-quoism, cannot rouse any enthusiasm or play any vital part. Only when at home India gives evidence of creative energy and proceeds to construct a new social order as described in this Platform that India's voice will become a clarion call.

The Socialist Party believes in a new world of equality, freedom and peace; a world in which there is no domination or exploitation of one nation by another, in which extreme poverty and backwardness do not lie side by side with dazzling wealth and technological progress, in which there are no race or other barriers, in which war has become obsolete.

Neither Russian leadership of the world nor American can ever create such a world. A Russian world would be a world ruled from Moscow, the dictates of which must determine the pattern of life all over the globe. An American world would have all the characteristics of a capitalist society in which a few exploit the many and inequality and injustice rule the lives of men. To the Russian and American world pictures, the Socialist Party presents a third alternative. In order to realize this picture of a new world the Socialist Party shall:

(i) abstain from involvement in the disputes between the Russian and American Camps, at the same time assuring the United Nations that Socialist India would in no event assist an aggressor;
(ii) strengthen the United Nations and its various agencies in all such efforts as might lead to a world of freedom, equality and peace;
(iii) endeavour to work for the collective security of that region in the world as keeps out of alliances of the Atlantic and Soviet Camps, in particular the belt that stretches from Indonesia to Egypt;
(iv) strive for friendly relations with all peoples and governments;
(v) support freedom movements of the yet unfree peoples, in particular

those of Africa, and attempt to keep them away from alliances with either Camp;

(vi) seek to revise all treaties and agreements and charters as have set up an international caste system of rich and powerful nations on the one hand, and of weak and poor nations on the other, and thus establish the principle of equality of all nations.

(vii) assist in all efforts to join the human race together, politically in a World Parliament and, economically through agencies such as a World Development Corporation and World Food Pool, so as to ensure that every human being, no matter what his country, is assured of a decent standard of living;

(viii) extend its support to Socialist movements all the world over and to all other popular movements as are striving to combat hunger and war with the weapons of socialism and democracy.

Kashmir

The State of Kashmir had lawfully acceded to India and the accession was wholeheartedly endorsed by the Kashmir National Conference, the largest representative body of the people of Kashmir. The whole of Kashmir is thus legally a part of the Indian Republic. The aggression of Pakistan, however, created a dangerous situation, and, while India resisted the aggression with all its strength, because of its anxiety to avoid a war with Pakistan, it sought the intervention of the United Nations. Unfortunately, instead of deciding the simple issues of aggression, the United Nations, due to extraneous reasons, further complicated the situation. Thus a stage has now been reached where it is necessary for the people of Kashmir themselves to settle their fate. The Socialist Party therefore endorses India's rejection of United Nations arbitration and fully supports the step taken by the Kashmir National Conference to convene a Constituent Assembly elected by the adult population of Kashmir.

The Socilaist Party feels that the Constituent Assembly should not only set up a representative Government, but also decide finally the issue of accesion, which decision should be taken by India and the world as final. As to how the rest of the Kashmir territory should be recovered from the hands of the aggressor can only be decided after the verdict of the Constituent Assembly. The Socialist Party believes that after that stage the issue should be settled between India and Pakistan themselves without any outside intervention.

The Prospect

Such is the first five years' programme that we propose for the reconstruction of our country. It is a coordinated programme, each part of which is to be understood in the context of the whole. And while it is a radical programme, it is also practical. Its fulfilment will mean more production and equitable distribution; it will mean more food and cloth, more employment; it will mean educational and technical progress, better health; it will mean the institution of a people's functioning democracy, more self-rule and less government; it will bring light and hope to millions of homes darkened today by poverty and ignorance; it will mean a miracle of rebirth.

The peasant, the worker, the man of the middle class, the technician, the small producer, the harijan, the adivasi, the backward people—each will have a new opportunity to march forward, without the impeding burdens of the past.

The *peasant* with the abolition of zamindari and landlordism, will become the owner of the land. Re-distribution of land will restore equality to village communities. Resuscitation of village panchayats, as the pivot of administration and economy, will enable the peasant to shape his way of life.

The *worker* will gain a new status industry. Social security and trade union rights will banish his fears, and partnership in production will impart work a new significance.

The *small producer* will be freed from cramping influences of monopolists and will be nurtured with State aid for legitimate expansion.

The *technician* and the *administrator* will get oppotunities for experimentation and development. The spirit of pioneering will revivify their activities.

The submerged people, like the *harijans* and the *adivasis*, will experience social reclamation, and injustices of centuries will at long last fade away.

The *community*, strengthened by egalitarian and social reforms, will turn to creative efforts. Cooperatives and industrial democracy will spell the end of exploitation.

Only a small section of the people will be stripped of their purple robes of privilege and deprived of the advantages of wealth and power. But they too in return may experience a new joy of participating in a community life uncursed by the envy and animosities of an unequal society.

These fundamental yet simple reforms will lay the foundation for that house of freedom wherein the peoples' fugitive hopes and questing desires will find their abiding mansions.

In all humility we invite the Indian people to give us their cooperation in this task of social reconstruction. We seek their cooperation and suffrage not only at the forthcoming elections, but also in the implementation of this programme. The Socialist Party has never believed that society could be reconstructed just by a party or a government. Both these have their parts to play, but it is the active participation of the people in the task of reconstruction, their never tiring initiative, their eternal vigilance, their ability to correct and command, that are essential for the success of this gigantic task. With such cooperation from the people we feel confident that this task will be accomplished and the picture of a new society that has been drawn here translated into reality. India will march to her destiny and a chapter will open in her long history that will be worthy of her great and ancient past.

APPENDIX 13

From Jawaharlal Nehru, 18 July 1951[1]

My dear Jayaprakash,

I returned yesterday from Bangalore and had immediately to face a very serious situation *vis-à-vis* Pakistan. There is also an accumulation of heavy and important work. I am however hastening to reply to your letter of the 17th July which I have just received.

2. I appreciate your writing to me. With reference to your last personal paragraph, I may have written to a friend that you were using strong language about me. I do not remember the exact word. Perhaps it might have been "abuse". I hope I have not become so thick-headed as to object to criticism, however strong it may be. What I meant was that repeatedly in your speeches, you had been fererring to me rather bitterly and with anger. I do not challenge your right to do so, but it did pain me that you were bringing down a high argument to a personal level and apparently challenging my *bona fides*. I felt a little hurt, not becasue of your criticism or condemnation, but rather because of this inference which seemed to flow from words. As you know, there is a very great deal of not only criticism but strong language used about me by various people and in various periodicals. I do not think I mind that very much and sometimes perhaps I profit by it. But it does hurt to know that I have fallen so low in your esteem.

3. I agree with you that it would have been better for me to issue an appeal to railwaymen at an erly stage.Unfortunately I was away for about ten days in Kashmir and for a number of these days I was even cut off from newspapers and other kinds of news. The very day I returned to Delhi I took this matter up and issued my appeal. Of course, I could have done this before I went to Kashmir also. But the matter was being dealt with by Gopalaswami Ayyangar and other colleagues of mine and I felt that perhaps I would not help by barging in.

4. It is a little difficult for me in this letter to discuss the details of the railwaymen's demands, which you have already discussed fully with Gopalaswami Ayyangar, Deshmukh and others. You know that Gopalaswami

[1] *J.P. Papers* (NMML).

Ayyangar has on past occasions gladly conferred with you and your colleagues of the AIRF. In fact he has refused to discuss these matters with other organisations, because he thought that the AIRF was the principal railwaymen's organisation. Whether he agreed with you or not, he certainly wanted to agree and try to find a way out. It was in no unfriendly spirit that he has dealt with you in the past. In the present case, you will at least appreciate that certain vital financial considerations put a strict limit to our ambition. I think this was put to you when you met Gopalaswami Ayyangar and Deshmukh. We have to consider the whole picture and cannot upset the apple cart even when something desirable is suggested.

5. You may be right in suggesting some vital change in our social structure. But, in existing circumstances, we cannot suddenly change that structure and have to deal with the situation as it is. We cannot go beyond our resources, unless we give up something vital, such as a river valley scheme, or just take to printing currency notes without backing and thus bring about progressive inflation. Prices rise again and the condition of the worker is as bad as before or worse. All our economy and schemes for development are shattered.

6. Because of all these considerations, which no doubt were placed before you and your colleagues, we could not add much more than we did to the burden on the exchequer. The problem is a difficult one and it is possible that you may not accept the argument put before you, or you may have other solutions. But you will at least admit that the matter is not simple and is full of difficulty. A government has to consider not only that particular matter but innumerable other factors which may be influenced by any particular decision.

7. Only two or three days ago, you must have seen Liaquat Ali Khan's complaint about our massing troops. One need not attach too much importance to Pakistan's complaint, but the fact is that for sometime past things have been coming to a crisis in the relations of India and Pakistan. We had to give serious thought to this many weeks ago. We saw a dangerous trend developing and we came to the conclusion that there was a fair possibility of Pakistan suddenly attacking us. They had been preparing for this for a long time and they had whipped up their people by a virulent propaganda of hate. Anything could happen. We could not take any risks or at any rate avoidable risks, and so we prepared for proper defence, if attacked.

8. Take this single factor, which we had constantly in mind for sometime past. I do not suppose that you have had this in mind except during the last two days or so. Yet we had to consider other matters too in relation to this. I could mention many other things which we had to keep in mind also.

9. You refer to the Ordinance. Nobody likes an ordinance and I hope few persons like any action taken against a *bona fide* strike. But I do not

understand how your Federation could expect Government to sit supinely and wait for a strike which might not only paralyse normal life all over the country but would also specially aggravate the food problem and weaken India so much at a critical time as to encourage Pakistan to invade it. I do not think any Government, including a socialist government, could take the risk of such a situation developing. If we have to take action, then surely that action should be effective. I do not myself see what alternative course we could adopt, after the strike had been resolved upon.

10. I agree with you that such suppression of the strike would leave deep wounds which take a long time to heal. It is for this reason that the idea of the strike has distressed me very greatly. You accuse the Government of trying to suppress the strike. Surely the responsibility of the consequences must rest very largely with those who advise a strike in such circumstances. The alternative to Government in suppressing such a strike is for the Government to resign and hand over the Government of the country to those who are responsible for the strike. Do you think that that would be in accordance with the wishes of the great majority of people in the country? Is it not true to say then that the Railwaymen's Federation, apart from the merits or demerits of its case, is bringing tremendous pressure on the community as a whole and trying to coerce it into doing something which it does not want to do or is incapable of doing?

11. You refer to the INTUC unions. It is true that some Congressmen are interested in them. But Government has, I believe, alwasy tried to accept the largest union in any industry, whatever it might have been. I do not think you are just or correct in describing the INTUC unions as merely company unions which cannot last a day without official support. I am not connected with them, but I know a number of these unions which are strong and independent. Would you call the Ahmedabad unions surviving merely because of Government support?

12. I am sending your letter to Gopalaswami Ayyangar for his information. I am sure that he is always willing to discuss matters with your Federation.

Yours affectionately,
Jawaharlal Nehru

APPENDIX 14

From Jawaharlal Nehru, 8 August 1951[1]

My dear Jayaprakash,

I have your letter of the 4th August. I have also received a copy of a letter you have sent to Gopalaswami Ayyangar dated August 7th.

Your impression that I was anxious for a settlement was certainly correct. I would gladly do what I can to bring this about. But I cannot take the matter out of the hands of the Railway Ministry which is dealing with it and take charge of it myself. That, as I said to you before, is physically impossible for me for some time at least, because of the grave situation that has arisen in regard to Pakistan and certain other matters which absorb all my time. Apart from this, surely the best way I can help is to give my full cooperation to the Railway Ministry in any matter of principle that may be discussed. They are as much part of the Government as I am, and they are primarily responsible. But such help as I can give, I shall gladly give. I recognise entirely that Railways are of vital importance.

You ask me for a "dentailed and definite" reply to various points that you have raised. These points not only involve principles but no doubt have to be considered in relation to many other matters. To consider them fully is to go deeply into the entire subject. No practical question of importance can be considered in vacuum, separated from other matters. If and when you discuss these matters with the Railway Ministry, I shall gladly try to make myself available, whenever I am needed.

You protest against my remarks about Pakistan being encouraged by the prospect of a railway strike in India. Those remarks have nothing to do with what your attitude or the attitude of the AIRF might be. I am sure that neither you nor the AIRF would like to encourage Pakistan in such a matter and that they would help in any national crisis. But what I said was that the Pakistan Government undoubtedly was encouraged by so much talk of a railway strike in India. Indeed I know this for a fact and I have had reports of it. That is quite natural for them. They are encouraged whenever they hear that we are in any kind of trouble, because they feel that weakens us in a conflict.

The situation *vis-à-vis* Pakistan, is very serious. I cannot obviously say whether it is bound to lead to war, and if so, when. We shall do our utmost to avoid it. But we cannot control the other party. Unfortunately they have received a good deal of encouragement from foreign sources and this makes them even more irresponsible. In my last letter to you, I appealed to you to give up the idea of the strike because of this serious situation. In your letter

[1] *J.N. Papers*: Files at Home (NMML).

to Gopalaswami Ayyangar you have clearly said that if the situation is a grave one, the railwaymen will stop the strike. I am glad you have taken up this clear attitude in this grave matter. I was sure that you would do so. Gopalaswami Ayyangar has sent you a telegram today with which I entirely agree.

Yours affectionately,
Jawaharlal Nehru

Copy to: The Hon'ble Shri N. Gopalaswami Ayyangar,
5 Queen Victoria Road,
New Delhi.

APPENDIX 15

From Gopalaswami Ayyangar, 26 September 1951[1]

My dear Shri Jayaprakash,

Thank you very much for your letter dated 13 September from Cuddapah. I have given my thought to the points you have referred to in your letter and indicate below my reactions.

With the Labour Relations Bill on the agenda of the present session of parliament, it was obviously not possible for me to come to a separate agreement with the AIRF as regards its immediate recognition as the sole bargaining agent for Railwaymen. It doesnot now seem likely that this will come up for consideration in this Parliament. As already agreed between us, we can, after the present session of Parliament ends, explore the possibility of considering this question separately for the railways.

At our last meeting it was agreed that the issue of participation of labour in management could not be tackled immediately under existing conditions as major questions of State policy were involved. I have, however, no objection to our having a further talk on this matter at our next meeting if you have any further suggestions to make in that connection. On the question of setting up an autonomous Corporation, you will remember we decided to put it aside for the present.

You ask me to reconsider what we agreed to as regards disciplinary matters. I am as anxious as you are that workers aggrieved by any disciplinary orders should be given the feeling that their cases have been considered fairly and impartially both at the original and the appellate stages. I am not enamoured of manning a disciplinary tribunal entirely or

[1]*J.P. Papers* (NMML).

predominantly by judges. I cannot agree with you that officers holding supervisory posts form a narrow minded Trade Union and their bias is always against the workers, and I am not so sure that at present you can think of any better machinery than we have agreed between us already. I shall certainly give further thought as desired by you to the question of whether that machinery could be improved upon in any way.

With regard to the question of dearness allowance, I am afraid, I can hold out no hopes in the immediate future for a modification of the decision taken by Government sanctioning a five rupee addition. The preliminary investigation of the question relating to the conversion of a portion of dearness allowance into basic pay is proceeding and I hope to be able to let you know, when we next meet, what decision the Government are in a position to take regarding the appointment of a Commission for enquiring into that problem.

I have read with interest the alternative suggestions you made in this regard. I am afraid they do not take us much further in view of the discussions we have already had. In the course of those discussions, Guruswami made the suggestion that the present concessional grainshops might be altogether abolished and that a full cash dearness allowance to all might be substituted with the concession that grain alone might be sold at fixed prices to all railway workers. It was pointed out in reply that such a suggestion could be considered only on two conditions, namely:

(i) that it should be made certain that those who are benefiting by the concessional grainshops would agree to such an arrangement; and
(ii) that the resulting change should not throw any additional burden on railway revenues.

Guruswami will be starting his talks with the Railway Board tomorrow. I am quite willing that you should meet me after those talks are over. I should prefer the third week of October to the second.

With regards,

Yours sincerely,
K. Gopalaswami

APPENDIX 16

From Evelyn Reynolds, 1 October 1951[1]

My dear Jayaprakash,

Ever since my return to England in June I wanted to write to you. But as I had promised to try and be of some little help, and had no progress worth mentioning to report, I thought I ought not to waste your time. However, after exercising so much self-restraint, I am going to sin to-day.

Well, on my arrival in London in June I made almost straight for Westminster and tried to unload some of my experiences and views upon a backbencher acquaintance and the Colonial Secretary, an affable ex-miner who joined us for some time, but I doubt very much if my efforts left any imprint on their minds, as they were, understandably, bent on relaxation rather than "serious talk". Later on, I had quite a long talk with Mr. Sorensen, one of the few, I imagine, who know something about India and take an interest in Indian affairs. He didn't seem at all surprised about my findings and said he had often heard such views expressed before, that that was how he himself imagined things in India to be, and that he would like to go there next year to see what you were doing. But, on the subject of closer co-operation between Socialists in India and here, he said he didn't see very much that could be done, because "our problems are so different from theirs". Well , that was that. He also said he would arrange for me to give a talk on my impressions of India in his constituency, where apparently he has been able to foster some interest for that topic, but I haven't heard from him since. And what with everything oozing out Persian oil and Bevanite treason and General Elections, it doesn't surprise me. So, when I returned to Nottingham, I felt I was in a dead alley, and for the next few weeks I didn't do much except try and acclimatize again. I did send a script to the BBC about the Village Reconstruction Conference, but they sat upon it until Bihar was no longer in the news and then returned it with regrets—possibly because they are allergic to anything with a political bias, especially when it concerns a foreign country.

At the beginning of August I went to Vienna for four weeks to see my parents, then my mother came on a three weeks' visit, and now, being back in peaceful solitude, I am trying out a new line—lecturing. You see, the trouble with writing is, that the big newspapers don't even take much of their own correspondents' stuff on India, except occasionally on Kashmir or Mr. Nehru, this or that, so they are even less inclined to take anything from a newcomer who doesn't even care about their policies. But there are quite a few meetings, though may be rather insignificant, where even a

[1] *J.P. Papers* (NMML).

nonentity such as myself can take advantage of a favourable personal impression made to put something across an audience that would not normally be so keenly interested in the topic. So this was my brainwave (unfortunately my brainwaves are few and far between), and I started off modestly enough talking to some of the good Nottingham housewives at the local YMCA, and although some of those in the back rows seemed to snooze off at times over their needlework, they rose to the occasion by refraining from asking, at the end: Now, did you ever see that famous Indian ropetrick? Or perhaps they hadn't heard about it. Anyway, a few said they would like to see India for themselves, and that they hadn't realized how fortunate they were in this country—so the basic reaction was all right. Then I went to the local Labour Party Office, and now I am "booked" for several talks in different wards after the General Elections. I had a useful recommendation from an old Labourite Alderman, a very well liked and prominent citizen, who was my boss for two years while I was working in the local Mineworkers' Union branch to save up for my Indian trip. Then I fixed up for a talk in November at the local Trades Council (TUC branch), and last week the Fabian Society wrote to say they had put me on to their panel of speakers for their London Branches, and there is also the local one. (I had suggested to give talks on India in general and the Socialists in particular—do I see you smiling?) Also, I have written to the National Peace Council, and to Jennie Lee (Mr. Bevan's MP wife) for an interview to enlighten her on your good cause—so, straight into the lion's den. By the way, I am sending you the two *Tribune* pamphlets (separate package No.1.) to elucidate the present Labour row, just in case you haven't seen them and would like to know about it. When the first pamphlet came out in July, I pricked my ears because one of Mr. Bevan's main arguments was not only against more rearmament, but far more for the "underdeveloped countries". *Tribune*, his platform, has since taken up the good cause again with an article on Point Four (I am sending that issue along with the two pamphlets) and since apart from the *New Statesman*, it is the only voice of reason in the wilderness, I thought that that rare iron ought to be beaten while it is hot. And, in the spirit of the *Tribune*, Jennie might lend a willing ear. I really dread the interview (if it comes off), because she is supposed to have a rather overawing personality, but I am at present trying hard to overcome my ingrained instincts of keeping away from everybody and out of everything. Things would be much easier if I lived in London, which is 250 miles away—so I can't go there very often. But maybe I can find some more willing victims in Birmingham and Manchester later on.

I found the whole Bevan affair rather promising and had hoped he would get support at the recent TUC Conference, but apparently the rank and file there, though rather sympathetic, was steamrollered by the good Attlee boys on the Executive by an ingenious presentation of resolutions, and any sparks of lightning were deflected upon the Commies, who seem to have come in rather useful as scapegoats. And the main argument over the measure of rearmament and its consequences didn't come to the vote at all. So it is difficult to say exactly what support Mr. Bevan enjoys. Now, with the elections at hand, he has concluded a temporary truce with the moderate camp. But if the Labourites were defeated, which is quite possible, and had to eat some humble pie, I think it would strengthen his hand and make him come out tops when they return—as they no doubt will when everybody has seen that the Tories can do no better, in fact somewhat worse, in the present circumstances. I have an inkling that some staunch Marxists may vote Tory this time. That would be outdoing Panditji's shock treatment methods.

There is not much of interest regarding India here. Occasionally the papers harp on her about Kashmir—the *Daily Mail* (I think) says, characteristically, that "it is difficult not to be prejudiced in favour of Pakistan" etc. etc. The *Statesman*—the only reasonable and intelligent paper apart from the less highbrow *Tribune*—came out recently with the hitherto most advanced view that while India ought not to yield on the two-nation theory argument, she should be more cooperative towards UNO and more understanding towards Pakistan's complexes. I vainly tried to enlighten the Editor further, and while I was at it I also presented *Tribune* with my views on Point Four—so there are always a good many pies into which to put my unwilling fingers. And while doing so, I am still pondering about whether and how to write that book on India which I had hopefully promised myself and the world on setting out. Well, one day perhaps I (and it) shall see the light. In the meantime, to get over my inhibitions, I jump before looking, but over harmless brooks only. And I can't help feeling that I have seen next to nothing of India.

Some weeks ago I read the announcement in the *Herald* that the Labour Party is going to fork out £1,000 to help Asia's Socialists. Well, well, I hope they don't overdo it. A statistical mind would no doubt derive much pleasure from the penny-splitting involved in the allocation to the respective beneficiaries. However, since Mr. Phillips has been so nice, which, I imagine, must have been due to Dr. Lohia's presence in Frankfurt, it might be useful to try and interest Jennie in following up the good deed. Incidentally, you must forgive me my flippant remarks here and there, I don't really mean to be flippant, but I just can't uphold the serious tone for long, no matter how near to my heart the problem.

Recently, on reading a review in the *Statesman* of a book on *India since Partition*, I discovered a kindred spirit in Mr. Brailsford, the Gandhi-biographer, who writes: "To this portent (the land problem), and to the negative legislative record of Congress, Mr. Mellor (the author) devotes only a few lines. Has he ever, one is tempted to ask, spent even a few days in a rack-rented and indebted village? There is a 'third force', the Indian Socialist Party, which may, before it is too late, succeed in winning the peasants. Its asset is the personal character of its leaders and the devotion of its active workers who learned their ethics (but not their politics) from Gandhi. Mr. Mellor does not mention the spectacular marches of peasant masses which it has organized with Delhi and other cities as their goal. These suggest that it is beginning to reach the villages. Congress, however, has its millionaires and its machine and the right to cover its degeneracy with Gandhi's halo and Nehru's name. It may win the coming elections only to lose Asia". Which sums up the problem quite nicely. I shall contact Mr. Brailsford after the elections.

So much, then, for politics from this side, in which I am now taking a dutiful interest,—trying to make amends for past indifference which I had conveniently mistaken for detachment. In my case, it is such a welcome pretext for writing you an inordinately long letter.

An Indian friend sends me his weekly edition of the *Statesman* (Calcutta), so I have been able to glean a few meagre facts about what you are doing. I was very anxious lest they should clap you into jail under that strike-prohibition ordinance, and was very relived to see that the issue had been postponed. I have the feeling it might have shaken people up, but rather in the way of a person who is woken up at 3 o'clock in the morning—the reception might have been unkindly. Assuming that one of the main problems is the unsatisfactory state of conciliation machinery, I am also sending you along with the *Tribune* pamphlets a copy of the new British Industrial Disputes Order. Perhaps you haven't got it at hand and might like to have a look at it. Incidentally, the Railwaymen's Union here has also just put in a claim for a 10 per cent increase for about 4,50,000 members, which is being referred to the Railway Staff National Tribunal, but the General Secretary of the Union has declared beforehand, just to make sure, that he will not consider their findings under the Disputes Order as binding.

Unfortunately I haven't been able to find any reports on the "Constructive Week" and the Delhi march, and I wonder what you think about the results. Probably you will by now be busy with arrangements for the election campaign. I wonder if you have got your symbol allocated now and how you are getting on with putting up candidates and finance. And how Rambahadur Lal is getting on in Bihar—I hope the matting-walled wells have proved a success and the dam for which we laid the "foundation bricks" is standing. You must have breathed a sigh of relief at the final secession of the hot-gospellers within your ranks, though why they should not have gone the whole hog and teamed up with the Commies I can't fathom.

Mr. Koestler aptly calls this type of revolutionaries the half-virgins,—the "not quite, but almosts". Unfortunately his sexy similes wouldn't lend themselves to Indian usage. Also, I imagine, you are by now reassured about the new Praja Party. I can't help being prejudiced against the Acharya [J.B. Kripalani], he looks the ascetic type, and I dislike ascetics, because one half of them is hypocritical and the other half out of this world, so what's the use? Unless a person has the stature of a saint, he should be just normal. So, in my prejudice, he looks to me a bit of a fraud, and he does say some silly catchpenny thing. It rather reminds me of those newfangled sculptors who try so hard to be different, and the harmless spectator is amazed to find that what he has taken to be the model of an atom structure, is really supposed to be a Madonna with Child.

And, of course, to put first things last, I should dearly love to know more about yourselves, where you are touring or staying, what your programme is, what you are thinking and reading, and how many hours' sleep you get nowadays. However, I can, fortunately, continue to exercise my imagination in that respect, and it's good to know at least that you are up and doing somewhere in this world.

I am also sending you (separate package No. 2) Mr. Koestler's latest, the *Age of Longing*, which please accept with my sincere thanks for the best memories of my stay in India. With this enjoyable bit of gloom he must have exhausted the topic of frustration, and perhaps he has by now hit upon a solution. Or perhaps he has laid his unsolved problems at the foot of the altar and entered the Catholic Church. He wouldn't be the first.

So far as personal news are concerned, I am partly enjoying being back to the cool and misty days, being able to do all my housework myself without being encumbered by servants and do's and don't and social prejudices, and having my fill of music and privacy. But only partly, and the other part is itching to go back to India. Well, I shall, later on, and I only wish I had sufficient courage to stay there. At the moment, having got used to living snugly in the Welfare State, I am scared of being at the mercy of a rather merciless society, and besides, I can't just see how I could make myself useful in India.

We are living in a very small flat, so I get through my chores in a jiffy and spend most of my days reading (about India mainly) and writing. Though my Indian trip has plunged me into debts up to my neck, my husband—the creditor—has kindly granted me a further moratorium, and so I am able to go on pondering about India and putting off the evil day when I shall have to go to work, repay my debts and save up for another escapade. I am thinking of going into a factory this time, it would be a new (and quite lucrative) experience, but first I am waiting to see if they are going to introduce equal pay for women. Though I bet they won't.

Social intercourse does not take up much time because we have hardly any friends here. Two of our Indian friends have gone home, rather reluctantly, and so the only visitors we have are an ex-hungarian ex-diplomat, who escaped from Budapest three years ago and is now happily settled as a textile worker, earning £14 a week (about Rs. 190) and re-reading his economics and politics in peace, and an English student eternally failing his B.A. and selling ice cream in his spare time. We assemble once a week round our fireplace for a few rounds of bad contract bridge and some animated discussions on how to look at the world without getting cross-eyed. I have cut down on relatives' visits to the bare minimum,—though they are all very kind and lovable people, they always give me the feeling, as Mr. Koestler quotes, of being in a "dry and weary land where no water is".

My husband is shortly going on a fortnight's training course for reserve officers, and I am looking forward to quite an orgy of reading. I shall sneak off to the lending library to borrow shamefacedly—guess what—*Das Kapital*, as I can see your eye rest on me reprovingly for walking about without fundamentals. However, I am not as enthusiastic about it as I should be, and regard it as a sort of mental khaddar-spinning—a matter of principle and discipline rather than an urge to do something indispensable to my, or anybody else's, salvation. Of necessity, I am soft-pedalling on my degree in Indian History, and have shelved indefinitely everything between the Vedic Age and the first Non-Cooperation Movement—there's no hurry.

It was rather a relief from the process of settling down to go to Vienna—we went at the beginning of August to spend my husband's annual holiday there. I had taken Mr. Palme Dutt's "*India Today*" for reading on the way, but as soon as we entered the Tyrol and the grand mountain ranges, I had to put it aside—it seemed somehow out of place, and even more so amid the threadbare elegance of Vienna. I would have loved to show you round all the palaces and churches and vineyards and forests—I do think you ought to come to Europe just once—and, of course, the blocks of workers' flats, though they seem somehow incidental and very much grown on to their utterly bourgeois surroundings. In fact, the whole of Vienna is comfortably "bourgeois" down to the marrow of its old bones, even, it seems, the socialists, and the atmosphere doesn't appear to lend itself very much to revolutionary belligerence, except for an occasional spasm. Despite a few hard words here and there, it's amiable compromise all over, somewhat resigned and a little complacent, and one just relaxes. So now you know why everybody calls us a spineless race. But at least we are nicely, and perhaps usefully, spineless—or so we think.

Some people thrive exceedingly on the proceeds of Marshall aid, others just manage more or less comfortably, and there are long clerical-looking queues at the Labour Exchanges. But almost everybody seems to get something or other to his hard-to-please taste from the foodshops, indecently crammed, and all the many popular winegardens thrive—I was idly speculating whether I could have got you to taste some of our harmless "grape juice". The impoverished patricians go on selling their jewellery and oilpaintings, promptly spending the meagre proceeds at the grocer's or the local coffee house, where many people seem to spend the better part of their lives, or on an occasional outing into the rarefied and delicious-smelling atmosphere of one of the leading confectioners (by Appointment Suppliers to the King Emperor). And the workers seem to manage to get their steaks and dumplings and their bottles of wine (which is cheaper than coffee), and ambitions don't rise very much higher. A pleasantly demoralizing atmosphere—very pleasant indeed and mellow, and understandable after the nervous exhaustion of the last 13 to 17 years, not to mention the future. Everybody, except a few forlorn comrades, is, of course, united in the common grouse No.1, the Russians, and what with Russia, hanging over poor little Austria like the sword of Damocles, one can't blame them. All the same, if the Russians did leave one day, the Viennese would find themselves bereft of their favourite topic of conversation. At the end of our stay, we spend a few days in the Tyrol and crossed one of the many glaciers into Italian territory, a chilly enterprise considering that I had to wade through snow and ice water for two hours in sandals—suicide plus sacrilege to the seasoned mountaineer. However, all went well, and the sandals were the only casualty.

And so now I am back again to meditate over my Indian impressions; some of them are rather like a Chaplin-film: comical at the first glance and sad at the second. The mood behind it all also seems to be one of longing—though perhaps a more elemental one than Mr. Koestler's sophisticated agonies.

While sorting out some ancestral documents the other day, I found a little souvenir from the French Revolution. I thought it might amuse you and so I am enclosing it with this letter for "good luck" during your strenuous campaign. It's one of those assignats, dated 8.2.1794, and it would have entitled you to £25 worth of nationalized Church lands, had you been on the spot at the time quickly enough to cash it in. Apparently that ancestor of mine hadn't, and kept the note as a sad reminder. Ominously, the word fraternity has been left out to make place for an untruthful description of the value of the note, which, even when it was printed, would have hardly redeemed what it promised. Well, I could never really warm up to the French Revolution or any other such bloody event, which is probably due to my, as yet, imperfect understanding of things. But perhaps it will be, to you, a reminder of the continuity of human endeavour to better the world, (not of national bankruptcies), so I am sending it along. Also, I am enclosing a hazy snap which I took of you on our tour of villages—please exchange it for one where I can see you more clearly. And another one of myself with a friend in Vienna, so that you may recognize the writer of this letter.

In case you have anybody around you who could oblige, I should very much like to have one or two things. One is your latest report (so far, the main fount of my knowledge is the Madras report of 1950) which I hope includes your thesis on Leftist Unity, and one or two press cuttings, if available, on the Constructive Week and the marches in May/June, and some pamphlet showing how the Socialists stand with the Indian trade unions. I am not very clear about the present all-India trade Union position and shall be on very thin ice when talking about it. And I have a little query about the membership of the Hind Kisan Panchayat—the Madras report says it is about 5,00,000, but a Janvani Divas Committee circular mentions specifically 2,00,000, probably that was a mistake.

But, dear Jayaprakash, if you don't happen to have anyone at hand, don't bother about these things (except the photograph, and I don't care if you say: well that's just like a woman)—I shall manage somehow. On the other hand, I should be more than happy if I could do something for you, whatever you may require—any reading, precis—or contact making, looking out for things, sending newspaper cuttings or any publications on any subject, or what have you—just let me have your instructions and they shall be executed to the best of my ability (limited).

Please remember me to Prabhavati Devi, Mr. Saran, Mr. Bhasin, Mr. Mehta, the jolly professor Mukut Bihari Lal, and Rambahadur Lal, if you see any or all of them. I sincerely hope you will forgive me this outrageously long letter, which will have made you look at your watch at least half a dozen times. It was very inconsiderate of me, but I had been looking forward so much to breaking the silence, though without good reason. Consequently I am selfishly unrepentant.

With my best wishes to accompany you always,

Very sincerely yours,
Evelyn Reynolds

APENDIX 17

From Sadiq Ali, 5 October 1951[1]

Dear Jayaprakashji,

I have received a letter from Shri Puratan Buch informing us that he had a talk with you about some adjustment in Gujarat particularly with regard to the seat Shri Morarji Desai is contesting but you expressed your inability to make any adjustment as you had made your selections and it was not possible for you to disturb them. We appreciate your difficulty but may I know if it is your settled policy not to disturb the selections you have already made. If that is the settled policy I do not see how it could be possible for us to make adjustment in various States and avoid triangular contests which perhaps is our common wish.

Yours sincerely,
Sadiq Ali

[1]*J.P. Papers* (NMML).

APPENDIX 18

From Jawaharlal Nehru, 7 February 1952[1]

My dear Jayaprakash,

Your letter of the 16 January only reached me about four or five days ago. I do not know why it took such a long time.

It was good of you to write to me to clear up a certain misunderstanding. I have naturally to rely on press reports. The press reports were, so far as I can remember, that four years of Congress rule had done more injury to the country than a hundred years of British rule. My name was not mentioned. What I said was this: If this statement is true, even partly true, then surely I am the guilty party because I am more responsible than anyone else for the Government's activities during these four years. I did not say that you had referred to me.

The new version that you give is somewhat different. You have every right to believe it. But as a statement, it seems to me completely misconceived.

You are welcome to see me or write to me when you choose to discuss any matter.

[1]*Brahmanand Papers* (NMML).

It is true that I have felt deeply pained at the numerous and continuous personal references made about me by the leaders of the Socialist Party.

Yours affectionately,
Jawaharlal Nehru

APPENDIX 19

From Jawaharlal Nehru, 14 February 1952[1]

My dear Jayaprakash,

I have received your letter of the 12 February. I have already replied to your previous letter.

I have enquired from the Bihar people in Parliament if they know anything about the slogan which you quote. They tell me that they have never heard it before. I cannot, of course, say whether anyone said it or not. Certainly it was a very improper thing to say.

The Bihar people tell me that much was said by Socialist candidates in Bihar and in particular by Rammanohar Lohia in some of his speeches, which they thought was very offensive and personal.

You refer to the Communists saying that the Indian Embassy in Washington was responsible for the statement that Lohia brought thousands of dollars from America for the Socialist Party's election campaign. The Embassy had said nothing about this to us at any stage and, on enquiry from the then Ambassador, I am told that the Embassy did no such thing. She adds, however, that there was certainly a rumour going around Washington to the effect that a part of the reason for Lohia's coming to the States was to raise finances for Socialist Party. In fact, she says that she tried to trace the sources of this rumour and personally contradicted it on several occasions.

You will remember that when Norman Thomas was in India, he stated repeatedly that the International Socialist Movement should help the development of the Socialist organization in India. I believe he said so even in an interview to *Janata*. In the newspapers something more was said. I have at present with me a cutting from the *Indian News Chronicle*, Delhi, dated 25 March 1951. In this Norman Thomas is reported to have said in New Delhi that "the Socialist all over the world should establish an international fund for aiding the Socialist campaign in India". I do not know if this statement was contradicted at any time.

[1] *Brahmanand Papers* (NMML).

Soon after this Lohia visited America, as the guest, I believe, of the World Government Movement. Probably all this led some people to believe that funds might be collected in America.

I do not know what you mean by saying that Lohia and the Indian Embassy did not get on well together. So far as I know, there was no contact between them at all and so there was no opportunity for getting on or not getting on well together. Indeed, at the time a report came to us that at some function one of the members of our Embassy staff met Lohia and invited him to come to our Chancery so that Indian officers might have an opportunity of talking to him. Lohia's answer was not a pattern of courtesy. After that naturally the staff of the Indian Embassy had no further contacts with him.

There was and is no question of the Socialist Party of India being objectionable in the eyes of the Indian Embassy. Our Mission abroad are instructed to show every courtesy to every Indian visitor, whoever he might be. They should have nothing to do with politics or other views of the individual. At the same time, Indian visitors are expected to show normal courtesies to our Missions abroad, regardless of any views that they might have. The mission is a symbol of their country. Any dishonour to that Mission by a foreigner would be deeply resented by our country, because that meant a dishonour to the country. Much more is it surprising that any Indian going abroad should treat his Embassy with discourtesy.

It is not customary in other countries for their citizens to go abroad to run down their own governments and people. They confine their controversies to their own countries and do not carry them abroad. I find that this salutary rule was not followed by Rammanohar Lohia and that his addresses abroad largely consisted in running down the government here and others.

You refer to what I am supposed to have said about "these people having entered into a pact even with the Jan Sangh". This is partly true, but on every occasion I made it perfectly clear that I did not refer to the party in this matter but to individual candidates who had made some local arrangements which came to my knowledge. In Rajasthan some persons calling themselves Socialists were cooperating with the Jagirdars. In Himachal Pradesh there was cooperation with the Jan Sangh; and a number of other instances came to my notice.

It is quite likely that some Congress candidates made local alliances which were undesirable. I have in fact taken action wherever I could trace these with some certainty. If you can draw my attention to any such cases, I shall certainly enquire into them.

As for what Asoka Mehta wrote to me about the Congress in Bombay and the Fourth Party, I enquired into this matter immediately and, in fact, I am still dealing with it. I see from the newspapers that S.K. Patil has issued a statement denying this.

Yours affectionately,
Jawaharlal Nehru

APPENDIX 20
From Ramanandan Mishra, 11 April 1952[1]

Dear Comrade,

Today's exchange of views has smashed my plans.[2] For the past two months I have been in a dilemma. On the one hand, I felt like removing myself for sometime [from the Bihar Party]. On the other hand, seeing the condition of the province I wanted to again do my bit.

Three years ago, at the time of the meeting of the General Council [of the Bihar Party] and especially at the time of the All India Conference of the Party [Patna, March 1949] I had decided that I should gradually remove myself from the provincial politics. This was in a way nearly implemented and the process would have been completed if I had joined the Council of States. Thus a portion of my heart wished that I should move to Delhi and settle there.

On the other hand, my heart would begin to crack seeing the condition of the Party [in Bihar]. Another voice echoed from the heart: 'The Party is dying. What will you achieve by going abroad or to Delhi?' I, therefore, wanted to put a shine to the Party again by working beyond my capacity. I had firmly made this decision after the rejection of [my] nomination paper [for election to the Council of States.]

[1] *J.P. Papers* (NMML). Original in Hindi.

[2] This refers to the exchange between J.P. and Mishra, one of the prominent leaders of the Socialist Party in Bihar, in the forenoon of the last day of the conference of the Socialist Party in Bihar (Patna, 9 to 11 April 1952). Mishra's supporters in the Bihar Party had started a compaign against the leadership of the Party soon after the announcement of the result of the General Elections of 1952, underlining the poor performance of the Party. It was generally understood in Party circles that the campaign had been started at the instance of Mishra himself. At the time of the Conference the latter came into the open and a pamphlet written by him was distributed among the delegates, accusing the leadership as responsible for the debacle of the Party in the election. On the third day of the Conference he orally presented his thesis. Although J.P. was not named by Mishra either in his written or oral presentation, it was clear that J.P. was the main target of the latter's attack. J.P. was emotionally very much upset by it and announced his decision to have nothing to do with the Socialist Party in Bihar and left the meeting.

However, there are two conditions for its success:

1. There should be a general feeling among the members of the Party that we had strayed afar from the revolutionary path and a great effort would have to be made by sharpening that sentiment. The picture of all our work should change. New comrades must enter the Executive. The structure of the organisation must change.

2. Your full cooperation must be available.

To fulfil the first condition I presented my views before the comrades, orally, in black and white, and in print. I encouraged the comrades to fully discuss and debate this matter at the time of the Provincial Conference. The workers should themselves decide how to make the Party effective.

I was myself apprehensive lest this should lead to groupism in the Party. I had told the comrades again and again that while the atmosphere must change, groupism should not be allowed to emerge. This seems difficult. Therefore, I wanted you and Ganga Babu to stay with me for four or five days, but this did not materialise. From today's talks [at the Provincial Conference] an impression has been created that a revolutionary propaganda is not being carried on in the province by you and Ganga Babu and that both of you should be removed from the Party.

As you yourself said, we cannot work together in such an atmosphere of lack of confidence. In the past there had been such things which created pain and shock, but still we suppressed those feelings and worked together. I thought in the present circumstances you would appreciate my actions, but that did not happen.

Whether you believe or not, I have no desrire to become a leader. The person who held the burden of the provincial leadership, especially at this time, would be crushed under its weight. I was prepared even for this, but without your cooperation it would not bring any result. Therefore, I am returning to Leheria Sarai [my home town]. Please extend my apology to the representatives attending the Conference. Believe me, in this situation I shall not make any effort to keep awake the feeling of opposition. I shall do all I can in the South Darbhanga Assembly constituency. I shall always be at your and the Party's disposal whenever you desire. I shall also resign from the National Executive on reaching Leheria Sarai.

Yours sincerely,
Ramanandan

APPENDIX 21

Rammanohar Lohia's Presidential Address at the Pachmarhi Convention of the Socialist Party, 23 May 1952[1]

We are meeting in a Special Convention at a grave moment in the life of our people and our Party. A shadow has fallen over the Party of socialism in our land. At the same time, the stage is set for a more purposeful striving after the ideal of socialism. What we do at this Convention will decide for some years at least, whether India divides into two sets of dreary and screeching chorus-boys of capitalism and of communism or adventures into creating a new civilization away from both. Acharya Narendra Deva, in whom many comrades have glimpsed a reflex of Mahatma Gandhi's glory and with whom the heart may commune even though the head disagrees, was to have presided over this Convention, but he is away. To deputise for him can give no pleasure to anyone, but the work must be done. May socialists in India and all the world over learn communion of the spirit in the midst of differences in opinion.

Socialism, the only hopeful doctrine of the age, is in a bad way. All Asia except Burma, all Europe without Scandinavia, Yugoslavia and a fitful England or Austria, and whole three continents have not yet felt the power of socialism or drawn its benefits. This lack of power moves alongside of lack of mind. Torn between the two worlds of capitalism and communism, socialism is unable to evolve into a doctrine, which would reconcile the claims of stability and of change, which would serve the needs of stability without strengthening the status quo as well as the needs of change without fomenting chaos. This lack of a socialist mind is revealed in sundry ways. In India, it leads to hesitancy in action, to frequent lagging behind the cohorts of capitalism or of communism. In Britain, it leads to an unresolvable tension between the need of austerity and the aim of increasing prosperity. In the US, it makes earnest socialists wait revengefully for misery during which they could carry their gospel to a depressed and responsive people. Internationally, it causes the going of separate ways by socialists of different lands, as for instance, the opposition between French and German Socialists on issues of coal and steel and the European army.

The Fundamental Quest

Socialism is a newer doctrine compared to capitalism or communism. That would explain some of its failings and also give hope. Faulty applications and organization are another cause. But the career of socialism is impeded

[1]*Report of the Special Convention of the Socialist Party*, Pachmarhi, 23-27 May 1952, pp. 132-70.

most by its inability hitherto to secure a doctrinal foundation. No living doctrine is ever fully founded or closed. That day will be dismal when socialists cease to complain of their confusions. But there must be adequate doctrinal foundation of consistent logic that gives socialism an autonomous direction in thought and action and save it from confusions that disperse and scatter. Socialism must ever be a doctrine that grows but it must also ever seek the principle that holds its various limbs together. Socialism should cease to live on borrowed breath. Too long has it borrowed from communism its economic aims and from capitalism or the liberal age its non-economic and general aims. An acute disharmony has resulted. To explore once again the economic and the general aims of society and to integrate them into a harmony should be a high endeavour of socialist doctrine.

The establishment of social ownership over existing means of production, their further development and mass production and some kind of a planned economy are acknowledged in varying degrees as the economic aims of socialism. The preservation of national freedom, democracy and human rights, and the securing of peace and of what are variously termed as the values of culture or the spiritual qualities of life, are believed to be the general aims of socialism. This grafting of one on the other is full of peril to the future of socialism, for it encourages the disastrous belief that economic democracy prevails under communism and political democracy under capitalism, and all that needs to be done is to join them. Even the otherwise felicitous concept of democratic socialism sometimes inclines men to seek one of its profiles in capitalist democracy and the other in communist dictatorship, and a general weariness of thought and action follows. Both capitalism and communism have their own integrations and, whatever disasters they might yet heap on mankind, they are at least logical monsters. Unless socialism is able to disintegrate the premises on which capitalism and communism are founded and arrange instead its own harmony of economic and general aims, it will continue to be an illogical doctrine that refuses to come of age.

Antagonisms in Capitalism

Capitalism is a doctrine of the individual and of free enterprise that leads to ever-changing application of science to industry and agriculture. In its economic aims, it seeks mass production and low costs and profit to owners. In its general aims it seeks democracy and morality through adjustment of diverse interests and peace through balance of power. This capitalist integration held good for one-third of mankind, to whom the benefits of its revolutionary technology have strictly been confined, although it has led even among them to periodic crises and wars. It has engendered the clash between owners of concentrated capital and their proletarian grave-diggers, the clash between forces of production and relations of production, but it has also produced the graver contradiction between massive means of production over one-third of the earth and the decaying apparatus of production over the rest. This contradiction has like a knife cut the world into two; peoples living upwards of forty degrees north of the equator have at least acquired bodily comfort while the much vaster numbers of others are submerged in misery, but the whole world bleeds. Capitalism imposed the peace of death on Asia and elsewhere, caused their population to grow and their economic apparatus to decay. While growth in population and in means of production proceeded alongside among the white or pink peoples, the more coloured peoples suffered a loss in arts and crafts together with an increase in population.

To this day, the pinks of Russia and America live under 50 to the square mile and, although some parts of Europe have reached high densities, they have their vast production apparatus and still have the vast colonial hinterland of Africa to fall back upon. The coloured peoples have already attained unbearable densities, for instance, 300 to the square mile in India and 600 in Java, and their productive apparatus is so woefully meagre as to compare Rs. 150/- worth of tools to the person with Rs. 5,000/- to Rs. 8,000/- to tools per person among the white peoples. To provide to such enormous populations the tools of agriculture and industry as would bring them on a level with Europe and the US is an impossible task for capitalism and its private property or mass production. Capitalism has ravaged the coloured peoples so much that they cannot now respond to its embrace however affectionate. The task of capital formation over two-thirds of the world is far too colossal for private capital to accomplish. Capitalism cannot even fulfil its primary function of providing capital to mankind. The effect to spread to capitalist integration, which has hitherto been of local application among the white peoples, to all mankind and make it universal is foredoomed to failure. Poverty and war have been the monstrous progenies of capitalism, poverty for two-thirds of mankind and war for the rest, and it is powerless to destroy its own children. In the midst of such appalling poverty of the coloured peoples, morality through free enterprise and democracy through adjustment of interests are impossible to achieve and national freedom is a precarious treasure however hard won. War continues to be the great temptress for the whites.

Limitations of Communism

Communism is a doctrine of social ownership and of release of means of production from their relations of private property. It foresees as high a general aim of culture as any other doctrine, when men will no longer need government and things will be administered, but, in the process, it brings into being a centralised party earlier and a centralised state later in order to release the forces of production and to develop them. To it, the morality of a stateless society is in no contradiction with the immorality of a dictatorial party and state, for it has achieved such a complete integration of economic and general aims that the latter inevitably flow from the earlier. It argues this immorality away with the plea that the fulfilment of economic aims will inevitably lead to the securing of general aims and, as the dictatorial mode of the party and the state are a condition for victory, the immorality of the process is actually a high servant of the morality in the ultimate. The whole communist doctrine and its general theory on human civilization is proving faulty, for capitalist relations of production are snapping where the forces of production are least clamorous. This defeat of communist theory may be left aside, but the practical disasters of communist victories in areas of high density and low technology must be keenly appreciated.

Communism inherits from capitalism its technique of production; it only seeks to smash the capitalist relations of production. Communism claims to be the continuator and developer of capitalist technology, when capitalism is no longer able to do so. What capitalist technology has meant to two-thirds of the world has not been digested in communist theory. There are paltry forces of production and huge populations. Communist rationalisation of these economies or a hot-house nurturing of productive forces is impossible except through mass murder unknown to history, and then too, almost impossible.

To turn a peasant of India, Java or China into a worker, a cultivator into a tractor-driver or to provide a factory worker of these areas with concentrated capital of modern technology may or may not be a high endeavour, but its achievement is impossible and it shall stay a barren and cruel effort. Lands averaged around 15 acres for every agricultural worker in Russia before collectivisation and the tractor brought them on somewhat at a level with American agriculture. Where lands average between one acre and one and a half as in India and China, the communist modernisation of agriculture would throw tens of crores of people out of work. They could not be absorbed in modern industry, for that too would require an un-achievable capital. That the process could be spread over a century or a half would not be possible in view of the tensions between the rationalised and unrationalised sectors of economy, between those privileged to receive the comforts and amenities of communist rationalisation and the vast unrationalised mass of people, and the growth in population.

Barrenness of High Rationalisation

By any standards of employment commonly called rational in Europe or the US, over half of the population living in two-thirds of the world is unemployed. This unemployment is indeed concealed, for almost everybody appears employed although they are all chronically underemployed. To secure employment to such great numbers, even according to lower European standards and not those of the US, a capital investment running into more than Rs. 50,000 crores for India and five times that amount for all the underdeveloped areas would be necessary. A mere statement of the requirements reveals its fathomless absurdity. On the basis of India's current Five-Year Plan and taking the multiplier factor into account, around 15 such plans or a period of 75 years would be needed. A bigger capital investment under communism made possible through ruthless suppressions may at best reduce the period to 50 years. During this period famine and other tensions would cause untimely death by tens of millions, unheard-of brutality and certain collapse.

Barring textiles and railways and such like industries, which too would need large capital renovations if they are to be brought up to European standards, every sphere of economy will have to be rationalised almost from scratch. Assuming that an annual capital investment of Rs. 500 crores for a First Five-Year Plan were somehow available to communist India, it could at best provide rational employment to one million persons on the basis of Rs. 5,000 worth of tools per worker. Very limited regions and small sectors of economy could benefit. Communism would indeed know how to abolish unemployment by concealing it under the guise of under-employment, a practice which it has followed in Europe and which is all too familiar in the underdeveloped two-thirds of the world. But it will not be able to conceal that a few more Calcuttas and Kanpurs it may build rest on the dry bones of tens of millions dying in the numerous hamlets and towns of the country. Is there then no way out? There is none, if the accepted modes of rationalisation, common to capitalism and communism, are pursued and the mind refuses to display its intelligence and ingenuity.

Technique of Decentralisation

A new mode of rationalisation and a corresponding mode of ownership will have to be devised. The small-unit machine run by electricity or oil is the answer. Only a few such machines exist; many more will have to be invented. Technology, which the modern age has kept ever changing, will have to make a revolutionary break with the present. The problem will not be solved by going back to earlier machines discarded by modern civilization but by inventing new ones with a definite principle and aim. This machine shall be available to hamlet and town as much as to city; it may be a maid-of-all-work or as many as possible; it shall be built on the principle of immediacy in operation and output; it shall not require a large capital investment. Such a machine is not the product of decentralisation in space, which modern civilization in Europe and the US has started talking about and which keeps the existing principle of technology intact, but it is the embodiment of the whole principle of decentralisation, in space and in time, so as to avoid complexity and achieve immediacy. This machine will not only solve the economic problem of the underdeveloped world; it will also enable a new exploration and achievement, of the general aims of society. This is not to deny altogether the heavier machine in steel-works or in river-training projects, but emphasis must heavily rest on the small unit machine. On the basis of investment assumptions made earlier with regard to five-year plans, rationalisation carried out through such machines may well provide employment to ten, instead of one, million persons annually.

This immediacy in science and planning must be matched with immediacy in ownership and political control. Private property must of course go, except such as does not occasion employment of one person by another. Ownership of property by the state exclusively at the centre goes with mass production and is disastrous both for bread and freedom; property of appropriate types must be owned by the village and the province as much as by the centre and by cooperatives. Socialism must irrevocably reject all doctrines of restricted capitalism and mixed economy. In this connection, the debate between redistributors of land and efficiency-mongers who fear a decline in production consequent upon increase in uneconomic holdings is interesting. The efficiency-mongers do not understand that there is no way to evoke volunteer zeal and labour for minor irrigation projects and so to achieve great capital formations without cost except through providing land in however small quantities to all tillers.

Aims: Economic and General

Even apart from the fact that general aims of society do not so inevitably flow out of economic aims as is proposed by communist theory, the pursuit of economic aims of communism in conditions of high population and low technology is a delusion and a disaster. By communist reasoning itself, fullness of freedom shall come after the achievement of fullness of bread but, as communism shows no way to rationalise underdeveloped economies, what tend to become permanent are the general aims it adopts in the process and not those it preaches as an ideal. The centralised party and state and all that they give birth to seem to be the only achievable general aims of communism. Communism can provide neither bread nor freedom to two-thirds of the world.

A widespread notion ascribes the cultural deficiencies of communism to certain elements and traits of the Russian people. It is argued that the older cultures of India and China or the democratic conscience of the British people would soften communism. The reverse may well be true. The Gita and similar philosophies which India has sung will perish at the first touch, when communism starts rationalising Indian agriculture which does not possess the wide scope that its Russian counterpart did. Already China's terror has surpassed in some ways that of Russia and, should the average of one or one and a half acre per agricultural worker be pressed into the moulds of communist rationalisation, there is no knowing to what lengths the spirit of man may have to be suppressed. Soviet Russia would then appear to have been civilized in its processes. This is not to deny the imperishable glory of the *Gita* or the old cultures, but to recognise their importance when contrary economic aims sway the government of the day. They are effective only so far as they make difficult the victory of a creed of cruelty or assist in the encouragement of later disobedience to it. These general aims and motivations of man have a fragile quality, which yield noble fruit when handled with devotion. They cannot amend conditions of economic contrariety, and then can only exist hypocritically without effect or provoke disobedience.

Relations of Production and Forces of Production

Capitalism and communism share a certain community of economic aims in so far as the latter inherits the former's processes and forces of production and alters only its relations. Mr. Ford and Mr. Stalin share each other's attitudes on mass production and efficiency and high wages and, although Americans may point out the significant difference of democracy and Russians the equally significant difference of social ownership, this community of outlook between them is of the most decisive import. The new world must go beyond them both, beyond capitalism and beyond communism, if for no other reason than that the techniques of mass production are inapplicable to two-thirds of the world. Communism alters alone the capitalist relations of production and seeks to reproduce its forces; socialism must alter them both. This is no rejection of the machine but it is a rejection of the situation in which the heavy machine and its counterpart the Leviathan State predominate. Nothing but failure lies at the end of a long trail of savagery, should ever the underdeveloped world decide to form itself in the image of the developed, an ambition common to capitalism and communism. Some persons reconcile themselves to the savagery in the hope of success at the end of it; they would ultimately be rewarded by the bitterness of defeat and the remorse of cruelty. Communism wants to move history backwards and to repair the ravages of capitalism, but imitating its ways of mass production. That cannot be done. Socialism must know how to move history forward.

About the need of early destruction of capitalism and feudalism in two-thirds of the world, there should be no doubt or hesitation. Capitalism must increasingly mean poverty of body and soul to this part of the world. It cannot even feed these populations; it must perpetually undernourish them and occasionally starve them to death. It can only produce for profit and there is no scope for profit in these undeveloped economies, not certainly in food and houses and tools that may make the small man produce wealth, but perhaps in margarine, medicines, cinemas, and, above all, in speculation. It is increasingly reducting man to the status and work of half-man, half-horse, for, in India and elsewhere, horse-carriages are dying out for want of returns and being replaced by men who pull men. Retail traders multiply and factories decay. The truest symbol of Asia today is the rickshaw and the man-horse, for capitalism cannot provide many other openings for a living. Imitative of the ways of its rich white cousins, capitalism in the undeveloped areas carves out little islands of security and luxury in an ocean of black misery. To do that, it excels in buying and selling and specialises in hoarding and speculation. It even speculates in people's food and health and children's textbooks, for textbooks are altered almost every year to yield profit to their privileged publishers and writers. In the developed areas, honesty may be a good policy; India and similar areas prove the impossibility of making an honest living. Over everything settles the smell of decay and death; decay of body and economic aims and death of soul and general aims. Such a capitalism can no longer be pruned or amended; it must be uprooted and there is not much time to lose.

Two Types of Class Struggle

No greater disaster could befall socialism if the historical peculiarities of its career in Europe were sought to be universalised and reproduced in the other two-thirds of the world. Socialism in Europe has been gradual, constitutional and distributive. Socialism henceforth and in the rest of the world must be drastic, unconstitutional when necessary, and lay the accent on production. The great deeds of European socialism in the sphere of the welfare state must remain an inspiration and a model, but Europe's socialism had a reservoir of mass production, which Europe's capitalism had built and from where it could distribute. Socialism in the rest of the world must build the reservoir as much as it has to distribute its contents justly. It has to set up the investing and capital-forming community, before it can achieve the welfare-state. Where such a productive apparatus has yet to be created, socialism must be drastic and, in order to be that, it cannot always adhere to the slow processes of constitutionalism. While European socialists have earned lasting credit for their refusal to misuse power of government in order illegally to defeat their opponents and for their faith that to lose democratically is better than to win dictatorially, and, thus, set up a model of constitutional action when socialism is in office, socialism in opposition must often adopt the ways of struggle. The processes of persuasion and law-making are not always available or timely; to them must be added the methods of class struggle, particularly in the undeveloped areas. Class struggle hastens and matures the destruction of capitalism, without which two-third of the world cannot even make the first move.

The class struggle against capitalism is expressed through two major types, that which destroys capitalism in one of its aspects and reinforces it in another and the other that achieves socialism. Depending on what one thinks should be the outcome of the struggle against capitalism, one chooses between the two types. Those who believe that capitalism should be destroyed in its aspect of private property but should be strengthened in the aspect of its own peculiar technology and forces of production are naturally fond of large concentrations, centralised control and apparatus in which everything gets done to the detail according to a master-plan. Such an approach inevitably strives for power to the exclusion of all else. All such struggles and forms of party organization are encouraged in which, no matter how much the general aims of society are sacrificed, power appears to ensue. Hatred becomes the chief motor of such struggles and organization. As this power will be unable to achieve its economic aim of the big machine in industry and the combine in agriculture in two-thirds of the world, it will be marked after victory by barren cruelty as it is based on barren hate in the period of struggle. Such a class-struggle, however fiercely waged, is reactionary, for it can at best destroy capitalism in its aspect of private-property but must restore it in its aspect of technology and, to two-thirds of the world, his technological restoration of capitalism will spell economic barrenness and general inhumanity.

Immediacy in Struggle and Organization

Socialism must devise forms of struggle and organization which destroy capitalism in both of its aspects. Its struggle and organization must correspond with its economic aims. It aims economically at a technology that rationalises economy, not sector by sector nor region by region, but, as far as possible, in all sectors and regions at the same time. This immediacy must also characterise its struggle and organization. Not remote but immediate tests should be applied to the expressions of class struggle. Immediate tests would ever keep in the foreground issues of democracy and culture. Remote tests often sacrifice these for the achievement of power. The aim of immediacy in science and planning should be matched with the aim of immediacy in democracy and power. Such forms of struggle and organization must be encouraged, which diffuse democracy and power to the smallest unit, which assist every being to travel on the road to initiative and responsibility. Remote tests have led to a situation in which no act of struggle contains its own justification, each act is sought to be justified by the outcome of the next, the chain of justifying acts lengthens and the outcome of it all is horror and the death of general aims of society. Each act of struggle should contain its own justification. Its immediate quality must be such as makes it pass the tests of general aims of society. It must not justify a present lie by future truth, an immediate bureaucratisation by remote democracy, a present sacrifice of national freedom by a remote one-world, an immediate murder by a future health. Man is today become victim to ideologies of remote success, so that the chain of acts of horror lengthens and the last link of the good act is never forged. The immediate test of the good act should characterise the class struggles of socialism. Only then will socialism amass power enough to destroy capitalism in both its aspects and to achieve the economic as well as the general aims of society.

Communist modes of action and class struggle completely fail the test of immediacy. High priests of communism have rejected all notions of absolute morality and have raised evil behaviour into a noble virtue as long as it serves the cause of revolution. Socialists of India are becoming familiar with the communist empire of lies. Although the Socialist Party in India took no money from the US or any other foreign source for its election campaign, the party of communism ably supported by conservatives carried the lie into the remotest village. Those who believed the lie should have known that the doctrine of socialism admits of no short cuts to success and relies exclusively on internal resources for its political action, while the doctrine of communism obligates the receiving of foreign aid and the telling of lies for the revolution. Communism also jumps from one lie to another, so that trying to catch upon it and deny it is a waste of effort. In similar wise, sacrifice of national freedom and treason becomes a commendable virtue if practised for the international solidarity of the working class as expressed through Russia or China. Democracy or parliament is utilised alone for its destruction and, what is perhaps worse, the hierarchical spirit and cult of complete obedience to the party leads to the abandonment of all responsibility and democratic conscience except such as is expressed through the highest committee. Mass violence and purges are a necessary instrument. Above all, communism denies reason and has no faith in the capacity of the people to reach a decisively clear judgement except through civil war or improbable conditions of democratic maturity as in England. It holds capitalist control over information, education and the army strong enough to prevent the people from giving a decisive verdict in its favour. A doctrine such as this, which does not trust the people fully, is never reciprocated with adequate confidence of the people. A communist government through the vote for a whole people is therefore a contradiction in terms. Until communism achieves its problematic victory through an insurrection, its chief role is to split the socialist vote thus to assist in the continuance of a conservative government.

Conservatism and communism have a strange identity of interests against socialism. Conservatism holds socialism as its democratic rival and does not fear communism except as a threat of successful insurrection. Communism prefer the continuance of conservative government and is mortally afraid of a Socialist Party coming to office, for its chances of an insurrection are then dimmed. Until communism revolts successfully, it is a doctrine of succour and support to the bourgeoisie. Even after a successful revolt, it does not cease to be a doctrine of evil behaviour, for its economic aim of mass production and abundant living is unachievable in two-thirds of the world, and consequently its general aim of a remote culture is an ideal that ever recedes. The class struggle of communism is a doctrine of deceit, lies, treason, tyranny, decay of culture, and also, of assistance to capitalism until a successful revolt takes place.

Three Qualities of Modern Civilization

The like debacle of capitalism and communism is easily understood when they are viewed as parts of a single civilization that appears to have neared the end of its voyage. All civilizations have aimed at comfort, culture, peace and the ideal kingdom and what distinguishes one civilization from another are the processes to attain them and their precise content. Every civilization is moved by certain purposes of life and certain specific drives. To seek to understand these human purposes through categories such as religious or secular, authoritarian or libertarian, rational or emotive, feudal or capitalist, spiritual or materialist is not an adequate venture. Modern civilization cannot be understood in terms of democracy or totalitarianism, private or state property alone. The distinguishing drives of modern civilization are continuous application of science to economy, rising standard of living and increasing social equality. What moves a modern society is the impulse for an increasing output, and a modern man the desire for rising standards and an improving home. No previous civilization entertained such impulses, for it did not possess a revolutionary technology. Nor was any previous civilization so powerfully influenced by the passionate urge for social equality, also now possible through this changing technology. The modern man, whether in the US or Soviet Russia, is moved by identical aims of increasing output through mass production and a beautiful home and wants these purposes to be placed within the reach of all, primarily within his own nation. At the end of the realisation of these aims lies heaven on earth and the ideal kingdom, equality, peace and the full life. But road-blocks are multiplying.

The three qualities of modern civilization, revolutionary technology, rising standards and social equality have run into trouble. Revolutionary technology is face to face with the demon of its own creation that it cannot slay, the terrifying poverty of two-thirds of the world. No matter to what amazing heights it is reaching in the US, or the USSR, it is unable to expand in West Europe, the first seat of its glory, where it has stayed constant in the past three decades. The hunger for rising standards is breaking its teeth on the stone of a constant or decreasing output. The anxieties, tensions and general emptiness arising out of the unsatiable hunger for increasing output and living standards are becoming unbearable. The relationship between man and things is reversed so that these use him rather than he them. West Europe, the prince of modern civilization, is showing the same irritation towards the US which India has been feeling against it, the irritation of a poor relation or, perhaps, the wisdom that comes after having been out-raced by a new comer that the race is anyway not worth running at all. The tensions and emptiness of modern life seem difficult to overcome, whether under capitalism or communism, as the hunger for rising standards is their mother and is common to both. Capitalist expected their ideal kingdom to arise out of each man's self-interest operating under a perfect competition; communists still expect their ideal kingdom to arise out of social ownership over means of production. Their common fallacy has now shown up that the general aims of society do not inevitably flow out of certain economic aims. An integrated relationship between the two sets of aims has to be set up by the intelligence of man. Likewise, social, political and economic equality, which has reached heights unscaled by any previous civilization and which has made the duchess and the laundress look almost alike, is cracking up because it did not at the same time explore spiritual equality. If previous civilizations broke down under the weight of a spiritual equality coupled to a social inequality, modern civilization appears to be cracking under the weight of a social equality coupled to a spiritual inequality. Collective life has become so callous and man is but the object of an experiment.

Irrelevance of Capitalism and Communism

The mind of modern civilization came to the end of its voyage some decades ago. The present century has known only one originator, Mahatma Gandhi, and only one discovery, the atomic bomb; the discovery is the culmination of modern civilization same as the originator came out of a womb not yet identifiable or strong. Modern civilization has placed idea entirely in the service of force and it cannot be otherwise as long as its three drives are not subjected to a relentless examination. The accusations against each other of capitalism and communism, of the US and the USSR, mount, but they are unable to slay the twin demons of poverty and war and what they say or do only serves to heighten their demonic quality. The have enveloped the world with fear and hate. Man is no longer at peace with himself. He must move away from existing civilization in both its aspects of capitalism and communism. Their kindred qualities and drives have made them both equally irrelevant to venture into a new civilization. This theory of equal irrelevance must not be confused with the doctrine of equal evil or the contemptuous wishing of plague on both houses. This theory does not set itself upon a high moral pedestal from where to judge and denounce; it is perfectly aware of the imperishable glory of the existing civilization and its achievement of social equality which was never before reached by any earlier civilization. There is much to learn from the thought and practices of the existing civilization and many of its features will inevitably go with due integrations into the new human effort. The theory of equal irrelevance is the decision of the traveller on a new road, who refuses to be tempted by the two other roads that go round and round and lead nowhere. Nothing is more fatal for such a traveller than to waste his time in comparisons between the two other roads; they are equally irrelevant to him and, if a language of overtones must be used, they are equally good or equally evil.

Systems and Peoples

Adherents of the Atlantic as well as the Soviet Camps are deeply hurt by the theory of equal irrelevance. They are correct in diagnosing the virus of the opponent but are singularly blind to their own. Concealment of such viruses denotes grave peril to mankind. There is no need to keep quiet over the suppressions and tyrannies of communism, the disaster of its economic aims when applied to the underdeveloped areas and the barren cruelty that it represents. There is equally no need to keep quiet over the Atlantic effort to act as world's policemen and instructors on behalf of decay, the girdle of firm dealing and reform they are trying to throw round all the world and their mad culmination of modern civilization. Nevertheless, it is said that possibilities of change in a democracy make it preferable in any event to a dictatorship. These possibilities are theoretical. Even property relations are exceedingly difficult to change, but a civilization has never yet been known to fly out of its skin to change its specific drives and purposes. A living civilization prospers or is relegated; it does not change. Should this rare display of human intelligence ever occur, those who achieve it will recognise that the theory of equal irrelevance was correct until then. It is true that possibilities of free conversation and debate enable contacts among like-minded people in all lands, which gives joy. Meanwhile, what an armed guard accomplishes under communism is generally obtained by the pressure of events and conventions, which outflank a heretic, in a democracy. Possibilities of change within the framework of the existing civilization are not altogether absent in communism. They come unheralded and without debate. A Yugoslavia may be a rare event, but it has happened once. Some socialists who detest communism find greater kinship with Yugoslav Communist Party than with socialist parties of many a land. After their break with international communism, Yugoslav communists are facing toward socialism, with their gallant instinct for national freedom and for a force away from the two camps and their taste for decentralisation.

The peoples of all lands have endearing qualities and they are all equally relevant to the new civilization. The two forms of the existing civilization, capitalist and communist, are equally irrelevant to a new creation, but not so the peoples living under them. Who will not be fascinated by the young vitality of the Americans and their direct virtues, the method and thoroughness of the Germans, and mellow manners of the British? Such Slavs and Chinese as one meets whet the appetite and the Slavs awaken nostalgic memories of the common ancestor of some centuries ago and cause regret that one cannot oftener make contacts with the great peoples of Russia and China. Communist governments have erected three barriers between their peoples and the outside world. None but communists live in these lands so that a meeting of like minds unless one is a communist is not possible. It is only natural that a socialist of India should feel a kinship with the socialists of Burma or Yugoslavia, France or Africa, Germany or America, which he cannot with the communists of Russia or China. The people to people relationships are further soured, because, only under communism does a whole people and its government form exclusive friendship with communist parties of all lands to the natural irritation of their non-communists. Lastly, calumny replaces argument and, although the Socialist Party of India is just as much pro-American as pro-Soviet, international communism has heaped lie upon lie in order to malign it as an agent and spy of America. The builders of a new civilization will not lose their self-assurance. They will criticise where criticism is due. They will not counter-balance every criticism of America with a simultaneous criticism of Russia or vice versa. An argument must take its course and lack of self-confidence must not mar its logic. Organized non-violence must be able to see both communism and capitalism in the face, without flinching but with pity, and without hate but with anger. Enmity may fade away.

Brigades of Reconstruction

There is now a remote possibility that the grim combatants of existing civilization may somewhat relax their tensions and cold war. They may be willing to listen to proposals for an international pool of resources and for international brigades of reconstruction. The pool will help underdeveloped areas create faster what they cannot do by themselves. If the developed areas help the underdeveloped world create what it needs, it will in its turn help them to conserve what they have already created. Creation and conservation will be joined together. The brigades will throw together men and women of all nationalities into a common effort of reconstruction and peace. National qualities may melt into one another and excesses may be cured. From the white world's activity may be shed its strife; from the dark world's poise its sloth. Activity may wed poise. A physical and cultural approximation of humanity may for the first time take place on design. The youth from Africa, America, China, Europe, India, Russia and other lands and continents working together on projects of well-being may create a temper for peace such as the tortured world of today cannot imagine. Some government should gather enough courage to keep on presenting proposals for World Brigades of Reconstruction and a World Development Authority through the UN and similar bodies. In any event, people's organizations must move as many young men and women as possible away from their habitual surroundings and make them labour and build in strange lands, not only to give what they know but also to take what they do not possess. The dark world may learn to be less slothful and the white world may give up some of its strife and this cultural approximation of various races may well prove to be one sure way to pluck the prize of peace. The cult of co-existence of hostile systems is fuzzy, but the doctrine of coexistence with approximation enforced by a higher world conscience may enable them to coexist, cure their excesses and approximate.

Outcastes, the Inheritors

Capitalism and communism are but two parts of the single complex of exisitng civilization. Often before, a civilization has split up into two warring prongs in a valiant effort to renew itself, and their shots are heard throughout the world so as to deafen men against the still small voice of the new civilization. The communist theory on human civilization is all upside down. If an earlier idealism seized upon the peak point of history attained in Prussia as man's fulfilment, the communist theory has similarly wanted to freeze the peak points attained in West Europe into eternal splendour. History does not move entirely within a civilization. If it did, no civilization would ever decay or be relegated and there would be no shifts of power from one region of the world to another. When a civilization flickers, the torch generally passes into the hands of its outcastes. The outcastes of the present civilization are the underdeveloped two-thirds of the world. But they are worthy of the torch only if they make a break with the old and devise their own forms of thinking and living. What may happen, for the first time on earth, is a joint endeavour of the human race to devise these new forms. That will be the rarest intelligence and a consummation to be devoutly hoped. Who likes these continual shifts, at least, not the Asians, who remember the ashen taste of having in the past sat on the peak points of history.

New Drives

Socialist parties in European lands and of the US will do well to link their thinking and action with this great drama of a change-over in human civilization. They have hitherto brought their peoples up on the desire for an ever-increasing standard of living and their action in that direction has been limited to their national frontiers. They should now venturesomely ask their peoples to help achieve a decent standard of living for everyone in the world, even at the cost of some sacrifice in their own standards. Their peoples will understand. They pay regularly the cruel price of war for national progress in their material standards. The reward for some sharing of what they possess in order to secure international progress in living standards may well be peace. Indoctrination into the demand for every rising standards of living within national frontiers is patently wrong. It leads to frustration when not realised as in England. Its thunder is stolen by the capitalist as in the US and it does not answer the American's need for peace of mind. Socialism should be a doctrine that thrives not alone in misery but also in conditions of comfort and comparative luxury. While decentralization of technology and political power may be exceedingly difficult to practise in West Europe and the US, their socialism should somehow inscribe on its bannner the demand for a life of poise and slower tempo. It must indeed campaign for such programmes as a nationalisation health service, civil disobedience against injustice and nationalisation as in England or the guaranteed annual wage as in the US While the twin demands for a decent standard of living to all mankind and for a life of poise and peace without hunger for ever-rising material standards to peoples of Europe and the US may give world socialism its new drives, a World Parliament and a World Law should also be sought to secure the freedom of the smallest nations and to abolish war. Furthermore, European socialism has had to become a part of the Atlantic Camp. Instead of trying to shape world socialism in its own image or persuade Asia's socialist to adopt its foreign policies, European socialist should wish for added strength to Asia's socialism in its striving to chisel the distinct features of socialism as the creator of a new civilization. While Asia's socialists should never tire of keeping away from both forms and caps of the existing civilization and of providing socialism with its own distinct face, they might treat Europe's socialist with consideration, whom the accumulation of past deeds and history seldom lets act except as a corrective.

An event of great significance is the projected full conference of Asian socialists. It is only proper that gallant little Burma, whose leadership rests in the wise hands of U. Nu, U. Ba Swe, U. Kyaw Nyein and which enjoys the benevolent presence of that rare treasure of Asia, Mrs. Aung San, should be the venue of this conference. While Asia's socialists will fulfil their pledge only to the extent that they become aware of the great problems of human civilization and therefore do not imitate Europe's socialists, they must ever prize the world unity of socialism as a high aim of their endeavour. No one is a socialist unless he is equally free and frank and friendly with socialist of all lands and skins.

The Right of Way?

The foregoing examination of economic and general aims reveals that they have both their autonomous existence, but that a doctrine of their integration is possible. This integration also provides the doctrinal foundation of socialism. The contemptuous theory, shared alike by capitalism and communism, that general aims are automatically secured after the fulfilment of certain economic aims must be rejected, if for no other reason than that the economic aims of both doctrines are impossible to fulfil. Another theory that any set of general aims can be superimposed by man's effort on any set of economic aims is somewhat more insidious. This theory grants an independence to both types of aims, which they do not possess. Their autonomy is valid only to the extent that they are integrated into a harmony; otherwise one must give the right of way to the other. Without integrated harmony, it is generally the economic aims which command the right of way, no matter what calamity they might thereby bring. The democratic and liberal faith, the great religions and the creed of organised non-violence must all give the right of way to whatever economic aims a society sets for itself, unless they take care to shape these in their own image. They may be remembered at prayer-time and on ceremonial occasions or when a person gives himself the luxury of contemplation. They may at best somewhat colour the personality and cleanse the main stream of life just a little, but they are powerless to alter the flow.

International socialism operates on the hypothesis that on the economic life of planning and mass production and rising standards can be grafted the general aims of society through an effort of the will. All that needs to be done is sanction to the charter of human rights, to democratic representation and workers' control and, generally, to the worth of human personality. The absurdity of such an imposition has been indicated. Some variants of the hypothesis of international socialism have shown up in Asia. The socialists of Burma, for instance, believe that Marxism and Buddhism are symmetrical doctrines, that Marxism satisfies the material needs of man while Buddhism answers the spiritual needs and that the two can and must go together. Such a belief is patently illogical and untenable. But this belief can under certain conditions produce beneficial results, which will in turn lead to the correct doctrine. Burma socialist will soon enough be faced with awkward situations in which they will be called upon to surrender either Marxism or Buddhism, but, if they fortunately prove true to both, they will be compelled to achieve the theory of integration of economic and general aims of society.

Forms of Action

While it is necessary to give a firm foundation to the theory of socialism, it is equally necessary to discover the appropriate forms of action through which the doctrine may be realised. An unfortunate emphasis has hitherto been placed on two modes of action, electioneering activity and insurrectionary activity, and opposition has been allowed to develop between the two. Socialists are often wont to reject the democratic process of the vote when unsuccessful and to resort to insurrectionary action at least in speech. To the extent that the Party's *Policy Statement* encourages, even though without meaning it, this polarity between the ballot and the bullet, it needs to be supplemented with a clarification.

All actions should be aimed at the expression and organization of the people's will and at reconstructing the national life in whatever measure possible. While doing good in the immediate, they should amass power enough for socialism in order that it may defeat capitalism. The organization of the people's will is of primary importance and its expression through the vote or revolt or other appropriate forms is a secondary question of passing value. The party of socialism must have power and organization enough so that it can use them in the service of whatever action may be deemed appropriate at the time. In order that such power and organization may be built up, the party of socialism should continually strive to become a spokesman of the people, organizer of its will, resister against injustice and accomplisher of reconstruction. It must be ready ever to take part in constructive action, to enlighten the popular verdict and be enlightened by it in turn and to resist injustice; three modes of action already symbolised by the spade, the vote and the prison.

Parties in office or such as depend on the maintenance of the status quo and those which use hate and fear for their growth have always found constructive action a dull and tardy affair but the doctrine of socialism cannot thrive except through constructive action. It must indicate to the people, even while in opposition and in however small and ineffective samples, what it wishes to accomplish when in government. It must do good even while in opposition so that it lives not alone on promises about the future, but also on accomplishment in the present. The Socialist Party has in the recent past attempted to unfold a whole range of constructive activities around agricultural reconstruction. It has attempted to move the people to dig for minor canals, wells, tanks, roads and other projects. This and other types of constructive action must become the primary and acknowledged modes of socialist action. A main reason why organization of the peasantry and factory workers, such as the Hind Kisan Panchayat or the Hind Mazdoor Sabha, have not grown as fast as they should is their neglect of constructive action. The Kisan Panchayat must be built to resist injustice, and equally so, to change people's habits with regard to food and the way to eat, raising of crops, making of manure and assist them in storing and marketing of produce and in finding good tools.

Organization, A By-Product

Such constructive action is also a chief instrument for organizing and educating the people. The Socialist Party must learn from its experience that mere enrolment of members does not lead to an organization nor do its persistent efforts for a volunteer corps or a youth movement bear fruit. Other parties that live on hate or fear may find it possible to train a volunteer corps through simple drilling or parading or through acts of fitful violence. The Socialist Party must learn that organization will come to it and its affiliates as a by-product of action and not as something which is aimed at directly. Only to the extent that its members and units are put to tangible work does organization result. As long as socialists aim at organization directly, they will be frustrated, but when they aim at some concrete reconstruction, organization will automatically come out of it. The problem of political education can be solved in a similar way. Propaganda meetings and the study circle are the two chief vehicles for political education. The Socialist Party has lacked in the study centre. Apart from the fact that efforts were not so persistent, a main reason why the programme of study centre has failed is the absence of concreteness and its lack of anchor. A network of study centres must be woven around a network of constructive centres.

The village or the unit that builds up a constructive and a study centre achieves two parts of a single activity and will prosper in both. Political workers as a rule lack in regional knowledge, no matter to what party they belong, or however much they may be able to mouth stale theory. That is why they are unable to withstand the encroachment of bureaucracy upon democracy. In order that democracy may achieve the greatest diffusion of power and active participation of the people, the politician down to the smallest unit must be equipped with regional knowledge as much as with theory. Unfortunately, however, a great deal of regionalism in spirit obtains while little or none at all in knowledge. Politicians of the village, as much as of the nation, are naturally prone to guard their preserve against outsiders not through better knowledge but through disastrous sentiments of exclusiveness. A study centre hinging on a constructive centre will equip such politicians as much with regional knowledge as with theory. Socialists must overcome their corrupting aversion to reading.

It may also not be forgotten that the Indian people are perhaps the saddest on earth and the element of delight is lacking in them and their politicians. Short temper, working at cross purposes, and intrigue mark politics in India more than elsewhere. Politicians in other countries do not take opposition and defeat quite so much to heart and engage in other pursuits of delight and joy. The Puritanism of the politician in India usually turns into sour intrigue, all in the service of the high deal he imagines to profess. Whatever, therefore, scatters this grey sadness and expresses the natural instinct of delight and joy must be acknowledged as a genuine type of constructive action.

Resistance to Injustice

Constructive action must be supplemented by resistance to injustice. Throughout the world, and more so in the underdeveloped territories, a doctrine and a party is judged not alone by what it professes but also by the extent to which it can struggle and suffer. The people are drawn to a faith that brings out the capacity to bear witness and to suffer. Apart from the political advantages of a struggle, it is difficult to believe how a genuine doctrine can stay unmoved in face of an injustice and, whenever a doctrine does so, there is something lacking in it. A propagandist agitation against injustice, if it is not fake, must necessarily lead to resistance.

The Socialist Party has in the recent past suffered generally from a miscalculation. Eager to organize the popular verdict in favour of socialism, it thought that a diffusion of activity into struggles would reduce its capacity to win votes. Such a mechanical conception of organization is wrong and socialism should never again repeat the error. It has now been established that areas where socialists undertook resistance to injustice have generally returned them to the legislatures, no matter how long they stayed in prison or how much their organization was apparently broken up. The spade, the vote and the prison are all interrelated activities and, whatever mode of action powerfully influences the people's will, its effect is undoubtedly felt in the other spheres.

Another error obstructs the free expression of *satyagraha*. It is commonly supposed that a call for resistance to injustice must go out from a higher committee before it can be undertaken by primary units and members.

Undoubtedly, situations arise in which a whole nation or a whole state is called upon to bear witness to its faith and to struggle against injustice. But there are other situations in which no such call can go out and where primary units and even the individual must shoulder the responsibility for an act of resistance. Whoever refuses to resist injustice, when other forms of agitation are not available or exhausted, becomes a party to it. To the extent that such potential *satyagrahis* increase in a nation, to that extent is the nation free. The best defence of freedom is the readiness of individuals and of primary units of organization to resist injustice. Of the two types of civil disobedience, that undertaken on the call of a high committee and the other carried out by a primary unit or individual, the latter requires a greater democratic awareness.

No society is completely free from injustice but India and the other underdeveloped territories abound in misery and repression. Various issues of chronic undernourishment, starvation and famine, land ownership, high prices, dismissal and unemployment, expensive medicine and education, high rents and no houses and, on top of them police repression are daily acquiring such proportions that the whole of India may well become a vast stage for intermittent practices in *satyagraha*. A day may come later when the whole nation is summoned to organize resistance against injustice and for the achievement of a new order.

Satyagraha and Class Struggle

A fancy opposition has been allowed to grow between *satyagraha* and class struggle. There is in fact no such opposition and a genuine class struggle is civil disobedience. It is commonly believed that the driving motive of stayagraha is to change the heart of the opponent, while the theory of class struggle admits of no such change of a whole class and therefore requires the overthrow of the exiting order. Whole civil disobedience is indeed a mode to change the heart of the opponent, it is even more so an effort to reduce his power and to increase the power of the good doctrine. *Satyagraha* and class struggle are but two names for a single exercise in power, reduction of the power of evil and increase in the power of the good. That a change of heart does take place is evident, more so in the ranks of the good doctrine in so far as they acquire greater determination and organization and capacity for action but also in the ranks of the opponents some of whom begin to be declassed. It must be repeated again that an act of satyagraha or class struggle must pass the test of immediacy and it must not make use of lies or deceit or violence. Crude practices should be eliminated.

The issue of force plays a large part in any socialist debate and some socialists believe that the ultimate overthrow of the existing order cannot be carried out except by force. This debate has proved harmful to the progress of the socialist doctrine and movement. Whether force is ultimately used or not is a secondary question and the primary issue is whether to organize the people's will on the basis of peaceful struggles or otherwise. The distinguishing feature of a movement should be whether it advocates and organizes violence and not whether it ultimately uses force. A brief instant may be reached in the life of the people when the existing order rests alone on bayonets and these bayonets are shaky and the vast mass is determinedly striving for the new order. In this brief moment, the people may well choose to exercise their majesty of power so as to end to agony of old and give birth to the new. This will be spontaneous violence of the people displayed only for a brief moment. One may hope that even this may not be necessary. In any event, such a momentary display cannot become the enduring basis of a theory of organization.

A mark of degradation of man is the extent to which he makes and listens to demagogue appeals of force. Such appeals to violence are a denial of reason and of the basis which may one day enable man to rear a decent life. Doctrines which ennoble violence are incapable of achieving a classless and casteless society. Socialism must learn to distinguish itself rigorously from such doctrines. Socialism must ever denounce the advocacy and organization of violence and it must strive to achieve such basis of peaceful struggles as will lead to increased individual initiative and responsibility and not to concentration of power. Organization of violence inevitably leads to concentration of power. The use of violence is a major issue in the world of today and large numbers are beginning to realise that the advocacy and organization of violence is bad even when used for good purposes.

Challenge to Violence

A tremendous difficulty has indeed shown itself. Violence is of two types, that which expresses itself in the relationship of two or more states and in wars, and the other which expresses itself in the internal politics of a people through murder and insurrection. Against the violence of wars, no method of peaceful struggle has yet been evolved, although some feeble and praiseworthy attempts are being made. But the internal politics of a nation need not now pollute itself with recourse to organized violence. Modes of peaceful struggle are available. All the good world must make a mighty effort to dramatise this issue of organization for non-violence *versus* organized violence in such a fashion that doctrines which glorify violence are stripped of their glamour.

The great continent of Africa is eminently suited for this drama in human affairs. Issues of national freedom and of discrimination between man and man on the basis of colour and creed have come to the fore. Shall these issues be decided by the organization of non-violence or by the use of organized violence? A great event of our times is the decision of the people of South Africa to practise civil disobedience. The rest of Africa is also striving for national freedom. There have been international brigades in the past to take part in wars. The time has now come for an international brigade recruited from all over the world to take part in this African endeavour for the organization of non-violence. If the socialist parties of West Europe may find it embarrassing to raise such international brigades, the socialist youth may well do so. There are any number of other liberal minded people, pacifists, religious men and democrats throughout the world who could assist in such an effort. Inside the great Republic of the United States, there is ample scope for the exercise of civil disobedience on the issue of discrimination between Whites and Negroes and on problems of citizenship. That is not to deny that similar scope is available on the issue of caste system and citizenship in India. The day may come when the exercise of civil disobedience in numerous countries of the world produces its effect on people living under communism. The whole world must be jostled out of a smug belief in the advocacy and organization of violence. Callousness and brutality whether on the part of the government or the people must go. Instead, must awake a world mind which holds violence in contempt and revulsion but which also knows how to resist injustice non-violently.

When socialism is able to unfold continuous programmes of construction and struggle, the winning of votes will naturally follow. No one should minimize the importance of the vote, for it is the grandest expression of the people's will. This expression may sometimes go counter to the doctrine and programmes of socialism, but it will not do then for the Party to blame the people or deride the vote. Both the people and the Party are at fault in such an event, for if the people are not sufficiently enlightened the Party too is not sufficiently mature. A main defect of socialist agitators is to look upon themselves as teachers of the people and they must realise that they are students as well. A two-way relationship of student and teacher should be established between the people and the Party. Whoever is aware of such a relationship will look upon an electoral reverse as a spur to further efforts for improving the party and enlightening the people. The majesty of the vote should never be derided, for there is no alternative to it. In another sphere the alternatives are between peaceful struggle against injustice and organization of violence, between peaceful revolution and armed insurrection. "Ballot or Bullet" is a wicked presentation made by capitalism and communism; the choice is "Satyagraha or Bullet".

The Party of Socialism must indeed learn to approach the people with a richer variety of programmes than hitherto. The accent on peasants' and workers' movement must continue but a more diversified approach should be made to other sectors of the population including the middle and professional classes. The Party must also become sensitive to general problems of the day and be able to sweep the whole people into movements that lift them up. While food and corruption are obvious issues on which to move the people and where the government may be forced to appoint high policy committees consisting of representatives of all major parties in the country and to take action, the great value of general and cultural movements should not be lost sight of. Such are, for instance, the great movements for world parliament and world peace and for the consolidation of socialist in Asia and throughout the world and for international brigades whether of reconstruction or peaceful struggles. The Party should also be able to play its part in the cultural, literary and artistic life of the people without wanting to establish a political dictatorship over it.

Social Reforms

Socialism should act more powerfully with regard to issues of caste and in relation to women. The Party of Socialism in India and some other underdeveloped territories has indeed resolved to destroy the system of caste and subjection of women, but it is generally inert on these issues. Some socialists have been slow on these issues for fear of hostility that they might arouse or in the belief that, after establishment of a socialist government, these issues would get resolved automatically. Some have also thought that there was no point in making a special appeal to women as they would go alongside with their men. Such notions are mischievous. Not only do they lose many valuable votes that would otherwise have come to socialism, they do greater harm by obstructing the Party in the fulfilment of its essential functions. The Party of Socialism must be brave enough to open a full-scale attack on social evils prevailing among the people. Should it appear for a brief moment to lose popular approval, it should be sustained by the hope and the knowledge that the people will come to it in increased numbers after obscuring clouds have been cleared away. No party wins if it is unwilling to risk temporary disapproval for right causes. The socialist legislators must seek out occasions in their various parliaments to remove social evils, to destroy the systems of caste and wedding expenditure and to control growth in population. Socialists must be willing to state outright that the decay attendant upon systems of caste and marriage settlements destroys far more than transitional excesses that may arise out of free social relationships. A socialist movement without the active participation of women is like a wedding without the bride. Not only are women ultimately responsible for the health of the race and the growth of the new generation, they are also the chief support of a movement for peaceful resistance. Every six out of ten men but every eight out of ten women are today undernourished. The Socialist Party and the women of India may both ponder the need of coming together.

Grass Roots

Every socialist organizer must strive to become the companion in life and in death of his locality. He must have fun and friendliness enough so that no festival or feast is complete without him; he must be ever ready and resourceful to have petty complaints removed; he must combat injustice; he must be comprehensively aware of all the constructive possibilities in the area and take part in their realisation. There has been a lamentable tendency to self-pity and to bemoan the lack of zeal and discipline among socialists. A socialist does not and should not possess the fanatical hate of the communal or communist reactionary, and we should be happy at this. But the socialist has at times shown the deep springs of loyalty and devotion that lie within him, he has risen to heights of sacrifice and works himself to the bone when the spirit moves him, he is indeed somewhat lethargic and lack concentration and is sometimes quarrelsome, and there is nothing the matter with the fine youth that forms the core of the Socialist Party. The time is come to try to free this gold of its dross.

There is nothing more important than educational and training programmes, an arm of the Party which has been so sadly neglected hitherto. In the absence of training into the doctrinal foundation of socialism and its combination of sympathy and anger, he imbibes the hate around him and feels frustrated when the Party's programmes do not enable him to express it. The socialist must learn to integrate the economic and the general aims of society. He must spurn the spurious doctrine of water-tight division between private and public life. While cruel and ignorant puritanism must be rejected, there is no need to countenance deceit and selfish intrigues and undemocratic behaviour. While each one must draw his own line on how far he could go without transgressing into vulgarity, this line must be drawn and a socialist code for conduct should voluntarily grow. There is also need for socialist ashrams, at least one in each state, to which members of the Party could repair in times of spiritual need and which would radiate an atmosphere of creative work and creative rest. These ashrams should be largely self-sufficient out of such crops and crafts as they can produce. It is in the Indian tradition to build ashrams for the training of the spirit and the spread of a doctrine, and every movement in the world has built its own centres in the name of the commune or some other. A sound doctrine and training into it will probably give the socialist movement an uplifting quality of the spirit, so that its acts of sympathy and its acts of anger are all passionate. Whosoever touches it will then be suffused with the joy of oneness.

Initiative and Discipline

Certain principles of organization must in addition receive the Party's assent. The inglorious centralization of initiative and decentralization of discipline must be rapidly reversed into the decentralization of initiative and the centralisation of discipline. While discipline is largely internal to a man and the outcome of a doctrine held with conviction and of training, it must also be externally enforced. Disciplinary action may be rare, but it must be quickly enforced and without fear and partisanship. Various limbs of the Party must be taught to help one another and their centres and the Party must grow a nervous system. Decentralized initiative will probably be the weightiest factor towards the growth of a disciplined party. Coordination in activities and choice of priorities must also be attempted. Much has been made of the difference in speech of those who are commonly called leaders of the Party. This difference in speech would have resulted into an orchestra, had there been a coordinated offensive on selected targets. Because of the country's vastness and other reasons, such a coordination has been lacking. It must anyhow be attempted. The leaders, needless to say, are tied with inescapable bonds that will not let them seek another companionship.

New persons will come into the Party. The people of India, in particular its intellectuals, are showing greater interest in the Party, probably because of a heightened sense of responsibility in view of the threat of stagnation and chaos. These newcomers should be welcomed with warmth. They must indeed not aspire for office straightway, for that makes them suspect in the eyes of others and does not provide them a period to qualify and make friends. The Party must learn adjustment. Not everyone should be expected to do every job. The Party must also learn to dismiss with contempt the maligning done by its opponents of newcomers and old comrades, with a view either to stem the expansion of the Party or drive a wedge into its leadership. A dirty political trick of opponents is to pick out persons from the Party, some for praise and others for denunciation.

Withdrawal and Return

Socialists must also learn to appreciate the principle of withdrawal. Withdrawal is not necessarily permanent; it may be temporary or from certain spheres. Either because a person has not been too successful or feels inconvenient in certain spheres or has just been there too long, or for clarity in policies, he may retire from relevant offices and executives and such temporary withdrawals should occasion no comment nor sorrow. His activity will not diminish, whether as crew or as captain. In this land of non-attachment, politicians retire only when they die, for they are either indispensable or greedy and the line between the two is not always easy to draw. The principle of temporary withdrawals will add freshness and zest of political life. New men will get trained; they will express their zest and also become responsible. This will minimize the chances of organizational disputes over personnel of executives turning into ideological disputes. People will cease to fight an unreal and disastrous battle of ideas, when they are actually fighting a battle of organization. The leadership of the Party, whatever it may be at any moment and from village right up to nation, must concern itself with policies and programmes and their execution and the display of manifold initiative at all levels and let the organization run its own course democratically within the limits of discipline, even if that course may appear to be somewhat unpleasant.

Awkward situations arise when judgements have to be made and opinions differ. Democracy knows no way other than that of debate and majority decision. Such judgements are not necessarily correct. But that is no reason why those who differ should go behind these judgements, seek out imaginary motives for the error and translate every difference of opinion into a crisis of principles. No party can live in a state of permanent crisis. At the same time, judgements should be made in the light of considered principles and after weighty consideration and not on grounds of expediency or under pressures. There should be no display of autocracy or compulsion. Decisions are being made every day, officially and unofficially, which appear eminently correct to some and equally incorrect to others. Such are, for instance, the unofficial decisions for the red cap and official decisions on the presidential election, prohibition, united front and on issues which cut into agriculture and industry at the same time. The red cap is in India's tradition of sectarianism and devaluation of deepest philosophies into outward symbols. While return to the white cap as a headgear of national unity may be somewhat difficult, the Socialist Party must cure itself of externalism and exercise itself on the evolution of a dress which will not reveal the wearer's politics or religion. Even after the Congress party had badly mismanaged the presidential nomination and in view of no socialist or superior candidate being in the field, the outstanding merit of President Rajendra Prasad as a freedom-fighter and of having later born himself with dignity and fairness should have met with recognition at the hands of the Socialist Party. On all such issues, there are bound to be debate and differences of opinion. One may hope for an earnest debate, but it should not degenerate into a crisis.

False Polarization

An incipient polarization between the Congress party and the Communist Party seem to have emerged as a result of the general elections. This poisonous seed must be scotched before it bears foul fruit and paralyses the nation's mind and activity. There are reasons to hope that the polarization is temporary and a timely warning to India's socialists to act. It would be a mistake to ascribe the gains of the Communist Party to its programmes or energy and to the illiterate belief that misery breeds communism. Misery may breed good and evil; there is no reason why, with faith and work, it should not lead to the belief into socialism. Two main reasons have resulted in communist gains. The Communist Party has been willing to act, however mischievously. Its belt of electoral victory is strictly co-terminous with the areas where it burnt and killed. Without going into the comparatively irrelevant question whether communist terrorism was a provocation for or a retaliation against governmental repression, it must be noted that the Communist Party was thoroughly trounced where it did not burn and kill, the big northern and central belt. The lesson of this remarkable happening must be drawn. Poverty and misery have so harassed the people that they are willing to lend their ear to whoever apparently suffers for them. They will be drawn to the communists when the government chases them and inflicts unmerited suffering on many innocent people in the process. The people have however shown their conclusive preference for peaceful struggle, wherever they were provided with the opportunity to judge and choose.

The fact of communist gains in areas of their violent activity also opens out a dangerous prospect. Having tasted victory, they are likely to repeat the adventure, which gave it, in other areas. Whenever the communist effort at consitutionalism exhaust itself, the adventure will start. This will naturally never give them the majority but it may well establish them in the estimate of around one quarter of the people, a vantage point from where they will expand their won army of liberation and hope for a turning of the regular army. The Socialist Party needs to devote its attention to the soldier whose loyalty and refusal to take part in shooting politics is a mainstay of India's democracy. The soldier must on the one hand be made aware of the forces now at large in the world and on the other his problems such as the monthly pension of Rs. 15/- to Rs. 30/- after he is crippled and disabled in a battle must be brought into the open. Much more than this, the Socialist Party must forestall adventure into violence by its own constructive action and peaceful struggles throughout the land. Communist gains must also be traced to the two temples of international worship which they have erected, Russia and China. Once a worship starts, all questions of right and wrong dissolve, as all wrongs are done for the greater glory of the temple. It is useless to expose communist tactics, their twists and turns and their acknowledgement after every four years that they were wrong in the earlier period, without exposing the true nature of their worship. Once the mind is seized with the idea that the Soviet temples are saviours of mankind and that they will inevitably grow, it does not matter whether a communist party allies itself with capitalism and the government of the day, whether it preaches democracy or dictatorship, for all that is a problem of tactics. India's intellecutals and government have in the recent past encouraged worship in one such communist temple but there are reasons to hope that they will not long continue to force silence on the telling of truth about such centres of worship.

Ironed Out? Never

Socialists of India must know that the reasons for their reverses are removable. Socialist candidates were the youngest in the country; socialist doctrine has not yet been firmly grounded; the Party has now and then adopted a facing-both-ways policy; its record of constructive work and struggles in the recent past has not been too impressive; it spent four annas to the vote while Congress and Communist expenditure averaged between Re. 1/- to Re. 1/8/- to the vote. Barring the lack of abundant money, all other reasons are removable. The Party shall never be able to command big money, whether from loot, foreign sources or the native rich. This lack of big money will eventually work to the Party's advantage, for the people of India will one day realise that some of its good work is not being done for lack of money. While there should be no attempt to conceal that the Party was unable to scale the heights it contended for in the general elections and was somewhat mauled in the process, no socialist should ever insult the nearly twelve million people who reposed their confidence in socialism by pooh-poohing the Party's vote. That is a good enough spring board for future action. The twelve socialists in parliament have each a million persons behind them. Even if the Communist Party had somehow been able to set up the same number of candidates as the Socialist Party, it could not have got that large vote, as is evident by its complete trouncing in U.P. and Bihar, where none of its candidates won, and it secured only 1/10 per cent and 1 per cent of the total votes cast.

The Socialist Party must definitely abandon its facing-both-ways policy in doctrine as well as in programmes. It should never be an auxiliary team of the Congress party, nor should it ever act as sappers and miners of the Communist Party. It is only fair to note that much of the criticism on this score is interested propaganda by opponents. The battle between capitalism and communism is so grim that, both nationally and internationally, socialism is regarded by both combatants a kink to be ironed out. These two holders of power possess enough resources in propaganda to ridicule successfully the Socialist Party from their angles. Communist wrath is old and too well-known but a recent example of suppression practised by the international capitalist press is the killing of a decisive and news-making statement in favour of the third camp by U. Kyaw Nyein, that alert mind of Burma who was once her Froeign Minister and has now chosen to be the Secretary-General of the party which rules the land. Such suppressions are common nationally. Both the Congress and the Communist Party would very much like to rub the Socialist Party out of existence, for it is their essential foe. Nevertheless, there is some truth in the accusation that the Socialist Party does alternate service to the Congress and the Communist parties.

An Enveloping Power

As long as the doctrinal foundation of socialism is not secured, the Socialist Party will continue to be a thorn between the Congress party, which will often appear as the instrument of democracy and national stability, and the Communist Party, which will as often appear to be a party of change. The frequency with which lables like rightist and leftist are used adds to confusion. The Socialist Party must be willing to take risks, to see in itself the expression both of national unity and of change and to act irrespective of immediate and apparent consequences. It would do the right act, even if that should appear for the time being to enhance the mischief of the Congress and the Communist Party and be willing to run the risk of temporary extinction.

The two elements of democracy and national freedom which go into the making of the Congress party give it an advantage over the Communist Party. In the long run, the Congress party is, without a doubt, superior to the Communist Party, for one may reasonably expect it to act democratically and nationally within certain limits. In the short run, however, the Congress party is the party of famine and corruption and disguised capitalism. Socialist support extended to such a party would defeat the very purpose for which it were intended. Such a policy of support would disable the Party from organizing the people's will and combating injustices and a section of the people would turn to the Communist Party in a state of mad frustration. The Congress party is indeed to some extent a coalition of conservatives and radicals. Contrary to popular estimate, such a coalition does more harm than good and confuses the public mind with regard to radical views and forces. The radicals in the Congress party do more harm than its conservatives. There can be no question of the Socialist Party treating them with consideration or wooing them. If a split occurs in this coalition within the Congress party, it would be due to the pressure of events in the country. The Socialist Party can increase this pressure by intensifying its own constructive action and peaceful struggles and initiating political moves in a big way. Socialists must overcome the temptation to liken the Congress party to the Kuomintang and to forecast a bloody revolution of a communist victory in the event of the Congress Government refusing to change its policies and programmes. This tends to awaken the mistaken belief that a communist government would act better than the Congress Government and, what is more disastrous, it makes the people look upon the Socialist Party as a helpless spectator and adviser. Between the stagnation of the Congress party and the chaos of the Communist Party, the Socialist Party must ever appear to intervene like an enveloping power.

Socialist speech-making and action often furthers the interests of the Communist Party, for it is sometimes difficult to distinguish between a socialist and a communist speech. The mistaken notion of a commonality in economic programmes of the two parties must be removed, before the Socialist Party is able to generate a people's force that would shun the Communist Party. Otherwise, the Socialist Party would suffer the continual ill-luck of the rewards of its labour going to the Communist Party. When socialists generate hate and immorality through their speeches and are unable to express it in their action, an addition to the strength of the Communist Party naturally results.

Overriding Unities

Certain unities of national life are above party. There must be full respect shown to the national flag and song. Unities of dress, food, habits, calendar and the like must grow. There must be a universal readiness to defend the nation in the event of outside attack. The element of violence should be eliminated altogether from the internal politics of the country. The Socialist Party must do all it can to further these national unities. When a climate of disgust against the use of violence grows in India as it has in the West European contries, even communists may find it profitable to act within the pale of democracy although under compulsion. The Socialist Party must awaken this repulsion against violence, not by moral exhortation but by the most manifold organization of non-violent resistance against injustice.

The general elections have for the time being resulted in the fragmentation of the nation's political life. Besides these three parties, a large number of other parties and groups have appeared on the scene. The electoral inability of the Socialist Party to challenge the Congress party as the only alternative agency of stability and change is doing some tricks to the minds both of the people and the socialists. In a situation such as this, it is only natural to look for scapegoats and to refuse to look for the real sources of failures, but socialists must resolutely overcome either temptation. There must be of course no short temper nor mutual recrimination and accusation, for every one of us has been guilty. The temptation to go back to a restricted membership must also be resisted and the healthier attitude to expand the organization and to remove its defects must grow. Another easy way is to look for coalitions and united fronts. Let there be no escape from duty and no fear of isolation. Much of this yearning for coalition or united fronts is the refusal to face reality and to struggle the hard way for removal of defects. The Socialist Party will be eternally cursed if it sought easy solutions and escapes from the duty to reinvigorate itself or feared isolation.

A Rational Realignment

There is no need to emphasise that a policy of coalition with the Congress or United Front with the Communists paralyses, for it leads to dishonesty in public conduct and to further fragmentation of political life. A main argument of upholders of United Front is that they could thereby expose the true character of their temporary allies. Such an attitude of exposure of one's own allies is basically dishonest. Communists are at the moment playing two separate tricks of United Fronts of Leftists and of National Democratic Fronts and they can afford to do so in view of the great temples of worship that they have built in Russia and China. Parties which do not command such temples of worship nor wish to do so should ever avoid trickery. Nevertheless, the Socialist Party must face the fact of fragmentation of political life and outline an honest political policy, which would serve to consolidate the nation. Its essential task is to rejuvenate itself and to develop its own constructive action and struggle, but it must not refuse to shoulder responsibility for an honest political line of consolidation.

Three broad types of political groups other than Socialists, Congress and Communists have appeared on the Indian scene. One type is represented by political groups like the Forward Bloc, RSP, the Peasants & Workers Party and the RCP which have, in varying measures, the twin impulses to be better communists than the Communist Party itself and also to be loyal to democracy and national integrity. It must be noted that every such political party has split up into two hostile and independent groups, one predominating in its sentiment for communism and the other unable completely to overcome its loyalty to freedom and democracy. These parties must soon enough realise that the absence of a considered doctrine and of a massive party embodying it will pulverize them further. The second type of political groups is represented by all parties like the KMPP, Jharkhand, Scheduled

Castes Federation, and the third type by parties like Ganatantra Parishad, Hindu Mahasabha and Ram Rajya Parishad; and the Jan Sangh seems to share the characteristics of both these types. While the second type has blurred the line between radicalism and conservatism, it may under favourable circumstances add its weight to the growth of a massive radical party and the third type may under similar pressures join the Congress party and the youth of Jan Sangh may travel either to socialism or communism and its leadership to the Congress. There is need now to work out a political line which would in time break up the coalition of the Congress party and send to it groups represented by the third type and some elements of the second type. The Congress party will then become in outward form what it is already in actual reality, a clean and outspoken party of Indian conservatism. This political line must also consolidate groups represented by the second type and elements of the first with the Socialist Party, so that this party becomes in time a clean instrument of Indian socialism and radicalism and is able to absorb all other radical elements when they split away from their various organizations. The Communist Party will in such an event lead, as it should, an isolated existence of extra-territorial loyalty, of doctrinaire hair-splitting and of unfructifying calls to general strike and insurrection. The Socialist Party must be able to unfold a political movement which with its wide sweep achieves such a consolidation.

Sarvodaya and Socialism

A recent movement of significance is Sarvodaya. Although the Sarvodaya Movement is no political party nor does it aspire ever to become one, it has been able to release a massive upsurge of national energy round a programme of land-redistribution. The Socialist Party may recall that the first act of voluntary land redistribution in recent years was carried out under its auspices by a socialist, Mohammad Zuhair, in the district of Lucknow. The Sarvodaya Movement has given to the programme of voluntary land-redistribution continuity and passion. Large numbers of poor farmers are offering to share their lands with still poorer and landless farmers. This arousing of a feeling to share and of good neighbourliness is of inestimable advantage both to the people of India and to the doctrine of socialism. While the limits of such a movement must never be lost sight of, socialists must continue to participate in it. Change of heart and change through laws or peaceful struggle are two sides of the same coin, both equally important. There is a point at which both types of change must coalesce, if barrenness is not to result. Many revolutions of hate have occurred before, but they have replaced one tyranny by another. The world has also awaited many a revolution of love but they never materialised. While communism is a doctrine of hate, Sarvodaya has hitherto been an inadequate doctrine of love. Only when love and anger, love for all and anger against injustice, find a combined expression through a revolution, will humanity be able to make the next onward move. There seems to be a spark in Acharya Vinoba Bhave, which has already led to this massive expression of love in collective life and which may one day lead to an equally massive expression of anger. While the Socialist Party should continue to support the Savodaya Movement in its programme of voluntary land redistribution, it may be noted that every party and movement expects socialist support without extending a like support in return. One may legitimately expect the Sarvodaya to extend its support to the Socialist Party in all its movement which express anger against injustice and sympathy for all.

Faith that Cannot Die

This Socialist Party has suffered a temporary reverse. If it frets and fumes and tries artificially to capture attention, it will be but one of many other parties, without rudder or compass. The great test for a party comes when it suffers adversity. Can the Socialist Party take it? To take it would mean to bide one's time and to prepare, to strengthen one's base and doctrine and further train the spirit. India is on the threshold of famine and is being continually stunted and deaths by the million may suddenly overwhelm it. Another test might come to the Socialist Party much before the next five years and in quite a different way. Meanwhile, it must construct whatever it can and struggle wherever it must. Possibilities of some big movement of ideas and national emotions may also come its way. Man's current civilization is cracking and nothing but Socialism can lead him into the new age. Victory belongs either to barbarism or to socialism and there is no middle way. There may be many defeats yet for socialism. Those who set out to build a new civilization must be ready for defeat, ready to struggle and be defeated and yet to struggle again. The Socialist Party may perish many a time in fighting its own clean battles without pollution from the twin monsters of the age. The Socialist Party will rise again, for man will live. Victory shall belong to Socialism.

APPENDIX 22

From Jawaharlal Nehru, 27 May 1952[1]

My dear Jayaprakash,

Thank you for your letter of the 25th May. This reply will probably not reach you before you come here. I am therefore sending it to your Delhi address. I shall fix up some time to meet you on the 29th May when you are here and will let you know by telephone.

I did not bring in what Norman Thomas said in order to blame or criticise but merely to suggest the origin of a tale.

You refer to what Harris Wofford wrote to Lohia about someone of our Embassy saying something to him. Obviously I can say nothing about this as no name is mentioned and I can make no enquiries about it. It is conceivable that some young man associated with our Embassy, and there are many of them, might have made a foolish remark. I have not heard of this before.

I have not yet received Harris Wofford's book which you have sent.

Lohia's letter, a copy of which you have sent to me, is so unbalanced that it hardly needs a reply. He refers to four criticisms which he has apparently made of me. I had not heard of any one of these previously either from Lohia or from anyone else. The fourth of these points relates to the Prime Minister's Relief Fund. This criticism too I had not heard previously from anyone. The Fund is not a Government Fund although a number of Government people, like the Finance Minister, are among the members of the Board of Trustees. Accounts are periodically submitted to the Board of Trustees. The whole purpose of this Fund is to afford quick and immediate relief where needed, without the delays involved in Government routines.

You say that I have done harm to socialism. I am no judge of that. But I think that I have never said a word against socialism. Rarely in the course of the election addresses I referred to the Socialist Party. This too was chiefly in connection with their foreign policy and their alliances in India. I do not pretend to be a socialist in any formal sense of the word but surely socialism is not the monopoly of any particular group.

Yours affectionately,
Jawaharlal Nehru

[1] *Brahmanand Papers* (NMML).

APPENDIX 23

From Jawaharlal Nehru, 8 July 1952[1]

My dear Jayaprakash,

I have hesitated to write to you during the ordeal which you have imposed upon yourself. You have made us very anxious and my thoughts have been with you. Nevertheless I had a feeling of embarrassment in writing to you and did not quite know what to say. You will, I am sure, understand.

I earnestly hope that you will pass through this ordeal successfully and that your health will not suffer because of it in future. It is some comfort that you have best advice and the conditions are as favourable as they can be for such a supreme test. Your life is too precious for all of us and for India.

With love,

Yours affectionately,
Jawaharlal Nehru

[1] *Brahmanand Papers* (NMML).

APPENDIX 24

From Jawaharlal Nehru, 12 July 1952[1]

My dear Jayaprakash,

I was happy to get your note and happier still to find from your letter as well as from the newspapers that you have been progressing well. By the time this letter of mine reaches you, you will have completed your fast and this successful conclusion of a terrible ordeal will lift a burden from innumerable people's minds. I hope that you will take full care of yourself for some time after the fast. There is always a risk of not taking this after-care and of trying to get back to normal life too soon. But Dinshaw Mehta will no doubt see to it that your are looked after properly during these subsequent days.

When you are well enough, I hope you will come here. Indeed you had promised to do so when I met you last. I would like you to come not just for a brief and rather hurried talk, but for something more.

Although you made your fast an entirely personal one and kept it quite

[1] *Brahmanand Papers* (NMML).

apart from other matters, nevertheless inevitably, it was connected in people's minds with the unfortunate controversy about the Postal strike long ago and the strike period pay which had been demanded. I would beg of you not to pay attention to these past events which, I have no doubt, were due to misunderstandings. The earnest desire and hope of Rafi Ahmed Kidwai to find a way out, no doubt, gave the impression to you and others that it was practically an assurance. However, I have said that we are perfectly prepared to consider any feasible proposal de novo. I shall personally do it. I would have been glad to discuss this matter with you. But as you cannot come for some time, I am prepared to do it with anyone else. I would only suggest that this approach should be a friendly one.

Love,

Yours affectionately,
Jawaharlal

APPENDIX 25

From Pyarelal, 21 July 1952[1]

Dear Jayaprakashji,

I have your letterof 16th July enclosing a copy your statement. Since then there has been the futher welcome news of a compromise settlement ot the old issue. It is of couse pure gain so far as you are concerned for you had written off the whole episode. But even on merits I call it a good compromise. This is how it very often happens in *satyagraha*. By voluntarily throwing away tained gains we recover with compound interest what we have lost.

In my opinion the Government's stand as regards the demand of wages for the strike period is intrinsically correct. I feel too that it would add to the strength and solidarity of labour to adot the principle for itself. It would be as fatal to pamper labour by holding out promises of wages for the period they are on strike as it would be to hold out promise to civil resisters of allowances from Congress funds or compensation from Government treasury for the period they may be in prison. The goal of labour even as in the case of civil resisters engaged in a struggle is to vindicate a principle. For that they must be prepared to make *willing sacrifices*. Do not promise them "salvation without tears". Demand for wages for the strike period may be good as a technique for "intensifying crises". But it will be a source of weakness if the object is to build up strength and mobilise mass support which clean sacrifice, cheerfully undergone always evokes.

All this has relevance only if I have understood your mind correctly. It

[1]*J.P. Papers* (NMML).

arises out of the logic of your fast. I have presented this line of reasoning not because the method of fasting can have any prescriptive sanctity for you, but because it embodies a principle which holds the key to power and enables you to obtain results which you cannot perhaps otherwise obtain.

I read your statement. It was nice. I think I can make use of it. For this Achint Ram ji will have to be contaced. You may be in good health. As a result of it this old disease may vanish. Hoping Prabhavati to be well.

Yours sincerely,
Pyarelal

APPENDIX 26

From B.P. Koirala, 21 July 1952[1]

My dear Jayaprakashji,

I have not written to you all these days when you were suffering the agony of body and soul. We have been wanting to go to Poona. Sushila was particularly anxious to be there when you broke your fast. But this could not be. Sushila is, however, going there within a fortnight. If the situation here eases, I may accompany her, otherwise she will go without me.

The situation here is deteriorating. The Government is a house divided; the Congress ministers themselves are pulling in defferent directions, the consequence of which has been that the authority of the Government is not felt at all. Law and order remains a constant problem. The Congress consequently is discredited. We are judged by the work of the Government which has nothing bright to show. Matrika Babu is in the grip of undesirable elements and is lacking in clear understanding of what is required to be done. Therefore our W.C. called upon here to reform the Government and suggested a team of the colleagues out of the present cabinet itself, which was not accepted by Matrika Babu. Hence this crisis.

Once I am free from the present pre-occupation, I will meet you.

With love,

Yours affectionately,
Bishweshwar

[1]*J.P. Papers* (NMML).

APPENDIX 27

From B.P. Koirala [Telegram], 24 July 1952[1]

Your telegram[2] held up by Prime Minister delivered this morning stop Through terrible bungling inefficieny and lack of cohesion in Govt. country drifting towards chaos and Congress suffering loss of prestige stop Many district committees seeking permission from Congress to launch satyagrah against Govt. stop Even Prime Minister admits this state of affairs and hence working committee takes control of situation and if Congress is made responsible for Govt. it must prevent fatal drift particularly when Prime Minister himself agreed to working committee suggesting cabinet personnel stop Prime Minister after accepting idea of working committee making necessary reduction in cabinet and recommendations of personnel backs out only when some individuals were sought to be dropped stop If Prime Minister was not prepared to shoulder responsibility with team suggested by working committee he could seek permission to come out of Government and not openly challenge authority of working committee stop Calcutta agreement does not preclude working committee stepping in to stop Congress disintegration stop Kindly await full report before judging

Yours,
Bishweshwar

[1]*J.P. Papers* (NMML).

[2]J.P.'s telegram to B.P. Koirala could not be traced.

APPENDIX 28

From Jawaharlal Nehru, 28 July 1952[1]

My dear Jayaprakash,

Thank you for your letter of the 25th July. I am very happy that you passed through, so successfully, the great ordeal of the fast. You should, of course, take things very easy till you recover fully. I confess that December seems a long way off and I rather doubt if this long stay might not itself become a burden to you. Rest, of course, you should have.

Environment counts for a great deal and I am always a little afraid of anyone staying too long in a hospital or clinic. I have myself stayed for nearly a year in a clinic (not as a patient, but with my wife in Switzerland). I found that life affecting me powerfully, as it was affecting much more the

[1] *Brahmanand Papers* (NMML).

patients themselves. I wonder if you have read a book called the '*Mountain*' by Thomas Mann.

Since then I have never advised anyone to stay too long in a clinic. My own inclination would be to go to the mountains and rest there after the preliminary stage of rest is over. I understand that the President has invited you to stay with him in Simla. Simla is, of course, very pleasant in September, but after all it is very official. There is a lovely cottage, 7 or 8 miles from Simla, totally unused except, perhaps, for two or three days in a year. This is at Mashobra and was a kind of week-end retreat of the old Viceroys. It is an ideal place for quiet rest.

But, of course, no place compares with Kashmir purely from the health point of view. The month of October in Kashmir is ideal and braces one up more than anything else. The air is invigorating. It may be that people who are used to the enervating climate of Bombay do not like this kind of nip in the air. For me two days of it is equal to a fortnight's rest elsewhere.

If you care to go to Kashmir, arrangements could be made very easily. A good solution would be for you to stay at Dinshaw Mehta's clinic till the middle of September, then go to Kashmir for a month, and then go back to the clinic for a final check up.

I am feeling terribly tired, both physically and mentally. If at all possible, I shall go to Kashmir for a week about the middle of August. If I do so, I shall not stay anywhere, but trek in the mountains for at least five days.

I am glad you have written to me about Rao Sahib Patwardhan. I entirely share your view about him. My recollection is that when I made some suggestions to him sometime back, he was not agreeable to them. I certainly hope that we shall be able to take advantage of his earnestness and ability.

Yours affectionately,
Jawaharlal

APPENDIX 29

From B.P. Koirala, 30 July 1952[1]

My dear Jayaprakashji,

I received both of your telegrams; and I am sure by now the picture of the situation in Nepal has emerged clearer even in the Indian Press. The Indian Press is under the patriotic impression that I am anti-India, and therefore whenever there is any controversy in which I figure it comes to the conclusion that I am wrong. It has not forgotten my previous stand against what was India's interference in our affairs, particularly my stand against

[1] *J.P. Papers* (NMML).

C.P.N. Sinha. I consider this attitude to be almost chauvinistic. On one occasion about two months ago when Sheikh Abdullah made some remarks with reference to Kashmir's relations with India, there was a chorus of condemnation in the Indian Press.

I owe it to you to write in detail about the present developments. The present Government suffered from aweful lack of cohesion, each minister pulling in different directions, as a consequence of which the Government had become ineffective. When the ministers started abusing each other publicy, so much so that one of them even accused his colleague of corruption from the Nepal Radio, the situation became intolerable. Administration was at a standstill, the Central Secretariat reflecting the antagonisms in the Cabinet. In some places district administration was almost non-existent, and even where it existed it was so loose and ineffective and corrupt that people are fed up with it. Lawlessness stalks the land, and the prestige of the Nepali Congress reduced to dust. Reactionary elements are raising their heads. We have been discussing all this for over last three months. Government of India too is perturbed with this state of affairs. Matrika Babu himself has been admitting that the situation is none too good and that there is no cohesion in the Government. When I came from the Janakpore Conference I called our Congress Ministers and told them what I felt about the situation. They all told me with one voice that Government was a house divided. Matrika Babu did nothing to correct the situation; he was too weak. Of late the situation grew still worse; some districts in the Terai came under the grip of extreme lawlessness. Murder, loot, arson were rampant.

From the districts the Nepali Congress units would send me reports of grave nature. It was growing difficult for Congressmen to appear in public as Congressmen, because all the blame of the Government directly attaches to the organisation. Some district committees sought permission of the Centre to launch Satyagrah Movement against the Government. I do not understand why the Congress can't step in to correct the situation.

The matter was discussed firstly in the Parliamentary Board. Matrika Babu himself suggested that Working Committee should meet to discuss it. In the Working Committee Matrika Prasad agreed to the idea of WC suggesting names to him for his cabinet. When we suggested names he backed out and started taking constitutional position. Ultimately he went to the extent of saying that he was not bound by the decision of WC and of challenging the very authority of the Committee. Now the position is—should WC meekly submit to the challenge or assert its authority?

I made every effort to reach a settlement with M.P. consistently with the dignity of the organization. I told him that even now matter could be amicably settled if he wrote to the WC stating that he had no intention of defying the authority of the WC Fortified by your authority, M.P. thought he could very well defy the authority of the WC. I cannot accept the position that anyone however important can challenge the Central Executive of the organization with impurity. He could have sought redress in the ANCC if he thought that WC was wrong.

Much noise has been created about our Calcutta Agreement. The agreement is before me as I write this. I don't see how I have violated that agreement. It is not the day to day affairs of the Government that the Congress is interfering in, and I don't remember if ever I agreed to the Congress always supinely watching the progressive deterioration of the situation in the country and remaining neutral and ineffective in the face of growing catastrophe. I am not a pettifogger, and I am a man of honour. I am bound by the agreement; but I hold that the agreement has no relevance to the point in issue.

Matrika Babu has let loose a reign of terror. Members of ANCC are being arrested. Men of Intelligence Deptt. are posted at my place. My letters and telegrams are published by the Government, even before they are delivered to me. Mahabir SS has become Home Minister and is functioning like a Maharaja of old. This is the situation. If I had not been held up here by serious developments, I would have paid you a speedy visit; but as it is, I cannot leave the place for some time yet.

How is your health? How is Shekhar progressing?

Sushila is here. She sends you her remembrance.

Yours affectionately,
Bishweshwar

APPENDIX 30

Questionnaire Prepared by the Land Redistribution Committee, 2 August 1952[1]

(1) Please give: Population of your state or region, area, rural population, urban population of those engaged in agriculture, density of population, proportion of the landless to the (a) total population (b) landed population, total area of cultivated land, estimated waste land (per district if possible), estimated fallow per year (per district if possible).

(2) (a) What is the proportion of big landlords those holding more than hundred acres) in your State?

[1] *J.P. Papers* (NMML).

(b) What is the size of the biggest holdings?

(c) What would be the number of proportion of such holders?

(d) What part of the total cultivated land is in the hands of those who have more than hundred acres each?

(3) (a) What is the average size of holdings in your State?

(b) What is the size of the smallest holding?

(4) Are there big capitalistic farms in your State? Give details as to size, location, ownership, labour wages etc.

(5) Do the big landholders in your State generally cultivate their lands with hired labour or do they sub-let them to crop-sharers, tenants etc.?

(6) Up till now has the Party done any work regarding redistribution of land in your state? If so, please give details.

(7) Is the Party in a position to undertake the land redistribution movement in the whole of your State? If not, in what district or areas is it possible? Be specific.

(8) Vinobaji already visited your State? If so, give all details: districts visited, total acreage given in Bhoodan (districtwise), state organization set up to conduct the movement; organization set up to distribute the gifted land; any state legislation enacted in behalf of the Bhoodan Movement (give salient features).

(9) If Vinobaji is to visit your State in the future, give details; when expected; targets fixed by Sarvodaya Samaj for your State (districtwise if available; organization set up (state and district level) to prepare for Vinobaji's visit and to obtain land gifts etc.

(10) Have you established any contact yet with the Sarvodaya organization for this purpose?

(11) Have members of the Party joined the Sarvodaya committees at the State or District levels formed in connection with the Bhoodan Movement?

(12) Are Party members taking any part in the Bhoodan activities? If so, what?

(13) Have you given away any part of your own hand (in case you have land) yet? If so how much and to whom?

(14) Have Party members given away their lands? Give details?

APPENDIX 31

From Devendra Prasad Singh, 22 August 1952[1]

My dear Jayaprakashji,

Your kind letter to hand. We are happy to know that you are doing well. When will it be possible for you to leave Poona and come to this side? How is Mahabir doing now, and how long will he be there? Kindly remember me to him, and to Prabhavati and Shekhar. Shekhar must have made good progress by now. Will he stay on in Poona after you have left it or go home?

Sushila is here at Patna. She is doing quite well and wishes to be remembered to you. She has been wanting to see you, but she can't undertake the journey to Poona with her young baby. Prakash is also at Patna, but we have put him in a boarding house. He seems to be doing quite well there, although it is fairly expensive to keep him there.

Shri N.G. Goray will have a seat reserved for him in the plane for the 26th. I also may be going with him the same day. In case I do not, I shall inform Bishweshwar to make suitable arrangements for his stay at Kathmandu. If he reaches here on the 25th, he will put up with Pannaji for the night.

There is one thing now I wish more than anything else. And it is that I should never be associated with anything political. I consider it to be my ill luck that some of my friends are interested so much in politics. I wish Bishweshwar gets out of politics and settles down to a decent life. His being in politics is an insufferable strain to Sushila and also to me.

There this finds you happy.

With warmest regards,

Yours affectionately,
Devendra

[1] *J.P. Papers* (NMML).

APPENDIX 32

From Sushila[1] Koirala, 23 August 1952[2]

My dear Jayaprakashji,

As I sit down to write to you I really do not know what to write. I know, you are very much dissatisfied with us. This is evident from your letter to Devendra Babu.[3] I pray all this may not harm our relations. You know we

[1]Sushila Koirala; wife of B.P. Koirala.

[2]*J.P. Papers* (NMML).

[3]J.P.s letter to Devendra Prasad Singh could not be found.

value your affection and friendship for us and I do not doubt whatever happens, we will continue to get them. So far as I am concerned your attitude, although very painful, has not made any difference to our regards for you.

Kindly remember me to Prabhavatiji.

I hope you are doing well.

Yours sincerely,
Sushila

APPENDIX 33

From Sushila Koirala, 27 August 1952[1]

My dear Jayaprakashji,

A few days ago I had written a letter to you. I think you must have got that. I am really very sorry I could not write to you from Kathmandu. That is because we were so much overwhelmed by the difficult circumstances and the recent happenings there, that inspite of our worries, I was not able to write to you. I hope you will excuse me.

I want to say something about B.P., if you please permit me to say. I saw your letter which you had written to B.P. and it was so painful to go through it. A friend like you should not have written that kind of letter. He has dedicated his life to his country and he will not hesitate to give his life even now if it is needed for the benefit of Nepal. An honest man like him can not become dishonest and tear all the reputation that he has earned all through his life. I am sure he can kick whole world's kingdom if he has to choose between the two. Please do not think he is trying for the Prime Ministership of Nepal. That is nothing at all. I know you have saved his life and have [been] a great help to him. But now you have taken away much more than you have given him. It was better he should have died long before with the name of a brave fighter. He could have challenged the whole world then, but now he can not. In the world's eye now he is a dishonest man craving for power. There is your letter as evidence. A friend's letter is more than evidence. Is it not? It is a pity you have not understood him and you have not cared to know him. Now let us watch where fate will take him. Please excuse me. I have no right to say anything to you about politics, because I do not know about it at all. All this I have written to you because I have a right to express my feelings to you. If there is anything objectionable, kindly excuse me.

I wanted to come to you but [it] is difficult to move about with a small child.

[1] *J.P. Papers* (NMML).

How is Prabhavatiji? I hope she is in good health. How is your health? Will you kindly write to me about you and Prabhavatiji.

Yours sincerely,
Sushila

P.S.: How is Shekhar?
Please remember me to him.

APPENDIX 34

From B.P. Koirala [not dated, but 29 or 30 August 1952[1]]

My dear J.P.,

Goray is going back. He has seen things with his own eyes, and must have come to some conclusions in respect of the situation of this place. I am really grateful that Goray came here to study the situation. At least now, my friends, whose opinion I value most and whose friendship I cherish so dearly, will not misunderstand me. I am unhappy; because even if I have not succeeded in anything that I undertook to achieve, I had always felt that my motives would not be questioned—this fond illusion has been suddenly lifted from my life. I am adjusting myself to this brutal realization. I now only wish that I won't be corrupted by this realization. I feel so lonely. Devendra also tells me that he is drifting away from me. I would have left politics long ago, but this, I feel, won't help. If I am bad, I will carry my badness to wherever I go, to whichever profession I may decide to join. If I decide not to do anything in life, will not the renunciation make me, perhaps, still worse.

Perhaps the situation is not as bad [as] I imagine. The sentiments that I am now expressing have most likely been prompted by the mood of dejection, which will pass off.

I will meet you shortly after I finish my work here. Sushila will also come with me. I propose to stay at Poona for a week with a day or two in Bombay for medical check up.

Yours affectionately,
Bishweshwar

[1] *J.P. Papers* (NMML).

APPENDIX 35

From Sadiq Ali, 10 September 1952[1]

My dear Jayaprakashji,

I have your letter of the 8th instant. I am sorry if the tone and temper of my letter have hurt you. In Delhi your statement caused quite a flutter. The press people and other friends soon started making inquiries about the fate of the merger. Their independent reactions were in no way different from the fears I expressed in my letter. In Bombay also I find independent observers expressing similar fears. It was in our anxiety to avoid any possibility of endangering the merger at this advanced and final stage of our negotiations that I thought it necessary to employ plain and unambiguous language in the letter. I wrote to Asoka Mehta and made our meaning clear. Nothing of course could be further from my intention than to be discourteous to you.

I do not think it would serve any useful purpose to subject your statement to a further dissection. We are all for the moment interested in seeing that nothing intervenes to put an end to the high hopes that we have roused in the country. We knew at the start that the Madras situation might prove the chief obstacle in our way and hence we took special pains to make clear our position and commitment to this regard. Our socialist friends knowing as we did how strongly they felt in the matter would have been justified in rejecting our position. In that event the negotiations would have terminated, but they did not terminate. Shri Asoka went to Madras and had talks with Shri Prakasam and some other leading members of our party. From Madras he came to Delhi where Acharya Kripalani and myself had detailed talks with him. To our explicit enquiry he said that Madras, that is the UDF, need not stand in the way of our negotiations as he was satisfied with his talks with Prakasam. He felt convinced from his talks with Shri Prakasam that the UDF after the merger would not last long. The impact of the new forces the merger would release, would in the course of a few months make short, work of the UDF. We had no quarrel at all with this hope and analysis.

The negotiations therefore started on the clear understanding that the UDF was not in our way. If that was in our way the negotiations would not have started, much less ended in the agreement which was arrived at in Lucknow between Acharya Kripalani and Acharya Narendra Deva and which was forthwith released to the press. Acharya Kripalani was bound by the mandate of our Central Executive which was to the effect that it welcomed the merger proposal and that Kripalaniji should subject to the continuance of the UDF, carry on further talks with leaders of the Socialist

[1] *Brahmanand Papers* (NMML).

Party about the lines on which the merger should be effected.

This, according to us, was the position when you issued your statement and almost the next day appeared Shri Asoka Mehta's article on the UDF which have made everybody doubt where exactly we are and whether the conference we are calling would at the very outset plunge into this controversy leading us to God knows where. After Lucknow our assumption naturally was that all controversy between us was at an end and the conference was being called as it were to put its final seal of approval on decisions reached at Lucknow and frame a programme of action and public education for immediate and vigorous execution. It appears these hopes of ours have now received a setback. It is for you to guide us.

I reached Bombay on the 8th and propose to be here till the end of the conference. I am thrashing out things afresh with Asoka and doing my best to see that no misunderstanding mars our deliberations at the proposed conference and they are brought to a successful conclusion.

We are all looking forward to meeting you here. I join your numerous well-wishers in wishing you full and speedy recovery.

With regards,

Yours sincerely,
Sadiq Ali

APPENDIX 36

From J.B. Kripalani, 12 September 1952[1]

My dear Jayaprakashji,

Thanks for your letter of the 8th instant received today. I am sorry the tone and temper of Sri Sadiq Ali's letter has offended you. We all have to be careful about our language. I have not seen anything in S.A.'s language that should give offence. As for suspecting a conspiratorial activity I do not suppose it even entered in S.A.'s mind. What he meant was that you both thought that your statement was necessary. I am glad it was not so. If you had only informed me that what I said at the Press conference about the UDF had not commended itself to you we could have discussed the matter and come to some understanding as I did with others. I am sure I have not been wanting in a spirit of accommodation and compromise. What I mind is our speaking to each other through Press Interview which give the Press and public an opportunity to think that there are hitches in the way of the merger when actually the merger has been decided upon.

[1]*Brahmanand Papers* (NMML).

Any way we have perhaps gone too far to retract. So far as I am concerned I have decided to remain silent in public. All that I may have to say will be said at the conference. I have even suggested if further talks are necessary the Conference may for the time being be postponed. However I have in this matter given full power to S.A. to act. For he is in Bombay and can meet you and is always meeting A.M.

You need not have mentioned anything about my visit to you. It was a pleasure to meet you and Prabha. Remember me to her.

With best regards,

Yours sincerely,
J.B. Kripalani

APPENDIX 37

From B.P. Koirala, 17 September 1952[1]

My dear Jayaprakashji,

I reached back [Patna] yesterday; will most probably go to Kathmandu tomorrow.

Matrika Babu has already left Kathmandu for Biratnagar; so if you have not already written to him at his Kathmandu address, you should write now to him at Biratnagar—"Koirala Niwas", Biratnagar P.O. Jogbani (Purnea).

I will write to you from Kathmandu.

With love,

Yours affectionately,
Bishweshwar

[1] *J.P. Papers* (NMML).

APPENDIX 38

From Jawaharlal Nehru, 23 September 1952[1]

My dear Jayaprakash,

As I am leaving Delhi tomorrow for about a week, I am writing to you rather early to send you all my love and good wishes on the occasion of your coming birthday, when you will complete half a centrury. I used to

[1] *Brahmanand Papers* (NMML).

think that age quite respectable. But now that I am 62, it appears to me very youthful. Anyhow, may you retain your youth for long.

I shall look forward to meeting you before long.

Love,

Yours affectionately,
Jawaharlal Nehru

APPENDIX 39

From Jawaharlal Nehru, 10 October 1952[1]

My dear Jayaprakash,

Your letter of the 3rd October has only reached me today in Madras. I do not remember getting any letter from S.K. Patil or Mridula about the Democratic Youth Conference. I am returning to Delhi tomorrow morning and after a few days there I am going to the tribal areas in Assam and Manipur. It is true that I am going to Nagpur on the 31st and Wardha on the 1st of November. I have to rush back for the Parliamentary Session and I do not see how I can fit in a visit to Bombay then.

I would of course have been glad to be present at this Youth Conference. But it does not seem to be feasible at all. I am certainly interested in this Conference and would like to help.

Yours affectionately,
Jawaharlal Nehru

[1] *Brahmanand Papers* (NMML).

APPENDIX 40

From Jawaharlal Nehru, 19 December 1952[1]

My dear Jayaprakash,

For months past I have been hoping to see you, but somehow this meeting does not come off. Meanwhile, things have happened which have both surprised me and distressed me. And now, I find that many of your colleagues are becoming increasingly associated with the most reactionary and communal elements in the country. It is possible, of course, for such association to take place in regard to a particular subject, but you will agree with me that this has dangerous potentialities. Indeed, the potential is becoming the actual step by step.

[1] *Brahmanand Papers* (NMML).

I have today written a letter to Kripalaniji. I enclose a copy of it. I would not have written this letter if I had not felt the gravity of the situation from many points of view. Socialism, which you have represented for these many years, would be submerged in communal cries and communal passion. The only groups that will profit will be the communalists on the one hand, and the Communists on the other.

In Jammu, the leaders of the agitation are a purely communal group which holds forth their ideal of a Hindu Rashtra all over India. Jammu is just a base of operations. Of course, the Jammu people have some legitimate grievances and they should be looked into. But the people who are leading the agitation care little for these grievances and are bent on their objectives. They want the Maharaja back as the leader of the Hindus against the Muslims of the Jammu and Kashmir State. They cannot of course succeed in that, but they may well succeed in creating a lot of trouble and in helping Pakistan over the Kashmir issue, as indeed they are doing now. The cry of fuller integration with India in reality means, in the present context, a break-up of the Jammu and Kashmir State and presenting a very large part of that State to Pakistan.

Each group has some different objective, although they may cooperate with others in a common attack on our Government. Master Tara Singh's record is well known. He is completely irresponsible and can think only in terms of war and chaos, out of which he thinks he will come out as the winner. He has done enough harm to the Sikhs already by his unwise leadership and, if he continues for long, he will no doubt do much more harm to them and to the country. The Hindu Mahasabha, the RSS, and the Akali Dal have joined hands in Jammu and propose to spread out in the Punjab.

Oddly enough, Master Tara Singh is cooperating with the Communists in PEPSU. There are no principles—only ambition and hatred.

In Bengal chiefly, and to some extent elsewhere, the East Bengal refugees question is kept in the front. Everybody sympathises with them and wishes to help them. It may be that opinions may differ as to how best to do this. But I do not think any reasonable or sensible person would like to bring about chaos in the hope that the East Bengal Hindus might be helped.

The banning of cow slaughter is a general cry, which naturally must appeal to most Hindus. That is the all-India front. All these three things are joined on to attract various types of people and the strings appear to be in the hands of the most bitter communal groups. I do not know where the Socialists come into this picture. And yet, they are giving them their moral and other support. Where will Socialism be if this continues? It would be a tragedy if we reverted to the barbarity of the post-Partition period, which ultimately led to the death of Gandhiji.

I am writing to you frankly as I feel you will not mind that. The matter is too serious for anything but frankness.

Yours affectionately,
Jawaharlal Nehru

APPENDIX 41

From Jawaharlal Nehru, 21 January 1953[1]

My dear Jayaprakash,

Thank you for your letter that you sent from Rangoon. It reached me in Hyderabad. I returned from Hyderabad yesterday afternoon.

I am glad you are coming here for three or four days from February 1st onwards. I suggest that you might come to my house on Sunday, February 1st at 6 p.m. and stay on to dinner. We can fix some time on February 2nd also then. On the 3rd, my day is partly occupied already. On the 4th, I shall be very full with the conference of Governors here which will last the whole day and part of the night. But, if necessary, I shall find time on the 2nd and 3rd February also. In any event, come on the 1st February at 6 p.m. and stay on to dinner.

Yours affectionately,
Jawaharlal Nehru

[1] *Brahmanand Papers* (NMML)

APPENDIX 42

From Jawaharlal Nehru, 17 March 1953[1]

My dear Jayaprakash,

I received your letter of the 4th March from Gaya some days ago. I did not reply to it as you were coming to Delhi, and yesterday we had a talk.

Reading your letter, I realised not only how much we had in common in regard to our basic outlooks, but also the differences in our approach. It may be that those differences are partly at least due to our viewing our problems from different angles. It is fairly easy to make a list of what we would like to have. It is more difficult to get that done in the proper order of priority. To attempt to do many things at the same time sometimes results in nothing being done.

[1] *Brahmanand Papers* (NMML).

After all, our Five-Year Plan is an attempt to look at the picture as a whole and lay down certain priorities. It is quite possible that Plan itself may undergo improvement and variation with experience and further consideration, but the basis of it will, no doubt, remain.

In your letter you complain that I have often dealt with some points repeatedly in the same language. Probably you are right, because one can only proceed to discuss a thing from one's own point of view. Of course, if, in the course of talk, other aspects come up, they are dealt with accordingly. I have a sensation of basic dynamic changes taking place in the world which are really affecting human life in every aspect—political, economic, social, etc. Mostly these result from the pace of technological advance. I do not think these changes are all to the good, but there they are. I have also the feeling that all of us, if I may say so, are apt to be left behind in our thinking by these changes.

Take the question of war. All of us want peace. But in spite of us war may come with all its terrific consequences. The communists shout loudly of peace. But there is little of peace in their shouting. The rival group also talks of peace and prepares for war. Whatever attitude we might adopt may not ultimately prevent some catastrophe from occurring which will upset the present day world and all our thinking.

You say that the goals and values of socialism are unalterably fixed for you and you define these goals as the creation of a new society in which there is no exploitation, in which there is economic and social equality, and in which there is freedom and well-being for all. Surely, there is hardly any intelligent person in the world who will not agree with that goal or those values. Certainly I accept them completely. I accept further the necessity for trying to achieve them in the soonest possible time. The question is how to proceed about it and there we come up against all manner of uncertain factors, including the human material we work with. I am inclined to agree with you that a sense of urgency is lacking in the country generally and in our policies also. I should like to increase that sense of urgency.

I confess that I have a feeling of groping forward step by step, even though the goal might be clear.

But I do not wish to argue these matters, because there is no end to argument and it does not usually lead anywhere. When people understand each other, even though they may differ somewhat, they do not require a novel argument.

My own purpose in having talks with you, as well as with Kripalaniji and Narendra Deva, was to bring about as large a measure of cooperation in our activities as possible. Also to infuse that very sense of urgency, as well as a clarification of our goals. You will remember that I have been trying to meet you for many months past. This was no new urge due to any new occurrence. Long before you undertook your fast, I wrote to you and suggested that you might see me. But this could not be arranged, because of your fast and subsequent convalescence. Thus my desire to discuss these matters with you was not related to any new happening, but had been present in my mind for a long time past. It was obviously due to a feeling that we have big things to do in this country and we should approach them with our joint effort. I feel that the next five or ten years are crucial in our existence. I am not satisfied, if I may say so, with the rate of our progress or advance. I wanted to hasten it and I wanted your help to do so.

I did not think of any precise method of doing so. It was rather the general approach that mattered. That is why when you or Kripalaniji asked me for greater precision all I could say was that I was prepared to consider this question at all levels. I had not really thought of it in that way. This was not a question of course of any offices being offered or accepted, but rather of a mutual realisation of the necessity of cooperation from which many things could flow. I had not thought even of what is called merger of parties.

Our talks have resulted in a good deal of speculative publicity, much of it wide of the mark. That should be cleared, though it is never possible to prevent people from giving vent to their own thoughts.

I feel after reading your letter and after my talk with you that, perhaps, any kind of a formal step at the present moment would not be helpful. We have to grow into things, not to bring them about artificially. You have sent me a draft programme which includes, among other things, basic constitutional changes. Now, obviously it is not easy for me to bring about these changes, even though I may not be opposed to them. You refer to all kinds of other changes of law and legal procedure and administration and reorganisation of the map of India, etc. To each one of these, considered separately, I have little objection and I would be happy to give thought to them. But, surely, it is beyond me both as Prime Minister and as the President of the Congress to deal with such vital matters and give assurances in regard to them. Many of these may be logically justifiable and yet there may be other reasons which come in the way. Again, one can hardly take all these things in a bunch.

At the same time, from your point of view, you are perfectly justified in putting forward what you consider your immediate programme to be.

There lies the difficulty, and it is because of this that I feel that it is better for us not in any way to tie each other down, but rather to try, to the best of our ability, to develop both the spirit and the practice of cooperation. I am quite sure that this is possible over a large field. That should not come in the way of your pursuing your particular aims and objectives or pressing for any changes in our programme. It is the spirit and the approach that count. If that spirit and approach are there, then we will influence each other in our policies and gradually come nearer. At a later stage we might be able to take further steps towards closer cooperation.

I agree with you, therefore, that for the present we should drop this idea in its more precise forms and make this clear to the public, in as friendly a way as possible, in order to put an end to public speculation. On the 20th of this month I am addressing a meeting of the U.P. Pradesh Congress Committee, as well as some office bearers of Congress committees, in Meerut. I might take advantage of that occasion to say something on this subject. I am separately noting down what I might perhaps say about this.

I do hope that we shall meet frequently to discuss common problems, and there are so many of them, and try to help each other to understand them fully. Certainly, I would welcome your help, as well as Kripalaniji's and Narendra Deva's. Indeed, perhaps, it might be better to do so without being tied down to any particular approach or formula.

Yours affectionately,
Jawaharlal Nehru

APPENDIX 43

Jawaharlal Nehru's Press Statement, New Delhi, 18 March 1953[1]

There has been a good deal of speculation in the Press and in the public mind in regard to some talks which I have had with some leaders of the Praja Socialist Party, notably with Shri Jayaprakash Narayan, Acharya Kripalani and Acharya Narendra Deva. Much of this speculation is entirely wide off the mark. I should like, therefore, to take into my confidence not only Congressmen but others also.

It has been natural for me to meet, whenever opportunity offered itself, my old colleagues, some of whom are leaders of the Praja Socialist Party. The fact that they are not in the Congress and, as members of another party, have often opposed the Congress, could not come in the way of my personal regard and affection for them. They are not only our old comrades but tried soldiers in the struggle for India's freedom. Whatever differences may have cropped up between them and the Congress in recent years, there has always been a very wide plane of agreement on basic issues. Indeed, that was natural because we have worked together for the greater part of our lives.

The formation of separate parties either with some ideological difference or placing greater emphasis on certain matters, is a natural development to which, I for my part, have no objection whatever. In a democratic set-up, it

[1] *J.P. Papers* (NMML).

is desirable that every opportunity should be given for the development of ideas and the education of the public in them. With the coming of independence, this development was perfectly healthy and natural, even though it brought some political conflicts in its train.

The parties, as they exist in India today, apart from the Congress, may be divided in four groups. There are certain political parties with an economic ideology. There is the Communist Party with allied organizations. There are the various communal parties under different names but essentially following a narrow communal ideology, and there are a considerable number of local parties and groups having only a provincial or even narrow appeal.

The Communist Party, with its views of a monolithic structure both of the party and the State, and its close association with methods of violence, is necessarily far removed for the basic structure and ideology of the Congress and its peaceful methods and democratic objective. The communal parties represent an outlook which is completely opposed to what the Congress has aimed at and struggled for during its long existence. They are disruptive and sometimes to some extent revivalist and totally reactionary. The provincial and local groups have no great importance from the all India point of view.

Of what might be called the political or economic parties, apart from the Congress, the Praja Socialist Party is far the most important. Whatever other differences there might be, there is a considerable field of common approach and methods between the Congress and the Praja Socialist Party. It is natural for them to cooperate in any field of activity, whenever opportunity offers itself. I have often thought, therefore, that we should enlarge these fields of cooperative activity. More particularly, when reactionary and communal forces divert people's attention into wrong channels, and when the country demands constructive work of all kinds to build up the new India, I have naturally thought that we should cooperate. I feel that the next five or ten years are going to be crucial in our country's history.

With these thoughts in my mind, I invited Shri Jayaprakash Narayan to meet me. The invitation was sent some six months ago or possibly more, but it was not possible for him to come to Delhi to meet me. When at last he came, we had long talks about all kinds of subjects. I discovered, what I knew already, that there was a wide area of agreement between us. I put it to him, therefore, that we should try to explore the possibility of closer cooperation. I had not thought of any precise ways of cooperation, because I wanted the background and the approach to be made clear. If this was cleared, then details could be discussed. I suggested that such cooperation could be at all levels, the popular level of course and also the Governmental level. We did not discuss any details about this and talked much more about wider policies. I did not suggest the merger of the Praja Socialist Party with the Congress. I thought that we should begin our cooperative efforts in a relatively small way, which could easily develop later, if circumstances proved to be favourable.

Jayaprakashji wrote to me at some length afterwards and we met also later. We felt that probably the time had not come for any commitments to be made at this stage about minimum programmes etc., although there might be a good deal of agreement between us. As a consequence we decided not to pursue this particular line of action at present. That of course does not mean that we should not cooperate to the largest possible extent wherever opportunity offers itself. Indeed I very much hope that this will be so and that we shall frequently meet and discuss common lines of action.

Our meeting have been exceedingly friendly and frank as they were bound to be between old friends and colleagues. There is no misunderstanding between us and I would greatly deprecate criticisms or any attempt to caste blame on anybody.

APPENDIX 44

From Jawaharlal Nehru, 18 March 1953[1]

My dear Jayaprakash,

I have been so fully occupied all day that I could not find even a few minutes to send you the corrected paragraph to which you referred this morning. On my return home rather late this evening, I read the statement which you had issued to the press today. I also got your letter of today's date. Of course, you can issue your previous letter to me to the press if you so wish it. I have no objection whatever. I am sorry that the press people should indulge in foolish criticism.

I had told you that I would speak about this matter at Meerut day after tomorrow, but in view of developments, that seems rather far off. I have, therefore, decided to issue a statement to the press. I enclose a copy of it. Probably, it will appear in tomorrow morning's papers.

As for the fourth paragraph at page 2 of my letter to you dated March 17th, I suggest the following change.

The original paragraph to be replaced by the following:

I did not think of any precise method of doing so. It was rather the general approach that mattered. I had not thought of, what is called, merger of parties. I felt that if there was a mutual realisation of the necessity of cooperation, other things would

[1]*Brahmanand Papers* (NMML).

flow from it. When you or Kripalaniji asked me for greater precision, I said that I was prepared to consider this question at all levels, including both popular and governmental. It was left at that and we did not discuss this particular matter any further.

If it is at all possible for you to see me tomorrow, I shall be happy. I do not wish to discuss the matter referred to in our correspondence. I would like to meet you any way. Apart from this, I should like, if that is possible for us, to meet you and some of your colleagues from time to time to discuss various policies, for instance, some things that you have mentioned in your suggested programme. Such discussions can prove helpful.

Yours affectionately,
Jawaharlal

P.S. If it suits you we can meet at 7.15 p.m. tomorrow—19th.

APPENDIX 45

Text of the Resolution Adopted by the Executive Committee of U.P. PSP, 31 March 1953[1]

The State Executive is definitely of the opinion that cooperation or coalition with the Congress is not only detrimental to the national interest but also a great obstacle in the growing strength and organization of the Party. In the past the people's democratic movements have been ruthlessly crushed by Congress Organization and the Government. Since taking over the charge of the country's administration, the policies of the Congress have been reactionary throughout, as a result of which not only the burning problems of the oppressed and the downtrodden masses were not solved; but employment, starvation and corruption are on the increase and have become the order of the day. Thus the Congress has strengthened the forces of reaction, capitalism and communalism.

The State Executive having firm faith in democratic socialism and the establishment of the casteless & classless democratic society is determined, with an uncompromising attitude, upon the policy of socialisation of the chief means of production.

Further, the Executive considers that PSP and the Congress are diametrically opposed to one another on all matters of socio-economic policy and the political structure of the state.

[1] Adapted from *National Herald*, 1 April 1953.

In the opinion of the State Executive, the Congress President has initiated this coalition or cooperation talks only to divert the attention of the people from the hard realities and due to this the PSP has suffered a great setback in the matter of growth. Therefore the State Executive affirms its opinion that this talk with the Congress must be stopped forthwith and forever.

APPENDIX 46

From Jawaharlal Nehru, 10 May 1953[1]

My dear Jayaprakash,

Thank you for your letter of 6 May.

I am sorry for the misunderstanding and mess made about Kripalani's candidature. I did not see Balvantray's statement before it was issued. I am sure he did not mean any ill, but he was trying to convince the Bihar people. However there it is.

I do not know if you saw a statement issued by some official of the Praja Socialist Party from Patna. This was, if I may say so, very offensive.

Now a new difficulty has arisen. In spite of all that has happened, Congress is not running a candidate against Kripalani. But this is a double seat, one of them being meant for Harijans. Harijans are contesting the other seat, one Congress and one Praja Socialist. The result is that there is a contest anyhow.

You refer to the Vindhya Pradesh MLA matter. You have no doubt judged of this from certain rather superficial facts. We have gone very deeply into this matter and consulted the best authorities we could. There is no question of our by-passing the Election Commission or the President. It is rather accepting their decision that we have proceeded. There are exact parallels to this in British practice which we normally follow. I know that, *prima facie*, this looks odd, but people forget that Vindhya Pradesh, as a Part C State, is governed by somewhat different laws than the other States.

Yours affectionately,
Jawaharlal

[1] *J.P. Papers* (NMML).

APPENDIX 47

General Secretary's (Asoka Mehta) Report to the Special Convention of PSP, Betul, 14 June 1953[1]

1. The Praja Socialist Party was formed by the merger of the Socialist Party and the Kisan Mazdoor Praja Party in September 1952. The documents connected with the merger have been published separately.
2. As a result of the merger, *ad hoc* committees composed of members drawn from both parties had to be set up from the national to constituency level. The committees have been formed by mutual consultations. District and lower committees have been organized by State Executives, which, in their turn, were set up by the National Executive. In nearly all the States, barring a few 'C' States, committees of the Party are functioning. In Rajasthan and Madhya Bharat the organization is in a rudimentary stage, and at the state level only co-ordinating committees exist. 406 district offices are functioning though we do not have in the Central Office the names of the members of all the district committees.
3. The merger has been smoothly achieved in most states. An overwhelming majority of workers of the two parties have accepted the merger.
4. The *ad hoc* arrangements are inevitably of a temporary nature; in the next four months elected committees have to be set up at all levels. The necessary elections can be held only when members have been enrolled, quotas of membership fees paid to the state and the Centre, and electoral rolls, through membership lists, are prepared constituency-wise. All this has to be done by September so that a duly constituted National Conference (of elected delegates) can meet in October 1953. The Convention might decide the venue of the Conference.

Membership

5. In all democratic States, political parties have mass membership. A certain relationship also exists between votes polled in elections, and the party membership. To broad-base our Party, at least a million members have to be enrolled. That would mean just one member out of every seventeen persons who voted for us in the last General

[1]*Report of the Special Convention of PSP*, Betual, 14-18 June 1953, pp. 162-70.
[2]Middle East Defence Organisation, under US Leadership.

Elections. The enrolment so far has not proceeded as briskly as was expected; my suggestion is that the last date of enrolment be extended from 31st May to 30th June 1953, and in that period determined efforts be made to fufil the membership targets for different districts and States.

6. While mass membership extends our influence and becomes a source of finance, the work of the party is carried on mainly by the *active* members. Separate efforts need to be made to organize them. The Bombay (City) Party has valuable experience to contribute in this direction. There the active members not only carry out the work assigned, but enrol at least a minimum number of primary members, collect funds, contribute a fee of eight annas a month and an additional voluntary contribution of 2 per cent of the income. They participate in periodical study camps and discussion groups on Party policy and organization. Only round the hard core of such members can the broad-based membership develop.

Organization

7. Politically and organizationally the Party is weak in those parts of the country where disruptive forces are in the ascendance. The question that we have to decide is whether we concentrate our efforts in states that are stable, where we are organizationally strong or we turn our efforts to areas where the disruptive forces are growing and are creating conditions of instability. Again, in the states, where we have been active for long, our strength is not uniformly spread all over. Here too the question to be answered is whether we develop intensively or extensively? My view is that for at least a year more we strengthen ourselves where we have a good base.

8. Since the General Elections, there have been twelve bye-elections to the House of the People. An analysis of the votes polled yields the same pattern of opinion as was revealed by the General Elections—Congress 50 per cent, PSP 17 per cent, Communist 6 per cent, Hindu Mahasabha 6 per cent and Independents etc., 20 per cent. The Hindu Mahasabha and the Forward Bloc (Marxist) retained their seats, the Independents won a seat in Rajasthan, the Congress retained seven seats and lost tow seats to the PSP. Though we contested five elections, our vote was good only in three places—Madhya Pradesh, Bihar and Bombay—the stable states where our organization is good. Elsewhere, either we did not contest or our vote was negligible.

9. In the sixty bye-elections held for State Assemblies, since the General Elections, the Congress won thirty, PSP twelve, Communist eight,

Jan Sangh and Hindu Mahasabha two each, Independents four and two regional parties one each. The Congress retained twenty-nine seats, lost nine and gained one. The PSP retained eight and gained four, the CP retained five, lost two and gained five. The PSP contested twenty-two bye-elections, and put up a good fight in seventeen of them, while it fared miserably in the remaining five. All the poor contests, as well as a majority of the thirty-eight contests from which the PSP kept out were in areas where the Communists or the Communalists are markedly active. In Hyderabad, in seven out of the eight bye-elections, the fight was straight between the Congress and the Communist PDF. Our intervention in a solitary case left us with a poor vote. In Madhya Bharat, Rajasthan and Delhi the communal forces continue to grow. In the Punjab the Communists won a spectacular victory and are emerging as a potent rival to the Congress in the state. These gains have to no small extent been due to their *entente* with the Akali Dal. The political map of India that the General Elections had revealed (*cf.* my *Political Mind of India*) has been generally confirmed by the bye-elections.

Political Consolidation

10. The situation can be changed by either (i) political consolidation, or (ii) mass upsurge, or (iii) intensive work. As far as political consolidation is concerned it has to be noted that four main parties have emerged out of the elections: the Congress, PSP, CP and Jan Sangh. All the four have been gaining through the process of consolidation. The KLP has virtually merged in the Congress, the near Communist parties in the Punjab, Uttar Pradesh and Bombay have merged in the CP. The Jan Sangh is striving to build up a combine of four communal parties—Hindu Mahasabha, Ram Rajya Parishad and Akali Dal—under its leadership. On marginal parties, such as the Ganatantra Parishad, the pull in that direction is growing. The left parties have temperamental aversion to consolidation, and any consolidation achieved will not materially alter the political map of India. Political consolidation, as we understood it after the General Elections, will no longer be a major factor. The only mass movement of significance to arise recently is Bhoodan. It too has developed in the stable states, like Uttar Pradesh and Bihar, and has, so far, played no part in reorienting political alignments. Whether other mass movements can be developed by our Party, particularly in what we have characterised as unstable areas, is a crucial question. Are there any forms of intensive work that can foster such movements?

Disruptive Forces

11. Communalism is evoking in North India popular interest and is now treading the path of *satyagraha* also. It is interesting to note that though over three thousand persons courted imprisonment in the Food Satyagraha in Bombay State in 1952, and over two thousand went to prison in Saurashtra in the recent anti-Sales Tax agitation, neither of the two movements received the attention that was given to the Praja Parishad *satyagraha* in Jammu and outside, though in it too just two thousand *satyagrahis* were involved. Communalism is becoming a stubborn emotion in various parts of North India and that emotion is impervious to the basic social and economic issues facing the country. The disturbing development is that communal influences are striving to reach the administrative personnel and the Armed Forces.
12. In the South, linguistic redistribution of States is receiving mounting attention. From a popular and vital movement like this we cannot keep aloof. It is equally our responsibility to guard against the pitfalls. Care must be taken to see that a language group has *one* state, as multiplicity of states must destroy economic viability. Any agitation on the part of a sub-language group to seek statehood must be resisted. Together with linguistic redistribution there should be moves towards strengthening the inter-States bonds. Zonal or multi-States Governors, as also Public Service Commissions and High Courts, are among the possible steps in that direction. This will help to achieve economy and maintain efficiency. The demand for linguistic states should necessarily be accompanied by the demand for the strengthening of the inter-states bonds. Gravest danger lies in linguistic *irredentism*. Controversies over disputed areas threaten not merely to prolong but intensify instability. Party members must scrupulously keep out of controversies on bilingual areas and boundary conflicts. The Government should be asked to appoint a high level Commission to demarcate the boundaries, that is to virtually re-draw the administrative map of India. Once the new boundaries are finalised no agitation for their revision should be countenanced. The linguistic question needs to be resolved *quickly and decisively*. Both communalism and linguism, till recently essentially urban movements, are seeping into rural areas. Hence decisive action is needed.
13. The Communist Party is fully exploiting the unstable conditions created by communal agitation in the North and the linguistic upsurge in the South. Forces that weaken the cohesion of India are being sedulously encouraged. In the North, the alliance with the Akalis is

being used for establishing deeper contacts with other communalists. If Pakistan joins the MEDO, Hindu communalists will be invited to lean on the rival Soviet *bloc*.

14. In India, today, the Congress is the governing party and PSP, CP and the Jan Sangh are the principal opposition parties. Because of fundamental differences, the PSP can have no truck with the CP or the Jan Sangh. If either of them wins power, the Socialist movement, as in China or Pakistan, would receive a terrible setback. It is therefore not surprising that when the democratic or secular foundations of the Indian Union are attacked, the PSP does not hesitate to fight back, even though the attack is ostensibly directed towards the governing party. Under these circumstances, the fringe parties are likely to develop a tendency to draw together. The Communists will consciously exploit the situation. They will also inflame linguistic passions and sedulously support linguistic fanatics like the Dravida Kazagham in Tamilnad. Linguisic redistribution of states will not, by itself, remove the stubborn economic difficulties; on the contrary, it is likely to create new difficulties and fresh frustrations. From them linguistic fanaticism will emerge, and the Communists will feed and foster it. Not agrarian unrest, but politics of unstability will be the main pre-occupation of the Communists.

Watch the Frontiers!

15. The Communists are concentrating their efforts in areas near our frontiers. In some of these border areas, as in Tripura, recent political changes have created a power vacuum that the Communists have shrewdly filled up. In the Punjab and PEPSU, forces of communalism, linguism and the frontier psychology overlap. There the Communists are characteristically most active. To influence and infiltrate in the South Indian troops stationed near the frontiers, Communist literature in southern languages is being distributed through south Indian contact men especially deployed for the purpose. To counter these subversive developments, it is necessary to work out, what Rammanohar Lohia has aptly called, a Himalayan policy. In it co-operation with democratic and socialistic forces in Nepal will form an important part. In Jammu and Kashmir, as the PSP is not able to endorse the actions of the State Government nor countenance the subversive moves of the Communists and Communalists, the Party must decide to function and rally round its banner healthy and forward-looking elements.

16. Another disturbing factor is the periodical exodus from East Pakistan.

To stop it and to provide security to the minorities in Pakistan, we have ceaselessly endeavoured to strengthen the secular character of our Union and have advocated, on the question of the exodus, a policy of firmness towards Pakistan. We even forged a broad-based united front on the issue and considered possibilities of direct action. The fact remains that an adequate policy has still to be worked out.

Political Compulsions of Backward Economy

17. Free India is to be built round three basic elements—national integrity, democratic freedom and social change. Whether as a government party or in opposition, patriotic forces strive to strengthen these basic elements and fight the forces that weaken them. It is for this reason that we find ourselves unable to support the Communists or the Communalists even in opposition, and cannot contemplate the possibility of either of them becoming the government party. The Congress believes that on the issues of nationalism, secularism and democracy we have more in common with it than with the other forces arrayed in opposition to the Government. It is for that reason that some weeks back the Prime Minister—President of the Congress—held discussions with the spokesmen of our Party. The correspondence and statements related to the talks have been published separately. The talks for cooperation, at all levels, between the Congress and the PSP, initiated by the Prime Minister failed, among other reasons, for divergence in policies on social change. He who initiated the talks terminated them. The matter therefore got dropped and the two parties are arrayed in Indian politics as before.
18. Even when the question of cooperation with the government party is dropped, certain difficult questions affecting our *policy of opposition* remain. The economic backwardness of India exerts inescapable compulsions on our policies. The backward economy has caused social stagnation: caste, communal and regional considerations and loyalties receive disproportionate support. As the problems of economic development are difficult of comprehension and execution, discontent as well as opposition tend to flow in channels of traditional allegiances. The Socialist movement not only can have nothing to do with such narrow and sectarian efforts but is organized to counter them. Its policies have to be in terms of social reform and social change and development. That development, in our under-developed country, depends on the acceptance of equality, austerity and hard work. The strain involved in such policies is considerable, and opposition based upon such policies has to strive

hard to prevent sliding into attitudes and actions that run counter to the basic needs. Economic development, for instance, demands higher taxation. An opposition party tends to oppose it, unless it is confined to the top few. Backward economy imposes strains of development and an opposition party, to built itself up, decries and resists the strains. Demand for swifter development, if it means added strain, rarely helps to build up an alternative focus of power. The result of the dilemma is that politics becomes somewhat unreal, and an all-round reluctance to embark upon bold policies emerges. The Congress party, because of the fear of opposition and its lack of understanding and purpose, hesitates to pursue in a state a bold policy of taxation and development; in the same state, the PSP, controlling a Local Body, notwithstanding its understanding and initiative, finds itself in no better position. Politics reach a point where, until structural changes are made from the Centre, activities at the periphery become unreal.

19. A major element in the development of a backward economy is co-operation of the people. Constant tug-of-war might weaken the springs of cooperation and make people apolitical. Totalitarianism, with its monopoly of power and compulsory coordination of all activities, has therefore been considered a suitable motor of social change in a backward country. That, of course, for a variety of reasons known to our members, is not true (*cf.* my *Socialism and Peasantry*). If totalitarianism is unwise, parliamentary democracy is not much helpful. Even if just two parties existed, the axiom of opposition's job to oppose would make economic development difficult. The existence of the Communists and Communalists as parliamentary and political forces makes our legislatures timid. Stagnation versus disruption threaten often enough to become the fundamental alternatives to the detriment of the forces of democratic social change. The compulsions of backward economy tend to push towards totalitarianism or timidity. The dilemma can be resolved by (1) so broad-basing the government that it gets power to move forward, because opposition is driven to the fringes, and (2) strengthening the forces of pluralism in authority and initiative.

20. In such a reorganistion, democratic rights—of speech, press, assembly and association—have not only to be cherished but strengthened. Only frequent changes in government, that parlia-mentary democracy assumes, would be replaced by a broad-based government holding power on a long-term tenure—in effect though not in law. Criticisms would be expressed through the usual democratic channels, the opposition, as distinct from criticism, would be confined

to those irreconcilables who are opposed to the fundamentals of the State. Such a readjustment might impart the needed drive to the government and open up the channels of popular co-operation in the process of development.

21. There is obviously no magic in broad-basing a government or in confining opposition to the fringes. The change can come only if the Government brings into existence an *institutional framework* wherein authority and initiative get widely shared, where rights get interwoven with responsibilities. Such a framework is obviously offered by compulsory village cooperatives and union-shop trade unions. The cooperatives and the unions will be effective because, though all-embracing, they will however remain *internally* wholly free and democratic. The cooperatives and trade unions, brought into being in a comprehensive way, would become new sources of authority and initiative. The rural co-operatives would not only revitalise the agricultural economy but play a crucial role in developing, say, state-trading. Compulsory unions of workers and of technicians would provide firm checks on capitalist enterprise and also foster industrial development. The two mass organizations would give new strength to the democratic foundations of a backward country striving for social transformation. The mass organizations will be better suited to evoke popular initiative and cooperation than political bodies. They would become new media of power besides administration, and thereby broaden the base of government in a new and a vital way. They would help to evoke the new atmosphere, and also forge the agency for social change. Functional pluralism is a powerful solvent of totalitarian tendencies.

22. It will be noticed that in the recent talks between the Congress and the PSP, the Congress was conceiving broadening of the government in a limited way while PSP spokesmen were thinking of a wider, functional and plural, expansion. It should be our endeavour to make the second set of considerations the fulcrum of people's political thought. Organs, other than the administration, have to emerge to safeguard the rights of the people and having the strength to accept responsibility.

23. The Five-Year Plan in the next two years, the final years of the Plan, will be facing widening deficits and increasing economic and financial difficulties. Either the Plan will have to be cut down below even its modest targets or fresh thinking will have to be done on the lines suggested above. The opposition too will have to rethink its strategies. Those with a stake in democracy cannot remain stagnant in thought or action.

24. In an under-developed country like India, there is always the danger of democratic and secular policy getting discredited because of the failure of a party like the Congress. The difficulty can be met by one of the two alternatives: (i) programmatic agreement between democratic parties, or (ii) delimitation of areas of agreement and of disagreement. Nation-building activities and partisan politics have to be demarcated. This consideration does not apply to situations where we can develop mass movements on *social* issues like unemployment and semi-starvation.

Local Bodies

25. From the point of view of devolution of authority or of developing a rival power, local bodies occupy an important position. As far as village panchayats are concerned, it is generally agreed that party differences should not be injected into the working of the panchayats. Political divisions at that level might tend to become deep-seated and create new obstacles in the way of village solidarity which is the basis of most plans of reconstruction. What attitude do we adopt towards the Local Bodies that intervene between the village panchayats and the State Legislature—towards District Boards and Municipalities? We occupy a majority in some of these Bodies, but we have yet to work out a distinctive socialist policy. Within the powers given by law to these Bodies, we must work out a policy that make them organs of democracy and development, then alone can we demand widening of powers and revision of the laws, even of the organic law of the land. Only if the Local Bodies function well can we hope to democratise administration at the crucial district level and thereby have all the four pillars popularly controlled. A socialist programme for Local Bodies is an urgent necessity.

APPENDIX 48

Rammanohar Lohia's Speech on General Secretary's Report, Betul, 15 June 1953[1]

I have been asked to speak before Jayaprakash Narayan. That enables me to ask you and him to forgive any sharp phrases that I may utter and to take note alone of the basic ideas which I will try to put before you.

The result of recent by-elections have been a subject of controversy here.

[1]*Report of the Special Convention of PSP,* Betul, 14-18 June 1953, pp. 39-49.

Do they indicate that coalition and cooperation talks with the Congress party have added to the prestige and influence of the Party? Or, are they the result of a continuing and deepening trend of popular dissatisfaction with the Congress Government? There is as yet no method of social and political analysis which can give a conclusive answer to such questions. It is hard to determine as to what is causal and what is coincidental. Two phenomena may appear together and there is no method to know finally whether they have appeared simultaneously and coincidentally or whether they stand in the relationship of cause and effect. In the answer to such questions, the individual's aspirations and creative outlook inevitably enter. However, I am trying to be as objective as possible and therefore concede readily that the vocal section of the Indian people, city-dwellers, publishers, traders, educated people and the like, have generally been wanting some sort of a cooperation between the Praja Socialist Party and the Congress party. This is not to say that the reactions of the Indian people as a whole are similar. To the Indian people as a whole, the unmasking of the Congress party is taking place gradually and, for all that I know, the increasing vote of the Party at the bye-elections is a result of this gradual unmasking than of any desire for coalitionist politics. Nevertheless, there is a considerable opinion in favour of coalition or cooperation and the non-cooperators must take note of it for they may have to swim against the current. No party ever did great things unless it was prepared from time to time to face popular disapproval in the service of causes that displease the people when they are new but are vital to the health of the people.

Public opinion is a matter of great importance, but it shifts. Who knows that the people of India are wanting to roll over to another side of the bed because they are feeling uncomfortable for having lain too long on the Congress side, but may it not be that they may want after some time to roll over to Communists and the Jan Sangh and similar forces? In addition to taking note of public opinion, a primary test for policy and action ought to be its effect on the Party, its refinement as an instrument of the good and of reconstruction. What use are temporary advantages if they blunt the capacity of the party for achieving its more enduring goals?

Arising out of the talks of cooperation, a political formula has been placed before us which would without doubt blunt the Party—the formula that because of their common adherence to nationalism, secularism and democracy, the Praja Socialist Party and the Congress party are sister parties as distinct from other parties in the land. If sch common features are to be detected from time to time, what would prevent some people from detecting common features with the Communist Party such as nationalisation of industries or redistribution of land? It is true that the social change that Socialists want differs in quality from the social change that Communists want, but that would also apply to democracy and nationalism and their varying qualities which Socialists and Congressmen desire. While some of our colleagues were leaning towards the Congress party, I confess that I was re-acquiring my affection for Aruna Asaf Ali and, if that can happen to me, what of others. I hasten to add that I am not yet drawn towards any male Communists. There is also this peculiar argument about democracy. This democracy, which is supposed to establish a sisterly relationship between the Praja Socialist Party and the Congress party because the two are distinct and rivals for people's favour, is now being utilised to undermine this distinctness so as to achieve cooperation between them and to make them cease to be democratic rivals for people's favour. Democracy is being made to eat itself and socialism must reject formulas with such results.

The Praja Socialist Party is committed to the view that it is as distant from the Congress party as it is from the Communists and the communalists. We have been asked if politics are static, if political parties do not change their character and whether we should stick to rigid formulas that would prevent us from influencing other parties. It has been suggested that the acceptance of the fourteen-point programme by the Congress party would have changed its character and it would then have stopped being a party of *status quo*, and the question has therefore been asked as to why people like us should object to such a beneficial act. I will go into the question of the fourteen-point programme and the character of political parties later, but I should first of all like to point out that reform of other political parties should never become an aim of one's political action. It should at best be regarded as an incidental outcome of other aims. A political party must set before itself the aim of its own reform and strengthening and that of the country. It may incidentally through such an effort achieve a by-product of reforming other parties. And why should we confine such an endeavour to the Congress party? Our actions may also achieve an incidental reform of the Communists and Jan Sangh. One the basis of this faulty reasoning about changeability of character of political parties, similar fourteen-point programmes may be suggested to other parties in order to change their character, but this is not how politics are done.

Too much importance has been attached to the fourteen-point programme and some persons have held the view that its acceptance by the Congress party would have changed its character and created conditions in which national reconstruction would be possible. This is taking too easy a view of successful programmes, and not one but three factors are necessary for the successful execution of a programme, (1) well-defined items which are concrete and time-bound, (2) appropriate agency, (3) corresponding milieu. It is unfortunate that some of our colleagues hold the view that merely by signing under the fourteen items of a programme, the Prime Minister would have qualified to receive socialist support both inside and outside the Government. Even with regard to the items in this suggested programme, there is considerable vagueness. How far this can go is further seen in the agreed programme for Andhra. Vagueness and meaninglessness is a characteristic fault of Indian thought. We are always fond of talking of first principles and of philosophy but seldom take good care to put meaning into our talk. For instance, the Congress party has aimed for classless society, Cooperative Commonwealth, a State without isms and a Welfare State at intervals of about six months. Such ideals may be very fine to debate and may even show a kinship among various parties but they are largely vapour and meaningless and even deceitful such as the ideal of the Welfare State. If you take one item from the programme regarding reform in administration, it needs no evidence to point out that the demand for decentralisation of political power and administrative authority would be easily acceptable to all political parties in the land.

The demand may mean everything to everybody and therefore it means nothing at all. Such demands do not educate the people politically and do not arouse in them any concrete desires. Their enthusiasm is not concretely awakened so that they neither grow in power today nor are they in a position to direct the government when they or their party come to power. If this demand were plainly stated as the abolition of the present administration through District Magistrates and its replacement by elected district and local bodies to whom police and appropriate welfare powers are conferred, it would provide the people with a concrete aspiration. A sufficient number of men and women would also get trained into the resolve to achieve this demand when a socialist government takes office. Today, even Socialists are not clear nor agreed as to what decentralisation means, what to talk of the people at large. This is only an illustration. There is paramount need today to come down from the high perch of vague and meaningless principles to concrete measures.

Outlining of such concrete measures will enthuse the people, make them strive for power and train up a body of determined local administrators for future use.

In addition to the factor of a well-defined programme, it is always necessary to remember that programmes depend for their successful execution on proper agencies, and by that I do not mean administrative agency only. Parliamentary agency is principally in question. With under 30 Socialists in Parliament against over 300 of the Congress party, such an agencies just does not and cannot exist. Frequent reference has been made here to European or other foreign experiences—references to France, Japan and Italy. An occasional socialist coalition or cooperation could have never been contemplated except when the country was actually invaded or when parliamentary government broke down and socialist legislators were in a position to make or unmake governments. Only in India could talks of such coalition or cooperation have emerged out of the air, with no basis at all. But then some would say that India is a strange country. In any case, let us do nothing in our country to form a mind out of which multi-party helplessness arises as in France or in Italy.

Then there is the question of milieu. When a programme is voted to power there already exists among the people a determination and an awareness so that the government is in a position to act. In the absence of such a determination and awareness the government will have to decide from the top, and, instead of acting on measures, it will first have to arouse the determination and awareness, which is an exceedingly difficult thing to do. In fact, the whole question boils down to that of perspective, as Bagaitkar has said—the perspective of governmental power leading to people's power or the perspective of people's power leading to governmental power. I do not think it is any use trying to secure an agreement with the Congress party at the top and thus to achieve a government which could enthuse the people. Such an agreement is hardly possible and, even if it were, it will not lead to any substantial results; for, to achieve these, all the three factors of programme, agency and milieu must be present. Let us strive instead to get people's backing for socialism and through that for a socialist government.

There has been talk here of the political compulsions of a backward economy. It has been suggested that in a backward economy heavy burdens have to be imposed on the people and unpopular taxation also, in order to make reconstruction possible. For such heavy sacrifices to be undertaken by consent and not through dictatorship, it is felt necessary to achieve co-operation among the two largest parties in the country. This is faulty and mechanical reasoning. The consent of the people depends not on top co-operation among the parties but on the nature of measures undertaken and the character of the Government. One might wonder why the Congress Government finds it necessary to extend such ridiculously frequent invitations to the people of India and their parties for cooperation. I am inclined to think that the less deserving a government is of people's co-operation, the more frequently does it extend invitations for cooperation. If the Government were deserving and undertook satisfactory measures in a satisfactory way, the people would not wait for invitations in order to co-operate with it, nor would their political parties do so. Even a single party government, and more so the Congress Government with its overwhelming parliamentary majority, would have the largest measure of consent if it only chose to undertake satisfactory measures. One may suspect that these frequent invitations for cooperation are either meaningless or, if they ever resulted in cooperation or coalition government, the situation will only have arisen in which there is sharing only of the discredit of administration rather than substantial reconstruction of the country.

Far more dangerous than the actual achievement of cooperation or coalition is the attitude of mind that it generates. The search for areas of agreement somewhat removes from sight the very much wider areas of disagreement. In a country where 100 million people have to live on one meal a day, where near-famine stalks from State to State and full famine is threatened, where ejectments, police repression, unemployment and other injustices continually prevail, the Party will only stultify itself by shutting its eye to the sweeping areas of disagreement with the government party. An illustration of where this attitude of areas of agreement may lead is provided by the suggestion regarding village and district councils. They have first to become capable of using such powers as they have advantageously and then to ask for more powers, so says this attitude. But we would say that acquiring greater ability and fighting for more powers should be not sequential but simultaneous pursuits. It is almost like the old British rulers wanting us to become able before we asked for greater powers. We have found from experience that acquiring of ability and fighting for greater powers are dependent on one another and we must use the same method also for future purposes.

A complaint has been made here regarding the work of the various limbs of the Party and I should think that legitimate self-criticism is always good. While we would like our legislators to go in for informed criticism than for meaningless generalities, let us also not forget that legislators like C.G.K. Reddy have frequently made the Prime Minister speechless. Furthermore, much of our analysis and many of our reactions depend upon our respective attitudes. There was, for instance, the incident of Rajnarayan, the leader of the opposition in the Uttar Pradesh Assembly, when he was forcibly removed from the Chamber by policemen. Some persons at that time reacted against such a flouting of the Speaker, while other persons reacted in favour of such an act to secure the non-partisan character of the Speaker in a democratic Assembly. Neither had the facts. These differing reactions resulted more or less from differing attitudes. A judge of the High Court in Uttar Pradesh has subsequently stated in the Law Court that if he had been the Speaker he would have acted differently. Let us not forget that we are still a young democracy and many democratic conventions and practices that are so natural to maturer countries have yet to be secured and in the process many protests and fights will have to take place, such that the European peoples no longer find necessary to undertake.

Mankind knows yet no analytical or objective method to decide all political issues. Take for instance the question of whether the Prime Minister should or should not have contested in the last general elections. Much evidence could be adduced for either view. In the ultimate instance everyone's judgement depends on one's attitude, whether the areas of agreement far outweigh the areas of disagreement and so forth, and that is the creative element in politics. Doing politics does not mean merely to analyse the political situation but also to introduce precisely this creative element into them. It will do us all good if we recounted not merely the lapses of the various limbs of the Party but also those of the leadership in failing to introduce precisely this creative element to the maximum possible degree. I am as much guilty as any other person.

We have not been able to do much in the past regarding famine or near-famine wherever it broke out. We should not be content by merely turning ourselves into famine relief committees. We should be able to strike peacefully at injustices and failings which lead to famine, for after a famine has actually broken out there is little initiative left among the people except for relief, and this only shows that the search for areas of agreement can be extremely enervating if it leads, as it does, to obscuring all the areas of disagreement. Let us by all means search for cooperative endeavour with all elements, wherever cooperation is possible, but let us not forget the constructive non-cooperation or opposition to the government is still our primary duty.

In addition to political compulsions which have already been talked of here, let us also refer to the moral and spiritual compulsions which are being talked about and which will probably also find expression here. It is being said that good people of all parties should come together, that the party system leads to wasting and frittering away of national energy, that a clash exists between party interest and national interest and that good people must therefore rise above party interest. All this has no meaning in politics unless it is meant to lead to a break-up of the existing parties and to the creation of a new one or to increase the strength of the party of one's choice. A no-party or an all-party effort inevitably leads to either some kind of a dictatorship or to the building up of a political party of one's choice. I can well understand the effort to remove the difficulties and weaknesses of a party, but I cannot understand the decrying of the party system altogether. I have in the past emphasised more than any other the defects of negativism, externalism, electionism and insurrectionism that obtained and still obtain in our Party. But then a party is only a way and to destroy the party is to destroy the way. I believe that Gautam Buddha must have been decried as a partisan, full of bitterness and jealousy, by his contemporaries when he made his first speech at Sarnath. But he and his party persisted in the chosen way. I do not wish to flatter our Partymen, I am only too well aware of their numerous failings, their indolence, their irregularity and their lack of discipline, but let me say this to their credit that they have persisted in their way and therefore lived in discomfort while many of them could easily have lived in comfort by leaving the way. And who are good people anyway?

I do not think there exists a clash between party interest and national interest unless the party has lost all its good content and is merely a ladder for power. A party inevitably arises when the existing ways have lost their value and a new way becomes necessary.

I can well understand the need for goodwill in life and the need to emphasise the politics of goodwill as distinguished from the politics of clash. But goodwill is both a philosophical concept and a political recipe and it would be dangerous to confuse one with the other. As a philosophical concept, goodwill must permeate every act as far as possible and be ever at the back of the mind. It is then a universal feeling and its effects must not be restricted. This philosophical or emotive background of goodwill must bring within its purview the Communist Party and the Jan Sangh as much as the Congress party. To restrict it to anyone party to the exclusion of others is to distort the feeling of goodwill and unconsciously perhaps to adopt it only as a political tactic. Such an emotive background of goodwill would apply as much to Russia as to America, to the peoples and parties living under capitalism as much as those under communism. But while I have said this much about the philosophical or religious aspect of goodwill, let me hasten to emphasise the politics of clash, for, in a sense, all politics and even the best of politics are clash. Politics must ever be an effort to wrest away new realms from tyranny to freedom, and that inevitably means clash.

The question may then be asked if these two compartments of human activity, philosophical goodwill and political clash, are watertight compartments and one does not flow into the other. I definitely maintain that the two must interpenetrate, but that they are two separate activities must never be forgotten, and that the philosophy of goodwill must ever colour the politics of clash. There is a grand illustration of what such mixing up of goodwill with clash leads to and that is civil disobedience or non-cooperative action against tyranny. We must however remember that love as well as anger were component parts of Gandhiji's action. Some would prefer to describe anger as vigour or lustrousness, but I would persist in calling it anger. To those who wish to walk on this razor's edge there is always an ever-recurrent danger of forgetting to be angry against injustice.

Some comrades are holding me responsible, so I am told, for recent happenings in the Party, because they believe that by seeking to destroy the Marxist basis of the Party, I, more than any other, have brought it to such a pass. I admit that I have been relentless in criticising Marxism, which some persons have taken to be, I believe wrongly, a Marxist effort to develop

Marxism. But it was not merely a negative criticism but a positive effort at building up of a new thought. In this effort I may have made the mistake of not emphasising adequately the possible failings of Gandhism and I should like to state here today that in addition to the forgetting of anger or to the perpetuating of undemocratic organizational principles of selected or one-man leadership, there are other undesirable elements as well. I am reminded of the controversy between Mahatma Gandhi and Poet Tagore when Gandhiji traced the Bihar earthquake of 1934 to the long-practised sin of un-touchabiltiy and Poet Tagore expressed his disapproval of this statement. I had at that time thought the Poet Tagore was indulging in mental luxury while Gandhiji was destroying a million-fold curse, but I now think differently. Not even for the highest and best of ends must there be such playing with the mind, for such a playing with the mind of man is among the worst means that can ever be adopted. If that could happen to Mahatma Gandhi, a man who arrives once in tens of centuries, it is well for those who choose to tread in his path to guard themselves against the unconscious temptation to play with the mind, and thus to practise the worst of frauds unknowingly.

Our opposition to recent talks with the Prime Minister has sometimes been misunderstood. I consider it vulgar to denounce the leaders of the Party on grounds of power-seeking but I also consider it equally vulgar to declare that they were no office-seekers in doing what they did and to make a demand for trust in their integrity. It is all a question of judgement and we are perfectly well entitled to doubt the political wisdom and understanding shown in this act. We are also asked if they should not meet Mr. Nehru when invited to do so. Of course they can, and they may also meet him uninvited as often as they like, but the question is one of what they should talk and settle, and the distinction between informal talks and formal talks must always be maintained. In any case, they must remember that the Prime Minister has at least as much intelligence as they.

Mr. Nehru was supposed to have made a definite offer of cooperation at all levels. But in his letter to Jayaprakash Narayan occurred these sentences: "I did not think of any precise method of doing so. It was rather the general approach that mattered. I had not thought of, what is called, merger of parties. I felt that if there was a mutual realisation of the necessity of co-operation, other things would flow from it. When you or Kripalaniji asked me for greater precision, I said that I was prepared to consider the question at all levels, including both popular and governmental." It is obvious that the Prime Minister had only made a very vague request for cooperation. He was not clear about the precise method. Our colleagues asked for greater precision. I am afraid that the Prime Minister may some day find it necessary to use this sentence against the Party. Even if a programme had been presented to them, there was no need for our colleagues to have so precisely offered their cooperation on the level of the government in the event of its acceptance. They could have offered cooperation on the people's level and decided to tolerate the Government in the event of acceptance of their programme.

Even as far as Andhra is concerned it is true that Mr. T. Prakasam has been entrusted with the authority of the National Executive to deal with the issue there. It will be no diminution of that authority but in fact its complementing, if the Convention were to make certain requests to him. There is an Executive in Andhra of the PSP and future action should be taken in consultation with that Executive. The Convention would also wish the policy of toleration as against the policy of coalition to be followed in Andhra. The PSP in Andhra will do well not to accept participation in the Andhra Government, but to tolerate it as long as it carried out worthwhile policies.

Much ridicule has been pureed on me for refusing to accept organizational responsibility. Let me state here very definitely that I have neither the taste nor the talent for organizational responsibility. But that does not mean that, although I do not have the talent, I should not want to express my taste for policy framing.

Chairman:

That means you want to inspire and want us to perspire.

Rammanohar Lohia: (continues)

That indeed would be a perfect combination. But as it is I am perspiring and you are under the fan, and that is not such an unusual event either.

It is indeed very strange logic that would prevent me from sharing in policy-making and all other work unless I were prepared to assume organizational responsibility. If I am called bad on that score, well that is how I am built. But I should like to issue a warning. There are differing trends and opinions in our Party as in any other party. No outsider should ever acquire a moral or ideological authority to help a party in deciding what kind of policy and men should control the party, not even if he is the Prime Minister of the country, and in fact even more so because he is one. Every party stands permanently under the threat of such a danger.

The Chairman was perfectly right in stating the democratic principle of resignation from the National Executive in case the Party chose policies with which he disagreed fundamentally, but whether he was right in doing so yesterday may be a matter of opinion. The Convention, I trust, understands this position very well. In any case, persons like Verghese, C.G.K. Reddy and Ram Chandra Shukla and others who intervened so capably in the debate must also be capable of assuming responsibility.

There is no need to adopt a resolution on what happened in the past but there is need to lay down the political policy of the Party and to state clearly some fundamental principles for its conduct. I hope that the Convention would be able to frame a resolution of such a character.

There is great need to appoint a commission for the purpose of framing programmes for the Party both when it is in opposition and when it is in office. Such programmes will be a political education of the people as a whole and of the Party in particular. They will also throw up a sufficient number of men and women, political leaders as well as determined administrators at all levels from the village to the nation, for the execution of these programmes, for what is necessary uppermost today is a programme that is a consistent unity in itself and leaves no room for doubt and which can be worked out instead of being woolly and extremist. It may be possible that when such a commission gets down to work what appear to be formidable theoretical differences may turn out to be very small differences in actual practice.

APPENDIX 49

From Jawharlal Nehru, 8 July 1953[1]

My dear Jayaprakash,

I have just returned from Agra. In today's papers there appears a statement by you, in which you say that the Kashmir authorities had been criminally negligent in looking after Dr. Syama Prasad Mookerjee's health. This appears in a number of papers. I enclose a cutting from the *Times of India*, Delhi Edition. I presume that this report is a correct one of what you said.

You accuse me in a public statement of pronouncing judgement on a controversial subject. You have yourself, however, categorically pronounced that judgement in stating that you had no doubt in your mind that "the Kashmir authorities were not only negligent but criminally negligent in looking after Syama Babu's health". Further you said that the life of this great Indian could have been saved by better care.

You have passed your judgement presumably on what Justice Rama Prasad Mookerjee told you. Obviously, Justice Mookerjee, at the time, had only fragmentary facts in his possession and was deeply moved by the

[1]*J.P. Papers* (NMML).

sudden death of his brother. I made the statement I did partly from personal knowledge and partly from examining both papers and persons who had some direct knowledge. From that evidence I came to a certain conclusion which I conveyed to Atulya Babu in answer to a letter to me.

I do not know whether you had read a statement issued by the Kashmir Government about three or four days ago. You make no reference to this statement. That statement itself was naturally fairly brief. I believe they are issuing a very detailed statement soon. But even that brief statement, I think, presented a clear case that the Kashmir Government were anxious to do, and did in fact do, everything in their power to show consideration for Dr. Mookerjee. I am naturally no judge of what medicines should have been given to him.

Having had a fairly lengthy acquaintance with prison life, as you have had, I do not know of anyone in prison having been given more confortable quarters to live in than Dr. Mookerjee. The place was an ideal one, climatically and otherwise. The surroundings were beautiful. Food and other conveniences were, it has been admitted, very satisfactory. The one complaint that Dr. Mookerjee made at some late stage was that he could not have long walks. There was a small garden attached to the house with flowers and fruit trees, but this was not big enough for a long walk. When he pointed this out, he was permitted to go for a walk to the adjoining Nishat Bagh, which is one of the loveliest of the Moghal Gardens. I believe he did go there once.

As regards medical attendance, apart from the usual doctors connected with the jail establishment, the Director of Medical Services, Colonel Chopra, visited him fairly regularly and kept in touch with his requirements and health. Unfortunately he went on tour just two days before Dr. Mookerjee's death.

Occasionally Dr. Mookerjee complained of some minor ailment which was attended to. There was no serious complaint and there was no apprehension in the minds of anybody. It was only the day before his death that, for the first time, his condition was not good. A little later he was removed to the hospital. As I have said above, I cannot say what a proper treatment in such cases should be. The men in charge were supposed to be competent and even in hospital there was no serious development. When the Doctors suggested that they would send telegrams to his relatives, Dr. Mookerjee himself said that he would prefer sending the telegrams himself telling them not to worry and that he was being well looked after. In fact, he was apparently fairly well till the very evening of his death and met people. No one thought that there might be a serious turn to his illness. Certainly the Kashmir Government had no reason to think so. It may be that some doctors might have taken a more serious view. Heart disease is naturally a serious thing, but people have it for years and then it may be that some sudden thing upsets them. Only three weeks ago, a friend of mine died of this very heart disease, "coronary thrombosis", which he had for a long time, while driving a car. He just collapsed at the wheel.

I really do not see where any negligence, criminal or other, comes in on the part of the Kashmir Government. It may be that the doctors should have been more wide awake. It may be also that they should have informed the Kashmir Government of the very serious nature of the case earlier. The Kashmir Government was as much taken by surprise by the sudden development in the course of the night as any other person.

However, I do not wish to argue this matter with you. I merely wish to point out that I did not make the statement I did without inquiring into the matter with some care and satisfying myself about the facts.

When Dr. Mookerjee was sinking, efforts were made to get doctors from the Indian Army Hospital. Distances in Srinagar are long. It took some time to get them out in the middle of the night. They came just too late.

Communications from Srinagar are not very easy. Efforts to telephone were not successful. Ultimately a telephone message came to Delhi. Some time later they got through to Calcutta, but it was impossible to hear or be heard. The result was that the message could not be given directly but had to be relayed by two telephone operators, who repeated very briefly what they liked and could not convey it in proper form or at length. That message as delivered by the telephone operator must have shocked Justice Mookerjee.

Letters from Kashmir have been delayed greatly during the last few weeks. They go by air and sometimes air services are held up for a week at a time.

It is a well known fact that a few days previous to his death, the Kashmir Government had given facilities for Sardar Hukam Singh, Mr. Trivedi, his lawyer, and later Prem Nath Dogra, the President of the Jammu Praja Parishad, to see Dr. Mookerjee. Prem Nath Dogra had been specially brought from his place of detention in Jammu and he had long talks with Dr. Mookerjee. The Kashimir Government knew that these talks related to the withdrawal of the Jammu agitation and were naturally anxious to facilitate them. In fact they had decided to release Dr. Mookerjee within a few days. I am mentioning these facts so that you might judge of the motive or intention of the Kashmir Government in this matter. The fact is that no one in Srinagar, and certainly not the Kashmir Government, had the least intimation or feeling that Dr. Mookerjee's illness was serious. This illness took a turn for the worse just five or six hours before the death took place.

You refer to an enquiry into this "whole affair". Personally I or the Government of India cannot have any objection to any enquiry. But it is not for the Government of India in such matters to by-pass the State Government.

It is for the State Government to take such action as they decide upon. More particularly, in regard to Kashmir, there is so much argument in regard to what the Government of India's relations are with the State Government, and it would be improper for us to take any such action directly. As you must know, Sheikh Abdullah invited Dr. Bidhan Roy to come and see for himself, as they have nothing to hide and welcome any friend going there to find out facts for himself. But they do object to being put in the dock and treated as if they were criminals and charged, as you have done, with criminal negligence when, according to their thinking, they went out of their way to show every courtesy and consideration to Dr. Mookerjee.

I might mention that after Dr. Mookerjee's death, when his body was being flown from Srinagar aerodrome, his two colleagues, who had been with him in detention and who accompanied the body, had not only no complaints to make but, in spite of their evident sorrow, expressed their appreciation of what the Kashmir Government had done in this matter. That was their immediate reaction.

Yours affectionately,
Jawaharlal

APPENDIX 50

From Jawaharlal Nehru, 12 August 1953[1]

My dear Jayaprakash,

Thank you for your letter of August 8 about Burnpur.[2]

What has happened in Burnpur is certainly most unfortunate. Whatever disputes there might be, it is tragic to see a great industrial plant suffering serious damages. No one yet knows the extent of this damage because of the go-slow policy,[3] but it is feared that this might be very serious indeed. Certainly if this continues, the plant is doomed.

To adopt any policy which may result in such serious damage to a plant which has cost a vast sum of money and which produces something of basic importance seems to me completely wrong.

[1]*Selected Works of Jawaharlal Nehru*, Vol. 23, pp. 159-60.

[2]Jayaprakash Narayan wrote that the "whole issue at Burnpur is one of domestic adjustment within the Congress Party" and "the dispute is between two groups of INTUC (i.e. Congress) workers". He felt that as the vast majority of the workers were opposed to Michael John, the President of the Union, Nehru should act in the matter not so much as Prime Minister but as President of the Congress.

[3]As a result of the go-slow strike the company suffered a loss of Rs. 3 crores in terms of sale, and the loss of production amounted to 1,00,000 tons of steel.

[4]As advised by the Action Committee, the workers had agreed to raise the production from 20 to 35 per cent from 1 August 1953.

You say that the dispute is one of domestic adjustment within the Congress. I am not quite sure if it can be entirely described as such, though partly you may be right. Anyhow there can be no two opinions about the desirability of a fair election. Such an election must be held and John, the President of the Union, has said so quite clearly. Obviously it cannot be held suddenly and in this excited atmosphere, but it should be held as early as possible.

You have sent me a copy of a telegram from Chhotelal Vyas, the President of the Action Committee at Burnpur. He is also the President of a Congress Committee. I do not know him personally, but I confess that I have formed no good opinion of him from such reports as I have had. He is a share broker exploiting labour and possibly even profiting by this. What is called his gesture amounts to his kindly agreeing to workers doing 35 per cent of their normal work.[4] Why should they do 35 per cent when both from the point of view of the plant and the wages they get, they are supposed to do 100 per cent. This can hardly be called any kind of a gesture.

So far as I am concerned, both as Prime Minister and as Congress President, I have tried to do my best.

I have communicated with Sri Babu on this subject, with Dr. Roy who is directly dealing with it as well as the Ministries here.

Yours affectionately,
Jawaharlal Nehru

APPENDIX 51

From Jawaharlal Nehru, 22 November 1953[1]

My dear Jayaprakash,

Need I tell you how happy I felt on receiving the message which you and Prabha sent me on the occasion of my birthday. It is a joy to have the affection of old comrades.

Yours affectionately,
Jawaharlal Nehru

[1] *Brahmanand Papers* (NMML).

APPENDIX 52

From Ellen Roy, 17 February 1954[1]

Dear Jayaprakash Narayan,

Your kind words. If you only knew how much Roy had improved since you saw him last, you could imagine how shocking was this sudden undoing of our long last battle against this illness, when it seemed all but won.

He had started writing and dictating letters and articles and walking exercises succeeded better every day. In the evenings already he was sitting again in his place by the fireside for a while before walking back to his bed, with support on one side.

These attacks of coronary thrombosis come like lightning without any previous symptoms. This one came ten minutes after we had changed his position in bed, and he said he was comfortable, when the nurse noticed a disturbed sound in the breathing and found the pulse already almost imperceptible. Half an hour later, he still replied to the doctor's question, that he had a pain in the chest and asked me to shift a pillow. But the doctor knew what had happened and would allow no movement nor even a touch, gave morphia, and in the following 22 hours of oxygen and many injections, he never showed a sign of awakening again. So I cling to the idea that he did not suffer and did not know what was happening to him nor have to think of what is now happening to me.

Yesterday it was three weeks since they took him away. Many friends came and some usually stay with me, and all that had to be done was beautifully and well. I still feel very much under his eyes, and shall always do so. So I know that I may not let myself go to pieces and must start doing some work. There is more of it than I shall be able to do in the rest of my life, but have to make a start somewhere.

The *Radical Humanist* will of course continue; there are stacks of unpublished lectures and discussions among my yet un-transcribed shorthand notebooks. There is the biography of those periods not covered by his written memoirs to be compiled and edited, for which I may have to go abroad some time. There are 9 heavy foolscap volumes of handwritten material for his big work on the Philosophical Consequences of Modern Science, all written in jail and not even yet copied out, and the American edition of some of his books under negotiation. A conference or reunion is to be held here in May and, last but not least an enormous correspondence. If work is only a kind of dope for the moment, perhaps in course of time it will help me to live again, although I am not looking forward to that, because what a poor life will it be compared to the one we had together.

[1]*Brahmanand Papers* (NMML).

It had been one of his last joys that you came to see him. He had been looking forward to the talks you were going to have, the very prospect of which was a confirmation to him of his vision that fruitful social change in our time must result from the penetration and movement of ideas, a movement which, to be effective—because if he had vision, he was yet no visionary—would create its own pattern of action and coordination, though not in the form of political parties, all of which, from left to right, whether they know it or not, are based on the pernicious Marxian doctrine of the capture of power, with its implied object of ramming even good things down people's throats, taking their reluctance or inability to will them and achieve them by themselves, for granted.

If ever you come this side again, don't fail to come here.

Sincerely yours,
Ellen Roy

APPENDIX 53

From Rammanohar Lohia, 30 March 1954[1]

Dear Jayaprakash,

Others may be writing to you. I don't write, but I am sure you would not have concluded anything from it. I write only when some emergency arises.

As a result of giving up *swadharma* [one's duty], I am catching several new diseases. I have, of course, heard that you too have caught some diseases. But in your life there is at least some discipline and it can improve further, but it is impossible for me. Now you should take over my place [as General Secretary of the Praja Socialist Party] at the time of the General Council meeting. According to my understanding, the time is approaching to shake the country and the Party. Nobody else can shake them like you. Of course, this is conditional upon the shaker himself not shaking between the Congress and Communists and the Atlantic and the Soviet Camps.

This work cannot be done by me. This time even the priests at Devaghar have closed my lineage record. Earlier it was already closed in Mathura. My way is different. To some extent your condition is the same. But you have got wife, brother, nephew etc. You have an emotional relationship with the nation and you alone can be a leader of the country and take it forward to socialism. There are hundreds of other reasons, but it is useless to mention them. My inner voice says that you should now take responsibility

[1]*J.P. Papers* (NMML). Original in Hindi.

of the Party and this is the greatest reason for me [for saying so]. It may not be so for you. But if you think a little more, with a sympathetic attitude towards me, you will also realise the importance of this reason.

If your reply is not appropriate, I may perhaps have to do something at the time of the General Council that may not be appropriate from all points of view.

Say *Pranam* to Prabha.

Yours,
Rammanohar

P.S.: I will be at Kanpur on the 7th and at Bombay on the 9th.

INDEX